MANAGEMENT DECISION SCIENCES
Cases and Readings

The Irwin Series in Quantitative Analysis for Business
Consulting Editor   **Robert B. Fetter**   *Yale University*

Management decision sciences

Cases and readings

William L. Berry
The Ohio State University

Charles J. Christenson
Harvard University

John S. Hammond III
John S. Hammond and Associates

1980 **Richard D. Irwin, Inc.**
Homewood, Illinois 60430

Irwin-Dorsey Limited
Georgetown, Ontario L7G 4B3

ISBN 0-256-02219-4
Library of Congress Catalog Card No. 79–88785

Printed in the United States of America

1 2 3 4 5 6 7 8 9 0 MP 7 6 5 4 3 2 1 0

Preface

This book provides materials for a management science course to emphasize the processes involved in construction and use of mathematical models. Our philosophy is that understanding the *processes* of management science is more crucial to most business school graduates than thorough knowledge of its *techniques*. Thus, our ultimate purpose is helping our students learn how to ask the right questions and use analytical results in managing, as opposed to teaching the technology of solving problems.

This is not to say that the technology of management science is ignored, however. Knowledge of techniques is essential to asking the right questions and sound use of results. Furthermore, a large part of our students' early careers will involve solving problems posed by others. Consequently, the textual material provides sufficient technical guidance for the student to understand the essentials of the management science topics covered and to resolve the quantitative issues of the cases.

But the pedagogy of this book looks beyond students' early careers to the more rewarding and demanding challenges of higher level management. As a management career advances, responsibilities shift from problem solution to problem definition, from choosing between alternatives to specifying alternatives, from optimizing constrained situations to imposing resource limitations. All of these activities require some technical ability. But more general skills are also needed for managers to see important implications in the results of analysis and to effectively interact with analysts. Analysts, in turn, are responsible for answering the manager's questions and solving problems defined by the manager. This book aims to provide the frameworks for a classroom experience that will develop the blend of general and technical skills required of future managers rather than the more elaborate technical skills future analysts will need.

These skills will develop primarily in classroom discussion of cases. In virtually every case in this book there are overt problems, usually of a quantitative nature, which must be solved. However, in cases there are also covert problems. The student's job is not complete until these "hidden" issues, too, are uncovered and analyzed. Typical of questions that bring these issues to light are:

Is the problem I've been analyzing really *the* problem in this case? Or is it a symptom of a different problem?

If I were the manager described in the case, what questions might I have for the analyst? If I were the analyst, what would I need from the manager?

Might the assumptions of the quantitative technique I have used to perform this analysis be unrealistic? How unrealistic are they? In what ways does this unrealism limit the usefulness of the analysis?

What specific actions does the solution to the problem suggest? Are those consistent with what I know about this firm from the case? With my understanding of this industry? With my common sense?

Is the data I've been analyzing of reasonable quality? If not, is my analysis really relevant to the problem faced by this company?

And so forth.

Students in classroom discussion of cases will raise these covert issues simultaneously with discussion of overt case problems. In this way they will gain skill and experience in searching for and uncovering the less obvious but often more meaningful issues. The classroom can thus become a forum where students begin to build their own base of experience. They can learn from these experiences to be more discerning about issues they raise. As classroom discussion nurtures the students' capacity to discriminate between relevant and irrelevant issues, penetrating and misleading questions, fruitful and barren paths of inquiry, a heightened ability to make effective classroom contributions evolves that signals emergence of the important skills of *asking the right questions and using analytical results soundly.*

This view of the role of discussion in the classroom underscores the authors' belief that an instructor's role is not to teach but to help students to learn. Learning is the students' responsibility. The responsibility of the instructor is to create an environment wherein learning can take place. The materials assembled herein are designed to help create that environment—that classroom ambience—that not only allows learning but encourages it.

Supplementing the text material and cases are nine readings. These readings appear together at the end of the book but are meant to be assigned and studied as the course progresses. Some are light and fun to read. Others are tougher sledding. Each of these readings, however, is highly relevant to the central theme of this text: describing and illustrating the managerial processes important to building and using mathematical models.

December 1979   William L. Berry
                                    Charles J. Christenson
                                    John S. Hammond III

Acknowledgments

Our book represents the merging of several streams of creative thought. Its most immediate precursor was an experimental course taught at The Ohio State University by Professor Berry from 1975 to 1977. In 1977 this course replaced a technique-oriented course in the Ohio State curriculum and is currently a requirement for the bachelors degree in Business Administration there.

Much of the material and many of the ideas in Professor Berry's course had been developed by Donald L. Wallace while teaching at The University of Western Ontario and l'Instituit pour l'Etude des Methodes de Direction de l'Entreprise (IMEDE). Professor Wallace's penetrating insights and continual quest for practical and effective pedagogy were an important inspiration. His willingness to share his materials with us has, to an immense extent, made this book possible.

Ohio State University faculty members William H. Bright, John C. Chambers, Biplab Dutta, and Lisa M. Sokol as well as teaching associates John W. Bradford, Daniel J. Bragg, Vicki L. Davis, F. Robert Jacobs, Edward R. Niedzwiedz, Charles F. Rauch, R. Daniel Reid, and William T. Stewart have also had a great influence on this book. They agreed to teach from these materials although their backgrounds were *not* case-oriented. Observing their development as case instructors helped us shape this book to make it useable by instructors of very diverse backgrounds in many types of business schools. We are truly grateful to them for attempting, for persevering, and for making a success of this pedagogical experiment, and we are pleased that several won teaching awards in the process.

Professor Christenson and Dr. Hammond contributed to Professor Berry's course through their advice to him and eventually became involved in co-authorship of this book through the quality and relevance of their writings. Most of their writings were articles and cases developed while they were teaching the Managerial Economics course at Harvard Business School. Some of these materials were published in a book by Professor Christenson, Richard F. Vancil, and Paul W. Marshall entitled *Managerial Economics: Text and Cases* pub-

x

lished in 1973 by Richard D. Irwin, Inc. That book was the revision of a 1962 text bearing the same title which listed Neil E. Harlan as author along with Professors Christenson and Vancil. Several of the cases as well as some of the material in Chapters 2, 3, 4, and 6 of this book appeared first in *Managerial Economics*. We gratefully acknowledge the influence of that earlier text and are indebted to the authors and to Richard D. Irwin, Inc. for allowing us to borrow from it.

In 1977 the authors decided to collaborate on this text. This effort involved preparation of several new cases and writing of considerable new textual material. Additionally, a substantial amount of material written by others was reviewed, a small fraction was class-tested at Ohio State University, and a select few items were included in this book. We are indeed grateful to the authors of cases, articles, and other materials and to our many Harvard and Ohio State colleagues who have shared with us the task of developing cases included in this volume. Those who have participated in these ways include: Barry Anderson, Robert N. Anthony, M. Edgar Barrett, Stephen P. Bradley, Stanley I. Buchin, E. Raymond Corey, Edward W. Davis, Thomas F. Funk, Stephen H. Goodman, C. Jackson Grayson, Jr., Neil E. Harlan, Robert H. Hayes, Simon A. Hirshon, Ray Hyman, Cullom Jones, Philip Kotler, Charles W. Krallman, Mitchell Lazarus, John D. C. Little, Martin V. Marshall, F. Warren McFarlan, Robert E. McGarrah, Richard F. Meyer, Juan P. Montermoso, William T. Morris, Wayne C. Pfeiffer, William F. Pounds, John W. Pratt, Howard Raiffa, Paul O. Roberts, Robert C. Ronstadt, Stephen R. Rosenthal, John K. Shank, Paul A. Vatter, Donald L. Wallace, James A. Wegge, Steven C. Wheelwright, Robert B. Wilson, Jr., and D. Daryl Wyckoff.

We are grateful to the President and Fellows of Harvard College, the Trustees of Boston University, the Board of Trustees of Leland Stanford Junior University, The Institute of Management Sciences, *Sloan Management Review*, Lord Publishing Company, *The Chronicle of Higher Education*, and Cahners Publishing Company for their permission to reproduce cases, articles and other materials to which they hold the copyright.

Our academic reviewers, principally Edward W. Davis of the University of Virginia but also others who are anonymous to us, provided timely, coherent and useful advice. These people, and Robert B. Fetter of Yale University, editor of the series this book appears in, have materially contributed to this work. We are very grateful for their help.

The authors were also fortunate to have the counsel and encouragement of our academic administrators in this project. We are thankful that Dean Edward H. Bowman and Associate Dean Robert E. Georges of The Ohio State University's College of Administrative Science helped provide an atmosphere that encouraged and rewarded pedagogical innovation. We also thank Dean Laurence E. Fouraker and Associate Dean for Research and Course Development Richard S. Rosenbloom of Harvard Business School for their help in this project and for their institution's continuing intense involvement in case development.

Finally, the authors want to express their gratitude to their former students at Harvard and at Ohio State who, through their discussions of the materials we put before them, taught us the meaning of what we had written.

Although many have contributed to this volume and a few have contributed greatly, the responsibility for error rests with us.

W. L. B.
C. J. C.
J. S. H. III

Contents

Introduction **1**

Chapter 1 Models and managers **11**

1-1 The development of the atomic model, 18
1-2 The development of the accounting model, 22
1-3 Bud Mathaisel, 24

Chapter 2 Cost analysis **37**

2-1 Analysis of a limited operation, 43
2-2 Bob Mogielnicki, 46
2-3 R. C. Blake Co., 49
2-4 Bill French, accountant, 54

Chapter 3 Linear programming **61**

3-1 Sherman Motor Company, 88
3-2 Red Brand Canners, 91
3-3 The law school question, 94
3-4 Super-Rite Meats, 97
3-5 Rubicon Rubber Company, 103
3-6 The Lockbourne Company, 112
3-7 McGowan Paint Company, 115

Chapter 4 Decisions under uncertainty **119**

Appendix 4-A Probability distributions, 142
Appendix 4-B Assessing probabilistic forecasts, 152
4-1 Warren Agency, Inc., 172
4-2 The *Nancy M. Hohman,* 173
4-3 Family Health Center, Inc. (A), 176
4-4 Family Health Center, Inc. (B), 185
4-5 Weston Manufacturing Company, 191
4-6 J. B. Robinson Fertilizer and Explosives, Inc., 195
4-7 Petro Enterprises, Inc., 202
4-8 Technotronics Corporation, 204

4–9   Hinkle Automotive Products, 205
4–10   Hawthorne Plastics, Inc., 210

Chapter 5   Preference theory **215**

5–1   J. B. Robinson Fertilizer and Explosives, Inc. (P), 237
5–2   Edgartown Fisheries, 239
5–3   Marketronics, Inc., 244
5–4   The *Stephen Douglas,* 248

Chapter 6   Simulation **256**

6–1   Weatherburn Aircraft Engine Company, 278
6–2   Synergistic Systems Corporation, 279
6–3   The grimbel, 282
6–4   Central Steel, 285
6–5   Hollingsworth Manor Apartments, 291
6–6   Tauride Transportation Corporation (A), 296
6–7   Tauride Transportation Corporation (B), 300

Chapter 7   Models and organizations **311**

7–1   The Engel Company (A), 326
7–2   The Engel Company (B), 333
7–3   ALPHA Concrete Products, Inc., 334
7–4   General Leasing Company (A), 346
7–5   Xerox Corporation distribution system (B), 359
7–6   DYCO Chemical Corporation (AR), 372
7–7   DYCO Chemical Corporation (B), 383
7–8   Transit maintenance, 396
7–9   Bennington Products, Inc., 422
7–10   Everclear Plastics Company, 431

Chapter 8   Wisdom from the experts **452**

Reading
8–1   Solving problems, 453
           Ray Hyman and Barry Anderson
8–2   The process of problem finding, 466
           William F. Pounds
8–3   On the art of modeling, 486
           William T. Morris
8–4   The wizard who oversimplified: A fable, 499
           Robert N. Anthony
8–5   Corporate models: Better marketing plans, 502
           Philip Kotler
8–6   Management science and business practice, 528
           C. Jackson Grayson, Jr.

8–7   Models and managers: The concept of a decision calculus, 539
        John D. C. Little
8–8   Let there be light (with sound analysis), 566
        Cullom Jones
8–9   To tell the truth, 569
        Charles J. Christenson

Title index of materials for discussion **577**

Index of text **579**

Introduction

MANAGEMENT SCIENCE

Management science, which is the application of scientific method and quantitative techniques to the management of enterprise, is often spoken of as a relatively new subject. Many authorities point to the development of operations research techniques during World War II and to the advent of the computer in the 1950s as the birth and weaning of management science. A broader definition of management science would place its birth much earlier in history. Certainly the work of Frederick Taylor in the latter part of the 19th century and the work of Charles Babbage in the middle of that century come within the scope of any reasonably broad definition of management science. So should the work of Alfred Marshall and the economists before him dating back to Adam Smith. All of these people—and there were earlier contributors too—were attempting to rationalize and generalize the activities of commerce. This is the fundamental hallmark of management science.

Perhaps, to keep the field of management science within reasonable bounds, the formal use of mathematics must be included as a defining characteristic. Nevertheless, it must be held that the early contributors did use formal mathematics—however simple—in their work. Arithmetic can make an analysis that is just as rational and just as scientific as can differential equations and matrix algebra.

What happened during World War II and the postwar period was not the birth of management science but the dramatic expansion of its techniques and uses coupled with the beginnings of widespread interest in it by the managers of industry. This expansion will no doubt continue, and widespread interest will be followed by widespread use.

At this stage in the development of management science what is needed is to convey to the prospective manager the *concept* of management science—its uses and limitations. Managers, whose primary skills must be in administration, should be familiar with what management science is and what it does. The task of managers is to analyze, to evaluate, and to implement the schemes of management science. To do this job adequately they must have some grasp of the totality of management science and its basic precepts. Managers may never be able to really understand the detail, but they must be able to comprehend the total framework within which the management scientist works.

In the article reprinted in the following section, Mitchell Lazarus expresses the idea that an applied mathematical education can be useful for most college students. These same ideas, transposed to the special case of business students, provide the foundation for this text.

THE ELEGANCE AND RELEVANCE OF MATHEMATICS[1]

Strikingly few people regard mathematics as a part of their intellectual lives. Most are afraid of it and avoid the subject whenever they can, which is hardly surprising, since most of the mathematics we teach in school and college is tedious, difficult, and without apparent purpose.

Consider, however, the people who do use mathematics easily and often. Oversimplifying, we can think of them in two broad groups: those who deal with mathematics for its own sake and those who use it for something else.

The first group includes professional mathematicians and the people who enjoy mathematical puzzles and games—together, a small fraction of civilized humanity.

The second group, much larger, includes everyone for whom mathematics is a tool, a means to other ends. Some, like scientists and engineers, have sophisticated mathematical needs. Others use simpler mathematics every day. And some need mathematics for public issues—and almost everyone for his personal affairs.

Mathematics-as-a-tool and mathematics-for-itself: The first is sometimes sloppy and "close enough," while the second tries to be clean, elegant, and more or less rigorous. The first centers on results, and the second on process. The first always expresses something in the real world, while the second occurs in an abstract realm.

It is fruitless to argue which is the better approach to mathematics. But we can compare the two for particular groups of students. Mathematicians-to-be need extensive and rigorous training, and so do some future scientists and engineers. But many college students, including most in the liberal arts, would find mathematics-as-a-tool more suitable and productive.

---

[1] This section is reprinted by permission from *The Chronicle of Higher Education*, December 1, 1975.

But the kind of mathematics that helps people understand real situations is now foreign to the liberal-arts curriculum. Instead, first-year students typically confront topics like permutations and combinations, simple probability theory, binomial work, algebra and equation-solving, and some trigonometry. Some college programs also present set theory, analytic geometry, and calculus.

To most students, these topics are neither interesting nor helpful. It is arguable whether they "improve their mind." Indeed, their disfavor leads to the familiar rejoicing whenever a college drops a mathematics requirement.

Instead of trying to teach mathematics for its own sake, colleges should teach it for their students' sakes. Not elaborate arithmetic, which is quickly becoming obsolete thanks to the pocket calculators. Not the beauty of mathematics, which leaves all but a few students cold. The focus should be on mathematics that can open the eyes and equip the hands, letting students look upon the world in new and fruitful ways.

Certain mathematical ideas can be extremely helpful. For example, the concept of rates of change is basic to thinking about most natural and manmade phenomena. A naturalist concerned about an endangered species of whale must look at the rate of decline as well as the actual number of whales. A shrinking population spells trouble, even if the numbers of whales are still large. And if the rate of decline itself is increasing, there is even more cause for alarm. Other familiar situations that involve rates of change include inflation, bank interest, gasoline consumption, and the steepness of a ski slope. Rates of change are the core of differential calculus, but the symbols of calculus are not necessary to understand the concept.

A second useful idea, dynamic equilibrium, arises when rates of change interact. Anyone who has an "In" basket tries to keep the papers moving out at the same rate as they move in—otherwise, all is lost. The total rate of change should equal zero. This gives an equilibrium—a steady number of papers, even though the papers are constantly changing. Society, economics, and countless minor phenomena are collections of shifting equilibria. The concept of equilibrium helps us see below the surface of many events and processes.

A third mathematical idea, saturation, arises when an equilibrium cannot be maintained. The job market ordinarily shows an uneasy equilibrium between the number of job openings and the people qualified to fill them. But occasionally the equilibrium edges over to the point where nearly all positions are filled, thus saturating the job market. The equilibrium can move no further; there is no way to take up the slack of more people looking for work. The result is usually increasing unemployment.

A fourth example, which cuts across the other three, is mathematical modeling: representing a situation in mathematics, working with the mathematics, and interpreting the situation back into reality. Modeling is a very powerful tool. It allows conclusions about events that have not occurred, about machines that do not exist, and about processes that are still developing. An engineer can use mathematical models to determine on paper whether an airplane will fly—long before it is built. And someone moving into a new apartment can determine whether his furniture will fit in his living room.

Mathematical models are especially helpful when rates of change are involved. It can be very difficult to calculate rates from experimental data. Often, it is easier to find a mathematical expression that mimics those data reasonably well, and then calculate rates from that. In many other situations, too, mathematical expressions can be simpler to work with than the original data, and still give highly useful results.

These mathematical ideas, and others like them, suggest a new content and style of mathamatics education for college students who do not plan to make mathematics a profession. We could call the new style the "mathematical arts," like the mechanical arts or the language arts.

The manipulation of symbols plays an important part in these plans, but a subordinate one. Abstract operations give mathematics its power, and one cannot speak of mathematics without them. But abstraction should not become an end in itself, unconnected with the needs mathematics can fulfill. In the mathematical arts, abstraction should serve the cause of useful purpose.

Thus, mathematics education should proceed in terms of reality, and perhaps realistic fantasy. The stress should be on the relationships between reality and mathematics, encouraging the idea of mathematical modeling to the point where it becomes almost automatic and intuitive. The student should come away with an armamentarium of mathematical skills and ideas that can help provide new and useful perceptions of the world.

Consider an analogy: If mathematics were music, professional mathematicians would be composers—the creators of new works in the medium. The composer's place is unique and special, for without him there is no music at all—and without the mathematicians, no mathematics. But not everyone need compose music. For most, it is enough to play an instrument a little, or perhaps just understand enough music to enjoy it. Likewise, not everyone has the talent, interest, drive, or need to create new mathematics. Those who do are a most important body of students, needing the close guidance of working mathematicians at every step in their education. But for most people, it is enough to know how to use mathematics, and, for some, enough to understand how others use it.

PURPOSE OF THIS TEXT

This text is meant to support a survey course in management science. This is not a course in the *techniques* of the field but one concerned primarily with the *direct application* of management science to business activity. The techniques are, of course, presented—as indeed they must be. Students must have some facility with the techniques if they are to understand the management science process. The emphasis, however, remains on the process. The question is not so much How should it be done? as What should be done? and Why should it be done?

The objectives of this text are threefold:

1. To convey the *concept* of management science and the *process* of building mathematical models.
2. To provide an opportunity to practice the analysis and evaluation of management science efforts.
3. To present a body of substantive information concerning the techniques of management science.

The objectives are listed in the order of their importance. First and foremost is to convey the concept of management science: what it is, how it works, why it is useful, where it is limited. Second, the objective is to permit development of *skills* in the analysis and evaluation of management science studies. This is *not* development of skills in the actual design and construction of management science models. Instead, the aim is for students to develop skills and nurture confidence in their ability to analyze and evaluate the work of others. Third, the objective is to present enough facts and terminology so that the students will be able to better understand the construction of existing models.

What will be done, in an overall sense, is to encourage students to use management science methods on the basis of sound understanding without having either to accept such methods without question or to reject them out of hand.

LEARNING BY THE CASE METHOD

The course taught from this book will rely heavily on what has come to be known as the *case method* of instruction. Simply stated, the case method calls for discussion of situations that have been faced by business executives. Cases will approximate the kinds of situations you will become accustomed to encountering in your future role as a manager. These situations have been written up by case writers who, as good reporters, have tried to present the information that is available to the business executives concerned. In an actual situation, however, a manager may not have all the information necessary to make a decision or to resolve a difficulty. On the other hand, he or she probably also has some data or knowledge that seems irrelevant to the problem at hand. The cases in this book often reflect these aspects of the real-life situations they depict. Sometimes, when analyzing a case, you will find that you need to make reasonable assumptions or speculations about missing information. Sometimes you will have to sort bits of useful information from data that are less useful. Sometimes, too, you will have to judge the reliability of information that may be presented as, for example, a case character's opinion. This may require that you consider the underlying motivations or aspirations of the character.

The realism of the cases can add a new dimension to this course that has not been present in many of your earlier courses—especially the ones dealing with quantitative techniques. That is, this course will give you the opportunity to make mistakes—and learn from them—in a very low-risk setting. Needless to say, the opportunity to err will occur repeatedly in your career but probably never again with such a low risk of penalty.

The educational purpose of the case method

The use of business cases follows a long tradition of professional education in fields like medicine and the law. For future business executives, case studies provide a pale substitute for actual business experience but usually a far better substitute than other pedagogical techniques. For a student, the case method of learning tends to develop a more professional sense of what management is, as the participant comes to recognize that the problems faced by a manager are not unique to one organization.

Study of the cases in this book will sharpen your analytic skills, since you must produce quantitative and qualitative evidence to support recommendations and decisions. In discussions, you will be challenged by instructors and co-participants to defend your arguments and analyses. The effect should be a heightened ability to think and reason rigorously.

Cases and the related discussions in class will provide the focal point for using your expertise, experience, observations, and prior training. The approach used by each class member in identifying the central problems in a case, analyzing them, and proposing solutions is as important as the content of the case itself. The lessons of experience are tested as you present and defend your analysis against those of class members who have different experiences and attitudes. It is in this process where common problems, interdependencies, differences of attitudes and organizational needs, and the impact of decisions of one sector of an organization on other sectors emerge and force the class to face and deal with them.

Perhaps the most important benefit of using cases is that they help you learn how to ask the right questions. An able business leader once commented: "Ninety percent of the task of a top manager is to ask useful questions. Answers are relatively easy to find, but asking good questions, that is the more critical skill." In suggesting *discussion questions* for each case, the instructor is not preempting your task of identifying the key problems in the case. You still must ask yourself: What really are the problems that this manager has to resolve? Too often, both in real life and in academic situations, facts and figures are manipulated without the real problem having been specifically defined.

There is one final benefit that will be achieved by using cases: The case method of learning renews the sense of fun and excitement that comes with being a manager. Participants should come to sense that being a manager is a great challenge—intellectually, politically, and socially.

How to prepare a case

The use of the case method first calls for you to carefully read and think about each case. There is no single way that works for everyone. Some general guidelines can be offered, however, and you can adapt them to the method that works best for you.

1. Read the first few paragraphs, then go through the case almost as fast as you can turn the pages, asking yourself: What is the case about broadly and what types of information am I being given to analyze?
2. Read the case very carefully, underlining key facts as you go. Then ask yourself: What are the basic problems this manager has to resolve? Try hard to put yourself in the position of the manager in the case. Develop a sense of involvement in *the manager's* problems.
3. Note the key problems on scratch paper. Then go through the case again, sorting out the relevant considerations for each problem area.
4. Develop a set of administratively workable recommendations for action, supported by your analysis of the case data and consistent with the central goals of the corporation studied.

Until now, your best results will come if you have worked by yourself. However, if you have time before class, it is useful to engage in informal discussions with some of your classmates about the cases. The purpose of this discussion is *not* to develop a consensus or a group position; it is to help each member refine, adjust, and amplify his or her own thinking.

What happens in class

In class, the instructor usually will let students discuss whatever aspects of the case they wish. However, it is the faculty member's role to prod you to explore fully the avenues of investigation down which you have started and to lead you into consideration of areas you may have missed. A healthy debate and discussion will ensue. You will benefit most if you take an active role in that debate. Sometimes the instructor will tell business "war stories" from other settings that relate to the situation under discussion and will encourage participants to do likewise. Finally, the instructor will summarize the discussion and draw out the useful lessons and observations that are inherent in the case problem and emerge from the case discussion.

A typical request at the end of a case discussion is: What is the answer? Except in certain specific situations where the purpose of a case is to highlight the workings of a mathematical tool (for instance), the case method of learning does not provide *the answer*. Rather, several viable answers will be developed and supported by various participants within the total group. As Charles I. Gragg wrote "Business is not, at least not yet, an exact science. There is no single, demonstrably right answer to a business problem. For the businessman it cannot be a matter of peeking in the back of a book to see if he has arrived at the right solution. In every business situation, there is always a reasonable possibility that the best answer has not yet been found—even by teachers."[2]

The instructor may suggest the pros and cons of various alternatives or tell what actually happened in a given situation. However, what actually happened or what any one person thought ought to be done is not of great significance; what is significant is that *you* know what *you* would do in a specific situation.

Learning results from rigorous discussion and controversy. Let each member of the class—and the instructor—assume responsibility for preparing the case and for contributing ideas to the case discussion. The rewards will be a series of highly exciting, practically oriented educational experiences that expose and analyze a wide range of topics and viewpoints.

Case ethics

Robert Ronstadt, in his book *The Art of Case Analysis*,[3] proposes a code of ethics for students in case-oriented courses. The following is reprinted by permission of the author and publisher.

The principal kinds of case-related ethical problems are:

1. Passing on case notes to students who haven't yet taken the course, thereby giving them an unfair and unearned advantage.

---

[2] Charles I. Gragg, "Because Wisdom Can't Be Told," *Harvard Alumni Bulletin*, October 19, 1950.

[3] Copyright © 1977 by Lord Publishing Co., Needham, Mass.

2. Discussing the case with someone who has not yet had the case in class but expects to have it at a later time.
3. Spending considerable effort attempting to find out "what happened in the case" in order to look good (as if what the company did was the correct answer, or that someone else's "right" answer is right for you).
4. Contacting a case company without permission to gather more information about the case situation.
5. Blowing the cover of a disguised case.
6. Taking advantage of other group members by letting them do the bulk of the work—the group parasite syndrome.

A professional code of ethics must be recognized and followed by students regarding their treatment of cases. I believe two principal elements of this code are:

1. You should not provide information on a specific case to people who have not yet had the case in class.
2. One does not seek or provide information about the case situation other than what is provided in the case, unless *explicitly* permitted by your instructor.

Cases represent a considerable investment in time and money. Generally, it takes about 30 to 40 days to research, write, and get a case approved for classroom use. Including expenses, I estimate the average cost of a case is approximately $2,500. Yet, many cases are written that are not used more than one or two times in class. For various pedagogical reasons, four or five cases may be written for each one that works well in class. If the costs of the less effective cases are included in the total cost, the approximate cost of developing a quality case rises to around $10,000.

While these figures are only rough estimates, they serve to illustrate the value of a good case. My impression is that most students do not realize the damage they can do by passing on notes, etc. No doubt your instructor will realize what has happened before too long. Unfortunately, the need to withdraw or shelve many good cases will have a direct impact on the quality of your course since the inventory of good cases is limited.

What should you do if your roommate approaches you and says, "You had XYZ Company yesterday, didn't you? How did your class handle it?" However you respond, I advise you not to act terribly offended. The situation is usually one where the person making the inquiry may not realize the nature of the inquiry and the position he/she places you. Unfortunately, the routine of obtaining packaged information from lectures has conditioned and confused some students into thinking they can always obtain prepackaged, spoon-fed answers. How they obtain the answer doesn't matter. After all, if you can buy course notes of Prof. X's lectures on the open market, what's wrong with asking a friend for information on a case?

Indeed, you can obtain "answers" about a case situation. Yet, this information gathering is *not* learning. Perhaps the most important step you can make in your educational career is the realization that you will "learn" *only* through your own efforts. A second step is the realization that you have a responsibility to help others to learn. Providing notes or extensive verbal information about a case is *not* helping an individual to learn.

Certainly professors can and should vary their case offerings and thereby reduce the temptation to obtain "inside" information on particular cases. But in the end, the case system can flourish only if students hold in spirit to an ethical code. And as recent scandals in business and government suggest, perhaps we require not only more classroom discussion of ethical conduct in professional life, but also more practice while in school.

Models and managers

If business executives were polled about their use of models, the results would likely be that most executives do not see themselves as heavy users of models. Using a narrow definition of the term *model* to mean a mathematical construct meant to provide quantitative "answers" under idealized conditions, these executives would probably be correct in their self-perceptions. After all, the people who build and manipulate these elaborate mathematical models are typically not at the executive level. With a slightly broader definition, however, executives would admit that models are very much a part of their daily business lives.

WHAT IS A MODEL?

One definition of the term *model* is *an abstract representation or copy of something real.* Now, this is a pretty broad definition that covers a wide range of possibilities from an architect's mock-up of a new building to a person hired to put on articles of apparel to display to customers. This definition will serve us well enough, however, because it includes the entire range of *mathematical models* from the executive's back-of-the-envelope rough calculations to the most sophisticated programming or simulation model. Notice that this definition also includes a host of very useful mathematics-based constructs that, although rigorous in derivation, tend to be a bit fuzzy in everyday application. Concepts like the learning curve, economic supply-demand relationships, the cost of capital, and so forth are examples of mathematical constructs that have become an integral part of every manager's collection of intuitive, instinctive models.

From this discussion one should get the notion that almost any consistent idea, thought process, form of analysis, or even prejudice can be conceived of as a model of something. That notion, we believe, is correct. At the same time, we recognize that it really says very little about models of the sort that find application in the administration of business affairs. What is the difference between models that are widely used and those that are largely ignored? In other words, why do business managers use models and why do they use particular ones?

First, let us dispel the idea that certain models are used because they are "more nearly correct" or "of a higher degree of elegance" than their competitors. Academic journals are full of examples of mathematical models that have been rigorously judged as being both correct and elegant and yet have never been used widely to solve business problems. Instead, the models that are used in business are the ones that provide insight for executives about the operation of their enterprises. This should not be particularly surprising. Put differently, business managers use those models that are useful. It is by this standard—usefulness—that models are judged by the ultimate user. If models aid executives in understanding a complex real-world problem or if they help in making a tough decision, then they are useful and will be used. Often repeatedly. The academic editors of learned journals, evidently, use a different standard.

FINDING USEFUL MODELS

How does a business executive go about discovering useful mathematical models? One might sort through many abstract mathematical constructs and compile a list of those that seem to have some potential utility. One might enroll in an educational program for exposure to a variety of presorted models. (Although executives should be highly suspicious of those who do the sorting!) One might assemble a corporate group of applied mathematicians to invent appropriate models.

More reasonably, however, most business executives might not even think of the usefulness of a mathematical model or modeling form until a particular business problem arises. Then, they could possibly rely on their judgment as already sharpened by their conceptual baggage, a collection of intuitive models. Often, however, and more often with increasing complexity or unfamiliarity of a particular problem, on occasions when previous intuitive analyses have been tried and are found wanting, or when the weight of a formal analysis may help make a point or sway a consensus, a mathematical statement or formulation of the problem will be used in hopes that the solution to the model will provide a prescription for administrative action. In short, mathematical models in the business world are used to help solve a problem at hand. They are not usually constructed and stored away against the possibility that they will find application on some rainy day. They are developed in response to a need and often against great time pressures. Frequently it happens that models can be used repeatedly to guide routine decisions. An example is the linear program that is used each month to schedule a large paper mill. The original impetus for development of this model, however, was the increasing complexity of the business and the inability of manual schedulers to keep pace. There is no such thing, in the pragmatic world of business, as a model looking for a problem. There are, however, many problems that can be better understood through judicious use of mathematical models.

THE MODELING UNIT

To this point we have developed a set of arguments that presents our viewpoint regarding the *what*, the *when*, and the *why* of mathematical models in business applications. If you are really "with us," you are probably saying to yourself that the authors are, themselves, engaged in developing a "model." You're right! Now we want to deal with the issues of *who* and *how*.

The principal actors in any modeling effort are classified as (1) the manager, (2) the model builder, and (3) the user. Sometimes these three roles are all in one person. Often, the manager is also the user and, in any event, is usually at least an indirect user. It is common also, that different persons or groups of persons occupy each role. And each actor has certain responsibilities if a particular modeling effort is to succeed.

The manager

The impetus for the development of a new model comes from the manager. This is the person who must recognize that *the problem* exists and that conventional methodologies are unlikely to provide a satisfactory resolution. This is also the person who has the most influence over the eventual success or failure of the modeling process. The manager must provide a succinct and accurate statement of *the problem* to the model builder and must also be sensitive to the model builder's understanding of *the problem*. The model builder who retires to the dark recesses of the laboratory with an incorrect (or incomplete) knowledge of *the problem* is likely to fill in the missing details personally and, in the final analysis, provide a great solution to the wrong problem. The burden of satisfactory communication, then, falls on the manager. The manager must be certain that he or she and the model builder are talking the same language and, failing that, should call in a translator.

A second prime responsibility of the manager is to *manage* the modeling project. Mathematical models like PERT charts are often helpful in overseeing modeling projects. As a minimum, project milestones and some sort of reporting system can be quite useful in almost any modeling project. If these managerial tools do nothing else, they help identify weaknesses in the manager's communication with the model builder at the earliest possible stage when it is perhaps not too late to apply a remedy.

Finally, it is the responsibility of the manager to insure that the model builder receives adequate cooperation from other people in the organization. This could be crucial in many instances. For example, if the model builder is to construct a means to automate some portion of, say, the purchasing department, it is likely that at least a segment of that department will regard the model builder with a degree of hostility. If the model builder needs data or information from these same people, one can only wonder about the data quality if the manager does not provide some indication of job security, for instance, to those in the purchasing department.

The model builder

This individual, interchangably called "management scientist" or "analyst," will perform the bulk of the mathematical formulation of the model. The analyst's responsibilities include understanding the manager's charge by asking questions and feeding back the problem statement to the manager until mutual understanding is reached. Typically, the model builder will select the form of the analysis—linear programming, or queuing theory, or simulation, etc.—by consideration of the problem, the information needs of the user, the time and money available to support the project, and so forth. The eventual successful outcome of a modeling effort will depend heavily on the builder's particular training, experiences, and skill.

Often, the model builder is someone from outside the organization, either from a corporate analysis group or a hired consultant. When this is the case, the model builder must guard against much richer opportunities for faulty communication. The model builder must be sensitive to the possibility of organizational jealousy or other interpersonal difficulties that could jeopardize the modeling project. Here, a dimension of diplomacy can be of great value to the model builder. Unfortunately, our limited observation indicates that diplomatic skills are not often mixed with analytic skills in the same individual.

The user

The responsibilities of the user are both simple and complicated. The simple part of the responsibility is that he or she must often provide data to the model builder and that should be accurate, in clear form, and as unambiguous as possible. The user must also be able to communicate with the model builder so that the latter gets a clear idea of the former's information needs. The complicated part of the user's responsibility is that she or he must be the final judge of the modeling effort. As mentioned above, the user's criteria is not something like: Does the model demonstrate its ability to provide an optimal solution to the set of linear inequalities that we use as input? The user is concerned with questions like: Does it help me conduct my affairs? Is it better than the procedure I currently use? Can "my people" read the output format?

The modeling unit

Taken together, these three types of actors—the manager, the model builder, and the user—form an interdependent team called the *modeling unit*. The manager provides impetus, communication, management skill, resources, and a cooperative environment. The model builder must have a commitment to provide a useful solution and the analytic ability to deliver it in a variety of quantitative milieus. The user must cooperate and eventually judge the outcome of the modeling unit's efforts. Responsibility for success or failure is a joint matter among the actors, with the credit or the blame usually divided unequally between them. In a successful modeling effort, however, the modeling unit has been an effective team. In failure, the entire team has failed.

The cases in this book will give you the opportunity to play each of these roles, frequently more than one per case. You should have all three "hats" ready whenever you read one of these cases. We can promise that you will wear each of them more than once.

THE DEVELOPMENT OF MATHEMATICAL MODELS

How does this modeling unit, this interdependent group of people, work to develop a mathematical model that has some degree of usefulness to their organization? There is an extensive body of literature concentrating on the internal functioning of small, task-oriented groups. These studies, while highly relevant, are outside the scope of this discussion, which will center on the interactions of the modeling unit with the outside world.

The process of building models, too, is described in various places in the literature. The essence of this process, however, can be captured in a few steps that occur, more or less in order, in an iterative or repeatable fashion. These steps are called *observation, abstraction, analysis,* and *testing.*

Observation

Observation is the primary interaction that the modeling unit has with its environment—the real world. Through this process the modeling unit first recognizes that a problem or unexplained phenomenon exists. Observation, however, is perhaps the most difficult phase of model development. The process is often random, governed by serendipity, and guided by what appears to be chance. On the other hand, some people have a genuine facility for observation. These people are able to examine the same real world as many others and discern relationships or differences that others miss. An element of creativity, which can be cultivated by practice, is required to see a familiar problem from a new perspective. To do this—to be an able observer—one must discard preconceived notions about a situation and be able to ask penetrating questions. The cases in this book are designed to provide practice in finding problems. Of course, cases are no substitute for experience, but they are better than many alternatives and allow the student to approach a large number of problems in a short period of time. Further, since case situations are likely to be approached differently by different class participants, there is an opportunity to enlarge your repertoire of possible approaches or points of view and judge their appropriateness to the problem type and your own style.

Abstraction

Abstraction is the process of specifying variables and estimating their relationships in a mathematical expression of the essence of a problem. Considerable judgment must be exercised in selecting variables that are both measurable and germane to the end use of the model. Much has been written about the importance of making useful assumptions at this phase of the modeling process. Making assumptions is complementary to abstraction in which extraneous detail is selected to be excluded from the model.

The process of abstraction, then, is deciding which aspects of the real world to mimic with the model and which to ignore. It is by this process that intractable real-world problems are simplified until they can be solved.

Analysis

If you can think of the abstraction process as the setting up of an equation, analysis is the process of solving the equation. Analysis takes place in an imaginary "model world" that is separate and distinct from the real world the model tries to imitate. Here the analyst can forget about the reality represented by the mathematical model and operate on the model as a separate construct until "the answer" is obtained. Here, too, is some danger. The analyst can become enchanted with the mathematical artifact until he or she begins to believe that the model is, in fact, reality instead of an abstract reflection of it. The hazard is that the analyst will become lost in the model world and never quite return to reality. This is only natural. To a management scientist the model world is a neat and orderly place. It is rational and logical. "If only managers were more intelligent," you can almost hear the analyst say, "the real world would then more closely approximate my model." It is clear that this sort of reasoning is absurd. But we can all cite examples of it. The analyst's potential attraction to the model world underscores the importance of the manager and user roles as integral parts of the modeling unit.

Testing

When an analysis is able to provide an answer, for example, a solution to a set of equations, the results need to be validated against the real-world situation the model was intended to represent. This step is one of the most crucial and one of the most neglected in the modeling process. It is in testing that the modeling unit is required to judge the value of the model. Here, questions pertaining to the analytic results are resolved:

Does the model behave as had been expected?

If not, can the surprises be understood?

Is the model "close enough" for our purpose?

Simultaneously, questions regarding the usefulness of the model are asked:

Does the result provide real guidance?

Does it help us understand the problem?

Is the output understandable by the users?

Providing answers to these questions involves a great deal of judgment on the part of the modeling unit, for it is unusual indeed that the testing process provides any clear-cut answers to these questions. After all, because of necessary abstraction, a model is never a perfect representation of reality. Similarly, a model seldom is judged completely useless.

At this point in the analysis, then, after the model's results have been brought back to the real world, the modeling unit can identify important points of difference between the model and the reality it represents. This, of course, is an *observation* and often leads to another cycle through the abstraction and analysis phases. Finally, the new results are tested against the real world and the iterative process of model building is repeated. At each cycle the model can be improved somewhat, made more applicable, able to explain more phenomena, and made more useful to the modeling unit's organization.

One of our students exclaimed, when this entire scheme had been presented, "But you are just giving us a model of the modeling process. I'll bet the *real* modeling process doesn't look like that at all." She was correct. But this model does turn out to be useful in many ways. Even though the *real* modeling process seldom follows the exact sequence described above in a consistent way, all of the steps described above *do*, in fact, occur. Put differently, the essential activities of model development may be classified according to this scheme. Further, this model is a useful aid to understanding what one does when building a model. Finally, it provides the basis for a consistent vocabularly that you, the student, will be able to use throughout this course.

case 1-1

The development of the atomic model*

The now familiar concept of the atom as a tiny planetary system of outer electrons whirling about a central core or nucleus had its beginnings at least as far back as ancient Greece. In Athens, about 420 B.C., Democritus first conceived the idea that there must be some form of tiny, indivisible building blocks of which all matter was composed. He called these building blocks "atoms" or "indivisibles." To the philosopher, this concept of indivisibles is appealing, since it avoids the possibility of being able to divide matter into ever-smaller and smaller particles—*ad infinitum*—an unsound idea at best.

Another Greek, Empedocles, extended the theory of Democritus in order to explain certain natural phenomena. He suggested that there were four different kinds of atoms: earth, air, fire, and water. All matter, according to Empedocles, was composed of these four "elements" in varying proportions. The rusting of iron could then be explained as the substance iron losing some of its fire atoms and returning to a state in which there was a higher proportion of earth atoms.

The teaching of the Greeks persisted, basically unchanged, for over 2,000 years. Through the Middle Ages and the early Renaissance, first the alchemists and then the great early scientists accepted the fact that matter was composed of atoms. The alchemists attempted to add a few more fire atoms to iron or copper so as to turn these base metals into gold. The scientists, Bacon, Descartes, and Newton among them, made no such attempts, to be sure, but they did accept the existence of atoms—primarily on philosophical grounds.

The "earth, air, fire, and water" theory of itself, however, began to collapse. Increasingly sophisticated investigations into the chemical composition of matter were conducted—most importantly, perhaps, by the Frenchman Lavoisier. Iron, for example, was found to *increase* in weight as it rusted—a phenomenon difficult to explain under the Greek theory. If atoms did indeed exist, they must be something other than earth, air, fire, and water.

In 1808 the concept of the atom was markedly advanced when an English chemist, John Dalton, proposed a more comprehensive theory about atoms. Dalton claimed that there existed a great many elements—many more than just earth, air, fire, and water. He claimed that each element (and he considered iron, copper, gold, etc., to be elements) was represented by its own brand of atoms unlike the atoms of any other element. Dalton went on to support his theory by showing that chemical compounds, in general, can be formed from and decomposed to small, simple proportions of the elements they contain. For example, exactly two parts of hydrogen and one part of oxygen form the compound water—H_2O. To Dalton this meant that two *atoms* of hydrogen were joining with one *atom* of oxygen to form a single molecule of water.

Although Dalton's atomic theory certainly helped to explain how various *chemical compounds* were formed, it did not explain how the atoms themselves were formed. It said nothing about *how* atoms of one element differed from those of another. Dalton asserted only that they *were* different and these differences gave rise to different properties (such as different weights, different densities, and different lusters) for each element. Dalton's theory was widely accepted, however, and an international conference was convened in 1860 to agree on the relative weights of all the various atoms. It was almost a century after Dalton's original contribution, however, before anyone suggested what it was that made atoms different from each other.

Michael Faraday laid the foundation for such an investigation as early as 1833 when he discovered that in some way (he didn't know exactly how) atoms had electricity associated with them. J. J. Thomson, an English physicist, determined this relationship a little more precisely in 1897 when he discovered the particle of negative electricity—the electron—and noticed that *all* atoms contained electrons. He then reasoned that, since the atoms themselves had no net electric charge, the electrons must be embedded in a mass of positive electricity, much as stones are embedded in cement to form concrete. As far as the differences between atoms? Quite simple: each type of atom had a characteristic number of electrons which, for the most part, determined its physical properties.

It was not long, then, before Thomson's new theory was even further extended. One of his own colleagues, Ernest Rutherford, who had also been one of Thomson's students, in 1911 made another bold advance in the atomic theory. Rutherford's great discovery stemmed from an experiment he conducted in which he bombarded a thin sheet of material with a stream of rapidly moving atoms. What he expected was that these high-speed atoms would, due to their high energy, pass directly through the thin sheet of material. What he got, however, was a phenomenon known as *scattering*. On passing through the sheet, the bombarding atoms flew off in all directions at all sorts of wide angles. From this, Rutherford reasoned that the individual atoms in the thin sheet were *not* of uniform consistency, as Thomson had suggested, but had dense centers and then thinned out toward their outer edges. Rutherford's experiment can be likened to a customs officer inspecting bales of cotton by firing bullets into them. If the bales of cotton are of uniform density (i.e., they contain no contraband), the bullets will pass directly through. If, however, there are dense centers within the bale (where the contraband is hidden), the bullets will ricochet at odd angles, revealing the contraband. Rutherford then proposed what he called the *nuclear atom* with a dense core or nucleus of positive electricity and a more rarified exterior of negative electricity.

As Rutherford had carried on the work of J. J. Thomson, his teacher, so Rutherford's own work was carried on by Niels Bohr, a Dane who had come to the Cavendish Laboratory to study and work under Rutherford. Starting with Rutherford's nuclear atom, Bohr worked out a detailed scheme of how the negative electricity revolved in exact, mathematical orbits around the positive nucleus, much as the planets of our own solar system revolve around the sun. Bohr's new proposal explained not only the phenomenon of scattering, the existence of electricity within the atoms, and the formation of compounds, but it went on to explain more complicated phenomena such as the formation of x-rays and optical spectra.

It had long been known that an incandescent gas composed of a single element in the pure state emitted light of only certain selected wavelengths. Hydrogen, for example, when incandescent, emits a series of wavelengths of ultraviolet light as follows:

Longest wavelength (λ_2) = 1,215.68 × 10⁻⁸ cm.
Next longest wavelength (λ_3) = 1,025.73 × 10⁻⁸ cm.
Next longest wavelength (λ_4) =   972.54 × 10⁻⁸ cm.
Next longest wavelength (λ_5) =   949.75 × 10⁻⁸ cm.

$$\cdot$$
$$\cdot$$
$$\cdot$$

Shortest wavelength (λ_∞) =   911.76 × 10⁻⁸ cm.

Curiously enough these distinct wavelengths, and no others in that vicinity, were emitted.

Although no one knew *why* such a series should be produced, the empirical evidence of its existence was well established. In fact, through painstaking effort Rydberg, Balmer, Lyman, and others had derived a formula which related the wavelengths of a given series and showed them to be distributed in a quite general pattern:

$$\lambda_n = K\left(\frac{n^2}{n^2 - 1}\right) \qquad n = 2, 3, 4, \ldots$$

where K is simply a constant of proportionality. Despite the existence of this formula, however, no *physical* significance had been proposed for the quantity "n" before Bohr presented his theory.

One of the great advances represented by Bohr's model was that it *did* afford physical significance to the mysterious quantity "n." The various "n's" in the Rydberg formula represented the numbers of the various electron orbits in the atom. When an electron "jumped" from one orbit to another it caused the emission of light energy of one and only one wavelength, which was determined solely by the number of the orbit the electron was "jumping" from and the number of the orbit the electron was "jumping" to. The formula given above, then, can be used to determine *all* of the wavelengths in the series resulting from electron "jumps" from any of the "n" orbits into the first orbit.

Since Bohr's time, of course, the work has continued. The atom has been split and put back together again, the electron microscope has been developed, countless new subatomic particles have been identified. Each researcher has tried to refine the model of the atom a little further so that, with each refinement, some additional natural phenomenon could be more adequately explained.

The development of the accounting model*

Economic record-keeping, at least in its most primitive form, goes back to the earliest civilizations. Babylonians, Assyrians, Egyptians— all have left behind examples of how they recorded their daily commercial transactions. These old economic records, although they are in different languages and even use different number systems, have one striking feature in common. They all use a *single-entry* system, taking note of what is happening to only *one* business resource, usually cash. For example, if a sale or purchase is made, only the cash received or paid out is recorded. In this way the single-entry system keeps track of the inflow and outflow of a single resource, again usually cash, into and out of the business entity.

The single-entry system, if it records only cash, can be called a simple cash model of the business. This simple model, however, has several serious weaknesses. In the first place the simple cash model gives no indication of whether or not the business is making a profit. A net inflow of cash can, in fact, be accompanying a loss if the business is, at the same time, running up its debts or allowing its property to run down through use or neglect. Conversely, a net outflow of cash can be accompanying a profit if the debts of the business are declining or the value of its property is increasing. A second weakness of the simple cash model is that it affords no way of recording anything but cash. Except possibly by the use of memoranda, no records are kept of what other property the business owns or what debts it owes. If, for example, a business should buy some land, the only record of it would be the cash spent. The existence of the land itself would go unrecorded. A third weakness of the simple cash model is that it provides no means of identifying errors. It is impossible to know when a mistake has been made in a long list of cash transactions unsupported by other data. In summary, the simple cash model *does* represent business activity, in that it gives a picture of how cash is flowing into and out of a business. It is, however, a very unsophisticated picture at best.

In the Middle Ages there began a steady expansion of trade and an increased use of "bills of exchange" (a form of promissory note). The simple cash model, under these conditions, became less and less useful as a system of accounting. There simply had to be a better way of keeping track of how the business was doing. Such a better way did, in fact, begin to develop during the 11th or 12th century. Although the exact date of its development cannot be accurately determined, by 1340 the House of Massari in Genoa was doing all of its bookkeeping in a new accounting system—the double-entry system. This new system was thoroughly examined and described, in 1494, in a textbook by an Italian monk, Luca Paciola.

The double-entry accounting model of the firm, as described by Paciola, can be pictured in the form of an equation in which everything of value, including cash, which the business has in its possession is set identically equal to the sum of its debts to its creditors and the equity of its owners. In other words the Assets of a business equal the sum of its Liabilities and the Ownership of the proprietors, or symbolically $A = L + O$. The power of the double-entry system, then, is that it keeps this equation in balance by always adding or subtracting the same thing to or from both sides of the equation or by adding and subtracting equal and opposite things to the same side.

The advantages of this double-entry accounting model over the simple cash model are many indeed. First of all, being based on the principle of exchange, the accounting model provides for *both* aspects of every exchange transaction to be recorded. This keeps track of all financial data relating to those things that the business either owns or owes—not just cash. In the second place, the accounting model provides a constant check on accuracy: the books have to balance. Last, but not least, the accounting model provides a way to measure the size of the ownership in the business and can be used to determine whether this ownership is increasing in size or decreasing in size. In general, the accounting model more accurately reflects what is actually going on in the business. It is a refinement and extension of the simple cash model.

Nor does the accounting model represent the ultimate in the abstract representation of a business entity. The model itself, since Paciola's time, has undergone many additional refinements. Methods of allowing for decreases in asset values, other than as a result of exchange transactions (e.g., depreciation) and methods of evaluating inventories, among other things, have been importantly changed in recent years and, in fact, continue and will continue to be changed as time goes on.

Bud Mathaisel

In October 1970 Bernard "Bud" Mathaisel, 26, was reminiscing with the case writer about his 3½ year career as a user of operations research in the airline industry and was discussing the possibility of a job change. A graduate of MIT, he had both a B.S. in aeronautical design (1966) and a M.S. in flight transportation (1967). His experience in airline operations research had been with American Airlines and more recently with Northeast Airlines.

"My ideas about the role of operations research and the operations researcher in management have changed a lot in my 3½ years of experience," he began. "While I am a strong believer in the power of operations research, properly applied, I can now see why management has a healthy suspicion about the techniques. However, I don't think my remarks will mean much unless I put them into perspective by giving you a little bit of my background.

A START IN AERONAUTICAL ENGINEERING

"I would never be where I am today were it not for a lifelong interest in airplanes and a bent for mathematics. When I was a kid I spent many an afternoon and weekend hanging around Logan Airport watching airline movements. My brother and I even used to stand on the observation deck with schedules and figure out the destinations of planes that were taking off.

"I suppose my interest in mathematics was linked to the fact that you could solve a problem logically and get one right answer. Although I have always had an interest in liberal arts, I was constantly frustrated in high school when my English teachers told me that my particular interpretation of Shakespeare wasn't one that they wanted.

"The prospect of working with airplanes kept me going through an extremely difficult freshman year at MIT. I guess the MIT practice of having examinations every Friday during the freshman year is well known. After freshman year I majored in aeronautical design, which nicely combined my interest in airplanes and math. I wallowed in equations; it was great!

"The beginning of my junior year marked the first turning point in my career. I had learned that by going to school for two summers I could enter a co-op program run by the Aeronautical Engineering Department and spend a full term in a job as an aeronautical engineer. It was with great excitement that I left to spend five months working in the DC-9 program at Douglas Aircraft Corporation in Long Beach, California. I was assigned to the Aeronautics Performance Department whose responsibility was to produce a flying DC-9.

"Personally, I was responsible for determining the second segment climb gradient for the aircraft at various airports. This consisted essentially of determining the rate of climb for the aircraft which depended upon the altitude of the airport, the air temperature, and many other considerations. The job was so repetitive that forms had been prepared for it and a procedure worked out such that all you had to do was to plot a curve based on several hours of calculator work using the characteristics of a particular airport.

"Frankly, it was boring, menial work. The only thing that kept me going was relating to the physical project. I used to spend several hours per week wandering around in the hangar where they were assembling the prototype DC-9.

"It was brought to my attention several times in conversations with my boss that I had been noticed wandering around the flight assembly line. Finally, as a result of wanderings of myself and other similarly interested engineers, the security people made the area a restricted one and I could no longer have the pleasure of association with the project. The final blow came when I locked myself inadvertently on the roof of a nearby building where I was to witness the roll-out ceremony of the new aircraft. The security people really gave me a tough time.

"The overall experience really concerned me. Fortunately, I had the perspective that came from knowing that I would be leaving in a few months. I developed a feeling that if I became an aeronautical engineer I would have to do such menial work all my life. I saw people around me who had been doing this for years and whose main claim to recognition was based on seniority. So concerned was I that I wrote a memorandum to the director of personnel; unfortunately, the memo 'leaked' and next thing I knew a Xerox copy of the memo appeared on the bulletin board with the words 'menial labor' and 'seniority' circled. Needless to say it ruffled my boss and fellow employees a great deal.

"Leading up to the work-study experience, I had been excited about the use of math in aeronautical design. I could look at the wing of an airplane and see equations skipping through my head. But I really didn't get to write many equations at Douglas—the calculation procedure had been all worked out. Besides, after two years of engineering school, the excitement begins to wear off.

A SHIFT TO FLIGHT TRANSPORTATION

"I had to report to Professor René Miller at MIT when I returned from the work-study program. I was ready to quit aeronautical engineering. Professor Miller introduced me to Bob Simpson who was then a graduate student in flight transportation. Flight transportation was an interdisciplinary program involving the Sloan School of Management, the School of Aeronautical Engineering, and other departments at MIT and it took a technical systems approach to air travel. It was essentially MIT's version of what a well-educated airline manager should know. Simpson and I worked out a program that would prepare me for graduate work in flight transportation. At that time I saw myself heading towards a career in airline management and wanted to apply my engineering background to the user end as opposed to the manufacturing end of the industry.

"I spent the summer between graduation from the bachelor's program and entry into the master's program working for Swissair in Switzerland. My work capitalized on my knowledge of the DC-9 gained at Douglas and involved determining performance characteristics of the DC-9 at various airports where Swissair was contemplating using the aircraft. As before, the work was routine, but it did get me to Europe for the summer. I took advantage of my position on the Continent and the airline passes that came with my job to visit the operations research departments of almost every major trunk airline in Western Europe. I wanted to find a thesis topic on a problem which was of concern to them. What I was originally thinking about, computerized flight planning across the North Atlantic, I found was essentially solved. I found that what was plaguing them was flight and crew scheduling.

"Upon returning to MIT, I settled on a thesis project in aircraft scheduling. My thesis topic was 'An Out-of-Kilter Approach to Multi-Commodity Aircraft Scheduling.' It was essentially an integer-linear programming, network algorithm applied to scheduling a fleet with many types of aircraft. When I graduated, I had compiled a grade point average of 4.8 out of a possible 5.

WORKING FOR AMERICAN AIRLINES

"As I was writing my thesis I learned of a career seminar in New York sponsored by American Airlines. I had heard good things about American as an employer and as a progressive airline so I decided to invest the $22 in plane fare to go to the conference. Its purpose was to introduce college students, who might be ignorant of the workings of an airline, to various phases of its operation to help them determine whether they would like a career working for American. Every major function of the airline had a representative there.

"I had an interview with the director of corporate planning who was beginning to form a technical long-range planning group to work on long-range planning in equipment and technology. This was an opportunity to apply my engineering background to airline management. As a result of this preliminary interview I returned to New York for more extensive interviews with the assistant vice president—technical planning, who made me a job offer.

"Not only was the particular job of interest but also American had a program which would allow me to spend six months learning all about the line. I know such management training programs frequently are looked upon with skepticism by students, but in this case I looked upon it as a golden opportunity to round out my technical background.

"When I joined American, I entered the training program and found it most worthwhile. A group of about 20 of us went through it and we really got an exposure to the company. We spent the first day with the president and chairman of the board and the second day with the various executive vice presidents. We took various field trips including ones to the Tulsa maintenance base and to the corporate data processing facilities. A two-week field trip was arranged for another trainee and myself to Los Angeles. There, we spent days and nights watching behind-the-scenes operations firsthand.

"While I was in the management training program I was reporting simultaneously to my new boss, so that I could keep abreast of the projects and be in a better position to dig in once the management training program ended. As the program came to a close, the Boeing 747 was a big airline issue. This aircraft would have an enormous physical impact on an airline, since it was different from anything in the existing fleet. For example, all of the airport facilities had to be modified for use with this huge aircraft; new loading gates, ground handling equipment, lounges, etc., had to be constructed or made available. In addition, new procedures had to be developed for pilots, gate agents, ground handlers, maintenance personnel, and stewardesses; new manuals had to be written, training programs implemented, etc.

"My boss was concerned that all these activities be coordinated so that when the first 747 was delivered, American would be ready for it. This phasing-in program was important both dollar-wise and publicity-wise. I was delighted when my boss put me in charge of it. He told me that we could get the computer group to handle the nitty-gritty and that I had other technical support available to me. I saw the problem as 'can we get PERT to work for us?' I had read a great deal about PERT and it seemed inherently logical. I wondered how the Polaris Submarine could ever have been designed and built without PERT. It seemed obvious that PERT was applicable to my problem.

"I thought to myself, 'this is a real opportunity to show my supervisor what I can do. I have an important job, a good approach to deal with it, people available to help me, and the authority to call meetings.' My boss's boss, a vice president, called the other VPs together in the board room and gave a big speech about the project. He then introduced me as the man in charge and asked for their support. I got up and gave a speech about my information requirements. I used as an example the purchase of a tow tractor for a 747 and used a GANTT chart to illustrate what was required to assure that it would be in place when needed. I ask everyone for their suggestions about my program and, receiving none, I asked everyone to set priorities among their personnel to support the activity.

"There was a wide gulf between the cooperative spirit evident in the board room and the actual implementation. The biggest problem was to get each management group to take time to supply the needed information. They had to explain their jobs to me so I could coordinate it with others. Although some cooperated fully, most gave only their half-hearted support and some wouldn't help at all. I kept plugging away and periodically published a detailed list of people who were behind. One of the problems was that I had very little authority myself and whenever I wanted to exert any pressure I had to go through my boss to his boss and then back down through the other fellow's boss, a long chain of command.

"After a while I began to discover that I wasn't in the mainstream. The decisions were being made without me and the plane was basically on schedule even though my PERT plan was not. I was just getting in the way and slowing things down. I never found out how my boss felt about it, but personally I think the whole project was unsuccessful. It took me a long time to realize this. However, I must have realized this subconsciously, because I became less and less enthusiastic about it and did a less and less proper job. I began to find diversionary jobs and new programs to work on so that gradually I became 'too busy' to carry out the PERT steps. Some vestige of the PERT project did remain until the very end, however.

"As time went on I looked back at the project and asked myself, 'How come it worked for the Polaris but didn't work here?' I concluded that American was an organization that was a closely knit working group and didn't need an outside force for coordination. Each individual knew who to get information from at critical times and who to feed it to. I had just designed a big system to do what each individual would have done as a normal part of his job process. The Polaris project, on the other hand, needed coordination essentially because different contractors in widespread geographical locations needed some efficient communication device. I suppose people didn't want to cooperate with me because I would slow them down, I wasn't needed, and perhaps I might have been a threat to their job security. Besides, I was just a young kid that had to learn about each of their jobs; I suppose the psychology of their reaction was like the reaction to a young guy wielding a bullwhip over them and then asking how do you crack this thing anyway?

"As a result of this perceived failure, I reverted back into engineering. I became an authority on vertical and short takeoff and landing aircraft (V/STOL) and worked on air bus selection. These were both engineering-type decisions.

"Toward the end of my career at American Airlines I drifted back into more management-oriented issues. A Harvard Business School alumnus, affiliated with the group, attended an HBS Alumni Association seminar and came back all fired up about time-sharing computing. As a result we got a time-sharing terminal and I reintroduced myself to this capability which I had used to some extent when I was an engineering student at MIT.

"It was with this tool that I built a simple financial profit and loss model to investigate whether it was economically advisable to convert the Lockheed Electras, currently in American's fleet, into cargo aircraft. The initial reasoning was that for many types of cargo it didn't matter that these planes were about 100 miles an hour slower than the pure jets, and it was thought that it would be cheaper to move cargo using them. My analysis took into account scheduling problems, conversion costs, operating costs, and the cost of taking these planes out of the current passenger fleet. Management acted on my recommendation and decided against the conversion.

"I also used time-sharing to analyze what American could afford to pay for leasing a 747 in order to have the plane in its fleet earlier than if it waited for the first plane to arrive from Boeing. The analysis had to take into account that the 747 would be displacing 707s currently in the fleet and would entail early crew training and early delivery of support equipment. Again, my recommendations were followed. I hadn't really thought about it until now, but I suppose that my assignment to this particular project was based upon my familiarity with the introduction of the 747 obtained through the PERT project; I was probably one of the few people in that department who knew about what it took to get the 747 into service sooner.

WORKING FOR NORTHEAST AIRLINES

"I was brought into Northeast Airlines in the early fall of 1968 as a senior analyst in corporate planning, by Robert Griffin, vice president of corporate planning. He had worked in the Planning Department of American Airlines but had left prior to my time at American. He was interested in my knowledge in V/STOL aircraft and my operations research background.

"I was attracted to Northeast by the prospect of returning to my native Boston and by the prospect of working with a group of bright, young, ambitious people who were really set on making the line go. Northeast had shown substantial growth in the previous several years.

"My first assignment was in V/STOL aircraft. Subsequently I became more and more involved in the application of modeling to marketing and operations problems. I was later promoted to manager of schedule planning and finally to director of operations planning.

"One incident that I particularly remember early in my days at Northeast was the hazing that I got from an individual who also worked in planning. I am not sure of the reason for his actions, although I know he thought I was brash for my age. It also might have been due in part to the management faction with which I seemed to be identified or to the type of analysis that I was noted for doing. At any rate, I was doing an incremental analysis of a problem and I was sent to him for some cost data. His response was that he didn't have the data—I should go and get them from a man he named in another department. When the man in the other department told me that the original fellow had the data, I came back to him and he acted a little surprised. 'So that's what you want,' he said. He dug out some data and handed them to me and trusting him fully, I used it in my analysis. After I filed my report, I learned that its conclusions were wrong. I subsequently found out that he had given me allocated cost data when I had clearly asked for incremental data. This man was experienced in airline costing and its use, and I later learned from my boss that he had given me the wrong data intentionally.

"When I realized the trick and the reason for it I was quick to change some of my behavior. Eventually I found that some of the group originally hostile to me were being much more sociable.

"I owe a lot of my ultimate success at Northeast to my familiarity with time-sharing. Because of my capabilities in modeling on a time-sharing system I was able to make myself useful to managers who had little computer background. My basic approach was to help the manager to do his job more quickly and thoroughly than he could manually. I always explained that a model was no more than a numerical representation of what he did anyway and tried to avoid a lot of technical language. Perhaps you could say that much of my approach was getting him to use a computer to help himself rather than to be dependent on me or other analysts.

"Using time-sharing, I got a lot more cooperation from management than I did with batch processing. Because the 'instant' feedback made it clearer that using models was simply an extension of their way of thinking, they had a tendency to get more personally involved in the modeling effort. Involvement meant understanding and commitment.

I don't think management will easily accept results that come from a 'black box' and are to be taken on faith.

"I have observed an interesting phenomenon, however. There seem to be two sorts of users. Both will work with me side by side in the development of the model, but while one will actually sit at the terminal and use a developed model, the other will always want me to interact with the terminal. He'll even look over my shoulder while I sit at the terminal, but he won't use the terminal, no matter what I do to try to convince him that it's easy and that the programs are foolproof.

"My modeling/time-sharing capability increased my visibility to senior management, to a level unusual for someone my age, I was frequently involved in helping them to solve their problems. I have even been in on a number of top-level staff meetings.

"Strange as it may seem, the same fellow who fed me the wrong data was responsible for giving my modeling 'business' the biggest boost. He was in charge of preparing an operating plan which was a statistical base for cost forecasting prepared with long-range (five-year) schedules. Given a proposed schedule, he was responsible for calculating the hours flown, number of departures, miles flown, etc., and all associated costs. It was a two-man-week project to produce one operating plan for a given schedule, using a desk calculator.

"On one particular occasion after he had prepared an operating plan, some very basic assumptions used in the plan were changed twice. By now, he had completed the plan for the third time and was wary of going through the manual calculations again. I wasn't very busy so I was assigned to help him out. I can't remember how I raised it with him, but I told him that while I was capable of pushing through the figures on a desk calculator, I really didn't want to do it that way. It was then that I proposed writing a computer program to do the job. I had it running on a preliminary basis in three days, and he was surprised that I could produce a working program in such a short period of time. However, he was still skeptical until he laid the hand-calculated results down side by side with mine and saw that there was agreement. He really became a believer when the schedule was subsequently changed again for a fourth time and I produced the new operating plan for him in a day. His next reaction was 'Now can I have more?'; he began to ask whether the program could be expanded to produce additional data such as airport activity lists, etc. When I produced this material for him, he really spread the word and there was soon a line at my door asking for my services.

"I learned from that experience that you can't artificially induce an environment that creates a demand for models. You really have to move in at the right moment where there is a need. This particular fellow was weary and desperate. Just a few weeks before I had sent a fellow in my department to school to learn how to interact with a computer system, but it didn't work. He was really an artist, not a technician, and he would say, 'My work is a product of my imagination and experience. No machine could do my work for me.'

BACKWARD REFLECTIONS

"Maybe I wasn't really listening in class when I earned that high grade point average at MIT, or maybe there was a weakness in my education, but I really wasn't well equipped to handle real problems when I graduated. What I meant when I said I understood PERT back at American Airlines was that I could take network representation of a problem, get the cards punched, and get computer results. What I didn't know (and I didn't know at the time that I didn't know) was how to represent a real problem as a diagram. I'm afraid that this is the problem with engineering types in general. They come equipped with fancy technical tools, slide rules, calculus, physics, and chemistry, but to confront a real-world problem and model it usefully is a horse of a different color.

"It would have been desirable to have a part of my education on problems looking for equations, rather than equations looking for problems, as is traditionally taught. If you took the brightest guy in linear programming and turned him loose in crew scheduling, 10 to 1 he'd produce a model, but it won't solve the real problem. If you could take an expert in crew scheduling and teach him mathematical programming, you'd really get a solution.

"I think that the hardest part of being a model maker is getting management to define the problem in analytic terms. You can design a model to do just about anything once you understand what he wants. Many requests are based on misunderstanding or on the PR value of using the computer. I have to determine whether there is a legitimate need for a model.

"For example, the 'in' thing today is management information systems. I have been asked three or four times in the last year for a management information system by people who haven't the slightest idea what they want or what one is. Once you talk to them you find that some think it's an elaborate information-gathering system and others think it's a simulation model. More often than not, what they really want is for the computer to generate a report for them regularly—say, quarterly.

"I hope I don't sound like I'm trying to be the supreme wizard in these remarks. I was brash and cocky when I started and I've mellowed a lot. I'm still learning, but I probably won't be fully mellowed by the time I retire.

THE JOB OFFERS

"I face a difficult decision in the next couple of weeks as a result of the potential acquisition of Northeast by Northwest Airlines. I have to decide whether to stick it out at Northeast or accept one of three job offers that I now have. I guess I am pretty lucky to have so many attractive possibilities in spite of a weak job market in this difficult period for airlines, but still I am not looking forward to making the decision. Besides staying at Northeast I have offers from a smaller airline on the West Coast, a large international carrier based in New York City, and a consulting firm near Boston specializing in transportation.

"This difficult choice culminates a three-month search that started by contacting the MIT Placement Office and responding to some *Wall Street Journal* ads. The interviews and the several offers that resulted got me thinking about my career objectives and better prepared to handle the job decision. One of the offers I declined was doing airlines work for an established consulting firm; the offer was accompanied by a big pep talk about future prospects. Then, a few weeks ago, I got a call from the fellow who made me the offer asking whether *I* knew of any job openings—he was out of a job due to a cutback. Needless to say, that experience makes me somewhat nervous.

"Regarding the choices I face now, let me start with Northeast. I have been very fortunate in my very rapid rise in that organization; although I was initially unsure of taking on an administrative position, it has worked out well. The people for whom I work have been very good to me, and the people who work for me are great. I have been given a real opportunity to prove myself and I have won the confidence of top management as a respected logician in the analysis of their problems. I don't have to push the numbers myself, but I'm the one who interprets them for management. As an example of their confidence and trust, my advice is sometimes sought on matters entirely outside my area of expertise. Further my salary has increased 140 percent in the last year. (Before you get too excited about that, I should say that the starting point was low.) As a result I feel a strong personal commitment to these people who have given me a chance; to leave Northeast at this time would be copping out on them.

"But frankly, I am nervous about the future. I have been told that my area of expertise would be needed at Northwest. I'm sure that my 'sponsors' at Northeast would continue to support me, but there is no assurance that they will be kept. Unfortunately, there's also a prospect that if I was kept by Northwest, I would get moved out of the Boston area.

"My contact with the small carrier on the West Coast came through two people whom I had known and respected at Northeast. The first is an older man who had been with Northeast for many years, had once been in a job very similar to the one I now have, and had left just before I joined Northeast. We had met subsequently and we knew one another by reputation. He had a position of considerable responsibility at the small carrier. The second fellow was a Harvard Business School grad who joined Northeast six to eight months after me and became a good friend of mine. He joined the West Coast carrier about four months ago and after getting established there, he gave me a call to see if I would be interested in several opportunities which came to his attention.

At his request I sent a resume and soon he called to invite me out for an interview. The opportunities, each of which had at least a slight operations research orientation, fell into scheduling, market planning, and operations. I talked to two vice presidents and the general manager while I was there, and the vice president–operations made me an on-the-spot offer. I would be his assistant and my responsibilities would include establishing and programming an action plan for the Operations Department and doing special projects for him. He asked what I was making at Northeast and then said apologetically, 'Unfortunately our Personnel Department has our positions pretty well cut out. We can't offer that much, but I can throw in a car.' I'm told, however, that these people pay well once you are established.

"There's a lot to be said for working for a developing carrier versus one with an uncertain future, and I liked the people I met there. It seemed to me that many of the things that I'm capable of doing had not yet been done, and the carrier was small enough that anything I would do would be quickly visible. The small size also meant more opportunity for real responsibility than I would get with a larger carrier and less competition for promotion. Of course, the West Coast location would be ideal.

"However, while I have a good relationship with and feel compatible with others in the organization, I don't know my potential boss as well, which makes me uneasy. Also I am leery about any 'assistant to' job. It seems that it would entail no managerial responsibility, but rather would be strictly staff. There would be no one working for me.

"At the international carrier, there is a large contingent of former bosses and colleagues of mine from Northeast. I received two or three inquiries from them and there was no formality of sending a resume. Instead it was a case of come-down-and-we'll-show-you-around!

"The job that I am offered is very, very intriguing—a real plum. If I had to choose the one job that I would most like at this point in my career, it would be this one. They want me to be manager of schedule development for the Pacific Region, with very good immediate promotion prospects. The people with whom I would be working are just the type that I enjoy: intelligent, respected in the industry, and personable. The salary offer is very competitive, about a 15 percent increase over my present one.

"But there is another side to the story, too, revolving around the size of the carrier and its location. I saw plenty of talented, ambitious, career-minded young people in the ranks of the organization, and it seems that it would be tougher for me as a young technician to work into higher management. Further, the location in New York is a distinct disadvantage. I had worked in New York once before and neither my wife nor I enjoyed it. I don't relish the thought of spending 3½ to 4 hours a day commuting and seldom seeing my wife and son except on weekends.

"The final offer I have is from a small consulting firm specializing in transportation. I had become acquainted with a young Harvard Business School graduate who had left a large consulting group to form a consulting firm with several others. I would work in his group and fill a gap as an airline expert, based on my experience using operations research in the airline industry. The group strikes me as extremely bright, capable, and aspiring—having all the qualifications necessary to achieve its goals. The location, in Boston, is attractive and so is the salary. Furthermore, I would also have the opportunity to do work outside airlines in the transportation industry, and perhaps, longer run, outside transportation. It seems that the firm has realistic plans for superdiversification, which provides all sorts of opportunities to younger members of the firm. Finally, the prospect of joining a newly organized, growing firm is a real opportunity to get in on the ground floor.

"I am really torn by this opportunity. Here is a real chance to diversify my career instead of being cloistered in one airline, and an opportunity to work with top-level management in many corporations. It is also a chance to become more versed in economic and financial criteria, such as cash flows, which I had not previously used in airline industry analysis. (Most of the decisions were based upon developing operating profit and loss statements for the decision at hand.)

"On the other hand, I had started to develop what seemed to be a very successful career in airlines and I would be leaving airplanes which I like so much. Should I diversify or should I stay with the airline industry? I wonder, too, at age 26, if I will have that much credibility to top management in a consulting capacity and I am wondering whether I should get more experience before I try to become a 'wise counsel.' There is little doubt in my mind that someday I would like to be in top management in the airline industry, and I am not sure entering consulting would help me or hinder me in this ambition.

There's also my preference, mentioned earlier, for line-oriented responsibility, mixed with analysis, and I'm not sure I'll find it in consulting.

"You know, there's an interesting thing that I've observed in my job-hunting. Only once in my career has an interesting job opportunity not come from personal contact. Each of the three offers and my current job all came to my attention from personal sources. All recent opportunities that came about due to other sources have not proved interesting."

Cost analysis

The word *cost* is a ubiquitous one in our language. In business usage, we speak of the cost of inventories or of equipment used for production, the cost of goods sold, the cost of operating the machining department, or the cost of making a certain part in-plant rather than purchasing it from outside.

The possibilities for confusion are compounded because the word *cost* is used in different ways by accountants and economists. Members of both these professions would agree on the most general definition of cost: a measure, usually in monetary terms, of the resources consumed in achieving a given objective.

The difference between the accountant's and the economist's concepts of cost involves the different principles they use to value the resources consumed. Accountants generally use the concept of *acquisition cost*, by which they mean the amount of cash or other financial resource that was originally paid out by the enterprise when it acquired the resource in question. Accountants, therefore, are basically historians, reporting on the results of past events.

Economists, on the other hand, measure resources in terms of their *opportunity cost*. By this they mean the return the resources would bring if they had instead been devoted to the best alternative opportunity. Economists have traditionally been interested in the optimal allocation of resources, which involves the decision-making function. No decision made today can affect what has already happened. Hence the costs economists consider relevant are *future* costs rather than the historical costs compiled by accountants.

Opportunity cost may be either greater or less than acquisition cost. Suppose, for example, that a firm is considering the production of an item that would require the use of material on hand for which $100 was originally paid; the acquisition cost, then, is $100. If the material could currently be sold on the market for $125, however, its opportunity cost must be $125, because the use of the material requires the firm to forgo the opportunity of receiving $125. If, on the other hand, the material currently has no market value or alternative use, its opportunity cost is zero.

The manager lives with both these concepts of cost. For decision-making purposes, the economist's concept of opportunity cost is appropriate; a rational decision must involve the comparison of alternative future courses of action. The accountant's role as a "scorekeeper" for outside investors is also important to the manager. Moreover, accounting records are often a primary source of information for decision-making purposes. For these reasons, it is important to understand both the differences and the similarities in the two approaches.

CLASSIFICATION OF COSTS

In order to sharpen our discussion of costs relevant for business decisions, we will first indicate two ways in which costs can be classified—by product identification and by variability.

By product identification

One way to classify costs, which is quite familiar to accountants, is by the degree to which the resources consumed in generating revenue can be identified with specific units of product. Under this scheme, total costs are divided into two classifications; *prime costs* and *overhead costs.*

Prime costs represent those that are supposedly identifiable with specific units of end product. These costs include *direct material* and *direct labor,* both of which are directly dependent on the products in such a way that it is possible to say that specific units of resource *input* were consumed in producing specific units of product *output.*

Overhead costs represent general support activities that are not directly identifiable with specific units of product. Overhead, in turn, is commonly classified further into three subclasses: factory overhead, selling expense, and general and administrative expense.

The distinction between prime costs and overhead costs is to some extent a matter of convenience. Some overhead costs could no doubt be directly identifiable with specific units of product given sufficient effort on the part of the accountant. The inclusion of such costs within the classification of overhead generally results from a determination that greater precision would require more effort than it is worth.

By variability

This second basis of classification is quite similar to the first. It also divides costs into two categories, this time depending on whether or not the total amount of cost incurred in a period of time varies with the quantity of product produced during that period.

FIGURE 2–1
Cost variability with volume

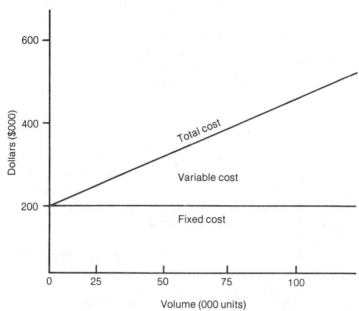

Direct costs, often called variable costs, are those costs whose total *does* vary. Direct costs generally include prime costs, as defined above, and also *direct overhead,* that portion of overhead costs that varies with the quantity of production.

The other category of cost is called *period cost.* These costs are so named because they are assumed to be constant relative to the quantity of production and hence can be expressed as so much "per period." Period costs are also often called *fixed costs.*

It is often assumed in practice that direct costs vary in direct proportion to production, which implies that the *average* direct cost per unit of production is the same regardless of the level of production. (In economic terms, marginal variable cost equals average variable cost at all levels of production.) This assumption, while not necessarily true under all circumstances, often turns out to be a satisfactory empirical approximation. When it is true, direct cost is a linear function of the quantity of production, as illustrated in Figure 2–1.

RELEVANT COST

These different cost classification schemes pose particular problems for managers or analysts who are formulating a model of a business situation. Which costs should be included in the model and which simply obscure the real issues they would like to deal with? The problem is rather like the old Mother Goose riddle:

> As I was going to Saint Ives
> I met a man with seven wives.
> Every wife had seven sacks.
> Every sack had seven cats.
> Every cat had seven kits.
> Kits, cats, sacks, wives;
> How many were going to Saint Ives?

If we are guided by the riddle's question, we can quickly and correctly answer one. In the same way, we can determine which costs or other factors are important to a particular model by concentrating on the purpose or intended use of that model. By excluding from consideration factors or costs that are not influenced by a manager's decision, an analysis may be considerably simplified.

In other words, only costs that are relevant to a particular managerial decision need be analyzed. This sounds simple, but since an important source of cost information is the firm's accounting records, which are basically historical documents, and since management action can influence only the future, some adjustments to accounting data are often needed to make them useful for management purposes. There are two closely related concepts that are helpful in this task: sunk cost and contribution margin.

Sunk cost

A sunk cost, by definition, is an unrecoverable past expense. Since management action cannot affect the past, sunk costs may be safely ignored in a managerial analysis. They will be included, to be sure, in any accounting record that seeks to determine the overall profitability of a business venture. That is not the aim of this course, however. Here we are concerned with managerial activities that have influence only on the future. Therefore, we need not confound and complicate our analytic work by trying to simultaneously generate a historical record.

Contribution margin

The most fundamental concept used to analyze relevant costs is the concept of *contribution to overhead and profit*. Consider, as a simple example, the following income statement for the Clinton Company in 1978:

Net sales	$500,000
Cost of goods sold	300,000
Gross manufacturing profit	$200,000
Selling, general, and administrative expenses	100,000
Net profit before taxes	$100,000

The Clinton Company manufactured only one product, and in 1978, it sold 100,000 units at a price of $5 each. For a single-product company such as this, the historical price and volume factors in the profitability equation may be relatively easy to establish. The cost factors, however, may require further analysis. The fact that the cost of goods sold was $3 per unit is not pertinent to our analysis because it reflects the combined effect of the total manufacturing costs for the year and the volume produced and sold. Some of these costs were incurred in order to create and maintain the company's production capacity; at different volume levels, the total cost per unit would reflect the spreading of these relatively fixed costs over a greater or lesser number of units. Let us assume that an analysis of the $300,000 of manufacturing costs reveals that $175,000 was spent for direct labor and materials, and $125,000 was for supervision, property taxes, insurance, and other fixed costs. A similar analysis of selling, general, and administrative expenses discloses that sales commissions of 10 percent of the selling price is the only item of demand-creating cost that is variable directly with the quantity sold. Thus, average variable costs at the 1978 volume were $2.25 per unit ($1.75 manufacturing cost and $0.50 sales commissions).

The difference between price and average variable cost is called *contribution per unit*. The average contribution earned on each unit sold by the Clinton Company in 1978, for example, was $5.00 − $2.25 = $2.75. The word *contribution* is intended to suggest that the price of each unit sold, after first being applied to cover its variable costs, is able to "contribute" to a pool of funds out of which the company's fixed costs will be met. Any residual in this pool of funds after payment of fixed costs then becomes the company's profit.

The concept of contribution may be illustrated by recasting the Clinton Company's income statement in the following instructive way:

Contribution to fixed overhead and profit:		
Selling price per unit	$5.00	
Average variable cost per unit	2.25	
Contribution per unit	$2.75	
Total contribution on 100,000 units		$275,000
Less: Fixed overhead		175,000
Net profit		$100,000

The simple concept of contribution to overhead and profit is a powerful analytic tool. Suppose, for example, that the management of the Clinton Company wished to explore the effect of reducing the price on its product from $5.00 to $4.50, an action that it expected might increase the sales volume to 125,000 units. A rough calculation of the effect of this change takes less than a minute:

Contribution at a price of $4.50:
Selling price per unit		$4.50
Variable costs per unit:		
Manufacturing	$1.75	
Sales commission, 10 percent	0.45	2.20
Contribution per unit		$2.30
Total contribution on 125,000 units		$287,500

Comparing this calculation with the preceding one, we see that the contribution to overhead and profit is $12,500 higher than it was at the $5.00 price; the price reduction would be a profitable one if 125,000 units could be sold. The value of the contribution concept lies in its efficiency as a calculating procedure; it is neither more nor less accurate than the estimates of cost variability on which it rests. But it is more efficient, as illustrated by the longer, more traditional accounting calculation shown in Table 2–1, which is based on the same estimates of cost and volume and, inevitably, arrives at the same conclusion.

A key factor in the decision to exclude fixed costs from your analysis (i.e., to use contribution margin rather than profit) is the nature of the

TABLE 2–1

CLINTON COMPANY
Evaluating the effect of a price decrease

	100,000 units at $5.00 price	125,000 units at $4.50 price
Net sales	$500,000	$562,500
Cost of goods sold:		
Variable costs @ $1.75.........................	$175,000	$218,750
Fixed factory overhead	125,000	125,000
Total cost of sales	$300,000	$343,750
Gross manufacturing profit	$200,000	$218,750
Selling, general, and administrative expenses:		
Sales commissions, 10 percent	$ 50,000	$ 56,250
Other fixed overhead	50,000	50,000
Total selling, general, and administrative expenses	$100,000	$106,250
Net profit before taxes	$100,000	$112,500

managerial action your analysis is intended to support. In general, one might observe that some decisions have mainly short-run implications. Short-run decisions tend not to have a major impact on the overall level of fixed cost of a firm, although they may affect the accountant's *allocation* of that fixed cost to specific units of output. Since by definition these fixed costs are not directly identified with any specific item, however, the accountant's allocation of these costs is often highly artificial. This allocation is to allow an estimate of the overall profitability of that item or unit of output. If short-run changes take place, as in the example of the Clinton Company above, the per-unit allocation of fixed costs will also change. But, since the *total amount* of fixed costs has not been affected by the short-run change, the analysis *for a manager's purpose* need not consider the allocation (or reallocation) of fixed cost.

The cases in this chapter will provide some practice in building and analyzing a few simple models in which recognizing the costs relevant to the specific management situation can considerably simplify the analysis. In approaching these cases as well as cases in ensuing chapters, be mindful of the need to identify and carefully examine the managerial need that the analysis is meant to fill. Doing this will help you to identify the crucial factors, as with the riddle of Saint Ives, and avoid much needless computational complexity.

case 2–1

Analysis of a limited operation*

BACKGROUND

William Allenson was 31 years old. He had worked for the past 13 years, since his graduation from vocational school, for a major manufacturer of household appliances in the U.S. Midwest. Starting as a maintenance technician, he had risen to his present post of manager of one of the company's assembly areas.

Although Allenson was quite happy with his present position and found that he could comfortably support his family of four on his sal-

---

ary, he saw little opportunity in the company for further advancement. In addition to what he conceived as a limited opportunity, Allenson had also long entertained the idea of going into business for himself. Thus far, however, although he felt he had adequate savings to both protect his family and support a business venture, he had not come upon a sufficiently interesting scheme. His present idea of becoming a supplier to the company he now worked for was the first such scheme that seemed to offer real promise.

A NEW ASSEMBLY TECHNIQUE

In the course of his job in the assembly area, Allenson had conceived of an idea that would increase productivity in one section of his area by 30 percent. The idea centered on a special fixture that he had designed and that would greatly facilitate the assembly of one particular part.

After he had carefully considered his original idea and perfected the design of the fixture, Allenson had suggested that the company's Industrial Engineering Department fabricate some sample fixtures and try the idea out in the assembly area. The Industrial Engineering Department, however, after reviewing the design of the fixture, was of the opinion that savings of the magnitude claimed by Allenson would not be forthcoming. They rejected the design and requested the Assembly Department to retain the present assembly procedures.

Allenson remained convinced that his new fixture would offer considerable savings. He went so far as to construct a wooden model of the fixture and to give it a preliminary trial. In Allenson's eyes the trial was a complete success. The industrial engineers remained unconvinced.

Feeling that the industrial engineers were rejecting his design merely because they hadn't thought of it themselves, it was at this point that Allenson began to consider supplying the company with assemblies for his own profit.

PRELIMINARY ANALYSIS

Allenson's first inquiries were made at a commercial tool and die shop. The shop told him that they would make the fixtures for him, guaranteed to perform to his specifications, for $400 each—provided he ordered at least ten fixtures. Allenson thought this price to be reasonable and, since his savings could cover such an investment, resolved to carry his investigation further.

His next step was to look for facilities. A few inquiries around town provided him with the information that he could obtain the unused second floor of a local retail shop for $450 per month—including rent, taxes, and all services such as heat, power, and water. Further investigation revealed that he could fully equip his "factory" with the necessary furnishings for $2,000.

Allenson's next step was to determine how much it would cost him to produce the assemblies. The required parts, which he could obtain at the same price that his present employer paid, would cost $0.41 for each complete assembly. Assemblers could be hired at a cost to Allenson of $5.40 per hour. Since he calculated that each assembler could produce 60 assemblies per hour—after all allowances for personal needs—the $5.40 per hour came to $0.09 per assembly. Shipping, including cases, sealing tape, and delivery, came to $0.03 per assembly. This made the total cost to Allenson of each assembly $0.53.

Other expenses that Allenson envisioned included his own supervisory salary of $2,000 per month, about $400 per month for various maintenance expenses and consumable supplies, and about $200 per month for administrative expenses such as telephone, stationery, and office supplies.

FURTHER CONSIDERATIONS

At this point Allenson contacted one of his friends in the Accounting Department and talked over his idea with her. The friend was enthusiastic about the idea and thought that the plan would be successful. She told Allenson that the company was presently carrying that particular assembly on its books at a cost of $0.66 and would certainly buy from Allenson if he could reduce that cost by 10 to 15 percent. She also assured Allenson that the company would want to procure approximately 1,200,000 assemblies per year, although this figure could vary by 25 percent in either direction. As a final caution, however, she warned Allenson that an additional $6,000 would be required, at a minimum, just to provide Allenson's venture with working capital. If additional funds were necessary, she suggested that Allenson could easily borrow them.

ALLENSON'S FINAL ANALYSIS

After his discussion with his friend, Allenson went over the figures again in his mind. To produce 1,200,000 assemblies per year, he would need exactly ten fixtures. He thought, however, that to guarantee to his present employer that he would cover all their reasonable needs, he would require 15 fixtures. This would afford him with both spares and excess capacity. At the quoted price of $400 per fixture, he would need $6,000 for fixtures alone. Added to this were the funds required for furnishings and working capital, bringing his total investment to

$14,000. Annual expenses, including his own salary, rent, maintenance, supplies, and administrative expenses would come to about $36,000 per year.

Reviewing these figures, Allenson was convinced that he could offer his present employer a price of $0.57 per assembly—almost 15 percent less than their present cost—and still make a good profit for himself.

Bob Mogielnicki

In June 1974, Bob Mogielnicki went to work for the Brandywine Corporation, a medium-sized manufacturer of electrical controls and electronic devices. What particularly attracted Bob to the job offer from Brandywine was the fact that it presented an opportunity to assume line responsibilities after a brief training period. The position in question was that of supervisor of the parts fabrication shop at the company's San Jose plant.

At that time, the staff of the parts fabrication shop consisted of ten machine operators and two clerks in addition to the supervisor. The shop was producing five parts which were used by other departments of the San Jose plant in the assembly of final products. A statement of costs incurred by the parts fabrication shop during the first week of Bob's supervision is shown in Exhibit 1.

EXHIBIT 1

Cost statement for week of September 16, 1974

Prime Cost	
Labor	$1,397.56
Materials	3,116.80
Total Prime Cost	$4,514.36
Departmental Overhead	
Departmental supervision and services	$1,002.16
Depreciation	1,200.00
Total Departmental Overhead	$2,202.16
General Overhead	$1,500.00
Total Costs	$8,216.52

When he took over the parts fabrication shop, Bob was told by the plant manager, Mr. Wallis, that it was Bob's responsibility to see that the five parts being produced by the shop were acquired at the lowest possible cost to the company. For this reason, he had the authority to buy all or any of these parts from outside sources if he found this to be more advantageous to the company.

In order to carry out his responsibility for make-or-buy decisions, Bob felt he needed more cost information than was supplied by the weekly cost statement (see Exhibit 1). He discussed his needs with the plant accountant, Mr. Dreyfus, and together they agreed on a format for a second weekly report, which would show the actual cost of producing 100 of each of the parts during the week in question. The first such report, corresponding to the cost statement of Exhibit 1, is shown in Exhibit 2.

EXHIBIT 2

Product cost report for week of September 16, 1974

	Cost per 100 units of part no.				
Cost element	101	102	103	104	105
Labor	$ 8.48	$13.30	$ 5.25	$ 7.33	$ 4.31
Materials	18.40	24.00	14.80	17.20	13.60
Total Prime Cost	$26.88	$37.30	$20.05	$24.53	$17.91
Overhead	22.42	35.15	13.88	19.38	11.39
Total Cost	$49.30	$72.45	$33.93	$43.91	$29.30
Production (100 units)	33	40	32	42	26

The figures in Exhibit 2 were obtained as follows:

1. *Direct labor/hundred.* Each machine operator kept a time sheet indicating the time (in hours and tenths of an hour) spent on each part. These times were accumulated for each part and costed at the direct labor rate of $3.50 per hour. The total cost for each part was then divided by the amount of production.

2. *Direct materials/hundred.* When materials were drawn from the storeroom, an issue slip was prepared indicating the amount drawn and the part on which the materials were to be used. The amounts were totaled for each part, and the totals were divided by the amount of production.

3. *Overhead/hundred.* The total of all departmental and general overhead costs was divided by the number of direct labor hours to produce a cost per hour. This figure was multiplied by the number of direct labor hours charged to each part, and the result was then divided by the amount of production.

After receiving the information in Exhibit 2 from Mr. Dreyfus, Bob Mogielnicki solicited bids on each of the five parts from several small shops in the San Jose area. The lowest bid received on each part was as follows:

Part no.	Lowest bid
101	$65.00
102	90.00
103	37.50
104	60.00
105	34.50

After studying these bids, Bob concluded that the company should continue to make each part in its own shop.

In the spring of 1975, demand for Brandywine's products fell sharply because of a business recession. This decline was reflected in the workload in the parts fabrication shop. Because of the reduced work load, Bob Mogielnicki had laid off one machine operator and had transferred another to performing maintenance of equipment that had been deferred during the period of higher production.

When Bob received his product cost report for the week of April 14, 1975, shown in Exhibit 3, he discovered that costs were up on all five parts, and that part 103, in particular, now cost more to make than the bid of $37.50 per hundred he had received in the fall. Bob called the owner of the shop who had made that bid and asked him for an updated bid. The owner responded with a bid of $36.00 per hundred, saying that his business was off and so he was willing to shave his earlier price a bit if it would help to keep his shop busy. Bob promptly accepted the reduced offer and asked the purchasing agent of the San Jose plant to issue a purchase order to the outside source for 4,000 units (about a two-week supply at the current usage rate). Bob estimated that his decision would save Brandywine about $140.

EXHIBIT 3

Product cost report for week of April 14, 1975

	Cost per 100 units of part no.				
Cost element	101	102	103	104	105
Labor	$ 9.02	$14.00	$ 5.60	$ 7.82	$ 4.33
Material	18.43	24.01	14.78	17.20	13.59
Total Prime Cost	$27.45	$38.01	$20.38	$25.02	$17.92
Overhead	30.92	48.00	19.20	26.80	14.86
Total Cost	$58.37	$86.01	$39.58	$51.82	$32.78
Production (100 units)	26	32	20	30	21

The cost reports for the week of April 28, 1975 (Exhibit 4) showed a further rise. Once again Bob checked with the sources of earlier bids, this time on parts 102 and 105, and learned that in both cases the bidders were sticking by their earlier quotes.

EXHIBIT 4

Product cost report for week of April 28, 1975

Cost element	Cost per 100 units of part no.				
	101	102	103	104	105
Labor	$ 8.68	$13.33	—	$ 7.50	$ 4.50
Material	18.43	24.00	—	17.20	13.55
Total Prime Cost	$27.11	$37.33	—	$24.70	$18.05
Overhead	37.60	58.00	—	32.14	18.00
Total Cost	$64.71	$95.33	—	$56.84	$36.05
Production (100 units)	25	30	—	28	20

case 2–3

R. C. Blake Co.

Brent Mullen, a mechanical engineer in the Process Development Department of the R. C. Blake Company's Spartanburg, South Carolina factory, was concerned about how to react to some criticism that had recently developed of a promising project in the company's Solvent Spread Department that he had been working on for the past several months.

The R. C. Blake Company produced adhesive tapes for the industrial and consumer markets and also manufactured a line of special adhesive products that were sold, through distributors, to hospitals. One product, a vinyl-backed finger bandage, accounted for about half of the sales of all hospital products and, while intense competition in the finger bandage market kept profits on this item low, finger bandages were considered to be an integral part of the total hospital products line, which was noted for its overall profitability.

THE SOLVENT SPREAD DEPARTMENT

The Solvent Spread Department consisted of two 80-foot-long machines, the "east" and the "west" solvent spread lines. These machines applied adhesive mixed with a volatile solvent to 40-inch-wide tape backing material. The coated backing material was then passed through an oven, which took up most of the length of the solvent spread line. Elevated temperature in the oven evaporated the solvent, leaving behind the adhesive firmly bound to the backing. The resulting tape was wound on "jumbo" rolls that were later rewound, slit to commercial lengths and widths, packaged, or, as in the case of most hospital adhesive products, further processed. Flesh-colored vinyl material was converted into finger bandages by a special machine that applied a gauze pad, cut individual bandages between the pad, covered the adhesive area with a silicone-treated nonstick paper, and encased each bandage in a wrapper.

The east solvent spread line theoretically could have supplied more than sufficient capacity for all of the R. C. Blake Company's adhesive products but, due to subtle differences in product characteristics, two different solvent spread lines were needed. For example, because the flesh-colored vinyl material used to manufacture finger bandages tended to soften when exposed to the heat of the oven, finger bandage material had to be produced on the west line, which had a supporting belt to transport the vinyl material through the oven. Also, because the vinyl would deform when subjected to pressure, an unconventional procedure was used to apply the adhesive–solvent mixture to the vinyl. The only other product manufactured on the west line was a plastic electrician's tape, which, despite its relatively low volume, was consistently profitable.

The east line handled a wide variety of cloth or paper tapes whose backings were not as flexible or sensitive to heat as vinyl. These product characteristics meant that the east line could run hotter (and thus faster) and allowed the use of a more precise method of applying the adhesive–solvent mixture to the backing than was used on the west line. Another characteristic of the east line was that there was no transport belt through the oven. Since products run on that line were able to support themselves, they simply passed over rollers spaced at about 3-foot intervals.

It took three workers to operate a solvent spread line. In 1976, the department was operating about one and a half shifts. That is, a daytime crew of six workers operated both lines and an evening crew of three workers operated one or the other of the lines according to instructions left by the overseer. In 1976, the evening crew had operated the west line about 850 hours and the east line about 1,100 hours.

R&D EFFORTS

Brent Mullen had been assigned the task of lowering finger bandage costs through the development of improved manufacturing methods in the summer of 1976. Since the cost of solvent spread processing amounted to about 50 percent of finger bandage costs other than those for materials, he felt that this was a logical place for his cost reduction program to start. Mullen concentrated on ways to manufacture finger bandage material on the east line and soon hit upon the idea of applying adhesive to paper coated with a silicone release agent, drying the adhesive by passing the paper through the oven, and laminating the vinyl to the paper at the end of the line. The release paper could then be removed and reused, and the adhesive would remain on the vinyl. He designed and had fabricated a special fixture to perform this operation. Experimentation with this new process was successful. It was found that there were several significant benefits to the new method:

1. The paper coated with adhesive could be run three times as fast on the east line as vinyl could be run on the west.
2. The vinyl retained more flexibility since it had not been exposed to heat. This could be viewed as either a desirable marketing feature or as a potential to begin purchasing a lower-grade vinyl.
3. The amount of adhesive applied could be reduced by 12 percent because of better control of adhesive application on the east line.
4. The east solvent spread line had a lower overhead rate.

In a report to management that summarized his experiments, Mullen estimated that the annual savings from this new method of running finger bandage material amounted to over $80,000 (see Exhibit 1). Initial reaction to this report was quite positive. The Production and Hospital Products Marketing Departments were convinced that Mullen's project represented some significant savings and could also provide some product improvements.

EXHIBIT 1
Summary of savings (costs) from applying adhesive to finger bandage vinyl on east solvent spread line (assumption of 400,000 linear yards per year of 40-inch-wide finger bandage vinyl, 1976 yardage plus 3.7 percent)

	East line (proposed)	West line (present)	Savings
Speed (ft./min.)	30	10	—
Temperature	270°F	155°F	—
Adhesive applied (lb./sq. yd)	0.563	0.630	—
Annual adhesive cost (@ $1.07/lb.)	$267,737	$299,600	$31,863
Machine hours/year	667	2,000	1,333
Labor ($12.75/hr./crew)	$ 8,504	$ 25,500	$16,996
Fixed overhead rate ($/hr.)	$ 25	$ 27	—
Total overhead	$ 16,675	$ 54,000	$37,325
Release paper @ $0.04/linear yd.,			
133,333 linear yd. (reuse twice)	($5,333)	—	($5,333)
Net savings			$80,851

Ms. Alice Duncan, head of the Cost Accounting Department, was less enthusiastic about Mullen's innovation. In a memorandum to Mullen, she expressed her feeling that Mullen's estimates of savings were overstated:

> . . . your reported cost reduction is largely illusory. While the reduction in overhead would indeed lower the standard cost of finger bandage material, there would be no reduction in the amount of actual charges to the overhead accounts. Therefore, your savings figure has to be reduced from $80,851 to $43,526 because that's the net impact of the change on the factory as a whole.

Duncan went on to detail some undesirable potential side effects of Mullen's project:

> In a few weeks we will be calculating overhead rates for the coming year based on the Marketing Department's projections of volume. If your proposal is adopted, there will be a significant impact on the standard cost of black electrician's tape which, as I understand it, would continue to be produced on the west line. Using 1976 volume on this product (170,000 linear yards at 10 feet per minute), we get about 850 hours of production on the west line. At that usage, the hourly overhead rate goes up to over $90 per hour. This is more than enough to completely wipe out the $35,000 or so in profit made on that product. Inevitably, management would decide to stop producing electrician's tape and the company would lose that profit. Not only would that completely wipe out the project's savings, but it would completely idle the west solvent spread line. If that happened, most of the overhead from the west line would have to be picked up by the east line, causing reduced profitability for all products there. If that happened, the overhead rate on the east line would go up to about $40 per hour (based on the 3,800 total hours that the east line would have been run last year had we produced finger bandage material as you propose.) For these reasons, I *strongly* recommend that product machine assignments remain as they have been in the past.

A few days after Duncan's memo was circulated, a meeting was held. Attending were the plant manager, Alfred Cathcart; Winifred Whyte, the manager of Hospital Products Marketing; Alice Duncan, the head of the Cost Accounting Department; and Brent Mullen. Cathcart opened the meeting with a review of the problem and added that the purpose of the meeting was to determine whether Mullen's project should be continued or scrapped.

Cathcart: Alice, I don't suppose there is any way that we could adopt Mullen's proposal and continue to assign the output to the west line so that its overhead would still be absorbed by the finger bandage material?

Duncan: Well, Fred, I gave that idea quite a bit of thought and, as I see it, there are a couple of relevant arguments against it. First, we would be violating a couple of pretty explicit corporate rules about overhead allocation that have been around a long time. Second, if we start to monkey with the way overhead is allocated in the Solvent Spread Department, then other departments will soon want to be doing the same sort of thing. We simply can't allow that to happen if we want to maintain the overall integrity of our cost accounting program.

Whyte: What you've been saying makes a lot of sense, but it seems a shame to just discard the results of Brent's good efforts because of an arbitrary sort of accounting convention. There must be another way to get those benefits. After all, the product is dramatically improved and about half of Mullen's savings are really there. Look, suppose everything goes as your scenario suggests. Couldn't we simply get rid of the west line and use that space for something else? And couldn't we run electrician's tape on the east line using the new release paper method?

Mullen: Actually, Winifred, you couldn't do either of those things. Unlike finger bandages, electrician's tape is sold in rolls. Thus, it is wound upon itself and, unless the adhesive is actually cured on the plastic by running it through the oven, it would delaminate or pull off when you used the tape. In other words, half of the time the adhesive would be on the "back" side of the tape when you unrolled it. Your other point, about finding another use for the space now occupied by the west line, is a good one except that the area around the spread lines is an explosive environment because of all the vaporizing solvent. We can't even run a forklift back there without risking a bad fire. Everything in that area has to be especially designed to be sparkproof. Furthermore, putting up a fireproof partition would cost over $100,000 and I don't even see why we'd do that—there is plenty of unoccupied space in this factory now.

There is, however, one alternative that I thought of only yesterday that might be worth exploring. Since we're on the subject, I may as well see how it strikes the group. Since Alice's memo came out, I've been thinking about ways that we could achieve the benefits of higher temperature and speed by using release paper on the west line. A few years ago I experimented using a similar concept on the west line. As I recall, there were only a few minor technical problems that should be pretty easy to overcome. Since the bulk of what you call the real savings come from more accurate application of adhesive, however, I'd have to make one major modification to the adhesive spreader on the west line. All in all, I

think that $40,000 in capital expenditure would let us run finger
bandage vinyl the new way and the electrician's tape the old way,
both on the west line. What do you think?

Duncan: That sounds like we can have our cake and eat it too! Great
idea!

Whyte: Terrific, Brent. How soon can you get this into operation?

Mullen: Within two or three months after a proposal is approved.
There's some design work and, of course, several weeks of fabrication and installation time.

Cathcart: Well, Brent, our capital budget is stretched a bit thin this
year but for a project with less than a one-year payback, I'm sure
we can get an extension from the corporate office pretty quickly.
Tell you what. Get your proposal to me in the next week or so.
Winifred, you and Alice give Brent all the support he needs. Let's
get this one off the ground!

Bill French, accountant

Bill French picked up the phone and called his boss, Wes Davidson,
controller of Duo-Products Corporation. "Say, Wes, I'm all set for the
meeting this afternoon. I've put together a set of break-even statements that should really make the boys sit up and take notice—and I
think they'll be able to understand them, too." After a brief conversation about other matters, the call was concluded and French turned to
his charts for one last check-out before the meeting.

French had been hired six months earlier as a staff accountant. He
was directly responsible to Davidson and, up to the time of this case,
had been doing routine types of analysis work. French was an alumnus
of a liberal arts undergraduate school and graduate business school,
and was considered by his associates to be quite capable and unusu-
ally conscientious. It was this latter characteristic that had apparently
caused him to "rub some of the working guys the wrong way," as one
of his co-workers put it. French was well aware of his capabilities and
took advantage of every opportunity that arose to try to educate those

around him. Wes Davidson's invitation for French to attend an informal manager's meeting had come as some surprise to others in the accounting group. However, when French requested permission to make a presentation of some break-even data, Davidson acquiesced. The Duo-Products Corporation had not been making use of this type of analysis in its review or planning programs.

Basically, what French had done was to determine the level of operation at which the company must operate in order to break even. As he phrased it, "The company must be able to at least sell a sufficient volume of goods so that it will cover all of the variable costs of producing and selling the goods; further, it will not make a profit unless it covers the fixed, or nonvariable, costs as well. The level of operation at which total costs (that is, variable plus nonvariable) are just covered is the break-even volume. This should be the lower limit in all of our planning."

The accounting records had provided the following information which French used in constructing his chart:

> Plant capacity: 2 million units
> Past year's level of operations: 1,500,000 units
> Average unit selling price: $1.20
> Total fixed costs: $520,000
> Average variable unit cost: $0.75

From this information, he observed that each unit contributed $0.45 to fixed overhead after covering the variable costs. Given total fixed costs of $520,000, he calculated that 1,155,556 units must be sold in order to break even. He verified this conclusion by calculating the dollar sales volume that was required to break even. Since the variable costs per unit were 62.5 percent of the selling price, French reasoned that 37.5 percent of every sales dollar was left available to cover fixed costs. Thus, fixed costs of $520,000 require sales of $1,386,667 in order to break even.

When he constructed a break-even chart to present the information graphically, his conclusions were further verified. The chart also made it clear that the firm was operating at a fair margin over the break-even requirements, and that the profits accruing (at the rate of 37.5 percent of every sales dollar over break-even) increased rapidly as volume increased (see Exhibit 1).

Shortly after lunch, French and Davidson left for the meeting. Several representatives of the manufacturing departments were present, as well as the general sales manager, two assistant sales managers, the purchasing officer, and two men from the product engineering office. Davidson introduced French to the few men that he had not already

EXHIBIT 1
Break-even chart—total business

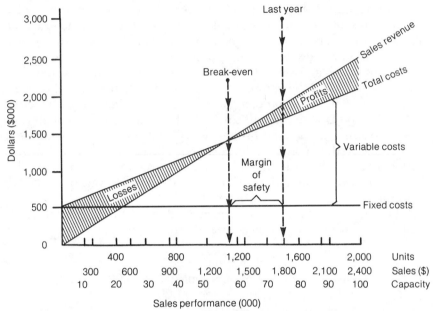

Break-even volume = 1,156,000 units, or $1,387,000

met and then the meeting got under way. French's presentation was the last item on Davidson's agenda, and in due time the controller introduced French, explaining his interest in cost control and analysis.

French had prepared enough copies of his chart and supporting calculations so that they could be distributed to everyone at the meeting. He described carefully what he had done and explained how the chart pointed to a profitable year, dependent on meeting the volume of sales activity that had been maintained in the past. It soon became apparent that some of the participants had known in advance what French planned to discuss; they had come prepared to challenge him and soon had taken control of the meeting. The following exchange ensued (see Exhibit 2 for a checklist of participants with their titles):

Cooper: You know, Bill, I'm really concerned that you haven't allowed for our planned changes in volume next year. It seems to me that you should have allowed for the sales department's guess that we'll boost sales by 20 percent, unit-wise. We'll be pushing 90 percent of what we call capacity then. It sure seems that this would make quite a difference in your figuring.

EXHIBIT 2
List of participants in the meeting

Bill French	Staff accountant
Wes Davidson	Controller
John Cooper	Production control
Fred Williams	Manufacturing
Ray Bradshaw	Assistant sales manager
Arnie Winetki	General sales manager
Hugh Fraser	Administrative assistant to president

French: That might be true, but as you can see, all you have to do is read the cost and profit relationship right off the chart for the new volume. Let's see—at a million-eight units we'd . . .

Williams: Wait a minute, now!!! If you're going to talk in terms of 90 percent of capacity, and it looks like that's what it will be, you damn well better note that we'll be shelling out some more for the plant. We've already got okays on investment money that will boost your fixed costs by $10,000 a month, easy. And that may not be all. We may call it 90 percent of plant capacity, but there are a lot of places where we're just full up and we can't pull things up any tighter.

Cooper: See, Bill? Fred Williams is right, but I'm not finished on this bit about volume changes. According to the information that I've got here—and it came from your office—I'm not sure that your break-even chart can really be used even if there were to be no changes next year. Looks to me like you've got average figures that don't allow for the fact that we're dealing with three basic products. Your report here (see Exhibit 3) on costs, according to product lines, for last year makes it pretty clear that the "average" is way out of line. How would the break-even point look if we took this on an individual product basis?

French: Well, I'm not sure. Seems to me that there is only one break-even point for the firm. Whether we take it product by product or in total, we've got to hit that point. I'll be glad to check for you if you want, but . . .

Bradshaw: Guess I may as well get in on this one, Bill. If you're going to do anything with individual products, you ought to know that we're looking for a big swing in our product mix. Might even start before we get into the new season. The "A" line is really losing out and I imagine that we'll be lucky to hold two thirds of the volume there next year. Wouldn't you buy that Arnie? [Agreement from the general sales manager.] That's not too bad, though, be-

EXHIBIT 3
Product class cost analysis (normal year)

	Aggregate	"A"	"B"	"C"
Sales at full capacity (units)	2,000,000			
Actual sales volume (units)	1,500,000	600,000	400,000	500,000
Unit sales price	$1.20	$1.67	$1.50	$0.40
Total sales revenue	$1,800,000	$1,000,000	$600,000	$200,000
Variable cost per unit	$0.75	$1.25	$0.625	$0.25
Total variable cost	$1,125,000	$ 750,000	$250,000	$125,000
Fixed costs	$ 520,000	$ 170,000	$275,000	$ 75,000
Net profit	$ 155,000	$ 80,000	$ 75,000	–0–
Ratios				
Variable cost to sales	0.63	0.75	0.42	0.63
Variable income to sales	0.37	0.25	0.58	0.37
Utilization of capacity	75.0%	30.0%	20.0%	25.0%

cause we expect that we should pick up the 200,000 that we lose, and about a quarter million units more, over in "C" production. We don't see anything that shows much of a change in "B." That's been solid for years and shouldn't change much now.

Winetki: Bradshaw's called it about as we figure it, but there's something else here, too. We've talked about our pricing on "C" enough, and now I'm really going to push our side of it. Ray's estimate of maybe half a million—450,000 I guess it was—up on "C" for next year is on the basis of doubling the price with no change in cost. We've been priced so low on this item that it's been a crime—we've got to raise, but good, for two reasons. First, for our reputation; the price is out of line class-wise and is completely inconsistent with our quality reputation. Second, if we don't raise the price, we'll be swamped and we can't handle it. You heard what Williams said about capacity. The way the whole "C" field is exploding, we'll have to answer to another half-million units in unsatisfied orders if we don't jack that price up. We can't afford to expand that much for this product.

At this point, Hugh Fraser, administrative assistant to the president, walked up toward the front of the room from where he had been standing near the rear door. The discussion broke for a minute, and he took advantage of the lull to interject a few comments.

Fraser: This has certainly been enlightening. Looks like you fellows are pretty well up on this whole operation. As long as you're going to try to get all of the things together that you ought to pin down for next year, let's see what I can add to help you.

Number one: Let's remember that everything that shows in the

profit area here on Bill's chart is divided just about evenly between the government and us. Now, for last year we can read a
profit of about $150,000. Well, that's right. But we were left with
half of that, and then paid out dividends of $50,000 to the stock-
holders. Since we've got an anniversary year coming up, we'd like
to put out a special dividend of about 50 percent extra. We ought
to hold $25,000 in for the business, too. This means that we'd like
to hit $100,000 *after* the costs of being governed.

Number two: From where I sit, it looks like we're going to have
to talk with the union again and this time it's liable to cost us. All
the indications are—and this isn't public—that we may have to
meet demands that will boost our production costs—what do you
call them here, Bill—variable costs—by 10 percent across the
board. This may kill the bonus-dividend plans, but we've got to
hold the line on past profits. This means that we can give that
much to the union only if we can make it in added revenues. I
guess you'd say that that raises your break-even point, Bill—and
for that one I'd consider the company's profit to be a fixed cost.

Number three: Maybe this is the time to think about switching
our product emphasis. Arnie Winetki may know better than I
which of the products is more profitable. You check me out on this,
Arnie—and it might be a good idea for you and Bill French to get
together on this one, too. These figures that I have (Exhibit 3)
make it look like the percentage contribution on line "A" is the
lowest of the bunch. If we're losing volume there as rapidly as you
sales folks say, and if we're as hard pressed for space as Fred
Williams has indicated, maybe we'd be better off grabbing some
of that big demand for "C" by shifting some of the facilities over
there from "A."

That's all I've got to say. Looks to me like you've all got plenty
to think about.

Davidson: Thanks, Hugh. I sort of figured that we'd get wound up here
as soon as Bill brought out his charts. This is an approach that
we've barely touched, but, as you can see, you've all got ideas that
have got to be made to fit here somewhere. I'll tell you what let's
do. Bill, suppose you rework your chart and try to bring into it
some of the points that were made here today. I'll see if I can
summarize what everyone seems to be looking for.

First of all, I have the idea buzzing around in the back of my
mind that your presentation is based on a rather important series of
assumptions. Most of the questions that were raised were really
about those assumptions; it might help us all if you try to set the
assumptions down in black and white so that we can see just how
they influence the analysis.

Then, I think that Cooper would like to see the unit sales increase taken up, and he'd also like to see whether there's any difference if you base the calculations on an analysis of individual product lines. Also, as Bradshaw suggested, since the product mix is bound to change, why not see how things look if the shift materializes as Sales has forecast.

Arnie Winetki would like to see the influence of a price increase in the "C" line, Fred Williams looks toward an increase in fixed manufacturing costs of $10,000 a month, and Hugh Fraser has suggested that we should consider taxes, dividends, expected union demands, and the question of product emphasis.

I think that ties it all together. Let's hold off on our next meeting, fellows, until Bill has time to work this all into shape.

With that, the participants broke off into small groups and the meeting disbanded. French and Davidson headed back to their offices and French, in a tone of concern, asked Davidson, "Why didn't you warn me about the hornet's nest I was walking into?"

"Bill, you didn't ask!"

Linear programming

Linear programming is one of the best developed and most frequently used management science techniques. In general, linear programming is a technique that allocates scarce resources to competing demands in an optimal way. This is a problem that has wide applicability in business situations. The general problem statement has three essential components; scarce or limited resources, competing demands for those resources, and an optimal or one best allocation of scarce resources to the competing demands.

No matter how large a firm might be, invariably some resources are in short supply. It is also common that some limited resources can be used in different ways, that is, applied to satisfy mutually exclusive demands. In other words, different uses of the same resource may interact to the extent that producing less of one end product (for example) frees some amount of scarce resources so that more of other end products can be made.

Achieving an optimal allocation or assignment of scarce resources to competing demands is the purpose of linear programming. To do this, a measure of the value or worth of each of the competing demands is necessary. Often, this is in the form of contribution margin per unit, or profit to be optimized (maximized). In other situations, the objective of a linear program is to minimize some negative factor like costs or lost sales. Taken together, the measures of worth for each of the demands for scarce resources are called the *objective function*. It is necessary that the objective function be expressed in mathematical terms for it to be useful in a linear programming problem.

Linear programming has been applied over a very wide range of problems that have been considered allocations of scarce resources to competing demands. It can provide helpful guidance in answering questions like: Should a single production facility manufacture more or less of one product or another, given that the constituent manufacturing processes are more or less efficient depending on the product made? How should investments be arranged in a portfolio to generate a desired rate of return? Given a limited supply of raw materials, how should they be combined to produce the most profitable mix of end items? What is the most effective way to schedule the assembly of different products in order to minimize inventories and stockouts? How can transportation costs from several factories to several warehouses be held to a minimum? What is the most effective combination of task assignments for each of a group of employees with different skills and work attributes?

Indeed, the applications of linear programming are seemingly limited only by the analyst's vision or ability to perceive a problem as one of allocation of scarce resources. In many situations, then, linear programming can be helpful. It is also true that, for problems of any size, the technique involves an incredible amount of computational detail. Despite this, the basic concepts underlying linear programming are few and simple. The reason linear programming is usually considered an advanced topic is because management science has developed more sophisticated tools to deal with simple problems involving linear relationships under conditions of certainty than it has for more complex problems involving uncertainty and nonlinearity. Some of these more complex problems are covered in later chapters in this text. Many students will find that the mathematics involved there will be less challenging than that encountered in linear programming. But nowhere will the concepts be so plain and straightforward as in linear programming.

To illustrate these simple concepts, let us consider an example of a classic linear programming situation—the two-product mix problem.

A SIMPLE EXAMPLE

Imagine yourself the newly appointed production manager of a factory that produces two styles of ball-point pens: retractable and non-retractable or "straight" pens. Your assignment is to use the assets under your control in such a way as to maximize the contribution margin of the products. For planning purposes you have been told that you may assume that there are no limitations on the amount of either product that may be sold, although you have determined that the contribution margin for retractable ball-point pens is $0.30 per dozen, while the margin for straight pens is $0.40 per dozen.

Your factory is divided into three departments: body molding, assembly, and filler manufacturing. The filler department manufactures the slim metal tube filled with ink and tipped with the "ball" that conveys ink to paper in the process of writing. The capacity of this department varies depending on the mix of retractable and straight pens produced. If all this department's capacity were devoted to retractable pens, the department could produce 3,000 dozen fillers per week. Since the straight-pen fillers are longer than the retractable, however, this department could produce only 2,000 dozen nonretractable pens if all of its capacity were devoted to that product. Because setting up a filler-making machine to produce either product is a simple matter, accomplished in a few seconds, and because there are several of these machines in the department, this relationship between manufacturing retractable versus straight fillers is essentially constant throughout. In other words, you can make 1½ dozen more retractable fillers for each dozen straight-pen fillers that you forgo (and vice versa) and still produce at the overall capacity of the filler department. You can portray this relationship graphically as in Figure 3–1.

FIGURE 3–1
Production limit set by capacity of filler-making department

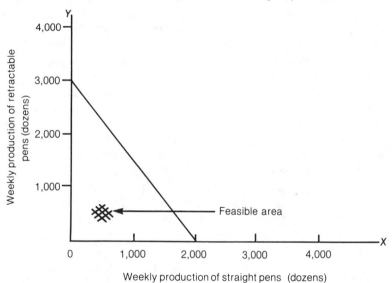

The line in Figure 3–1 drawn between 3,000 dozen pens on the retractable pen axis and 2,000 dozen pens on the straight pen axis represents the filler department's capacity. At any point on that line, the department is producing as many fillers as it is capable. Of course, production would be feasible at some mix of retractable and straight-pen fillers in the area bounded by the axes and the filler department capacity line. Notice, however, that outside of this *feasible area*, production is impossible. It would be infeasible, for example, to produce 3,000 dozen fillers of both types in the same week because that product mix would clearly exceed the capacity of the filler department. For this reason, the line representing the capacity of the pen filler department is called a *constraint:* It represents a maximum amount of production that may not be exceeded in the normal course of operations.

The equation that describes this constraint is $Y + 1.5X = 3,000$.[1] This means that, for any combination of X's (number of straight pens produced) and Y's (number of retractable pens produced), you (the production manager) can readily tell how the department is loaded with respect to its capacity. For instance, if a weekly production plan calls for 2,500 dozen straight pens and 1,500 dozen retractable pens ($X = 2,500$; $Y = 1,500$), you can tell that this plan exceeds the capacity of the filler department because 1,500 plus 3,750 ($1.5 \times 2,500$) equals 5,250, which is greater than 3,000.

Suppose your immediate predecessor as production manager had set the quantity of production at 1,000 dozen straight pens and 900 dozen retractable pens. This falls within the feasible area and does not violate the filler department capacity constraint, since 900 plus 1,500 (1.5×1000) equals 2,400, which is less than 3,000.[2] Your initial reaction to this discovery, no doubt, is that your firm could immediately realize an increase in total contribution simply by producing at capacity. In this situation, for instance, you could substantially increase the level of production. To oversimplify, you could either produce 400 dozen more straight pens or 600 dozen more retractable pens. To decide which of these actions to take, you might refer to your initial task statement—". . . maximize total contribution margin." Then, you might calculate that producing 400 dozen additional straight pens at $0.40 contribution margin per dozen equals $160, whereas producing 600 dozen retractable pens at $0.30 contribution margin per dozen equals $180. Your choice, then, should be 600 dozen more retractable pens for a resulting product mix of 1,500 retractable pens and 1,000 straight pens.[3] (See Figure 3–2.)

---

[1] You should be able to verify this result. A typical instructor's assumption is that all students in this course have mastered the elementary topic of writing linear equations given data of the sort presented in Figure 3–1. The authors have discovered that this assumption is not always fully justified. Perhaps you recognize a deficiency in your preparation at this point (i.e., maybe you can not write the equation of a straight line). If so, you are advised to put aside this text and repair this deficiency at once. We suggest referring to any basic algebra text. Your ability to write and understand linear equations is crucial to understanding this chapter and the cases that follow.

[2] Note that, while this product mix doesn't *violate* the constraint, neither does it *satisfy* the equation we wrote earlier. For this reason, constraints of this sort are typically written as *inequalities* (i.e., $Y + 1.5X \leq 3,000$) indicating that, while production of more than 3,000 dozen equivalent retractable pens is not possible, it is feasible to produce less than that number.

[3] This, of course, leaves you producing on the line representing the capacity constraint. In linear programming problems of this sort, you will always find that the most favorable total contribution will be located at some point along the perimeter of the feasible region. Further, so long as the contribution margins of the products are positive, that point will not be at the feasible point where nothing is produced.

FIGURE 3–2
Increasing contribution margin by increasing production up to capacity

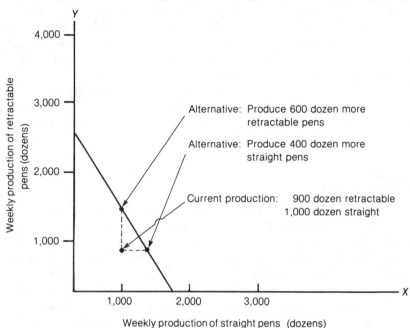

But, does this product mix (1,500 retractable, 1,000 straight) maximize total contribution to overhead and profit? Our intuition tells us that, indeed, this is not very likely to be the optimal mix of product. In the sense that the optimal product mix is the *one* product mix that will return a maximum contribution to overhead and profit of the firm, it would seem to be an incredible coincidence if this mix, arrived at by 95 percent history and 5 percent analysis, were that point. But we do believe that the optimal point is one that uses the total capacity of the department. So, instead of starting fresh, you might decide to improve on the solution you have already achieved by trading off production of one kind of pen for the other, while keeping a product mix that totally utilizes the capacity of the filler manufacturing department. For example, if you produce 10 fewer dozen of the straight pen, you can produce 15 dozen more of the retractable model. The filler manufacturing department is still at capacity $[1,515 + (1.5 \times 990) = 3,000]$ and you have added \$0.50 to total contribution $[(15 \times \$0.30) - (10 \times \$0.40)]$. This increase in total contribution, however modest, is a clear signal that you are moving in the direction of the optimal solution. You could make another similar trade-off by dropping another 10 dozen straight pens and replacing them with 15 dozen additional retractable pens. If you did, you would again notice a $0.50 increase in total contribution margin. Or, you could perform the trade-off on a large scale, dropping 500 dozen straight pens to add 750 dozen retractable, which would increase total contribution by $25. You could look carefully at the filler manufacturing constraint and conclude that similar trade-offs of straight pens for retractable pens are possible (and will increase total contribution) up to the point where you are producing 3,000 retractable pens and no straight pens at all. It is at this point that total contribution is maximized if we consider only the constraint imposed by the filler manufacturing department.[4]

Other constraints

Of course, before you ordered all of your pen production into retractable pens, you checked on the impact this would have on the rest of your operations, namely, the body molding and assembly departments. And it's a good thing you did. When you inquired about body molding, you found that the body molding department could produce only enough plastic parts to support a weekly production of 2,000 dozen retractable pens per week if the entire resources of that department were devoted to retractable-pen body production. If the output were concentrated on straight pens, 2,500 dozen bodies could be produced per week. Investigating the capacity of the assembly department, you found that retractable pens are much more difficult to assemble than straight pens. The capacity of the assembly area reflects this differential, being 1,500 dozen per week retractable and 9,000 dozen straight per week, if all assembly efforts were devoted solely to one model or the other. In both departments, production amounts between these extremes could be achieved by proportionately reducing the output of one design and increasing the output of the other. So now you have collected data as described in Table 3–1.

One way to proceed would be to request capital expenditures and increased work force to expand these departments to achieve a more appropriate balance with the filler manufacturing department. But this action would take at least several months and would require the approval of your boss. Your boss, incidentally, is not inclined to make

---

[4] This is true despite the fact that contribution margin per dozen for straight pens is 33 percent higher than contribution margin per dozen for retractable pens. This surprising result underscores the fact that it is not contribution margin per unit of output that is important in cases of competing demands for scarce resources; rather it is contribution margin per unit of scarce input that determines the optimal or most profitable product mix.

TABLE 3-1
Maximum capacities of production departments
(dozens of pens per week by model)

	Model	
	Retractable	Straight
Filler manufacturing.....................	3,000	2,000
Body molding..........................	2,000	2,500
Assembly	1,500	9,000
Contribution margin	$0.30	$0.40

major investments in productive capacity or expansions in the work force in the near future. You, it seems, must do as well as you can with what you have.

This is a more complicated situation than you imagined earlier. Suddenly, you are comfronted with three constraints instead of just one. How can you analyze *this* situation? One way to begin is to write the inequalities that each of these constraints represents, as in Table 3–2.

TABLE 3–2
System of linear inequalities describing constraints of the production system for retractable and straight pens*

Filler manufacturing	$1.5X + Y \leq 3{,}000$
Body molding	$0.8X + Y \leq 2{,}000$
Assembly department	$X + 6Y \leq 9{,}000$
Objective function	$0.40X + 0.30Y = $ Maximize

* X = number of dozens of straight pens produced weekly; Y = number of dozens of retractable pens produced weekly.

Displayed graphically, these constraints appear as in Figure 3–3. Looking at this graph, you can see clearly that your tentative plan to produce 3,000 retractable pens is not possible because that number exceeds the capacity of the body molding and assembly departments. Perhaps, if you are fortunate, you have also learned a lesson about defining the problem completely before plunging into an analytic effort. But all is not lost. You should at least review the two important lessons that you learned from your earlier analysis because they are principles that hold for any linear program. These principles are:

1. An optimal solution will be located on the perimeter of the feasible region and not inside it. Translated, this means that the par-

FIGURE 3–3
Graph of the constraints of the expanded problem

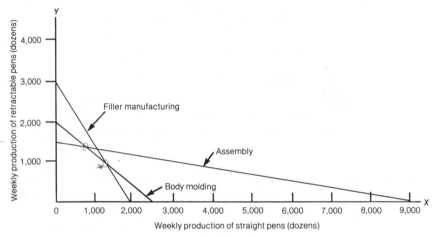

ticular product mix that contributes the most to overhead and profit will be found where some scarce resource is fully utilized.

2. Along the frontier of the feasible region, it is possible to trade off one product for another according to the slope of the constraint that makes up that part of the perimeter. As the product mix is thus changed, total contribution also changes. If the change in contribution is negative, you are progressing *away* from the optimal product mix. If the change is positive, you are progressing toward the optimum.[5] Since the perimeter is made up of segments of straight lines, the favorable trade-off can be continued until the slope of the feasible region changes. This occurs where two constraints intersect. Now, the trade-off procedure can continue according to the rule imposed by the slope of the newly encountered constraint. If *that* trade-off is favorable, then you can proceed to the next place at which the slope of the perimeter changes, i.e., the next constraint intersection, in a similar way. If unfavorable, then you are progressing *away* from an optimal solution. Hence, the optimal solution will be at the intersection of some two constraints. Translated, this means that not only will an optimum occur

---

[5] There is no change in the total contribution as you trade off one product for the other when the added contribution of the increased product just balances the reduced contribution of the other product. Where this is the situation, that entire segment of the perimeter of the feasible region represents a range of equally attractive optimal solutions. Choosing among these solutions is either arbitrary or involves invoking some other criteria than the stated objective function.

on the perimeter, but also it will occur where *more than one* scarce resource is fully utilized.

Knowing these principles, you can simplify your search for an optimal solution by considering only the perimeter of the feasible region and systematically evaluating each constraint intersection. The origin of the graph in Figure 3–3 is one such constraint intersection—the unmentioned constraint that a negative number of pens could not be produced. Let us arbitrarily choose the origin as a starting point for this analysis. Of course, at the origin your factory would produce nothing and hence earn no contribution. As long as the contribution per unit of some product is positive, the origin will not be the optimal solution. And so let us add some units of production—say, straight pens since they have the highest per-unit contribution. We can move along the X-axis in Figure 3–3 until we encounter a change in the slope of the perimeter. This occurs when we reach the point where the filler manufacturing department is at capacity. At this point we could produce 2,000 dozen straight pens and no retractable pens. Our total weekly contribution here would be 2,000 dozen straight pens times $0.40 per dozen plus 0 retractable pens times $0.30 per dozen, or $800. Not bad. Can we do better by trading off straight-pen production for retractable-pen production according to the rule imposed by the slope of the filler manufacturing constraint? Suppose you made only 1,900 dozen straight pens? Then, with the filler department capacity you have freed up, you could make 150 dozen retractable pens. At this point your total contribution is $(1,900 \times \$0.40) + (150 \times \$0.30) = \$805$, which is more than the $800 we were making before. Thus, we are moving toward an optimal solution and can improve total contribution by continuing to make this trade-off until the slope of the perimeter changes.

This happens at the point on Figure 3–3 where the filler manufacturing constraint intersects the body molding constraint. Can we proceed further? Try the trade-off of straight pens for retractable pens according to the rule imposed by the slope of the body molding constraint. Here, we could produce 20 dozen more retractable pens by forgoing production of 25 dozen straight pens. Since 20 dozen times $0.30 per dozen minus 25 dozen times $0.40 per dozen is *negative* $4.00, this trade-off moves away from the optimal solution. In other words, any movement further around the perimeter from the body molding/filler manufacturing constraint intersection will *reduce* total contribution. The coordinates of this intersection, then, represent the optimal product mix for straight and retractable pens. To identify the coordinates of that point (and, incidentally to compute the total contribution margin there), you must find the one point that these two constraint lines have in common. You can do this by solving the equations of these lines simultaneously.[6] That point is $X = 1,428.57$ and $Y = 857.14$. Maximum total contribution, then, is $828.57.

A technical digression

The process that you worked through to get to this optimal product mix of straight and retractable pens is, in essence, identical with the ritualized procedure known as the *simplex method* of solving linear programs. Because the simplex method is like a formal recipe (for optimal solutions), it has been routinized and programmed for use on digital computers. Just as there are many different recipes for apple pie, so there are many different computer routines that solve linear programs using the simplex method. But just as every apple pie requires similar ingredients (i.e., apples, sugar, flour), so each simplex computer program will require similar inputs. The aim of this section is to provide you with the background to recognize and collect the ingredients for the various simplex recipes.

The process of arraying information in a format useful for a simplex computer routine is called *formulation*. By writing the system of linear inequalities for the ball-point pen product mix problem in Table 3–2, we have made a good start toward the formulation of that problem. We shall, therefore, use that as an example of formulating a linear program and identifying the four basic ingredients in the simplex recipe: variables, constraints, available resources, and objective function.

Variables. The term *variable* is used to represent the basic choices that we want the linear programming computer routine to make for us. Variables, therefore, represent the competing demands for the scarce resources represented by the constraints. In this example, the choices are X, the number of dozens of straight pens to be produced weekly, and Y, the number of dozens of retractable pens to be produced weekly.

Constraints. Each of the three inequalities in Table 3–2 represents a constraint. For a simplex formulation these constraints are written in a tabular format. This is done, according to convention, by writing the names of the constraints along the left side of the table, writing the variables across the top, and entering the coefficients of the variables in the body of the table. This table of coefficients is referred to as the *technical coefficient table* because these numbers describe the allowable product trade-offs of the production technology.

---

[6] Reread footnote 1.

Resources. Each constraint inequality from Table 3–2 is a statement of the relative amounts of a resource required to satisfy one unit of each competing demand (variable). The amount of resources available to allocate to these demands is simply the number appearing on the right-hand side of the inequality.

Objective function. The objective function is an expression of the value attached to each unit of output. Usually it is written below the constraint set and includes the instruction "maximize" or "minimize."

Table 3–3, depicts an acceptable formulation of the ball-point pen product mix problem.

TABLE 3–3
Simplex formulation of ball-point pen product mix problem

	Variables			
Constraints	X	Y		Resources
Filler manufacturing...............	1.5	1	≤	3,000
Body molding......................	0.8	1	≤	2,000
Assembly	1	6	≤	9,000
Objective function...............	$0.40	$0.30		Maximize

For most simplex computer routines, when this information is put in the proper format, it is sufficient to find the optimal solution. For a few programs, an extra set of variables called *slack variables* must be added to the formulation so that the constraint inequalities can be rewritten as equations. For example, the filler manufacturing inequality:

$$1.5X + Y \leq 3,000$$

may be written:

$$1.5X + Y + S_1 = 3,000$$

by defining:

$$S_1 = 3,000 - 1.5X - Y$$

In a similar way, slack variables S_2 and S_3 can be added to the body molding and assembly constraint inequalities so that they can be restated as equations.

These slack variables are artificial constructs that represent unused capacity. Adding them to the formulation (as most simplex computer routines do automatically) restricts the search for an optimal solution to the perimeter of the feasible area by allowing restatement of the constraint inequalities as equations. The simplex formulation of the problem now appears as in Table 3–4. Notice that there is one slack variable associated with each constraint. Also notice that the slack variables have been assigned a contribution margin of $0.00 in the objective function. This corresponds with the notion that contribution is associated with the production of some product.

TABLE 3–4
Simplex formulation

Constraints	Variables						Resources
	X	Y	S_1	S_2	S_3		
Filler manufacturing...............	1.5	1	1	0	0	=	3,000
Body molding....................	0.8	1	0	1	0	=	2,000
Assembly	1	6	0	0	1	=	9,000
Objective function..............	$0.40	$0.30	$0.00	$0.00	$0.00		Maximize

Unused capacity, therefore, contributes nothing to the maximization of the objective function. The mathematical process of the simplex method starts at an arbitrary initial solution. In problems like this example that solution is the origin, where nothing but slack (having 0 contribution) is "produced." Proceeding systematically around the perimeter of the feasible region, slack is replaced by variables representing products that have a positive contribution margin per unit until an optimal solution is reached. Referring to the graph of Figure 3–3, you will see that at the optimal constraint intersection, no slack is "produced" in the departments that are at capacity, while the slack variable for the assembly operation takes on a positive value.

Results

Return now to your role as production manager of the ball-point pen factory. You have formulated the problem as in Table 3–4 and submitted it to your firm's computer, which indicated the optimal product mix exactly as you had calculated earlier. There are two additional pieces of information on the computer output that relate to the departments that are producing at their capacity. These are (for each department at capacity, or for each constraint having a slack assignment of 0) the *shadow price* (sometimes called the *dual value* or *implicit cost*) and the *range* over which this shadow price applies.

Shadow price. The shadow price information is a by-product of the simplex procedure that reports the value, in terms of total added contribution, of one additional unit of capacity for each constraint. In our example, for instance, if the capacity of the body molding department had been 2,001 dozen retractable pens instead of 2,000, the optimal product mix would have been 1,427.14 straight pens and 859.28 retractable pens.[7] Total contribution, then, would be $828.64, compared with $828.57 when the body molding department capacity is 2,000 dozen retractable pens. That extra unit of capacity, then, is "worth" about $0.07 per week. By comparing this shadow price with the cost of actually adding the capacity to produce another dozen retractable pen bodies, then, you can make some judgments about the desirability of such an investment.

Range. Of course, you are unlikely to want to move a constraint so slightly. It may be difficult to add just one more unit of capacity. You would probably want to add as much as you could if the shadow price indicated that the investment was worthwhile. The standard simplex option of ranging tells you how many units of capacity you can profitably add. In other words, ranging involves the process of moving constraints outward from the origin (in this example) until they are no longer limiting the solution. For instance, the body molding constraint could be moved outward on the graph of Figure 3–3 until it passes through the intersection of the filler manufacturing constraint and the assembly constraint.[8] Further additions to capacity beyond that intersection are meaningless unless additions to other constraints are also made. In the example, ranging will tell you that you may add capacity to produce as much as 212.5 dozen more retractable pens per week. If you did this, the equation for the body molding constraint would read:

$$0.8X + Y = 2,212.5$$

and would pass through the coordinate $X = 1,125$ and $Y = 1,312.5$, the intersection of the filler manufacturing and assembly constraints.

Similar results are also found for the filler manufacturing constraint. Interestingly, the shadow price for filler manufacturing is $0.23. This is logical, because if you had one additional unit of filler manufacturing capacity *and* one additional unit of body molding capacity, you would be able to produce one additional dozen retractable pens for a total increase in contribution margin of $0.30. At the current optimum, of course, you would be unwilling to expand your assembly department's capacity at any price, no matter how low, because adding to the

---

[7] Reread footnote 1.

[8] It must remain parallel to the original constraint, of course. Since this movement does not involve changing the technological coefficients of the equation but simply adds to the available resources, it is often referred to as *right-hand-side ranging*.

assembly department would not increase total contribution margin at all. In fact, since the slack variable associated with the assembly department has a positive value at the optimal product mix, there is currently some unused capability in that department.

The management meeting

Armed with your analysis of the production situation, your determination of an optimal production point, and plans for increasing plant capacity, you attend the weekly Wednesday morning managers' meeting for the first time. Your boss introduces you to the other managers present and promptly announces that your report will be the final agenda item for the morning.

The purchasing agent begins the session with a summary of new procurement policies and states that a new problem has arisen: "Because of a strike at the ACME Spring Factory, where we purchase the springs for our retractable pens, we'll be limited to 500 dozen springs per week until further notice. Unfortunately, our inventories of this item are pretty low right now, so I guess we'll have to live within that constraint for a while. I'm trying to develop an alternative source but that may take a few weeks."

At this point, little beads of perspiration begin to form on your forehead as the marketing manager begins to describe the plans for a new product: "The ZLP writing rod is ready to go. It should be introduced to production next week. The design people tell me that it should use the same filler as our retractable model, about half the assembly time, and, if the entire output of body molding is devoted to ZLP, we should be able to make 3,000 dozen per week. Contribution margin for ZLP is pegged at $0.35 per dozen. Oh yes, there's one more thing, I would like to request that at least half of our total production be this new model for the next several months as we'll need to build up our field inventories in preparation for initial market penetration. Is there any problem in that?"

The question was addressed to you. As you begin to formulate your response, the boss's secretary interrupts the meeting to say that headquarters is calling. The boss exits, saying: "Why don't you folks take a 30-minute break for coffee. We'll continue when I get those people in New York calmed down."

Pleased by this respite, you stand and are approached by a kindly old accountant who says: "I guess you'll be going to the computer for a little while. How do you take your coffee?"

Summary

As we take leave of the ball-point pen factory for the last time, we might wonder whether the new production manager will go to the computer to update the formulation (the student should do this as an exercise) or whether the manager will go and update his or her resume. In either case, it is useful to review a few salient features of this linear programming problem and to enumerate some of the assumptions of the technique in a more formal way before proceeding further.

Reality versus our simple example. The product mix problem such as faced by the production manager of the pen factory is a common situation in industry. Here, it was convenient to assume unlimited demand for the product. In a more realistic situation, limits to demand will be encountered. These can be conceived as added constraints in the model's formulation, as can the purchasing agent's supply limitation. Another kind of constraint can be the manager's judgmental limits to product mix. The manager may feel, as the marketing manager did, that some minimum portion of product output should consist of a particular product for longer-range reasons that transcend the immediate effect on contribution. Where this is the case, an analyst using linear programming will be able to tell how much such longer-range policies would cost (if anything) in terms of forgone short-run contribution margin.

Another important aspect of the ball-point pen product mix problem was its short-run nature. No long-run commitments were made or implied in deciding what the optimal mix should be for the next month. Still, the linear programming model was useful because it provided the basis for some managerial judgments regarding the effects of potential longer-run decisions on maximization of immediate total contribution. Of course, not all linear programming applications share this short-run orientation. When using the technique, however, the analyst should be alert to the implications of the concept of relevant costs developed in Chapter 2.

The ball-point pen example was useful for another reason. Since only two products were involved in the decision, it could be represented on a two-dimensional graph. Problems of this sort are frequently encountered in explanatory exposition as they help the student grasp the technique's essence and visualize the solution process. In the real world, things are seldom so simple. Many products might compete for the productive resources. For instance, in the example, addition of the new product made two-dimensional graphical analysis impossible. This is because, in problems like these, each production variable is represented by an axis of the graph. This is fine for two products, but it becomes increasingly difficult or impossible to visualize as the dimensions of the problem increase beyond three or four products. But the mathematical abstraction is easily solved by the identical methodology as used for the two-product problem. Regardless of whether the optimal constraint intersection involves two, or ten, or a thousand coordinates, the simplex method (or one of its more efficient offspring) can and will locate and report its exact location. Your main task, in dealing with linear programming models, is to formulate the problem correctly and interpret and use the results.

ASSUMPTIONS OF LINEAR PROGRAMMING

As with all models, the process of abstraction for linear programming problems requires making assumptions about the real-world system so that the technique can indicate a solution. In part, the process of testing involves close examination and judgment of how well the real-world system matches the assumptions of the technique. The major assumptions of linear programming are certainty, linearity, additivity, continuity, and independence.

Certainty

Every item in a linear programming formulation must be known with certainty, or you must be willing to *assume* that you know the precise values of all data for certain.

Linearity

The constraints and objective function of a linear program must be expressed as linear inequalities. This implies that there are no economies of scale in purchasing, production, selling, etc. Cost, price, technological coefficients, and other factors are, therefore, assumed to be constant over the entire range of production possibilities.

Additivity

The total usage of each resource is the sum of the amounts of that resource used in the production of each of the various products or activities. The effectiveness of any unit of resource is the same as any other unit of the same resource, no matter how it is used.

Continuity

Production or activity variables are assumed to be continuous; that is, they may take on fractional values.

Independence

Complete independence is assumed between variable coefficients and resource amounts. For example, the amount of one resource has no effect on the amount of another.

TRANSPORTATION PROBLEMS

Transportation problems are a class of linear programming problem for which finding an optimal solution is very much simplified. Frequently, transportation problems that would require a computer to solve by the simplex method can be solved manually using the transportation method.

The transportation method is named after the kinds of problems it was first used to solve. For example, a good may be available from three sources (manufacturing plants, mines, etc.) in predetermined quantities and required at four destinations (warehouses, steel mills, etc.), again in predetermined quantities. These quantities constitute the constraints of the problem. Since each source can ship to each destination, there are a total of 3 × 4, or 12 possible routes over which a quantity of the good may be shipped. These routes are the variables (or the activities or choices). The cost of shipping one unit of the good over each of the routes is the objective function. Determination of the minimum cost of shipping the good from the three sources where it is available to the four destinations where it is required is the objective statement of the problem.

To illustrate the transportation method, we will use a classic example. The essential details of the example are summarized in Table 3–5.

TABLE 3–5
Transportation problem example

Sources	Per-unit cost of shipping to destinations				Total available
	A	B	C	D	
I	$10	$15	$ 8	$20	7
II	$ 3	$ 2	$ 7	$15	5
III	$ 8	$11	$12	$18	3
Total required	4	2	3	6	15 15

There are three sources—labeled, I, II, and III—of a good that is to be supplied to four destinations—labeled A, B, C, and D. The quantities available at each source and required at each destination are given in the right and bottom margins, respectively, while the unit shipping costs (in dollars) over each of the 12 routes are given in the body of the table.

Simplex formulation

As suggested above, this problem has 7 constraint equations and 12 variables. Notice that the quantities available and the quantities required add to the same grand total. If this were not the case, some of the constraint equations would be written as inequalities, and slack variables would have to be introduced in order to achieve equalities for those constraints. If there were excess requirements, these slack variables would be added to the destination constraints. If there were excess capacity, slack variables would be added to the source constraints. The objective data for these slack variables, representing either unfilled requirements or unused capacities, are zero. The simplex formulation of this problem is shown in Table 3–6.

Notice that this resource allocation problem has a peculiar feature: All of the technological coefficients in the simplex matrix have the value of either zero or one. That is, a variable either enters an equation at its full value or it does not enter it at all. In more common language, a route is either used to ship a quantity of good or it is not used. It is this feature of the transportation problem (as signaled by the matrix full of zeros and ones) that lets us use the *transportation method* of linear programming to find the optimal solution to the shipment problem.

The first step is to set up a matrix as in Table 3–7. The constraint equations from the simplex formulation in Table 3–6 have been compressed to exclude the zero entries. Some constraints (the ones relating to destinations) now read from top to bottom, while others (relating to sources) read from left to right. Each box in the matrix represents one of the simplex variables, hereafter referred to as a *route*. Each route, as in the simplex formulation, therefore, enters two constraint equations: one a source and one a destination constraint. The objective data (cost) for each route are recorded (by convention) in the upper left-hand corner of the box representing the route.

The initial solution

Solving a linear programming problem, whether it is a transportation problem or not, is an iterative procedure starting from an arbitrarily selected initial solution. Recall that the simplex example presented earlier used the origin as an initial solution because the origin is sure to be part of the feasible region in problems of that sort. Notice that the origin in this case is not feasible. In fact, to ship nothing over any route would violate all seven constraints. Hence another way to select an arbitrary starting point is necessary. Several methods have been developed to do this, some more "efficient" than others. We will present

TABLE 3-6
Simplex formulation of transportation example

Constraints	Variables												Resources
	I-A	I-B	I-C	I-D	II-A	II-B	II-C	II-D	III-A	III-B	III-C	III-D	
Source I	1	1	1	1	0	0	0	0	0	0	0	0	7
Source II	0	0	0	0	1	1	1	1	0	0	0	0	5
Source III	0	0	0	0	0	0	0	0	1	1	1	1	3
Destination A	1	0	0	0	1	0	0	0	1	0	0	0	4
Destination B	0	1	0	0	0	1	0	0	0	1	0	0	2
Destination C	0	0	1	0	0	0	1	0	0	0	1	0	3
Destination D	0	0	0	1	0	0	0	1	0	0	0	1	6
Objective function	10	15	8	20	3	2	7	15	8	11	12	18	Minimize

TABLE 3-7
Initial program for transportation example

Sources	Destinations				Available
	A	B	C	D	
I	10 **4**	15 **2**	8 **1**	20 **0**	7
II	3 **0**	2 **0**	7 **2**	15 **3**	5
III	8 **0**	11 **0**	12 **0**	18 **3**	3
Required	4	2	3	6	

the "northwest corner" method which, in our opinion, is the easiest to master. There is only one restriction that must be observed in selecting an initial program for a transportation problem: The number of routes used must not be greater than $(m + n - 1)$, where m is the number of sources and n is the number of destinations. An initial solution that usually satisfies this requirement can be found by applying the northwest corner rule, to wit: Starting with the route I-A in the northwest corner of Table 3-7, set the amount of the commodity to be shipped over this route at either the requirements of A or the availability of I, whichever is smaller. Proceed across the table in a general northwest to southeast direction, exhausting the availabilities of one row before moving down to the next, and fulfilling the requirements of one column before moving on to the next. The initial program obtained for our example by using this northwest corner method is shown in Table 3-7. The shipments over each route are given in the center of the cell representing that route. The total cost of this shipping program can be determined to be $191 by multiplying the cost per unit on each route by the number of units shipped over each route and summing these costs over each route.

Pricing of alternative combinations

The initial program illustrated in Table 3-7 uses six routes $(3 + 4 - 1)$ at a positive level of shipment (I-A, I-B, I-C, II-C, II-D, and III-D) and six routes at a zero level. The six routes used at a positive level will be called *included* routes, and those at the zero level will be called *excluded* routes.

The *alternative combination* to an excluded route is defined as the combination of changes that would be required on *included routes*[9] if one unit were shipped over the excluded route. (Changes would be required because of the constraints.) Let us take the excluded route I-D as an example. If one unit were to be shipped over this route, it would be necessary, because of the restrictions on availabilities and requirements, to:

1. Decrease shipments over I-C by one unit.
2. Increase shipments over II-C by one unit.
3. Decrease shipments over II-D by one unit.

If one unit were shipped over route I-D, there would be a net saving on the alternative combination of $16, calculated as follows:

> Decreased costs:
> Route I-C .... $ 8
> Route II-D   15
> $23
>
> Less increased costs:
> Route II-C   7
> $16

Thus, $16 may be considered as the cost of shipping one unit over the alternative combination to route I-D rather than over route I-D itself. It is instructive to think of this $16 as the *opportunity cost of leaving route I-D unused,* since this cost could be saved on the alternative combination if route I-D were used. Since the cost of not using route I-D ($16 per unit) is less than the cost of using the route ($20 per unit), the route is better left unused; each unit shipped over the route would raise total costs by $4.

The costs of the alternative combinations to other excluded routes may be calculated in the same way. These costs are shown in Table 3–8 in the lower right-hand corners of the cells. The alternative combination in terms of included routes to any included route is, of course, that route itself. To represent the cost of this alternative combination, therefore, we simply transfer the cost given in the upper left-hand

---

[9] *Not* other excluded routes! Notice that there is one and only one alternative combination of included routes for each excluded route. This will always be true when the number of included routes equals $(m + n - 1)$. When the number of included routes exceeds $(m + n - 1)$, then some excluded routes will have more than one alternative combination of included routes, and a solution is impossible. In the course of the transportation method solution procedure, this will happen *only* through analyst error. When the number of included routes is fewer than $(m + n - 1)$, then some excluded routes will have *no* alternative combination of included routes. This occurs occasionally and is referred to as *degeneracy.* A way to handle degenerate transportation problems is described below.

corner of any cell representing an included route to its lower right-hand corner.

Substitute method of determination of opportunity costs

In the transportation method, the most tedious step is the determination of the costs of shipping over alternative combinations to excluded routes. Of course, the tedium becomes more pronounced the larger the problem is, since the number of excluded routes increases much faster than the number of included routes. These costs can be calculated by the shortcut procedure described below.

TABLE 3–8
Costs of alternative combinations of excluded routes for the initial program for transportation example

Source	Destinations				
	A	B	C	D	Available
I	10 **4** 10	15 **2** 15	8 **1** 8	20 **0** 16	7
II	3 **0** 9	2 **0** 14	7 **2** 7	15 **3** 15	5
III	8 **0** 12	11 **0** 17	12 **0** 10	18 **3** 18	3
Required	4	2	3	6	

1. First enter in the lower right corner of each *included* route the cost of shipping a unit of product over those routes. At this point, the transportation matrix will appear as shown in Table 3–9. (It is suggested that you follow the steps as given by entering the resulting numbers in Table 3–9.)
2. Select an *arbitrary* value for any one row (or column) and enter it in the column headed "Row values" (or the row labeled "Column values.") For example, select a value of 0 for row I.
3. For every *included route* in the row to which a value was assigned, determine a value for its column in such a way that (Row value) + (Column value) = (Cost of included route). With a value

TABLE 3–9
Student work sheet for substitute method of calculating costs of alternative combinations of excluded routes for the transportation example

Sources	Destinations				Row values
	A	B	C	D	
I	10 **4** 10	15 **2** 15	8 **1** 8	20 **0**	
II	3 **0**	2 **0**	7 **2** 7	15 **3** 15	
III	8 **0**	11 **0**	12 **0**	18 **3** 18	
Column values					

of 0 assigned to row I, for example, the value of column C must be 8; the value of column B, 15; and so forth.

4. Now use the column values just assigned to find unassigned row values in the same way; that is, for every included route in a column with a value assigned, determine a value for its row in such a way that (Column value) + (Row value) = (Cost of included route). With a value of 8 assigned to column C, for example, the value of row II must be −1.

5. Continue alternating between steps 3 and 4 until a value has been assigned to each row and column.

6. Now, for each *excluded* route, obtain the cost of its alternative combination of included routes by adding together the appropriate row value and column value. Enter this value in the lower right corner of its cell. If you have carried out these steps on Table 3–9, you should now compare that table with Table 3–8. The bodies of the two tables will be seen to be identical.

Improving the solution

If the cost of using an excluded route is less than the cost of using its alternative combination, then total costs will be reduced by substituting the excluded route for its alternative combination. In Table 3–8, four excluded routes satisfy this standard: II-A, II-B, III-A, and III-B.

The method of solution of a transportation linear programming problem requires, however, that *only one excluded route at a time be introduced into the program*. If a choice must be made, the rule customarily followed is to select the route for which the unit advantage from substitution is the greatest. In Table 3–8, this would be route II-B, since its cost is only $2 per unit, while the cost of its alternative combination is $14 per unit; a savings of $12 per unit can therefore be realized on every unit substituted.

Since $12 will be saved for every unit moved over route II-B, it is desirable to use the route to the maximum extent feasible. Because of the constraints, the factor controlling the number of units to be shipped over route II-B will be the amounts shipped over routes that will be reduced as a result of the substitution; the substitution can be made only until one of these quantities has been reduced to zero. Only two units are being shipped over routes I-B and II-C, both of which are in the alternative combination to II-B. Hence, only two units can be transferred to route II-B from its alternative combination.

The revised program obtained by transferring two units to route II-B from its alternative combination is shown in Table 3–10. The cost of this program is $167, as can be verified either by direct calculation or by subtracting $2 \times \$12 = \$24$ from $191, the cost of the program represented by Table 3–8.

Degeneracy. Table 3–10 illustrates a difficulty that may arise in the solution of a transportation problem. In going from Table 3–8 to Table 3–10, both routes I-B and II-C were eliminated from the program, while only route II-B was added. As a result, the revised program involves only five included routes. A program that includes fewer than $(m + n - 1)$ routes (six in this case) is said to be *degenerate*.

TABLE 3–10
First revised program for transportation example

Sources	Destinations			
	A	B	C	D
I	10 **4** 　　9	15 **0** 　　10	8 **3** 　　8	20 **0** 　　22
II	3 **0*** 　　3	2 **2** 　　2	7 **0** 　　1	15 **3** 　　15
III	8 **0** 　　6	11 **0** 　　5	12 **0** 　　4	18 **3** 　　18

The reason a degenerate program presents difficulties is that it is no longer possible to find alternative combinations for each excluded route. The student may verify in Table 3–10 that excluded route III-B has an alternative combination in terms of included routes but that none of the other excluded routes does. Thus we cannot perform the test to determine whether an excluded route should be substituted for its alternative combination.

Fortunately, the difficulties created by degeneracy can be overcome by a remarkably simple trick: We simply *pretend* that one of the excluded routes is included. In Table 3–10, for example, we have pretended that route II-A is included and have indicated this fact by starring it; any excluded route could have been selected. When this has been done, we have the required $(m + n - 1)$ included routes and are able to carry through the procedures of evaluating the costs of alternative combinations of included routes and improvement of the solution as before.[10]

Final program. A further improvement is possible in the program represented by Table 3–10, since route I-D has a unit cost of $20 while its alternative combination has a unit cost of $22. Substituting route I-D for its alternative combination involves decreasing traffic on routes I-A and II-D while increasing traffic on route II-A (which we have pretended to be an included route). Route I-D can be substituted for its alternative combination to the extent of the three units being shipped over route II-D. The resulting program is given in Table 3–11.

The cost of this shipping program is $161, which may be obtained by direct calculation or by subtracting $3 \times \$2 = \$6$ from $167, the cost of the preceding program. When the costs of the alternative combination to all excluded routes have been calculated, it is found that no further improvement is possible; in no case is the cost of using an excluded route less than the cost of using its alternative combination. Hence Table 3–11 represents an optimal program.

In one case, however, the cost of an excluded route (III-A) and the cost of its alternative combination are equal. This implies that route III-A could be substituted for its alternative combination with no change in total cost. The resulting program, Table 3–12, also costs $161.

In the final program, it will be noted that the two most costly routes (I-D and III-D) are both used. This is a result that very easily might

---

[10] Suppose route II-C had been starred in Table 3–10 rather than route II-A. Following through on the procedure of substituting an excluded route for its alternative combination when the route is less costly, it would be found that no such change in Table 3–10 would be feasible. In such a case, another route (such as II-A) should be starred and the procedure attempted again. When *all* excluded routes in a degenerate solution have been tried in this way and no improvement (or cost reduction) opportunities have been uncovered, the degenerate solution is optimal.

TABLE 3–11
Final program for transportation example

Sources	Destinations			
	A	B	C	D
I	10 **1** 10	15 **0** 9	8 **3** 8	20 **3** 20
II	3 **3** 3	2 **2** 2	7 **0** 1	15 **0** 13
III	8 **0** 8	11 **0** 7	12 **0** 6	18 **3** 18

have been overlooked by a traffic manager operating without the benefit of formal methods.[11]

Interpretation of the row and column differences

Notice that the costs in the lower right cells of the table representing any program always differ by a constant amount from row to row and from column to column. In the optimal program for our example (Table 3–11), the second row is uniformly $7 less than the first, and the third row is uniformly $2 less than the first. Similarly, column D is always $10 more than column A.

In the optimal program, these row and column differences have an important economic interpretation: They represent the *relative locational advantages* of the sources and destinations. A unit of the commodity is worth $2 more at source III than at source I, for example, because source III is closer on the average to the destinations, so it is able to supply them at a lower shipping cost (compare routes I-D and III-D, which are both used in the optimal program). Similarly, it costs $10 more to have a unit delivered at destination D than at destination A (compare routes III-A and III-D).

These values, which appear as by-products in the determination of

---

[11] Once we know the result, we can rationalize it: If we had supplied destination D from its cheapest source, II, that source would not have been able to ship over routes II-A and II-B, the cheapest routes. Overall optimization, therefore, requires use of the costliest routes in this case.

TABLE 3–12
Alternate optimal program for transportation example

Sources	Destinations			
	A	B	C	D
I	10 **0** 　　10	15 **0** 　　9	8 **3** 　　8	20 **4** 　　20
II	3 **3** 　　3	2 **2** 　　2	7 **0** 　　1	15 **0** 　　13
III	8 **1** 　　8	11 **0** 　　7	12 **0** 　　6	18 **2** 　　18

the optimal shipping program, are identical in concept with the shadow prices in the ball-point pen simplex example and thus have managerial significance of their own. From them we can determine, for example, that if the market at destination D is to be as desirable as that at destination A, the price must be $10 per unit higher. If we could expand capacity by one unit at some source, we should prefer to do so at source II, since this would enable us to reduce shipping costs by $7 by shipping one less unit from source I and one more from source II. You may want to verify this conclusion as an exercise.

THE CASES IN THIS CHAPTER

The cases in this chapter present you with opportunities to apply linear programming to problems that have been conceived of as constrained linear optimization. Most of these cases will require you to write the formulation of the problem. Some will require a computer routine to solve. Others, like Sherman Motors Company (case 3–1), Lockbourne Company (case 3–6), and McGowan Paint Company (case 3–7), are amenable to manual solution. For all of these cases, however, it will be necessary to interpret the results of the linear program in relation to the real world described by the case. This step, the process of testing the model's results, is most crucial. An optimal answer to the mathematical problem is useless unless accompanied by a reasonable set of managerial recommendations designed to transform "the answer" into operational reality.

Sherman Motor Company[1]

The Sherman Motor Company manufactured two specialized models of lightweight trucks in a single plant. Manufacturing operations were grouped into four departments: Metal Stamping, Engine Assembly, Model 101 Assembly, and Model 102 Assembly. Monthly production capacity in each department was limited as follows, assuming that each department devoted full time to the model in question:

| | Monthly capacity | |
Department	Model 101	Model 102
Metal Stamping	2,500	3,500
Engine Assembly	3,333	1,667
Model 101 Assembly	2,250	—
Model 102 Assembly	—	1,500

That is, the capacity of the Metal Stamping Department was sufficient to produce stampings for either 2,500 model 101 trucks or 3,500 model 102 trucks per month if it devoted full time to either model. It could also produce stampings for both models with a corresponding reduction in the potential output of each. Since each model 102 truck required five-sevenths as much of the capacity of the department as one model 101 truck, for every seven model 102 trucks produced it would be necessary to subtract five from the capacity remaining for model 101. If, for example, 1,400 model 102 trucks were produced, there would be sufficient stamping capacity available for 2,500 − (5/7)(1,400) = 1,500 model 101 trucks. Thus, the capacity restrictions in the four departments could be represented by the straight lines shown in Exhibit 1. Any production combination within the area bounded by the heavy portion of the lines was feasible from a capacity standpoint.

---

[1] Adapted from an example used by Robert Dorfman in "Mathematical or 'Linear' Programming: A Nonmathematical Approach," *American Economic Review*, December 1953.

EXHIBIT 1
Diagram showing production possibilities

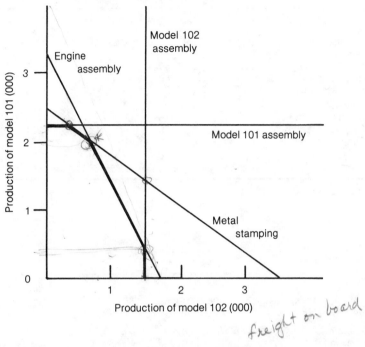

The prices to dealers of the two models, (f.o.b.) the Sherman plant, were $2,100 for model 101 and $2,000 for model 102. Sherman followed the price leadership of one of the larger manufacturers in the industry.

As a result of a sellers' market, Sherman currently was able to sell as many trucks as it could produce. The production schedules it had followed during the first six months of the year resulted in a monthly output of 333 model 101 trucks and 1,500 model 102 trucks. At this level of production, both the Model 102 Assembly and the Engine Assembly Departments were operating at capacity, but the Metal Stamping Department was operating at only 56.2 percent of capacity and the Model 101 Assembly Department was at only 14.8 percent. Standard costs at this level of production are given in Exhibit 2, and further details on overhead costs are given in Exhibit 3.

At a monthly planning session of the company's executives, dissatisfaction was expressed with the company's profit performance as reported in the six-month income statement just prepared (see Exhibit 4). The sales manager pointed out that it was impossible to sell the model 101 truck to yield a profit and suggested that it be dropped from the line in order to improve overall profitability.

EXHIBIT 2
Standard costs of two truck models

	Model 101		Model 102	
Direct materials		$1,200		$1,000
Direct labor				
Metal stamping	$ 40		$ 30	
Engine assembly	60		120	
Final assembly	100	200	75	225
Overhead*		*300*		*337*
Metal stamping	$216		$169	
Engine assembly	130		251	
Final assembly	445	791	175	595
Total		$2,191		$1,820

    * See Exhibit 3.

EXHIBIT 3
Overhead budget

Department	Total overhead per month*	Fixed overhead per month†	Variable overhead/unit	
			Model 101	Model 102
Metal Stamping	$ 325,000	$135,000	$120	$100
Engine Assembly	420,000	85,000	105	200
Model 101 Assembly	148,000	90,000	175	—
Model 102 Assembly	262,000	75,000	—	125
Total	$1,155,000	$385,000	$400	$425

90,000 (handwritten below Fixed overhead total)

  * Based on a planned production rate of 333 model 101 trucks and 1,500 model 102 trucks per month.
  † Fixed overhead was distributed to models in proportion to their degree of capacity utilization.

EXHIBIT 4
Income statement for six months ($000)

Net sales	$21,950
Cost of goods sold	20,683
Gross margin	$ 1,267
Selling, administrative and general expenses	1,051
Net income before taxes	$ 216
Taxes on income	115
Net income after taxes	$ 101

The controller objected to this suggestion. "The real trouble, Dick, is that we are trying to absorb the entire fixed overhead of the Model 101 Assembly Department with only a small number of units production. Actually these units are making a contribution to overhead, even though it's not adequate to cover fixed costs, and we'd be worse off without them. In fact, it seems to me quite possible that we'd be better off by *increasing* production of model 101 trucks, cutting back if necessary on model 102 production."

The production manager pointed out that there was another way in which output of model 101 trucks could be stepped up, which would not require a cutback in model 102 production. This would be through purchase of engines from an outside supplier, thus relieving the present capacity problem in the Engine Assembly Department. If this course of action were followed, Sherman would probably furnish the supplier with the necessary materials but would reimburse him for his labor and overhead.

At this point the president entered the discussion. He asked the controller, the sales manager, and the production manager to get together to consider the two questions raised by their comments and to report their recommendations to him the next day. The two questions were: (1) Assuming no change in present capacity and demand, what would be the most profitable product mix? (2) What was the maximum labor and overhead charge Sherman could afford to pay for engines if it purchased them from an an outside supplier?

case 3–2

Red Brand Canners*

On Monday, September 13, 1965, Mr. Mitchell Gordon, vice president of operations, asked the controller, the sales manager, and the production manager to meet with him to discuss the amount of tomato products to pack that season. The tomato crop, which had been purchased at planting, was beginning to arrive at the cannery, and packing opera-

* Reprinted from *Stanford Business Cases 1977* with the permission of the publishers, Stanford University Graduate School of Business. Copyright © 1977 by the Board of Trustees of the Leland Stanford Junior University.

tions would have to be started by the following Monday. Red Brand Canners was a medium-sized company which canned and distributed a variety of fruit and vegetable products under private brands in the western states.

Mr. William Cooper, the controller, and Mr. Charles Myers, the sales manager, were the first to arrive in Mr. Gordon's office. Dan Tucker, the production manager, came in a few minutes later and said that he had picked up Produce Inspection's latest estimate of the quality of the incoming tomatoes. According to their report, about 20 percent of the crop was grade "A" quality and the remaining portion of the 3,000,000-pound crop was grade "B."

Gordon asked Myers about the demand for tomato products for the coming year. Myers replied that they could sell all the whole canned tomatoes they could produce. The expected demand for tomato juice and tomato paste, on the other hand, was limited. The sales manager then passed around the latest demand forecast, which is shown in Exhibit 1. He reminded the group that the selling prices had

EXHIBIT 1
Demand forecasts

Product	Selling price per case ($)	Demand forecast (cases)
24–2½ whole tomatoes	4.00	800,000
24–2½ choice peach halves	5.40	10,000
24–2½ peach nectar	4.60	5,000
24–2½ tomato juice	4.50	50,000
24–2½ cooking apples	4.90	15,000
24–2½ tomato paste	3.80	80,000

been set in light of the long-term marketing strategy of the company, and potential sales had been forecasted at these prices.

Bill Cooper, after looking at Myers's estimates of demand, said that it looked like the company "should do quite well (on the tomato crop) this year." With the new accounting system that had been set up, he had been able to compute the contribution for each product, and according to his analysis the incremental profit on the whole tomatoes was greater than for any other tomato product. In May, after Red Brand had signed contracts agreeing to purchase the grower's production at an average delivered price of 6 cents per pound, Cooper had computed the tomato products' contributions (see Exhibit 2).

Dan Tucker brought to Cooper's attention that, although there was ample production capacity, it was impossible to produce all whole tomatoes as too small a portion of the tomato crop was "A" quality. Red

EXHIBIT 2
Product item profitability

			Product			
Costs ($)	24–2½ whole tomatoes	24–2½ choice peach halves	24–2½ peach nectar	24–2½ tomato juice	24–2½ cooking apples	24–2½ tomato paste
Selling price	4.00	5.40	4.60	4.50	4.90	3.80
Variable costs						
Direct labor	1.18	1.40	1.27	1.32	0.70	0.54
Variable overhead	0.24	0.32	0.23	0.36	0.22	0.26
Variable selling	0.40	0.30	0.40	0.85	0.28	0.38
Packaging material	0.70	0.56	0.60	0.65	0.70	0.77
Fruit*	1.08	1.80	1.70	1.20	0.90	1.50
Total variable costs	3.60	4.38	4.20	4.38	2.80	3.45
Contribution	0.40	1.02	0.40	0.12	1.10	0.35
Less allocated overhead	0.28	0.70	0.52	0.21	0.75	0.23
Net profit	0.12	0.32	(0.12)	(0.09)	0.35	0.12

* Product usage is as given below.

Product	Pounds per case
Whole tomatoes	18
Peach halves	18
Peach nectar	17
Tomato juice	20
Cooking apples	27
Tomato paste	25

Brand used a numerical scale to record the quality of both raw produce and prepared products. This scale ran from zero to ten, the higher number representing better quality. Rating tomatoes according to this scale, "A" tomatoes averaged nine points per pound and "B" tomatoes averaged five points per pound. Tucker noted that the minimum average input quality for canned whole tomatoes was eight, and for juice it was six points per pound. Paste could be made entirely from "B" grade tomatoes. This meant that whole tomato production was limited to 800,000 pounds.

Gordon stated that this was not a real limitation. He had been recently solicited to purchase 80,000 pounds of grade "A" tomatoes at 8½ cents per pound and at that time had turned down the offer. He felt, however, that the tomatoes were still available.

Myers, who had been doing some calculations, said that although he agreed that the company "should do quite well this year," it would not be by canning whole tomatoes. It seemed to him that the tomato cost should be allocated on the basis of quality and quantity rather than by quantity only, as Cooper had done. Therefore, he had recomputed the marginal profit on this basis (see Exhibit 3), and from his results, Red Brand should use 2 million pounds of the "B" tomatoes for paste, and the remaining 400,000 pounds of "B" tomatoes and all of the "A" tomatoes for juice. If the demand expectations were realized, a contribution of $48,000 would be made on this year's tomato crop.

EXHIBIT 3
Marginal analysis of tomato products

Z = Cost per pound of "A" tomatoes in cents
Y = Cost per pound of "B" tomatoes in cents
(1) (600,000 lbs. $\times Z$) + (2,400,000 lbs. $\times Y$) = (3,000,000 lbs. $\times$ 6)
(2) $\dfrac{Z}{9} = \dfrac{Y}{5}$

Z = 9.32 cents per pound
Y = 5.18 cents per pound

Product	Canned whole tomatoes	Tomato juice	Tomato paste
Selling price	$4.00	$4.50	$3.80
Variable cost (excluding tomato costs)	2.52	3.18	1.95
	$1.48	$1.32	$1.85
Tomato cost	1.49	1.24	1.30
Marginal profit	($0.01)	$0.08	$0.55

case 3–3

The law school question

In November 1978, Mr. Charles Krallman, an MBA student at The Ohio State University, was trying to decide which law schools he should apply to for the school year beginning in September of 1979. Although he felt that a law degree (in addition to his MBA) was necessary to achieve his objective of working in antitrust law, he was not convinced that a law degree from "just any school" would be worth the investment of three years of his time, not to mention income forgone plus the steep tuition of most law schools. Nonetheless, he was committed to the notion of applying to a variety of law schools. After the results of their admissions decisions were known, he could evaluate each school that admitted him on its relative merits. He would include, at that time, potential financial support, tuition, and school reputation in another analysis to decide which school to attend or even whether he should attend law school at all.

As an undergraduate economics major, Chuck had accumulated a grade point average (GPA) of 3.74 (out of 4.0), which placed him in the upper 3 percent of his graduating class at Ohio State. He had taken the LSAT (Law School Admissions Test) and received a score of 627, better than 82 percent of others taking that test. Mr. Krallman commented:

> My chances of being accepted by *some* law school are virtually 100 percent, but my chances of getting accepted to a top school are very low. Still, the payoff from a top school could be quite high. On the other hand, if I applied only to the top schools, I might not be accepted by any of them. The logical answer would be to apply to all of the top schools and several "backups." Unfortunately, each school requires a nonrefundable application fee of $10 to $35, and I just couldn't afford to apply to all of the schools I would like to. I have about $150 to spend on this venture and that's it. So I decided that I would try to maximize my chances of getting into a good law school by trading off the probability of acceptance (which I could estimate from the *Law School Handbook*) against the marginal value of the law degree from the various universities. To get that value, I first estimated a stream of earnings I would receive as an MBA without the law degree. Then I generated comparable figures assuming I had the law degree from different universities. After discounting this back, subtracting tuition and forgone income, and accounting for different costs of living in each city, I estimated the payoff associated with each school I was interested in. Finally, I multiplied that payoff by the probability of being admitted to each school given my GPA and LSAT score and came up with a marginal expected value for each university's law school.
>
> That may sound like a lot of work, and it was, but I had limited myself at the outset to some 22 schools that seemed to represent a broad spectrum of law school opportunities. These included several very prestigious Ivy League-type universities, a number of large state universities, and a few schools of lesser reknown as "backup" possibilities. I was satisfied that these 22 schools were enough for me to look at, especially since, after all, I can only actually go to one of them.

Exhibit 1 shows, in summary form, the results of Krallman's analysis. He decided that, since he was really trying to allocate scarce resources (his $150 budget) to competing demands (law school application fees), he could formulate his question as a linear program,

EXHIBIT 1
Basic data

Law school	Application fee	Probability of acceptance	Payoff	Weighted payoff
Capital University	$20	0.99	$10,000	$ 9,900
University of Chicago	15	0.05	20,000	1,450
University of Cincinnati.....................	25	0.99	11,000	10,890
Columbia University.........................	25	0.32	26,000	8,320
Cornell University	25	0.18	24,000	4,320
Georgetown University	25	0.25	20,000	5,000
George Washington University	25	0.36	18,000	6,480
Harvard University	35	0.04	30,000	1,200
Indiana University	15	0.50	16,000	8,000
University of Michigan	15	0.05	29,000	1,450
New York University.........................	20	0.13	24,000	3,120
Northwestern University	20	0.30	24,000	7,200
University of Notre Dame	15	0.60	16,000	9,600
Ohio State University........................	10	0.85	19,000	16,150
University of Pennsylvania	20	0.10	26,000	2,600
University of San Diego	25	0.96	12,000	11,520
Stanford University..........................	25	0.02	29,000	580
Washington University (St. Louis)	15	0.97	16,000	15,520
Yale University..............................	30	0.04	30,000	1,200
UCLA	20	0.30	25,000	7,500
University of California at Davis	20	0.45	13,000	5,850
Duke University	25	0.10	25,000	2,500

maximizing the payoffs weighted by the probabilities as the objective function coefficient for each law school variable.

As he wrote the formulation, he realized that his framework might eliminate *all* of the top schools because of their low probabilities of acceptance. Consequently, he decided to add constraints that would *positively* include *at least* one top school (Yale, Harvard, Columbia, University of Chicago, University of Michigan, Stanford) and at least one, but not more than two, "backup" schools. Additionally, he added two more constraints to insure that Columbia (because its literature promised "careful consideration" to applicants with GPAs higher than 3.5) and Ohio State (because he was a dedicated Buckeye) would appear in the final solution. He discovered, upon first submitting his program to the computer, that he also had to formulate a set of constraints to make certain that a single school would not be chosen more than once.

The results of the program indicated that Chuck should apply to the following schools:

University of Chicago
Columbia University
George Washington University
University of Notre Dame

Northwestern University
Ohio State University
UCLA
Indiana University
Washington University (St. Louis)

The total cost of applying to these schools was \$160—\$10 above his budget constraint (the solution included seven schools at a 1.0 level and one \$25 admission fee school at a 0.60 level). The extra \$10 investment didn't bother Chuck, but as he studied the results he began to wonder if his analysis had produced a worthwhile result. Wasn't this all pretty subjective stuff, even *with* the neat computer output? Wasn't he guilty of overanalyzing some pretty squishy numbers? And yet, reviewing the steps he had taken in this analytic effort, he couldn't positively identify any single spot where he could have been more rational. He was convinced that the procedure he had followed in deciding on this set of law schools was far more logical than any other method he had heard of. On the other hand, Chuck's roommate (who was also a law school applicant) had accused him of "turning the decision over to a machine" because Chuck was "afraid to use his own judgment."

case 3–4

Super-Rite Meats*

Dave Jackson, the production manager of Super-Rite Meats, recently attended an industry conference on the use of management science techniques in the meat-packing industry. At this conference Jackson was particularly intrigued by the potential use of linear programming in the planning and control of packing house operations. Upon returning to his office he assembled his team of production analysts and asked them to develop an appropriate linear programming model for trial use in the company's Table-Ready Meats (TRM) Division. If successful in this division, Jackson thought the model could easily be expanded to include other company operations. But because the con-

---

* This case was prepared by T. F. Funk and W. C. Pfeiffer of the University of Guelph, Ontario, Canada. Reprinted by permission.

cept was new to Super-Rite, he thought it prudent to start on a small scale and gradually build it up to include additional areas.

Heading the team of production analysts assigned to this job was Ken Norton. Although a meat scientist by training, Norton had become familiar with linear programming and was very excited about the possibility of using this technique in the planning and control of the TRM Division. He thought this was a particularly good area for an initial application because of the poor history of this division in cost and profit performance. Since the market for TRM products was expanding rapidly, poor performance in this division could become a major company problem in the near future.

In analyzing the operations of the TRM Division, Norton found that over 80 percent of the division's annual production could be accounted for by four major products—mince, salami, franks, and bologna. Thus he decided to concentrate his attention on these products in building his initial model.

The operation of the TRM Division was such that the major ingredients used were by-products from other company divisions. Five ingredients in particular were used in formulated meats. These were: pork trimmings, skinned jowls, pork cheeks, beef trimmings, and bull meat. Although usually sufficient quantities of these ingredients were available from other divisions within Super-Rite, occassionally these would be purchased from other suppliers. The prices for these ingredients were established in outside trading and varied considerably from week to week.

Of the four formulated products produced by Super-Rite, two products—mince and salami—were manufactured according to fairly rigid formulas in order to maintain high product quality standards. For example, mince could be produced by either one of two basic formulas. The ingredients used in mince production and the percentages of these ingredients in each formula were:

Ingredients	Percentage in formula 1	Percentage in formula 2
Pork trimmings	0.312	0.388
Skinned jowls	0.250	0.240
Pork cheeks	0.267	0.201
Beef trimmings	0.171	0.171
	1.000	1.000

Similarly, salami could also be produced by either one of two basic formulas. The ingredients used in salami and the percentages of these ingredients in each formula were:

Ingredients	Percentage in formula 1	Percentage in formula 2
Pork trimmings.....................	0.250	0.300
Skinned jowls	0.175	0.178
Pork cheeks	0.175	0.178
Beef trimmings....................	0.400	0.344
	1.000	1.000

Unlike mince and salami, the production specifications for franks and bologna were fairly flexible. Based on a substantial amount of product research, the company knew it could produce franks and bologna which would have essentially the same taste, color, and texture by using a wide range of kinds and amount of ingredients. Thus, for example, the specification for franks was stated as follows: Any combination of pork trimmings, skinned jowls, beef trimmings, bull meat, and water can be used so long as the following conditions are met:

1. Total fat must not exceed 31 percent of the finished product.
2. Total moisture must not exceed four times the protein content plus 10 percent of the finished product.
3. The amount of pork trimmings used must be greater than 15 percent but less than 35 percent of the finished product.
4. The amount of skinned jowls used must not exceed 25 percent of the finished product.
5. The amount of bull meat must be greater than 15 percent of the finished product.

In the case of bologna production, the production specification stated that: Any combination of skinned jowls, beef trimmings, bull meat, and water can be used so long as the following conditions are met:

1. Total fat must not exceed 26 percent of the finished product.
2. Total moisture must not exceed four times the protein content plus 10 percent of the finished product.
3. The amount of skinned jowls used must not exceed 30 percent of the finished product.
4. The amount of beef trimmings used must be greater than 35 percent but less than 60 percent of the finished product.

In order to meaningfully apply the above formulation guidelines, the company analyzed each incoming lot of ingredients for its biochemical composition, particularly for its percentages of fat, protein, and moisture. Although some variability was noted from lot to lot, the standards developed by Super-Rite over a considerable period of time for each of the ingredients were:

Ingredient	Fat	Protein	Moisture
Pork trimmings	62.6%	7.0%	29.0%
Skinned jowls	69.4	6.3	24.3
Pork cheeks	7.3	19.6	71.7
Beef trimmings	7.7	19.8	71.7
Bull meat	3.8	21.2	73.6

The company's traditional approach to the formulation problem, particularly for the flexible formula products of franks and bologna, was to use basic accounting data in selecting weekly formulas. This involved building a library of alternative product formulas that could be used in comparing the ingredient costs of various formulas as ingredient prices changed. An essential weakness of this approach for the flexible formula products was the almost infinite number of possible ingredient combinations that could be used. Using this approach, management had no way of knowing whether it was actually using the least-cost formulas. The number of alternative formulas was simply too large to be calculated and catalogued by conventional methods. Norton was convinced that his linear programming system would solve this basic problem.

In preparing to build his linear programming model for the TRM Division, Norton began by determining, in consultation with operating managers in the division, the planning and control data required for a weekly planning period. This information, shown in Exhibit 1, is broken down into reports for the division's three major functional units—procurement, formulation, and sales.

The ingredient procurement report shown in Part A of Exhibit 1 lists the five ingredients used in formulating table-ready meats, the optimal purchase quantities, and the expected purchase prices. The

EXHIBIT 1
Planning and control data required for weekly operations

A. Raw material procurement

Ingredients	Purchase amount (cwt.)	Purchase price ($/cwt.)
Pork trimmings	_____	_____
Skinned jowls	_____	_____
Pork cheeks	_____	_____
Beef trimmings	_____	_____
Bull meat	_____	_____

EXHIBIT 1 (*continued*)

B. Formulation guide

1. Mince

	Formula 1		Formula 2	
Ingredients	Amount (cwt.)	Percent of finished product	Amount (cwt.)	Percent of finished product
Pork trimmings	_____	_____	_____	_____
Skinned jowls	_____	_____	_____	_____
Pork cheeks	_____	_____	_____	_____
Beef trimmings	_____	_____	_____	_____
Total	_____	_____	_____	_____

2. Salami

	Formula 1		Formula 2	
Ingredients	Amount (cwt.)	Percent of finished product	Amount (cwt.)	Percent of finished product
Pork trimmings	_____	_____	_____	_____
Skinned jowls	_____	_____	_____	_____
Pork cheeks	_____	_____	_____	_____
Beef trimmings	_____	_____	_____	_____
Total	_____	_____	_____	_____

3. Franks

Ingredients	Amount (cwt.)	Percent of finished product
Pork trimmings	_____	_____
Skinned jowls	_____	_____
Beef trimmings	_____	_____
Bull meat	_____	_____
Water	_____	_____
Total	_____	_____

4. Bologna

Ingredients	Amount (cwt.)	Percent of finished product
Skinned jowls	_____	_____
Beef trimmings	_____	_____
Bull meat	_____	_____
Water	_____	_____
Total	_____	_____

C. Product sales guide

Product	Minimum sales (cwt.)	Maximum sales (cwt.)	Optimal sales (cwt.)	Market price ($/cwt.)
Mince	_____	_____	_____	_____
Salami	_____	_____	_____	_____
Franks	_____	_____	_____	_____
Bologna	_____	_____	_____	_____

optimal purchase amounts were to be determined by the linear programming model given the Procurement Department's best estimate
of purchase prices for the planning week.

Part B of Exhibit 1 gives formulation guides for each product. In the
case of mince and salami, separate formulation guides were prepared
for the two formulas. In all instances, the formulation guides show the
amount and percentage of each ingredient used in each product.

Finally, Part C of Exhibit 1 provides product sales guidelines. The
first two columns of this report were included to allow the sales management people to specify minimum and maximum sales quantities
for each product. Although Norton realized these restrictions might
lead to a suboptimal product mix, he felt it necessary to include these
because many times the Sales Department would work out special
deals with retailers in which they would guarantee the supply of a
certain minimum quantity. Furthermore, in other cases, particularly
because of seasonal sales trends, certain maximum sales limits on
products would have to be permitted. In addition to this information,
the product sales guide also included the optimum sales quantity, as
determined by the linear programming model, and the expected market prices supplied by the Sales Department.

In his consultation with the managers of the various departments,
Norton also determined a need for some additional information. The
procurement people, for example, were concerned with what they
should do if the expected purchase prices for the various ingredients
would change during the planning week. If this were to happen, they
wanted to know whether they should change their optimum purchase
quantities in light of the price changes. Norton wasn't sure how to
handle this problem, but thought his model might provide some clues.

In addition, the formulation people were very concerned with the
costs of the restrictions they were forced to meet. For example, in the
production of franks, one restriction they thought had a significant
impact on overall profitability was the restriction that total fat could
not exceed 31 percent of the finished product. They wondered what
the cost of this restriction really was, and if it could be reduced, how
this might affect profitability. Although they were very concerned
about the fat restriction, they also felt that the cost of all restrictions
should be investigated to determine their relative importance. Again,
Norton was not sure if he could handle this problem in his model, but
said he would look into it.

Finally, the sales people were concerned about the cost and/or
value of the maximum and minimum sales restrictions they placed on
the weekly planning system. Because this problem was so similar to
the problem of the costs of formulation restrictions, Norton thought it
should also be investigated.

With all of his information at hand, Norton began the task of constructing the linear programming model for the TRM Division of Super-Rite. Upon completion he planned to test the model using the data shown in Exhibit 2.

EXHIBIT 2
Data used for model testing

1. **Plant capacity:** 1,300 cwt./week

2. **Ingredient prices**

Ingredients	$/cwt.
Pork trimmings	20.00
Skinned jowls	15.50
Pork cheeks	33.50
Beef trimmings	41.00
Bull meat	50.00

3. **Product prices and sales requirements**

Product	Price ($/cwt.)	Minimum (cwt.)	Maximum (cwt.)
Mince	40.33	—	—
Salami	38.05	—	—
Franks	36.68	350	—
Bologna	35.11	300	—

case 3–5

Rubicon Rubber Company

On Friday, February 13, 1970, Mr. George Nelson, manager of the Tire Division of Rubicon Rubber Company was boarding a plane enroute to a New York meeting with representatives of Eastern Auto Stores to negotiate a final contract for the delivery of automobile snow tires. A preliminary version of the contract called for the delivery of 15,000 medium-grade nylon-cord tires and 11,000 high-grade fiberglass-cord tires over the three-month summer delivery period. Prices had tentatively been set at $7.00 for the nylon tires and at $9.00 for the fiberglass.

Mr. Nelson had approximately two hours of time during the flight in which to review his notes and to examine the analysis prepared for him by Jim Leader, a new member of the staff and a recent MBA. Nr. Nelson felt that there were a number of things which he had to resolve before he felt secure in finalizing the contract, so he was anxious to get to work quickly to avoid the possibility of a conversation with the fellow in the next seat.

BACKGROUND

Rubicon Rubber Company is a small company located in Independence, Ohio. It manufactured a variety of rubber products including tires for forklift trucks and small tractors. Founded in 1950, the company had grown rapidly in its early years and more slowly recently. Sales last year were $3 million. Future growth for the company appeared to be closely linked to the development and sale of specialty tractors and forklift trucks by the manufacturers of this equipment in western Ohio. Although most of Rubicon sales were tires for the small-tractor industry and rubber specialty products, Rubicon had for the past two years taken contracts to manufacture small runs of regular automobile snow tires for Eastern Auto Stores, one of the larger distributors of auto replacement tires. These small contracts supplemented larger ones placed with the major tire manufacturers elsewhere in Ohio. Those produced under the contracts bore the Eastern trademark and were to Eastern's specifications.

Rubicon had found it advantageous to take these short-lead-time contracts to utilize surplus capacity. (Expansion of plant and facilities in 1967 had left Rubicon with excess capacity that was expected to be fully utilized in time.) Normal production planning allowed tire machine utilization to be determined relatively accurately eight months in advance.

The contract with Eastern called for a staged delivery schedule of the two types of snow tires over the three summer months as indicated in Exhibit 1. The major problem in planning the production of these tires was the availability of sufficient tire machine capacity to insure that the contract could be satisfied. Only two types of machines could potentially be used in molding tires of the sort covered by the contract, the Wheeling and Regal machines. Virtually no time was available on either type machine until the first of June. After that time unused capacity was available spasmodically between other contracts. A table of anticipated machine availability as prepared by Joe Tabler, the production supervisor, is shown in Exhibit 2.

The two types of molding machines were similar except for their speeds. That the Wheeling machine was somewhat faster for both

EXHIBIT 1
Delivery schedule

Date	Nylon	Fiberglass
June 31	4,000	1,000
July 31	8,000	5,000
August 31	3,000	5,000
Total	15,000	11,000

EXHIBIT 2
Molding machine production hours available

	Wheeling machine	Regal machine
June	700	1,500
July	300	400
August	1,000	300

types of tire than the older Regal machines is shown by the production figures of Exhibit 3. This had tended to complicate production planning in previous years.

There was also a difference in productivity between nylon and fiberglass. This was due primarily to mold fastenings. The molds for

EXHIBIT 3
Production capacity for each tire (hour/tire)

	Nylon	Fiberglass
Wheeling machine	0.15	0.12
Regal machine	0.16	0.14

the nylon tires were somewhat more difficult to work with than those used for fiberglass tires. Since Eastern provided the molds, there was no easily made modification to basic equipment that was feasible in the short run. A machine shop modification was possible to improve efficiency, but it had never seemed practical in view of the short-time duration of the contract.

Costs (shown in Exhibit 4) were prepared by the Accounting Department for use in production planning. The difference in costs between the two machines shown in Exhibit 4 was due primarily to a

EXHIBIT 4
Production planning costs

Wheeling machine	
Initial cost: $50,000	
Depreciation method: straight line	
Life: five years	
Machine amortization	$ 4.17/hr.
Operating labor	3.75/hr.
Supervision	0.25/hr.
Overhead =../2..machine..+..½..office..........	2.00/hr.
Total	$10.07/hr.
Regal machine	
Initial cost: $45,000	
Depreciation method: straight line	
Life: 5 years	
Machine amortization	$ 3.75/hr.
Operating labor	3.75/hr.
Supervision	0.25/hr.
Overhead	2.00/hr.
Total	$ 9.75/hr.

difference in initial equipment purchase price. Material costs for the nylon tire were estimated to be $3.10 and for the fiberglass tire $3.90. Finishing, packaging, and shipping were not expected to exceed $0.23 per tire. Costs were based on actual costs last year adjusted for price increases.

Warehouse space was not expected to be available within the company, since inventory would be at a seasonal high and the company would be receiving materials for fall production of new tractor tires. However, tires could be stored at a local warehouse at a cost of approximately $0.10 per tire per month. There was a storage area adjacent to the production shop where up to one month's production could be kept until delivered to the warehouse or to Eastern. Monthly storage costs at the warehouse were assessed on the tires as they were placed into storage and space had to be reserved ahead of time. Shipping was scheduled three days prior to the end of the month for delivery the last day of the month.

THE DECISION PROBLEM

As Mr. Nelson sat down he pulled the Eastern Auto file from his briefcase and thought back over the short meeting with Jim Leader that he had managed to squeeze in before rushing to the airport. He had assigned the job of planning the production schedule to Jim even though he was new with the company, because Jim was bright and appeared to be an independent thinker. Since time was short, Mr. Nelson remembered the misgivings he had experienced when he found that Jim had formulated the problem as a linear program. Now he was forced to think back to his own exposure to this subject in his attempt to understand what Jim had done. At the same time he remembered that he had often thought the problem "looked like" a programming problem but there never seemed to be time to work out the details. Jim had prepared a short memo attached to the computer output which Mr. Nelson planned to study (see Exhibit 5).

EXHIBIT 5
Memorandum

TO: George Nelson
FROM: Jim Leader
SUBJECT: Scheduling for Eastern Auto Tire Contract

I have formulated the equipment and scheduling problem for this contract as a linear programming problem. I could see that there was not time to do what you wanted without taking this approach and also I believe the answers to be better than I could do by hand.

The problem is one of minimizing the cost of producing and storing tires. (See the LP tableau of Attachment 1.)

From the tableau you can see that there are two kinds of choice variables:

1. The number of each type tire to be scheduled on the Wheeling machine and the number on the Regal machine in each month. I have designated these as follows:

   W_n = Number of nylon tires to be produced on the Wheeling machine

   W_g = Number of fiberglass tires to be produced on the Wheeling machine

   R_n = Number of nylon tires to be produced on the Regal machine

   R_g = Number of fiberglass tires to be produced on the Regal machine

2. The number of each type placed to be in inventory at the end of the month. For the inventory variables:

   I_n = Number of nylon tires to be carried into inventory at the end of each month

   I_g = Number of fiberglass tires to be carried into inventory at the end of each month.

Note that I have used the subscripts n = nylon and g = fiberglass. I have also used superscripts above the numbers to indicate the month, since most of the variables are defined in all three time periods; 1 = June, 2 = July, and 3 = August.

EXHIBIT 5 (*continued*)

Thus, the variable W_g^3 stands for the number of fiberglass tires to be produced in August on the Wheeling machine. (Please note that these superscripts are a symbolic way of distinguishing between the months; W_g^3 does *not* mean raise W_g to the third power.)

The constraints are of two types:

1. The constraints on the available machine time in each month.
2. Demand or delivery constraints in each month.

To determine the machine availability constraint in each month, I took the number of nylon tires made on Wheeling equipment times the hours per nylon tire plus the number of fiberglass tires made on Wheeling equipment times the hours per fiberglass tire. This gives the total number of Wheeling machine hours for the month, which must be less than the Wheeling hours available in that month. For July:

$$0.15W_n^2 + 0.12W_g^2 \leq 300 = \text{Availability of Wheeling hours in July}$$

The demand constraints stipulate that the tires produced in a month plus the tires in inventory from the last month less the amount returned to inventory at the end of this month must equal the amount demanded in that month. Thus, for July the nylon tire equation is:

$$W_n^2 + R_n^2 + I_n^1 - I_n^2 = 8,000 = \text{Demands for nylon tires in July}$$

The program seeks to minimize the total cost* of operating the tire machines and storing inventory over the entire three-month period. The computer output for the problem is shown in Attachment 2. For your convenience, I have also indicated the principal results from the computer output on the tableau itself.

---

* The costs of operating the tire machines are taken to be the sum of operating cost and supervision plus half the overhead charge.

EXHIBIT 5 (continued)

Attachment 1: The Linear Programming Tableau*

	June Nylon W_n^1	R_n^1	June Glass W_g^1	R_g^1	June Inv. I_n^1	I_g^1	July Nylon W_n^2	R_n^2	July Glass W_g^2	R_g^2	July Inv. I_n^2	I_g^2	Aug Nylon W_n^3	R_n^3	Aug Glass W_g^3	R_g^3	RHS	Dual variables
Machine time constraints																		
June {Wheeling	0.15		0.12														≤ 700	−0.333
{Regal		0.16		0.14													≤ 1,500	
July {Wheeling							0.15		0.12								≤ 300	−1.166
{Regal								0.16		0.14							≤ 400	−0.625
August {Wheeling													0.15		0.12		≤ 1,000	−0.333
{Regal														0.16		0.14	≤ 300	
Demand constraints																		
June {Nylon	1	1			−1												= 4,000	0.8
{Glass			1	1		−1											= 1,000	0.64
July {Nylon					1		1	1			−1						= 8,000	0.9
{Glass						1			1	1		−1					= 5,000	0.74
August {Nylon											1		1	1			= 3,000	0.8
{Glass												1			1	1	= 5,000	0.64
Objective	0.75	0.80	0.60	0.70	0.10	0.10	0.75	0.80	0.60	0.70	0.10	0.10	0.75	0.80	0.60	0.70	Minimum	
Optimal solution	1,866.6	7,633.3	3,500.00		5,499.9	2,500.0	2,500.9	2,499.9					2,666.6	333.3	5,000.0		Optimal value of objective $19,173.33	

* All blanks are zeros.

Hours available

Number of tires demanded

Handwritten annotations: 0.75¢/lb; 4000 1000; 1500 1500

EXHIBIT 5 *(concluded)*
Attachment 2

LINEAR PROGRAMMING SYSTEM—RELEASE 6
INSTRUCTIONS (TYPE YES OR NO)? *N*
OPTION? *OPT*
DATA SET NAME? *RUBIC*
TITLE: RUBICON RUBBER
PROCEED, DISPLAY, OR REJECT? *P*
MAXIMIZE OR MINIMIZE? *MIN*
OPTIMAL SOLUTION FOUND.
  COST   19173.3
OUTPUT OPTION? *U*
ALL ITEMS NOT LISTED IN SECTIONS 1–4 HAVE THE VALUE ZERO.
1 DECISION VARIABLES

1.	WN-1	1866.67
2.	RN-1	7633.33
3.	WG-1	3500.00
5.	IN-1	5500.00
6.	IG-1	2500.00
8.	RN-2	2500.00
9.	WG-2	2500.00
13.	WN-3	2666.67
14.	RN-3	333.333
15.	WG-3	5000.00

2 SLACK(+) AND SURPLUS(−) IN CONSTRAINTS

2.	+R-1	278.667
6.	+R-3	246.667

3 SHADOW PRICES FOR CONSTRAINTS

1.	W-1	−.333333
3.	W-2	−1.16667
4.	R-2	−.625000
5.	W-3	−.333333
7.	N-1	.800000
8.	G-1	.640000
9.	N-2	.900000
10.	G-2	.740000
11.	N-3	.800000
12.	G-3	.640000

4 REDUCED COSTS FOR DECISION VARIABLES

4.	RG-1	.600000E-01
7.	WN-2	.250000E-01
10.	RG-2	.475000E-01
11.	IN-2	.200000
12.	IG-2	.200000
16.	TG-3	.600000E-01

OUTPUT OPTION? *N*
OPTION? *TER*

He also thought back to the meeting with Tabler. Tabler had mentioned when he produced his equipment schedule that an additional Wheeling tire machine was due to arrive the last of August. For a $200 fee it could be expedited to arrive a month earlier. Tabler had estimated that early arrival would make available 172 additional hours of Wheeling machine time in August.

Normally vacations were scheduled during the three summer months with approximately one third of the staff gone during each month. Mr. Nelson felt he would be able to put together the required manpower, though it would almost inevitably involve delaying some vacations until Christmas and hiring a few temporary men. Providing supervisory staff would present similar problems.

About one half of overhead costs was equipment depreciation and the other half was due to office expense. Overhead was allocated on the basis of direct labor and amounted to 50 percent of labor and supervision. The company had not computerized its clerical operations, so the presence of the Eastern contract would call for considerable office work.

As he prepared to go over the material, Mr. Nelson ticked off in his mind a few of the things that he would like to have at the conclusion of his analysis, whether or not he found Jim's linear programming approach satisfactory.

1. A summary of costs and revenues that he could show his boss John Toms, president of Rubicon, when he returned from the meeting with Eastern.
2. Materials for drafting a memo to Joe Tabler, telling him which machines to schedule for what, when, and whether to expedite the new machine.
3. A schedule of warehouse needs so that he could reserve space at the Bekson Warehousing Company.
4. A tentative schedule for the Maintenance Department indicating when the yearly maintenance check on the various machines could be performed.

One final worry he hoped to resolve before going into the meeting involved what his strategy should be if Eastern asked for more fiberglass tires. The Eastern representative to whom he had talked on the telephone the previous day had suggested that Eastern just might want more, since sales had been very good the previous year. As he turned to the task of analysis, he noted the weather outside and thought to himself that if there were time due to delays in landing at the Kennedy Airport he would like to explain to himself what was going on with those dual variables, but the other matters seemed more important at the moment.

Solve using Tran   case 3–6

The Lockbourne Company

The Lockbourne Company was one of the country's leading manufacturers and distributors of a line of packaged goods which it sold nationally under the trade name of Burn-Lock Products. The company operated three factories from which it shipped to regional warehouses or directly to large outlets.

In 1977, demand for Burn-Lock Products was 3,200,000 "equivalent" cases, distributed as follows according to the five sales regions:

Sales region	Forecast demand (100,000 cases)
Atlanta	5
Los Angeles	4
Dallas	4
Chicago	11
New York	8
	32

One-shift production capacity in each of the three plants was as follows:

Plant	Production capacity (100,000 cases)
Home city	12
Branch 1	7
Branch 2	15
	34

Estimated freight costs per case from each of the factories to each distribution center are given in Exhibit 1. While not all shipments were routed through regional warehouses, on the average the freight cost on direct shipments to outlets was quite close to the cost which would have been incurred if the shipment had been routed through the servicing warehouse.

Lockbourne followed a philosophy of decentralized management. Top executives favored this approach for a number of reasons. First, by enriching the experience of subordinate managers, it provided better training for ultimate top management responsibility. Second, it in-

EXHIBIT 1
Schedule of freight rates (dollars per case)

Factory	Regional warehouse				
	Atlanta	Los Angeles	Dallas	Chicago	New York
Home city	$0.95	$1.05	$0.80	$0.15	$1.00
Branch 1	0.35	1.80	1.40	0.80	0.30
Branch 2	0.90	1.80	1.60	0.70	0.85

sured that, insofar as possible, operating decisions were made by those persons most familiar with the detailed circumstances which would determine the success or failure of the decisions. Under the decentralized approach, subordinate managers were held responsible for the profitability of operations under their control.

Consistent with the policy of decentralization, each of the five regional warehouses was under the direct supervision of a regional sales manager. The warehouses were not assigned to a particular plant for servicing, since demand shifts made a certain amount of flexibility necessary. Rather, the regional sales manager or a delegated subordinate decided upon which plant to place an order. The price paid by the warehouse was $6.25 per case f.o.b. the plant. This price was set to recover costs plus a reasonable return on investment for the manufacturing division.[1] Since the regional warehouse was required to absorb the freight costs, it was expected that the regional sales managers would place their orders so as to minimize their own freight costs and hence those of the company as a whole.

Over a period of time, this procedure had led to increasing amounts of organizational friction, and in early 1978 some officials of Lockbourne were beginning to question whether the procedure was even achieving the objective of minimizing freight costs. Because Branch 2 was not the closest plant to any of the regional warehouses, it was never deliberately selected as a source by a regional sales manager. Rather, the managers would initially order from the home city or Branch 1, whichever was closer. Since these plants had inadequate capacity to meet all sales demands, it was then necessary for the plant managers to reject some orders. No consistent procedure was followed in determining which orders would be accepted, but it was largely a matter of "first-come-first-served." The regional managers whose orders were rejected were then usually forced to take them to Branch 2, typically at a considerable increase in freight cost. This aspect of the situation resulted in much grumbling by the regional managers.

---

[1] Variable costs of manufacture were quite similar in the three plants.

Moreover, since the orders placed with Branch 2 were not placed there in a conscious effort to minimize freight costs, there appeared to be a strong possibility that the resulting overall shipping program was not optimal. For this reason, some executives felt that the practice of leaving shipping decisions to the decentralized judgments of regional managers should be discontinued. They proposed instead that all orders be routed through a central office which could then determine an optimal shipping program from an overall company point of view. The actual quantities shipped over each possible route in 1977 are given in Exhibit 2; total shipping costs that year were about $2,275,000.

EXHIBIT 2
Shipping program in 1977 (100,000 cases)

Factory	Regional warehouse					
	Atlanta	Los Angeles	Dallas	Chicago	New York	Total
Home city	0	1	2	9	0	12
Branch 1	3	0	0	2	2	7
Branch 2	2	3	2	0	6	13
Total	5	4	4	11	8	32

Other executives were concerned about the effect such a proposal would have on the general effectiveness of decentralized management. They also observed that one result of the proposal would be to saddle the regional sales managers with freight costs over which they could exercise no control.

Introduce Dummy Warehouse (6 total)
Reg. Warehouse in Rochester Cost = 0

case 3–7

McGowan Paint Company

The McGowan Paint Company operated four factories and five warehouses located in the New England, Middle Atlantic, and Midwestern states. Eighty-five percent of McGowan's paint was for interior and exterior household use. Except for 15 company-owned stores in the greater New York City area, distribution at the retail level was through 600 independent, franchised dealers.

In recent years, the company's share of the market had dropped six percentage points. Fifteen of McGowan's best retail accounts had shifted to competitors' paints because they said their margin had grown too slim. Mr. B. A. Vernon, sales manager, made an intensive study of the situation and had this to say in his report:

> Quality-wise and delivery-wise our performance has been as good or better than most of our competitors. It's price where we've been losing out. Our list prices are the highest in three of the four largest selling types of paint. I'm convinced that to boost our share of the market, we'll have to cut our list prices across the board by a minimum of 5 percent, and preferably 7 percent. I also recommend that we open up more of our own retail stores in all territories. This will help to offset effects of price cuts on our margin, while boosting our total volume to where it should be.

After discussing Mr. Vernon's report with his brother, H. B. McGowan, president and treasurer, Mr. T. A. McGowan, executive vice president, said: "You're probably right about pushing cost reduction instead, Hank. Our margin is slim enough already. You're closer to the financial market than I am, and if you say we can't get the money for reasonable terms to expand our retail chain beyond New York, then we'll have to try to offset a price cut by cutting costs."

Each of the four plants was equipped to manufacture all types of paints sold by McGowan. For a variety of reasons, average direct unit costs were not uniform at all plants. Pigment dispersing mills and blending equipment were 20 years old in one plant and only three, five, and six years old in the other three plants; hence, hourly productivity and labor costs of operating and maintaining the older equipment were higher in the oldest plants. The f.o.b. plant costs of purchased materials (pigments, chemicals, and blending vehicles) varied because freight distances and costs were different for each plant. There were also slight differences in wages among the plants.

Briefly, the manufacture of paint in McGowan's plants involved a three-stage process. First, pigments were thoroughly dispersed in paste-like form by running them between two large, rotating steel cylinders until they reached the desired color, uniformity, and consistency. Next, the dispersed pigments were blended with selected "vehicles" (usually oils or lacquers) in large tanks equipped with mechanical agitators. Finally, the paint was packaged in a variety of standard size cans. After being dispersed, pigments had to be moved promptly to the blending stage; however, after being blended, the paint could be temporarily stored in tanks, before being packaged. Economic batch sizes were set by estimating the minimum sum of inventory carrying and equipment changeover costs for a year.

Freight costs of shipments from plants to warehouses varied significantly with distances from plants to warehouses. Accordingly, McGowan's "distribution policy" was to keep shipping costs at a minimum. Mr. T. A. McGowan had divided the multiplant-warehouse system into geographical units in such a way that each plant supplied only the nearest warehouse(s). (Of course, there were minor, temporary exceptions to this policy, when inventory levels were out of balance.)

Mr. T. A. McGowan discussed ways he approached his cost reduction problem: "One of my first considerations was to cut costs by replacing the old equipment in our Philadelphia and Springfield (Mass.) plants. But this would have meant major capital expenditures we couldn't afford. Another alternative would have been to have our purchasing agent shop around for better prices on materials we buy. There are probably big savings opportunities here because materials are 58 percent of our unit cost. But I don't think this would have been a way to realize the savings quickly enough. Besides, we might have jeopardized our quality and delivery performance by changing suppliers. What we needed was a way to cut the costs of utilizing the resources we already have. This led me to reconsider our method of assigning plants to meet our warehouse requirements. We've decided to try linear programming, which, as I understand it, is a technique that guarantees to minimize the variable costs of producing and shipping products."

Mr. McGowan requested the controller and traffic manager to obtain the shipping cost data shown in Exhibit 1. To obtain data measuring plant capacity available, he telephoned each of the five plant managers to explain what he wanted, and then sent a memorandum to confirm his request.

EXHIBIT 1
Data required to program operations at McGowan's four factories and five warehouses

Shipping cost ($ per 100 gallons)

	Factory				Warehouse requirements (gallons per
Warehouse	I	II	III	IV	day × 100)
A	$1.30	$0.80	$2.10	$1.70	29
B	1.90	1.30	2.60	2.30	50
C	1.70	1.10	2.80	1.90	22
D	1.80	1.40	2.60	2.20	19
E	1.50	1.80	2.30	2.10	35

Factory capacity (gallons per day × 100)

	Factory			
	I	II	III	IV
Single shift	55	90	35	105
Overtime	15	20	9	30

Manufacturing cost ($ per 100 gallons)

	Factory			
	I	II	III	IV
Normal	$21.80	$22.40	$23.10	$27.50
Overtime	25.60	26.10	27.80	32.90

. . . For us to use the transportation model of linear programming, we need a single measure of plant capacity in gallons per day. I realize that actual output rates vary for different types of paints made on the same equipment, and also that total output per day depends on the downtime for cleaning and adjusting the equipment between runs. However, the capacity figure I need will be accurate enough if you will compute it in the following manner:

1. Consider your (pigment) dispersing mills to be the key determinants of factory capacity, and calculate the average gallons per hour of equivalent blended paint the mills can produce. This average should be weighted by the forecasted product mix as follows: 40 percent for series 1,000 paints (flat-coat outside paints); 35 percent for series 3,000 paints (semigloss, inside paint); 25 percent for series 5,000 paints (inside, glossy enamel paint).

2. Estimate the average amount of time (in hours) you shut down a mill for run changeover work, including cleaning out the materials, set-

ting and adjusting the rolls, and putting in the first load of new materials to be dispersed in the next run. Also, estimate the average number of such changeovers per mill per day. Multiply this number of changeovers by the number of mills in your plant, and then multiply this result by your above estimate of average changeover time per mill. This figure should be the average hours per day for mill-run changeover time for your plant. Subtracting this from eight hours leaves the average productive time available for your mills.

    3.   Plant capacity in gallons per day is then (1) × (2). . . .

Requesting manufacturing cost data, Mr. McGowan said to Mr. R. A. Fetter, controller, "Bob, the cost data we need for each plant has to represent the average of the variable expenses per 100 gallons produced at that plant. I'd like your data to reflect whatever differences we have to pay for freight on purchased materials. Use your own judgment about the mix of materials you include in the input-output unit of equivalent standard 100 gallons; I told the plant managers to assume a 40-35-25 percentage breakdown of our three basic types of paints. You'll probably want to analyze the mix further, but I leave that to you. As far as labor and overhead costs are concerned, you know better than I that less than half our factory payroll is a strictly variable expense. I would like to have two sets of cost data, though; the cost per 100 gallons produced at each plant on straight time and the other the cost on the basis of overtime."

Mr. Fetter's cost data are summarized in Exhibit 1.

For demand data, Mr. McGowan used the latest monthly shipping forecasts furnished by Mr. Vernon's assistant sales manager. These data are also summarized in Exhibit 1.

Decisions under uncertainty

THE PRINCIPLE OF UNCERTAINTY

In the late 1920s a German scientist named Werner Heisenberg addressed the question of the positions of electrons orbiting around an atomic nucleus. He claimed that it was both theoretically and practically impossible to pinpoint the exact location of an electron in its orbit. Heisenberg reasoned that to determine the exact position of an electron, one had to "see" it—had to see, that is, *exactly* where it was. But in order for something to be seen, it must be exposed to at least a single ray of light. In the case of an electron, the thing being seen is so small that the light ray knocks it out of the way. Where the electron *is*, then, can never be seen. All that can be seen is where it *was* before the light ray struck it.

At first glance this conclusion, called the *Uncertainty Principle*, was a pretty disconcerting piece of information for atomic scientists. The principle states that it is theoretically impossible to know exactly where an electron really is at any given time. Scientists are rescued from this embarrassing impasse, however, by the existence of a mathematical equation that gives the *probability* that a given electron will be in a given place at a given time. Although they cannot know for sure that an electron will be in its proper position according to the Bohr model, atomic scientists do know for sure the *probability* that it will be in that position. Naturally this probability is quite high, while the probability that it will be far removed from this position is quite low.

It is a fact of nature, then, that it is impossible to know the exact position of an electron. It is also a fact of nature, however, that the probability that an electron will be in any one position *can* be determined exactly. Atomic scientists deal with the uncertainty in their science by describing the uncertainty in mathematical terms.

The businessperson constantly faces this same problem of uncertainty. It is impossible to determine exactly, for example, what the demand for a certain product will be next year. The very best that could be done is to determine what it would be if one did not person-

119

ally take action to change it—say, with new product features or stepped-up promotions. Even this sort of estimate, however, is not really possible because there are so many factors influencing demand. Everything from the take-home pay of heads of families to the whims of Paris fashion designers might conceivably affect the demand for a certain product. Business executives, like scientists, face uncertainty as a fact of nature. The problem, then, is: Can business executives *rationally* deal with uncertainty? Can they describe the uncertainty they face in rational, mathematical terms?

Many business firms, of course, do deal with uncertainty in a rational way. Life insurance companies, although they know for sure that every individual will eventually die, cannot know exactly *when* any one individual is going to die. Instead, they calculate the probability of that person dying in any given year. These calculations, of course, have become the very basis of the life insurance business.

Companies engaged in research and development cannot know which R&D projects will be successful or how successful they will be. They can and do, however, estimate the likelihood of success and the likelihood of various degrees of success. In this area, though, the uncertainty is so great that it is extremely difficult to deal with it on a rational basis.

Uncertainty, then, is just as much a part of business as it is of science. It is a fact of nature and nothing is ever going to make it go away. No one really wants it to go away because it is the very foundation of business and economics. The thing to do, then, is to recognize uncertainty and deal with it as rationally as possible.

Historically, businesspeople have dealt with uncertainty by using good judgment. They looked at the past to see what had happened in similar cases, and they used their intuition to determine what would happen in the future. The quality of their experience and the quality of their intuition spelled the difference between success and failure. To improve decision making under conditions of uncertainty, modern business executives *quantify* their experience and their intuition. They develop probability models of business that can be analyzed and tested for answers to such questions as: Is this what I really mean? Is this what the world is really like?

DECISION DIAGRAMMING

We have all been faced with decisions involving uncertain outcomes and have tried to adopt strategies or courses of action that would tend to improve the likelihood of a favorable outcome. For instance, most of us applied for admission to more than one college or university so as to maximize our perceived chances for admission to at least one.

Decision diagramming is a technique that involves building and analyzing simple models of decision problems that involve uncertain outcomes. The model, commonly referred to as a "decision tree," is a representation of the interrelationships of choices and uncertain events that must be considered in analyzing a decision. Drawing a decision diagram is often a useful step to take in analyzing a complicated decision problem. This chapter summarizes the more important points to be kept in mind when constructing a diagram and then illustrates the use of a decision diagram in solving a decision problem with uncertainty.

The basic element of a decision diagram is a fork, as shown in Figure 4–1.

FIGURE 4–1
Act and event forks

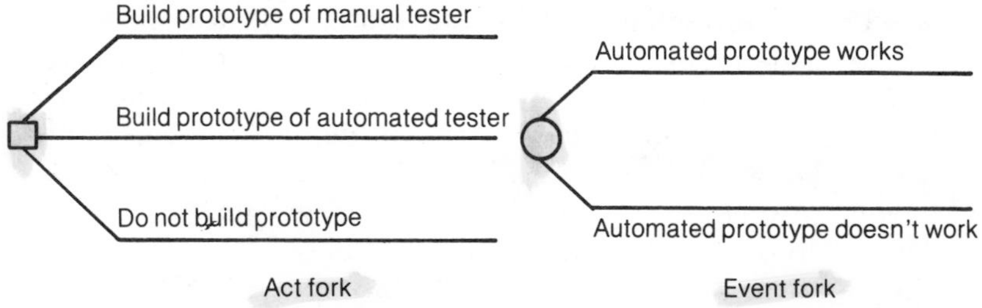

Build prototype of manual tester

Build prototype of automated tester

Do not build prototype

Automated prototype works

Automated prototype doesn't work

Act fork

Event fork

There are two types of forks; the difference between them involves whether or not the decision maker has control over which of the branches will be selected.

A fork representing a point at which the decision maker has a choice is called an *act fork*. The individual branches of the fork represent all the options that the decision maker wishes to consider in making the choice. For example, the act fork shown in Figure 4–1 shows the three options that a project manager might wish to consider in preparing to develop a new piece of test equipment.

A fork representing an event with an uncertain outcome that is out of the control of the decision maker is called an *event fork*. In this case, the individual branches of the fork represent each of the possible outcomes of the uncertain event. The event fork shown in Figure 4–1 represents the uncertainty about whether the previously mentioned automated equipment will work; either it will or it will not work as indicated by the fork.

A fork is either an event fork or an act fork; any situation that might appear to be a mixture of choice and chance should be represented by two or more forks, including at least one act fork and one event fork.

Structure of the diagram

This method of analyzing decision problems is based on arranging the act forks and event forks in sequence. The "base" of the tree represents the decision nearest the present, and the tips of the "branches" represent the most distant future to be considered.

A reasonable procedure for determining the structure of a decision diagram is as follows:

1. Identify the possible decisions or choices to be considered, and describe each of them in terms of the *alternative courses of action* that are available and the *point of time* when a choice must be made between these alternatives.
2. Identify the uncertain or chance events that can occur, and describe each of them in terms of the *alternative consequences* that can occur and the *point of time when the decision maker will discover in fact which consequence actually occurred.*
3. Compile a rough *time sequence* or calendar of decisions and events, so that all possible decisions and events are ordered according to the points of time identified above.
4. Now draw a decision diagram with time proceeding from left to right. The first decision or choice that can be made will almost always be the first fork in the diagram, followed by all the uncertain events and decisions that are relevant to each "branch" of the diagram, in their proper sequence.

AN EXAMPLE OF A DECISION UNDER UNCERTAINTY

To focus our discussion it will be useful to have a simple decision problem for consideration. Jane Owens must decide whether or not to introduce a new novelty toy into the Owens Novelty Company product line. Owens already offers many other novelties and therefore does not believe this is a major strategic decision, but she does want to be systematic and careful in her analysis, since her success depends on the cumulative outcomes of many decisions of this type. Because of the short life of most novelties, she is willing to consider only one year into the future.

Owens has determined that this particular novelty can be made by one of two manufacturing processes; one uses a standard machine, and the other a highly automated machine. In either case, she has decided to lease the manufacturing equipment. The standard machine rents for $1,000 a year and will result in directly variable costs of $1.00 per item produced. The automated equipment can be leased for $5,000 per year and will result in directly variable costs of $0.50 per item produced. She knows that this novelty is similar to some already on the market and that the existing price for this type of toy is $1.50 net to the manufacturer. Since she does not wish to try and change the price structure of this market, she has decided that if she introduces this product, it will be at the $1.50 price.

The forecast of possible sales has occupied most of Jane Owens's recent thinking on this problem. She knows that there are many possible sales volumes; however, she has decided to concentrate on only two typical situations. She thinks that there is a possibility that the novelty will be a failure and she will sell only about 1,000 items. If everything goes well, she could sell 12,000 items. In summary, Owens is willing to assume that sales will be either 1,000 or 12,000 units.

How to select acts

There is very little that can be said about how to select acts to be analyzed in a decision problem. This depends on the creativity and imagination of the decision maker. It is generally best to include as many relevant acts as can be imagined at this stage of the analysis. The cost of ignoring an act with a good outcome can be very steep, whereas the cost of including several inferior choices is limited to the time spent analyzing and rejecting them. No analytic technique will generate the alternatives to be considered; this can be accomplished only by careful evaluation of the situation by someone familiar with the basic problem. One general point can be made, however, concerning what is often not thought of as an act. To take no action should always be evaluated as an alternative. Doing nothing has consequences in the future; and doing nothing is under the control of the decision maker— therefore, to do nothing is an act.

In Jane Owens's problem, the acts are: (1) do nothing, that is, do not introduce the novelty; (2) introduce the novelty and use the standard machine; and (3) introduce the novelty and use the automated machine.

The selection of events

Selecting which events to consider in a decision problem is also a matter of judgment. It is not possible to include everything that is beyond your control. For example, Owens might consider whether or not her competition will react to the introduction, and if so how soon. She might worry about government policy on taxation and whether this will increase or decrease the disposable income available to buy toys, and so on. All of these factors may influence the forecast of the future sales. If they do, she must think about them, but it would be useful to have a simpler framework for actual analysis. This can be achieved if she follows some simple rules in selecting events.

First, for a specific analysis the decision maker should recognize only those events that will result in different consequences for the actions being considered. For example, if Owens is able to finance this project without borrowing, then she can ignore all the possible future interest rates. Whatever the rate is in the future, it will influence all of her acts in the same way, and thus for the purpose of this decision, interest rates can be ignored.

The second rule is to define the event in such a way that its consequences can be measured by the decision maker in an unambiguous way. This can be done if the decision maker thinks of an event as an occurrence at some point in time and then thinks of the possible outcomes of the event at that time. In this example, Jane Owens really only has to think of the event: demand for the novelty in the next year. There are many factors that will influence this event, but at some time in the future the combined influence of all these factors can be measured by counting the number of orders received. This *event* can have many *outcomes,* all of which must be measurable. In this case, outcomes of demand can be 1,000 or 12,000 items. In thinking about the possible outcomes of an event, two rules should be observed:

1. The outcomes should be *mutually exclusive.* This means that the consequences of each outcome can be measured in an unambiguous way. It would not be useful for Owens to talk about the outcome: demand equals more than 1,000 units, because she could not clearly measure the consequences of her various actions against this outcome.
2. The outcomes should be *collectively exhaustive.* This means that all of the possible outcomes should be determined. This rule is to ensure that all factors that can happen are being considered.

In summary, Ms. Owens can define as the only relevant event: demand for the novelty next year. The outcomes of this event are 1,000 units or 12,000 units.

We can now construct a decision diagram to help organize our thinking about Jane Owens's problem. As the decision problems you face become more and more complex compared with this simple example, you will find this technique increasingly helpful. A decision diagram is particularly useful in the analysis of a sequential decision problem in which the decision maker can take various actions after he or she

FIGURE 4–2
Jane Owens's basic problem

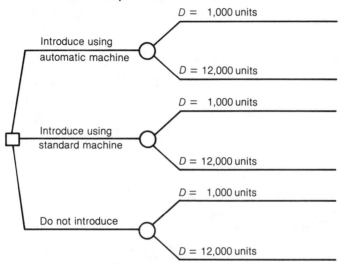

learns the outcome of some event. Figure 4–2 is a decision diagram for Jane Owens's basic problem.

This diagram illustrates several convenient conventions. First, act forks are represented by a small square with one branch drawn for each possible course of action. Event forks are denoted by a circle with a branch representing each possible outcome. Second, the decision diagram follows a time sequence from left to right. The first step in time is the decision on the type of machine, after which demand occurs at the various levels. The diagram ends at a cutoff date in the future beyond which the decision maker does not wish to structure the problem. In Owens's case, this is one year. For every sequence of choices and outcomes there is an end point on the diagram. Collectively, these end points represent every possible terminal position that Owens thinks is relevant to her decision.

Evaluating the consequences

From Figure 4–2 we see that there are six terminal positions in Ms. Owens's basic problem. Each of these positions has a particular dollar value to Owens based on the cash flows associated with each act and event leading to the terminal position. To evaluate the worth of these terminal positions, it is often helpful to note on the diagram the costs and revenues associated with each choice or outcome. Each terminal position then may be evaluated by summing the costs and revenues that occur on the path leading from the initial decision point to the terminal position. For Owens's problem, this is done on Figure 4–3.

FIGURE 4–3
Calculation of terminal position values

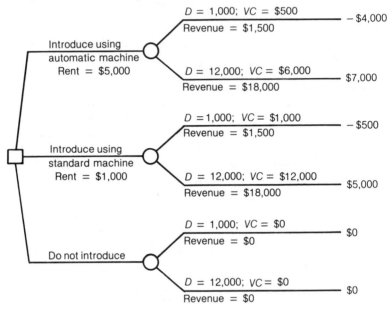

Notice that all of the costs and revenues in Figure 4–3 have one thing in common: They are all to be encountered in the future. No costs that Owens has already incurred in her preliminary investigation or development of the novelty are included in the analysis. There are at least two reasons for ignoring any such "sunk" costs. First, they were incurred in the past, and our current decisions can affect only the future. Hence, we cannot influence our past actions. Second, since any sunk costs, if they occurred, occurred in the past, they will have an equal effect on all future cash flow positions evaluated by the decision diagram. This last rationale also holds in the case of an equal *proportional* influence on all terminal problems. For example, Owens can safely ignore the effect of taxes as long as the consequences at the terminal positions are all taxed (or create tax losses) at the same marginal rate. If, however, Owens would be placed in a different tax bracket or if her firm has no other income to apply the losses to, she should evaluate her decision on the basis of after-tax income.

In other words, when analyzing a decision problem it is important to remember that the purpose of constructing a decision tree is to help make a decision, not to construct an accounting report. Factors that affect all terminal positions in a like way, such as sunk costs and usually taxes, can be safely ignored. The eventual outcome of the analysis, the selection of the best alternative, will not be altered by including such items.

Probability

Any ranking of the acts open to Jane Owens should take into account both the consequences that could result from the various outcomes of relevant events and the likelihood that these various outcomes will occur. The consequences usually can be described in some economic unit, like dollars of profit or opportunity cost. A quantitative measure of the relative likelihood of a particular outcome is the *probability* of its occurrence.

It is useful here to make some observations. First, for the purposes of business decision making, there is usually no meaning to the term *true probability* or *correct probability*. The language of probability is used in this context to describe an attitude about the relative likelihood of various occurrences in the future. Thus, a manager's probability assessment is a personal statement about the future. Two reasonable people can view a similar set of facts and assign different probabilities to future outcomes of events. If this were not true, there would never be any wagers on horse races. This does not mean that probabilities can be arbitrarily assigned or that they are unimportant. Instead, much hard thinking should be associated with the assigning of probabilities. This leads to a second observation, which is that decision makers should not allow their judgments to be replaced by techniques when they assign probabilities. There are many aids, some simple and others quite complex, to assist decision makers in assessing probabilities. These techniques may be appropriate in many cases, but decision makers must realize that in the final analysis a probability assessment is a *personal judgment* about future outcomes. This judgment can be guided and often improved with techniques, but it cannot be replaced.

Now we can return to Jane Owens and ask her to assign probabilities to the various outcomes of the event: demand for the novelty next year. We do this by asking her to think hard about the various factors that influence demand and to summarize her judgment in a quantitative way by assigning probabilities.

Owens is willing to do this, and the results of her efforts are shown in Table 4–1. From this table we can see that she has not changed her mind about considering only two outcomes, since she assigned zero

TABLE 4–1
Probability of outcomes for the
event: Demand next year

Outcome	Probability
1,000	0.5
12,000	0.5
	1.0

probability to all other possibilities. She has also observed the second rule and made the sum of all outcomes equal to 1.0. We can see that she now thinks that the outcomes of 1,000 units and 12,000 units are equally likely.

The decision diagram is completed by placing Jane Owens's probabilities on each event fork branch. Figure 4–4 is a decision diagram for Owens's problem with the end points and probabilities included. In addition, the act fork is broken into two parts. This is to demonstrate the fact that acts can be represented sequentially or jointly as long as there are no intervening events. In fact, in this case it would be possi-

FIGURE 4–4
Ms. Owens's complete decision diagram

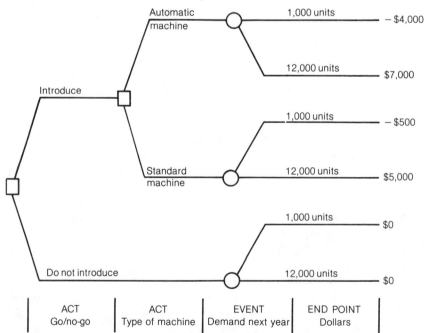

ble to put the decision about the type of machine first and then follow it with an act fork for whether or not to introduce the machine, since no event of interest occurs between these two acts.

Making the decision

Once the problem has been structured with a decision diagram, the process of making the decision begins. In order to decide which branch is preferred at each fork, the decision maker must decide on the worth of being at the end of each branch. This usually means that he or she must decide what a complete event fork is worth. This is a complicated exercise because it requires the decision maker to simultaneously consider the consequences and their likelihood. It can be further complicated if one considers the global meaning of the term *consequences* and not merely the monetary value of the terminal positions. If, for example, the loss of $4,000 would jeopardize Jane Owens's business, she may wish to avoid that event fork altogether, however slim the chance of incurring that loss. A technique called *preference theory* has been developed to incorporate a manager's varying attitude toward risk into a decision tree model. This topic will be dealt with in a later chapter. For the time being, let us assume that Owens is willing to "play the averages" in making her decision about introducing this novelty. This is not an inaccurate assumption if the consequences are small relative to Owens's total assets and if she makes decisions of this sort frequently.

If Ms. Owens is willing to play the averages to evaluate this decision, she can use the *expected monetary value* (EMV) of each event fork as the worth of being at that fork. The EMV of an event fork is calculated mechanically by computing the weighted average of the terminal values using the probabilities as weights. Table 4–2 illustrates the calculation of an EMV for Owens's problem for the act: introduce novelty using standard machine.

TABLE 4–2
Calculation of expected monetary value for the act: Introduce using standard machine

Outcome for event: Demand next year	Consequence (C)	Probability (P)	Consequence times probability (C × P)
1,000	−$500	0.5	−$250
12,000	$5,000	0.5	$2,500
		Expected monetary value =	$2,250

The expected monetary value of $2,250 can be regarded as equivalent to the center chance node in Figure 4–4 as long as Owens is willing to play the averages (or, in shorthand, be an EMVer). Computing the expected values of the other event forks allows us to reduce Owens's decision problem to the one shown in Figure 4–5.

FIGURE 4–5
Jane Owens's problem with expected monetary values replacing event forks

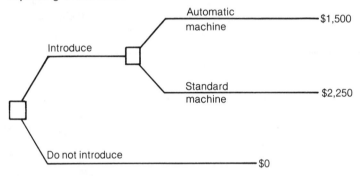

Jane Owens controls the choice of branches at the act forks, and therefore she would go ahead with the standard machine because it has the highest EMV.

In summary, a decision can be obtained from a decision diagram by going to the far right-hand side and working backward, with each event fork being replaced by an expected value. At each act fork, the branch with the highest EMV is selected. This expected monetary value is then used to replace the entire act fork. This process is continued from right to left until the best choice is determined at the initial act fork. This process is called *backward induction* and is used to reduce complex decision diagrams so that the best initial act is selected.

Sensitivity analysis

If Jane Owens is a reasonable person, she will probably admit to some lingering doubts about the above analysis of her decision problem. While she may be comfortable with the analytic technique, the costing of outcomes, and other mechanical aspects of the analysis, she is probably not totally at ease with some of her subjective inputs. One of these inputs was her assessment of the probabilities that the outcomes would actually occur. Assuming, for the moment, that she is willing to restrict her analysis to the two possible outcomes she has already considered, Owens can perform a *sensitivity analysis* to answer the question: How far off could I have been in my original probability assessments without changing the decision analysis outcome? Owens can approach this problem by first considering that her assessed probability of success (selling 12,000 units) is too optimistic for comfort. The question then becomes: At what probability P of selling 12,000 units would the act of not introducing the novelty have the highest EMV?

Let the probability of demand equaling 12,000 units be P and the probability of demand equaling 1,000 units be $(1 - P)$. Jane Owens's problem now appears as in Figure 4–6.

FIGURE 4-6
Jane Owens's problem when the probability of next year's demand equaling 12,000 units is represented by P

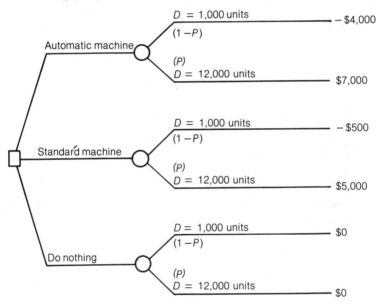

Owens can now calculate the value of P for which she would be indifferent between doing nothing and introducing the novelty using the standard machine. That value of P is derived from the expression:

$$5,000P + (1 - P)(-500) = (0)(P) + (1 - P)(0)$$

which simplifies to:

$$5,500P = 500$$

or:

$$P = 0.091$$

In other words, as long as the probability of success is greater than 9.1 percent, the decision to introduce the product would have the higher EMV. Since this value is far removed from the 0.5 probability Owens assessed earlier, she should feel reasonably comfortable with the decision to introduce the product.

Table 4–3 presents the results of a complete sensitivity analysis of Owens's probability assessments. The student may wish to verify these results as an exercise.

TABLE 4–3
Sensitivity of Jane Owens's decision to probability of event: Demand for novelty equals 12,000 units

P = Probability of demand equals 12,000 units	Act having highest expected monetary value
If $P < 0.091$	Do nothing
If $0.091 < P < 0.6364$	Introduce; use standard machine
If $P > 0.6364$	Introduce; use automatic machine

A MORE COMPLEX PROBLEM

The decision diagram is most useful when the decision problem has sequential choices of acts. Jane Owens's basic problem is not such a case. In order to show the value of diagramming, we will consider the following extension of the basic problem. Ms. Owens has a friend, Mr. Fischer, who is in the market survey business. Fischer has offered to do an exhaustive survey on the novelty Owens is considering introducing, and he absolutely guarantees that he can predict what market there will be for this toy. He plans to visit several toy wholesalers to discuss the characteristics of this product, and on the basis of this and other general economic indications, he will be able to determine what will happen. Owens has been trying to decide what this service would be worth and whether she should make an offer to Fischer. In order to analyze the problem, she has constructed the decision diagram shown in Figure 4–7.

Several features of this diagram should be noted. The initial act has two forks representing the basic alternatives of whether or not to buy the survey. If the survey is not purchased, the decision problem is exactly like the problem we have already diagrammed, and thus the portion of the diagram following the "no survey" fork is exactly like the basic problem diagram shown in Figure 4–3.

The major advantage of buying the survey is the ability to delay the decision on machine types until the results of the survey are known.

FIGURE 4–7
Decision diagram for Jane Owens's expanded problem

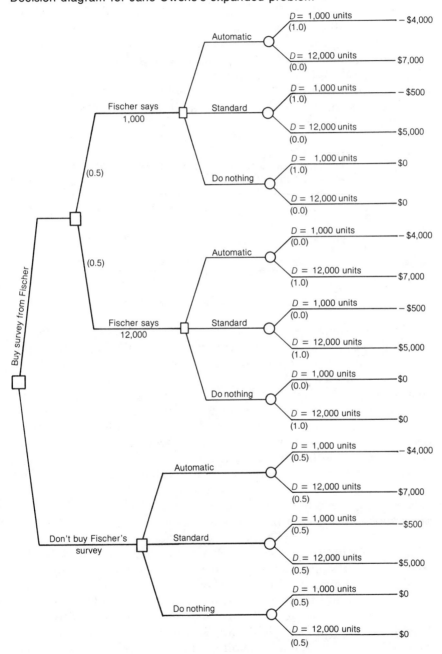

Therefore immediately following the act fork "buy survey," there is an event fork representing the results of the survey. The probabilities assigned to this event fork depend on two things: the decision maker's feelings about the real world and her feelings about how good the survey is at revealing the real-world conditions. For the sake of simplicity, let us assume that Mr. Fischer is a perfect forecaster. This means that when Fischer finally predicts an outcome, Owens will assign a probability of 1.0 to this outcome actually occurring. If this assumption is true, we can assign probabilities to the first event fork according to Table 4–4.

TABLE 4–4
Probabilities of outcome to event: Results of
Fischer's survey

Outcome	Probabilities
Fischer says 1,000	0.5
Fischer says 12,000	0.5
	1.0

As you can see, these are the same probabilities that Owens initially assigned to the outcome of the event: demand next year. If Owens believes that Fischer is perfect, then she will assign these same probabilities to the survey outcomes. Fischer has not promised that he will change the world, only that he will accurately reflect what is there. Since Owens's judgment about what would happen was reflected in her original assessment of the probabilities, she should not alter them because a survey is being taken. This concept is often hard to appreciate, so we will discuss an example.

Assume that there is a roulette wheel hidden from your view. You have previously inspected the wheel and you believe it is fair. This means you believe that half the time the metal ball will end up in a black spot and the other half the time you believe it will end up in a red spot. This wheel will be spun and stopped, and then you will place your bet on what color came up. Remember that you cannot see the wheel when it stops, so you would want to assign a probability of one-half to the outcome red. Now suppose you have a friend who can see the wheel and tell you where the ball stopped before you must place your bet. How often will this friend tell you the outcome is red? If he is honest and not color-blind, he will say red half of the time. Thus you would assign a probability of one-half to the outcome: my friend says the outcome is red. This analogy is like Jane Owens's problem. She can hire Fischer to tell her something about the world. but Owens already has a feeling about her "roulette wheel," and she should include this feeling in her decision making.

Returning to Figure 4–7, after each of the two outcomes of the survey result event fork, there is an act fork that represents the three basic alternatives available for manufacturing. Each of these act forks is followed by an event fork representing the event: demand next year. You can see that we have assigned zero probabilities to the outcomes not mentioned by Fischer in each part of the diagram. This is the result of our assumption about Fischer's forecasting ability. We could have eliminated all outcomes that have zero probability from the diagram, but for illustration they were included. After each branch on this final event fork is the value of the consequence of that particular path through the diagram. No cost has been charged for the information because we are attempting to determine the value of such a survey. If the cost were fixed and known, we could include it here.

To analyze this diagram, we would start at the far right. We will assume that Jane Owens is still willing to play the averages and will, therefore, use the expected value of each event fork as the equivalent of the fork itself. The EMVs for the event forks on the survey portion of the tree are easy to calculate because all probabilities are either 0.0 or 1.0. If Fischer says 1,000, the act with the highest expected value is no-go, with a value of $0. If Fischer says 12,000, the best act is the automatic machine, with a value of $7,000. Figure 4–8 is a reduced diagram representing the conditional decisions mentioned above. The action planned, given each of Fischer's responses, is shown in parentheses, and the expected monetary value is shown at the end of each branch representing an outcome.

If we continue to reduce the diagram by replacing each event fork with its expected monetary value, we will produce the circled numbers at the bases of the event forks in Figure 4–8. Owens should use the standard machine if she does not buy the information because this act has the highest EMV of the three choices. Thus, as we concluded before, the expected value for the entire no-information strategy is $2,250. The expected value for the buy-survey strategy is $3,500. Owens can conclude that the difference between these two EMVs is a measure of the value she would assign to having the information. This value is $1,250.

It is often practical to perform an analysis of hypothetical acts like "buy Fischer's survey" in Jane Owens's problem. The outcome of $1,250 is called the *expected value of perfect information* (EVPI). This measure is significant because it places an upper bound on the amount a decision maker (who is an EMVer) would be willing to spend to reduce the uncertainty he or she faces. Of course, EVPI is an upper

FIGURE 4–8
Reduced decision diagram for expanded problem

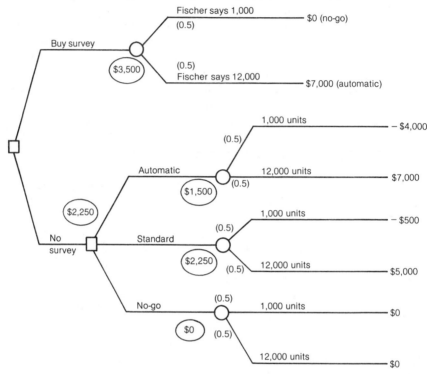

bound because, in the real world, perfect forecasters like Mr. Fischer are extremely difficult to find!

THE IMPERFECT TESTER

Suppose now that Mr. Fischer quoted Ms. Owens a price of $2,000 for perfect information about the size of the market for her novelty. Since $2,000 is greater than the EVPI of $1,250, Owens would decline to hire Fischer to acquire perfect information. Fischer then might describe a limited market test costing $500 that could indicate the size of the market but could not predict the eventual outcome with certainty. Since Fischer has had some experience with the limited test on other projects similar to that of Jane Owens, he can say that when demand is actually low, the test would have predicted that outcome 90 percent of the time. When demand is high, that outcome would have been predicted 70 percent of the time. The predicting capabilities of this test are summarized in Table 4–5.

TABLE 4–5
Conditional accuracy of Mr. Fischer's $500 market survey

Outcome that will occur	Test says 1,000	Test says 12,000
Demand next year = 1,000	0.9	0.1
Demand next year = 12,000	0.3	0.7

Jane Owens should note with caution that the figures Mr. Fischer cites are conditional upon knowing the level of demand. Owen's best assessment of demand is still the 50–50 chance of either 1,000 or 12,000 units she made earlier. Owens's information can be summarized as in Figure 4–9.

FIGURE 4–9
Schematic probability tree of Ms. Owens's information regarding Mr. Fischer's imperfect test

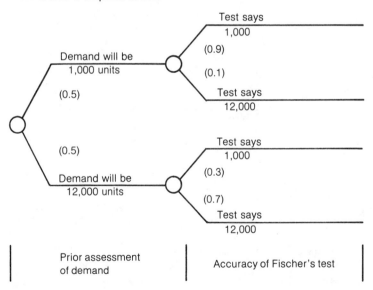

Should Ms. Owens accept Mr. Fischer's new proposal? Part of the answer lies in her ability to place the test and the outcomes (what demand actually is) in the proper order. Logically, if Owens decides to use the test, she should have the results of the test before she finds out what the level of demand actually is. But, unlike the situation where Mr. Fischer was to provide perfect information, Ms. Owens's estimate of the probability that the test would say 12,000 is not readily apparent. Further, the probability of demand being, in fact, 12,000 units given that the test said 12,000 is not clear, since part of the time the test says 1,000 when demand is actually 12,000 units.

The first step for Owens's analysis of Fischer's proposal should be to calculate the *joint probabilities* of each test outcome and demand level. This is done by multiplying the probabilities together and combining the outcomes of the two events into one event fork as done in Figure 4–10.

FIGURE 4–10
Probabilities of joint outcomes derived from Ms. Owens's assessments and Mr. Fischer's test claims

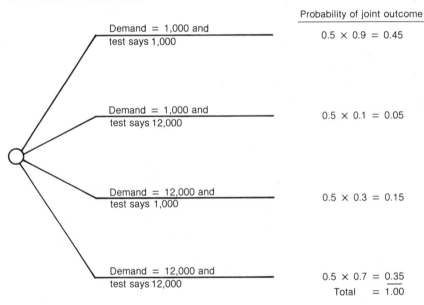

Jane Owens can now find an estimate of the probability of the test saying 12,000 that is consistent with her earlier probability assessment and with Mr. Fischer's test accuracy data. She can do this by adding up the joint probabilities associated with each branch for which the test says 12,000. These are branches 2 and 4 from Figure 4–10. Their joint probabilities sum to 0.4, which is the probability of the test saying 12,000. Similarly, the probability that the test will say 1,000 is 0.6.

Now, what proportion of the time that the test says 12,000 will demand actually be 12,000 units? Since the joint probability of branch

4 (demand = 12,000 *and* test says 12,000) is 0.35, the answer is 0.35 divided by 0.4 or 0.875.[1] Figure 4–11 shows the results of the completed analysis, giving probabilities of demand levels conditional on test outcomes.

FIGURE 4–11
Demand level probabilities conditional on outcome of imperfect test

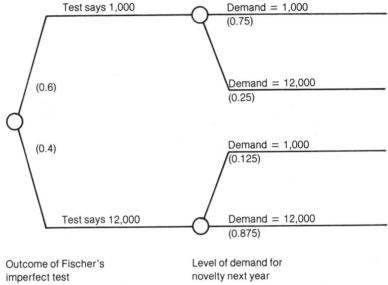

Outcome of Fischer's
imperfect test

Level of demand for
novelty next year

Ms. Owens may now decide whether to accept Mr. Fischer's proposal to conduct the limited market survey. Figure 4–12 is identical with Figure 4–7 with the exception of the probabilities and the cost for the imperfect test being included. The circles at the base of each event and act fork represent the expected monetary value at each point.

Since the EMV of the act: buy imperfect test from Mr. Fischer, is higher than the EMV of proceeding without that information, Owens would presumably purchase Fischer's services. Because the results of the analysis were so close, however, Owens may seek further information from (or about) Fischer, such as inquiring more closely about the comparability of the sources of Fischer's test accuracy information to the case of Owens's novelty. Or, Owens may conclude that the analytic results were so close that she would decide whether to purchase Fischer's services on some subjective issue not included in the analy-

---

[1] This process of reversal of order of events forks follows the rules of *Bayes theorem*, which is treated in detail in most statistics textbooks.

FIGURE 4–12
Decision diagram for Ms. Owens's problem using Mr. Fischer's imperfect test survey

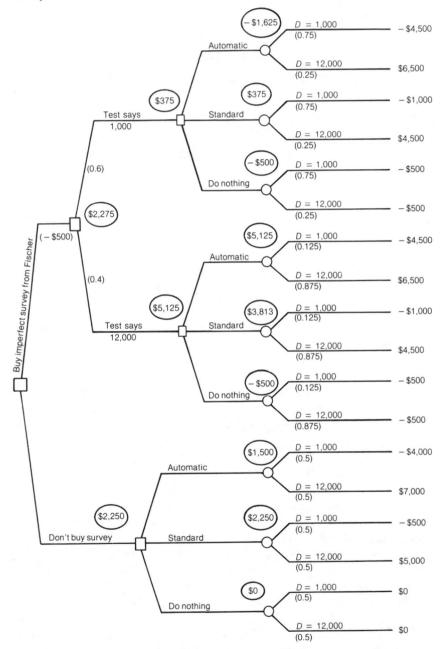

sis. For example, Owens may conclude that, although Fischer's test was not particularly economical for this problem, it may be valuable in the future. Hence, Owens might buy Fischer's survey for this novelty to more clearly assess its worth for future projects.

SUMMARY

This chapter has proposed the following process for analyzing decisions when the future is not known with certainty:

1. Determine the possible actions that can be taken.
2. Determine the events in the future that can result in different consequences for the various actions.
3. Determine all the possible outcomes of these future events.
4. Assign some value to the consequence of each act and each outcome.
5. Assess the decision maker's probability for each outcome of each event.
6. Determine the decision maker's expected monetary value for each action in the problem. If he or she is willing to "play the averages," the expected value of an act is the weighted average of the consequences for the outcomes of the following event using the probability of each outcome's occurrence as the weights.
7. Select the act with the best expected monetary value.

If the problem has sequential decision options, then steps 6 and 7 must be repeated starting at the far right of the decision diagram until the expected monetary values for all alternatives on the initial act fork have been determined.

8. In addition, the decision maker may find it useful to calculate the expected value of perfect information (EVPI) to determine the maximum amount that should be spent to collect more information. The EVPI can be calculated by *assuming* that one alternative is access to a source of perfect information. The EVPI is the difference between the EMV of the real problem and the EMV of the problem with the source of perfect information as an alternative.
9. Sensitivity analysis may often be helpful to the decision maker as a means of assessing how stable a decision is in light of variations in some of the assumptions or subjective probability assessments.

There are two technical appendixes to this chapter. Appendix 4–A on probability distributions describes different ways to represent distributions and a simple means to handle problems involving continuous or many-valued distributions. In Appendix 4–B on assessing probabilistic forecasts, procedures for making probabilistic forecasts are outlined. Appendix 4–B will be useful both to help you make assessments about uncertain events and to help you understand the procedure that underlies much of the data in the cases following this chapter.

These cases will give you an opportunity to practice and gain familiarity with the process of building and analyzing models for decisions made under conditions of uncertainty. Recognition of the uncertain nature of the business world in these cases is an important step toward reality, when compared with the cases of the preceeding chapter. However, it is still crucial for you to remember that these models are, after all, highly simplified representations of the real world, and the added realism is far from a panacea. These models, like those analyzed earlier, will require considerable judgmental interpretation to turn the results of an analysis into a recommendation that is useful to a manager.

APPENDIX 4–A
Probability distributions

When Jane Owens assigned probabilities to the various levels of demand for her new product, she was assessing a probability distribution for the outcomes of the event: demand next year. The word *distribution* can be confusing; it is easier to understand if you recall that when you assign probabilities you are distributing a set of weights across the various outcomes of an event. There are two ways of representing probability distributions that we will find useful. We will call these the discrete distribution and the cumulative distribution. Ms. Owens's assessment was a discrete probability distribution.

To distinguish between these two representations of probability distributions, it is necessary to remember how we defined an event and its outcome. An event takes place at some point in time and has outcomes that can be measured after the occurrence of the event. In a way, an event is the general description of a point in time, while an outcome is one of many specific measurements that can be made at that point in time. An example of an event is the demand for a product next week. There may be six outcomes for this event: no demand, one unit, two units, three units, four units, and more than four units. Another example of an event is the condition of a part after manufacturing. The outcomes of this event may be that the part is good or that the part is defective. The set of outcomes for an event *must* be mutually exclusive and collectively exhaustive. This means that the definition of each particular outcome is unique and that the set of all outcomes takes into account everything that can happen at the point in time for which the event is specified. In the first example given above, the outcomes are zero, one, two, three, four, and more than four. This last outcome is acceptable because it has no overlap with the other outcomes; therefore, the outcomes are mutually exclusive, and the entire set of outcomes is collectively exhaustive. It is not required by the definition of outcomes that their description be quantitative. In fact, the second example above has outcomes entitled "good" and "defective."

THE DISCRETE DISTRIBUTION

A discrete probability distribution assigns a probability to the possibility that when the event has actually taken place, the result will be exactly equal to an outcome. This distribution assigns a probability to each outcome, and the sum of these probabilities for all outcomes of an event is 1.0. For example, suppose a retailer wishes to assess the probability for tomorrow's sales for one product. He knows that it is impossible to sell more than ten units because that is all he will have in stock. He also knows from experience that he may not sell any units of this product. After much thought and analysis, he assigns the probabilities in Table 4A–1. This is a discrete probability distribution for the outcomes of the event: sales tomorrow, because it assigns to each outcome a probability that sales will exactly equal that outcome. The sum of these probabilities is 1.0.

The headings in Table 4A–1 are also shown in symbolic form. The general name for the outcomes is: number of units sold, and the symbol for this is N. N can be any of the integers from 0 to 10. The name of the event is: sales tomorrow, and its symbol is $\tilde{S}$. The tilde over the

TABLE 4A–1
Discrete probability distribution for the event:
Sales tomorrow

Outcome: number of units sold N	Probability that sales = outcome $P(\tilde{S} = N)$
0	0.05
1	0.10
2	0.20
3	0.15
4	0.15
5	0.10
6	0.10
7	0.05
8	0.04
9	0.04
10	0.02
Total	1.00

symbol means that it represents an event and has a probability distribution associated with it. The symbol for the discrete probability distribution is $P(\tilde{S} = N)$ and is read: the probability that the event $\tilde{S}$ will have an outcome exactly equal to the value N. The probability for any specific outcome can also be written symbolically. For example, the probability that sales tomorrow will exactly equal 5 units is 0.10. This is written as

$$P(\tilde{S} = 5) = 0.10$$

The discrete probability distribution for our example can be drawn on a graph like the one shown in Figure 4A–1. The vertical axis repre-

FIGURE 4A–1
Discrete probability for retailer's event: Sales tomorrow

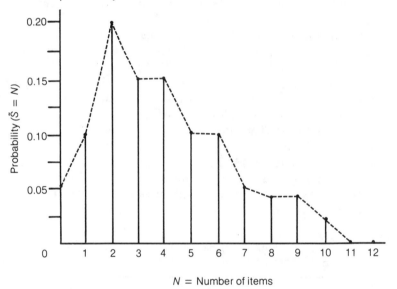

N = Number of items

sents the probability, and the horizontal axis represents the list of outcomes.

The discrete probability distribution has a positive value only for the possible outcomes of the event and has a value of zero for any numbers other than these outcomes. Therefore, the graph of the discrete distribution in our example is actually a row of vertical lines at the integers. For graphical presentation, a curve is often drawn across the tops of these vertical lines like the one shown in Figure 4A–1. This representation should not cause any problems as long as you remember that the only meaningful values on the curve are those directly above the possible outcomes of the event.

THE CUMULATIVE DISTRIBUTION

A cumulative probability distribution assigns a probability to the possibility that, when the event has taken place, the result will be equal to or less than an outcome. Taking the example of the retailer, we can construct the cumulative probability distribution shown in Table 4A–2.

TABLE 4A–2
Cumulative probability distribution for the event: Sales tomorrow

Outcome: Number of units sold N	Discrete distribution: Probability that sales equal outcome $P(\tilde{S} = N)$	Cumulative distribution: Probability that sales equal to or less than outcome $P(\tilde{S} \leq N)$
0	0.05	0.05
1	0.10	0.15
2	0.20	0.35
3	0.15	0.50
4	0.15	0.65
5	0.10	0.75
6	0.10	0.85
7	0.05	0.90
8	0.04	0.94
9	0.04	0.98
10	0.02	1.00
Total	1.00	

The first two columns of this table are identical with those in Table 4A–1; the third column, however, shows the cumulative distribution. The symbol for the cumulative probability distribution is $P(\tilde{S} \leq N)$ and is read: the probability that event $\tilde{S}$ will have an outcome equal to or less than the value N.

The value of the cumulative distribution for a specific outcome can be obtained by adding the values of the discrete distribution for all outcomes equal to or less than that specific outcome. As an example, the value of the cumulative distribution for the outcome of 5 units, written $P(\tilde{S} \leq 5)$, is 0.75. This can be obtained by adding the values of the discrete distribution for all outcomes of 5 or less. This calculation is shown in Table 4A–3.

Using this approach, you can calculate the cumulative distribution whenever you have the discrete distribution for an event. In a similar way, it is possible to calculate the discrete distribution if you know the cumulative distribution. The probabilities assigned by the cumulative distribution to two adjacent outcomes can be subtracted to obtain the

TABLE 4A–3
Calculation of cumulative probability
for outcomes of 5 units

Outcome, N	Discrete distribution, $P(\tilde{S} = N)$
0	0.05
1	0.10
2	0.20
3	0.15
4	0.15
5	0.10
	$P(\tilde{S} \leq 5) = 0.75$

probability that the discrete distribution would assign to the larger of the two outcomes. For example, Table 4A–4 shows the calculation for the probability that sales tomorrow will exactly equal 8 units.

TABLE 4A–4
Calculation of discrete
probability for outcome
of 8 units

$$P(\tilde{S} \leq 8) = 0.94$$
$$-P(\tilde{S} \leq 7) = 0.90$$
$$0.04 = P(\tilde{S} = 8)$$

The cumulative distribution can be drawn on a graph with the vertical axis for cumulative probability and the horizontal axis for outcomes. Such a graph for the retailer's distribution is shown in Figure 4A–2.

This cumulative distribution has a nonzero value for every number on the graph to the right of zero. As an example, the probability that sales will be less than or equal to 3.62 units is 0.50. It is obvious that sales cannot equal 3.62 units, but they can be less than 3.62 units, and therefore the graph of the cumulative distribution has a positive value over the 3.62 value on the horizontal axis.

As in the case of the discrete distribution, a smooth curve can be drawn to provide better graphical representation; such a curve is shown with dotted lines in Figure 4A–2. This smooth curve is only an approximation to the real curve, which is shown in solid lines. For events with hundreds or thousands of outcomes, the smooth curve will be almost exactly the same as the real cumulative curve.

FIGURE 4A-2
Cumulative probability distribution for retailer's event: Sales tomorrow

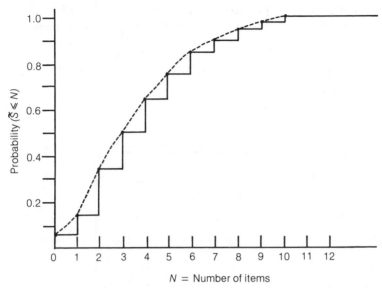

N = Number of items

APPROXIMATING A CUMULATIVE
PROBABILITY DISTRIBUTION

In many cases the event for which a forecast is being made will have many possible outcomes. Think about Jane Owens, the novelty manufacturer described earlier. The event: sales next year, could have many possible outcomes; however, she was willing to think about only two typical outcomes for that event. This simplification was necessary so that Owens could calculate the expected value for the various actions. A decision tree could have so many branches that calculation of expected values would become impractical. For these reasons, Owens thought about only a few typical outcomes and assessed a discrete probability distribution for them. This simplification results in an approximation to the "true probability distribution;" if the typical outcomes are selected carefully, this approximation can be used in calculations of expected values.

In analyzing realistic decision problems, the question of which few outcomes should be chosen as representative of the many possible outcomes is difficult to answer. We propose that for situations where the event has many outcomes you assess the cumulative probability distribution and then use it to guide your selection of representative outcomes. Assessment of the cumulative probability distribution will be discussed later in Appendix 4–B. Now we want to discuss how to select representative outcomes once you have a cumulative distribution.

Figure 4A–3 is a cumulative graph for the outcomes of some event. This distribution can be approximated with several representative

FIGURE 4A–3
Method for approximating cumulative probability distribution

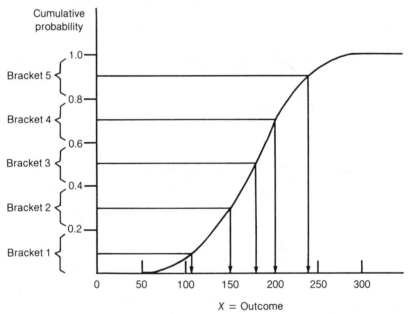

outcomes. Let us use five such outcomes to approximate this cumulative distribution. To select these five, mark off the vertical axis in five equal brackets as shown in Figure 4A–3. Starting at the midpoint of each of the brackets, draw a line parallel to the horizontal axis until it intersects the cumulative graph. At these points of intersection, draw a line directly down to the horizontal axis. The values thus selected on the horizontal axis are the representative outcomes. In Figure 4A–3, these values are 108, 153, 179, 203, and 242. Each of these outcomes is a representative for the entire bracket; therefore, you would assign the probability encompassed by each bracket to its representative outcome. This would result in the discrete distribution shown in Table 4A–5.

You should remember that this is only an approximation to the actual discrete distribution and is used only to facilitate calculations in a

TABLE 4A–5
Discrete distribution approximation
for actual cumulative distribution

Outcome, N	Discrete distribution, $P(X = N)$
108	0.2
153	0.2
179	0.2
203	0.2
242	0.2

decision analysis. If you wish to make a better approximation, the number of brackets selected on the vertical axis can be increased. There is no reason why the brackets need to be the same width. In fact, in some cases it is advantageous to make the sizes of the brackets different. There are other ways to approximate this distribution. Just remember that the goal of whatever method used should be to achieve a good approximation without requiring excessive calculations in the decision analysis.

In summary, we suggest the following approach for approximating a cumulative probability distribution with a discrete probability distribution:

1. Divide the vertical axis of the cumulative graph into brackets. In most cases five brackets of equal size are sufficient.
2. Start at the midpoint of each bracket and read over to the cumulative curve and down to the horizontal axis. The value selected is the representative outcome for that bracket.
3. Assign the probability of the entire bracket to its representative outcome. This will result in a discrete probability distribution for a few outcomes which approximates the actual probability distribution for the many outcomes.

MEASURES OF A PROBABILITY DISTRIBUTION

We have seen that there are two basic ways to describe the probabilities for the outcomes of an event: either as a discrete distribution or as a cumulative distribution. Each of these distributions can be presented in a table or a graph. These presentations are effective although clumsy descriptions. Other measures have been developed for describing the probability distribution more concisely. In this section, we shall define some of these measures.

The most common measure is the *mean* of the probability distribution, also called the *average* of the distribution. The mean of a probability distribution is calculated by taking the discrete probability for each outcome and multiplying it by the value of that outcome and then summing all these products. Table 4A–6 shows this calculation for the retailer's probability distribution we have been using as an example.

TABLE 4A–6
Calculation of the mean of the retailer's distribution

Discrete probability distribution, $P(\tilde{S} = N)$	Outcome, N	Product, $P(\tilde{S} = N) \times N$
0.05	0	0.00
0.10	1	0.10
0.20	2	0.40
0.15	3	0.45
0.15	4	0.60
0.10	5	0.50
0.10	6	0.60
0.05	7	0.35
0.04	8	0.32
0.04	9	0.36
0.02	10	0.20
		3.88 = Mean

The mean of a probability distribution is the weighted average of the outcomes using the discrete probability distribution to do the weighting. In Chapter 4, this same process was used to obtain the expected value of an event fork on the decision diagram. For this reason we will also use the phrase: the expected value of the distribution, to describe the mean of the distribution. It is impossible to read the mean of a distribution directly from the graphs of either the cumulative or discrete distribution; it must be calculated as described.

Another common measure used to describe a distribution is the mode. The mode of a probability distribution is the value of the most likely outcome or, in other words, the outcome to which the distribution assigns the largest probability. In the retailer's distribution, for example, the mode is the outcome of two units because this outcome has a probability of 0.20, which is larger than the probability for any other outcome. If two or more outcomes have an equal probability that is also the largest probability in the discrete distribution, then all of these outcomes are called *modes*.

The mode can be read easily from the graph of the distribution because it is the highest point on the curve. It is more difficult to read the mode from the cumulative distribution because the mode is the outcome over which the cumulative curve is rising most rapidly.

A third measure of a probability distribution is the median. There is a 0.50 chance that the final result of the event will exceed the median, and, likewise, there is a 0.50 chance that the final result will be equal to or less than the median. In general terms, the median is the midpoint of the cumulative distribution. The median can be read easily from the cumulative graph. Start at the 0.50 point on the vertical axis and move parallel to the horizontal axis until you hit the graph. Then come straight down from the graph to the horizontal axis and that point is the median. Figure 4A–4 shows such a procedure for the retailer's example. The median for this distribution is three units.

The median is really only one of many measures for the distribution that can be read directly from the cumulative graph. These measures are called *fractiles*. For example, the 0.25 fractile is the outcome for which there is 0.25 probability that the final result of the event will be equal to or less than that outcome.[1] The 0.25 fractile is found by start-

FIGURE 4A–4
Cumulative distribution for retailer's event: Sales tomorrow

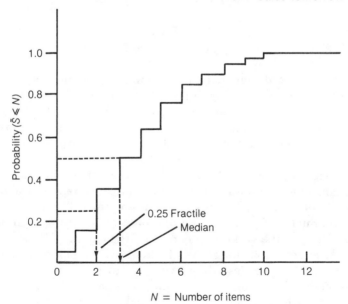

N = Number of items

<hr />

[1] The fractile of a probability distribution is the same as the percentile ranking used by some nationwide testing services. If you rank in the 25th percentile, this means 25 percent of the people taking the test had a score less than or equal to your score.

ing at 0.25 on the vertical axis of the cumulative graph and reading over to the graph and then down to the horizontal axis. The 0.25 fractile is also shown in Figure 4A–4 and has a value of two units.

If you understand the definition of median and fractile, you should see that the median is merely a special name for the 0.50 fractile. All fractiles of the probability distribution can be read directly from the cumulative graph. Try to read the 0.75, 0.01, and 0.99 fractiles from Figure 4A–4. You should get 5 units, 0 units, and 10 units, respectively, as the values.

There are other measures for a probability distribution, but we will not need them in our work. In summary, we have presented three measures or shorthand descriptions for a probability distribution:

1. The *mean,* which must be calculated using the discrete distribution.
2. The *mode,* which can be read directly from the discrete distribution.
3. The *fractiles,* which can be read directly from the cumulative curve. One frequently used fractile is the 0.50, and it is called the *median.*

APPENDIX 4–B
Assessing probabilistic forecasts

This appendix is designed to help you forecast the outcomes of a future event. An event of much interest to most business managers is the demand for some product at some time in the future. Although our examples will concentrate on demand forecasting, there is no reason that the techniques cannot be used to make probabilistic forecasts for other events.

A probabilistic forecast is for *a range* of possible outcomes instead of a single outcome, and you should express your belief about the relative likelihoods of various outcomes within this range actually occurring. Such a forecast can be obtained by assessing a probability distribution over the various outcomes for the event. This forecast will then be used within the framework for analysis presented in Chapter 4. In Appendix 4–A we described two ways to represent a probability distribution: discrete distribution and cumulative distribution. One representation can always be used to calculate the other; thus, the problem of forecasting can be stated as assessing either the discrete or cumulative probability distribution over the outcomes of the event being considered.

In Appendix 4–A we defined the fractile as a measure of a probability distribution. There are many fractiles for each distribution, and one special fractile is called the *median*. The final result of the event has a 50 percent chance of being less than the median outcome. In general terms, the Xth fractile can be defined in the following way: There is an X percent chance that the final result of the event will not exceed the Xth fractile. The concept of a fractile is the basis of the approach we will use for assessing the probability distribution for an event. We will ask the decision maker to think about some specific fractiles for an event. Once he or she has made these assessments, we can construct a graph of the entire cumulative probability distribution. Following this approach, the decision maker has to think about only a few well-defined outcomes, like the median, instead of trying to conceptualize the entire distribution. Judgment can be focused on a specific part of the distribution, thus allowing the manager to express more accurately his or her knowledge of the event. Once again, however, we remind you that any probability distribution or forecast is an expression of judgment. Any procedure that accurately reflects the assessor's judgment is therefore correct.

It is easier to discuss assessment if we think about several situations. The first situation occurs when no relevant data are available to assist in making the assessment. A second situation exists when there are relevant historical data available from previous events similar to the one under consideration. A third situation is when relevant data are available about a previous event dissimilar from, but related to, the event under consideration.

ASSESSING A PROBABILITY DISTRIBUTION FOR THE OUTCOMES OF AN EVENT WHEN NO DATA ARE AVAILABLE

Quite often a decision problem will include an event fork and the decision maker will feel that no relevant data are available to guide his or her judgment in assessing the probabilities for the various outcomes. This lack of data may be because no effort has been made to collect data or because none is available to be collected. In the first case, it may be worthwhile to make an assessment and prepare an initial decision analysis to see whether the value of information is great enough to make the collection of any data that may be available worthwhile.

If the event has only a few known outcomes, for example, if a test can be only good or bad, then the best approach is to think about the relative likelihood of each of the outcomes occurring and assess the discrete probability distribution. You should assign relative weights to each possible outcome, and if these weights sum to one, you have the desired discrete probability distribution. If they do not, you can add all

154

the weights and divide each individual weight by the total to get the discrete distribution.

When the number of outcomes is small, you can think about each outcome individually and assess the discrete distribution. This is not easy. However, when the number of outcomes exceeds five or ten, this approach seems hopeless. Try to imagine assessing the probability of a demand for exactly 118 units when you believe that demand could be anywhere from 0 to 1,000 units. For most practical situations, the outcomes for an event are numerous, and it is more realistic to think about the cumulative probability distribution. It should be easier to think about demand being less than 118 units in the above example than about demand being exactly equal to 118. Not only is it easier to think about the cumulative distribution, but it is also possible to obtain a satisfactory cumulative distribution by thinking about only a few points on the distribution as opposed to thinking about them all. Once you have assessed several points on the cumulative probability distribution, you can plot them on a graph and then connect the points with a smooth line. In most cases five points are sufficient for plotting a cumulative distribution: the median, the 0.25 and the 0.75 fractiles, and two extreme fractiles.

The median is by definition the outcome of the event that has a probability of 0.50 of being exceeded. This should be the first point assessed. In order to think about the median, picture a wheel with a spinner as shown in Figure 4B–1. You believe the spinner is just as

FIGURE 4B–1
A wheel with half the
area shaded

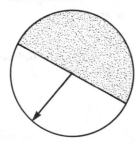

likely to stop at any one point on the wheel's circumference as any other, and you have examined the wheel and believe half of the area is shaded. The spinner on this wheel will be spun and you will receive a prize if the spinner stops in the shaded region. You will receive nothing if it falls outside the shaded area. Now think about the event for which you are assessing the probability distribution. Assume you would get the same prize if the event has an outcome equal to or less than X. Which of these two gambles do you prefer—the one based on the spin of the wheel or the one based on the outcome of the event? If you prefer the wheel, then think of an outcome larger than X. If you prefer the event, think of an outcome smaller than X. By going through this repeatedly, you should finally find some outcome of the event such that you do not care whether you take the wheel or the event as a gamble for receiving the prize. In other words, there is some outcome that makes you indifferent between a 0.50 chance of receiving a prize with the wheel gamble and a gamble in which you receive the same prize whether the final result of the event is less than or equal to that particular outcome. This outcome that makes you indifferent is your median for the probability distribution for the event under consideration.

The hypothetical wheel we described represents a concept called an *equivalent gamble*. The idea is to think of a situation in which you clearly understand the chances of winning, like a fair roulette wheel or a fair coin, and to use this device to structure a gamble with a prize of your own choosing. The next step is to structure another gamble with the same prize, but in which the winning of the prize depends on some outcome of the event for which a distribution is being assessed. By changing the value of the outcome, it should be possible to find one for which you do not care which gamble you would play for the prize. At this point, in your judgment, the gambles are the same. If this is true, we can then assign the probability of the equivalent gamble to the value of the outcome at which you expressed indifference. Figure 4B–2 shows two event forks representing two gambles.

The equivalent gamble provides a prize if the spinner in Figure 4B–1 stops in the shaded area and provides nothing if the spinner stops in the unshaded area. Since you believe the wheel is fair and has half the area shaded, you should assign 0.5 to the top branch and 0.5 to the bottom branch of the equivalent gamble. The second gamble has the same prizes and no probabilities. However, there should be some value for the outcomes of the event, call it Z, that makes you indifferent between the two gambles. This value Z is the *median* for your distribution.

The next step in obtaining the forecast is to assess the extreme fractiles. Most people believe that it is not difficult to think about the extreme values of the probability distribution. However, the results of some experiments have indicated that this belief may be unfounded. Part of the difficulty is in defining what is meant by an extreme value. One approach is to ask for the value of the 0.01 and 0.99 fractiles. By definition, the outcome of the event should be outside these two values only twice in 100 occurrences. This is not easy to conceptualize. In

FIGURE 4B–2
Two event forks between which you must be indifferent for
some outcome, Z

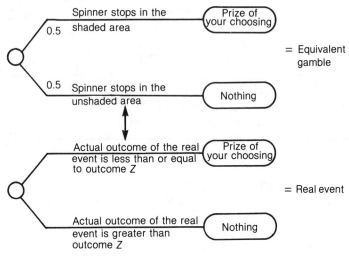

experiments, most people do not distinguish between the 0.99 and the 0.999 fractile or the highest possible outcome. Also most people tend to *underestimate* the deviation of the extreme points of the distribution from the median. For this reason, we recommend that you think with care about the highest possible outcome and the lowest possible outcome for the extreme points of the cumulative distribution.

With the median and extreme points assessed, you should think about some fractiles between these values. A common practice is to think about the 0.75 and 0.25 fractiles. To do this we suggest again the use of an equivalent gamble. For the 0.25 fractile (often called the *lower quartile*), think about the wheel shown in Figure 4B–3 with 25 percent of its area shaded.

FIGURE 4B–3
A wheel with 25 percent
of the area shaded

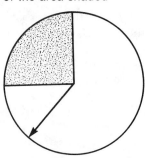

Think about a prize you would receive if the spinner stopped in the shaded area. Now think of some outcome of the event, call it Y. Imagine you will receive the prize if the final result is less than or equal to Y. The value Y that makes you indifferent to which gamble you play is the 0.25 fractile of your distribution. A similar process can be used for the 0.75 fractile (the *upper quartile*), only the wheel should have a 75 percent shaded area.

Other fractiles can be assessed using this equivalent gamble approach. Additional effort may improve the quality of the assessment, but it may only serve to confuse the assessor. If you stop after assessing the five points, you can do some checking on yourself. You should believe that it is just as likely that the outcome of the event will be between the 0.75 and 0.25 fractiles (called the *interquartile range*) as it is that the outcome will be less than the 0.25 or greater than the 0.75 fractile. If this is not true, you may wish to move the five points to make them more consistent with your best judgment.

Now plot your five points on a cumulative graph. The lower extreme point should be less than 0.01 but greater than 0.00 on the vertical axis; the upper point should be between 0.99 and 1.00. Now connect the points with a smooth line. This process may indicate a curve that you do not believe represents your best judgment. It may have an irregular shape in some sense that you believe is not representative of your feelings. Do not think that the five original points cannot be moved. Adjust the points until you believe the *entire curve* is more to your liking. Be careful in this process. You are not seeking some artistic prize for which symmetry is rewarded. If you really believe the lower and upper half of the distribution are symmetrical, then plot it that way, but *only* if you believe that a symmetrical distribution is representative of the event under consideration.

This entire process usually leaves one feeling uncertain. Remember, that is where you started. The uneasiness may be caused by the fact that you *do not really know* the outcome of the event, not because you are trying to quantify your feelings about this uncertainty.

You may find that this approach is not workable for you and that you feel more comfortable assessing the distribution in some other manner. This is quite appropriate. The only point to keep in mind is that your assessment should reflect your judgment about the possible outcomes of the event, not your likes and dislikes for the outcomes or your fears and wishes.

Summary for forecasting with no data

In summary, when you must assess the probability distribution for an event with no relevant data, there are two approaches: one for an event with few outcomes and the other for an event with many outcomes. In the first case, you should attempt to assess the discrete distribution of the event. The approach is to think about the relative likelihood of each of the few outcomes occurring. Once a set of relative weights is assigned, you should add them and divide them by their sum. This will assure that the resulting probabilities add to one.

In the second case you should attempt to assess the cumulative probability distribution of the event. The approach is outlined below:

1. Assess the median.
2. Assess the extreme points.
3. Assess the 0.75 fractile.
4. Assess the 0.25 fractile.
5. Check to see whether you believe that a value in the range between the 0.75 and 0.25 fractiles is as likely to occur as a value outside the range.
6. Plot the assessed points on a cumulative graph.
7. Smooth a curve through the points.
8. Adjust the shape of the curve to reflect your overall judgment.

ASSESSING A PROBABILITY DISTRIBUTION FOR THE OUTCOMES OF AN EVENT USING HISTORICAL DATA FOR AN INDISTINGUISHABLE EVENT

In the above section we presented an approach for assessing probability distributions when no relevant data were available. This is a difficult process and leaves most people with the desire to collect some data to help guide their judgment. You should keep clearly in mind, however, that even with data you are expressing a *judgment* when you make an assessment. The choices of what data to collect, how much to collect, which data should be discarded after being collected, and how to use the data not discarded are all judgmental. Too often a feeling of security is associated with data because the decision maker believes he or she can rely on past experience to forecast the future. This may not be true. The responsibility for deciding when data are a good guide to the future and when they are not should be taken as seriously as the responsibility for making a completely subjective assessment.

To approach the use of data systematically, it is useful to define an *indistinguishable event*. An indistinguishable event is one for which the decision maker has no reason to believe that the outcomes of the event are any more or less likely to occur for a given trial than they would be on any other trial. For example, the event may be the toss of a coin. The outcomes are heads or tails. Now if the decision maker believes that on the fifth toss the outcome heads is just as likely as it is on the 29th toss or any other toss, then this event is indistinguishable from occurrence to occurrence. Note that it is not necessary that the coin be fair (i.e., that the probability of heads be 0.5), only that each toss has the same probability of coming up heads. If the event is indistinguishable from occurrence to occurrence, then the outcome of previous occurrences can be used to forecast the outcome of the next occurrence.

In most cases it is possible to find some distinguishable characteristic for various occurrences of the same event. For example, an event of interest at a newsstand may be the number of newspapers that will be sold tomorrow. The various outcomes for this event are numbers of papers. The decision maker might feel differently about this event depending on the day of the week, because he or she knows, for example, that Sunday papers sell better (or worse) than weekday papers. In this case you would say that the event is distinguishable from one day to the next.

In assessing the probability distribution for an event, one major judgment required is whether you have data on events that are indistinguishable from the one under consideration. In a strict sense, this is never true, but in many cases the distinguishing characteristics are small enough so the decision maker is willing to treat the data as indistinguishable. In the newsstand example, the forecaster may exclude historical data on Saturday and Sunday sales when forecasting the number of papers that will be sold on Monday. However, the forecaster may be willing to use historical sales data from previous Mondays, Tuesdays, Wednesdays, Thursdays, and Fridays because he or she is willing to assume that all weekdays are indistinguishable when it comes to newspaper sales.

A classic example of a case where you would have data on indistinguishable events is the gambling table. Suppose you are shown a fair die and are asked to play a game in which the payoffs depend on the outcome of the roll of this die. What should you assess as the probability of each outcome?

You must decide first whether you believe this is really a fair die. You can hold it and observe that it is a perfect cube and has no abnormal distribution of weight, etc. On the basis of this observation, you are willing to conclude that it is a fair die. What would your probability distribution be for this die if you had to decide? A great number of people would assess a discrete distribution that assigns one-sixth probability to each of the six possible outcomes. This assessment is usually based on previous experience with fair dice. In fact, the amount of historical data is usually so large that the assessor is willing to assign the historical relative frequencies of the outcomes as the probabilities of these outcomes on the next roll.

Maybe you are not quite sure that this die is fair, so you ask for a chance to roll it a few times. You are now really checking to see that this die is in fact indistinguishable from the others in your background. Suppose the results of your first ten rolls are as shown in Table 4B–1. There are not much data here; however, you are now required to assess your probability distribution. What would it be?

TABLE 4B–1
Results of ten rolls

Face	Number of times showing in ten rolls
1	3
2	2
3	1
4	0
5	2
6	2
	10

Many people would still say one-sixth for each of the six faces. Their main reason would be that a fair die could give these results on ten rolls, and they would be unwilling to discard all the historical data they have collected on other fair dice. However, if you were convinced that this die was unfair and therefore your historical data were useless, then you might assess the discrete distribution in Table 4B–2.

TABLE 4B–2
Discrete distribution for the event-next roll of die, if the only relevant data are from the ten rolls

Outcome	Probability
1	0.3
2	0.2
3	0.1
4	0.0
5	0.2
6	0.2

The process followed to obtain this assessment was to assign the historical relative frequency of each outcome as the probability of that outcome on the next roll. Note that only the data from indistinguishable events (the ten rolls of *this* die) were used to calculate the relative frequencies.

If there was major uncertainty in your mind about the fairness of this die, you would roll it a large number of times. Suppose that in 10,000 rolls, the data in Table 4B–3 were obtained.

TABLE 4B–3
Results of 10,000 rolls

Face	Number of times showing in 10,000 rolls
1	2,980
2	2,020
3	1,010
4	3
5	2,497
6	1,490
	10,000

Now it is clear that the die is unfair. Using the historical data on the indistinguishable event: roll of this unfair die, you should feel comfortable with the discrete probability distribution for outcomes of the next roll shown in Table 4B–4.

TABLE 4B–4
Discrete distribution for the event-next roll of die, using data from 10,000 rolls

Outcome	Probability
1	0.30
2	0.20
3	0.10
4	0.00
5	0.25
6	0.15

In this example the major decision has been how much data resulted from a process that was indistinguishable from the event currently under consideration. When there was a large amount of data on an indistinguishable event, the *long-run relative frequency* for each outcome was assigned as its probability. This was true before rolling the die, or after 10,000 rolls. In both situations, there was some comfort in assigning relative frequencies because of the large amount of data considered to be relevant. Even after ten rolls, if you were still willing to assume the die was fair, you could invoke all your experience with dice to support the assigning of one-sixth probability to each face. The uncomfortable situation was when you believed the die was unfair and only had ten historical data points. This most uncomfortable situation unfortunately is also the most typical in the real world.

Making an assessment using a small amount of data

Suppose you have been keeping track of daily sales in your new business, which has been serving customers faithfully for ten days. Your historical sales records are shown in Table 4B–5.

TABLE 4B–5
Sales records

Number of items	Number of days that amount was sold	Number of items	Number of days that amount was sold
12	1	22	0
13	0	23	1
14	0	24	0
15	0	25	0
16	1	26	1
17	2	27	0
18	0	28	0
19	1	29	0
20	2	30	0
21	0	31	1

You are preparing to forecast the number of items that can be sold on the 11th day. Your first decision is whether you believe the first ten days are indistinguishable from the 11th. Let us assume you are willing to believe this. If you don't, you should ignore the data and assess the probability distribution for the next day's sales judgmentally.

If you used the data and followed the approach of assigning relative frequencies as probabilities, you would assess the discrete probability distribution shown in Table 4B–6.

It seems odd that you would assign a 0.2 chance to sales being 17 and a 0.1 chance to sales being 19 but no chance to sales being 18. In fact, you probably believe that 18 units could be sold tomorrow. If this distribution were based on 10,000 days of sales records, and 18 items had never been sold, then a probability of 0 for 18 might be believable. However, with ten days of data such a conclusion is doubtful.

A more useful approach is to calculate the cumulative relative frequencies of the historical data, as shown in Table 4B–7. The cumula-

TABLE 4B-6
Discrete probability distribution for event:
Sales on 11th day

Outcome, N*	Probability that Sales = Outcome, $P(\hat{S} = N)$
12	0.1
16	0.1
17	0.2
19	0.1
20	0.2
23	0.1
26	0.1
31	0.1

* Zero probability to all other sales levels.

tive relative frequencies can then be plotted on a graph. Such a graph for the data in Table 4B–7 is shown as the stairsteps in Figure 4B–4.

Now, using the stairsteps shown in Figure 4B–4, you can draw a smooth curve for the cumulative probability distribution. This smooth curve should not be drawn without careful thought, since the stairsteps are only a guide based on limited data. The curve should reflect your judgment about tomorrow's sales, and this judgment can be aided, but not replaced, by the historical data.

You would probably want the curve to extend below 12 and above 31 items. There is no reason to believe that in the first ten days you have seen the highest or lowest possible sales that may result on day 11. How far beyond these points you should extend the curve is

TABLE 4B-7
Historical cumulative relative frequency of sales

N = Items sold	Fraction of the days N or fewer items were sold	N = Items sold	Fraction of the days N or fewer items were sold
12	0.1	22	0.7
13	0.1	23	0.8
14	0.1	24	0.8
15	0.1	25	0.8
16	0.2	26	0.9
17	0.4	27	0.9
18	0.4	28	0.9
19	0.5	29	0.9
20	0.7	30	0.9
21	0.7	31	1.0

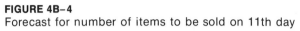

FIGURE 4B-4
Forecast for number of items to be sold on 11th day

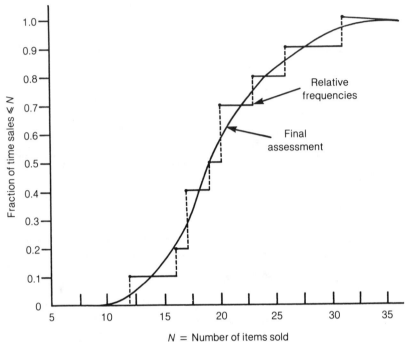

N = Number of items sold

judgmental. It might be useful for you to think about the highest and lowest sales you think are possible and plot them as the 0.001 and 0.999 fractiles before you draw the smooth curve. Note that the stairsteps are steepest between 15 and 20 items. This means that more historical occurrences were in this range. In fact, 60 percent of the historical data is between 15 and 20. This gives you some idea about where you might want to put the mode of your assessed distribution (remember the mode has the steepest slope on the smooth cumulative curve). After thinking about the shape of the curve, draw it in over the steps. One possibility for the smooth curve is shown in Figure 4B-4. At this time it may be useful to erase the stairsteps and begin to think about the overall shape and position of the curve. Once the curve satisfies your judgment, you can change the vertical axis scale from cumulative relative frequency to cumulative probability.

Summary on forecasting using data on indistinguishable events

In summary, two approaches have been suggested for situations in which you have data from indistinguishable events. These two approaches are classified for situations with much data and situations with little data.

1. With much data for indistinguishable events, you can assign the long-run relative frequency of each outcome as the probability of that outcome on the next occurrence of the event.
2. With little data for indistinguishable events, you can:
    a. Plot the cumulative relative frequency of the data.
    b. Think about the general shape and position of a cumulative probability for the event.
    c. Smooth a curve through the stairsteps of the plot, keeping in mind your ideas about shape and position.
    d. Use the smooth curve as your cumulative probability distribution for the event.

ASSESSING A PROBABILITY DISTRIBUTION FOR THE OUTCOMES OF AN EVENT USING HISTORICAL DATA FROM A DISTINGUISHABLE EVENT

In the preceding section we presented an approach for assessing a probability distribution for the next occurrence of an event when data were available for indistinguishable occurrences of the event. Unfortunately, in most cases the available data are not for indistinguishable events. This section will present two approaches for using data that are from events that can be distinguished by some characteristic.

For example, suppose on a Monday you are trying to forecast tomorrow's demand for a recently introduced item in a wholesaler's line of goods. The wholesaler has been offering this item to grocery stores in a large metropolitan area for the past three weeks and has collected the order data shown in Table 4B–8.

Looking at the daily averages for the three weeks it is clear that there is a definite daily trend. Orders are higher in the early part of the week and fall sharply on Saturday. The wholesaler feels that this fact is

TABLE 4B–8
Wholesaler's order data

	Actual number of items ordered			Average daily orders
	Week 1	Week 2	Week 3	
Monday	133	126	146	135.0
Tuesday	110	131	130	123.7
Wednesday	126	82	79	95.7
Thursday	84	119	73	92.0
Friday	88	102	95	95.0
Saturday	52	55	61	56.0

consistent with the behavior of his grocery store customers on other items. In fact, he has kept track of dollar sales to the grocery stores for each day of the week and has developed the average daily orders shown in Table 4B–9.

TABLE 4B–9
Wholesaler's average daily orders

	Average daily order	Adjustment factor
Monday...............................	$682,349	1.4
Tuesday	584,392	1.2
Wednesday	487,207	1.0
Thursday	438,962	0.9
Friday	439,005	0.9
Saturday........................	292,477	0.6
All days..........................	487,399	1.0

You now have a choice in making the forecast for Tuesday's orders for the item. It is clear that Tuesday is distinguishable from the other days. Thus one choice is to discard all data on the other days and use only the three previous Tuesdays' data as a guide to your forecast. The second choice is to try to adjust the other days to make them indistinguishable from Tuesday and then use all 18 adjusted pieces of data to guide your judgment. If you make the first choice, you would plot the three data points as a cumulative relative frequency graph and draw a smooth curve through them, which would be your probability assessment.

The second approach is more attractive if there is some reasonable basis for making the adjustment to the other days. It can be argued that the only reason for the daily pattern in ordering might be the policy of grocery stores to let their stock run down by the weekend. This ordering pattern is reflected in the average daily dollar orders collected in Table 4B–9.

If this line of argument is acceptable to the wholesaler, then you can proceed in the following way. First, define the event you believe is indistinguishable: in this example, the basic daily demand for this item. Second, define a relationship between this event and the data available. In this example, *Basic demand = Actual demand ÷ Adjustment factor*. Finally, adjust the available data to make them indistinguishable. Adjusted data are shown in Table 4B–10.

The data in Table 4B–10 were obtained by taking the actual orders shown in Table 4B–8 and dividing them by the adjustment factors for each day shown in Table 4B–9. This procedure is possible because we

TABLE 4B-10
Basic demand for item (adjusted for ordering policy)

	Week 1	Week 2	Week 3
Monday	95	90	104
Tuesday	92	109	108
Wednesday	126	82	79
Thursday	93	132	81
Friday	98	113	105
Saturday	86	91	101

believe that the basic demand on Mondays is increased by a factor of 40 percent strictly because of the ordering policy of the grocers and that the basic demand on Fridays is decreased by 10 percent because of this ordering practice.

Once the influence of the ordering policy is factored out, the data are treated as indistinguishable. Table 4B-11 shows the cumulative

TABLE 4B-11
Cumulative relative frequencies of basic demand

D	Fraction of the times sales were less than D	D	Fraction of the times sales were less than D
79	0.056	98	0.555
81	0.111	101	0.611
82	0.167	104	0.667
86	0.222	105	0.722
90	0.278	108	0.778
91	0.333	109	0.833
92	0.389	113	0.889
93	0.444	129	0.944
95	0.500	132	1.000

relative frequencies of the basic demand. Figure 4B-5 shows a plot of these cumulative relative frequencies. A smooth curve has been drawn through the stairsteps to represent what might be a final assessment of the probability distribution for the event: tomorrow's basic demand. However, since tomorrow is Tuesday, this forecast of basic demand must be readjusted to take into account the ordering policy. This readjustment is accomplished by multiplying the basic demand on the horizontal axis by 1.2, which is Tuesday's adjustment factor from Table 4B-9.

In this example it is possible to take into account all the factors we believe make the data distinguishable, that is, the ordering policy of

FIGURE 4B-5

Plot of cumulative relative frequencies of basic demand and cumulative probability distribution for sales on Tuesday

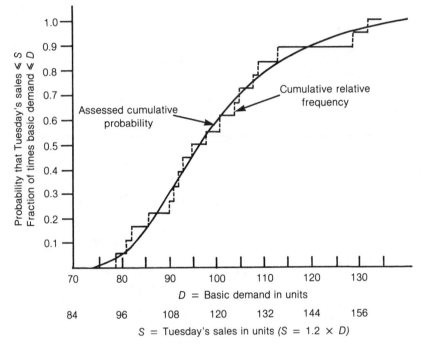

customers. In other cases there may be so many factors that distinguish the basic data that all the needed adjustments cannot be made. For example, if the wholesaler had run promotional deals in the first week and advertised heavily in the third week, it would have been necessary to adjust the data of the first and third weeks for these differences. However, there might not be adjustment factors that you would be willing to use for advertising and promotion. If this were true, then the first and third weeks' data should not be used to forecast orders on days when different promotional or advertising policies are in effect.

THE USE OF FORECASTING MODELS

Many situations change so rapidly or are influenced by so many different factors that it is virtually impossible to adjust for all of the distinguishable characteristics in the data. In these cases it may be possible to use a forecasting model. Such a model may be an elaborate mathematical abstraction or the judgment of an experienced employee. The basic assumption in using a forecasting model is that the model will account for all major distinguishable characteristics and be subject only to errors that are not attributable to any one particular factor. Whether this assumption is valid in any given case is a major *judgment* to be made by the decision maker.

Consider the first eight quarters of data for a product, as shown in Table 4B–12. The last entry of 190 units is the forecast for the first

ABLE 4B–12
orecasted product demand

ear	Quarter	Forecasted demand	Actual demand	Absolute error, Actual − Forecast	Relative error, Actual ÷ Forecast
977	1	100	94	−6	0.94
977	2	450	459	9	1.02
977	3	860	920	60	1.07
977	4	1,300	1,196	−104	0.92
978	1	110	122	12	1.11
978	2	430	421	−9	0.98
978	3	890	854	−36	0.96
978	4	1,240	1,426	186	1.15
979	1	190	?	?	?

quarter of 1979 made by the same model that had made the previous eight forecasts.

It is clear that there is a seasonal trend in actual sales data. The general level of the economy was changing during the period considered. In addition, it would be fair to assume that the marketing policy of the company selling the product and its competitors' policies may have changed during the period. All these factors make the actual sales for any quarter distinguishable from those for any other quarter. Our assumption is that these major factors were considered in the forecasting model and resulted in the changing forecast from quarter to quarter. In addition, we assume that the new forecast has been made by the same model after considering all major factors for the next quarter. The problem is how to use this model's forecast.

First, look at the fifth column, the absolute error in the data. This error is obtained by subtracting the forecasted sales from the actual sales. It should be clear that the error is quite distinguishable from quarter to quarter. When the actual sales are low (quarters 1 and 2), the errors are small. When the actual sales are high (quarters 3 and 4), the errors are large. This is a fairly common occurrence with forecasting models (human or otherwise) and indicates a tendency to make relative errors rather than absolute errors.

TABLE 4B–13
Cumulative relative frequency of relative error for forecasting model

X	Fraction of time $A/F \leq X$
0.92	0.125
0.94	0.250
0.96	0.375
0.98	0.500
1.02	0.625
1.07	0.750
1.11	0.875
1.15	1.000

Because the size of the absolute error changes with the actual sales level, it is more useful to look at the relative error. A measure of this relative error is shown in the sixth column of Table 4B–12. This column is the actual sales divided by the forecasted sales, or the A/F ratio. The A/F ratio in this example does not have any recognizable pattern

FIGURE 4B–6
Plot of cumulative relative frequencies of relative error and cumulative probability distribution for sales in first quarter of 1979

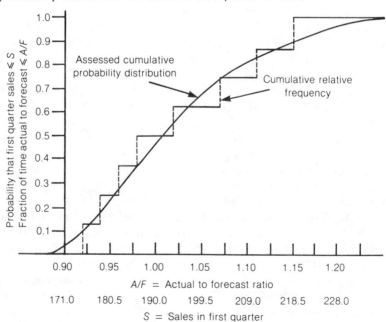

relating it to the actual sales levels; for example, it is not always greater than 1.0 for low or high actual values. If there is no distinguishable characteristic to the A/F ratio from period to period, then it becomes the undistinguishable event to be forecast.

Table 4B–13 shows the cumulative relative frequency of the A/F ratio, and Figure 4B–6 shows a plot of these data.

After thinking about the shape and position of the error curve, you might draw in a smooth curve like the one shown in Figure 4B–6. This would be your probability assessment of the relative error that the forecasting model will make in its next forecast. What you are interested in, however, is a sales forecast for next quarter. This can be obtained by taking the model's point forecast of 190 for the next quarter and multiplying it by the probability distribution you have just assessed for the error of the model. This is accomplished by taking 190 times the A/F values on the horizontal axis in Figure 4B–6. The result of this multiplication is your probability distribution for next quarter's sales.

Summary on forecasting data on distinguishable events

In summary, there are two forecasting approaches that use historical data on distinguishable events:

1. When there is some way to adjust the data to remove the influence of the distinguishing characteristics:
   a. Determine the relationship between the distinguishing factors and the data.
   b. Adjust the data using this relationship.
   c. Forecast using the data that are indistinguishable.
   d. Readjust the forecast for the particular event under consideration, using the relationship developed in step a.
2. When some forecasting model exists that you believe takes account of the distinguishing characteristics:
   a. Obtain the next point forecast from the model for the event of interest and the historical data on the model's previous forecasts and the actual outcomes of the event when the model was used to forecast.
   b. Determine whether the model has an indistinguishable error pattern (either absolute or relative errors).
   c. Use the indistinguishable data on historical error to forecast the probability distribution for the error in the next forecast.
   d. Adjust the point forecast by adding the probability distribution of the historical relative error you have assessed. The result will be a probabilistic forecast for the event of interest.

Warren Agency, Inc.

Mr. Thaddeus Warren operated a real estate agency which specialized in finding buyers for commercial properties. Warren was approached one day by a prospective client who had three properties in and adjoining Cambridge, Massachusetts, which he wished to sell. The client indicated the prices he wished to receive for these properties as follows:

Property	Price
Allston	$ 25,000
Belmont	50,000
Cambridge	100,000

Warren would receive a commission of 4 percent on any of the properties he was able to sell.

The client laid down the following conditions for an exclusive listing: "Warren, you have to sell the Allston property first. If you can't sell it within a month, the entire deal is off—no commission and no chance to sell the other properties. If you sell the Allston property within a month, then I'll give you the commission for Allston and the option of (a) stopping at this point, or (b) trying to sell either the Belmont or Cambridge properties next under the same conditions (i.e., sell within a month or no commission on the second property and no chance to sell the third property). If you succeed in selling the first two properties, you will also have the option of selling the third."

After the client had left, Warren proceeded to analyze the proposal which had been made to him to determine whether or not to accept it. He figured his selling costs and his chances of selling each property at the prices set by the client to be:

Property	Cost	Warren's assessment of probability of sale
Allston	$800	0.7
Belmont	200	0.6
Cambridge	400	0.5

He believed that sale of a particular property would not make it any more or less likely that the two remaining properties could be sold. Selling costs would have to be incurred whether or not a particular property was sold but could be avoided by deciding not to attempt to sell the property.

Since the Allston property would have to be sold before any further action could be taken, Warren prepared the following table showing the profit under various circumstances in an attempt to determine whether or not to accept the Allston property:

		Act	
Event	Probability	Accept Allston	Refuse Allston
Allston sold	0.7	$200 ?	$0
Allston not sold	0.3	−800	0
Expected value		−100	$0
Total	1.0		

Thus, based on expected value, accepting Allston would be unprofitable by itself. Warren was not very happy with this conclusion. However, he reasoned that success in selling the Allston property would entitle him to offer either the Belmont or Cambridge properties, and it looked as if either of these properties would result in an expected profit. He felt that somehow or other the value of this opportunity should be taken into consideration.

case 4–2

The *Nancy M. Hohman*

At 4:00 P.M. on the 14th of July, 1972, Captain Virgil Sandford, master of the oil tanker *Nancy M. Hohman*, was considering what action he should take regarding a malfunction of his ship's engine. The *Nancy M. Hohman*, a ship of British registry with 28 crew members, had been bound from Rotterdam, The Netherlands, to the Persian Gulf to take on a load of 200,000 tons of crude oil. At the time the engine malfunctioned, the *Nancy M. Hohman*'s position was 9 miles off the coast of South Africa, just out of Port Elizabeth. Port Elizabeth, however, was too small and shallow a port for a ship the size of *Nancy M. Hohman*, even when empty, to enter. The nearest port with repair facilities capable of accommodating a ship of the *Nancy Hohman's* size was Durban, South Africa, about 380 nautical miles to the east. Captain Sandford, who was known for "doing things by the book" and "running a tight ship," immediately broadcast an advisory of his ship's location and condition as a warning to other marine traffic to avoid her. Almost immediately, the captain of the *Ann-Marie*, a large seagoing tug, sent a message to Captain Sandford:

> We have heard your broadcast and advise that we are standing by to offer our services to assist you to Durban. We lie at Port Elizabeth and can reach your position within an hour of your call.

Captain Sandford acknowledged the *Ann-Marie's* message without either accepting or rejecting her offer. He knew that tugboats like the *Ann-Marie* often cruised these waters hoping to find an oil tanker or other commercial vessel in difficulty. With the closing of the Suez Canal in 1967, the passage around southern Africa had become the most heavily traveled sea route in the world. Also, since the days of the legendary *Flying Dutchman*, the waters off the South African coast had been known as a graveyard for ships. Indeed, the complex currents and severe southern winter storm season from April to September had claimed a number of oil tankers in recent years with resultant loss of life and widespread pollution of the local seas by their cargos.

While Captain Sandford was relieved that the *Ann-Marie* was available, he felt that there was still a good chance of taking his ship into Durban under her own steam. This was desirable because, if he commissioned the tug to tow the *Nancy Hohman* to Durban, he would be giving the *Ann-Marie* a claim to his ship. In other words, accepting the tow was tantamount to abandoning ship. Under international law, then, the *Ann-Marie* could gain legal salvage rights to the *Nancy Hohman*, a $40-million vessel less than one year old. In practice, however, salvage tugs were rarely awarded the salvaged ship in cases like this. More commonly, the owners of the towed ship paid an indemnity to the owners of the tug. This tended to avoid lengthy (and very costly) international litigation. The size of the indemnity that would be paid was subject to negotiation between the owning parties and usually took several months after the fact to settle. Some recent settlements of this sort had amounted to about 15 percent of the cost of the ship.

Captain Sandford paused to take stock of the situation. Gordon O'Donnel, chief engineer of the *Nancy Hohman*, reported that he felt that there was an 80 percent chance that he could make temporary repairs to the engine which would hold until they reached Durban.

Top speed with these repairs would only be about 8 knots, about half of normal top speed. Captain Sandford estimated that, under these conditions, he could put the *Nancy Hohman* into Durban in three days.

The weather that the *Nancy Hohman* could expect to encounter over the next three days was very important to Captain Sandford's decision. Consulting the South African weather service in Port Elizabeth, Captain Sandford found that the forecast for the next three days was for continued fair weather. His previous experience with the reliability of nautical weather forecasting made him uneasy, however. Sandford felt that, despite the favorable forecast, there was still about one chance in five that bad weather would develop sometime during the next three days. In the event of bad weather, sufficient power was required of the engines to maintain steerage in rough seas. Captain Sandford felt that, given bad weather, the *Nancy Hohman* stood about one chance in four of being unable to maintain steerage. If she couldn't maintain steerage, the result would be the same as if the engine stopped completely in a bad storm. That is, the *Nancy Hohman* would very likely be sunk by the storm's heavy seas, with some loss of life. If steerage were lost, the probability of the ship pulling through bad weather was only about one in ten. Sandford commented on the situation to his first officer.

"If the weather holds, we'll make it to Durban if O'Donnel can get a patch job done on the engine. If he can't, we'll stand a 50–50 chance of foundering on the South African coast or drifting off into the Indian Ocean toward Australia. Of course, we could put into lifeboats if we approach the coast or otherwise, wait for a tow. If the weather turns bad, however, then I've got to decide whether to abandon her or try to ride it out. We should have enough time to make the coast in lifeboats if rough weather approaches and, if O'Donnel can't get the engine fixed, that's what we'll do. If we wait till a storm is upon us before abandoning ship, then half the crew would likely perish. Of course, if we tried to ride it out on the repaired engine and were unable to maintain steerage we'd all be lost as the ship went down. In any event, it's a good show that tug is lying in Port Elizabeth. If the weather turns or if O'Donnel can't get the engine going, I'll call her in."

At 10:00 P.M., about six hours after the engine malfunction occurred, the tug *Ann-Marie* pulled alongside the *Nancy M. Hohman* and signaled that she was sailing for Cape Town to take a Liberian freighter in tow. The message continued:

> If you want us to tow you to Durban you'd best say so now for we'll be gone several days. Also, Captain Sandford, there are no other tugboats in this area that are large enough to be of any help to your ship save the *Ann-Marie*.

With that, the *Ann-Marie* opened her throttle and moved westward toward Cape Town.

Captain Sandford quickly called the engine room. He found that engine repairs would be completed within three hours—too late to recall the *Ann-Marie* if they were not successful. Further, Mr. O'Donnel was standing by his 0.8 probability estimate that repairs would be successful. Sandford knew that the master of the *Ann-Marie* was telling the truth about there being no other tugboats in the area to help the *Nancy Hohman* but he was not so sure about the story of a commission near Cape Town. If the *Ann-Marie's* message were a ploy to get Sandford to accept a tow, then the tug might still be available in the event Mr. O'Donnel's engine repairs wouldn't hold or if the weather deteriorated unexpectedly. If the master of the *Ann-Marie* had been truthful (and Sandford felt that there was about one chance in four that the *Ann-Marie* did actually have another job), then the *Nancy Hohman* was left to her own resources. As Sandford watched the receding lights of the *Ann-Marie* from the bridge of his ship, he knew that the responsibility for action in this situation was entirely his. He also knew that he would be held accountable for his decision before a shipowner's board of inquiry back in London if he either accepted a tow or if the *Nancy Hohman* were lost. For a moment he wondered how these financiers, sitting in their plush London offices, would react in this situation. Then, realizing that he had only about 30 minutes to recall the *Ann-Marie*, he began to concentrate on his decision.

case 4–3

Family Health Center, Inc. (A)

Dr. Morris Sinnick was carefully reviewing the pages of rough calculations he had generated on a proposed "Family Health Center." Although these numbers were preliminary, he mused, they would provide a sound basis for this evening's discussion with his long-time friend and colleague, Dr. Anthony Collado.

Dr. Collado had called Dr. Sinnick earlier in the week and enthusiastically proposed the creation of a family-oriented group practice in a suburban community near Boston. He described the group as one designed to provide a full range of ambulatory health services to the community, including specialists in internal medicine, pediatrics, obstetrics and gynecology, general surgery, and dentistry with supporting laboratory and radiology facilities. It would indeed be a center for family health with all essential services located in the same place. Dr. Sinnick had agreed to discuss the proposal further with Dr. Collado, after he had time to research and analyze it properly.

The doctors had become close friends as medical students at the University of Rochester. In fact, their first joint effort grew out of repeated requests for copies of Dr. Sinnick's notes in medical school. Dr. Collado had suggested that it would be a great income supplement if the notes were printed and sold to their classmates, but Dr. Sinnick was characteristically less optimistic. Nonetheless, following considerable discussion, they agreed to give it a try. After each had invested $500 of his meager savings in initial typing and printing, however, problems with pricing and overoptimistic demand forecasts developed, causing the entrepreneurial effort to terminate in six months.

Over the years, each had gained considerable respect in the medical community. They had often collaborated on journal articles which were well received by their colleagues. It was their book, however, which won them wide recognition. In it they combined their specialties (obstetrics and pediatrics), explaining how to provide total care for mother and child.

The joint ventures plus their personal practices provided them sufficient personal wealth so that during the late 1960s they could afford to turn their attention toward the mounting problems of health care delivery. From 1966 to 1970 they had devoted about one quarter of their professional time to efforts to found clinics and health care plans in lower-income urban areas, working through a large New England medical school.

Their biggest success had provoked the greatest controversy between the two friends. Dr. Collado had envisioned a neighborhood health center located in an inner-city community designed to provide maximum social impact, while removing all the usual barriers to access: distance, time, cost, impersonality, complex eligibility requirements, etc. However, Dr. Sinnick had fought the whole concept, producing numerous calculations clearly showing that the proposal couldn't make it financially. The idea culminated in the Commonwealth Community Neighborhood Health Center, an unprecedented success, which was used as the national model for the funding of 41 such centers.

When Dr. Collado arrived at Dr. Sinnick's home, he joined him in the library. After warm greetings, Dr. Sinnick started right in.

"Tony, I've reviewed the plan for the Family Health Center carefully. In fact, I've thought about it so much I've been having dreams . . . no . . . nightmares over it. I know we agree conceptually, but if we're going to bring it to fruition, then we will have to pin down some of the important parameters. You know, location, type of equipment, patient population. . . ."

Dr. Collado was so encouraged at this initial sign of approval from his colleague, that he grew impatient with his friend's unimpassioned manner.

"Morris, this will be the culmination of our efforts in community health—to deliver comprehensive health care to the family unit. We can create an organization, incorporating the flexibility to meet the needs of the family and to serve its members in their own style and in their own environment. Instead of doctors of the same specialty practicing as a group—which is great professionally but not well suited for the medical consumer—we'll have the essential specialties in a single location."

"I understand the grand design," Dr. Sinnick responded, "but what about reality? Where will it be located? How many will it serve? What kind of staffing and equipment will we require?"

Dr. Collado looked annoyed. He just didn't like thinking about these "details." Nevertheless, he knew Dr. Sinnick was asking some important questions, just as he had so many times in the past.

"I think we can start with the nucleus of people I have described. Eventually, we can build on the organization, adding psychiatric services, a cardiologist, a specialist in every area, providing total care for the family in one place. Think of it!"

"Hold on, hold on," Morris pleaded. "In order to support such a staff and its associated overhead, what volume of patients do you foresee?"

"Well sure, Morris, it will be small at first, but you have to start somewhere. Eventually who knows, maybe the whole community will be knocking on our door."

At this point, Dr. Sinnick handed Dr. Collado the calculations he had been working on, showing him the information he collected on the communities of Brookline, Newton, and Weston, the locations they were considering (see Exhibit 1). He explained that by leasing the building and equipment, they would reduce the risk during the start-up period. He also said that he had discussed with potential landlords and equipment lessors the possibility of two-year leases, so that if things weren't successful, they could gracefully retire at the end of the lease. For this reason he felt they should confine the analysis to the two-year outlook.

He then began to explain the specific revenues and expenses at each of the three locations (see Exhibits 2–4).

EXHIBIT 1
Map and demographic data for the three potential locations

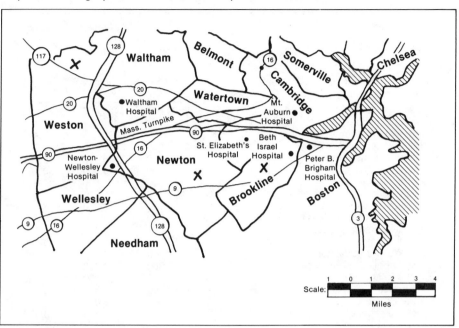

Key:
    X—possible FHC location
    •—hospital

Vital statistics

	Brookline	Newton	Weston
Population	58,689	91,263	10,870
Median age	38.6	32.3	28.4
Median family income	$13,701	$15,381	$23,530
Number of physicians*	380	165	22
Number of dentists*	No data available	80	6

* The number of physicians or dentists *residing* in each community; the community is not necessarily where their practice is located.
    Source: Commonwealth of Massachusetts, Department of Commerce and Development, Bureau of Research (DATA: 1970).

"Tony, let's take a look at the patient population in these communities: Newton, Brookline, and Weston. We could conceivably have any number of patient visits from 5,000 to 50,000 per year depending on where we locate and how fortunate we are. To get a rough idea where we stand, I picked three representative volumes of patient vis-

EXHIBIT 2
Annual revenues and expenses for Brookline

	Volume		
	Low	Medium	High
Operating revenues			
Number of patient visits/year	20,000	30,000	40,000
Average charge per visit	×$16	×$16	×$16
Gross income	$320,000	$480,000	$640,000
Operating expenses			
Salaries and benefits			
Physicians and dentists	$200,000	$200,000	$200,000
Doctors' benefits	25,000	25,000	25,000
Administrative	30,000	45,000	60,000
Paramedical	15,000	22,500	30,000
Technician	7,500	11,000	15,000
Employee benefits	9,000	13,000	18,000
Laboratory and x-ray fees	2,500	3,500	5,000
Medical and surgical supplies	12,000	18,000	24,000
Building and occupancy	50,000	50,000	50,000
Furniture and equipment	4,500	4,500	4,500
Office supplies and services	6,000	9,000	12,000
Legal and accounting	2,000	3,000	4,000
Telephone	3,000	4,500	6,000
Insurance	5,000	5,000	5,000
Other	8,000	8,000	8,000
Total expenses	$379,500	$422,000	$466,500
Net income (loss) before tax	($59,500)	$ 58,000	$173,500

its for each location, which I have called low, medium, and high. For example, in Brookline (he pointed to Exhibit 2), I used 20,000, 30,000, and 40,000 patient visits per year, where 20,000 is really a stand-in for 5,000 to 25,000 patients, 30,000 is a proxy for 25,000 to 35,000 patients, etc. Are you with me?"

Dr. Collado nodded.

"Furthermore, I had to choose an average charge per visit for each location, and the numbers I have selected have taken into account an allowance for laboratory and x-ray charges, the types of patients we are likely to see in each location, and the level of fee we can legitimately charge, based on the income level and medical competition in each town. The building lease figures reflect the high prices of office space in Brookline and the relatively low rates we can get in Weston due to surplus space there.

"Now, what's your feeling on how likely it will be for achieving volumes of these patient visits in the three locations we are considering? Keep in mind that each figure is a proxy for a range of values."

"I understand," Dr. Collado replied. "Well, first of all, excluding the transient student population (and they are all on the Student

EXHIBIT 3
Annual revenues and expenses for Newton

	Volume		
	Low	Medium	High
Operating revenues			
Number of patient visits/year	10,000	25,000	40,000
Average charge per visit	×$18	×$18	×$18
Gross income	$180,000	$450,000	$720,000
Operating expenses			
Salaries and benefits			
Physicians and dentists	$200,000	$200,000	$200,000
Doctors' benefits	25,000	25,000	25,000
Administrative	16,000	40,000	64,000
Paramedical	8,000	20,000	32,000
Technician	4,000	10,000	16,000
Employee benefits	5,000	12,000	19,000
Laboratory and x-ray fees	1,500	3,000	5,000
Medical and surgical supplies	6,500	16,000	25,000
Building and occupancy	45,000	45,000	45,000
Furniture and equipment	4,500	4,500	4,500
Office supplies and services	3,000	8,000	13,000
Legal and accounting	2,000	3,000	4,000
Telephone	1,500	4,000	6,500
Insurance	5,000	5,000	5,000
Other	8,000	8,000	8,000
Total expenses	$335,000	$403,500	$472,000
Net income (loss) before tax	($155,000)	$ 46,500	$248,000

Health Plan, anyway), Brookline has a primarily aged population. I believe they're a pretty tight-knit group, set in their ways. In fact, I'm not sure our family approach even fits there. Furthermore, the elderly would be all too reluctant to leave their personal physicians. I would guess that start-up would be very difficult, with a low volume being most probable, say, 50 percent. There might be up to a 30 percent chance at medium and only a 20 percent long shot at a high volume, if at all. Think of the competition from all the physicians and medical institutions already located there."

"I agree, Tony. What about Newton and Weston?"

"Well, Newton is more residential and spread out. Their good schools attract lots of new families each year, so I would guess the FHC would do extremely well there eventually. Initially—that is, within the first two years—I would guess the chances are fairly high for small volume, say, 40 percent because of the diversified demography in the ten separate subcommunities. However, the growth potential there is just unbelievable and I would say we have a 50 percent shot at a really sizable volume within two years."

"And what about Weston?"

EXHIBIT 4
Annual revenues and expenses for Weston

	Volume		
	Low	Medium	High
Operating revenues			
Number of patient visits/year	10,000	20,000	30,000
Average charge per visit	×$22.50	×$22.50	×$22.50
Gross income	$225,000	$450,000	$675,000
Operating expenses			
Salaries and benefits			
Physicians and dentists	$200,000	$200,000	$200,000
Doctors' benefits	25,000	25,000	25,000
Administrative	20,000	40,000	60,000
Paramedical	10,000	20,000	30,000
Technician	8,000	16,000	24,000
Employee benefits	9,000	16,000	23,000
Laboratory and x-ray fees	1,500	3,000	5,000
Medical and surgical supplies	8,000	16,000	24,000
Building and occupancy	35,000	35,000	35,000
Furniture and equipment	4,500	4,500	4,500
Office supplies and services	4,000	8,000	12,000
Legal and accounting	2,000	3,000	4,000
Telephone	2,000	4,000	6,000
Insurance	5,000	5,000	5,000
Other	8,000	8,000	8,000
Total expenses	$342,000	$403,500	$465,500
Net income (loss) before tax	($117,000)	$ 46,500	$209,500

"Well, since both our private practices are located there, we would have a broad base to draw from. I'm reasonably certain that we have a 60 percent chance of capturing a medium-sized practice. Sure, there's still a significant risk of the whole concept being a flop, say, 20 percent. But, Morris, numbers-schmumbers. This is ridiculous! These numbers don't mean anything."

"Tony, we just cannot allow ourselves the luxury of just thinking about how wonderful it is to deliver health care in a new, revolutionary way. I know I don't have to remind you of the class notes distribution fiasco we had in medical school. Just because we didn't run the numbers, we had to eat beans for months afterwards."

"Well, Morris, I don't intend to take all the blame for that. We had an idea, and it failed. Sure, it was difficult recovering from those losses, but what an idea—the concept of helping our classmates make it through school. Dammit, I'm willing to take some personal risks if it appears as if we can help so many people. What about the Commonwealth Community Health Center?"

"OK, Tony, OK, calm down."

EXHIBIT 5
Adjusted income statements

	Brookline volume			Newton volume			Weston volume		
	Low	*Medium*	*High*	*Low*	*Medium*	*High*	*Low*	*Medium*	*High*
Operating revenues, first year									
Number of patient visits/year (75 percent)	15,000	22,500	30,000	7,500	18,750	30,000	7,500	15,000	22,500
Average charge per visit	×$16	×$16	×$16	×18	×18	×18	×$22.50	×$22.50	×$22.50
Gross income	$240,000	$360,000	$480,000	$135,000	$337,500	$540,000	$168,750	$337,500	$506,250
Operating expenses Fixed	$292,500	$292,500	$292,500	$287,500	$287,500	$287,500	$277,500	$277,500	$277,500
Variable (75 percent)	62,250	97,125	130,500	35,625	87,000	138,375	48,375	94,500	141,000
Total expenses	$357,750	$389,625	$423,000	$323,125	$374,500	$425,875	$325,875	$372,000	$418,500
Net income (loss) before tax, first year	($117,750)	($29,625)	$57,000	($188,125)	($37,000)	$114,125	($157,125)	($34,500)	$ 87,750
Net income (loss) before tax, second year	(59,500)	58,000	173,500	(155,000)	46,500	248,000	(117,000)	46,500	209,500
Total net income (loss) before tax	($177,250)	$28,375	$230,500	($343,125)	$ 9,500	$362,125	($274,125)	$12,000	$297,250

"All right, Morris, but there is one thing that still disturbs me about your numbers. Have we allowed for patient buildup? In other words, the volume of patient visits that we estimated may seem reasonable for the second year of operations, but wouldn't we be somewhat naive to expect to achieve those same results in the first year?"

"That's a good point, Tony, though it shouldn't cause us too much difficulty. Let's make a conservative estimate as to how well the FHC can do the first year relative to the second. How does 75 percent sound? That implies we will do one-third better the second year."

"Sounds reasonable."

Dr. Sinnick continued: "Then, we will have to adjust the revenues proportionally and also those expenses which vary with volume. The costs which do not vary with volume, of course, remain fixed. Certainly, this will make each alternative look less attractive. The question really is by how much. If you'll give me a couple of minutes, I'll make the calculations so we'll know where we stand."

While Dr. Sinnick made the calculations shown in Exhibit 5, Dr. Collado reviewed the relative merits of each location, including socioeconomic status, proximity to hospitals, and accessibility by public transportation and major thoroughfares.

"Here it is," Dr. Sinnick said when he finished his calculations. "What I have done is to calculate new income statements for the first year, using the approach I outlined a few minutes ago. To each first-year result, I've added the second-year figures which I previously calculated (see Exhibits 2–4) to get the net income before tax for the two-year period. How does it look to you now?"

As they mulled over the figures, Dr. Sinnick was more convinced that an opportunity really did exist. But, he still wondered which location would be best, and, more basically, whether he should give up his $50,000+ per year personal practice for this venture.

case 4–4

Family Health Center, Inc. (B)

Dr. Anthony Collado had just arrived at his office when his secretary announced that Dr. Morris Sinnick was on the phone. While he had anticipated a reaction from Dr. Sinnick following their meeting the night before [described in Family Health Center, Inc. (A), case 4–3], so rapid a response was hardly expected. Picking up the phone, he was greeted warmly, and then the conversation turned to business.

"Tony, as I reviewed my notes on our meeting after you left, I realized that there were still several points which required clarification. Further discussion of these points, I hope, will allow us to focus better on the location decision. For one thing, it seems to me that it is clear that we can immediately reject Brookline. Considering the high probability of financial loss, the large aged population, and the stiff professional competition, there is just too great a chance of failure. The decision then really boils down to a choice between Newton and Weston."

"I agree, Morris. As I drove home last night, the more I thought about Brookline, the more pessimistic I became about its possibilities. But another thing that bothered me was the possible $340,000 loss (over two years) in Newton. That just seems too risky for me."

"Well, that bothered me too. But do you realize that the largest part of our operating expenses, over 75 percent, would be for personnel? That's right, and nearly 80 percent of that—$200,000—is comprised of doctors' and the dentists' salaries! I wonder if there isn't some way in which our colleagues could share some of that risk with us."

Dr. Collado reflected for a moment and replied:

"Well, back in our Commonwealth Community Neighborhood Health Center experience, I recall that the salary issue was quite a controversial one. Three methods of remuneration which are still in use in group practices were considered:

1. Straight salary: This furnishes income security to the physician but provides little incentive to achieve higher patient volumes.
2. Fee for service: Here, a strong incentive for seeing more patients is provided, but quality of care is bound to degenerate. Furthermore, during periods of low volumes, like startup, the physician's salary is likely to suffer. Thus, this method is least attractive to him.
3. Base salary plus fee: This is the obvious compromise. A small base

salary provides the stable component while the fee per visit provides incentive to see more patients and to raise their total income.

Furthermore, various bonus plans have been described in the literature which provide remuneration based on volume and contribution to profits. I'll send you a summary of all the methods currently in use." (See Exhibit 1.)

EXHIBIT 1
Salary alternatives in group practices: Distribution of clinic income

Distribution of clinic *net* income is a complex procedure for which there is not one best method available. The method for distribution of income that results in compatibility within the group is recommended as the one to use.

While group practice may be less remunerative to the physician than a highly successful solo practice, the group physician is generally assured an income at least as high as the average solo practitioner. The AMA's Periodic Survey of Physicians (1968) showed solo practitioners earned a mean net income in 1967 of $29,771 while group practitioners earned a mean net income of $31,000. It must be noted that the physician should consider factors other than income, such as professional stimulation and practice satisfaction.

A study conducted by Medical Group Management Association concerning methods of income distribution in medical groups revealed almost as many plans as there were clinics involved. The oldest, but presently the least employed, method of distribution is for each partner to share equally in the net income of the medical group. The advantages of equal distribution are the ease of description and administration. The disadvantages concern its tendency to minimize incentive. This usually operates to create friction between physicians who wish to work at a different pace than their more easy-going colleagues.

In some cases medical groups employ a formula for distributing or sharing net income which may be based on:

Total bookings.
Total collections.
Length of service.
Formal training.
Other similar factors.
Combinations of the above.

Such plans encourage incentive and recognize both seniority and training. The disadvantages include difficulty in establishing values to be assigned to the several elements of the formula and the omission of some elements that could seem important to an individual but not

EXHIBIT 1 *(continued)*

necessarily to the group, thus creating friction between that individual and the rest of the group.

Other medical groups have established point rating systems with points assigned to:

New patients seen.
Seniority.
Group value.
Professional standing in community.
Drawing power.
Patient volume.
Patients referred to other clinic physicians.
Professional charges.
Publications and research.
Administrative ability.

The advantage of this system is that theoretically it encourages individual physicians to greater effort in the public relations area. Disadvantages are the difficulty of establishing the plan, selecting the factors to be included, and complexity of administration. The use of arbitrary factors to the exclusion of others opens the way to friction within the group. The complexity of a point system may make it quite difficult for the average physician to understand. This has caused some groups to abandon this system even though earlier it had been thought successful.

Some groups distribute net income precisely in accordance with each member's contribution, or on the basis of individual bookings less a share of the expense, or individual collections less a share of the actual expense. The disadvantage of a plan or system of this kind is that it tends to maximize competition within the group by emphasizing the element of incentive. It could be questioned whether such a method of compensating physicians represents a true group practice.

Studies of medical groups conducted by Medical Group Management Association found that most income distribution plans represented combinations or variations of those mentioned here. Some, for instance, distributed the net income of the group in a manner calculated to recognize equality, longevity, and effort by allocating a portion of the net income to each of these categories. For instance, the amount allocated to be distributed equally could be 40 percent of the whole amount available, 10 percent of the whole net earnings or income may be allocated in some relationship to longevity or seniority, and the balance on the basis of the individual contribution and effort of each physician. This may be measured by bookings or collections, with the simplest method the use of net bookings of each physician, that is, gross bookings less discounts, adjustments, and bad accounts. Such a plan may encourage

EXHIBIT 1 *(concluded)*

---

the cooperative "group" sense, allow prestige recognition, and still create incentive for the aggressive group members.

Actual figures in one study of over 300 medical groups showed 25 percent shared income equally, 50 percent used predominantly an incentive system, 15 percent used a salary plus other arrangements, and the remaining 10 percent combined the salary and the incentive distributions.

With the advent of the professional corporation, each physician employee of the corporation is paid a salary that is fixed by the governing group of the corporation. All factors mentioned earlier, with adjustments reflecting the economic fortunes of the corporation during the year, may be used to fix this salary.

It will be noted that no mention is made of the individual investment of each physician in the group facilities or assets. It was found that the physical assets of the group were usually owned by a separate organization—a corporation, foundation, or partnership. The amount of the investment of the individual in such a business corporation, while it would influence his return from the operations of the proprietary organization, would not affect his income from the practice of medicine as a group physician.

Most income distribution formulas contrived by physician associates in medical groups have one thing in common: they are seldom permanent. Plans have been altered as many as three or four times in a ten-year period—retaining the best features of the old and substituting new provisions for those that have proved inadequate or unsatisfactory. A good part of this can be influenced by the changing philosophy of a group. If the practice is growing and there is a need to attract new associates, modifications may be adopted that are calculated to interest new physicians. If the group prefers to remain stable in size, change is not so apt to occur. Change merely for the sake of change or experimentation—or because a minority of the group physicians may advocate a change—is not advisable.

In conclusion, it must be noted that, while the method of distribution of net income or net earnings in a medical group may seem to present a problem, the variations of plans to achieve a desired result or a satisfactory arrangement are limited only by the imagination, ingenuity, and resourcefulness of those charged with the responsibility for creating the income distribution formula.

Source: *Group Practice—Guidelines to Joining or Forming a Medical Group,* published by American Association of Medical Clinics, American Medical Association Medical Group Management Association.

Dr. Sinnick had been hurriedly writing notes on Dr. Collado's comments. He made a few quick calculations concerning a reasonable base salary and fee per visit in the two locations, and then continued the conversation.

"Of course, our analysis last night was only a rough cut. We can now refine it to some extent for the Newton and Weston locations by including the salary options. I'm quite sure that for the first year we'll have to offer the $40,000 salaries just to attract our colleagues to join us. However, for the second year, I suggest we consider not only the $40,000 straight salary but also include the possibility, at our option, of converting at the beginning of the second year, to a $20,000 base salary plus a fixed fee of say $4 per visit in Newton and $5 per visit in Weston. I think we can eliminate the fee-for-service option because it would be inconsistent with our goal of high-quality care and would also provide too much risk for the physicians. Furthermore, I believe we should include the possibility of closing down after the first year, which could save us the operating expenses, but would cost us $15,000 to cover a penalty fee for breaking our leases on the building and equipment. Certainly, the possibility of closing down or converting to base salary plus fixed fee per visit at the end of the first year will make it somewhat harder to attract as good people as the three colleagues we had in mind, but I think I know of several good candidates who would still be interested in joining us."

"You know, Morris, I'm always skeptical of your numbers. However, the refinements you propose make the analysis more complete. On the other hand, I still question the validity of the probabilities we discussed last night. Remember you said that when a given patient volume occurred in the second year of operations, you assumed that 75 percent of that volume occurred in the first year?"

"Right."

"Well, can we really assume that if we had a given patient volume at the end of the first year, we could be *assured* of an increase of 33 percent in the second year?"

"Of course not, Tony," replied Dr. Sinnick, "but that's not a bad approximation for a rough-cut analysis."

"Well it made me feel a little uneasy yesterday and now with the latest proposal I'm even more uneasy. It would say in effect that we could size up the situation at the end of the first year and forecast the second-year results perfectly based on the 'trend.' Yet, couldn't it occur that we might, for example, get off to a good start and then fail to grow or even have a downturn in the second year?"

"You're absolutely right," replied Dr. Sinnick. "What we should do is to have probabilities for *each* year and then reflect the fact that if we hit 75 percent of high volume in the first year, for example, the chance of high in the second year goes way up, but isn't a certainty. For instance, we forecasted that the chances of achieving high volume in Newton was 50 percent. If we should attain 75 percent of high volume in the first year, then I'll bet the probability of achieving high volume in the second year would go up to something closer to 80 percent or 85 percent."

The discussion continued for another half-hour until all the probabilities were reevaluated. The results are shown in Exhibit 2.

EXHIBIT 2
New second-year probabilities given first-year outcomes

First year		Second year	
Volume	*Probability*	*Volume*	*Probability given first-year outcome*
Newton			
75 percent of high	0.5	High	0.85
		Medium	0.1
		Low	0.05
75 percent of medium	0.1	High	0.4
		Medium	0.3
		Low	0.3
75 percent of low	0.4	High	0.1
		Medium	0.1
		Low	0.8
Weston			
75 percent of high	0.2	High	0.7
		Medium	0.2
		Low	0.1
75 percent of medium	0.6	High	0.05
		Medium	0.90
		Low	0.05
75 percent of low	0.2	High	0.1
		Medium	0.2
		Low	0.7

Dr. Collado closed by cautioning that the long-term growth prospects should be considered also. Initial losses, he felt (or at least hoped), would be made up by future gains.

Hanging up the phone, Dr. Collado knew that the new information would provide a more complete analysis. Hopefully, sometime in his busy schedule during the day, he would have a chance to reevaluate the Newton–Weston decision.

case 4–5

Weston Manufacturing Company

At their quarterly meeting held on November 5, 1965, the directors of the Weston Manufacturing Company were informed that the company would probably finish the fiscal year ending December 31 with an operating loss of nearly $50,000 on sales of approximately $1.8 million. This would be the second year in succession of unprofitable operation, the only two such years in the company's 57-year history. The loss of $49,971.48 in 1964 followed a profit of more than $150,000 in 1963.

The financial statement for the period ending October 31, 1965 showed a loss of $48,915.56. This compared with the loss of $73,059.68 for the same period in 1964. Scott Howell, the chairman of the board, expressed disappointment in October's profit of $15,261.58 on net shipments of $217,245.97. Unfortunately, one big order did not come out as expected due to final design changes.

Shipments for November were projected to be $85,000, resulting in a loss of approximately $14,000. If shipments in December reached $240,000 as estimated, a profit of $13,000 was expected.

After dispensing with the financial projections for the remainder of the year, Scott Howell began to inform the directors of the background of negotiations with the Sheridan Electric Products Corporation. Sheridan was a national manufacturer of heavy-duty industrial electrical appliances, and the company's headquarters were in Dayton, Ohio, less than 100 miles from Weston.

"In 1958 Sheridan asked us to determine whether a flat-bed car with 330-ton capacity and a bed height of 26 inches could be built. The car was needed to move one of a series of new transformers from the construction area to the testing shop, a distance of 2½ miles on the company's track. The low bed height was required because of vertical clearance constraints in the area of the construction shop. John Sanders did some figuring and wrote them that such a car could be built for about $20,000.

"It seemed to us that Sheridan was on the verge of placing the order but then decided instead to rent a car from the Baltimore and Ohio Railroad each time one of the large transformers needed to be moved. No reason was given for this decision, but I do know that we were the only people Sheridan had contacted with a view to having a car built for them. Over the next five years, Don Archer occasionally stopped by the Sheridan plant and found their interest in the purchase of the flat-bed car to vary from time to time.

"Last year Sheridan indicated interest in resuming serious talks. Bert Stokes drew up some plans according to the gauge, capacity, height, and other specifications received from Fred Shillkof, Sheridan's chief engineer. Shillkof approved the plans and, as usual, we took this as an assurance that the track was a normal, level, industrial installation, permitting the proposed simple nonoscillating design for the car. In spite of a general increase in costs in the interim, John was able to submit the original bid of $20,000. The production costs were actually $15,000. The order was placed, and the car was shipped March 23, on schedule.

"Unfortunately, Sheridan's track foundation was not adequate, and the car derailed on a banked portion of the track. Sheridan would not accept the car and returned it, at a cost of $550 to us. Bert then undertook an engineering restudy and concluded that the cost of rebuilding the car with oscillating trucks would be about $16,000. A further review of costs developed no useful shortcuts. On July 18, a revised total price of $36,000 was offered to Sheridan. If we decided to rebuild the car, the modifications could be completed in less than a week.

"As you know, I was more or less out of action for most of the fall due to a prolonged serious illness in the immediate family. Shortly after I returned, early in October, having received no reply to our July proposal, I sent a wire requesting that Bert and I meet with Sheridan's chief engineer, the purchasing agent, and the general manager.

"I have asked Bert to report to the board on that meeting. He will be along in a few minutes. In the meantime, has anybody any questions?"

"Yes, Scott, there is one point I'd like to clear up," said O'Brien. "Did anyone from Weston see the Sheridan track?"

"Bert and I inspected the track when we visited in October," replied Howell. "It was totally unsuited for a nonoscillating car. It turned out that Sheridan's people thought the car would flex, but any engineer could see that that would be impossible for a car with 330-ton capacity."

There was a knock at the door and Albert Stokes entered. No introductions were necessary, so Howell asked Stokes to proceed immediately with the report of their joint visit to Dayton.

"On October 22, Scott Howell and I met at Dayton, Ohio, with Sheridan's purchasing agent, Mr. Robert Casey, and Mr. James Woodruff, their general manager. Mr. Woodruff informed us that according to a report from his Traffic Department dated October 8, there had been four instances since March when the Weston car could have been used if it had been operating satisfactorily. In each case it was necessary to pay the B&O Railroad $300 demurrage charges. However, they foresee that a car of 330 tons capacity could be used about 12 times a year—equivalent to $3,600 demurrage charges.

"Woodruff expressed the feeling that on the basis of a car life of 20 years, $36,000 was a greater investment than the company would consider. They felt that a suitable car should cost about $25,000. This figure was based on savings that would accrue to them if they did not have to pay the demurrage charges.

"We left the meeting with the understanding that we would review the design to see if costs could be reduced below the quotation of July 18. Scott had also suggested that they consider whether this car would not serve additional uses for Sheridan in moving and storing the new large transformers. We said we would keep in touch, although Woodruff and Casey indicated that there was 'no great rush.' "

"Bert, why wasn't Fred Shillkof at this meeting?" asked Hall.

"I don't know, Max," Stokes replied. "Neither Woodruff nor Casey gave any reason for his absence. He hasn't been fired, and he wasn't off sick. I know because we walked past his office on our way from the meeting; the door was open, and he was working at his desk."

"One more question, Bert," said O'Brien. "If we rebuild the car with oscillating trucks according to the revised design, what are the chances that it will again derail?"

"Very small, even though that track of theirs is not so hot. I'd say not more than one chance in a hundred."

There being no further questions forthcoming, Stokes collected his papers together and left the room.

"Well, gentlemen," said Howell, "where do we go from here?"

The ensuing silence was broken by Sanders: "We quote them a figure of $36,000 based on the present estimate of the costs of modification and the production cost of the original car. Now though, with an indication that a suitable car at $25,000 might be acceptable to them, we could reconsider. But I would like to remind you that it would have been impossible to have built an oscillating car originally for $25,000. Maybe we should split the difference and make a bid of $30,000. However, I would say that we would have less than an even chance of getting the order at $30,000, say, around two in five; whereas at $25,000 the odds would be about nine to one in our favor. By the same token, at $36,000 we'd be lucky to have one chance in ten."

"What about trying to sell the car to someone else, if Sheridan turns us down?" asked Hall.

Don Archer shook his head: "Not very good—as is we might have a one-in-20 chance of selling the car. If we can find a customer, we might get between $10,000 and $18,000, and my best estimate is about

$15,000. The market is pretty small, so I don't think our selling costs would run over $200. We should be able to survey this market in less than two weeks.

"If we rebuild the car with an oscillating trunk, there are more firms who might be interested, and the chances are about one in five of finding a customer. We should get between $17,000 and $25,000 with an average of about $20,000, but, in this market, the selling costs would be around $500, with all prospective customers contacted in less than four weeks.

"Those are very reasonable prices, but that would be about the most we could expect in either case."

All agreed that the possibilities of bargaining further with Sheridan were nil. Sanders summarized the situation: "As I see it, we have two choices: Make them a firm bid for the rebuilt car on a take-it-or-leave-it basis or absorb the loss ourselves. As scrap, the car might be worth about $3,000 to us. If we rebuild the car with oscillating trunks and it still doesn't work, its scrap value might go up to around $4,000."

"I think that just about says it, John," said Howell. "I certainly don't want to absorb any loss in view of our recent poor profit picture but would do so in preference to a legal battle. Our lawyers have assured me that we could force Sheridan to pay a substantial cancellation charge on the grounds that the track was substandard. Another and perhaps stronger reason for demanding a cancellation charge would be the claim that Shillkof could have warned us when he saw and approved the plans. Legally, we are on sure ground, but this is our first contract with Sheridan, and possible future business from such a large company could substantially help us to halt, even reverse, our present sales decline. Besides, getting your name involved with a wrangle in court never does you any good in this business, no matter how right you are in the eyes of the law. For the same reason we have to give Sheridan the right of first refusal on a modified car. Only if they turn down our bid, can we consider selling it elsewhere. Anyway, the next move seems to be ours, and should be made soon. The sale of this car could significantly alter the profit projections discussed earlier. Given Bert and Don's estimates, I see no reason why we cannot resolve this transaction before the end of the fiscal year. I would like you to give some intensive thought to this matter, and for us to reach a decision before the end of the week. Now, John, let's have that general report of yours."

Sanders opened his briefcase and took from it four copies of his general report. He passed one copy to each of the other three directors, so that they could refer easily to the quantitative data contained in the report. Having cleaned his spectacles and taken a drink of water, John Sanders, reading from his own copy, went to the next report on the agenda.

case 4–6

J. B. Robinson Fertilizer and Explosives, Inc.

The J. B. Robinson Fertilizer and Explosives Company manufactures and sells fertilizers and explosives in the southeastern United States. The company was founded in 1910 by J. B. Robinson to sell fertilizer in Alabama, but over the years sales expanded and gradually the company found itself serving customers all over the southeastern part of the country.

Throughout its history, ownership of Robinson was closely held. Its management also stayed within the family, the current president being J. B. Robinson III, grandson of the founder. The Robinson family was a prominent one, active in community affairs in the city where the company's headquarters were located.

HISTORY OF THE COMPANY'S INVOLVEMENT IN EXPLOSIVES

Like many fertilizer companies, J. B. Robinson's entry into the explosives business came as a result of a major disaster which occurred in the late 1940s. In April 1947, a ship containing ammonium nitrate (AN) fertilizer caught fire at its berth in Texas City, Texas. After attempts to extinguish the fire failed, the captain ordered the hatches to be battened down in the hope of smothering it. Instead of the fire going out, the ship exploded, resulting in a disaster that took over 400 lives and did millions of dollars in property damage.

The repercussions of this explosion were soon to rock the entire explosives industry. Prior to the disaster, most explosives were based on nitroglycerin and TNT, mixed with limited amounts of AN; explosives were then selling at $20–$30 per 100 pounds. Subsequent to the explosion, various parties attempted to develop an AN-based explosive. Among them was Robert L. Akre, a blasting foreman for Maumee-Collieries Coal Company. In 1955, he and Hugh B. Lee were issued a patent for an explosive consisting of "ammonium nitrate and carbonaceous fuels. . . ."[1] Referring to the Texas City fire, part of their patent reads:

> The theory of the cause of this explosion which we developed is that the gases generated by the raging fire which were trapped beneath the

---

[1] U.S. Patent 2,703,528, March 8, 1955.

hatches caused the ship itself to explode and that this explosion, owing to the high pressure inside the ship, caused the detonation of the ammonium nitrate. It was conceived that, if the conditions of this Texas City explosion could be duplicated in the blasting of rock strata and the like, it would be possible to make substantial savings in the cost of blasting explosives since the company with which we are associated had been purchasing blasting explosives at a price several times that at which ammonium nitrate was being sold to farmers as fertilizer, for example. This conclusion led to an extensive series of experiments during the course of which the present invention was developed.

The resulting new products offered users at least a 50 percent cost reduction. In the late 1950s companies that had not previously been in the explosives business, such as fertilizer and oil companies, rushed in and the traditional explosives manufacturers scrambled to adapt to these new competitive and technological developments. The original patent proved to have narrow coverage and within a few years of its issue most manufacturers found a way to get around it.

Robinson entered the explosives market in 1956. As it overcame distribution problems and succeeded in hiring technical personnel to solve customers' individual blasting problems, its business grew. By the early 1960s, however, the industry began to be plagued by overcapacity and competition grew intense. Success then hinged on getting a technological or service edge on competition. In 1964, the company's chief blasting engineer, J. A. Dawes, developed a formulation of AN-based explosives and a detonation system which offered a temporary edge in certain market segments. The firm marketed the system under the trade name DIREX. A new system, developed in 1966, superseded DIREX.

THREAT OF A PATENT SUIT

In early 1967, Saunders Explosives, one of the larger independent manufacturers, was sued for patent infringement by American Explosives. American's suit alleged that Saunders had been infringing on a patent, granted to American six months previously, that covered an AN-based formulation and detonation system. Examination of American's patent revealed that the patent application predated Dawes' development and that DIREX fell under the claims of the patent. This news caused great concern to Mr. Robinson.

He asked Mr. Robert Mather, executive vice president, to consider the patent question, assemble expert opinion, and suggest a course of action which the company should take regarding this potential threat. In assigning this responsibility to Mr. Mather, Mr. Robinson suggested that the company's attorney on retainer be brought into the situation as early as possible, rather than after things were out of the company's hands entirely.

As Mr. Mather saw the problem, American's move on Saunders was a strategic one. After talking to his marketing manager, he found that Saunders had had sales second only to American in products related to the patent. If American could get a ruling against Saunders, it would be armed with a powerful precedent when it came to other firms infringing on the patent. If American won its case, there was little doubt that J. B. Robinson would be the next target.

CONVERSATION WITH THE FIRM'S COUNSEL

Mr. Mather next consulted the firm's counsel, Mr. Arthur Grant, about the possible consequences to J. B. Robinson should it be pursued by American. Mr. Grant's answer was that American would set a tough initial bargaining position; it would seek to collect substantial back royalties based upon the gross sales of DIREX. If no agreement satisfactory to both parties could be reached, the case would then go to court. Unless the amounts were quite large, the case usually terminated with the decision of the court. The total cost of any of these possible outcomes would depend on the legal fees and court costs as well as the final payment, if any.

When asked about the chances for any of the outcomes, Mr. Grant replied that he had not had time to survey the related patents, laws, and precedents sufficiently but that certain generalizations could be made about this type of situation. The most important consideration was timing.

For instance, Mr. Grant continued, if Robinson were to initiate negotiations with American before the outcome of the Saunders case was clear, it could probably get a lower payment than if it waited and the Saunders case was decided unfavorably. On the other hand, if American could not prove patent infringement, Robinson might have settled needlessly. By waiting for the outcome of the Saunders decision, Robinson would be in position of either having no problems if American lost or having an almost certain suit, with a high probability of losing its case, if American won. If American lost the Saunders case, it probably would not make further attempts to enforce the patent, whereas if it won, its bargaining position would be considerably stronger.

In the eventuality that Robinson waited for the outcome of the Saunders case and the decision went against Saunders, Robinson could pursue its case in court if it felt that American was asking too much in direct settlement. Once in court, Robinson could either contest the validity of the patent or merely fight the amount of the settlement. If it contested the patent decision, the consequence of losing would probably be a more stringent settlement than if it had not contested. If it won, no back royalties would be paid.

The rationale for going to court, not to contest the decision but to fight the payment, was that Robinson might get a lower settlement than American was willing to offer out of court. While it was possible to appeal the court ruling if it turned out unfavorably to Robinson, Mr. Grant advised against it. His advice was based on the fact that the costs of proceeding, weighed against the chances of a reversal of the decision, were generally justified only for very large amounts of money.

Given this information, Mr. Mather asked the counsel to review the existing laws on matters similar to this, and to think about the chances of various events occurring. In addition, he scheduled a meeting where Mr. Grant, Mr. Cooper (the controller), and he would be present to discuss the possible actions and consequences of the problem.

CONVERSATION WITH THE CONTROLLER

After discussing the matter with Mr. Grant, Mr. Mather next contacted Mr. Cooper, the company's controller, to apprise him of the situation and to suggest a data-gathering plan which would provide the information needed to describe the consequences of various outcomes.

He asked Mr. Cooper to prepare a schedule of yearly sales of DIREX. Mr. Cooper said that it would take a little time but that he could have it ready for the meeting with Mr. Grant. He also hoped that he could come up with a few more numbers that would be of interest in deciding what to do.

MEETING OF MESSRS. ROBINSON, MATHER, COOPER, AND GRANT

In preparing for the proposed meeting, Mr. Mather realized that he could avoid much needless work by including Mr. Robinson in the early stages of the analysis; consequently, Mr. Robinson was present when the three men met in the company's board room.

At the meeting, Mr. Cooper presented figures (see Exhibit 1) showing DIREX sales. He pointed out that this had been a very profitable line because variable production and distribution costs had averaged about 50 percent of sales. He remarked that the amounts concerned were substantial but that they constituted less than 10 percent of 1967's revenue. Next, he presented additional figures on Robinson's corporate sales and profits. He concluded by saying that the company's cash balance was $500,000, which appeared to him to be more than enough to handle even the worst possible outcome.

EXHIBIT 1
Schedule of revenues received from DIREX sales

Year	DIREX sales revenues	Robinson sales	Robinson after-tax profits
1964	$120,000	$13,387,000	$1,080,000
1965	430,000	11,290,000	257,000
1966	390,000	15,713,000	1,241,000
	$940,000		

The estimates of legal fees for different possible actions were then given by Mr. Grant. (These are shown in Exhibit 2.) When questioned about the very high cost if Robinson contested the patent decision (approximately $25,000), he replied that court costs would be higher and that outside legal help would be necessary to prepare the case properly.

EXHIBIT 2
Estimates of legal fees and court costs for different preparations*

Settle out of court now	$ 3,600
If Saunders loses case—settle with American out of court	3,000
If Saunders loses case—prepare Robinson's case for contesting decision	25,000
If Saunders loses case—prepare for fighting amount of settlement payment	13,000

* All figures include $600 already expended for preliminary legal search to draw up these estimates.

He was also asked why settling out of court after the decision on the Saunders case had been handed down was less costly than doing so before it was made. He replied that he knew no reason for this, adding, "My guess is that the $3,000 is a typographical error and that $4,000 is really the correct number."

At this point, Mr. Robinson interrupted to comment on the various outcomes. He was quite concerned that an adverse court ruling might reflect on his personal reputation. Settling out of court, he went on, was bad enough, but the stigma associated with a court-directed settlement was worse, and fighting the decision and losing was the worst possible outcome. He felt that the monetary costs did not really reflect the undesirability of these various events.

After everyone agreed that they wished the whole thing had not come up, Mr. Mather tried to get a feeling for the strength of Mr. Robinson's opinions about different outcomes. For a while there was confusion among those present about how this might be done. Mr. Mather suggested considering fictitious payments which might be made in lieu of certain of the outcomes. He asked Mr. Robinson to think hard about what he would be willing to pay to have the stigma completely removed.

After reflecting for some time, Mr. Robinson decided that, although he would prefer having Saunders win its case, he could assign the costs he would be willing to pay to avoid a "patent infringer" black eye. For instance, he said that he would be willing to pay $5,000 to avoid the reputation damage associated with settling out of court now.

After more questions, Mr. Robinson decided on the following as the amounts he would be willing to pay to avoid reputation damage if various events occurred.

1. Settle out of court now: $5,000.
2. Saunders loses, Robinson settles out of court: $12,000.
3. Saunders loses, Robinson fights payment: $15,000.
4. Saunders loses, Robinson contests patent and loses: $20,000.
5. Saunders wins or Robinson contests patent and wins: $0.

The meeting then turned to Mr. Grant's analysis of the possible strategies and the chances of various events occurring. The men used the concept of a lottery to think about chances of outcomes. First, Mr. Grant spoke of what he called the "two-outcome events." These events included for/against verdicts, and the chance that American would pursue Robinson if it won the Saunders case. His assessments are given in Exhibit 3. When asked why it was not a virtual certainty

EXHIBIT 3
Assessed probabilities of two-outcome events

Probability of American pursuing case with Robinson should it lose its case against Saunders	0
Probability Saunders loses case	0.6
Probability of American pursuing case against Robinson, given that it wins case against Saunders	0.9
Probability of Robinson winning its case, given Saunders loses and Robinson contests decision	0.25

that Robinson would be pursued if American won, Mr. Grant replied that the cases were not exactly the same; there was enough difference to make it possible that American would not.

Mr. Cooper asked why Robinson shouldn't include the possibility of taking its case to court before the outcome of the Saunders case was known rather than limiting itself to an out-of-court settlement. To this, Mr. Grant said that they had not yet been contacted by American.

American would have to initiate the proceedings; however, Robinson could settle out of court with the sufferance of American.

Based on the position taken by American in the Saunders case, Mr. Grant went on, American would start with an initial demand that Robinson pay back royalties equal to 10 percent of DIREX sales. However, this position would probably soften as the bargaining proceeded. "As their bargaining position changes, so does their settlement amount," was Mr. Grant's summary.

As an aid to the analysis of the problem, Mr. Grant considered the possible final settlement in increments of 1 percent, although he explained that the final settlement could in reality take on any of a very large number of values. Realizing that the settlement would be greatly influenced by the circumstances under which the agreement was reached, Mr. Grant assessed several distributions of percentage settlements, which are shown in Exhibit 4.

EXHIBIT 4
Probability of settlements as a percentage of sales revenues given various outcomes

Probability of settlement percentage if Robinson settles out of court now

Percentage	Probability
3	0.1
4	0.2
5	0.4
6	0.3

Probability of settlement percentage if Robinson settles out of court after Saunders loses case

Percentage	Probability
7	0.2
8	0.4
9	0.3
10	0.1

Probability of settlement percentage if Saunders loses; Robinson goes to court; contests decision; loses

Percentage	Probability
7	0.1
8	0.3
9	0.4
10	0.2

Probability of settlement percentage if Saunders loses; Robinson goes to court; fights payment

Percentage	Probability
5	0.2
6	0.3
7	0.4
8	0.1

The remainder of the meeting was spent explaining the various figures and on the implementation procedures necessary if different strategies were adopted.

MR. MATHER'S PROBLEM

Armed with the various judgments and evaluations, Mr. Mather felt he had all the information necessary to proceed with an analysis of the problem.

case 4–7

Petro Enterprises, Inc.

In mid-December 1977, Mr. William Snyder, president of Petro Enterprises, was trying to decide whether to commit his company to drilling for oil on a parcel of East Texas land. Petro had bought a short-term nontransferable option to drill on the land which expired on December 31, 1977. Snyder had two weeks in which to commence drilling before the option expired. This was the only deal that Petro was currently involved in or that Snyder expected to consider before the option expired.

Petro Enterprises had been formed nearly five years before, in 1973, for the purpose of wildcat exploration of the Texas oil fields. Through a combination of good judgment and good fortune, Petro had enjoyed two highly profitable years in 1974 and 1975. With his share of profits, Snyder bought out the two "silent partners" who had provided initial backing for the venture. In 1976 and 1977, however, Petro had drilled a number of dry holes. Snyder had been more careful in selecting sites for exploration as the asset position of Petro was reduced by unsuccessful attempts to locate oil and felt that the site represented by the current short-term option was more likely to be a producing well than any Petro had attempted in the previous year. Recent dry holes elsewhere had reduced his company's net liquid asset position to $130,000. Nonetheless, Snyder felt that the location of this site, on the fringe of a producing field, made it a reasonable risk. He commented: "This option cost me $4,000 but it is well worth it because of the location. Many of our efforts in the past two years were

directed toward finding oil in places that seemed promising, geologi-
cally speaking, but that no one had looked at before. It is clear now
that we dissipated our resources in the effort to find a major new field.
Drilling this site represents a return to our previous strategy of simply
trying to *extend* an already known oil field rather than trying to find a
completely new one. It is well known that the payoffs aren't as high
with this strategy, but the outcomes are far more certain."

Petro had retained the services of a professional geologist who had
examined the surface geology in the area near the site. The geologist
expressed the opinion that there was a 0.55 probability that if a well is
sunk, oil will be discovered. Snyder knew that a seismic test could
determine the subsurface structure with greater accuracy and allow a
better determination of whether or not oil was present. A seismic test
cost $30,000 and could be conducted in a few days by one of several
contracting firms offering this service. The cost of drilling the well was
estimated at an additional $100,000. The general experience of the oil
exploration industry with seismic tests was that, if the test results were
positive, the probability that a well would strike oil in commercial
quantities would increase to 0.85. However, even if the seismic test
results were negative, the probability that oil was present was still one
in ten.

Due to Petro's precarious financial situation, Snyder had decided
that, if oil were struck, Petro would not try to exploit the find. Instead,
Snyder had entered into discussions with a major oil company that had
agreed to purchase Petro's rights to any oil discovered for a flat
$400,000.

Snyder knew that a decision regarding drilling on this site would
have to be made soon. He recognized that if he chose to drill, Petro
would be brought to the brink of ruin and the possibility of obtaining
further financing on favorable terms would be very slight. Further, he
was convinced that he could not obtain additional funds before beginning to drill because of the short time remaining before the option
expired.

Technotronics Corporation

Technotronics Corporation of Waltham, Massachusetts, was organized to exploit the technical talent of Dr. Robert F. Rutledge, who, until becoming president of Technotronics, had been professor of electrical engineering at a nearby university. As was typical of many of the small companies in the electronics industry, Technotronics derived the major part of its revenues from subcontracts placed with it by larger companies who held prime contracts to produce military electronics systems.

One such subcontract held by Technotronics called for the production of a component which was later incorporated into a complete system by the Babson Aircraft Company, the prime contractor on the job. The subcontract provided for a fixed price for each unit delivered to Babson. Experience with this component had indicated that with the manufacturing process then being used, about 30 percent of the components produced were faulty. The flaw was not detectable by the inspection procedures then being used. When Babson subjected the completed system to its final test, however, the flaw in the component would result in failure. Babson would then be forced to disassemble the system. Under the terms of the subcontract, Babson was permitted to charge the cost of these operations, amounting to $65 per defective unit, back against Technotronics.

By adding another operation to its own manufacturing process, Technotronics could ensure that none of the components would be faulty. This additional operation would add $15 to the manufacturing cost per unit, however, and since only 30 percent of the units actually required this operation, it was not clear that the additional cost would be justified. Dr. Rutledge had discussed the problem with the purchasing agent of Babson and had learned that Babson would not be particularly concerned if the defective rate stayed at the 30 percent level, since it was being adequately reimbursed for its extra costs. Hence, it seemed to Dr. Rutledge that the decision should depend on which course of action would be least costly to Technotronics.

As an alternative to performing the additional operation on each component, it would be possible to subject each component to a test and to decide whether or not to perform the additional operation on the basis of the results of this test. Testing would add $5 to the manufacturing cost. Unfortunately, the test being considered was not capable of making a perfect discrimination between good and defective components. The test resulted in one of two possible outcomes—positive or negative. The conditional probabilities of these outcomes for both good and defective components are given in Exhibit 1.

EXHIBIT 1
Conditional probability of test results

	State of component	
Result	Good	Defective
Positive	0.75	0.20
Negative	0.25	0.80
	1.00	1.00

Thus, while good components were more likely to give a positive test result than defective ones, 20 percent of all defectives would also give that result, so that it was not possible to say that a positive test result was a definite indication that the component was good.

case 4–9

Hinkle Automotive Products

In September 1978, Mr. Jerry Hinkle, president of Hinkle Automotive Products, was describing his pending decision to enter the automotive electronics business: "Our first product in this line will be the GAS-MIZER, an add-on computer that monitors gas mileage and feeds back data to a cruise-control device. It will automatically select the most efficient speed for the automobile to cruise at in freeway-type driving. Of course, there are failsafe devices built in that would prevent operation of the GAS-MIZER whenever the accelerator or the brake is operated manually. The device operates just like a computer, with several readout options and so forth, but the technology involved is about what is in some of your simple hand calculators today.

"I first had the idea for the GAS-MIZER as an undergraduate engineering student when our school entered a car in an economy contest back in the late 1960s. Nothing came of the idea then, basically because the electronics technology wasn't there, but also because I didn't have the technical skill to pull it off. But a few years ago, at the time of the gas crisis, I thought of the concept again and we hired a full-time electronics engineer to work on it. He's done a great job of making the idea practical. The core of the GAS-MIZER is a small plastic box with about a dozen purchased components wired together inside. Of course there are a couple of sensors—depending on the options selected—that also are needed, but the total cost will be only $200 or so, installed. For anyone who does 10,000 miles per year of freeway driving, that should pay itself back in about a year."

COMPANY BACKGROUND

Hinkle Automotive Products was founded after World War II by Mr. Hiram P. Hinkle as a supplier of machined parts to the automotive industry. Jerry Hinkle, son of the founder, joined the firm in 1969 upon graduation from college with a bachelor's degree in mechanical engineering. In 1975 he assumed the presidency when his father suffered a disabling heart attack. That same year development of the GAS-MIZER began in earnest and, in 1977, a working prototype was installed on Jerry Hinkle's personal automobile. A patent application was filed in mid-1978. Several additional features had been added to the GAS-MIZER, including a digital readout of fuel level, a speed limit monitor/override, and an elapsed-time trip clock.

MARKETING THE GAS-MIZER

In August 1978, Jerry Hinkle had been approached by representatives of the Pilgrim Corporation, a major domestic automobile manufacturer. They had heard about the GAS-MIZER and were very impressed with the completeness of its development. After a series of meetings between Hinkle's and Pilgrim's lawyers, the Pilgrim Corporation made an offer of $100,000 for exclusive rights to manufacture the device and include it as an option on their luxury line of automobiles. Jerry Hinkle commented on his decision to reject that offer: "It was quite gratifying to me personally to receive Pilgrim's offer but, actually, it wasn't all that attractive. If we did the manufacturing ourselves and sold the device through the add-on market for $100, we'd make about $40 per unit in contribution margin. Also, if it were really to take off, we'd be out in the cold. I'm looking for a deal that will at least give us some royalties. We have another offer from Clayton's, a consumer retailing firm that runs a large number of auto repair shops around the country. They propose to do all the marketing and even install the

GAS-MIZER for a consumer cost of $200 and pay us $100 for the hardware. Their initial purchase would be for 2,500 units, but there would be no guarantee that there would ever be enough demand to justify further orders. That's where we stood two weeks ago. Our problem was that we just didn't have a very good feel for the size of the market or the appeal of a product like the GAS-MIZER to the general public.

"Finally, I did what I should have done in the first place, I hired a consultant. This woman, Ms. Janet Barnes, was a well-respected individual who had been hanging around the fringes of the auto industry for decades. Her report was almost insulting at first but, when I think about it, she's probably right. She classified the GAS-MIZER as an "automotive novelty" or fad that would have a market life of about five years. Her feeling was that the GAS-MIZER would sell fairly well in that very limited segment of the market that buys things for their "show" value and not for economic reasons. One thing she based this on was the fact that an auto travels at a lower speed with the GAS-MIZER than is normal on freeways, even with the reduced speed limits these days. Still, she wasn't completely discouraging. She said that if the editors of automotive magazines liked the GAS-MIZER and got behind it in their product reviews, we'd likely sell 10,000 units per year. If they didn't, we'd be lucky to sell 500 a year.

"Other than this, Ms. Barnes wouldn't offer any estimate of how large the market might eventually be for the GAS-MIZER, but she did suggest that we get in touch with a marketing research firm called Marketronics, Inc., that would estimate the size of the market we could expect. Also, she said that we should get the research done right away, since once the news of the development of GAS-MIZER is leaked to the editors, they would announce it in their magazines and, if they were unfavorable, it would probably kill any deals that we hadn't signed up to that point. When I pressed her for an estimate of the likelihood of the editors being favorable about the GAS-MIZER, she said that she felt very uncomfortable about assessing such a probability because she didn't want to encourage us unduly. Finally, however, she said that the chances for a favorable review were about six out of ten."

MARKETRONICS, INC.

Marketronics, Inc., was a Detroit-based consulting firm that had considerable experience in estimating consumer demand for automotive option products like the GAS-MIZER. Mr. Hinkle contacted Leslie Ecks, president of Marketronics, immediately after receiving Ms. Barnes's report, and Mrs. Ecks visited Hinkle's office later that afternoon. After describing the need for urgency and secrecy, Hinkle explained that he needed to know the approximate size of the market for the GAS-MIZER. Would annual sales be closer to 10,000 units or 500 units? Mrs. Ecks responded that Marketronics, Inc., could perform consumer panel research in three locations around the country during the coming week that would indicate either favorable or unfavorable market acceptance for the GAS-MIZER if it were sold in the automotive after-market. Mrs. Ecks emphasized that, since the automotive magazines were very sensitive to market desires, this was about the same thing as asking Marketronics to predict a favorable or unfavorable editorial response to the GAS-MIZER.

Mrs. Ecks continued: "Of course, due to the rush nature of this job, we can't be 100 percent certain of our results. Ideally, we'd like to have a month or more to study the product's chances, but we agree that in the case of the GAS-MIZER, that may be too long to wait. The cost of the study will be $50,000, which may seem a bit high, but there has to be a premium for the quick results. To do this job by the end of next week, we'll have to pull some analysts off of other jobs. In any event, we should be able to tell you whether the GAS-MIZER will approach Ms. Barnes's high estimate or not with a fair degree of accuracy. Marketronics has done a large number of studies similar to the one you request and, based on the results of those studies, I can say that if you go ahead and market the GAS-MIZER and are successful, and if we had done the study, the odds are nine to one that our report would have been favorable. On the other hand, we are not quite as good in the opposite direction. If you try, and the market for the GAS-MIZER turns out to be small, and if we had done a survey, the odds are only three to one that we would have reported an unfavorable result to our study."

At this point Mr. Hinkle called in Mr. Keith White, Hinkle's vice president of marketing and had Mrs. Ecks repeat the information about the accuracy of the proposed study. Shortly thereafter, Mrs. Ecks departed with the understanding that Hinkle would contact her the next morning to give her the go/no-go decision on the market survey. The following discussion ensued:

Hinkle: Well, Keith, what do you think?

White: I don't know about those numbers she was throwing around, but there must be some way to use them in an analysis of this situation. There was another matter regarding GAS-MIZER that I wanted to report to you, though. I got a call from Pilgrim Corp. just a few minutes ago and it looks like they're ready to sweeten the pot a bit by pushing their offer up to $400,000 for exclusive rights to the GAS-MIZER. How about that!

Hinkle: I don't know. Will they go any higher?

White: I doubt it. Evidently they're about at the limit of what they think they'd have to spend to develop something like the GAS-MIZER without infringing our patent application.

Hinkle: Interesting. That's only about ten times what we've got sunk in it. Anyway, we've got to figure out what to do next. The new Pilgrim offer is pretty attractive and we've got to be able to include it in our analysis, but there are a couple of important things that accepting the Pilgrim offer would deal us out of. One, of course, is the upside potential of the GAS-MIZER. The other is the experience of producing an electronic automotive product. You've known all along that I consider GAS-MIZER as an initial entry to the electronics field. If we sell the rights to it now, we may as well sit back and resign ourselves to being just another job shop making patterns and molds for the "big three." On the other hand, one thing the Pilgrim offer will do for us is let us avoid the $150,000 investment in setting up a production line for GAS-MIZER.

White: That's just the first year, too. If demand goes high, we'll eventually have $450,000 in the line and maybe another $100,000 in inventories and so forth.

Hinkle: Well, if we can sell 10,000 per year for five years, we can afford it. Especially if we can get a couple of other electronic gadgets going that can use some of this equipment as GAS-MIZER winds down in 1983 or 1984. What I'm worried about is spending the first $150,000 in the face of all this uncertainty.

White: Let me get a few things straight, Jerry. It looks like there are three basic choices we can make: (1) sell the GAS-MIZER to Pilgrim, (2) sign with Clayton's and begin manufacturing, or (3) buy the Marketronics survey first and then do one of the other two. Couldn't we both sell the idea to Pilgrim *and* manufacture for Clayton's?

Hinkle: No. Both firms have been insistent on an exclusive. And based on what Ms. Barnes told me, we don't really have time to generate other alternatives. She guessed that the editors would be on to us inside of a couple of weeks. We'll have to have gone one way or the other by then.

White: And I don't suppose we could sign with Clayton's, wait for the editors' reaction, and pull out if its unfavorable?

Hinkle: I'm sure we could, but there's a nonperformance penalty clause in that contract that would cost us at least $100,000. I guess it's a good thing that I own this company outright. I'd never be able to explain this deal to a board of directors!

Hawthorne Plastics, Inc.

Hawthorne Plastics, located in Hawthorne, California, specialized in the fabrication of plastic parts as a subcontractor to companies marketing plastic products, such as manufacturers of toys, kitchenware, fishing tackle, etc. Most of its production involved the molding or extrusion of plastic raw materials and over half of its production was for two major manufacturers of toys, located nearby. The vast majority of its customers were located in southern California, with a few in Arizona, Nevada, and northern California. In its market area the company was known for its high-quality, low-cost products. Its low cost was based on extremely efficient production methods, so efficient that on some items it produced at prices lower than the costs of the company for which it was subcontracting. Other items were produced for companies lacking their own production facilities. Still others (about 40 percent of total dollar volume) were produced as "overflow" for companies whose own production facilities were operating at capacity.

The high percentage of overflow sales had always been a matter of concern to William Campanella, Hawthorne's president and founder. His concern was based on the fact that in economic downturns, the overflow business tended to decline quickly, making Hawthorne's sales revenue more cyclical than he desired. Mr. Campanella and his marketing manager, John D. Stein, had lately been considering the possibility of developing several proprietary lines which Hawthorne could produce and market. This would eliminate some of the uncertainty that resulted from being exclusively a subcontractor. It would also, however, require expansion of the company's three-man sales force.

THE POLYPROPYLENE STRAPPING SUBCONTRACT

On October 10, 1969, Mr. Stein had just completed negotiations on a subcontract proposed by the David F. Pynes Strapping Co., located in nearby Gardena, California. Pynes produced and sold a line of plastic strapping, the fastest growing part of which was used for bundling such items as magazines and newspapers. Plastic was rapidly displacing bailing wire in this segment of the strapping market. The costs of wire and plastic were comparable but plastic was more flexible than wire. Its use resulted in fewer newspapers or magazines being torn by the strapping material when the bundles were thrown during shipment.

Pynes had discovered that in spite of the obvious advantages of plastic strapping over bailing wire, few newspapers and magazines were aware of it. However, with an aggressive personal selling effort, the company had succeeded in converting many users to plastic. So successful was its marketing effort that sales were running nearly twice what had been projected, with the result that Pynes's plant was operating three shifts and orders were being turned down. Pynes had sought to advance the starting date on a plant expansion originally scheduled to be completed in a year, but the best that could be done was completion by April 10, 1970. Consequently Pynes contacted Hawthorne to see if it could handle some of this "overflow" production.

The request came at an opportune time for Hawthorne, since capacity had just been freed up after heavy production for the Christmas toy season. The negotiations proceeded to the point where Hawthorne agreed to deliver 100,000 pounds of polypropylene plastic strapping per month to Pynes for the next six months; capacity problems at Hawthorne prevented larger shipments, although Pynes would have liked to buy more.

The price per pound that Pynes would pay depended on the quality of the strapping that Hawthorne delivered. The industry distinguished between "low-camber" and "high-camber" strapping: low-camber strapping was much straighter and thus was suitable for use in automated bundling machines; high-camber strapping would cause automated equipment to jam and thus was suitable for use in manual equipment only. Because low-camber strapping was sold at a higher price on the market, it was frequently referred to as "high quality," whereas the high-camber strapping was referred to as "average quality."

Pynes had agreed to pay Hawthorne $0.60 per pound for high-quality strapping and $0.50 per pound for average quality. It did not matter to Pynes which quality strapping it received, because by adjusting its own production process it could provide itself with relatively more high-quality strapping if Hawthorne provided average-quality strapping in a given month, and vice versa. Pynes would provide the production dies and Hawthorne would deliver the strapping on spools bearing the Pynes trademark.

After consultation with his production engineer, Ralph Nelson, Mr. Stein signed a contract agreeing to the above terms on behalf of Hawthorne.

Mr. Stein was also influenced in his decision to take the contract by the apparent attractiveness of plastic strapping as a potential proprietary line for Hawthorne; for example, Pynes's selling price was about $1.00 per pound for high-quality strapping and about $0.75 per pound for average-quality strapping, which, given Hawthorne's production efficiency, would yield a nice markup. While Pynes seemed to have a strong position in the magazine and newspaper market, Stein had read of other applications of plastic strapping pioneered by other companies; for example, the Signode Corporation of Chicago, Illinois, had developed a scheme for compressing and bundling automobile tires with plastic strapping. Mr. Stein felt that with an imaginative applications engineer other markets might be opened.

THE PRODUCTION DECISIONS

During the contract negotiations, Mr. Nelson was considering how he would produce the polypropylene strapping. It would have to be produced by extruding polypropylene resin, which cost between $0.20 and $0.25 per pound, and in 100,000-pound batches because of scheduling considerations.

One of the most important unanswered questions was what production equipment to use. This issue was clouded by the fact that the quality of the strapping produced depended on what extrusion equipment was utilized and on a key characteristic of the raw material. If the average length of the chemical chain forming the molecules of the raw material exceeded a critical length, then production of high-quality strapping was possible if the right equipment were used. From raw material with shorter chains it was impossible to obtain high-quality strapping with any process available to Hawthorne.

Nelson had three manufacturing processes available to him, whose production costs increased with their ability to produce high-quality strapping. Process 1 involved the use of a simple extruding machine and produced average-quality strapping regardless of the raw material. Process 2 used a different machine which could utilize better temperature controls than Process 1, but which had no means of controlling pressure. Consequently Process 2 was capable of producing high-quality strapping from long-chain raw material, but only if the extrusion pressure remained above 150 pounds per square inch (psi) during the processing of a batch. Process 3 involved adding pressure controls to the temperature controls used in Process 2, which guaranteed that long-chain raw materials would be converted into high-quality strapping. The capabilities of the three processes are summarized in Exhibit 1.

Any one of the three processes could be used on any batch of raw material, but Mr. Nelson knew that once he decided on the process for any given batch, the other machine would be used for other production

EXHIBIT 1
Type of finished strapping for various combinations of chain length and process

	Length	
Process	Long-chain molecule	Short-chain molecule
1..............	Average quality	Average quality
2..............	High quality if pressure maintained above 150 psi	Average quality
3..............	High quality	Average quality

processes. He planned to decide on the process for the Pynes job first since the equipment had equal costs on the alternate jobs coming up in the next six months, jobs which were far less demanding than the strapping job. However, because of scheduling problems, he knew it was impossible to use more than one process on a given batch of strapping; further, because of the continuous nature of the process, once started it was expensive to stop and restart.

Process 1 had a variable cost of $0.13 per pound of finished strapping plus a $200 setup cost per batch, whereas Process 2 cost $700 setup plus $0.15 per pound variable cost. The most expensive process, Process 3, cost $1,200 setup plus $0.17 per pound variable cost. The difference in operating costs was due to a difference in the number of operators required in each case, and differences in costs of setting up dies, sensing, and control equipment. These costs excluded the cost of raw materials; all three processes required 1 pound of raw material per pound of strapping. However, the Process 2 and Process 3 setup costs did include an allocation of $200 per production run, which Mr. Nelson had added to recover $1,200 that was spent in experimenting with the sensing devices and controls on the two processes. Further, the setup figures included an allowance for the nominal cleanup costs for each process. However, Mr. Nelson knew that on a few types of products, the machine used for Processes 2 and 3 required considerably more cleanup labor—up to $250 more than nominal. He was not sure whether extra cleanup would be required in the production of strapping.

Nelson had pressure data from other production runs of polypropylene on Process 2 for conditions nearly identical to those required to produce the Pynes's strapping. These data are summarized in Exhibit 2.

Mr. Nelson planned to purchase raw material in batches large

EXHIBIT 2
Minimum pressures observed on ten production runs using Process 2

Date of run	Minimum pressure (psi)	Date of run	Minimum pressure (psi)
2/ 7/68	153	9/12/68	154
3/17/68	147	12/ 1/68	146
4/30/68	153	3/ 5/69	153
6/19/68	151	3/13/69	148
7/25/68	146	8/21/69	154

enough to produce 100,000 pounds of strapping. To him, the choice of production process would be an easy one if the chain length of the particular batch of raw material were known for sure at the time of choice. Unfortunately, this was not the case; although the manufacturer of the polypropylene resin could assure uniformity within a given batch of raw material, he could only tell Hawthorne that the chance was 50–50 that any batch of raw material would be of the long-chain variety. Since the manufacturer made no claims that the chain length of a particular batch was long, polypropylene that turned out to be short chain could not be returned.

Accurate determination of chain length required a series of very expensive chemical tests. However, using a standard piece of test equipment in the Hawthorne lab, it was possible to perform a rough measurement of average molecular weight which would be an indicator, albeit imperfect, of chain length. It was only possible to tell from the test whether the molecular weight was "large" or "standard."

As a service to its customers, the manufacturer of the test equipment distributed various technical bulletins about the accuracy of its test equipment. One bulletin described the results of a series of experiments on samples of polypropylene that had been subjected to the elaborate and expensive chemical tests necessary to determine molecular weight accurately. The following results were obtained:

> For batches known to be of long-chain material—96 percent tested out as "large molecule" and 4 percent tested out as "standard molecule."

> For batches known to be short-chain material—24 percent tested as "large molecule" and 76 percent tested out as "standard molecule."

Performing the test would cost $200 per batch; its inaccuracy was an inherent feature of the test which could not be improved by repeated testing of a given batch.

Mr. Nelson felt that the pressure resulting in Process 2 was unrelated to both molecular weight and chain length.

chapter 5

Preference theory*

Most formal analyses of business decisions involving uncertainty assume that every individual or every company has (or ought to have)
the same attitude toward risk. The underlying assumption is that a
decision maker will want to choose the course of action that has the
highest expected value of profit. (The expected value of mathematical
expectation is the weighted average of the possible results anticipated
from a particular course of action, where the weights are the probabilities.) In other words, the analysis usually assumes that decision
makers will want to play the averages on all deals, regardless of the
potential negative consequences that might result. But in fact very few
business managers take this attitude toward risk when they make important decisions.

You can convince yourself of this by answering the simple question:
What is the maximum amount that you would be willing to pay for a
50–50 chance at winning $500 or losing $100? If you are the sort who
plays the averages, your answer is $200 [i.e., (0.50 × $500) − (0.50 ×
$100)], the expected value of the venture. But if you are like most
people, your answer is less than $200, and perhaps considerably less,
reflecting quite properly your attitude toward risk.

What is lacking, then, is a scheme for tailoring the decision-making
technique to the risk-taking attitude of the decision maker. It is possible to make a precise statement about a person's attitude toward risk in
the form of a utility or preference curve, and then to make direct use of
the curve to incorporate this attitude in many important types of business decisions involving uncertainty. The terms *utility theory* and
preference theory can be used synonymously, but whereas the former
is used more frequently in the literature, it is also used to describe
another subject in economics; hence the term *preference theory* will
be used here.

---

* This chapter was developed from John S. Hammond's article, "Better Decisions
with Preference Theory," *Harvard Business Review*, November–December 1967, copyright © by the President and Fellows of Harvard College; all rights reserved.

This chapter describes a procedure for determining a graph that summarizes a decision maker's risk-taking attitude and how to incorporate this *preference curve* into a decision tree analysis. To do this concretely, we focus on a simple case about an oil wildcatter.

PETRO ENTERPRISES

Petro Enterprises was a fledgling organization founded to wildcat in the Texas oil fields. Petro has a nontransferable short-term option to drill on a certain plot of land. The option is the only business deal in which the firm is involved now or that it expects to consider before December 31, the time drilling would be completed if the option were exercised. Two recent dry holes elsewhere have reduced Petro's net liquid assets to $130,000, and William Snyder, president and principal stockholder, must decide whether Petro should exercise its option or allow it to expire. It will expire in two weeks if drilling is not commenced by then. Snyder has three possible choices:

1. Drill immediately.
2. Pay to have a seismic test run in the next few days, and then, depending on the result of the test, decide whether or not to drill.
3. Let the option expire, i.e., do nothing.

To conserve capital and maintain flexibility, Petro subcontracts all drilling and seismic testing; also, it immediately sells the rights to any oil discovered, instead of developing the oil fields itself. It can have the seismic test performed on short notice at overtime rates for a fixed fee of $30,000, and the well can be drilled for a fixed fee of $100,000. A large oil company has promised that if Petro drills and discovers oil, it will purchase all of Petro's rights for a flat $400,000.

The company's geologist has examined the geology in the region and states that there is a 0.55 probability that if a well is sunk, oil will be discovered. Data on the reliability of the seismic test indicate that if the test result is favorable, the probability of finding oil will increase to 0.85; but if the test result is unfavorable, it will fall to 0.10. The geologist has computed that there is a 0.60 probability that the result will be favorable if a test is made.

This decision problem involving uncertainty can be structured in the form of the decision tree shown in Figure 5–1. The tree shows the probabilities for the various events, based on the judgment of the company geologist, the cash flows encountered under different alternatives, and the economic valuation of the nine terminal positions representing the nine possible sequences of acts and events.

The economic quantity that the decision maker has used to describe the result of a particular path on the decision tree is called his or her *criterion*. In this case, Snyder has chosen a criterion of net liquid

FIGURE 5-1
Complete decision diagram showing Petro Enterprises' assets at each end position

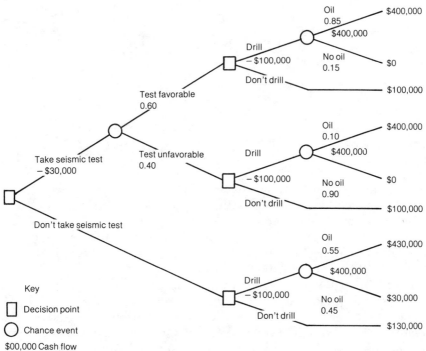

Key

☐ Decision point

○ Chance event

$00,000 Cash flow

assets, since his liquid asset position determines his ability to consider future deals. Other business executives in other situations might well select earnings, net cash flow, or some other criterion. Obviously, the use of different criteria can lead to different decisions in some situations.

Regardless of the criterion he has chosen, Mr. Snyder may reduce the decision diagram in Figure 5–1 by replacing the event forks with their expected monetary values (EMV) and selecting the highest EMV alternative at each act fork. The result, which should be confirmed by the student using the methodology outlined in Chapter 4, is depicted in Figure 5–2.

Does it make sense?

We can now speculate on how Snyder might react to these results. Surely he is pleased that the expected value of his asset position following immediate drilling is $250,000—much higher than if he does nothing and stays with a sure asset position of $130,000. Also, he would be very pleased if he struck oil and ended up with $430,000 in

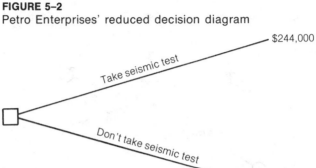

FIGURE 5–2
Petro Enterprises' reduced decision diagram

Take seismic test → $244,000

Don't take seismic test → $250,000

assets. However, he is quite disturbed by the fact that there is a 0.45 chance that he will end up with only $30,000 in assets, which for practical purposes would put him out of business. (This contingency is summarized in Figure 5–1, where the drilling action following omission of a seismic test is followed by a 0.45 chance of no oil discovery. Since drilling costs $100,000, the company's original asset position is reduced by that amount.)

Snyder then looks at the strategy: take seismic test and drill only if favorable. Although it has a slightly lower expected value than the chosen option ($244,000 versus $250,000), he notes that the chance of ending up with a low asset position is considerably reduced, from 0.45 to 0.09 (i.e., 0.60 × 0.15). Like many business managers, he is conservative. In fact, because of his firm's weak financial position, he is extremely conservative, and he is rather skeptical of the course of action recommended by the expected monetary value analysis. His intuition tells him he *should* take the seismic test, but this decision analysis tells him he is wrong.

Snyder, like many business managers, is caught in a dilemma. Because uncertainty is a major factor in his decision, he is aware of the need to recognize it explicitly in his analysis; he has, quite properly, structured his analysis with a decision diagram. He feels he has correctly assessed the economic consequences of various contingencies. He also feels that the probabilities used in his analysis reflect his best judgment of the chances that the events will actually occur. Yet his intuition seems to be telling him that the conclusion of the analysis just isn't for *him*.

QUESTIONABLE ALTERNATIVES

It is worth noting that Snyder is not alone in his doubts about using a mode of analysis designed to maximize mathematical expectation.

Many business managers find that such an approach does such a poor job of reflecting their attitudes toward risk that they resort to other analytic approaches. Unfortunately, their alternatives often are equally questionable.

For example, many people flatly refuse to consider uncertainty explicitly in their analyses. Instead they make padded or "conservative" estimates of the unknown quantities that will affect the success or failure of the venture being analyzed. They then pretend that the world will be like their estimates and, in essence make their decision under assumed certainty. This sweeps uncertainty, an important dimension of the problem, under the rug and in most cases is clearly an unsatisfactory approach.

An extreme example of this behavior is "worst case" analysis. To be "conservative," some companies will not market a new product unless it can be demonstrated that it will be profitable under the worst foreseeable combination of circumstances: highest production costs, highest distribution costs, greatest competition, lowest demand in each of the next few years, and so forth. They do a profitability calculation, assuming that all costs and revenues have their worst possible values. Then if the resultant calculation shows a profit, they go ahead; if not, the venture is dropped.

Closer examination often shows that the chance of all variables simultaneously taking on their worst values is extremely small— perhaps a thousand to one or even a million to one! As a result only riskless (and often low-yield) ventures are accepted, whereas ventures that have a small chance of unprofitability but a high chance of great profitability are dropped. For a small and acceptable amount of additional risk, much greater profitability would result, but the padded estimate approach will never show this. Only with explicit recognition of uncertainty and of one's attitude toward risk can the right combination of risk and return be found.

Other business managers recognize the need to consider uncertainty in their analyses, but they take account of their conservatism by increasing the probabilities of those events that can lead to unfavorable consequences. For example, in a decision tree analysis of a new product venture, the probabilities assigned to unfavorable costs, unfavorable levels of competition, unfavorable demand levels, and so forth, will be arbitrarily increased. The resultant probability does not represent the decision maker's best judgment on the chance that the event will occur; it is distorted by the attitude toward risk. Unless the decision maker in such a case has some magically consistent way of adjusting the probabilities, this distorted approach is also unsatisfactory, for there is no assurance that the resultant analysis properly reflects the degree of conservatism desired by the decision maker.

Another approach some companies use to take risk into account starts with the decision tree structure. However, instead of using the analytic technique just described, the analysts determine the probability distribution of outcomes associated with various complete descriptions of action, called *strategies*, described on the tree. Using Snyder's oil-drilling problem as an example, you can see that the strategy: don't take the seismic test—drill immediately, has a 0.55 chance of making $300,000 and a 0.45 chance of losing $100,000. This is compared with the strategy: take seismic test—if it is favorable, drill, and if not, don't drill, which has a probability of 0.40 of losing $30,000, a probability of 0.09 (i.e., 0.60 × 0.15) of losing $130,000, and a probability of 0.51 (i.e., 0.60 × 0.85) of making $270,000, and with other possible strategies.

The distributions of outcomes associated with the strategies are then compared and a choice is made according to some criterion. For example, it may be decided that the second strategy is preferable because there is a much smaller chance of losing a large sum of money. Or the first strategy may be preferable because there is less chance of losing money and the amount to be gained is larger.

The Snyder case is extremely simplified; for each strategy there are only a few possible outcomes. In more realistic cases the number of strategies to be compared usually becomes extremely large, as does the number of possible outcomes. In these cases decisions are sometimes made on the basis of comparison of the expected value and the variance of the various distributions of profit, of the expected value and the coefficient of variation (the coefficient of variation is the square root of the variance divided by the expected value), of the probability distributions of those outcomes corresponding to a loss, or of other criteria.

Major difficulties arise because of the very large number of alternatives to be compared in most situations. Other difficulties arise when there are alternatives with conflicting characteristics. For example, using the first of the criteria just mentioned, one would like to choose the strategy with the largest expected value and the smallest variance.

However, very seldom does one find an alternative that simultaneously has both characteristics. Therefore some companies decide on a maximum acceptable variance and then select the course of action with the highest expected value. The danger in doing this is that an alternative with a much higher expected value and a variance only slightly above the limit may be passed up—an alternative that on reflection may be preferable to others. As a matter of fact, it is even possible to find two alternatives with the same expected value and the same variance but with different intuitive attractiveness to the decision maker.

This catalog of ways that business managers deal with risk is by no means exhaustive. The main point is this: Although there are clearly times when some of these techniques will work satisfactorily, there are many situations, especially ones involving complicated decisions, where the methods are likely to take improper account of the decision maker's risk-taking attitude.

Now let us consider an approach that does not require the business decision maker to play the long-run averages if he or she does not want to. This approach begins with an examination of basic attitude toward risk.

DEFINING RISK ATTITUDE

If the decision maker is not a player of long-run averages, we must replace the event forks on the decision tree by numbers *other* than mathematical expectations. The new numbers must simultaneously take three things into account: probabilities, economic consequences, and an attitude toward risk taking that is different from playing the long-run averages.

For an example, let us go back to Figure 5–1. The top terminal event fork has a mathematical expectation of $340,000. This is the minimum sure asset position that a player of long-run averages would be willing to accept in place of the gamble represented by the fork. If the player were more conservative, however, the fork would be "worth" less than $340,000. The exact amount can be decided only by the decision maker, since it is his or her attitude toward risk that we wish to reflect in the analysis.

Just what do we mean by "worth," and how is it determined? Let us tackle both questions together. Suppose we ask Snyder the following questions regarding the event fork under discussion: Imagine you have committed your firm to drill on land where you believe there is a 0.85 chance of striking oil. If oil is struck, your firm's asset position will increase to a sure $400,000; whereas if you get a dry hole, you will be left with nothing (zero assets). Imagine further that a wealthy investor is interested in paying you cash for the rights to any oil that may be discovered, before either of you learn the results of the drilling. In other words, the investor will take over the risk of the drilling and the rewards, too, if there are any. You'll be free of the risk and keep the amount you are paid for your rights. If the investor offers to buy your rights for an amount that will increase your assets to $150,000, will you sell out?

Snyder's reply is an emphatic *no!* Thus he has told us that, as far as he is concerned, $150,000 in hand is less valuable than a 0.85 chance of assets of $400,000 and a 0.15 chance of nothing. If he is offered assets of only $150,000, in other words, he would rather take his chances with drilling.

Next we ask Snyder if he will sell out for $250,000 of assets, and his answer is *yes*. We now know that he prefers a sure $250,000 to running the risk of proceeding with drilling—in spite of the fact that the venture has an expected value equivalent to $350,000 of assets.

We now ask a third question: What if there is only one potential bidder and the maximum offer is equivalent to only $225,000 in assets to you? Will you still sell out? Snyder thinks a bit and answers *yes*.

Snyder's answers to our three questions tell us that the gamble represented by the event fork is worth somewhere between $150,000 and $225,000 in sure assets to him, where the word *worth* is used in a special sense. It means the rock-bottom asset position that Snyder would accept in exchange for the risky outcome of drilling. In other words, there should be some amount that, if offered to him, would make him indifferent as to whether he should go ahead with the venture or sell out. If he were offered just a few dollars more, he would sell out; if he were offered just a few dollars less, he would prefer to take the risk of drilling.

We refer to this amount or worth as Snyder's *certainty equivalent* for the event fork. This certainty equivalent is a precise measure of his attitude toward risk in this particular situation. It should be obvious that the lower his certainty equivalent, the more conservative he is, and vice versa.

By asking Snyder just a few more questions, similar to the ones already asked, we should be able to zero in quickly on his certainty equivalent. Once he understands the concept being applied here, we should be able to ask for his certainty equivalent in a single question rather than in a series of questions.

PRACTICAL APPLICATION

To take the decision maker's attitude toward risk into account, we must find for each event fork a certain (sure) amount that is equivalent in the decision maker's mind to running the risk represented by the event fork. This certain amount, his certainty equivalent for the event fork, is measured in units of the decision maker's criterion and can be used to replace the event fork in a decision diagram. So far, as in Chapter 4, we have used mathematical expectations (EMV) as certainty equivalents.

One way in which the analyst can obtain the decision maker's certainty equivalents for event forks is to ask the decision maker to supply them fork by fork working backward through the tree. While this is relatively easy in decision problems as simple as the Petro Enterprises example, it would be out of the question in more realistic problems. There are two reasons for this: (1) in more realistic problems the number of event forks is so large that the process would become hopelessly time-consuming; and (2) event forks with many branches would likely be encountered, and it is difficult to think sensibly about certainty equivalents for such complicated uncertainties.

USING PREFERENCE CURVES

The answers to the problems just mentioned lie in the use of a *preference curve*. This curve is a complete summary of the decision maker's attitude toward risk over the range required to solve a particular business problem. The curve can be used to determine the certainty equivalents for the event forks in a problem (including those forks with many branches) in a straightforward, mechanical way. In fact, we will see that it is possible to use preference values, derived from the decision maker's preference curve, as "proxies" for certainty equivalents in a decision tree analysis. Fortunately, the decision maker's preference curve can be determined by finding his or her certainty equivalents for just a few very simple two-branch gambles.

Let us now examine the characteristics of preference curves and the means of obtaining them. Snyder's preference curve (see Figure 5–3) will serve as an example.

FIGURE 5–3
Snyder's preference curve

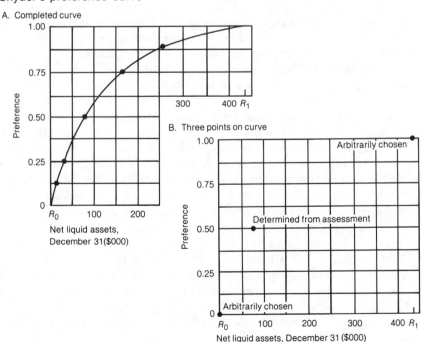

Salient characteristics

The horizontal axis in Figure 5–3 displays the consequences of the decisions, measured in units of the decision maker's criterion, on a certain date. In Snyder's case the units are net liquid assets on December 31. For other decision makers in other situations, they might be earnings or net cash flow for the period ending on a particular date, or something else.

One of the most important things to notice about the horizontal axis is the range that it covers. Since the curve is to be used to analyze the drilling decision problem, it must (and does) cover the range of consequences possible in the problem, $0 to $430,000. More generally, *a preference curve must accurately reflect the decision maker's attitude toward risk over a range of consequences encompassing at least the worst and best results that can arise in a given problem.* Of course, it is all right (and occasionally advantageous) to measure the attitude over a range *greater* than that needed, but it is not all right to cover a shorter range.

The end points of the range have special status, which is signified by calling them the *reference consequences.* The symbol R_0 has been assigned to represent the lower reference consequence, and R_1 represents the upper reference consequence. In Snyder's case, R_0 must be less than or equal to $0, and R_1 must be greater than or equal to $430,000. Provided they encompass all consequences, the selection of reference consequences should in no way affect the result of a decision analysis such as the one we will do on Snyder's problem.

Turning now to the vertical axis, two points on the curve may be chosen arbitrarily. Assigning a preference value of 0 to R_0 and a preference value of 1 to R_1 allows us to interpret the preference index in a similar way as interpreting a cumulative probability. The vertical axis thus ranges from 0 to 1, while the horizontal axis ranges from R_0 to R_1.

Knowledge of the exact meaning of the vertical axis is not necessary for use of the preference curve in analysis. It is sufficient that the decision maker simply understands that it is an index of his or her attitude toward risk and knows how it is used in practice. For the specialist, however, the following technical note may be useful.

A preference, $P(C)$, assigned to consequence C means that the decision maker is indifferent between having an amount C for certain or having a chance $P(C)$ of achieving R_1 and a chance $[1 - P(C)]$ of achieving R_0. Thus in part A of Figure 5–3, for example, Snyder has indicated that he is indifferent between achieving an asset position of $100,000 for certain or having a 0.60 chance of getting $430,000 and a 0.40 chance of ending up with nothing, since the curve passes through the point ($100,000, 0.6).

Obtaining the curve

The process of obtaining the decision maker's preference curve, called *assessment*, consists of two stages: (1) the assessment of a preliminary curve, and then (2) the verification and correction of that curve (that is, checking its behavioral implications to see whether it truly reflects the decision maker's risk-taking attitude).

It is not the purpose of this chapter to present an exhaustive discussion of ways to assess preference curves; there are many ways, and each has advantages and disadvantages.[1] The method to be described has been selected because it is very easily understandable (although the reader should be warned that in practice it often results in irregular-shaped preliminary curves that require correction in the process of verification). This method consists of obtaining points on the decision maker's curve by asking for his or her certainty equivalents for a series of simple 50–50 gambles and then drawing a smooth curve through the points. Let us focus on the details by imagining that we are obtaining Snyder's curve.

To begin, suppose that Snyder, like most business managers, has never heard of a certainty equivalent. Since it plays a pivotal role in what follows, an essential first step is to make sure he understands exactly what we mean by the term. Once the concept is understood, we can proceed to get his preliminary curve.

Assessing the preliminary curve.   Since we have already assigned preference values of 0 and 1 to the two reference consequences, we have two points on Snyder's curve. To obtain the third, we ask for Snyder's certainty equivalent for a 50–50 chance of assets of $0 or $430,000. Let us suppose that Snyder thinks carefully about the question and finally answers $72,000. Since this is the first certainty equivalent we have obtained, we will call it CE_1.

Snyder's conservatism is already quite apparent. If he were an averages player, his response would have been the mathematical expectation of the gamble: $215,000 [i.e., (0.50 × $430,000) + (0.50 × $0)]. But since he is conservative, his response is $72,000. We call the difference between the mathematical expectation for a gamble and a decision maker's certainty equivalent the *risk premium;* in this case the risk premium, $143,000, is substantial.

To obtain the preference corresponding to $72,000, we make use of the following principle: The preference of a gamble is the mathematical expectation of preferences corresponding to the consequences of the gamble. Thus:

---

[1] For a more complete discussion, see Robert O. Schlaifer, *Analysis of Decisions under Uncertainty* (New York: McGraw-Hill Book Company, Inc., 1967), chap. 5.

$$\text{Preference of } CE_1 = (0.50 \times \text{Preference of } \$0)$$
$$+ (\$0.50 \times \text{Preference of } \$430{,}000)$$
$$= (0.50 \times 0) + (0.50 \times 1) = 0.50$$

We now have three points on Snyder's preference curve: the two arbitrarily chosen points and a third that we have just inferred from his answer to our question. Let us plot these as shown in part B of Figure 5–3.

We obtain another point by asking him a similar question involving the third point on the curve and one of the reference consequences, such as: What certain asset position in dollars would make you indifferent between a 50–50 chance at asset positions of $72,000 or $430,000?

Suppose he replies that his certainty equivalent is $163,000. Then, using the same principle, we can determine the preference corresponding to $163,000 as follows:

$$\text{Preference of } CE_2 = (0.50 \times \text{Preference of } \$72{,}000)$$
$$+ (0.50 \times \text{Preference of } \$430{,}000)$$
$$= (0.50 \times 0.50) + (0.50 \times 1) = 0.75$$

We might ask a similar question about a 50–50 chance at asset positions of $0 or $72,000. Suppose Snyder's reply is $28,000, which can be denoted as CE_3. His preference for $28,000 is 0.25 [i.e., $(0.50 \times 0) + (0.50 \times 0.50)$].

We would continue in this manner until we obtained a sufficient number of points through which we could draw a smooth curve (see part A in Figure 5–3).

Summary of procedure. By now the pattern must be clear, so let us tie it together.

1. We first selected reference consequences R_1 and R_0, encompassing the best and worst consequences that could arise in the decision problem. We arbitrarily assigned a preference value of 1 to R_1 and of 0 to R_0 and plotted them as the first two points on our preference curve.

2. Next we asked the decision maker a series of questions about his certainty equivalents for 50–50 gambles involving various consequences in the range between R_1 and R_0. We started by asking for his certainty equivalent for a 50–50 chance at the extreme case, $430,000 or $0 (i.e., the two reference consequences R_0 and R_1). We determined that the preference corresponding to this certainty equivalent was 0.50 and plotted this point on the graph. Then we obtained the certainty equivalents for two more gambles, CE_2, having a preference of 0.75, and CE_3, having a preference of 0.25, and plotted these points on our graph.

3. We started with only one pair of points on our curve, R_0 and R_1,

and assessed CE_1. Next, we used the two new pairs of points generated by the assessment of CE_1 (i.e., R_1 and CE_1, and R_0 and CE_1) to assess CE_2 and CE_3. Now, CE_2 and CE_3 gave us *five* new pairs of points (R_1 and CE_2, R_1 and CE_3, R_0 and CE_2, R_0 and CE_3, and CE_2 and CE_3), which we could have used to assess five more certainty equivalents; and these in turn would have generated a large number of possibilities for more assessments. This "boot-strapping" process would end quickly, however, for soon we would have enough points through which to draw a smooth curve, as is done in part A of Figure 5–3.

Verification of curve. Before using the preference curve, it is imperative to make consistency checks to see that it correctly reflects the decision maker's attitude. If it is to be useful, it must correctly represent the manager's attitude toward risk for *all* gambles in the range between the reference consequences. If it does not do this, inconsistencies exist. Inconsistencies are best illustrated by example, so let us return to Snyder.

Using his preference curve (see Figure 5–3, part A), we would determine his certainty equivalent for a 50–50 chance at assets of $100,000 or $350,000. First we compute the preference of the gamble:

$$(0.50 \times \text{Preference for } \$100,000)$$
$$+ (0.50 \times \text{Preference for } \$350,000)$$
$$= (0.50 \times 0.60) + (0.50 \times 0.95) = 0.775$$

We then read the certainty equivalent corresponding to 0.775 from the preference curve; it is $180,000.

Now suppose we ask Snyder to assess his certainty equivalent for the same gamble, and his reply is $210,000. Then clearly the attitude toward risk implied by his preference curve is inconsistent with that expressed by the assessment just described. Something has to give; if the problem is due to improper smoothing of the curve, the solution is easy. If not, either part of the preference curve must be reassessed or the new assessment does not truly reflect Snyder's attitude.

As a general rule, such checks for inconsistency should be made after the first plot of a preference curve is done; and, if necessary, changes and additional checks should be made until the decision maker is confident that the curve is a correct reflection of his or her attitude toward risk. Only then is it appropriate to make some of the practical uses of the curve that will be described later on in this chapter.

Some analysts argue that the inconsistencies that often result in the assessment of preference curves are a reason for avoiding their use. On the contrary, the fact that the decision makers are inconsistent in their attitudes toward risk is one of the strongest reasons for the use of the preference theory model. The process of assessment points up these inconsistencies and permits their resolution—*before* they can adversely affect a decision.

AN IMPORTANT DISTINCTION

We mentioned earlier that without the use of preference theory, some decision makers tend to distort their probability assessments by increasing the probabilities assigned to events that have particularly unattractive consequences. This is undesirable because it confuses the decision maker's judgments about probabilities with attitude toward risk.

With the use of preference theory in decision tree analysis it is not only possible but *necessary* to separate the two or there will be danger of double counting. It is absolutely essential that decision makers think only about the chances of occurrence of an event when assessing a probability, paying no attention whatever to the desirability or undesirability of the consequences that might result if the event occurred. Similarly, in assessing a preference curve, it is absolutely essential that decision makers think only about what their attitudes would be if they ever face a gamble of the sort for which they are being asked to assess a certainty equivalent. They should pay absolutely no attention to the chances that they will ever face such a gamble.

Benefits achieved

In principle, the assessment procedure is extremely easy; but in practice it is extremely difficult, especially the first few times it is tried. Strangely enough, the reason for the difficulty is the simplicity of the process. And the simplicity is, in turn, the source of the power of the technique. By isolating attitude toward risk from the other aspects of a complex decision problem and eliciting the attitude by simple questions, we force the decision maker to be explicit about his or her attitude. Formerly the manager could take refuge in the complexity of a decision; attitude toward risk was muddled in with the risk itself and all the other complexities. The painful soul-searching required to answer the question; *Exactly* how big a risk taker am I? was avoided. Now, however, the attitude is forced out in the open.

A common misconception (or perhaps it is an escape) is that the certainty equivalents can be treated as "estimates." Because the decision maker has never been faced with such questions, he or she thinks it is impossible to answer them exactly. But this can and must be done. Managers make difficult and precise quantitative decisions all the time, and they can learn to make the decisions described here, too. A certainty equivalent of "about $75,000" is as inappropriate as writing a check for "about $100"!

If one wishes to make rational decisions consistent with attitude toward risk, one must make the attitude precise. These "small" decisions are the stuff of which the larger decision is made; if they are made vaguely or carelessly, the quality of the larger decision will be affected. Even if one were not planning to make explicit use of the resultant preference curve in a formal analysis (as we are about to do here), one's intuitive decision-making powers would be enhanced by the better self-awareness that results from this process.

ANALYSIS WITH PREFERENCES

To get the certainty equivalent of an event fork in a decision diagram, we use the following procedure, based on a principle of preference theory:

1. *Convert the consequences of the gamble to their corresponding preferences.*
2. *Compute the mathematical expectation of these preferences.* The resultant number is the preference for the event fork.
3. *Go to the preference curve and find the criterion value corresponding to the preference of the fork.* This value is the certainty equivalent of the gamble.

The procedure can be illustrated with the event fork in the upper right corner of Figure 5–4.

1. From the preference curve in Figure 5–3, part A, we know that the preference of $400,000 is 0.98 and the preference of $0 is 0.
2. The mathematical expectation of these preferences is 0.83 [i.e., $(0.98 \times 0.85) + (0 \times 0.15)$].
3. Returning to the preference curve, we see that the certainty equivalent of the fork is $215,000, considerably less than the mathematical expectation of $340,000 computed earlier. We can use this certainty equivalent to continue the analysis by moving back to the drilling act fork; since $215,000 is greater than $100,000, the act chosen would be to drill.

We could complete the analysis in this manner, but it can be done more simply. After obtaining the preferences of the event forks, it is not necessary to convert back to certainty equivalents before making the act choices. Instead, the same results can be obtained if the act choices are made to maximize preference.

Thus, use of the preference curve with decision trees requires only a simple modification of the procedures described in Chapter 4 for maximizing mathematical expectations. The basic principle is this: *If the decision maker wishes to make the best decision consistent with attitude toward risk, he or she must choose that course of action that*

230

FIGURE 5-4
Analysis using preferences

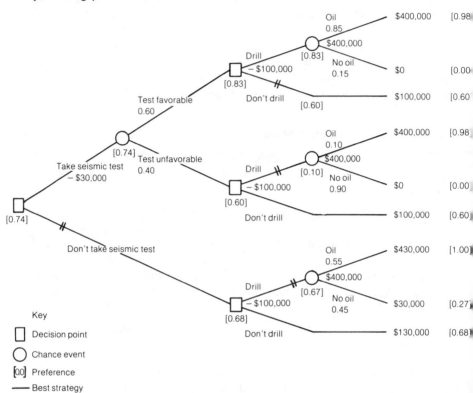

Key

☐ Decision point

◯ Chance event

[00] Preference

—— Best strategy

has the highest preference. To implement the principle, the following procedure should be followed:

1. *Convert all of the end positions of the decision diagram into preferences,* as in Figure 5–4. For example, at the uppermost end position, the preference of $400,000 is 0.98 (taken from the preference curve in Figure 5–3).

2. *To find the decision maker's preference for an event fork, take the mathematical expectation of the preference values at the end position of the fork.* In other words, instead of multiplying the dollar values by probabilities, as in a decision tree analysis using expected monetary value, multiply the preferences by the probabilities. Thus at each event fork take a weighted average of the preferences, where the weights are the probabilities. For example, at the uppermost event fork representing "oil/no oil," the prefer-

ence is 0.83 [i.e., $(0.85 \times 0.98) + (0.15 \times 0)$]. Write the preference
in brackets at the base of the fork, as in Figure 5–4.

3. *At each act fork, choose that act with the highest preference.* For
example, at the uppermost decision fork in Figure 5–4, the choice
is between drill with a preference of 0.83 and don't drill with a
preference of 0.60, so the choice is to drill. Write the preference of
the act chosen, 0.83, in brackets at the base of the fork and cross off
the act not chosen (as shown by the double bar on the rejected
choice in Figure 5–4).

4. *Continue backwards through the tree, repeating steps 2 and 3
until the base of the tree is reached.* For instance, the preference of
the decision to take the seismic test is 0.74 [i.e., $(0.60 \times 0.83) +
(0.40 \times 0.60)$], whereas the preference of the decision not to take
the test is 0.68.

The analysis using preference theory therefore indicates that
Snyder's best strategy is to take the test and, if it gives a favorable
result, drill; if it gives an unfavorable result, don't drill.

How does the foregoing conclusion compare with that reached by
maximizing EMV? As might be expected, the two answers are sharply
different; the mathematical expectation approach tells Snyder to drill
immediately and thus to run a 0.45 chance of ending up with an asset
position of $30,000. The preference theory approach, which takes into
account Snyder's conservatism, tells him to take the seismic test first
and drill only if it is favorable, with a mere 0.09 chance at a low asset
position (in this case, $0). The seismic test, then, is a form of "insurance
policy," which is a good buy for a person as conservative as Snyder but
not worth its price to an averages player, an EMVer.

Added interpretations

You may wonder whether any interpretation can be given to the
preference value assigned to the best strategy (in Snyder's case, 0.74).
A preference value is not an index of desirability in any absolute
sense; we cannot say that a strategy with a value of 0.74, for example, is
twice as attractive as a strategy with a value of 0.37, any more than we
can say that 74°F. is twice as hot as 37°F. Yet certain interpretations can
be made that are occasionally useful in the decision-making process.

Worth of option. If the decision maker will read from the preference curve the criterion value corresponding to the preference of the
best strategy, he or she will know the certainty equivalent for the
entire decision tree. In other words, the manager will be indifferent
between receiving the certainty equivalent amount for sure and taking
a chance on following the best strategy. In Snyder's case, the certainty

equivalent corresponding to the best strategy is found by locating on part A of Figure 5–3 the asset position corresponding to 0.74 on the preference curve. That position is $160,000, which means that Snyder is indifferent between a sure $160,000 in assets and going ahead with the best strategy.

We could go a step further and use this result to get an implicit minimum selling price for the option, if it were transferable. We know that Petro's current asset position is $130,000; this implies that Snyder should be willing to consider any offer for his option to drill that is greater than $30,000 (i.e., $160,000 − $130,000).

Need for complete diagram

In the extremely simple case we have been studying, the only business deal under consideration concerns the option. Our diagram correctly summarizes the possible acts and uncertainties necessary to deal with the problem; that is, everything that might possibly affect net liquid assets on December 31.

What if things were more complicated? For example, suppose there were several other deals under consideration (e.g., the purchase of other options) and perhaps other uncertainties (e.g., a pending lawsuit regarding rights to oil in another pool) that might be resolved before the completion of drilling on the land under option? Each of these uncertainties and deals has a potential impact on the value of Snyder's criterion on December 31. How would these complications change our analysis?

The temptation is to treat each as a separate problem. In fact, the potential asset positions and risks associated with one package of deals may be sharply different from those of another combination. For example, exercising some risky option *by itself* may seem worthwhile, and the same might hold true of another option *by itself*. But the two options *together* may entail a considerable risk of very negative consequences, an exposure the company may not wish to take.

Therefore, it is necessary in theory to include in the diagram all decisions and uncertainties that can have a significant effect on the decision maker's criterion in the time period under analysis. Preference theory applied with a decision tree analysis will then result in the combination of decisions that is most consistent with the decision maker's attitude toward risk.

While a complete diagram is necessary theoretically, in most situations it is impossible to be so comprehensive without unduly complicating the analysis. The tree would become hopelessly large. Thus, as is the case in most mathematical modeling situations, real art and skill are required to capture just enough detail for the analysis to be useful.

An impression may have been created that every time a new decision is faced, a new preference curve must be assessed. This is not necessarily so. Suppose, for example, we have assessed a curve that applies to net liquid assets on June 1, and we use it to make a group of decisions that will affect assets on that date. Then, a few weeks later, we find ourselves faced with an important and unanticipated new decision that also will affect assets on that date. Suppose the reference consequences on the old curve were $R_0 = \$500{,}000$ and $R_1 = \$2$ million. If the results of the earlier decisions *and* the new decision together will fall within this range, and there have been no essential changes in the decision maker's attitude toward risk, the earlier preference curve can be used. On the other hand, if the reference consequences no longer encompass the best and worst consequences, a new curve must be assessed.

The main point is this: It is often advantageous to place the reference consequences a bit farther apart than necessary to encompass the consequences of a particular decision problem. Any unanticipated new decision then can be analyzed without having to obtain a new curve. The reference consequences should not be too broadly spaced, however, for then the values of real interest will be such a small portion of the curve that they cannot be assessed or read with the accuracy needed to analyze the problem.

COMMONLY OBSERVED CURVES

Although a preference curve is a highly subjective expression of a decision maker's attitude, certain types of curves are observed frequently enough to warrant being classified. Awareness of these various types will help business managers to verify their own curves as well as understand the significance of other persons' curves. Three curves corresponding to three different risk-taking attitudes are illustrated in Figure 5–5.

1. **Risk averter.** The conservative person's curve is concave as viewed from below. This is equivalent to saying that the decision maker has a positive risk premium for all gambles in the range covered by the curve. (Recall that the risk premium is defined as the mathematical expectation of the gamble less the certainty equivalent of the gamble.) Curves showing varying degrees of risk aversion are the type most commonly observed in practice; most of us are conservative to a degree. The executive who is in this class will want to be sure that his or her curve is concave at all points as viewed from below.

2. **Averages player.** This person's curve is the straight line in Figure 5–5. The risk premiums are zero for all gambles in the range covered, which means that the manager wishes to play the long-run averages. A linear preference curve may be observed when a person

234

FIGURE 5–5
Three commonly observed types of preference curves

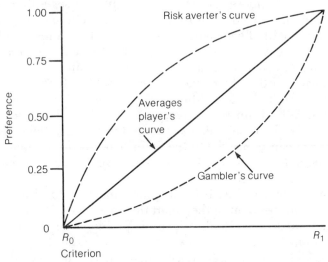

makes a decision with consequences that are small compared with the total asset position of the company.

The person with a linear preference curve is the person for whom analysis by EMV was designed. For this reason, such managers have no need at all to use a preference curve.

If a decision maker faces a decision with consequences that are small compared with the total asset position, the assessment of a preference curve may possibly be avoided. If he or she feels that the certainty equivalent for every gamble in the range covered by the decision is (for practical purposes) equal to its mathematical expectation, then the manager can proceed directly to an expected monetary value analysis.

3. Gambler. This person is the rarest of the three types. The preference curve is convex when viewed from below and is characterized by a negative risk premium for all gambles. Such a manager is, in effect, willing to pay a premium above the mathematical expectation for the "thrill" of gambling or for other reasons.

Sometimes preference curves are observed that are composites of the types just described. For example, a curve might show risk aversion in its upper region and gambling inclinations in its lower region, resulting in a curve shaped like an "S."

Decreasing risk aversion

Referring to Snyder's curve (see Figure 5–3, part A), we can easily see that he is a risk averter. However, his curve is a very special type of risk averter's curve—yet one often observed in practice. We say that it displays *decreasing risk aversion*, by which we mean that the decision maker becomes less conservative as his or her asset position increases.[2]

To see that this is so, compare the risk premium for several 50–50 gambles in which the consequences differ by $100,000. For example, consider the following 50–50 gambles, which we will call Gamble A and Gamble B.

Gamble A's consequences are $0 and $100,000. The expected value is therefore $50,000. To find the certainty equivalent, compute the preference of the gamble, in this case 0.30 [i.e., (0.50 × 0) + (0.50 × 0.60)]. Then read the certainty equivalent corresponding to 0.30 from the curve—$35,000. The risk premium is thus $15,000 (i.e., $50,000 − $35,000).

Gamble B's consequences are $300,000 and $400,000. The risk premium, computed in the same manner as for Gamble A, is $5,000 (i.e., $350,000 − $345,000). This is considerably less than the $15,000 risk premium of Gamble A. It is easy to show that for Snyder the risk premiums for 50–50 gambles decline as the size of the asset position increases, provided that the difference in consequences remains constant.

What is the explanation of decreasing risk aversion? Many people tend to get braver as their criterion increases in value or, conversely, more conservative as it shrinks. People who feel they are decreasingly risk-averse should, as a part of the verification of their curve, check to see whether their preference curve bears out the notion. The phenomenon of decreasing risk aversion is one reason that Snyder expressed the consequences of his decision in terms of assets rather than incremental cash flows.

The zero illusion

A frequently observed phenomenon is the so-called zero illusion, illustrated in Figure 5–6. As shown here, the zero illusion consists of a rather sharp break in the slope of the preference curve over zero on the horizontal scale. This means that the decision maker reacts very aversely to the asset position going negative. (Instead of asset position, it could be cash flow, earnings, or another criterion.)

While this phenomenon is perfectly understandable and in no sense wrong or irrational, many people whose preference curves initially display the zero illusion decide later to modify them when the behavioral implications of the sharp break in the curve are pointed out. A person can check a curve for the zero illusion by seeing whether his or her risk aversion takes a sudden jump for gambles having both positive

[2] For a technical discussion of risk aversion, see John W. Pratt, "Risk Aversion in the Small and in the Large," *Econometrica*, January–April 1964, p. 122.

FIGURE 5–6
Preference curve illustrating the zero illusion

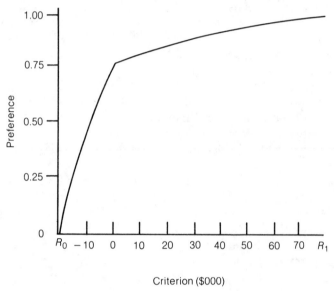

Criterion ($000)

and negative consequences near zero (e.g., a 50–50 chance at assets of $5,000 or a net liability of $5,000), as compared with gambles near zero involving only negative consequences (e.g., a 50–50 chance of a liability of $1 or of $10,001) or only positive consequences (like a 50–50 chance of $1 or $10,001). Behaviorally, this means extreme conservatism around zero and much smaller conservatism for positions that are slightly positive or negative. Few people say they wish to adhere to such a preference curve once this implication has been pointed out.

LIMITATIONS ON USE

It should be noted that while there are many important classes of business decision problems to which preference theory applies, there are other classes to which it does *not*. It applies to most short-term problems, but it does not apply to longer-term problems in which there are uncertain receipts and expenditures significantly separated in time, and in which the date of resolution of the uncertainty is very important to the decision maker. If the date of the outcome of the uncertainties is important to the decision maker, the necessary adjustments for time differences in receipts and expenditures cannot be made simply by discounting. Unfortunately, many capital budgeting problems fall into this class because some alternatives allow the decision maker to obtain strategic information sooner than others do.

Research is being done that aims at extending preference theory to cover such problems, but so far the theoretical results have been too complex for practical application.

SUMMARY

Preference theory is an important refinement of decision analysis that significantly extends the applicability of those analytic techniques to more relevant and realistic problems. In the same way that decision analysis introduced rational and explicit consideration of uncertainty to the list of problems we may consider, preference theory allows us to evaluate situations in which nonlinear risk attitudes contribute to the complexity of the problem. The cases in this chapter are designed to give you some practice with the technique of preference theory. They will also give you some additional experience in building decision diagram models, since the two methodologies are inextricably linked.

case 5–1

J. B. Robinson Fertilizer and Explosives, Inc. (P)

Mr. Robert Mather, executive vice president of the J. B. Robinson Co., engaged a consultant to review his analysis of a legal problem faced by his firm. [See J. B. Robinson Fertilizer and Explosives, Inc. (case 4–6), for a description of this problem.] This consultant, Dr. Harvey Rodger, had been a college classmate of Mr. Mather. Dr. Rodger was employed as a professor of business statistics at a nearby university. Mr. Mather and Dr. Rodger spent a full morning reviewing the problem. At length, Dr. Rodger concluded that Mr. Mather's proposed recommendation was supported by his analysis.

Over lunch, Dr. Rodger commented that there was one extension to Mr. Mather's decision model that he would suggest: use of preference theory to reflect Mr. Robinson's risk-taking attitudes. At this point, Mr. Mather exclaimed (after briefly choking on a bite of salad): "Don't you realize that I've got to present this to Mr. Robinson at 1:30 this afternoon? How can we redo the whole analysis by then? And what's this preference theory thing anyway?" In quick order, Dr. Rodger explained that it was all very simple, would require Mr. Robinson's inputs anyway, couldn't hurt anything, was up to date and would help explain "why you hired me." This final argument convinced Mr. Mather, who invited Dr. Rodger to his afternoon meeting with Mr. J. B. Robinson III, president of the firm.

In the meeting, Mr. Mather presented his recommendations to Mr. Robinson, who watched and listened intently and without comment although his distaste for the subject was evident to all present. Upon concluding his remarks, Mr. Mather turned the floor over to Dr. Rodger. Dr. Rodger, using a few examples, explained the concept of preference theory and expressed his desire to apply it to J. B. Robinson's problem.

Mr. Robinson agreed to cooperate with the comment: "We need all the help we can get in this situation."

"Fine," said Dr. Rodger. "Now let me ask you a few questions. How would you feel about a 50–50 gamble between. . . ."

After two hours of questioning, Dr. Rodger and Mr. Mather returned to Mather's office. Dr. Rodger requested a sheet of graph paper from Mr. Mather's secretary and began to convert Mr. Robinson's certainty equivalents into the chart shown in Exhibit 1. Mr. Mather re-

EXHIBIT 1
Mr. Robinson's preference curve

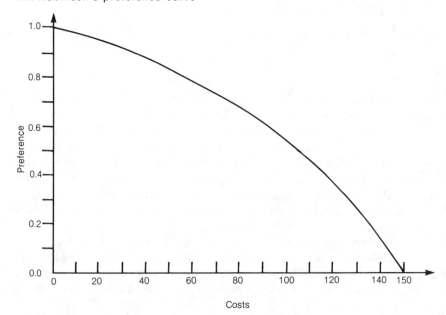

quested a couple of aspirin and, after swallowing them, began a lengthy diatribe against Dr. Rodger: "Harvey, that was the most foolish waste of time I've ever experienced. I hired you for one day to check out my math and you changed the whole point of the analysis. I mean, who cares if the old man is indifferent between some make-believe coin-flip and whatever. This whole afternoon was a royal pain. I've got a good mind to send you back to that ivory tower of yours, slam the door, and throw away the key!"

Dr. Rodger, who had been ignoring Mather's comments to this point, completed his graph of Mr. Robinson's preferences and interrupted: "Now, Bob, I know you don't mean that and I can't take it at all seriously. Mr. Robinson turned out to be an excellent subject and I think he was interested in the preference theory approach. This is a very interesting preference curve. Look at this. I'll not be a bit surprised if it completely changes your recommendation."

Mather, suddenly attentive, said, "Really? Tell me how it works."

case 5-2

Edgartown Fisheries

PART A

On a rainy day in March 1969, Lars Dyson, MBA '48, businessman and adventurer, president of Edgartown Fisheries, faces a difficult and preplexing decision problem.

Edgartown Fisheries is in the shark-fishing business and operates one fishing boat especially equipped for sharking in the North and Middle Atlantic. The company was formed in order to exploit a technique which had previously been little used for shark fishing, a technique called "long-line" fishing, in which arrays of long, baited lines are suspended from buoys. Dyson has now had a few years' experience using this technique, and he and his crew feel that they have acquired substantial skill in catching shark this way. Nevertheless, he feels anxious about Edgartown Fisheries' future, largely because of uncertainties about the size of the catch and the price the fish will command.

On this particular rainy day, Dyson has just received a letter from an Italian shark importer who offers to make a one-season contract with

Edgartown Fisheries for 300,000 pounds of shark at $0.55 a pound, delivered in Italy. The shark is to be delivered by October 10, 1969, but Edgartown Fisheries may, under the terms of the proposed contract, divide the 300,000 pounds into partial shipments in any way it desires. Dyson has to decide whether or not to accept the contract within the next few days, and he has assembled the following information to help him with his decision.

Shark production and market

The Atlantic sharking season runs from April 1 through October 31. However, Edgartown Fisheries ordinarily obtains only about 120 days of active fishing, the other 90 days being spent either in port or traveling to and from the fishing grounds. (The travel and port time is somewhat affected by various factors, particularly the weather.) There are two distinct types of season. In a good season, Edgartown Fisheries can catch about 600,000 pounds of shark; in a bad season, about 480,000 pounds. The variation in the size of the catch from day to day is small enough to be ignored, so that Dyson is willing to think of his catch as being a constant 5,000 pounds per fishing day if the season is good or 4,000 pounds per fishing day if the season is bad. Thus it is possible to determine, after the first few weeks of the season have passed, whether the season will be good or bad. Unfortunately, it is impossible to tell ahead of the start of the season what kind of a season it will be.

Shark is caught not only in the Atlantic but also in the Pacific, primarily by the Japanese. The price for Atlantic shark, therefore, depends not only on whether the Atlantic catch is large or small, but also in the size of the catch in the Pacific. Exhibit 1 shows the price per pound which Dyson expects for shark landed in New Bedford (his home port) under each of the four conditions that may occur. For example, if Dyson encounters a large catch (5,000 pounds per day) and

EXHIBIT 1
Anticipated price per pound
of shark landed in New
Bedford

Pacific catch	Atlantic catch	
	Large	Small
Large	$0.30	$0.35
Small	$0.40	$0.45

the Pacific catch turns out small, Dyson expects to receive $0.40 per pound landed in New Bedford.

As with the Atlantic catch, it is impossible to tell before the start of the season whether the Pacific catch will be large or small. However, after the first few weeks of the season have passed, the size of the Pacific catch to date provides a reliable indication of the rest of the season. Dyson's wife can obtain this information and radio it to him.

As he looks forward to the season, the four possible conditions that may occur all seem equally likely to Dyson, so he assigns them the probabilities given in Exhibit 2.

EXHIBIT 2
Probabilities of various
catch sizes

Pacific catch	Atlantic catch	
	Large	Small
Large	1/4	1/4
Small	1/4	1/4

Shipping to Italy

Dyson can store shark already caught in a cold-storage warehouse for as long as one season at essentially no cost. He is therefore not constrained to ship the fish to Italy as soon as they are caught. He can ship fish from New Bedford to Italy at a cost of $0.19 per pound by a standard freighter service offering weekly departures. Any one freighter will take all or any part of the 300,000-pound order.

Alternatively, Dyson could ship the 300,000 pounds by sending his own vessel to Italy. His boat can carry only 150,000 pounds of shark packed in ice, so that two trips of his own boat would be required to deliver the entire shipment of 300,000 pounds. In each round trip to Italy, his boat would lose the equivalent of about 20 fishing days. (Note that the 300,000 pounds must be delivered before the end of the season.) In comparing the cost of operating his boat for fishing with the cost of operating his boat for transporting fish to Italy, Dyson finds that the additional fuel required to transport the fish just about balances the cost of the bait that would have been used in the corresponding time spent fishing. Use of the boat to transport the fish will actually reduce the cost of tackle, since no tackle will be used in a transport operation, whereas tackle is regularly lost while fishing.

Costs and assets

On April 1, 1969, at the start of the season, Dyson will have assets which, besides his boat and some office equipment, include $20,000 cash and 40 miles of ready-to-use tackle. Excluding tackle, his total costs for the entire fishing season (interest payment on boat mortgage, crew's wages, office rent, etc., and fuel and bait) will be about $160,000. Regarding tackle, in his normal fishing operations, Dyson carries 20 miles of tackle on board his boat; the other 20 miles he has are stock he carries for replacement purposes. Loss of tackle turns out to depend directly not on the number of days of fishing, but rather on the number of pounds of shark caught. Based on past experience, Dyson knows that he will have to replace about 1 mile of tackle for every 50,000 pounds of shark caught. The cost of ready-to-use tackle (including hooks, buoys, radar reflectors, etc.) from Dyson's regular supplier is $1,000 per mile. However, 30 miles of Dyson's present tackle were purchased used from the estate of another shark fisherman in New Bedford at a cost of $22,500. This is the only instance that Dyson has ever encountered of used tackle being for sale, and he considers future availability of used tackle to be a virtual impossibility.

PART B

On a clear day in March 1969, following a rainy day and sleepless night spent worrying about an Italian shark importer's contract offer, Lars Dyson calls in a decision consultant by the name of Ayre. Ayre listens to Dyson's problem and decides to value Dyson's possible terminal positions at the season's end relative to an artificial tackle stock base of 0 miles. He obtains from Dyson the information concerning Dyson's preferences shown in Exhibit 3. They analyze Dyson's problem and Dyson goes home to a good night's sleep.

The next day, however, Dyson receives another letter which sends him back to Ayre again. This letter is from a Japanese tackle manufacturer who offers to become his permanent supplier of tackle at $500 per mile. Dyson is satisfied that the Japanese tackle will be of the same quality as the tackle he currently uses, and Ayre and Dyson reason that since they now have a lower replacement cost for tackle, they should revise their adjustment of the monetary end positions for the stock of tackle on hand. When they actually do this, however, they are puzzled by the result. It looks as if all the end positions become less desirable after this adjustment, and yet Ayre and Dyson both feel that the prospects of Edgartown Fisheries have improved as a result of the availability of cheaper tackle. They begin to wonder whether the availability of cheaper tackle, none of which they expect to buy during the 1969 season, should affect the way they adjust their end positions for the stock of tackle left over at the end of the 1969 season.

EXHIBIT 3
Lars Dyson's preferences

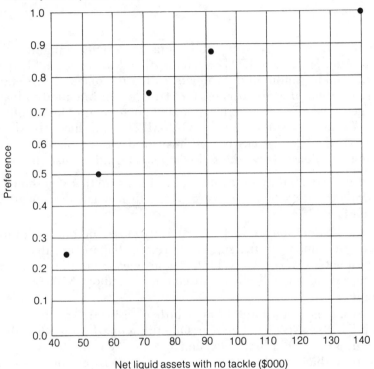

Net liquid assets with no tackle ($000)

Marketronics, Inc.

At 8:00 A.M. on the morning following the events reported in the Hinkle Automotive Products case (case 4–9), Mr. Jerry Hinkle, president of Hinkle Automotive Products, called the office of Mrs. Leslie Ecks, president of Marketronics, Inc. Hinkle had intended to leave a message to the effect that he had decided not to retain Marketronics to perform a market survey for the GAS-MIZER product. Hinkle was surprised when Mrs. Ecks herself answered the telephone. After an exchange of pleasantries, the following conversation ensued:

Ecks: I'm sorry about your decision, but I am glad that you thought of Marketronics when you were trying to manage the uncertainty you faced.

Hinkle: The decision was actually a pretty close one but, as it turned out, we came up with a simple alternative that insures that we'll at least not lose any money. If we'd gone ahead with the survey we'd have stood a small chance of coming out about $100,000 in the hole.

Ecks: Yes, I know. Last night I ran a little decision tree analysis myself on the GAS-MIZER situation. One thing puzzles me, though. My figures showed a higher expected monetary value for buying our survey than for the other two choices. You say you developed another possible action?

Hinkle: It beat the survey by about $7,000. And I don't have any further worries about even a small chance of losing $100,000.

Ecks: But $7,000 isn't much. I still think our service would help you make your basic Pilgrim/Clayton choice. But you seem pretty concerned about losing the $100,000. Is that a lot of money for your firm?

Hinkle: I'll say it is! That's close to our pretax profits this year. If we were to lose that much money in one deal, it'd make our bankers very unhappy.

Ecks: Then it sounds to me like you should have used some form of preference theory in your analysis to account for your attitude toward risk.

Hinkle: Funny you should mention that. Keith White, my marketing vice president, said something along those lines about midnight when we were finishing up our analysis. Neither of us knew much about those ideas and so we just ignored it. I doubt if it would make any difference, though.

Ecks: I'm not so sure. Tell you what I'll do. Let me come over with Mr. Hamilton Evans, one of our new young analysts. He's been bending my ear lately about this risk attitude stuff. He'll spend about an hour with you and we'll see how that might affect your decision.

Hinkle: Well, I don't know. . . .

Ecks: Listen, Jerry, this will be no charge and it won't be a high-pressure selling job either. In fact, I can promise you that I won't try to change your mind by lowering my bid, although I think that if I came in at $40,000 I'd get your business. I just want to be sure that your attitude toward risk is as logical and rational as the rest of your analysis. Anyway, I want to see this preference stuff myself. Perhaps we will both learn something.

Hinkle: Alright, Leslie. You've sold me on rethinking that part of the analysis. Would 10:00 A.M. suit you?

At 10:00 that morning Mrs. Ecks, Mr. Hinkle, and Mr. Keith White listened while Mr. Hamilton Evans made a brief presentation about how preference theory could be used to assess a decision maker's risk attitude. After about 20 minutes, Mr. Evans asked if there were any questions, and the following conversation began.

White: I seem to recall learning this in a business school class, but I'm not sure if it really applies here or not. Are you saying we were wrong to select the alternative with no possible losses if we are risk-averse?

Evans: I don't think I was passing judgment on your decision. Only you or Mr. Hinkle can do that. And judging a decision wrong depends mainly on the criterion you select to evaluate the decision. Mr. Hinkle expressed a fairly strong risk-aversion to Mrs. Ecks in his conversation this morning. What I am proposing is an alternative criterion to monetary expectations that takes his risk aversion into account. As yet, I can't guess how the analysis might turn out.

Hinkle: Where do we go from here, Ham? You've convinced me that we should at least give this preference analysis a whirl.

Evans: OK, let's begin. First, I'd like you to put the GAS-MIZER decision out of your mind for a moment and concentrate simply on the dollar figures I will give you and the probabilities of achieving them.

Hinkel: Is this that certainty equivalent concept you were talking about?

Evans: Yes. First, I'd like you to assess a certainty equivalent for a one-shot lottery in which you have a 50 percent chance of winning $2 million and a 50 percent chance of losing $250,000.

Hinkle: Wow! You don't fool around, do you? Those are big numbers in either direction. In fact, aren't they a bit beyond the bounds of the GAS-MIZER decision?

Evans: Yes, and that is on purpose. I want you to think about the money involved in this hypothetical gamble rather than the specifics of the GAS-MIZER decision. What amount for certain would you exchange this lottery for?

Hinkle: If "exchange" means I have it and what would I sell it for—then I guess I'd take what the market would bear. If "exchange" means how much would I pay for a ticket in your lottery, I don't think I'd pay very much at all. In the sense that I'd be just indifferent to playing your game or taking some amount for certain . . . hmmm. That'd be like flipping a coin, right?

Evans: Right. A fair coin.

Hinkle: Well, I think those two numbers look a lot alike to me on different ends of the scale. Winning $2 million would make me just about as happy as losing $250,000 would make me unhappy. I guess my response would be that I'd be indifferent to entering your lottery or not for no compensation either way. Zero. That's my certainty equivalent for a 50–50 chance at plus $2 million or minus $250,000.

Evans: Do you mean that you'd have a hard time choosing between these alternatives? (Mr. Evans showed Mr. Hinkle his note pad with the diagram shown in Exhibit 1 written on it.)

Hinkle: Well, since you put it that way, it does look awfully funny, doesn't it? Keith and I spent a long time looking at diagrams like

EXHIBIT 1
Diagram on Mr. Evans's note pad

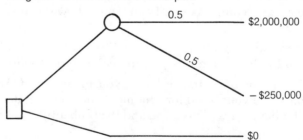

that last night and, then, there was no question about which alternative to choose. But, yes, that's how I feel about it. I wouldn't pay anything to get into a gamble like that and I'd give it away to anyone else who wanted to play.

Evans: Would you pay any amount to get out of that gamble? Would you pay me, for instance, to take it off your hands?

Hinkle: No—if you wanted it, I'd give it to you but I wouldn't pay you to get rid of it. After all, there is a 50 percent chance of winning.

Evans: Good. I think we're getting the hang of this. Now, Mr. Hinkle, what about a 50–50 gamble between winning $2 million or nothing?

The interview with Mr. Hinkle continued for another hour and resulted in certainty equivalents being assessed for several gambles as shown in Exhibit 2.

EXHIBIT 2
Mr. Hinkle's certainty equivalents for 50–50 gambles

50–50 gamble consequences		Hinkle's certainty equivalent	Hinkle's preference value
−$250,000	+$2,000,000	$ 0	0.5
0	+ 2,000,000	+ 350,000	0.75
− 250,000	0	− 170,000	0.25
+ 350,000	+ 2,000,000	+ 700,000	0.875
0	+ 350,000	+ 140,000	0.625
− 170,000	0	− 100,000	0.375
+ 700,000	+ 2,000,000	+ 1,100,000	0.9375

By 11:30 that morning the certainty equivalent assessment process was completed. Hinkle felt that he "hadn't worked so hard in a long time," and all parties agreed that it had been a productive session. After Mr. Evans assured himself that Mr. Hinkle and Mr. White knew how to use the new data in their analysis, Mrs. Ecks thanked Mr. Hinkle and excused herself and Mr. Evans.

On their way to the Marketronics, Inc., staff car parked in the Hinkle Automotive Products visitors' lot, Evans remarked that it was near lunchtime.

Ecks: No—we'll send out for sandwiches if you like. We're going back to the office to pull together a field team for this Hinkle job.

Evans: But—we don't know how their analysis will turn out. Maybe they'll still not hire us.

Ecks: No they will. And I want to be in the office when Hinkle calls in the next 20 minutes or so. Here, look at this (handing Evans her notebook). I finally figured out what their unannounced alternative was. They may still have a few questions and I'll want you there to answer them, but I'll bet you lunch that they'll hire us.

Evans (looking at Ecks's notes): No thanks. That's one gamble I won't take.

case 5–4

The *Stephen Douglas*

William Babcock, a successful Philadelphia real estate entrepreneur, was excited—yet concerned—about a venture in which he had recently become involved.[1] This venture had nothing to do with real estate and was considerably more risky than any of his previous business dealings. On the other hand, the potential rewards were substantial and the enterprise appealed to his sense of adventure. He was considering the feasibility of salvaging cargo from a sunken Victory ship at a 240-foot depth in the Irish Sea.

Victory ships were used in World War II for convoy duty. They were relatively fast for their day (capable of 15 knots). They had a length of approximately 455 feet, beam of 62 feet, loaded draft of 28 feet, and dead-weight tonnage of 10,850. Together with the Liberty ships, they provided a vital link in sustaining the logistics of the Allied effort.

During the war, a number of these ships were torpedoed en route to England from Canada and the United States. As a result, the British government took over several tugboat companies to tow damaged vessels to the nearest friendly port. Frequently, vessels were so badly damaged that they sank while in tow. Of particular interest to Mr. Babcock was the *Stephen Douglas,* one of seven vessels lost in the period of 1942–1944 while under tow by the tug *Christopher J. Lovelock.* To the best of his knowledge, no successful major salvage operations had been conducted on these vessels.

Mr. Babcock had learned about the *Stephen Douglas* during a business trip to the Bahamas in November 1969. He had struck up a friend-

---

[1] This case was made possible by a businessman ("William Babcock") who prefers to remain anonymous and who requested that some case information be disguised.

ship with Andrew Greer, a salesman for a Bahamian land company, and during the week that they jointly investigated a property, they became well acquainted.

The salesman mentioned that he had been in the underwater salvage business for several years prior to moving to the Bahamas. As he described some of his salvage operations, he mentioned the story of the seven vessels which sank in international waters while under tow by the *Christopher J. Lovelock*. One of the seven, the *Stephen Douglas*, had the most attractive cargo. According to Mr. Greer, when it left New York for Liverpool it contained some $3 million worth of planes, tanks, and ammunition. In his opinion, subsequent salt water corrosion and changing technology made these items valueless. In addition, however, it reportedly contained bismuth metal, chrome ore, and blister copper, which if fully salvaged at 1970 market prices would be worth approximately $6 million; these metals would not be affected by corrosion. (Vessels frequently carried such a mixed cargo in wartime to minimize risk to the war effort as a result of the loss of any individual vessel.

Salvage rights to this vessel had been purchased from Lloyd's of London in 1945 by a British firm. Its salvage ships had traveled back and forth across the area where the vessel allegedly sank, but never were able to locate its position. Subsequently, the firm had made no further attempts at salvage operations. Its difficulties in locating the ship, according to Mr. Greer, resulted from the vagueness with which the coordinates of the sinking were registered in the Ministry of Transport. Virtually all of the detailed reports and other records of World War II sinkings had been destroyed in a fire in the Archives a number of years earlier.

Mr. Greer claimed that he knew more about the location of the ship than the salvage company because he had located Captain Wiley who was in command of the tug *Christopher J. Lovelock* at the time of the sinking. Wiley had kept a private diary during World War II which contained, among other things, the precise coordinates of all vessels under his tow at the time of sinking. He had kept the diary for the purposes of writing a book, something he had never done. Nonetheless, he turned the diary into personal profit when Mr. Greer persuaded him to sell it for $5,000.

Using the coordinates provided by Captain Wiley, Mr. Greer had located three of the ships—including one at the location where the *Stephen Douglas* was alleged to have sunk—and had salvaged a safe from one of them. Because of the high cost involved in conducting a salvage operation at 240 feet in an area known for its severe currents, Mr. Greer had been unable to continue. Eager to begin again, he asked whether Mr. Babcock wanted to join him by backing a salvage venture. A detailed background check of Mr. Greer revealed that while he had mixed financial success in past ventures, he was considered to be of unquestioned integrity. Subsequently, Mr. Babcock paid him $6,000 to form a partnership, the terms of which gave Mr. Babcock 90 percent of the first $1 million dollars of net revenue, 85 percent of the second $1 million, 80 percent of the third $1 million, 75 percent of the fourth $1 million, and 50 percent of everything else. Net revenue was to be adjusted for legal expenses but not for the salvage expenses, which were to be borne by Mr. Babcock.

At this point, Mr. Babcock was concerned about how to proceed, since there was substantial uncertainty associated with many aspects of the proposition. First, he was not sure that the ship had in fact left New York with the indicated cargo of metals. In a book written in the mid-1950s describing the history of the British tug and steamship companies, the *Christopher J. Lovelock* was written up in some detail. Reference was made to the $3 million worth of planes, ammunition, and tanks on the *Stephen Douglas,* but no mention was made of the ore. Mr. Babcock felt this was an oversight due to incomplete research on the part of the author.

Exact copies of the manifests of the seven Victory ships were available from the British Ministry of Transport; however, Mr. Babcock was reluctant to contact the ministry since this might draw renewed attention from other salvage firms and particularly the firm that owned salvage rights to the *Stephen Douglas.* The query might also raise some uncomfortable questions from the Ministry of Transport, which might claim he was unlawfully withholding vital information from the Crown (i.e., the coordinates in the diary). This could lead to protracted legal proceedings, which he wished to avoid at this early stage of his venture. Weighing all these factors, he decided to proceed without seeing the manifest. He believed that there was an 80–20 probability that the vessel had left New York with the ore and metal aboard and that the cargo on the vessel in 1943 had either contained the 6 million worth of ore and metal or none at all.

He decided his first action should be to hire a boat with divers to relocate the sunken vessel and to put the divers on the deck. They would be instructed to recover the wheel or some other vital element of the boat to ensure positive identification. In early December, he made a quick half-day trip out to sea aboard a fishing vessel, but the sea had been so rough that the fathometer of the fishing vessel was unable to work with sufficient precision to spot any unusual formation on the bottom. Mr. Babcock was encouraged by an offhand remark during the trip by the owner of the fishing vessel who did not know the purpose of the trip. The owner had mentioned that some large object seemed to be submerged nearby, as his deep-water fishing nets had repeatedly snagged in this vicinity.

Weighing the evidence, Mr. Babcock assessed a 95 percent chance of being able to locate a sunken vessel near the coordinates given in the diary. This discovery probability referred to finding a Victory ship near these coordinates. Given discovery, the odds of it being the *Stephen Douglas* were in his opinion roughly 0.75 in favor and 0.25 against. He did not anticipate that the cargo from any ship other than the *Stephen Douglas* would be worth salvaging. Further, he felt the probability of two Victory ships being sunk in this area was infinitesimal.

The cost of the search designed to locate and identify the ship could vary from $1,000 to $5,000 because of uncertainty about the time required to locate the ship and the high daily cost of the search vessel and divers. If it was not on the precise coordinates, a grid search pattern would be used to cover the general area. A fathometer and grappling irons would be employed to locate the ship; once an object was snagged by the irons, a diver would be sent down the line to investigate. The minimum cost of the search would be $1,000, but Mr. Babcock felt that there was a 25 percent chance of it costing $1,500 or less, a 50 percent chance of it costing $2,000 or less, a 75 percent chance of it costing $3,000 or less, and absolute certainty of the cost being $5,000 or less. Thus, the cost of conducting a thorough search and not finding a vessel would be $5,000.

Because of the weather conditions, even this initial search could not commence until April. If he located the *Stephen Douglas,* he then would retain a larger team of divers to survey the ship. The survey would reveal whether the ship contained metal, whether the cargo was intact, and how much of the cargo could be salvaged. It would also allow an estimate of the salvage cost.

This survey would cost between $8,000 and $16,000, with amounts in between judged to be equally likely. The large expense was due to the need for a series of complicated dives. At 240 feet a diver can work on the bottom for only ten minutes without going through a complex decompression sequence. Further, divers would have to breathe a special mixture of oxygen and helium. Because the tidal currents were so strong, the dives could take place only twice a day during periods of one-hour duration. It was also very difficult to place explosives on the deck of the ship to open it for examination to determine the position of the cargo, assessment of the difficulty of getting the cargo out, its physical condition, etc. Finally, this work would be further hampered by the 15-foot visibility at this depth.

Of particular concern was whether the cargo was intact. The tides and the currents in this particular location were among the swiftest and most complex in the world and even small cracks in the vessel could have resulted in the contents being scattered over the bottom of the ocean in the course of 27 years. Mr. Babcock thought there was about a 15 percent chance, given that the ship originally contained metal, that none would appear to be salvageable.

Mr. Babcock next turned his attention to forecasting the value of the cargo that would actually be salvaged if the *Stephen Douglas* were located and the survey reported that there was ore and metal on board that appeared to be salvageable. He recognized that divers were notoriously optimistic and that in this situation, particularly serious problems could be encountered in any salvage attempt. Babcock therefore indicated that in his judgment there was a 20 percent chance that even if the divers reported salvageable ore and metal from the survey, none would be recoverable during the attempted salvage. Taking into account his uncertainty about the value of the original cargo as well as the uncertainty of what percentage would be recoverable, Babcock assessed the distribution shown as Exhibit 1. More specifically, this exhibit shows his distribution for the value of the cargo recovered given that at least some of the cargo is salvaged.

In Babcock's opinion, conducting the actual salvaging operation would be relatively expensive. He would have to commit in advance approximately $125,000 for the necessary diving and dredging

EXHIBIT 1
Cumulative probability distribution for the amount of cargo recovered given that some is salvaged from the *Stephen Douglas*

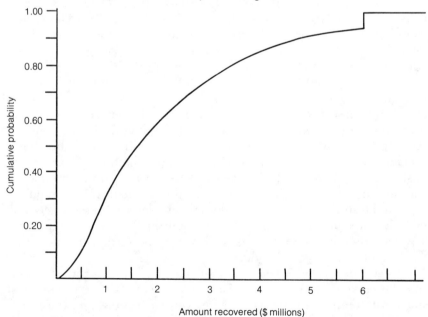

Amount recovered ($ millions)

equipment and about $50,000 in salaries during a two-month period to conduct the operation. He felt that he could raise $75,000 of the $125,000 for equipment from outside leasing companies who would be willing to take the equipment as security, and that he would be able to dispose of the equipment at the end of the operation for about $75,000.

If he were able to raise the cargo, Mr. Babcock expected a legal battle from the company that owned salvage rights to the ship. Lawyers informed him that a salvager had strong claims on salvaged material, even if he did not own the salvage rights, but he could be successfully sued for as much as 10 percent of the salvage revenue minus expenses. Mr. Babcock felt that there was a 15 percent probability the lawsuit would be thrown out entirely since the owners of the salvage rights had, in effect, abandoned search for the vessel. If he did have to pay a percentage, he indicated his uncertainty could be described by a symmetrical probability distribution with median 5 percent and with lower and upper quartiles at 4 percent and 6 percent, respectively. He stated, however, that, "this set of estimates is really off the top of my head." He further noted that the tax consequences of the operation would be negligible, since he and his partner could set up a Bahamian Corporation to handle the deal.

Because of the risk involved in the salvage operation he considered the possibility, if he relocated the ship, of selling its coordinates to the company that owned the salvage rights or to another salvage company. Being in possession of a part of the ship that clearly established its identity, such as its wheel, would make his claim to knowledge credible to a potential buyer. It was his opinion that he might get as much as $50,000 for the coordinates or as little as $5,000, with the values in between being equally likely. Without evidence of credibility, he thought he could get very little for the information.

Another way of reducing the risk of a salvage operation was to enter into an agreement with a large salvage company. He wondered whether, given credible evidence of the ship's location, a salvage company would accept the job on a contingency basis, charging nothing if no cargo was salvaged and taking a percentage if cargo was salvaged. He had no idea what percentage a firm would want, but he suspected that a larger firm could recover a greater percentage of the cargo than he could with his own efforts. Such a firm would probably want to conduct its own survey of the wreck, rather than rely on others' information.

In examining the proposition in terms of his personal financial position, Mr. Babcock felt some concern about the amount of financial risk to which he was exposing himself. He thought preference theory might be useful, but what he had learned about the subject at an executive program in a nearby university was a bit rusty. After a 30-minute discussion with the case writers, during which Mr. Babcock learned a great deal more about preference theory, the data labeled "first assessments" in Exhibit 2 were collected. Mr. Babcock felt uncomfortable about the results, and when some of the implications of his initial assessments were pointed out, he apologetically asked to start over again. The discussion continued for another half hour and resulted in the data listed under "second assessments" in Exhibit 2.

EXHIBIT 2
William Babcock's two preference curves

First assessments: certainty equivalents for 50–50 gambles with the following incremental cash flows:

Gamble consequences		Certainty equivalent
+$6,000,000	−$ 200,000	$ 500,000
+ 6,000,000	+ 500,000	3,500,000
+ 500,000	− 200,000	− 75,000
+ 500,000	− 75,000	100,000
+ 6,000,000	+ 3,500,000	5,000,000

Second assessments: certainty equivalents for 50–50 gambles with the following incremental cash flows:

Gamble consequences		Certainty equivalent
+$6,000,000	−$ 200,000	$ 300,000
+ 6,000,000	+ 300,000	1,400,000
+ 300,000	− 200,000	− 100,000
+ 300,000	− 100,000	0
+ 6,000,000	1,400,000	2,400,000
− 100,000	− 200,000	− 160,000

Some of the more interesting comments made by Mr. Babcock during the conversation were: "Real estate may sound like a high-risk business, but it really isn't. By using a good lawyer, selecting appropriate deals, using personal contacts, and carefully studying situations, I am able to eliminate most of the uncertainty. I have only been in on a losing proposition once in the last seven years. That was when I went into a partnership with a recent graduate of the Harvard Business School. I lost $5,000 and he lost $30,000. I won't make that type of mistake again.

"The frustration of this deal is that I don't know the subject well. If I had been in the salvage business as long as I have been in real estate, I would be more comfortable with my ability to size up the situation. . . .

"I don't want to be known as someone who made it and then blew it. I know too many of that type. On the other hand, it would be a real feather in my cap if I could pull this one off."

chapter

6

Simulation

You have all undoubtedly witnessed a simulated environment at some time in your experience. Much of your learning—from driver education classes at the wheel of a driving simulator, to military exercises using blank ammunition, to discussing cases in the classroom—has involved experiencing a simulated environment. This use of a close-to-real environment provided you with a chance to interact with a situation at very low risk. You cannot crumple the fender of the driving simulator; blanks involve considerably less hazard than live ammunition; and your recommendation to raise bonuses and increase advertising, no matter how inappropriate, won't push the ABC Corp. into bankruptcy.

Simulation, in the analysis of business decisions, serves exactly the same purpose: It allows low-risk experimentation, testing a variety of policies on a reasonable facsimile of the real world. Of course, any mathematical model is a simulation of some real-world phenomena. The main distinction that sets the more general approach of simulation apart from other mathematical approaches to problem solving is that analysis of a simulation model is based on experimentation rather than on a set of fixed computations. Simulation models also differ from other mathematical models by being more expensive to build and analyze. In the face of this disadvantage, it is surprising that simulation is one of the most widely used approaches to analyzing business problems. Reasons for the popularity of simulation include the fact that simulation models usually can be made to conform much more closely to reality than other mathematical models, which often require unrealistic or unappealing abstractions to force reality into an analyzable format. Put differently, simulation can produce useful models of more complex situations than can alternative modeling approaches.

The characteristics of any simulation model are determined by the uses to which it will be put. In other words, if the purpose of a simulation model is to perform a variety of sensitivity analyses in response to a number of "what if" questions, these questions will determine in part the scope and orientation of the model. It is therefore unlikely that any two simulation models, even of the same system, will closely resemble each other unless they are built for similar purposes. Indeed, this is often cited as a drawback of the simulation approach to modeling: Since simulation models are usually highly specific to a certain problem, they have limited transferability to other situations. On the other hand, the custom-made approach that simulation models require makes them potentially the most relevant mathematical decision-making tools.

Simulation is particularly useful in evaluating decision problems that include several interacting uncertain events. Rather than handling uncertainty by calculating expected values (as in a decision analysis problem), however, simulation involves collecting a random sample of values, computing the implications of each sample value, and reporting a frequency distribution of the sampled implications. This procedure provides a more meaningful result than an expected value analysis, especially since the interactions of two or more uncertain quantities may result in irregular distributions that could not be communicated well by a single value.

Many, if not most, simulations involve tracing a sequence of recurring events through time and recording the responses of the system to each occurrence. A very common problem of this sort involves waiting-line situations when new arrivals to the system occur at irregular intervals and the number of service channels is relatively fixed. Examples of both of these kinds of simulation problems as well as the mechanics of the sampling procedure are in the following section.

A DECISION PROBLEM EXAMPLE

We will now consider the problem facing the Peach Company: whether or not to raise the level of advertising by $30,000 in the next year on one line of consumer products. Betty Thomlinson, sales director for the Peach Company, thought that a continuation of present advertising policies would result in sales of between 75,000 and 120,000 units, with the cumulative likelihood of any intermediate outcome distributed as shown in Figure 6–1. Thomlinson, a vigorous proponent of the additional advertising expense, felt that the increase in advertising without any change in price would result in an increase in sales. She was unsure of the exact amount that sales might rise but estimated that the increase would be between 10 and 40 percent above the sales level that would have been experienced otherwise. Her assessment of this cumulative probability distribution is shown in Figure 6–2. Competition in this product's market was keen, however. Ms. Thomlinson therefore tempered this estimate by adding that if their

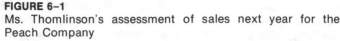

FIGURE 6–1
Ms. Thomlinson's assessment of sales next year for the Peach Company

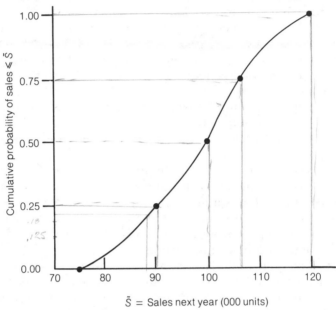

$\tilde{S}$ = Sales next year (000 units)

major competitor responded by increasing its own advertising, and there was about one chance in four that such a response would be forthcoming in the next year, the sales increases for Peach's product would be only about half of her earlier assessment. This is schematically displayed by the lower horizontal axis on Figure 6–2.

Production limitations at Peach's factory were that 120,000 units could be produced by workers on straight time and up to 150,000 units could be made if overtime was used. Contribution per unit was $3.00 for production on straight time but dropped to $2.50 per unit for units produced by workers on overtime. Additionally, overhead costs associated with the product line would increase by about $9,000 per year if overtime were used.

Figure 6–3 is a decision diagram for the problem facing the Peach Company. Each event fork represents a major uncertainty. Not all possible outcomes are shown on these event forks because the resulting confusion would make the diagram useless. Instead, the extreme outcomes are shown on the edges, and the continuous nature of the distribution is denoted by the arc concentric to the event node.

For problems like this it is, of course, possible to calculate the ex-

FIGURE 6–2
Ms. Thomlinson's assessment of sales increases resulting from $50,000 additional advertising expense

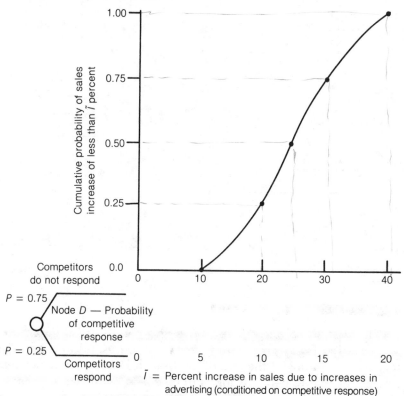

pected value of each set by approximating each probability distribution for each event with five representative outcomes as we did in Appendix 4–A. As the number of continuous probability distributions increases, however, this can represent a rather large computational effort. If there were four continuous distributions of uncertain quantities to be approximated, for instance, each act would result in 625 end points. An alternative way to handle problems of this sort is to use simulation to sample the end points. In much the same way that public opinion surveys can predict public attitudes from the interviews of a small sample of people, by random sampling of a few end points, we can calculate a special probability distribution called a *risk profile* that measures the outcomes and their likelihood in terms relevant to the decision maker.

FIGURE 6 –3
Decision diagram of Peach Company's Problem

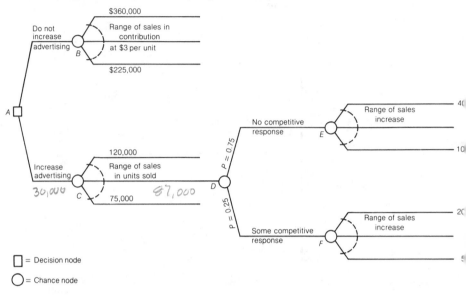

☐ = Decision node

◯ = Chance node

Random sampling of end points

Rather than sample end points directly, we will use a method that selects a value from each event fork. It may be useful to think of an interviewer standing at the end of the branch labeled "range of sales increase" in Figure 6–3. His job is to calculate enough end points so that he can approximate the risk profile associated with the act: increase advertising. He has a road map of the territory before him represented by the event forks of the decision diagram. What we must do is to tell him how to proceed along this road map to an end point. Once at an end point, he can calculate the annual contribution margins and return to the starting point. This process we will call making a trial sample. He will continue this process until he has performed enough trials to allow him to make an accurate approximation of the risk profile.

How should the interviewer proceed down the diagram on each trial? His goal should be to calculate the value of a "typical" end point. Suppose he comes to an event fork with only two branches and a probability of 0.50 on each branch. We can tell him to flip a fair coin, and if it comes up heads go along one branch and tails go along the other. During his many trials, we would expect him to go along each branch on about 50 percent of the trials following the coin-flipping rule. This is an accurate reflection of the likelihood of encountering each branch when the actual event occurs, and therefore using this rule should result in "typical" end points. If the probabilities on the two branches were 0.33 and 0.67, we would want to use a different rule. We could tell the interviewer to roll a fair die, and if this roll resulted in 1 or 2 he should go down the branch with the 0.33 probability, otherwise go down the branch with the 0.67 probability. In many trials, he would expect about one third of his sample end points to be after the one branch on the diagram and two thirds to be after the other branch on the diagram.

The process of selecting outcomes from the event forks for a trial calculation can be generalized for events with many outcomes. To do this we need what is known as a *random number generator* to replace the fair coin and fair die in the examples above. A random number generator must do the following:

1. Provide an equal probability of generating any number in its range on each given trial.
2. Be independent from trial to trial. In other words, the number generated on this trial has the same probability of occurring on the next trial as all the other numbers.

A fair coin is a random number generator for two numbers. A die is a random generator for six numbers. Lists of random numbers have been generated to avoid having to think up combinations of coin tosses and dice rolls. The appendix to this chapter is such a list. If you want a random number between 00 and 99, you merely read a two-digit number from somewhere in this table. As an example, if you took the 55th and 56th columns and the 7th row, the random number would be 50. You can now proceed from this point in the table to read a list of two-digit random numbers by moving in some systematic manner. If you read down the columns, the next five numbers are 80, 12, 22, 27, and 30. You can start anywhere and move in any systematic manner from that point, as long as you do not cycle back on the same sequence, and be assured that this list of numbers you generate will be random.

Now that we have a process for creating a random number generator, we can replace the coins and dice in the instructions we give the interviewer.

Now if he comes to an an event fork with two branches and probabilities of 0.68 and 0.32, we could give him the following rule:

1. Draw a two-digit random number from the random number table.
2. If the number is between 01 and 32 inclusive, go along the branch with the 0.32 probability.
3. If the number is between 33 and 100 (100 is represented by 00), go along the branch with the 0.68 probability.

If the random number generator is working correctly, there is one chance in 100 of drawing any number between 00 and 99. If the interviewer follows this rule, we would expect him to get a number between 01 and 32 about 32 percent of the time, and we have achieved a good sampling procedure.

Most event forks have more than two outcomes; in fact, most of the events in our sample problem have many outcomes. Since it is easy to generate two-digit random numbers, we will follow a procedure of using 100 typical outcomes to represent an event with many outcomes.[1] We can divide the vertical axis of the cumulative probability graph into 100 equal divisions and read over to the cumulative graph and down to the horizontal axis to get the 100 typical values for these outcomes. Now when the interviewer is making a trial and comes to this event fork, we can give him the following sampling rule:

1. Draw a two-digit random number.
2. Count the list of typical outcomes for the event starting with the smallest until your count equals the random number.
3. The outcome where you stopped is the value for this trial.

The probability of any random number between 01 and 00 is 1/100. This rule should select, in many trials, each outcome about 1 percent of the time, and this accurately reflects the 1/100 chance for each of the 100 typical outcomes actually occurring.

A typical end point

We will now follow this procedure for a typical trial through the Peach Company decision diagram in Figure 6–3. Ms. Betty Thomlinson's forecasts shown in Figures 6–1 and 6–2 will be used as the basis for selecting outcomes leading to a typical end point. First, a random number was selected to determine the outcome for sales next year; this number was 20. We could have divided the market size probability distribution into its 100 representative values and counted up to the 20th value. Instead, the same value can be obtained by going directly to the cumulative graph for the market size probability in Figure 6–1 and reading the 0.205 fractile. This value of 87,000 units is the same as would be obtained by following the counting procedure; it represents the number of units of product that would be sold in the coming year without any advertising increase. Thus, for the act: do not increase advertising (node B on Figure 6–3), 87,000 units represents a sample end point, and the contribution of this point, $261,000, may be calculated directly by multiplying by $3.00 per unit. The value of 87,000

---

[1] For a description of this procedure, see Appendix 4–A.

units is also a sample from the distribution that follows the act: increase advertising (node C on Figure 6–3), but in this case it is not an end point. We must include the effects of nodes D and E or nodes D and F before we reach an end point comparable to the one at node B. We now draw a second random number to determine competitive response. According to Ms. Thomlinson, there is a 75 percent chance that there will be no response during the coming year. This outcome can be represented by the digits 01–75, whereas the outcome: some competitive response, is represented by the digits 76–00. The second random number generated is 98; since it falls in the range 76–00, this indicates that our third random number will sample from the distribution represented by node F on Figure 6–3. The third random number generated was 10, and this caused a selection of a 7.4 percent increase in sales due to the increase in advertising. Total sales for this sample end point, then, are 87,000 × 1.074, or about 93,400. At $3.00 per unit, this translates into a total contribution of about $280,200. However, $30,000 must be subtracted from this total contribution to account for the cost of increased advertising to arrive at an end point valuation comparable to that sampled earlier from node B.

This process is also represented by the flowchart in Figure 6–4. It has generated one sample end point for each act. When compared, these sample points disclose that, for the conditions of this trial, more contribution was generated by not increasing advertising. Of course, it is necessary to calculate more typical end points before we can approximate the risk profile for each act. Table 6–1 shows the calculation of 20 pairs of typical end points.

The question of how many end points should be sampled is a difficult one to answer. It is clear that the larger the sample size, the better the approximations will be. The major constraint on the sample size is an economic one, and when the cost of making a single calculation is large, it is important to determine the sample size carefully. Techniques for calculating the sample size accurately are beyond the scope of this book. However, in most cases where the sampling and calculation are being done in a computer model, the cost of a single trial is small, and therefore less care is needed in determining the sample size. A rule of thumb in this situation is to take anywhere from 50 to 1,000 trials in the sample.

Figure 6–5 shows the risk profile resulting from the 20 trials in Table 6–1. These risk profiles are simply cumulative distributions of the results of the end-point sampling process. They were constructed by assuming that each sampled point would occur with an equal probability, thus implying a discrete probability distribution for each act. The risk profile cumulative distributions were then constructed from these discrete distributions.

FIGURE 6–4

Flowchart for Peach Company's simulation

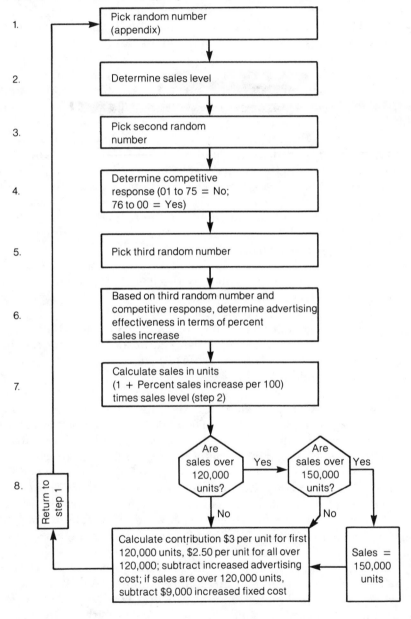

TABLE 6–1
Twenty-trial simulation of the Peach Company's advertising decision

(1) Trial	(2) First random number	(3) Sales level (000)	(4) Contribution ($000)	(5) Second random number	(6) Competitive response (node D)	(7) Third random number	(8) Sales increase (percent)	(9) Total units sold (000)	(10) Contribution ($000)	(11) Added expense ($000)	(12) Net contribution ($000)
1	20	87.0	261.0	98	Yes	10	7.4	93.4	280.2	30	250.2
2	01	75.3	225.9	49	No	16	17.5	88.5	265.5	30	235.5
3	64	101.4	304.2	55	No	53	25.4	127.2	378.0	39	339.0
4	21	87.2	261.6	23	No	21	19.0	103.8	311.3	30	281.3
5	80	107.0	321.0	62	No	31	21.2	129.7	384.3	39	345.3
6	50	100.0	300.0	82	Yes	90	18.2	118.2	354.6	30	324.6
7	38	96.0	288.0	90	Yes	84	16.3	111.6	334.9	30	304.9
8	82	107.3	321.9	54	No	63	27.4	136.7	401.8	39	362.8
9	72	104.5	313.5	45	No	46	24.1	129.7	384.3	39	345.3
10	36	95.0	285.0	80	Yes	35	11.2	105.6	316.9	30	286.9
11	94	114.0	342.0	11	No	51	25.2	142.7	416.8	39	377.8
12	77	106.0	318.0	51	No	37	22.3	129.6	384.0	39	345.0
13	99	120.0	360.0	69	No	01	10.0	132.0	390.0	39	351.0
14	68	103.7	311.1	64	No	52	25.4	130.0	385.0	39	346.0
15	94	114.0	342.0	55	No	97	38.0	157.3	435.0*	39	396.0
16	85	109.0	327.0	30	No	47	24.3	135.5	398.7	39	359.7
17	49	99.8	299.4	16	No	67	28.3	128.0	380.0	39	341.0
18	25	90.0	270.0	51	No	09	14.7	103.2	309.6	30	279.6
19	63	102.5	307.5	76	Yes	10	7.4	110.1	330.2	30	300.2
20	44	98.5	295.5	87	Yes	29	10.7	109.0	327.0	30	297.0
			Expected value = 302.7								Expected value = 328.5

* Based on maximum production of 150,000 units.

FIGURE 6–5
Risk profiles for the Peach Company's two alternatives

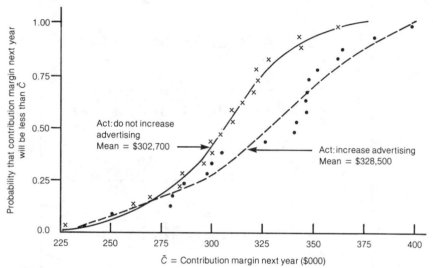

$\tilde{C}$ = Contribution margin next year ($000)

The means of these risk profiles are $328,500 for the act: increase advertising, and $302,700 for the act: do not increase advertising. If the Peach Company is willing to play the averages, they can use the mean of the risk profile as their certainty equivalent for each alternative, and

FIGURE 6–6
Differential contribution margins for act: Do not increase advertising, subtracted from act: Increase advertising

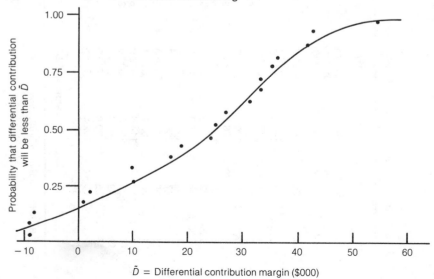

$\tilde{D}$ = Differential contribution margin ($000)

then they would decide to accept Ms. Thomlinson's proposal to increase advertising.

Because this is a major commitment of resources, however, the company may be unwilling to play the averages. If this is the case, we cannot say for sure which alternative is best. However, the information needed by the company to make the comparison is contained in that risk profiles of Figure 6–5. For example, a manager might notice that, while the act: increase advertising, produces greater contribution margin over most of its range, on 3 trials of the 20 the act: do not increase advertising, generated greater contribution. This situation can be clarified by calculating the difference between each alternative's contribution margin on every trial of the simulation. The results of these calculations can then be used to approximate a probability distribution for the differential contribution between the alternatives. Such a probability distribution is shown in Figure 6–6. From this you can still determine the probability of one alternative being better than the other. This probability is shown at the zero differential cash flow on the cumulative curve, and from Figure 6–6 you can see that it is about 15 percent. However, in addition, this distribution presents information more clearly than Figure 6–5 about how much better or worse one alternative is than the other.

A WAITING-LINE EXAMPLE

A slightly different kind of problem that is frequently approached using simulation involves analysis of waiting lines. The Felton Tool and Die Company has such a situation in the operation of its central stockroom. The Felton Company is a medium-sized job shop that produces machined parts to customer orders. The firm employs about 100 metal working machine operators who are paid $10 per hour, including fringe benefits. When a new order arrives at the shop, it is assigned to one or more of the machine operators. Their first action is usually to go to the stockroom to get the bar stock, metal plate, and other materials necessary to fabricate the order. Machinists also visit the stockroom to get special tools for their job or to replace broken drill bits, and so forth.

The stockroom is staffed by two workers who are paid $6 per hour. These workers respond to requests by machinists and maintain stockroom inventory records.

The problem facing the Felton Company is that long lines of machinists waiting for service sometimes form outside the stockroom. On the average, a machinist arrives at the stockroom every 15 minutes, although there can be as much as 30 minutes between these arrivals, and occasionally several machinists arrive at once. Figure 6–7 is a

FIGURE 6-7

Cumulative frequency distribution of machinist interarrival interval at stockroom of the Felton Company

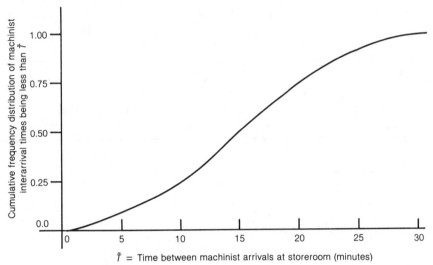

$\bar{T}$ = Time between machinist arrivals at storeroom (minutes)

cumulative frequency distribution of the time between machinist arrivals at the stockroom.

The amount of time required for the stockroom workers to service the machinists also varies randomly between 5 minutes for a small request to about 45 minutes for requests that involve cutting bar stock or moving a lot of heavy steel. The average time to service one of these requests is 30 minutes. Figure 6–8 is a cumulative frequency distribution of the amount of time required to service a machinist's request.

An expected value analysis of the Felton Tool and Die Company data would indicate that, on the average, there should be no waiting line. This is because the average service time (30 minutes) divided by the number of service channels (two stockroom workers) is just equal to the average time between machinist arrivals (15 minutes). Clearly, this simple expected value model does not accurately reflect the real-world observation of long waiting lines. Since the waiting line is the focus of concern in this situation, it is important that a model reflect that aspect of the problem. Hence, the expected value analysis is not very useful here. What is probably needed is a technique that takes the entire frequency distributions of Figures 6–7 and 6–8 into account. One such technique is simulation.

Approaching the Felton Company problem, as with most problems that simulate moving forward in time, the analyst is faced with an

FIGURE 6–8
Cumulative frequency distribution of stockroom servicing times at the Felton
Company

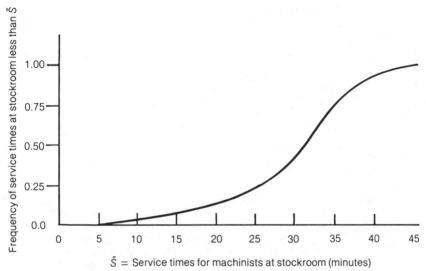

$\tilde{S}$ = Service times for machinists at stockroom (minutes)

arbitrary choice as to how to deal with time. Should she track each
machinist arrival and servicing time, or should she look at each unit of
time (say, each minute) and evaluate the probability of an arrival or
service completion during that interval? The first approach is called an
event-based simulation and will result in moving forward in uneven
increments of time, skipping over periods when "nothing new is happening." The second approach is called *time-slicing* and involves
moving the simulation through time in equal increments. In the Felton
Company example, the problem and the data appear structured in
such a way as to favor an event-based simulation, although it would be
possible to transform these data to perform a simulation based on
time-slicing. As an exercise, you should examine the frequency distributions of Figures 6–7 and 6–8 and imagine what the data would
look like if structured for a time-slicing simulation. Although it is difficult to generalize in situations such as this, time-slicing is most frequently used to simulate continuous activities, and event-based simulation is usually used where significant discontinuities exist. For example, a game of American football, with its set plays and time-outs, is
most suited to an event-based simulation, whereas European football
(soccer) with its more or less continuous action, lends itself to time-
slicing.

Figure 6–9 is a flowchart for an event-based simulation of the Felton

FIGURE 6 –9
Flowchart for the Felton Company's simulation

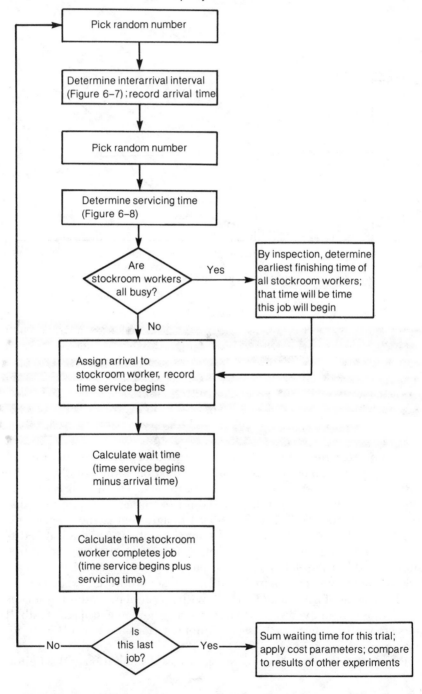

Company's stockroom waiting line. By following the procedure outlined on this chart, the analyst will simulate the arrival of one
machinist and his or her service by the stockroom workers.

Another somewhat arbitrary decision the analyst must make is the
time horizon for each trial. In this situation, a "natural" time horizon is,
perhaps, one shift. At the Felton Company a shift is eight hours long,
from 8:00 A.M. to 4:00 P.M. Table 6–2 shows one eight-hour simulation
trial based on the frequency distributions of Figures 6–7 and 6–8. To
get a frequency distribution of machinist waiting times analogous, to

TABLE 6 –2
One-day trial simulation of the Felton Company's stockroom—two stockroom workers

First random number	Arrival interval	Arrival time	Second random number	Service time	Stockroom worker 1		Stockroom worker 2		Wait time
					Start	Finish	Start	Finish	
38	13	8:13	83	37	8:13	8:50			0
37	13	8:26	27	27			8:26	8:53	0
97	27	8:53	51	31	8:53	9:24			0
93	25	9:18	13	20			9:18	9:38	0
35	12	9:30	64	33	9:30	10:03			0
96	26	9:56	51	31			9:56	10:27	0
22	9	10:05	58	32	10:05	10:37			0
32	11	10:16	28	27			10:27	10:54	11
72	20	10:36	25	26	10:37	11:02			1
30	11	10:47	84	37			10:54	11:31	7
09	6	10:53	13	20	11:02	11:22			9
26	10	11:03	56	32	11:22	11:54			19
94	25	11:28	88	38			11:31	12:06	3
02	1	11:29	19	24	11:54	12:18			25
09	6	11:35	19	24			12:06	12:30	31
20	9	11:43	74	35	12:18	12:53			35
87	23	12:08	93	40			12:30	1:10	22
17	8	12:16	72	35	12:53	1:28			37
25	10	12:26	94	41			1:10	1:51	44
33	12	12:38	34	29	1:28	1:57			50
35	12	12:50	46	30			1:51	2:21	51
58	16	1:06	50	31	1:57	2:28			51
45	14	1:20	54	32			2:21	2:54	61
98	27	1:47	70	34	2:28	3:02			41
62	17	2:04	72	35			2:54	3:29	50
13	7	2:11	03	7	3:02	3:09			51
87	24	2:38	07	13	3:09	3:22			31
33	12	2:50	44	30	3:22	3:52			32
36	13	3:03	43	30			3:29	3:59	26
78	21	3:24	81	37	3:52	4:29			28
31	11	3:35	59	32			3:59	4:31	24
39	13	3:48	37	29	4:29	4:58			41
17	8	3:56	06	12			4:31	4:43	35

Total wait time = 816 minutes
= 13.6 hours

the Peach Company's risk profile shown in Figure 6–5, many such trials could be run and their results tabulated as a risk profile.

We notice from Table 6–2 that this model, unlike the expected value analysis, reflects the observation that machinists often have to wait in line.

At this point, when the analyst is satisfied that the model adequately represents the real-world phenomena of interest, he or she is ready to perform some experiments. These experiments should be designed to answer some of the "what if" questions. For example, what if a third

TABLE 6–3
One-day trial simulation of the Felton Company's stockroom—three stockroom workers

Arrival time	Service time	Stockroom worker 1		Stockroom worker 2		Stockroom worker 3		Wait time
		Start	Finish	Start	Finish	Start	Finish	
8:13	37	8:13	8:50					0
8:26	27			8:26	8:53			0
8:53	31	8:53	9:24					0
9:18	20			9:18	9:38			0
9:30	33	9:30	10:03					0
9:56	31			9:56	10:27			0
10:05	32	10:05	10:37					0
10:16	27					10:16	10:43	0
10:36	26			10:36	11:02			0
10:47	37	10:47	11:24					0
10:53	20					10:53	11:13	0
11:03	32			11:03	11:35			0
11:28	38	11:28	12:06					0
11:29	24					11:29	11:53	0
11:35	24			11:35	11:59			0
11:43	35					11:53	12:28	10
12:08	40			12:08	12:48			0
12:16	35	12:16	12:51					0
12:26	41					12:28	1:09	2
12:38	29			12:48	1:17			10
12:50	30	12:51	1:21					1
1:06	31					1:09	1:40	3
1:20	32			1:20	1:52			0
1:47	34	1:47	2:21					0
2:04	35			2:04	2:39			0
2:11	7					2:11	2:18	0
2:38	13	2:38	2:51					0
2:50	30			2:50	3:20			0
3:03	30	3:03	3:33					0
3:24	37			3:24	4:01			0
3:35	32	3:35	4:07					0
3:48	29					3:48	4:17	0
3:56	12			4:01	4:13			5
						Total wait time =		31 minute
								= 0.52 hour

stockroom employee were hired? What would the result on the machinist's waiting time be? Or alternatively, suppose Benny, the lead stockroom worker, were sick for a week and no replacement were available? Table 6–3 shows an eight-hour trial with three stockroom workers. To be comparable with the trial using two workers (see Table 6–2), the identical sequence of arrival intervals and service times was used. Comparing the results of these experiments shows that the per-shift savings in mechanic waiting time valued at $10.00 per hour ($130.90) far outweighs the cost of the additional stockroom employee ($48.00).

The issue of evaluating machinist waiting time in this situation, however, is not necessarily this simple. If a reduction in waiting time were to reduce the amount of overtime in the shop, the amount of savings would be understated by using the straight-time rate of $10.00. If the shop is at capacity, reducing mechanic waiting time could allow Felton Tool and Die to accept additional jobs. Where this is the case, it may make sense to evaluate the cost of the stockroom worker against the additional contribution margin that could be earned. If the shop is not at capacity, the analyst must consider the probable behavior of the machinists. Will the time saved waiting in the stockroom line translate into increased productive time? In short, evaluating waiting time savings at the straight-time machinist wage rate gives only a crude measure of the actual benefits that might come from adding a third stockroom worker.

COMPUTERS AND SIMULATION

The development of simulation as an analytic technique has closely paralleled the development of the electronic computer. This is because the tedious nature of simulation (when carried out with pencil and paper) severely limits the scope of the problem that can be addressed. This also hampers manual calculation of a number of trials sufficient for reasonable confidence in the result. In the two example problems worked through in this chapter, you will notice the extremely simplified nature and the small number of trials conducted.

These problems are mitigated when the simulation model is computerized, but they still exist. In building a computerized model, there is still the problem of where to draw the system boundaries, i.e., what to simulate and what to ignore. And the appropriate number of trials to run is still a trade-off between cost and reliability. Of course, we know that judgmental issues of this kind exist with any analytic technique. Because there are fewer formal rules for simulation, however, the judgment skills of the analyst, the manager, and the user of the model assume even greater importance than when they use other analytic techniques.

SUMMARY

Simulation is a technique that is useful in analyzing decision problems that have a large number of events and problems involving system performance over time. The analyst should be careful to remember that simulation is only a part of the analytic process. It is still necessary to: (1) structure the problem, (2) assess probability distributions for all events either completely judgmentally or with the aid of some historical data, and (3) determine what criterion will be used to measure output value.

There are several problems with using simulation that should be mentioned. First, it is important to make sure that all the probability distributions are assessed to meet the needs of the real decision problems and not to meet the convenience of the simulation model. In many real-world problems, the probability distribution for one event will depend on the outcome of some other event. As an example, consider a market in which one of your competitors is very large and is the price leader in that market. That price is an event in your decision problem, and it is possible for you to assess a probability distribution for that price. The size of the total market is also an event in your decision problem, and you can assess a probability distribution for this event. However, you would be foolish to make these two assessments unrelated, for clearly the leader's price will have a direct influence on the market size. In fact, you should assess one probability distribution for the market size for each of the possible outcomes to the price event. This is true whether simulation or some other method is used to obtain the risk profiles. However, in many cases model builders have ignored such interrelationships. This can be hazardous because it will eliminate many of the interesting outcomes in the sampling process and thus give a distorted basis for decision making.

In the Peach Company analysis, for instance, we made the assumption that all of Ms. Thomlinson's assessments are independent of each other. This may not be a particularly useful assumption. For example, one appealing interrelationship we have ignored in our sample analysis is that the competition is more likely to respond to Peach Company's advertising initiative if the increase in advertising is effective. Furthermore, if competition does not respond in the current year, what is the chance that it will respond in the following year? Will the Peach Company then have to increase its advertising budget further? Concerns of this sort, which are part of the process of testing a model against the real world it represents, are particularly appropriate in a simulation effort. Other managerial questions might examine the source of the probability assessments—Ms. Betty Thomlinson. As sales director, she is interested in increasing her advertising budget. Has this colored her assessments? Is she perhaps a bit optimistic? Before the Peach Company commits the additional $30,000 to an advertising campaign, these issues should be resolved and perhaps a more extensive analysis performed. On the other hand, it may be reasonable to ignore some relationships or make extreme simplifying assumptions about them in the early stages of a modeling effort in the interest of getting a simulation model "off the ground." As the model develops, then, these assumptions can be modified or replaced as part of the fine tuning or enrichment of the model.

A second major problem with simulation is the cost of building the model. The amount of computation needed in simulation is large enough so that any practical use requires a computer. The building of computer simulation programs can be aided by special simulation languages and subroutines, but it still requires a substantial investment of time. If the model is to be effective, some of this time must be spent by the decision maker. Therefore, some thought should be given to this cost before simulation is proposed.

A final problem worth mentioning is psychological. Because simulation requires such an elaborate computational scheme, it is possible to begin to believe that this alone adds special credibility to the results. This belief should be avoided, and you should remember that the final result is no better than the initial inputs to the model. You must still define alternatives and make assessments for the events in the problem. No amount of computational massaging can take bad assessments or sloppy problem definition and create good decision making.

THE CASES IN THIS CHAPTER

On the following pages are a series of cases for which simulation is an appropriate solution technique. Most of these cases are designed to allow the student to perform a small number of trials by hand for the purpose of achieving a better "feel" for the technique than one usually gets from computer-based problems. Computer models may be used with any of these cases, however, and for some a computer model is the only reasonable way to proceed. In either case, when you get your "answer," you should not be too surprised if it is different from the results achieved by other class members. These differences usually will be resolved in class, often by aggregation of the results of different class members or perhaps by reconciliation of technical differences in different approaches to simulation of the case problem. The crucial factor, however, is still the conversion of your technical answer into advice or recommendations to the manager: Thus, you must (as always) test the reasonableness of your result against the case's "real world."

APPENDIX*
Random digit table

C- 4	5- 9	10-14	15-19	20-24	25-29	30-34	35-39	40-44
25251	28614	92995	38300	48205	75604	19773	93563	21276
81383	29C79	42026	62640	42210	82713	16390	84951	17792
14774	3C927	70C95	91419	54924	31062	85270	C0988	00639
79798	C4590	4C428	87688	31201	53375	39438	18397	17585
65703	83735	42154	23591	24304	64579	37662	37973	19946
99623	47137	41573	87348	18854	13423	1763C	7819C	65828
66003	24820	23815	68C87	63113	28C37	2449C	01392	78341
33907	29356	42873	34222	81620	50647	93592	C5723	54156
1C712	45891	65366	1C243	73165	02161	85551	18144	69973
86568	64681	86377	C5320	16667	84134	14319	59776	16213
73949	68521	85029	47418	43536	96597	56681	26072	15226
25568	13194	73338	76640	61940	75C93	2417C	24545	91419
13481	51552	74411	13564	96612	81285	2338C	13216	93162
38502	30461	98393	54063	9420C	78627	17179	50790	19053
03747	97466	44290	43904	26957	04458	27891	91573	36273
44459	17662	43693	20699	68811	13C04	58726	21749	70890
51215	25690	31057	03702	80555	74301	14024	14972	26623
41409	22557	00515	24363	27972	79639	5501C	15449	99743
66409	80855	18519	38778	65993	46951	8C982	63335	44383
71863	19C16	22691	40708	57535	C9904	22669	16872	21499
40138	49611	67490	89514	60745	83126	83124	14822	49887
10181	10754	66112	55244	29670	18677	24680	557C1	29585
72929	92342	28763	27932	15510	65958	30830	25980	26985
96583	38832	19105	27287	22846	98278	83039	29959	87762
01999	34240	73877	51468	46183	76030	40535	83223	58113
55865	28455	58341	35721	82471	42262	35622	95517	21428
09687	27139	17606	23523	58398	25108	18279	55212	67214
01444	955C3	53239	15266	81368	06172	3579C	45621	82690
33238	50189	84547	96115	77908	26702	59039	26063	97936
53640	27805	13124	52783	8501C	35C07	00313	24669	31627
93468	72989	21011	69164	12312	51395	83990	41379	16653
3C781	50812	45341	76882	53225	20623	37927	41952	41443
52136	58349	83019	04044	30069	06963	C9012	84615	50870
22029	23472	31C91	06365	96225	71521	58576	00979	78684
57676	48551	34366	31381	40105	18964	50297	35854	24595
27327	41C90	18095	04715	95862	25947	79356	11541	86114
59509	38667	89635	58732	69966	22279	28263	C0136	84305
41234	54504	18038	49111	18751	63721	82493	52540	97085
14050	51C16	66075	68379	77741	13177	10463	374C0	16660
26942	29325	82049	97295	07470	31311	22723	72762	00993
89454	22421	6C508	47686	17228	82511	99442	16193	64319
96313	53876	11799	54840	09277	31C25	20158	485C7	27126
27452	64377	25621	98618	98975	99506	99471	94490	64911
45493	18649	95671	33537	41376	77489	92552	20051	18406
32938	20787	90418	93281	26391	30352	93163	23666	89961
13830	55791	96704	78C99	22547	32390	24125	64513	38879
19550	27831	22103	88922	89961	17495	35144	70915	09189
69284	24151	45633	56436	58992	08171	18092	28230	99767
10309	09864	59620	24302	58098	64433	2586C	44193	49916
77528	03315	53210	44785	51964	39792	33219	03324	58829

45-49	50-54	55-59	60-64	65-69	70-74	75-79	80-84	85-89	90-94	95-99
16657	57028	61183	15990	89998	18766	89C44	C3225	80093	75820	27294
72901	32634	63978	90159	96225	28060	88767	17918	95037	25567	02207
88160	16419	91506	25676	29181	37218	09256	58428	22622	77106	41577
71C06	50069	18698	3049C	C7873	28184	60385	26160	82418	49680	63625
40C64	60867	14906	26913	20541	05315	71307	39355	66412	44279	61178
84471	45446	36726	73485	10371	60391	92463	21809	29528	11954	17514
97851	15484	50655	51001	12254	83438	23257	83597	47626	57673	48470
28785	78518	8C967	41280	43259	19107	18526	71237	31186	70266	82050
96985	81614	12080	57933	25306	99362	23776	10539	73538	01737	79652
28216	40885	22433	04487	49311	20266	67161	06999	37544	48701	85376
80994	C428E	27852	01172	79269	89355	84850	98123	87228	33471	71135
06286	77C84	30217	61160	29435	95093	61C00	34452	50925	26556	38863
64315	71714	13593	36133	11962	84431	23216	34778	30793	78540	80537
5042C	31C39	7C3C6	28911	65C02	29809	62758	25773	58738	37071	29208
48840	97649	30243	19789	70833	31388	36969	70389	89610	35231	60256
16026	58145	91064	23073	05294	30892	24135	28928	32059	80579	63868
42496	02935	86112	14546	43338	96432	45490	60411	84122	92106	57679
83704	28819	19578	25982	40471	26486	56822	02555	03934	93819	20725
89497	19719	60174	52501	35584	91794	29299	80716	07032	46818	04050
70363	15116	57430	94965	52921	18200	01834	71490	36721	01199	94064
52351	27266	3C288	84909	05786	C6115	97972	26014	60766	30467	04838
97707	66541	44170	59363	89714	13580	29181	07084	14183	14559	52922
59157	12074	93670	88157	79122	74537	28335	99176	95397	73008	03764
25865	964C0	0C971	62427	45548	17557	88626	11600	62388	84863	78758
55503	72143	64402	30337	71326	41357	30491	17515	10318	11051	66661
31054	86687	27063	13265	60309	28898	99537	92496	52353	88766	85895
37447	31896	34005	48032	13221	15961	69992	31659	84309	89849	42454
85546	312C7	72689	24196	23C42	94215	95768	19891	19573	31634	31145
08405	31145	28726	98836	89839	42727	03170	03401	85086	04196	21543
98810	46073	42508	02536	01569	79807	89C08	77925	59689	50022	25075
20722	50161	78247	68143	97848	04873	38154	56321	66038	20411	52414
33165	48514	23673	43264	64025	25848	47785	71584	30505	51319	07514
67975	81086	91536	03685	60425	84743	95704	73677	050C8	98027	36307
87582	79477	81842	37899	65C39	23313	78812	82590	94127	83592	47619
87029	38673	C4136	67941	27897	17078	75679	55728	46468	39398	80319
37103	C2953	21645	20794	26533	52786	95417	97430	19038	99499	49940
28895	07330	19151	42703	25408	30265	83992	C0491	09158	83581	85143
09652	46286	77277	4709C	11330	13095	69817	56405	03290	12097	70365
25503	51055	16521	32845	48378	25737	56872	27C98	19665	98396	37679
82172	08384	41826	61929	26214	68845	63578	24003	96099	98422	18851
26606	49695	76214	29613	87404	26831	05418	60615	94800	23259	72786
64045	26563	07258	19774	17255	56631	53417	72966	88109	42570	19561
63345	58013	40115	11787	47541	65592	96756	21279	19009	72037	28256
78547	43484	78271	78265	27292	14728	49523	51013	22514	28857	48776
64628	024C8	32795	61526	73996	21313	17268	18576	49259	38665	98815
45870	56383	56534	93901	54601	73579	18268	47397	03810	53000	39068
16898	36186	65032	64515	63946	65185	77740	20783	27073	06460	01760
99888	94635	62035	44782	03589	87419	16500	43297	28781	20867	90459
32832	25995	66956	36705	27892	15343	37678	05487	31672	27077	69333
78418	7212C	20171	71947	40838	64455	19183	59288	52009	40606	37699

* This table prepared by Stanley I. Buchin.

Weatherburn Aircraft Engine Company

In June 1977, the Weatherburn Aircraft Engine Company received an order for ten spare ring gears from Sierra Airlines. The ring gear was the largest and most expensive of the gears in the system that drives the propeller.

The Weatherburn Company carried in stock part no. 21573, the gear blanks from which the ring gears would be made. This gear blank was a standard size used in many airplanes. The number of teeth, however, was nonstandard. When Sierra Airlines bought the airplanes in which these gears were used, its management had decided that flying requirements peculiar to this airline necessitated a gear ratio slightly higher than standard, and Weatherburn had designed a special gear train accordingly. No other airlines used this ratio, and Sierra was on the point of converting its fleet of aircraft to jet operations. Upon inquiry, the production manager of Weatherburn Company learned that the lot of ten ring gears would almost certainly last until Sierra's current aircraft had been entirely replaced.

The gear blanks cost Weatherburn about $50 each to make. The first step in the machining process was hobbing. Setup for this operation was very expensive, costing about $500, but the direct cost of hobbing an extra gear was negligible so long as the machine's capacity of 25 gears at one time was not exceeded. After hobbing, each gear was individually subjected to a series of drilling, grinding, and finishing operations, the total cost of which was $90 per gear. In addition, there was a setup cost of $250 associated with these operations. The machined gears were then heat-treated at a cost of about $10 per gear, after which they were subjected to a hardness test, the cost of which was negligible.

After hobbing and before the remaining operations, the gears were subjected to a 100 percent inspection. In the past, an average of 4 percent of all the hobbed gears failed to pass this inspection and had to be scrapped. The heat-treating operation was much more difficult to control. The test for hardness had had considerable difficulty in meeting standards on this type of gear in the past; only 80 percent of the gears had proved acceptable.

case 6–2

Synergistic Systems Corporation

Mr. Norman Jenkins, manager of office equipment at Synergistic Systems Corporation, one of the top seven government contractors, was reasoning with Mr. George Wilson, manager of the contract typing pool. "George, I can't approve your request for a third copying machine just because you say you see typists waiting in line practically every time you're near your two machines. Back in 1966, I could have approved without question, but this is 1970. You know that we aren't doing as well these days due to the government cutbacks in aerospace spending. The word has come down from upstairs that we have to cut expenses wherever possible.

"As a matter of fact, we have been running a survey on usage of the machines in the building, hoping to reduce costs by eliminating unnecessary machines. Let me show you our results for your machines, George. This first table (Exhibit 1) shows that you average 16.17 pages per contract. This second table (Exhibit 2) shows that the average time between users arriving at the machines is 16.48 minutes.

"Previous surveys have shown that it takes one minute to make the required 20 copies of each contract page. Therefore, the average user should be on a machine 16.17 minutes. Since secretaries arrive to use the machine an average of 16.48 minutes apart, but only use the machine an average of 16.17 minutes, one machine should be adequate for your copying needs. Each machine costs us $110 per month or $5 per working day. How can I approve your request for a third machine with these facts in front of me? In fact, I was thinking of taking away one of your machines."

George Wilson puzzled over the tables a bit and then asked, "Why are all the times even numbers? Don't the users arrive three minutes apart, or five minutes apart?"

"Yes, but we found that it was convenient and accurate enough to record the information to the nearest two minutes. Anything up to one minute was recorded as zero, anything from one to three minutes was recorded as two, etc. (By the way, here's the form we used to record the results," he added, showing Mr. Wilson the form shown in Exhibit 3. "We just used two of the machine columns in your case since you only

EXHIBIT 1
Pages per contract

Pages	Percentage of contracts
6	1
7	1
8	2
9	2
10	2
11	3
12	4
13	6
14	8
15	9
16	11
17	12
18	11
19	9
20	7
21	5
22	3
23	2
24	1
25	1
	100

had two machines, and we recorded 20 all the time in the "Number of copies" column.) We fitted a smooth curve to what we recorded on both the pages and times between arrivals."

"Well, I don't really care how you recorded that data," said Mr. Wilson, "The important point is that secretaries are waiting in line and that's costing us money.

"You're familiar with our system of assigning typists to only one contract at a time and having them make their own copies when the typing is finished. The worst drawback of our present system is that the time anyone spends waiting to use a machine is wasted time, and typists with the speed and accuracy that we need don't work for peanuts. The 15 secretaries who work for me cost us about $5 an hour each, including variable overhead, and that's $40 per working day. That's why I worry when I see them waiting in line at the machine."

Mr. Jenkins asked, "Why don't you hire someone just to make copies? You ought to be able to get someone to do that for only $2 an hour. You would save the time your typists spend making copies, and eliminate all waiting time, and still get by with only one machine."

"I fought that battle last year with Bob Johnson in security. He agreed that we could save money by hiring someone just to run the copying machines, but he won't allow it. Most of the contracts are

EXHIBIT 2
Time between arrivals

Time since last arrival	Percentage of arrivals
0	17
2	8
4	7
6	6
8	6
10	5
12	5
14	4
16	4
18	3
20	3
22	3
24	3
26	2
28	2
30	2
32	2
34	2
36	2
38	2
40	2
42	1
44	1
46	1
48	1
50	1
52	1
54	1
56	1
58	1
60	1
	100

classified secret or top secret, and he's scared stiff of what the government security inspectors will say about any procedure where extra personnel handle the documents," Mr. Wilson replied. "Now the problem is worse. With the aerospace spending cuts, we've got a hiring freeze. We wouldn't be allowed to hire a copying machine operator, even if we thought it was desirable."

"George, I understand your concerns, but I just can't help you when the numbers show that I should take a machine away from you rather than give you another one. Take this copy of our survey with you. If you can show me that I'm wrong, you'll get your machine."

Mr. Wilson folded the copy of the survey, put it in his shirt pocket, and walked out dejectedly.

EXHIBIT 3
Data sheet

Time of arrival	Number of pages	Number of copies	Machine 1		Machine 2		Machine 3		Machine 4	
			Time on	Time off	Time on	Time off	Time on	Time off	Time on	Time off

case 6–3

The grimbel

In February 1979, Ms. Susan Connolly, general manager of Rutabaga, Inc., was evaluating a new freight rate recently proposed by one of the transcontinental airlines serving New England. If Rutabaga, Inc., would guarantee to ship a fixed amount of a single commodity to a particular destination each week for a year, lower rates would be offered on the fixed-shipment amount. The airline stated that such an arrangement would be justified from its standpoint as it would allow better planning.

Rutabaga, Inc., was a specialty food company that sold delicacies such as lobsters, fresh oysters, ripe fruit, and various fresh salad items. One of Rutabaga's most popular items was the grimbel, a small freshwater shellfish found only in certain unpolluted rivers in Maine. The Rutabaga factory was located along one of these grimble-rich streams. In 1972, Ms. Connolly perfected a technique of raising grimbels in an artificial environment, which assured her of a reliable year-round supply of the shellfish. Grimbels and other perishable products were shipped via airfreight to customers (mainly large restaurants) throughout North America.

Ms. Connolly decided to evaluate shipments of grimbels to her San Francisco customers in order to investigate the economics of the airline's proposal. Grimbels were shipped in cartons of ten dozen each to three large San Francisco restaurants on a flight that left Boston's Logan Airport each Tuesday. The contribution margin per carton was $300. The present airfreight cost from Boston to San Francisco was $90 per carton. Currently, therefore, the net contribution margin was $210 per carton.

The airline had offered Rutabaga, Inc., an annual contract under which the cost of shipping a guaranteed carton to San Francisco would be only $50. In other words, by agreeing to ship a certain number of cartons to San Francisco every week for a year, the cost of shipping each carton would be $50. However, Rutabaga must pay for the contracted number of cartons even though fewer cartons might actually be shipped. Further, any cartons shipped in excess of the guaranteed shipment size would go at the regular cost of $90 per carton.

Ms. Connolly tabulated the shipment records to San Francisco customers over the past two years (see Exhibit 1). These records verified what she already knew—that the number of cartons shipped per week was never less than four or more than eight. Apparently, however, the actual number shipped varied randomly between these limits. It seemed obvious that Rutabaga, Inc., could save money if it would guarantee a four-carton shipment each week on the Tuesday flight. At

EXHIBIT 1
Weekly San Francisco demand for grimbels,
January 1977–January 1979

Demand (cartons)	1977	1978	1979 (Jan.)
4	5	4	0
5	9	11	1
6	11	10	0
7	22	24	2
8	5	3	1

the same time, Ms. Connolly suspected that she might be able to save more money by guaranteeing a larger shipment, but she was unsure of how to go about determining the best number of cartons to guarantee.

As Ms. Connolly thought about this problem, it occurred to her that the San Francisco market for grimbels was one of her least attractive due to the high cost of air shipment. Further, there may be times in the coming year that Rutabaga, Inc., would be unable to completely satisfy San Francisco's grimbel demand because the recent addition of grimbels to the menu of a popular Boston restaurant had pushed total demand very close to capacity. For the coming year, Ms. Connolly estimated that while she would always be able to supply as many as five cartons per week to San Francisco, half of the time she would be unable to supply more than five cartons, and two thirds of the time she would not be able to supply more than six cartons.

Only about one sixth of the time during the coming year, Ms. Connolly estimated, would Rutabaga, Inc., be able to supply as many as eight cartons of grimbels to her San Francisco customers. Although Ms. Connolly could estimate this frequency distribution (shown in Exhibit 2), she felt that it was impossible to predict grimbel availability ahead of time due to the uncertainties of demand in closer (and thus, more desirable) markets and the uncertainty of the size of her grimbel harvest week to week. Although she was planning to build new grimbel beds that would alleviate this situation, they would not become sufficiently productive to commence harvesting until December 1980.

EXHIBIT 2
Estimated availability of grimbels
for San Francisco

Number of cartons	Percent of time available
4	100
5	100
6	50
7	33.3
8	16.7

EXHIBIT 4
Costs associated with changing and grinding one set of work rolls

	Fixed cost*	Variable cost †
Roll stock loss	$ —	$148.00
Labor	9.00	42.50
Repair and maintenance	6.25	9.75
Grinding wheels	—	10.00
Utilities	1.50	1.00
Miscellaneous supplies	0.25	1.75
Depreciation	20.00	—
Total	$37.00	$213.00

Note: At the end of a comedown, work rolls are removed from the mill and sent to the roll shop for grinding before reuse. In 1978 the roll shop had operated at capacity and ground 24,000 sets of rolls. It was estimated that to increase roll shop capacity by 10 percent would require a capital investment of $1 million.
* Fully absorbed per set of rolls at capacity (24,000 sets per year).
† Per set of rolls.

EXHIBIT 5
Time needed to replace steel work rolls on tandem mills

Number of sets of rolls to replace	Minutes to replace rolls	
	52 inch	80 inch
1	30	15
2	38	19
3	46	23
4	52	26
5	60	30

tandem mills varied from less than 100 tons to more than 2,000 tons of steel processed. Some analysis had been carried out at Central Steel to try to determine the reasons for this wide variability in roll life. Apparently, however, roll life varied randomly between these limits. Exhibit 6 shows a frequency distribution of roll life as a function of the number of tons of steel processed on the tandem mills.

Mr. Strawser, after reviewing these data, discussed the suggested revision in maintenance procedures with Miss April Atwood, his assistant. After explaining the problem and reviewing the data he had collected, Mr. Strawser admitted he was unsure about how to proceed with an analysis. The following conversation then took place.

Atwood: Well, Jerry, I'm not certain but I think it could be handled with a pretty straightforward simulation model. As you know, I'm

EXHIBIT 6
Cumulative frequency distribution of work roll life between grindings

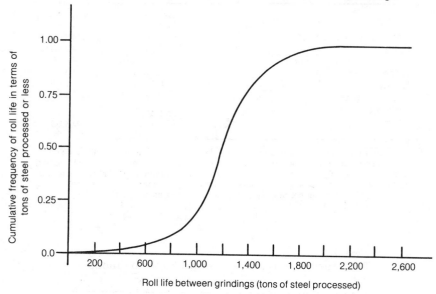

Roll life between grindings (tons of steel processed)

enrolled in a night-school MBA program and I seem to recall problems that looked a lot like this in a course I took last term.

Strawser: Great! Why don't you take this stuff (handing a pile of papers to Atwood) and get to it then? Tell you what. To simplify your work, concentrate on the 52-inch tandem mill, at least initially. It's the one that's at capacity and any slowdown there should show the largest negative impact. Also, I think you should ignore the impact on the roll shop for the purposes of the simulation—if we overload that shop we can always get rolls ground by an outside job shop.

Atwood (under her breath): Wow! Did I get hooked!

Strawser: What's that, April?

Atwood: Er . . . I said I'd give it a look, sir.

Strawser: Good. Check back with me on Friday so I can see what progress you've made.

case 6–5

Hollingsworth Manor Apartments

In April 1971, David Rockman, a second-year MBA student was considering the purchase of a four-unit apartment building located in Cambridge, Massachusetts. When he had first investigated the property three months before, the asking price had been $150,000, but Dave felt that he could now purchase it for considerably less.

BACKGROUND

Dave Rockman was a Massachusetts native and a Yale graduate. After a stint in the Air Force, he had worked for several years in a bank, married, and entered the MBA program at Harvard with a strong interest in both real estate and financial planning.

During his second year, Dave had more or less decided to stay in the Boston area after graduation. Consequently he considered investing part of his $40,000 assets in Boston area real estate. Not only would such a move provide useful firsthand real estate experience, but it also appealed to his entrepreneurial spirit to run a small side business while pursuing a full-time career. Further, given the perennial shortage of housing in metropolitan Boston, real estate appeared to be a good investment. He felt that returns in the neighborhood of 12–15 percent would be necessary to make a real estate investment worthwhile.

In January 1971, Dave heard that a Cambridge apartment house was available for $150,000. He contacted the owner, Mrs. Judy Percy, and made an appointment to see the property.

VISIT

Located at 36 Hollingsworth Lane in a quiet, upper middle class residential section of Cambridge, the apartment structure itself was a five-story converted "brownstone." The largest apartment unit occupied the basement and first floors, while the other three units occupied only one floor each. (The basement could not be converted into a separate apartment due to the low ceiling and other construction constraints.) Dave referred to his potential purchase as the Hollingsworth Manor Apartments because it and the three adjoining buildings originally had been a single apartment complex built 50 years previously and called Hollingsworth Manor. About 15 years ago it had been converted into separate apartment buildings. Although there were no special parking facilities, the building was conveniently located near shopping areas and public transportation.

Dave learned from Mrs. Percy that the building had been purchased two years previously for around $80,000. To cover substantial improvements she had made since then and to allow for increases in values, Mrs. Percy was asking $150,000 for the property. Because of these renovations, Dave felt that no major repair work would be needed in the foreseeable future.

Glancing at the schedule of current monthly rents (Exhibit 1), Dave

EXHIBIT 1
Schedule of monthly rentals by floor, 1971

Unit 1 (basement and first floors)	$ 550
Unit 2 (second floor)	375
Unit 3 (third floor)	390
Unit 4 (fourth floor)	350
Total	$1,665

quickly calculated annual, full-capacity revenues of almost $20,000. While the rental figures accurately reflected current market conditions, Dave realized that generally the annual occupancy rate (as a percentage of 12 months) would vary between 75 and 100 percent. On the expense side, Mrs. Percy showed Dave her most recent records for 1970, when occupancy had been 100 percent (Exhibit 2). Mrs. Percy emphasized that the utility costs (except water) of the individual apartments were covered by the tenants themselves, with the landlord being responsible only for lighting the stairs, heating the hallways, heating hot water, etc.

EXHIBIT 2
Annual expenses, 1970*

Taxes	$3,000
Heat and hot water	700
Insurance	800
Electricity	300
Maintenance	1,500
Water	150
Total	$6,450

* These expenses, which the landlord assumes, exclude certain utility expenses that tenants pay themselves.

Although he was favorably impressed with the building and location, Dave told Mrs. Percy the price was too high. For example, the price violated the rule of thumb that an apartment's value was six or seven times gross rents. So after chatting a while longer about the apartment business, the two parted with the understanding to get in touch with each other if anything should change.

INTERLUDE

During February and March, Dave conducted further investigations regarding the acquisition of the Hollingsworth Manor Apartments as well as other apartments. In investigating the prices of other apartments in the area, he found out that a similar property nearby had just been recently sold for $120,000.

Dave consulted with several banks and other financing companies for mortgages. The best deal came from a bank that offered a 20-year first mortgage of up to $100,000 provided it was 75 percent or less of the purchase price. The interest would be 8.5 percent per annum on the outstanding balance at the beginning of each year. According to mortgage tables, the annual payments would amount to $104.16 per $1,000 of loan.

Dave estimated that, after graduation, he would be in the 30 percent tax bracket for the foreseeable future. Depreciation that would apply to only the building could be handled on a declining balance basis at 125 percent of straight line spread out over 30 years. Dave could depreciate the book value of the building to zero. Mrs. Percy had said that since the land area was small, city officials currently valued the building at around 90 percent of the total property assessment. Consequently, the IRS would accept 90 percent of the purchase price as a basis for depreciation for income tax purposes. Since an accelerated depreciation method was used, any gain from resale of the property would be handled in two parts. The part of the gain that was the difference between the net resale price and the book value of the building measured on a straight-line depreciation basis was taxed at the capital gain rate of half of the ordinary income rate. The additional gain due to the accelerated depreciation measured by the difference in book values using the straight-line and accelerated depreciation alternatives was taxed at the ordinary income rate.

In thinking about the riskiness of the venture, Dave pinpointed three major uncertainties: the occupancy rate, inflation, and rent control.

While the apartments were all occupied in January, Dave felt that during the summer it might be harder to rent them. Cambridge, however, was never short of apartment seekers. He finally decided that for the 12 months of the year, there was a 45 percent chance of full-time occupancy, a 20 percent chance of 11 ½-month occupancy, a 15 percent chance of 11-month occupancy, a 10 percent chance of 10 ½-month occupancy, a 5 percent chance of 10-month occupancy, a 4 percent chance of 9 ½-month occupancy, and a 1 percent chance of 9-month occupancy.

As far as inflation went, Dave felt it could conceivably affect both rental income and expenses. He believed there was a 50–50 chance of 5 percent inflation or less per year. Further there was only a one in four chance of having inflation at 3.5 percent or less or as high as 7 percent or more, and only one chance in a hundred that inflation would become 1 percent or less or 10 percent or more.

With the uncertainties of local politics, there was also the "hot issue" of rent control legislation. There was currently a law that froze rents at March 1970 levels until 1975. While costs and tax increases could be passed on to tenants, the Rent Control Administration had not yet worked out adjustment formulas so that, effectively, owners and landlords were absorbing all increases in expenses.

Relief from this control could come from either the courts or the rent control board. Dave doubted that the courts would overturn the current legislation. However, he did feel that there was some chance rent increases based on the previous year's inflation rate would be granted. Specifically, Dave reckoned there was only a one in a hundred chance of getting a rent increase to match the percentage increase in expenses. Similarly, he thought the possibility of getting no relief was just as remote at one in a hundred. He further judged that there was only a one in four chance of getting a rent increase above one half of the inflation rate or below one fifth of the inflation rate. It also seemed that the rent increase would just as likely be more than 40 percent of the inflation rate as less than that. Dave also thought that, given the present situation, he would not get an increase in 1971.

DEADLINE

While Dave weighed these various considerations during the Easter holidays, he received a phone call from Mrs. Percy. She explained that the Hollingsworth Manor property was still available and asked him if he was still interested. When Dave replied in the affirmative, Mrs. Percy said she would be willing to hear Dave's offer. Because she needed cash for some other deals, and because she had another interested party, Mrs. Percy added that she could wait only two or three days for Dave to respond.

That afternoon Dave gathered his notes and did a rough pro forma based on a minimum purchase price of $120,000 (see Exhibit 3). He

EXHIBIT 3
1971 Pro forma*

Income		$19,980
Less:		
Expenses	$6,450	
Interest	7,650	
		14,100
Profit before taxes and depreciation		$ 5,880
Less: Depreciation		4,500
Profit before tax		$ 1,380
Tax		414
Profit after tax		$ 966
Less: Amortization	1,724	
Plus: Depreciation	4,500	
Cash flow		$ 3,742

Return on investment = $3,742/$30,000 = 12.5 percent

* Assumptions:
1. Full occupancy rental for 12 months.
2. No inflation effect in 1971.
3. No rent control in 1971.
4. Building is valued at 90 percent of $120,000 = $108,000 for depreciation purposes.
5. Mortage is for $90,000 and 20 years at 8.5 percent annual interest.
6. Annual debt service payment is $104.16/$1,000 × $90,000 = $9,374.
7. $30,000 is equity investment.

felt it was inadequate, however, and began an analysis to get a better feel for the risks. For this analysis, he made the following assumptions:

1. The occupancy rate would be applied to the whole building, not individual apartment units.
2. Fifteen percent would be his target of return, but he would also try 12 percent.
3. If he wanted to sell out in five years, he could get a minimum resale price of 6½ times gross (i.e., full-occupancy) rents.
4. Working capital needs would be on the order of $200–$300.
5. Inflation would boost up both expenses (including taxes) and rents unless rent control limited rental income.
6. That the final negotiated purchase price would be $130,000.

case 6–6

Tauride Transportation Corporation (A)

In July 1973, Mr. Peter Fox, president of Tauride Transportation Corporation, was reviewing the company's past history of growth in order to gain a perspective on the strategic needs of Tauride in the 1970s, particularly in reference to developing a plan for growth through acquisitions.

CORPORATE HISTORY

Tauride Transportation was a regulated general commodities carrier with 1972 revenues in excess of $70 million. The firm had been founded in 1927 by two brothers, Edward and John Tauride, to serve regional markets in California. Tauride expanded rapidly in the years immediately following its founding and established a route structure that ran from California through the Midwest and Southwest to Chicago, Pittsburgh, and Birmingham (see Exhibit 1).

EXHIBIT 1
Simplified route system, 1973

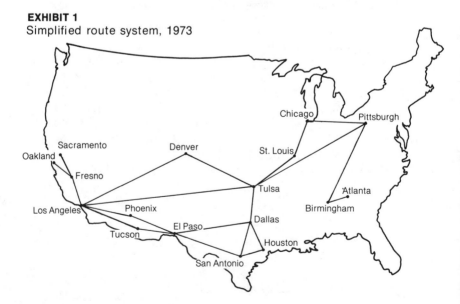

Management of the firm had remained in the hands of the Tauride family through the first 30 years of the company's operation. In 1959 Edward Tauride died and his brother decided to retire from a position of active management. Thus, Peter Fox, whose entire career in the trucking industry had been spent with Tauride, was made president of the firm, while John Tauride became chairman.

While John Tauride continued to influence the firm's policies both as a founder and major stockholder, effective control of the company passed to Fox. Immediately upon taking control of Tauride, Fox, who had gained a reputation as an innovator during his previous career, found himself confronted with a number of serious problems. Firstly, the firm had failed to adopt an aggressive sales policy and had exhibited virtually no revenue growth in the 1955–1959 period. In addition, Tauride faced a host of highly competitive common carriers on its routes and seemed vulnerable to actual revenue declines in the near future. Secondly, operating margins were extremely low due primarily to the lack of internal controls on operations and dependence on old equipment requiring excessive maintenance. Thirdly, the firm lacked a strong financial base due primarily to the fact that the Tauride family had avoided long-term debt or a public equity offering; capital expenditures had been financed solely by internally generated funds. Finally, Tauride Transportation lacked managerial depth in almost all areas of operations and middle managers lacked any real profit performance incentive.

Beginning in 1959, Mr. Fox began a program designed to build Tauride into a growing—and profitable—factor in the industry. Initial emphasis was placed on the expansion of revenues on existing routes through an emphasis on service and aggressive selling. A profit-sharing and incentive system was developed to increase motivation among salaried employees. In 1962, Tauride made a public issue of its stock, and the funds generated were used for the modernization of the firm's fleet and terminal facilities. As the 1960s progressed, Tauride rapidly developed into an efficient and competitive firm.

THE SITUATION IN 1973

By 1973, Tauride had become a trucker concentrating on long-haul shipments with a modern set of terminal facilities and a large fleet. Fiscal year 1972 revenues had set a new high, as had net income (see Exhibit 2). The institution of a strong service program, supported by an enlarged sales force, had allowed the firm to substantially enhance its share of the market within its established routes. A secondary public offering of common stock had taken place in 1967 and a portion of the funds generated had been utilized for the installation of a com-

EXHIBIT 2
Selected financial data, 1970–1973 ($000)

Fiscal year	Operating revenues	Income before taxes	Income after taxes	Earnings per share	Dividends per share	Market price common stoc High	Lo
1970	$50,140	$3,860	$2,010	$1.71	$0.40	22¼	13
1971	60,170	4,590	2,340	1.98	0.50	29⅞	17
1972	71,000	5,990	3,053	2.54	0.55	38⅜	25
1973*	40,115	3,215	1,640	1.36	0.30	22⅜†	

* Six months ended June 30, 1973.
† As of June 15, 1973.

puter system that allowed effective control of operations and improved operating margins.

Mr. Fox firmly believed that Tauride had emerged as an innovative firm within the industry. Tauride's incentive and bonus system had, Mr. Fox felt, contributed directly to its success and this program was considered one of the most progressive among trucking firms. In addition, a management development program, designed by an outside consultant, had remedied Tauride's initial lack of managerial depth, and a crop of talented young managers had been produced. The computer system, once debugged, had proved highly successful, and Tauride had developed the personnel required to monitor and operate the system at maximal efficiency. Finally, Tauride had developed a strong financial base and had been an industry leader in the aggressive use of unsecured bank debt to finance operations (see Exhibit 3).

Yet, Mr. Fox felt that one major unresolved problem continued to confront the firm. It had become apparent that Tauride would find it difficult to maintain its rate of revenue growth within its current route structure. Tauride's service strategy had produced a growing saturation of existing routes and, in addition, increased pressure was being felt from private fleets and shipping associations. Continuation of rapid revenue and profit growth was a cornerstone of Mr. Fox's managerial philosophy. In 1971, speaking to the New York Society of Security Analysts, he had stated:

> Tauride Transportation believes firmly that the key to success in the trucking industry is sustained growth in revenues, and even more importantly, profit. Our recent history has, I believe, clearly demonstrated our commitment to this belief and we feel that future results will display a strong upward thrust in these critical—and crucial—variables.

In addition, Mr. Fox had been informed that several mutual funds had purchased shares of Tauride. He felt that any reduction in growth

EXHIBIT 3
Summary balance sheet, December 31, 1972 ($000)

Assets:		
Cash	$ 4,030	
Accounts receivable	5,610	
Inventory	1,360	
Prepaid expenses	1,530	
Current assets		$12,530
Carrier operating property (cost)	$39,730	
Accumulated depreciation	14,960	
Net carrier operating property		24,770
Other assets		5,270
Total Assets		$42,570
Liabilities and Stockholders' Equity:		
Accounts payable	$ 4,510	
Miscellaneous payables/accruals	2,380	
Taxes payable	1,050	
Current maturity of long-term debt	680	
Current Liabilities		$ 8,620
Long-term debt		12,350
Stockholders' equity		
Common stock ($1 par)	$ 1,200	
Paid-in surplus	5,800	
Retained earnings	14,600	
Total Stockholders' Equity		21,600
Total Liabilities and Stockholders' Equity		$42,570

would induce sale of these holdings, depressing the price of the firm's stock and making it much more difficult to raise future equity capital.

Mr. Fox was keenly aware of the fact that many major trucking firms had developed strong acquisition programs to support their growth goals. Due to his concentration on improving Tauride's performance within its established routes, Mr. Fox had never seriously considered acquiring another firm in the industry. Now, as he considered methods to sustain future expansion, a policy of selected acquisitions seemed worthy of detailed consideration. At the same time, he realized that an acquisition strategy required an ability to select the right firm, in terms of capability and potential, to acquire, as well as the skill of determining the correct price to pay. Also, attention had to be given to smoothly integrating acquired operations with the existing operation; Mr. Fox knew of several rather sophisticated firms that had had difficulty in doing this.

As he considered these factors, Mr. Fox realized that he would have to decide whether acquisitions were to be an integral part of Tauride's growth strategy. Recent conversations with knowledgable outside directors of Tauride and the firm's financial executives had convinced Fox that an acquisition program was almost inevitable. Thus, he felt that it was imperative that Tauride develop a system for evaluating proposed acquisitions and their impact on the firm.

case 6–7

Tauride Transportation Corporation (B)

Mr. Peter Fox, president of Tauride Transportation Corporation, was considering, in August 1973, the possible acquisition of Ballard Trucking, Incorporated.[1] Ballard was a general commodities carrier, serving the Florida and Gulf Coast regions (see Exhibit 1), that had been founded, and was controlled by the Ballard family (see Exhibit 2).

EXHIBIT 1
Ballard Trucking, Incorporated, 1972 simplified route system

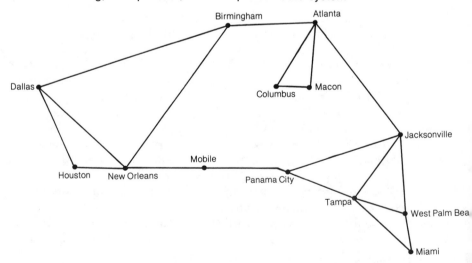

---

[1] See Tauride Transportation Corporation (A) for background (case 6–6).

EXHIBIT 2
Ballard Trucking, Incorporated, organization chart, 1972

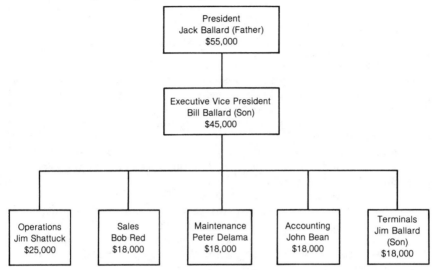

Source: Constructed from discussions with management.

Fox had taken the opportunity to send Mr. John St. Clair, Tauride's executive vice president, to meet with Mr. Jack Ballard, president of Ballard Trucking. Upon his return, St. Clair had prepared a memorandum containing financial and operating information on the potential acquisition candidate (see Exhibit 3). In addition, Mr. St. Clair had prepared a summary transcript of his conversation with Mr. Ballard. Mr. Fox now realized that he would have to consider whether Ballard was a good candidate for acquisition and what terms Tauride should offer.

302

EXHIBIT 3

TO: Peter Fox   August 17, 1973
FROM: John St. Clair
RE: Financial/Operating Data on Ballard Trucking, Inc.

I have assembled the attached financial and operating statistics on Ballard Trucking after discussions with management, examination of company records, and on-site inspection of facilities.

Ballard's accounting is conservative and the data presented are an accurate representation of the firm's condition. I have run a spot check on the firm's receivables. In addition, it should be noted that outstanding bank loans contain no unusual covenants or restrictions. Finally, I am of the opinion that it will be possible to write up the value of Ballard's Florida assets by approximately $250,000.

I have also contacted Teamsters' officials in Atlanta who indicate that the last election at Ballard was very close indeed. Management barely kept the union out. They plan to try again in November and, the way I see it, it could go either way. Our best bet, in my opinion, is to accept organization without contest if we go ahead with the acquisition.

EXHIBIT 3 (continued)

Ballard Trucking, Incorporated, balance sheet data, 1970–1972 ($000)

	1970		1971		1972	
	Dollars	Percent	Dollars	Percent	Dollars	Percent
Cash/working funds	$ 788	13.1%	$ 739	9.3%	$ 863	10.5%
Notes/accounts receivable	579	9.6	760	9.5	722	8.8
Other current assets	1,534	25.4	848	10.6	548	6.7
Total current assets	2,901	48.1	2,347	29.4	2,133	26.0
Net carrier operating property	3,065	50.8	3,994	50.0	4,441	54.1
Other assets	69	1.1	1,641	20.6	1,633	19.9
Total assets	6,035	100.0	7,982	100.0	8,207	100.0
Notes/accounts payable	$ 609	10.1%	$ 540	6.7%	$ 410	5.0%
Debt due within one year	—	—	—	—	—	—
Other current liabilities	1,030	17.1	1,387	17.4	1,132	13.8
Total current liabilities	1,639	27.2	1,927	24.1	1,542	18.8
Deferred credits/ reserves	111	1.8	—	—	—	—
Debt due after one year	657	10.9	1,241	15.5	607	7.4
Stockholders' equity	3,628	60.1	4,814	60.3	6,058	73.8
Total liabilities and stockholders' equity	6,035	100.0	7,982	100.0	8,207	100.0

EXHIBIT 3 *(continued)*

Ballard Trucking, Incorporated, income statement data, 1970–1972 ($000)

	1970		1971		1972	
	Dollars	*Percent*	*Dollars*	*Percent*	*Dollars*	*Percent*
Operating revenues	$16,963	100.0%	$19,057	100.0%	$21,320	100.0%
Expenses:						
Equipment maintenance						
expense.................	$ 1,124	6.6	$ 1,254	6.6	$ 1,279	6.0
Transportation expense	7,930	46.7	8,379	44.0	9,385	44.0
Terminal expense..........	3,184	18.8	3,653	19.2	4,269	20.0
Traffic expense	244	1.4	310	1.6	333	1.6
Insurance and safety						
expense.................	400	2.4	349	1.8	412	1.9
Salaries, general						
officers.................	97	0.6	94	0.5	108	0.5
Salaries, revenue						
accounting and						
other...................	161	1.0	169	0.9	181	0.9
Other administrative and						
general expense	660	3.9	662	3.5	714	3.4
Depreciation and						
amortization.............	460	2.7	570	3.0	841	3.9
Taxes and licenses						
expense.................	1,023	6.0	1,115	5.9	1,246	5.8
Total expenses	$15,283	90.1	$16,555	86.9	$18,768	88.0
Net operating revenue	1,680	9.9	2,502	13.1	2,551	12.0
Net before income						
taxes...................	1,711	10.1	2,508	13.1	2,525	11.8
Net income after taxes	848	5.0	1,358	7.1	1,449	6.8

EXHIBIT 3 (continued)
Ballard Trucking, Incorporated, selected operating and financial data,
1970–1972

	1970	1971	1972
Operating ratio	90.1%	86.9%	88.0%
Current ratio	1.77 : 1	1.22 : 1	1.38 : 1
Debt as percentage of stockholders' equity	18.1%	25.8%	10.0%
Return on stockholders' equity	23.4%	28.2%	24.0%
Personnel			
Number	1,006	981	893
Compensation (000)	$ 9,192	$ 9,792	$ 11,159
Revenue equipment owned			
Trucks	120	120	60
Truck trailers	59	86	148
Trailers	149	178	236
Cost, book (000)	$ 2,313	$ 3,229	$ 3,720
Total power units, average	275	321	317
Rented with drivers	—	—	—
Rented without drivers	214	242	233
Ton-miles, (000)	151,771	167,904	189,803
Rev. freight (billed weight) (000 tons)	506	521	554
Truckload (TL) (000 tons)	195	196	223
Less truckload (LTL) (000 tons)	311	325	331
Originated, terminated (000 tons)	301	333	373
Interlined			
Originated (000 tons)	85	81	76
Terminated (000 tons)	81	82	82
Intermediate (000 tons)	29	25	23
Average haul (miles)	302	322	342
Average load (tons)	9.8	10.6	11.1
Freight revenue (per ton)	$33.50	$36.55	$38.40
Per vehicle (cents/mile)	108.4	120.2	124.5
Per ton (cents/mile)	11.10	11.33	11.21

EXHIBIT 3 (concluded)
Ballard Trucking, Incorporated, sources and uses of funds, fiscal year 1972 ($000)

Sources of funds
Net income after taxes $1,449
Depreciation and amortization 841
Reduction in other assets 8
Total sources $2,298

Uses of funds
Increase in working capital .... $ 171
Increase in carrier operating property 1,288
Reduction in debt due after one year 634
Dividends 205
Total uses $2,298

DISCUSSION WITH MR. BALLARD

St. Clair: Could you briefly describe the history of Ballard Trucking?

Ballard: Two of us have really put this thing together. I started off working out of the Macon-Columbus-Atlanta area. In the early days, I did a lot of agricultural hauling into Florida and built up some pretty good relationships and got established in Jacksonville. About the time that the Interstate Commerce Act was passed, we were able to demonstrate that we had some properties and routes that did go into that area on a regular basis, so we got some "grandfather" rights from Georgia into Jacksonville. Actually, I wish we had gotten a bit more of that, because we could have saved ourselves a heck of a lot of money. After World War II, we were able to find an opportunity to move into operations in Tampa, Panama City, West Palm Beach, and Miami—that pretty well filled out our Florida operations.

As you may realize, Florida is a very directional traffic—there are a lot more manufactured goods that go into Florida than come out and that's always represented an operating problem for us. In the 1950s we continued to expand across to Birmingham and it has been only recently, just about two years ago, that we were able to get a piece of authority that ran from Dallas through Houston, New Orleans, and Mobile, and we could also tie in to our Panama City operation in the South and the Birmingham operation in the North. The result of all this expansion is that we are now doing over $20 million in revenues and almost $1,500,000 in profits.

St. Clair: To what degree are members of the Ballard family involved in management?

Ballard: Well, my oldest boy Bill is the most active—he has sort of grown up in the business. He's 45 now and is executive vice president. I'm 67 years old and serve as president. While Bill handles day-to-day operations, I make the major decisions—new financing and that type of thing. My other boy Jim, he's 37, handles our terminal operations.

The stock of the company is completely held by the Ballard family. We've been transferring the stock, over time, so that the estate won't be too cumbersome. Somewhere along the line I won't be with the company and I want that transition to take place as simply as possible.

St. Clair: How would you characterize your competitive position along your routes?

Ballard: We probably get more than our share. We think of ourselves as being pretty aggressive. See, in this part of the country it's the people you know that counts. In addition, we do a good piece of business interlining with other carriers, such as yourselves. Something like 20 percent of our interlining comes from Tauride, the other 80 percent from your competitors and other firms that want to serve the Florida and Gulf Coast areas but don't have that authority.

Our selling effort is very aggressive, but very personal. A lot of our effort goes into building relationships with companies like Tauride, because the interlining business is so important to us.

St. Clair: To what degree is the firm computerized?

Ballard: Well, computers are a very tricky business. We have done a little of that—we've put some of our accounting on computers. My son Bill has looked into the situation and our accountant, John Bean, has studied some at the school that IBM gives. Frankly, we're not convinced that we are up to the size where we need that yet.

St. Clair: What type of management incentive system does the company use?

Ballard: The way we work on that is we look at how we've done each year and, just before the books are closed, we make a distribution to certain key employees—members of the family; our operations manager, Jim Shattuck; Bob Red in sales; our maintenance man, Pete Delama; and John Bean.

St. Clair: How would you rate your labor relations?

Ballard: We have had what I would call very peaceful labor relations. We're not organized by the Teamsters—they're not too strong down here. Not being a national carrier, and by being close to our employees, we managed to avoid being organized. It has come to a vote several times and our boys have just turned it down.

St. Clair: What is the current condition of your fleet?

Ballard: We have gone through a period, until recently, where we have tried to own our own equipment. Bill did some very smart maneuvering recently. We had gotten into some pretty heavy expansion of the fleet associated with the tie-in of what we call our Texas run. We were able to turn that around pretty well when Bill cut an attractive sale-and-leaseback deal. So, in terms of the ownership of our fleet, much of it is leased and very modern.

In terms of our terminals, we haven't headed for very big terminals. The one thing we have done, in each case where we've been able to buy a terminal, is to try to locate in an area which we thought would be a growth area and we speculated on some interesting pieces of property, particularly in the Florida area where it's pretty hard to get stung.

St. Clair: Do you see the need for major financing in the near future?

Ballard: We've made heavy use of revolving credit. What we plan to do is to keep the same financing mix as we currently use. Our debt ratio is now pretty low—we tend to be pretty conservative—and we would aim to keep it that way. I think that we can finance our continued growth in a pretty smooth manner. Of course, if we merged with another firm, we might want to move a little closer to the edge and add more debt.

St. Clair: I have noted several significant changes in your balance sheet over the past few years. Could you explain these changes?

Ballard: First, there are the obvious changes associated with our sale-and-leaseback deal. Also, we had tended to build up a certain volume of cash which was being kept in certificates of deposit. When we made our Texas acquisition, we utilized these current assets and increased our other long-term assets through the purchase of the routes and some goodwill.

St. Clair: Do you feel that you can sustain your growth rate in the future?

Ballard: Yes, if we were left alone, I think we can sustain it. I don't want to brag, but I think that we could easily maintain an annual growth rate of 15 percent in revenues. If everything worked out really well, the best we could probably do is 25 percent. The lowest growth rate—if we were doing all sorts of terrible things—would probably be about 5 percent per year. I think there is a 50–50 chance it will be between 10 percent and 20 percent.

St. Clair: What do you think the major problems facing the firm are?

Ballard: I'm getting old—that's one big problem. I have to say, and I'm sure that you folks realize this too, that our main difficulty is going to be that our labor costs are going to increase relative to our revenues. I suspect that we will have to match the Teamsters' wages within the next few years. This will probably put our wages up to around 60 percent of revenues, near the national average for truckers our size.

Right now, our wages are running about 52 percent of revenues, the same as last year. Over the past few years, I have really put on some pressure for higher productivity and I've had some success in reducing the number of persons employed, even as our revenues increased. I don't know how much more of this we can do, but it has been important in keeping wage expense down. All in all, if I had to guess, I would expect our wages to approach 60 percent of revenues by 1977. That's an average increase of—let's see—2 percent per year. Probably the best we could expect to do would be to hold the line at 52 percent. If things really got bad, the increase could be as much as 3 points per year or so. There is probably a 50–50 chance that the rate of increase will be between 1 and 2½ percentage points per year.

The increase in compensation is our most significant cost trend. This will cause some of our other accounts, like terminal expenses, to drift up also. The most important issue is whether we can keep our rates moving equally with our labor costs.

St. Clair: Would you be interested in merging with another firm?

Ballard: Yes, I'd be interested. Yet, I would want to point out that it would be silly for any potential buyer to ignore the fact that the Ballard brothers, my two sons, have developed into a close working team. I would like to stress that they should be kept on as the managers of this company. Also, I think it would be smart, because of the volume of interline business that we do, that we not be just integrated into the buyer. I think we should be kept intact and separate, just as we always have, since many people down here like to deal with a family business.

Also, on this interline business, I think it's important that since we are dependent on a number of your competitors, there is more of a chance to hang on to this business if we are kept separate. I think you would agree with that.

At the same time, I would think that there is a lot we could gain from being merged. It certainly would help for my estate purposes. Also, you could bring to us the new marketing skills that you have developed. Much of our growth comes from the growth of the southeast region and, although we've done better than the average, some of our competitors are linking up with national carriers and starting to give us a harder run for the money. We are also at the point where we could use some of the financial and computer skills that you have. Frankly, the job of expanding this firm is getting to be a big job for the Ballard family resources and maybe it's time for some new support for our mutual benefit.

St. Clair: In general terms, what type of deal would you have in mind?

Ballard: Just recently, a number of investment banking firms have contacted us about making Ballard Trucking a public company. They think that we might get 12 times our next year's earnings—certainly 12 times our historic earnings. Just the same, I'm not the sort of man who would enjoy the process of taking my company public.

I've gotten to know your company pretty well from our interline relationship and I've watched your stock. I know that it trades about 16 times earnings but, and no offense to you or your fine president, it looks a little overpriced to me. In a deal, I think I'd rather have cash money than stock. My boys feel that there are some real advantages to getting stock, especially from the tax angle, so the best idea might be for you to make a cash offer and a stock offer; frankly I want more stock than I would cash. Make an offer, then let us consider the two alternatives.

There is another consideration that is part of this. I'd hate to see the name Ballard disappear from the trucks and the terminals. We've built up something here that I'm proud of and I would think it would be to your benefit to continue it and maintain our name. That would have to be part of any deal.

We've been approached by several carriers interested in acquiring us, but I look with some favor, if terms can be settled, on the idea of merging with Tauride, because I think we can work with folks like you.

chapter

7

Models and organizations*

In recent years the use of mathematical models in corporations has expanded rapidly. This expansion has paralleled the growth in formal quantitative analysis in most corporations and has led to management recognition that models can make exploration of the implications of strategic and environmental assumptions easy and fast.

Models can deal with complex interactions involving large quantities of data and can show how various decisions in one part of an organization affect the rest, thus facilitating integration and coordination. They can also show the risk and timing implications of alternative actions. Better insights into the corporation can arise from using models to understand its sensitivities to numerous internal and external variables.

In spite of these important advantages, management experiences with models have not been totally satisfactory. Models have proved expensive, many have taken longer than expected to create, and data requirements have been extensive and often unrealistic. Many have improperly represented business realities and, in general, they have been inflexible. Consequently, management has refused to accept a large number of models or has used them less often or differently than originally planned.

With such great promise, why have so many models been only partial successes or outright failures? Evidence seems to indicate that the problems are more managerial than technical: Few models fail because the technical state of the art is inadequate or because they are improperly implemented from a technical point of view.[1] It is true that some early failures were due in part to a lack of qualified modelers and to lengthy programming efforts in conventional programming lan-

---

* This chapter was developed from an article by John S. Hammond, "Do's and Don'ts of Computer Models for Planning," *Harvard Business Review*, March–April 1974. Copyright © by the President and Fellows of Harvard College; all rights reserved.

[1] Naomi Seligman, "Free for All," *Management Science*, vol. 14, no. 4, December 1967, p. B-145; and John W. Drake, *The Administration of Transportation Modeling Projects* (Lexington, Mass.: D. C. Heath, 1973).

guages. Both conditions, however, have since been remedied; there are now a number of programming languages for modeling purposes, and the number of people qualified to develop such models has greatly increased.

If the full potential of mathematical models as aids to managerial processes is to be realized, both managers and model builders need some guidelines for deciding how and whether to use them. Unfortunately, most of the literature on mathematical models is not particularly helpful—it concentrates on technical rather than managerial issues. The purpose of this chapter is to begin to fill this void.

THE TEN STAGES OF MODELS

Subjective judgment and skill must be brought to bear on all the parts of the process by which models are conceived, created, and used. This process can be broken into ten steps, which are listed below in the approximate order in which they occur.

One danger, however, of presenting the process as a sequence of steps is that such presentation masks its iterative nature. The reader should keep in mind that much looping back occurs when inadequacies or inconsistencies stemming from earlier steps are uncovered in a later step.

1. Decisions must be made as to where a model may be useful. To see where models might be beneficial requires a review of the company's activities.
2. A decision must be made whether to use a model. After a list of possible applications is generated, a decision must be made whether to go ahead with one or more of them. This decision depends on three considerations: Technically, is it possible? Economically, is it worthwhile? And, will the organization accept and use it?[2]
3. Specifications must be fixed. This step consists of defining the purposes of the model exactly, its primary inputs and outputs, the main aspects of its structure, and how it would be used. These specifications, in turn, determine the resources required to bring it into being.
4. A proposal must be prepared. If the required resources are significant and the procedures of the particular organization demand it, a formal proposal must be made to get (or grant) the approval to proceed. As part of the proposal preparation process, a decision

---

[2] McKinsey & Company, Inc., *Unlocking the Computer's Potential* (New York: McKinsey & Company, Inc., 1968).

must be made as to who shall be the modeler if the company concludes that a model will be beneficial. This person might be inside or outside the company.

5. Actual modeling and data gathering must go forward together. Modeling usually jumps back and forth between detailed conceptualization and computer programming. Tests of early versions of the model lead to modifications to suit refined conceptualization. Collecting the required data for the model almost always parallels model construction in this respect.

6. The model must be debugged. This step consists of checking thoroughly to see that the model does what it is supposed to do on two levels: (a) Does the computer program correctly implement the intended concept? (b) Judging from the output itself, does the concept require modification?

7. The users must be educated, and the model must gain acceptance. Most of the model's users will have had little experience or education in formal quantitative techniques, and their knowledge and background must be augmented. Even more important, they must be filled in on the specifics of the model in question. This educational process requires an understanding of the human and organizational obstacles to acceptance, such as resistance to change, and of the actions appropriate to overcome them.

8. The process of user validation must be established. Before a model can be considered ready for use, the users must check to see that it is valid for the purposes for which it was intended. Of course, the users will have been involved in the previous steps, so that validation will be a process that continues throughout the sequence, rather than a one-shot exercise.

9. The model must be put into actual use. Successful use requires an understanding of the model's capabilities and limitations so that its output can be creatively and intelligently used.

10. The model must be updated and modified. If the model is used on a recurring basis, several kinds of updates and modifications will be required. These modifications include changes made to (a) correct errors unearthed as a result of use, (b) modify the model as a result of the experience of actually using it, (c) refine the model to reflect new sophistication on the part of the users, (d) expand or adapt the model for new applications, and (e) incorporate up-to-date data.

With this multistage modeling process in mind, let us now turn our attention to ways that managers can increase the likelihood that their companies will use it successfully.

ORGANIZATIONAL CLIMATE

Managers must identify organizational and managerial settings in which models are more likely to succeed. They must also define the actions and behavior on the part of the modeling unit, the manager, model builder, and user, that will help to ensure success.

The situation is akin to that faced by farmers. They must first decide whether to plant a certain crop; naturally they will want to take into account climate and soil conditions—the givens of the situation. Once they have decided to plant a crop, they must focus on things within their control, such as seed strain, fertilizer, insecticides, and so on, to maximize the harvest.

Thus the first question a manager must face is whether the climatic conditions are favorable for mathematical models. These conditions are given, by and large—the manager can do little to alter them, at least in the short run. The following is a list of the organizational conditions that, if fulfilled, most greatly increase the probability of success in developing and using mathematical models.

Operations are well understood and data are ample

To make a useful model, the area or aspect of the business to which it will be applied must be well enough understood so that relationships that reflect operational realities can be written down. Then one must have the data necessary to "parameterize" those relationships.

Often these requirements can be met for marketing and production processes in older, more established industries—for example, steel, oil, and food processing, all well-understood industries with plenty of historical data. These industries also have large production runs requiring well-known proportions of raw materials; such continuous-flow processes are relatively easy to model.

On the other hand, an electronics company is less likely to be a "natural." It is likely to be a young company in a relatively new and rapidly changing industry.

The relevant data are easily accessible

This point sounds like part of the previous one, but it is not. The mere *existence* of data is not sufficient. Data must be readily *accessible* to the modelers. Often they are available only in a form that requires a great deal of massage to be useful. And, of course, certain data points required by the modeling process may be missing.

Sometimes the difficulty in getting the data is due to organizational considerations. For example, a modeler might be able to work rapidly on aspects of the company within his or her jurisdiction, but only slowly on the facilities outside this jurisdiction because the necessary information is hard to obtain. Also, political considerations respecting jurisdiction over "intimate" information have often kept models from being useful.[3]

Budgets, plans, and control systems are well defined and quantified

The use of models implies a highly quantitative, structured way of thinking. If the company's systems are all loosely defined, then two transitions are necessary: from loose to well-defined quantitative approaches and from not using models to using them. The second transition is seldom an easy one and is far more difficult if the first has not yet been made.

Models have management support

If there is support or enthusiasm for a model, more people will be committed to "make it happen." For example, at a steel company, the vice president of planning championed models; he encouraged their use, oversaw their implementation, and supported their existence. In a food processing company, the controller and top management fully supported the use of models, and another manager filled the role of champion.

Indeed, one consultant has remarked that he would only bid on modeling projects that have the support of the very highest level of management.

Management scientists accept responsibility for successful implementation

Several people have found a correlation between the success of a modeling project and the desire of the client and modelers to make it succeed.[4] Of course, a difficulty here is that the measure of success, or lack of it, in an area like this is usually set by a person involved. If someone really wants something to succeed, it is quite natural for that person to see it as a success afterwards, even though those less committed might feel otherwise. Unfortunately, objective measures of success are difficult to define.

---

[3] E. Eugene Carter, "What Are the Risks in Risk Analysis?" *Harvard Business Review*, July–August 1972, p. 72; and Rex V. Brown, "Do Managers Find Decision Analysis Useful?" *Harvard Business Review*, May–June 1970, p. 78.

[4] Drake, *Administration of Transportation Modeling Projects;* and Allan Harvey, "Factors Making for Implementation Success and Failure," *Management Science*, vol. 16, no. 6, February 1970, p. B-312.

Innovations and formal techniques have prospered in the past

Allen Harvey found that the highest correlation between any organizational factor and successful implementation was management's confidence in management science solutions to company problems, and he found a high correlation between success and prior experience using sophisticated problem-solving techniques. He also found that, for the 31 companies he studied, all 11 of the successful applications were in companies in which management had created a climate that encouraged innovation, whereas for the 8 unsuccessful projects, a generally negative attitude toward innovation prevailed.[5] (The remaining 12 were considered partial successes.)

Manager and modeler share status and background

Modeling and managing require very different types of knowledge and skills and usually attract very different types of people.[6] Sometimes the difference is so great that communication and an effective working relationship are difficult. Therefore, it helps when there is as much correspondence in background as possible.

One very successful modeler in a large chemical company is a veteran line manager turned staff member. As a result of that experience, this person has very strong rapport with line clients. In another company—a large diversified manufacturer—a modeler reports great success in working with line managers who are chemical engineers with Ph.D.'s, and who consequently have had training and experience in quantitatively modeling chemical processes.

This listing does not mean to imply that if all these organizational conditions are present, success is assured, or that if all are absent, failure is inevitable. But by comparing this list with a given situation, a manager can make a more informed judgment about whether to proceed.

FACTORS WITHIN THE MANAGER'S CONTROL

While the manager or the modeler can do relatively little to change the basic working conditions, there is still a great deal that can be done to help ensure success.

---

[5] Harvey, "Factors Making for Success and Failure."

[6] C. Jackson Grayson, "Management Science and Business Practice," *Harvard Business Review*, July–August 1973, p. 41; and John Hammond, "The Role of the Manager and Management Scientist in Successful Implementation," *Sloan Management Review*, Winter 1974.

Involve potential users in the development process

The decision makers—the users—must be drawn into the development process right from the start. From a survey that studied the success (or the lack of it) of 36 large corporations in using computers, McKinsey & Company concluded that user involvement is widely neglected and that this neglect is costly.[7]

Users should play an important role in the determination of modeling objectives. When designing the inner workings of the model, substantial attention should be paid to their perception of the situation being modeled. People tend to trust and use something they have had a hand in developing; they may not trust or use something they must accept on faith. Finally, involving the users during model development enhances their understanding and decreases the educational effort required after the model is completed.

Obviously, involvement of the ultimate users must be managed judiciously so as not to consume too much of their time. If critical milestones at which they need to be involved are identified, this is easily accomplished.

Define the model's goals explicitly, with a view to the decisions it will assist

The initial problem is to resolve these issues: What decision is the model designed to influence? Who will use the model? For whom is the output information intended? Consequently, what information must it provide to the users? What input variables will be used to permit the user to test alternatives and environmental assumptions? How often will it be used? How timely must the input information be?

The answers are crucial, for they define the model operationally. They become the specifications that the technicians must implement. Obviously, there will have to be some give-and-take between what is desired and what is technically possible. But the first thing is to define the operating characteristics from the point of view of the user. One ambitious modeling project was well specified technically but had gone two or more worker-years down the road before these crucial issues were faced. As a result, this model contained elaborate and irrelevant detail in several areas.

Express input and output in familiar formats

This is just another way of saying that the model should be easy to communicate with. Through years of dealing with problems, man-

---

[7] McKinsey, *Unlocking the Computer's Potential.*

agers have developed habits of thought, vocabulary, report format, and so on with which they have become extremely comfortable. Instances in which the model's output was in a sharply different format from what the user had come to expect were at best qualified successes as far as usefulness to managers was concerned. Other cases in which the outputs were not identified in English but rather were flagged by mathematical symbols were failures.

To ensure easy communication, many modelers prepare mock-ups of the output for the user's review early in the modeling effort.

Be opportunistic

Right from the start, be shrewd in choosing projects and methods. It is well known in marketing, for example, that a new product introduction is more likely to succeed if it fulfills an obvious felt need. The same principle applies to models. An operations research department in an electronics company failed miserably and was later dissolved because it tried to peddle new procedures rather than to solve managers' perceived problems. The solutions-in-search-of-problems approach has enjoyed broad failure.[8]

On the other hand, a mathematical modeling technique was successfully introduced in a major oil company partly because of the timing. The introduction occurred when management was facing a major operating crisis precipitated by the closing of the Suez Canal in 1967. The top managers had a need and called on the management scientists to help satisfy it—and the technique worked.[9] This was the beginning of successful use of models at this company.

Start simple and keep it simple

Initially, modeling projects should be kept as straightforward and uncomplicated in design as possible. Allowances must of course be made for increased sophistication and for changing needs, but simplicity is the rule; and modelers must never be allowed to go overboard.

John Little, who has had much experience observing managers using planning models, has said it well:

> The manager carries responsibility for outcomes. . . . We should not be surprised if he prefers simple analysis that he can grasp, even though it may have a qualitative structure, broad assumptions, and only a little relevant data, to a complex model whose assumptions may be partially hidden or couched in jargon and whose parameters may be the result of obscure statistical manipulations. . . .

---

[8] Drake, *Administration of Transportation Modeling Projects.*
[9] Carter, "What Are the Risks?"

> The best approach is to lead the potential user through a sequence of models of increasing scope and complexity. . . . Often a user, having learned a simple model, will start to ask for just the additional considerations found in the advanced models.[10]

The modeler, too, needs to grow in understanding of the particular situation that is being modeled. In one airline, a technically adept modeler, who knew relatively little about airlines forecasting, produced a complicated and elaborate sales forecasting system. It went unused. Later a much simpler model was created at a fraction of the cost of the first, and it was heavily used. Companies should beware of channeling effort to the development of a mammoth model before understanding has been firmly established by both managers and modelers and scope and feasibility have been made clear.

It is far better to get a simple version of a model up and running as soon as possible, use it for a while, and then expand it on the base of enhanced understanding. A certain self-restraint is advisable in such expansions, since the tendency is to err in the direction of too much machinery and detail.

Specifically, it is wise to resist all suggestion of an "all-purpose model." A massive, general-purpose model is unwieldy, is difficult to control, and requires huge amounts of data. Often, many facets of such a model are entirely extraneous to particular applications; equally, much detail in individual applications may be lost in the push to create a general-purpose model. Finally, these models are much more difficult to comprehend and therefore much more difficult for users to accept. A company that goes overboard in this direction is almost sure to regret it.

Often the top-down approach is a good way to start simple. The top-down process starts with representations of the market, company operations, and so forth, joined together in a very rough aggregate—the kind of broad-brush picture seen from the top of the company. Later, if more detail is required, some variables can be disaggregated and the description enriched. By using this approach, there exists a working model at all points, which is a great advantage.

The reverse—the bottom-up approach—requires tedious acquisition of data and modeling by product line, division, market area, and so on—or some other subdivision of the company's operation—and ultimately combining these to reflect the corporate picture. But the working model emerges quite slowly, and it frequently ends up being difficult to debug and too detailed for the purposes intended.

---

[10] John D. C. Little, "Models and Managers: The Concept of a Decision Calculus," *Management Science*, vol. 16, no. 8, April 1970, p. B-466.

Beware of creating misimpressions

The first trap here is to promise delivery on a more optimistic schedule than can be met. Computer programs notoriously take longer than planned, and an unrealistic schedule can damage both the work and the sponsor's reputation. Worse yet, the revelation that a project is behind schedule often comes too late for remedial action to be taken. To reduce this risk, it is useful to schedule in units of a worker-month of effort, with constant review of the whole schedule.

Second, the user frequently gets the incorrect impression that the model is intended to be the sole guide to decision making rather than an additional and important source of insight into a problem.

Put a manager rather than a modeler in charge

Ideally, the person in charge is both a manager and one who is skilled in modeling and in using the computer. However, even this person should function as a manager first, to ensure that the planning goals of the model are met and that the whole effort reflects a sensitivity to the motivations and priorities existing in the organization.[11]

Unfortunately, this ideal situation is rare. In a Diebold Research Program Survey, 61 percent of the 2,700 executives responding said that suggestions for new computer applications were coming from technicians, not from managers.[12] The Diebold study concluded that senior management's abdication of its responsibilities to technicians was one of the prime reasons that companies have not realized the true potential from their data processing investment.

Define roles clearly

It is vital to recognize that managers make decisions and management scientists make models and that their roles must be defined accordingly. One researcher has said that this recognition is the single most important element distinguishing successful from unsuccessful projects.[13] Obviously, some overlap between roles is required, but trouble arises when decision makers abdicate decision-making responsibility to modelers or when modelers attempt to usurp the decision maker's responsibility.

Score an early victory

Model creation is time-consuming and often expensive before demonstrable results are achieved. Understandably, management gets

[11] Harvey, "Factors Making for Success and Failure."
[12] Seligman, "Free for All."
[13] Drake, *Administration of Transportation Modeling Projects.*

impatient with long projects or is reluctant to fund them in the first place. Therefore, it is wise to arrange matters so that some *managerially* useful results—although not necessarily the final product— can be demonstrated as early as possible.

For example, one piece of a developing model may be useful in its own right. Alternatively, victory can be achieved through picking a small, simple, but high-impact project as the first effort.

Two contrasting anecdotes illustrate its value. First, in a large milk processing company, the modeler chose a simple, straightforward project for planning transportation as the initial effort. The benefits of the model were easy to measure and showed a clear improvement. The modeler soon was overwhelmed by requests for additional models.

Second, and in contrast, the modelers for a tire manufacturer looked at a production planning problem and proposed a new production planning system. But, they pointed out, it would not be fully productive unless new timing devices were installed on the production machines, and "by the way, some of the machines should be replaced, too." The price tag was $3 million plus a renegotiated labor contract. The response was rejection.

Build the model within the user's organization

The modeler must understand both the company and its industry and what is wanted by the managers who will use the model. If a modeling effort is to make good progress in the right direction, then the modeler ideally will be an inside person.

The closer the modeler and the user are organizationally, the more easily control, mutual understanding, and communication are maintained. As others have pointed out, this strategy enables the user to keep his most prized information close to his vest, where he wants it.[14]

Obviously, there are situations in which the absence of internal expertise dictates going outside for help. If this occurs, then control, communication, and mutual understanding are even more important.

Learn how to use the model effectively

Most managers' ways of thinking have been based on intuition, or at best on the time-consuming process of pencil-and-paper exploration of alternatives. Hence the number of alternatives they explore and the extent to which they analyze them have been relatively limited. With the computer have come expanded capabilities and speed, thus many more alternatives can be explored quickly. Consequently, users must develop a new style of thinking about problems to make the best use

---

[14] Brown, "Do Managers Find Decision Analysis Useful?"

of the model. They should realize that decisions are seldom based on a single run of a model. Often the result of a series of runs is a clarification and updating of their original intuitions and understanding of the problem.

Further, if users are to have an effective dialogue with a computer model, they must have fast access and fast response. This strongly argues for putting the model on a time-sharing system or a high-priority batch system, where results are available virtually instantaneously.

While the users need not become computer experts, it is nonetheless of the utmost importance that they receive some education in the use of computer planning models to ensure that they will be able to interact with models effectively and understand the kind of information they must supply in order for the model to run.

In addition, an educational approach can generate considerable enthusiasm, as the experience of a major accounting firm illustrates. The partner in charge of planning had developed a time-sharing model that could be used for planning by the managing partners at each of the branch offices. It was received coldly until he made a personal tour to introduce and explain it. Great enthusiasm followed; some of the managers became so fascinated that they stayed late at night exploring alternatives and analyzing consequences.

Finally, while the users ordinarily supply a model's most important data, some vital pieces of information must come from nonusers. These people must also be educated about the assumptions they are to make in supplying their inputs, so that their data will be consistent with the input of others.

Develop expertise to manage and update the model

The battle is not over once a model is put into use, unless it is a one-shot model. Ordinarily, when it goes out of date, its credibility and usefulness deteriorate. A model built for continuing use must be kept current by someone who knows the model, the company, and the industry—a person more likely to be found inside the company than outside it. The process of keeping a model up to date might be called *managing* the model.

A good example of effective model management comes from a major U.S. chemicals corporation. Originally built by outside consultants, the model is the responsibility of one of the corporate planners who has become skilled in keeping it up to date and improving it. Through the use of adjustment factors, the manager can allow for certain important considerations that are not specifically programmed into the model—for example, the receipt of a large government contract.

Treat the development and use of models as a process, not as the creation of a product (the model)

Distinguishing between product and process is critical; otherwise, one cannot create the frame of mind, in the modelers and the users, essential to realizing the full benefits of modeling. Unfortunately, the product approach is the more usual; its goal is to create a working model, and those involved find it difficult to see beyond that stage in their effort. (They generally cannot see beyond the debugging stage.) For the process approach, the creation of the model is an important step along the way toward using the model to affect planning favorably.

First of all, by working with the modelers, managers and users usually gain a great deal of insight into the company and its relationship to the business environment. In the product approach, these insights are by-products; in the process approach, however, they are recognized as valuable benefits to be sought out, and the fact that they must be sought out increases the chances of acquiring them.

Second, the longer view of the process approach fosters a give-and-take in model design and improvement that usually continues beyond the first use; it helps everyone to look ahead to how a model will be used in the future, to see how the organization is likely to respond to it, and to take this information into account in its design. In particular, the process approach anticipates the need for educational and organizational change in model introduction.

Finally, the process approach ensures that someone who knows the model's capabilities will be standing by to see that the model is used to full advantage. For example, one of the largest U.S. manufacturers had just completed a long-range planning model when its top management became seriously concerned about a lagging earnings trend. At first glance, the long-range planning model would not seem to be applicable to such a short-term issue, but the person responsible for it saw an application. It was usefully pressed into service to explore various plans to shore up short-term earnings—plans that would have minimal long-run effects.

Recognize that the process is individualistic and dependent on people

Initially, one might assume the opposite; for many, models and computers are the very symbols of impersonal processes. But they depend on both the modeler and the user as individuals. Many organizations witness the demise of a model with the departure of the chief modeler or the programmers responsible for it. Good documentation can do a great deal to reduce the chances of this happening, but the documentation process is time-consuming and ultimately ineffective, since everything cannot be written down. Even with documentation, it is easy to underestimate the time another technician needs to become familiar with a computer model.

The user has grown up with the model and has heavily influenced its character; often the original user is the only one with sufficient understanding and confidence in the model to use it. For example, a sophisticated and comprehensive planning model was built for a new division of a communications-based conglomerate. The person who served as division manager at the time the model was built used it regularly. When he was promoted, one of his subordinates became division manager; since he had been involved with the model from the start, he too used it. Finally, a third division manager from outside the division took over. The model is now gathering cobwebs.

Beware of misuses of models

Once users overcome old thought patterns and really begin to take advantage of the capability of models, a series of *misuses* often appears:

1. Sometimes work with a model becomes a substitute for good hard thinking about assumptions and alternative courses of action. It becomes an unimaginative ritual, just as the annual planning cycle often becomes the "rite of fall."
2. The fact that the results are printed out on the computer lends an air of accuracy to the anticipated impact of plans. This may be *just an air* of accuracy.
3. If many alternatives are tested with the model, the one that finally is selected sometimes takes on vaunted status because it has been so rigorously tested. Thereafter it may be followed too rigidly under changed conditions. In fact, rigid use represents a failure to use a model to its full advantage; after all, one main reason for building a model in the first place is to test the implications of a modified plan under changed conditions.
4. In many organizations, planning is an advocacy process. In such settings, models are sometimes used to justify, rather than to explore, the implications of actions.

THE CASES IN THIS CHAPTER

Some of these points of advice are more applicable to one organization than another, or to one kind of modeling than another; each situation is, after all, unique. To tie some of the points together, the cases in this chapter have a different emphasis than cases studied up to this point. Cases in earlier chapters have focused on some analytic technique and helped to teach that technique by placing the analytic burden on you, the student. In the earlier cases, while there was usually room for interpretation and a need for casting analytic results back into the real world, this was not usually the main theme. In this chapter, the cases may still involve some numerical analysis, but this is a relatively trivial part of the overall case. What you will be doing here is putting on the hat of the manager or the user and making some judgments about the job an analyst has done for you. Has the work been useful? Has it accomplished its objective? Why? Why not? Where should the model go from here?

These questions are indeed worth asking for any kind of analytic effort. In academic settings, however, we usually restrain ourselves to making judgments about the simpler issues like the model's "correctness" or "accuracy." It is our feeling that this academic kind of question provides too narrow a focus to adequately prepare you to evaluate the mathematical models you are likely to encounter after graduation. These cases, then, are intended to fill this gap. They provide a richer organizational description and thus a better sense of what the entire organization is about than cases earlier in the book.

In some of this chapter's cases the most meaningful issues are not readily apparent. Often, unearthing these issues will require a bit of enterprising speculation on your part—or some clash of points of view in discussion. Once these issues have surfaced, however (and it is important that they should), the significance of the modeling process as an integral part of management can be understood more fully.

There is no specific analytic technique illustrated by cases in this chapter. Instead, you will find the technical content of these cases a bit of a mixed bag. Several deal with simulation, others with decision analysis or linear programming. Some even illustrate techniques not otherwise covered in this text.

On the other hand, there is a common thread. It is not the quantitative technology but the *management* of quantitative technology that binds these cases together. The management skills that are important to the success of any kind of project are also important to projects that deal with quantitative methods. Specifically, the issues raised in this chapter will be important in dealing with these cases. We hope that by illustrating these concepts with case examples, you will learn them more surely than by simply reading the text. If this indeed happens, your ability to function in the increasingly model-oriented managerial world will be significantly enhanced.

The Engel Company (A)

The Engel Company was founded in Cincinnati in 1967 by Mr. Abraham M. Engel, an engineer, for the purpose of developing, building, and marketing machinery to be used in the manufacture of paper-covered wire ties of the type used with plastic garbage bags. Near the end of development work on the prototype machine, however, Mr. Engel concluded that manufacture of the ties would be a far more profitable venture than sale of the machines. The ensuing years had proved this judgment to be sound and the firm prospered. Bag ties were sold at an average price of $3 per 1,000 to manufacturers of blown polyethylene bags and to firms employing such bags as packaging of bakery products. By early 1973 the firm employed 125 people and had recorded profits in 14 consecutive quarters. Several promising new products had been added to the Engle Company's line in recent years but the bag ties still accounted for over 90 percent of sales and close to 98 percent of profits.

In February of 1973, Mr. Engel observed that his firm was becoming too large for him to personally supervise all of the functional areas as he had in the past. After considerable thought he decided that if he could hire a competent production manager, he would be taking a step toward freeing himself from the day-to-day routine, which should allow him to devote more time to the other functions of management. With this in mind, Mr. Engel placed advertisements in several leading newspapers and, at length, hired a young man named Brian Maxwell.

Maxwell had graduated from a prominent southern technical university with a degree in industrial engineering and had six years of industrial experience, the last three as production supervisor for a large chemical company. Mr. Engel decided that he would suggest that Brian look into the maintenance function of the bag tie machines as a way of getting his feet on the ground.

THE BAG TIE PRODUCTION OPERATION

Bag ties were produced at a rate of 500 per minute on each of 24 identical machines which were currently being operated on a three-shift, five-day-week basis. Each shift was punctuated by two ten-minute breaks and a 30 minute lunch period during which the machines were not running. Every machine was tended by an operator who maintained raw material supplies, cleared jam-ups, packed finished goods, and monitored the quality of the finished product. The machines had been designed by Mr. Engel, who had incorporated a series of modular subsystems for ease of maintenance. Each machine consisted of a framework, an electric motor, and several mechanical modules which could be removed and interchanged with a like module on any other machine. When a machine breakdown occurred, the operator would signal the maintenance crew by means of a red light mounted on the machine. Each shift was served by three mechanics whose only responsibility was to repair the breakdowns of the bag tie machines. Service of breakdowns was on a first-come-first-served basis to avoid long delays in returning a machine to service. Repair usually consisted of replacement of one of the modules or adjustment of feeds. When a module had to be removed from a bag tie machine, it was sent to the company machine shop for overhaul and was subsequently returned to the pool of spare modules for eventual reuse. Mr. Engel felt that the use of modules in the design of the machine had been a prime factor in achieving an exceptionally low downtime rate which, in turn, was considered to be instrumental to the overall success of the company.

The choice of having Mr. Maxwell study the bag tie maintenance function as an initial assignment was motivated not only by the conviction that the project would provide a means to acquaint him with the operations of the plant. The bag tie business was still expanding rapidly and lately the lack of production capacity had been a limiting factor, causing Mr. Engel to refuse some potentially attractive contracts. Three new machines were being built in the company machine shop at a cost of about $7,000 apiece, and still further expansion was contemplated. Mr. Engel knew that eventually he would have to add another mechanic to each shift, but he was uncertain as to when he should do so. He intuitively felt that he should have one mechanic for every ten machines or so, but his observation of the bag tie department often made him uneasy about this judgment. He knew that the mechanics were frequently idle for considerable periods but he had also seen the department at times when as many as ten red lights were on at once. Since the work rules of the union labor agreement prohibited the operators from performing maintenance themselves, they usually congregated in the coffee break area when their machine was waiting for a mechanic to complete a previous job. During periods when there were few breakdowns, the mechanics were often seen reading popular magazines. In an attempt to determine what to do about this situation, Mr. Engel suggested that it was a problem area of some importance to the new production manager, Mr.

EXHIBIT 1
Income statement, 1972 ($000)

Sales	$8,776
Cost of sales	
Direct labor	889
Material	3,636
Gross margin	$4,251
General, selling, and administrative	1,996
Depreciation	85
Other expense	679
Profit before tax	$2,291
Tax @ 52 percent	1,192
Profit after tax	$1,099
Dividends	250
Retained earnings	$ 849

Maxwell. Mr. Engel gave Maxwell the Engel Company income statement for 1972 and the standard cost sheets for the most popular product, the 3-inch bag tie, as background information (see Exhibits 1 and 2).

EXHIBIT 2
Standard cost data, 3-inch bag tie

Item		Cost per 1,000 ties ($)
Material costs		
Wire		$0.7954
Paper		0.4779
Direct labor @ 7.50/hour	$7.500	
Plus 10 percent waste	0.750	
	$8.250	
Plus 11.12 percent nonproductive	0.923	
	$9.173	
Times 0.0333 (1,000/30,000)		0.3058
		$1.5791
Plus packaging material		0.0500
Total		$1.6291

MR. MAXWELL'S STUDY

As an industrial engineer by training, Maxwell felt that the problem was subject to analysis by use of a waiting-line model. Gathering precise data for input to such a model could be a rather time-consuming process. Maxwell decided that, to conserve his time for other activities as production manager, he would ask the mechanics to report the details of each maintenance call on a simple form. He discussed the project with the first-shift lead mechanic, Ray Jeffries, and was given a cooperative reaction, since Jeffries felt that the results of such a study would show the need for at least one additional mechanic on each shift.

Maxwell had several small pads of a reporting form (see Exhibit 3) printed and distributed to the mechanics. He determined that the

EXHIBIT 3
Mechanic's self-reporting form

```
┌─────────────────────────────────────────┐
│                                         │
│     Machine no._____                  │
│                                         │
│                                         │
│                                         │
│     Start time_____                │
│                                         │
│                                         │
│                                         │
│     End time_____                  │
│                                         │
└─────────────────────────────────────────┘
```

recording of service calls should begin at noon on Tuesday and end at noon on Thursday. Brian explained the recording scheme to each mechanic individually, and he was sure that each man understood his task. The reporting was carried out only on the daytime shift in order that he and Mr. Engel could observe the men and determine that the data collection was being carried out conscientiously. At noon on Thursday, Maxwell collected the completed forms, and that afternoon he tabulated the service time and breakdown interval frequency distributions shown in Exhibits 4 and 5. He was somewhat disturbed to find that the data clustered around "convenient" numbers, but he felt that they were usable if he could assume that the mean value of the data was close to the mean value of the actual service times.

Maxwell went to one of his old engineering textbooks to review queuing theory. He found that, although the mathematical basis for the theory was quite complex, the essence of the difficult calculations was captured by several simple tables. The formulas and tables (see Exhib-

EXHIBIT 4
Distribution of service times

Service time (minutes)	Number of occurrences
1	1
2	5
3	14
4	9
5	69
6	4
7	7
8	6
9	1
10	36
12	1
13	1
15	25
20	11
21	1
22	1
25	1
30	2
40	2
50	1
60	1
105	1

Total service time = 1,967 minutes
Number of service calls = 200

EXHIBIT 5
Breakdown interval distribution (entire bag tie department)

Interval between breakdowns	Number of observations
0	4
1	7
2	16
3	27
4	40
5	36
6	20
7	23
8	8
9	11
10	2
11	2
13	3
15	1

EXHIBIT 6
Queuing theory parameters and formulas

N	= Number of machines in system
T	= Average service time per breakdown
U	= Average time between calls for service—one machine
M	= Number of service channels (mechanics)
X	= Percent of total time spent in service = $T/(T + U)$
D	= Probability of delay in service for any breakdown
B	= Percent of total time spent in waiting line = $(1 - F)/F$
F	= Efficiency factor
Lq	= Mean number of machines in waiting line = $N \times B \times F$
Wq	= Mean waiting time per breakdown = $(T + U) \times B$
H	= Mean number of units being serviced = $F \times N \times X$
J	= Mean number of units running = $N \times F \times (1 - X)$

EXHIBIT 7
Finite queuing tables*

$N = 24$ $X = 0.095$				$N = 26$ $X = 0.095$			
M	D	F	B	M	D	F	B
5	0.065	0.998	0.002	6	0.028	0.999	0.001
4	0.193	0.991	0.009	5	0.090	0.997	0.003
3	0.474	0.964	0.037	4	0.245	0.989	0.011
2	0.875	0.831	0.203	3	0.554	0.953	0.049
				2	0.926	0.790	0.265

$N = 28$ $X = 0.095$				$N = 30$ $X = 0.095$			
M	D	F	B	M	D	F	B
6	0.040	0.999	0.001	6	0.055	0.999	0.001
5	0.119	0.996	0.004	5	0.153	0.994	0.006
4	0.302	0.985	0.015	4	0.363	0.980	0.020
3	0.633	0.938	0.066	3	0.709	0.921	0.086
2	0.961	0.747	0.339	2	0.982	0.704	0.420

*Derived from: L. G. Peck and R. N. Hazelwood, *Finite Queuing Tables* (New York: John Wiley, 1958).

its 6 and 7) for application of queuing theory seemed straightforward, and Brian anticipated no difficulty in analyzing the problem.

ANALYSIS OF THE SYSTEM

Mr. Maxwell studied the queuing theory formulas intently (see Exhibit 6). It was obvious that N, the number of machines, equaled 24 currently, and that N could be varied so that the expanded system could be modeled. The average service time, T, for the period studied was the total service time divided by the number of service calls, 1,967/200, or about 9.8. Maxwell reasoned that this average would be independent of the number of machines and also independent of the number of mechanics. Therefore, this figure would not change as the number of mechanics or the number of machines was varied. U, the mean time between service calls for an individual machine, was more difficult for Maxwell to derive. It finally became apparent, however, that that number must be the total number of minutes available to run divided by the total number of service calls. Since there were 480 minutes in a shift and 50 of those minutes were nonrunning minutes anyway (for lunch and scheduled breaks), there must be 10,320 minutes available for machine running per shift (430 minutes times 24 machines). Reducing this figure by the time spent in maintenance, 983 minutes per shift, gave 9,337 minutes available for running, and dividing that by 100 breakdowns per shift gave an average of about 93.4 running minutes between breakdowns for a single machine.

Since the mean time between service calls, U, was the characteristic of an individual machine, it also was independent of the number of mechanics or the number of machines. Because T and U were both independent of the effects of changes in mechanic manning level or machine population, X, the ratio of the average service time to the sum of the average service time and the average running time must have also been a single value independent of changes in these factors. Therefore, X must have been equal to 0.095 [i.e., 9.8/(93.4 + 9.8)] for any number of mechanics serving any number of machines.

Turning to the finite queuing tables (see Exhibit 7), Maxwell saw that X, M, and N were needed to identify a value for F, the efficiency factor, and B, the percent of their total time that machines spent in the waiting line. Once F and B were known, the problem was reduced to computing values for the remaining elements and comparing the costs of the various mechanic alternatives for different machine population situations. Since it had gotten late, Maxwell put the analysis in his drawer and went home feeling that he could easily complete the study the next morning, the end of his first week of employment at the Engel Company. On his way out of the office he stopped by the personnel desk and found that mechanics were paid $9 per hour including fringe benefits.

case 7–2

The Engel Company (B)

The Engel Company, manufacturer of paper-covered wire ties used with plastic garbage bags, had recently employed a young industrial engineer, Brian Maxwell, as production manager. Maxwell's first assignment had been to study the maintenance function of the bag tie machines which made up the bulk of the Engel Company's manufacturing capacity (see case 7–1). Maxwell had used a technique called *queuing theory* to determine the effects of adding additional maintenance mechanics as capacity was expanded through the addition of new machines. He had arrived at a solution which appeared satisfactory and which seemed to please Mr. Engel, the owner of the business.

Nonetheless, Maxwell felt uneasy with the queuing theory approach to this problem. He felt that the assumptions which he had made concerning the service time distribution and the breakdown interval distribution might not be completely representative of the real system. Also, he was uncertain of the sensitivity of the results to the differences between the real system and the approximations which he had made to push the system into the queuing theory format. Finally, he felt that he could have used observational data to simulate the bag tie maintenance function and that he would have been more comfortable with a simulation model of the system.

The computer service firm that maintained the Engel Company's accounts also provided technical services at nominal additional expense. Mr. Hal Swift, the service manager of the computer firm, was sure that his machine held a "canned" program to solve a queuing problem. Maxwell gave Swift the results of his mechanic survey.

One week later Mr. Swift sent Maxwell a 75-page report that detailed the results of the simulation, a copy of the computer program that performed the analysis, and an invoice for $1,000.

ALPHA Concrete Products, Inc.*

Early in the spring of 1973, Mr. Rick Woodbury, secretary-treasurer of ALPHA Concrete Products, was anticipating how he might evaluate the long-range forecasts of company sales and profits that had recently been prepared by a local consulting firm. He realized that the other members of top management at ALPHA were expecting him to make a formal presentation of his projections within the next week so that as a group they could complete their five-year plan. Thus, he wanted to determine the limitations and strengths of the consulting firm's approach, perform any additional analysis that might be required, and determine just what his presentation should cover.

ALPHA was in the business of manufacturing concrete pipe and reinforced concrete boxes used in highway, utility, and farm construction. The company maintained three production facilities, one each in Utah, Colorado, and Idaho. Sales were handled through the company's own distributors located throughout the intermountain area. Approximately two thirds of the company's sales had gone to the major intermountain public utilities in recent years, with the balance going to mostly agricultural construction in the Idaho region and to about an equal mix of highway and agricultural construction in the other regions. In 1973 total annual sales came 60 percent from Utah, 22 percent from Idaho, and 18 percent from Colorado.

While the company generally submitted bids on all of the major projects in its marketing area, it was only awarded about 30 percent of those contracts. In aggregate, such major contracts accounted for over 80 percent of its volume. The company had noticed in the past that the total volume of bid requests was growing at a modest rate each year. However, the fraction of bid requests from each of the major market segments—utilities, highways, and agricultural—varied substantially from year to year.

Rick Woodbury had asked a local consulting firm to prepare a set of sales and profit forecasts for ALPHA through 1980. The consultant who actually conducted the project had spent several hours with Rick at the outset, asking questions about the firm and its skills, products,

---

* This case was prepared by Associate Professor Steven C. Wheelwright of Harvard University.

customers, and competition. The consultant also obtained from Rick a set of ALPHA's annual reports covering the past 15 years. The following report had been given to Rick following a summary presentation made by the consultant.

Pro forma sales and profits report, 1974–1980

CONTENTS

A. Executive Summary
B. Development of a Sales Forecasting Model
    Figure B1: Definition of variables
    Figure B2: Historical data variables
    Figure B3: Simple correlation matrix
    Figure B4: Results of four-variable regression model
C. Forecasts of ALPHA's Sales
    Figure C1: ALPHA sales forecasts, 1974–1980
    Figure C2: Confidence intervals on sales forecasts
D. ALPHA Pro Forma Income Statements
    Figure D1: ALPHA's historical cost structure
    Figure D2: ALPHA pro forma income statements, 1974–1980
    Figure D3: ALPHA 1980 pro forma income statements

A. EXECUTIVE SUMMARY

The major impetus for the preparation of this study was the need that ALPHA's management felt to prepare more accurate forecasts of both sales and income statements. Thus, rather than simply relying on linear extensions of past growth rates, the company decided to determine some of the basic relationships between economic factors and sales and then base prediction on these fundamental relationships.

The approach taken in this study involved the application of regression analysis to the sales forecasting problem at ALPHA. There were three main reasons for selecting this approach to forecasting. First is the fact that it is a systematic approach that has been tested in a wide range of situations and has been found to give significant results when the proper requirements are met. Second, this approach provides not only a best-estimate forecast for each of several years into the future but also allows the computation of confidence intervals so that management can determine the uncertainty that surrounds such estimates. Finally, this approach uses the historical data available to determine causal relationships between the dependent variable (sales) and the several independent variables that are felt to be the most important determinants of sales.

The results of applying this statistical approach to sales forecasting were indeed satisfactory. The model actually used explained 95 percent of the historical variation in ALPHA's sales. Thus, if this model had been used in the past 15 years in forecasting sales, on average the actual sales value would have deviated from the forecast value by less than $500,000. This would appear to be a fairly accurate model, at least on an historical basis.

This model, which bases the sales forecast on population growth, new dwelling unit permits, and construction employment, was then used to prepare forecasts of sales for each of the next seven years (through 1980). Of course, the basic assumption in such usage of the model is that those relationships that have determined the company's sales in the past will continue to do so in the future. In addition to giving a single sales forecast for each of the next seven years, this model was also used to determine a 90 percent confidence interval around each of those forecasts. This interval delineates the range of values within which it is 90 percent certain that the actual outcome will fall. Thus, this provides management with a measure of the uncertainty in these forecasts.

The final step was to take the sales forecasts and use these in preparation of pro forma income statements for the past six years of company operations. Thus, the assumption is that the cost structure will remain the same in the future as it has been in the past. (In fact, the cost structure has been very stable over the past six years.)

Since this is a first application of statistical forecasting at ALPHA, it will be necessary for management to explain the basis of this forecast to those who will actually use it. It will undoubtedly be the case that as the forecast is used, other variables and sources of data which might be used in the future will be recognized and thus the application of this technique can be continually improved.

B. DEVELOPMENT OF A SALES FORECASTING MODEL

While there are several alternative sales forecasting methods available, the one that was selected for use in forecasting ALPHA's sales was that of regression analysis. This technique develops a basic model using historical data and then applies this model to forecast future sales values. The model itself is a causal one in that the dependent variable (ALPHA's sales) is stated as a function of several independent variables on which data can be collected. Thus, in very elementary terms, the essence of this approach is to identify those factors (variables) that are felt to have the greatest impact on ALPHA's sales and then determine the relationship between these factors and company sales based on historical data. This relationship is then used to predict future values and sales.

Through discussions with ALPHA management, several factors were identified that might have a possible impact on ALPHA's sales.

These included:

1. Construction activity.
2. Expansion by major utilities.
3. Highway construction.
4. Agricultural expansion.
5. Interest rates.
6. Population.

Based on these factors, a number of variables were identified for which historical data could be collected and which could also be projected into the future. Figure B1 indicates the nine variables that were identified for possible use in this study. All of these variables are defined in Figure B1 and should be clear, with the possible exception of variables 8 and 9. Variable 8 is the number of new dwelling unit permits from the previous year. That is, this variable takes *1970* dwelling unit permits and uses them as an indicator of *1971* sales. The reason for this is that dwelling unit permits generally precede the actual construction activity. Thus, the issuance of such permits would be a leading factor in predicting ALPHA's sales. Variable 9 is what is referred to as a lag variable and is based on construction employment. Here the assumption is that actual construction employment will effect ALPHA's sales in a prior year. For example, ALPHA's sales in 1970 would be effected by 1971 construction employment.

FIGURE B1
Definition of variables

Variable	Definition (and source of data)	Units*
Time	The year, with 1959 = 1	1s
Population	Total Utah population (*Utah Stastistical Abstract*)	100,000s
Residential units	Total residential units in Utah (Mountain Bell)	100,000s
New dwelling unit permits	Total of new housing permits for Utah (*Utah Real Estate Facts*)	100,000s
Construction employment	Total employment in Utah construction industry (*Utah Statistical Abstract*)	100,000s
Mountain Bell telephone mains	Total Mountain Bell telephone mains in Utah (Mountain Bell)	100,000s
ALPHA's sales	Total annual sales of ALPHA (accounting statements)	100,000s
Lead—dwelling unit permits (8)	Same as variable 4	100,000s
Lag—construction employment (5)	Same as variable 5	100,000s

* Units used in regression model.

The actual data collected on each of the variables to be considered for use in this model are shown in Figure B2. These data cover the 15-year period from 1959 through 1973. One of the attractive features of the technique of regression analysis is that using a computer, several different models (that is, models that include different combinations of the variables) can be tested without much difficulty and then the most appropriate model (the one that makes the most sense and gives the best results) can be actually selected for use in forecasting. This approach of trying several models is the one that was followed in this study.

The results of this statistical analysis can first be seen by examining the simple correlation matrix shown in Figure B3. This shows the extent of the relationship (correlation) between each pair of variables. The value of any correlation is between −1.00 and +1.00. A correlation of 0 indicates no relationship between the two variables; a correlation of +1.00 indicates perfect positive correlation (an increase in one variable is always accompanied by an increase in the other); and a correlation of −1.00 indicates a perfect negative correlation (an increase in one variable is always accompanied by a decrease in the other variable).

From Figure B3 it can be seen that all of the variables show a high positive correlation with ALPHA's sales, with the strongest correlation being with population (0.922) and the weakest correlation being with new construction permits (0.689). It will also be noted that previous year's building permits (variable 8) correlates more highly with ALPHA's sales (0.727) than does the current year's building permits (0.689), and next year's construction employment (variable 9) correlates more highly with ALPHA's sales (0.715) than does the current year's construction employment (0.709).

The approach actually used in determining which set of variables gives the best model for forecasting ALPHA's sales is to try a variety of combinations (using a computer-based analysis) and then to select the best of those. In practice the computer uses a systematic approach to formulate the most promising combinations of variables. For purposes of this written analysis, it is only necessary to state that this has been done and that from the many alternative models available, the one shown in Figure B4 has been identified as being best in this situation.

The model shown in Figure B4 bases the prediction of ALPHA's sales on three variables:

X_2 = Population
X_5 = Construction employment
X_8 = Lead construction permits (previous year's permits)

This model was chosen as being best based on its ability to explain ALPHA's sales over the past 15 years. Some of the measures used in selecting this model are shown in Figure B4.

FIGURE B2

Historical data variables

Year	Time	Population	Res. units Mtn. Bell	New dwelling unit permits	Constr. empl.	Mtn. Bell tel. mains	ALPHA's sales	Lead–new dwelling permits	Lag–constr. Employment
1959	1	868,000	227,000*	8,272	15,715	218,500*	$ 2,904,000	8,000*	14,851
1960	2	890,627	232,627	6,700	14,851	226,600	2,868,000	8,272	15,569
1961	3	936,000	237,700*	8,030	15,569	234,400*	3,303,000	6,700	17,790
1962	4	958,000	243,200*	8,420	17,790	242,100*	4,888,476	8,030	17,549
1963	5	974,000	248,600*	8,744	17,549	249,900*	5,879,591	8,420	17,035
1964	6	978,000	253,800*	6,494	17,035	257,700*	5,947,587	8,744	15,971
1965	7	991,000	259,100	5,657	15,971	265,400	5,905,301	6,494	15,507
1966	8	1,009,000	264,800*	3,982	15,507	275,000*	5,442,447	5,657	13,420
1967	9	1,019,000	270,500*	5,116	13,420	285,000*	4,327,223	3,982	13,689
1968	10	1,029,000	276,200*	5,490	13,689	294,700*	6,237,503	5,116	13,964
1969	11	1,047,000	281,900*	5,964	13,964	304,300*	5,921,922	5,490	14,583
1970	12	1,059,000	287,700	9,070	14,583	314,000	7,619,577	5,964	16,951
1971	13	1,099,000	276,100	12,777	16,951	330,500	7,863,210	9,070	20,669
1972	14	1,128,000	313,800	17,320	20,669	349,100	9,853,870	12,777	22,100
1973	15	1,157,000	323,800	13,450	22,100	369,100	11,979,262	17,320	20,000*
Mean	8.0	1,009,660	266,347	8,364	16,358	281,033	$ 6,082,720	7,947	16,763
Std. Dev.	4.47	81,242	28,169	3,623	2,459	45,542	$ 2,506,079	3,345	2,821

* Approximate.

FIGURE B3
Simple correlation matrix

Variable		Time	Population	Res. units	New constr.	Constr. empl.	Bell Tel. mains	ALPHA's sales	Lead (4)	Lag (5)
Time	1	1.000								
Population	2	0.983	1.000							
Res. units	3	0.963	0.965	1.000						
New constr. (permits)	4	0.509	0.581	0.566	1.000					
Constr. empl	5	0.349	0.483	0.481	0.794	1.000				
Bell Tel mains	6	0.987	0.986	0.978	0.607	0.465	1.000			
ALPHA's sales	7	0.878	0.922	0.917	0.689	0.709	0.917	1.000		
Lead (4)	8	0.396	0.502	0.532	0.790	0.943	0.526	0.943	1.000	
Lag (5)	9	0.491	0.593	0.538	0.947	0.845	0.591	0.715	0.843	1.000

FIGURE B4
Results of four-variable regression model

Model

$$Y = B_0 + B_2X_2 + B_5X_5 + B_8X_8$$

where: Y = ALPHA's sales
X_2 = Population
X_5 = Construction employment
X_8 = Lead (one year) building permits (i.e., building permits in previous year)
B_0 = Constant factor
B_2, B_5, and B_8 = Coefficients for independent variables

Measures of goodness of fit

Multiple R = 0.9725
R^2 (percentage of variance explained) = 0.9457
Standard error of estimate = $658,820

Coefficient values (based on 15 years' historical data)

B_0 (constant) = −208.69
B_2 (population) = 22.91
B_5 (construction employment) = 157.69
B_8 (lead—building permits) = 155.78

Residual values (using model to predict past 15 years sales)

Time	Residual*	Time	Residual*
1 (1959)	$252,687	9	−$954,523
2	−284,433	10	573,518
3	−754,892	11	−256,115
4	−293,394	12	988,885
5	352,426	13	−534,986
6	359,352	14	−372,551
7	972,812	15 (1973)	155,020
8	−203,823		

* Residual = Actual − Forecast.

1. R^2 = 0.9457. This value indicates that the model explains 95 percent of the variation in ALPHA's sales.
2. Standard error of estimate = $658,820. Approximately two thirds of the actual values are within $658,820 of the value predicted by this model.
3. Positive coefficients. All three of the coefficients (B_2, B_5, and B_8) are positive, indicating positive correlation with sales. This is what one would expect.

4. Residual values. These values are the difference between the sales value predicted by the model and the actual sales value. On the average the error over the past 15 years is less than $450,000.

In summary this model fits very well with the historical data of the past 15 years and, assuming the same basic relationship in the future, provides a good model for forecasting ALPHA's sales for the next several years.

C. FORECASTS OF ALPHA'S SALES

Having selected a regression model to be used in sales forecasting, the next step is to obtain projected values for each of the independent variables. Since the three variables we are using are ones of major interest to the government and several businesses, these projections are readily available. Figure C1 indicates the values used for 1974–1980 for the variables—population, construction employment, and new dwelling unit permits. Based on these independent variables, the ALPHA's sales projections shown in Figure C1 can be made simply by substituting the appropriate values for each year into the forecasting equation.

FIGURE C1
ALPHA sales forecasts, 1974–1980

Model

$$Y = B_0 + B_2X_2 + B_5X_5 + B_8X_8$$
$$= -208.69 + 22.91X_2 + 157.69X_5 + 155.78X_8$$

Predicted values

Year	X_2*	X_5†	X_8†	Y
1974	1,168,000	23,800	13,450	11,738,000
1975	1,194,000	25,490	15,800	12,966,000
1976	1,221,000	26,250	15,000	13,580,000
1977	1,248,000	27,000	15,300	14,364,000
1978	1,276,000	27,750	16,000	15,232,000
1979	1,304,000	28,500	16,000	15,993,000
1980	1,333,000	29,260	16,500	16,854,000

* Based on Mountain Bell forecasts.
† Based on Bureau of Economic and Business Research, University of Utah estimates.

As indicated in Figure C1, ALPHA's sales are expected to reach $16,854,000 by 1980. Again, however, it must be remembered that these projections assume that the basic relationships that have affected sales in the past will continue into the future.

Additional information on future ALPHA sales can be obtained by computing a 90 percent confidence interval for each of these annual sales forecasts. This is done in Figure C2. The basis for this computation is the standard error of estimate that was determined when computing the coefficients for this regression model (see Figure B4). The notion is a statistical one which determines the range around any forecast such that the actual value will fall within that range (that confidence interval) 90 percent of the time. For example, the 90 percent confidence interval for ALPHA's sales in 1980 is $15,537,000 to $18,171,600. This means that assuming the same relationships that have held in the past continue to hold in the future, there is a 90 percent chance that actual ALPHA sales in 1980 will fall within this range. Of course, one must also remember that it means there is a 10 percent chance that the actual sales will fall outside of this range.

FIGURE C2
Confidence intervals on sales forecasts

Year	Sales forecast	Confidence interval (90 percent)
1974	$11,738,000	$10,538,000–$12,938,000
1975	12,966,000	$11,746,000–$14,187,000
1976	13,580,000	$12,200,000–$14,860,000
1977	14,364,000	$13,084,000–$15,644,000
1978	15,232,000	$13,900,000–$16,530,000
1979	15,993,000	$14,687,000–$17,300,000
1980	16,854,000	$15,537,000–$18,171,600

D. ALPHA PRO FORMA INCOME STATEMENTS

With the sales forecasts in hand, pro forma income statements can be prepared for 1974–1980. The one additional prerequisite to doing this is determining ALPHA's cost structure. Figure D1 indicates what this cost structure has been for each of the past six years. This figure also includes a composite set of figures which is based on the historical data *and* ALPHA management's judgment as to what can be expected in the next few years. It is this composite set of figures that has been used in preparing annual pro forma income statements through 1980.

Figure D2 indicates the income statements that ALPHA can expect based on the sales forecasts of Figure C1 and the composite cost structure of Figure D1. The short-term downturn in profits is due to the fact that the 1973 cost structure gave considerably higher profits (as a percentage of sales) than does the composite structure used in these projections. This simply underscores the fact that the cost structure is a major determinant of profitability, as are sales.

The relative effects of cost structure and sales can be seen from Figure D3. This figure shows the projected income statement based on sales being at either the upper or lower value of the 90 percent confidence interval. From these figures it should be clear that if ALPHA is to accomplish its long-term goals, it must manage both its sales and costs effectively.

FIGURE D1
ALPHA's historical cost structure*

	1968	1969	1970	1971	1972	1973	Composite
Net sales	100.0	100.0	100.0	100.0	100.0	100.0	100.0
Cost of sales	66.1	66.1	65.5	66.2	62.7	65.5	66.0
Gross profit	33.9	33.9	34.5	33.8	37.3	34.5	34.0
Selling, G & A	24.8	28.0	22.3	23.1	20.9	20.8	23.0
Operating profit	9.1	5.9	12.2	10.7	16.5	11.7	11.0
Interest expense	2.3	2.8	2.3	2.4	1.8	2.2	3.0
Pretax income	7.1	4.6	9.2	7.9	15.3	13.0	8.0
Income taxes	3.4	2.3	4.6	3.7	7.3	5.8	3.8
Net income	3.7	2.3	4.6	4.2	8.0	7.2	4.2

* Costs as a percentage of sales.

FIGURE D2
ALPHA pro forma income statements, 1974–1980 ($800)

	Composite*	1974	1975	1976	1977	1978	1979	1980
Net sales	100.0	$11,738	$12,966	$13,580	$14,364	$15,232	$15,993	$16,854
Cost of sales	66.0	7,747	8,558	8,963	9,480	10,053	10,555	11,124
Gross profit	34.0	3,991	4,408	4,617	4,884	5,179	5,438	5,730
Selling, G & A	23.0	2,701	2,982	3,123	3,304	3,503	3,678	3,876
Operating profit	11.0	1,291	1,426	1,494	1,580	1,676	1,760	1,854
Interest expense	3.0	352	389	407	431	457	480	506
Pretax income	8.0	939	1,037	1,087	1,149	1,219	1,280	1,348
Income taxes	3.8	446	493	516	546	579	608	640
Net income	4.2	493	544	571	603	640	672	708

* Costs as a percentage of sales (see Figure D1).

FIGURE D3
ALPHA 1980 pro forma income statements

	Low sales value*	Sales forecast	High sales value*
Net sales	$15,537,000	$16,854,000	$18,171,600
Cost of sales	10,254,000	11,124,000	11,993,000
Gross profit	5,283,000	5,730,000	6,179,000
Selling, G & A	3,574,000	3,876,000	4,179,000
Operating profit	1,709,000	1,854,000	2,000,000
Interest expense	466,000	506,000	545,000
Pretax income	1,243,000	1,348,000	1,555,000
Income taxes	590,000	640,000	690,000
Net income	653,000	708,000	865,000

* Based on 90 percent confidence interval for the sales forecast (see Figure C2).

case 7–4

General Leasing Company (A)

John Turnbull pulled his chair up next to the desk of the president of General Leasing Company as the president began to explain why he had called John up to his office so late on Wednesday afternoon. (General was a wholly owned subsidiary of a large Chicago-based manufacturing corporation with over $3 billion in sales in 1971.)

"We have to do something about the price of used aircraft, John. The subject has been bothering me ever since we lost money on that Boeing 707-120 we had to take back from Globeaire when they went bankrupt last fall. Even though that airplane was in excellent condition, it was underpowered and had very short range compared to the later model 707s. When we sold it we got only 40 percent of its new price, and the head office in Chicago didn't like the charge against our last quarter earnings at all.

"Luckily, the only other airplane we've taken back was that 707-320 we took back the year before last and then sold for a lot more than we figured it would be worth when we put the lease together.

"The problem seems to be that we have a hard time predicting the market price for used aircraft at the time we make a lease. If we could do better than we've been doing, I'd certainly sleep a lot sounder, especially since we have over $300 million in aircraft leases out."

"I'm surprised that this has suddenly become a problem with aircraft," John reacted. "Wasn't the value of used equipment a problem back in the days when most of General's leases were in trucks, railroad cars, and buildings?"

"It wasn't critical then," the president replied. "It was in the middle 60s that the idea of leasing 'portable' equipment came into its own. Before that, we always examined the quality of the lessee company as protection for our lease. Then, as the 'portable' idea took hold, we looked at the quality of the equipment for our protection. An airplane is very portable and can be leased to someone else if the first lessee defaults. On top of that, the airlines are required by regulation to adhere to rigid maintenance standards on aircraft. Unlike railroad cars and trucks, which might be poorly maintained, we figured we would be in good shape regarding the maintenance of our airplanes."

"I can see why you didn't see the problem at first and why you have a problem now," John responded. "Even though a plane is portable, the disposition of it is tied to the used aircraft market. I imagine that in re-leasing a used plane, the lease has to be competitive with purchasing the plane in the used aircraft market."

"That's right. I've been with this outfit since it was an independent company and helped it grow to where it is today, but all those airplanes out there are giving me fits. Can you imagine what would happen if we got ten 707s back?"

"If a carrier is in weak financial condition, going to court to enforce the lease would be tantamount to administering a coup de grace to the airline, so we would generally declare a moratorium on lease payments and leave the airplane with the carrier to generate revenue, hoping the carrier's financial strength improved. If we went to court to take a plane away from an airline or enforce lease payments, the other airlines would take a dim view of our action and might make it difficult for us to obtain new business."

"It looks as though we are locked in," John said as he shifted his chair to avoid the late afternoon sun streaming in through the president's corner window.

"In a sense we are, and I suppose we ought to be worried about a range of problems. First of all, what have we gotten ourselves into? What would happen if we have to take some more of those airplanes back? I want to have an idea about how risky our current position is rather than just theorizing about what might happen.

"To some extent the first problem is crying over spilt milk, I guess. What really matters is the future. How can we benefit from our past experience when making future leases? A case in point is that DC-10 we're going to lease to Pacific Airlines. What might it bring on the used aircraft market in a few years?"

"Would you recommend that I start by checking out the current used aircraft market?" John asked. "Maybe we could get some trends by comparing the price of certain aircraft now with prices of several years ago. But that DC-10's going to be a tough one. Only a few are in test flying now and none are in service, but from what I've heard it sounds like a great airplane."

"The controller had some ideas about used plane prices last fall and maybe he could help you. We had a crisis meeting when the Globeaire bankruptcy broke, and we talked a lot about doing a better job of allowing for used aircraft prices. Larry (the controller) expressed the opinion that there ought to be a wealth of data that might help us out at the Civil Aeronautics Board (CAB) in Washington. As you may know, all the scheduled passenger carriers are required by law to report equipment purchases. He thought that he could go through the CAB's records and pick out used aircraft purchases and use them to try to discover some trends.

"He was so excited about doing it that he went right to Washington to look through the airline reports to the CAB. He'd been there two days when he called to let us know that he would be there three more days to find the data he wanted. Then, when he got back he said the thing was such a can of worms that he was sorry he had opened it. I wouldn't be surprised if he still has the data though, and I know he's thought a lot about the problem. Maybe he can give you a hand, but I'd approach him with some care. I'm sure he's still interested in solving the problem, but he's taken a lot of ribbing from us and he may be rather sensitive about the whole thing.

"I'm afraid I can't give you much time to look into the problem. As I mentioned before, Chicago is upset about that last quarter charge on the 707-120, and the corporate controller and treasurer are coming down here next Wednesday to talk about the problem. They want to be reassured that we have the problem in hand. If you can come up with something fast, it will really take the pressure off me. In fact, you might as well make the presentation of the results to them yourself.

"On your way out, John, if Rose hasn't gone home yet, have her schedule a meeting for us first thing Monday morning so we can discuss your ideas."

John got up, pushed his chair back into the sun in front of the president's desk and walked quickly out of the office. Rose, the president's secretary, had apparently left for the day, so John wrote his name in the 9:00 Monday time slot on the appointment calendar she kept for him. Then, he walked down the hall to see if the controller was still there.

He was just putting his coat on as John looked into his office. "Can you spare a minute?" John asked.

"Sure," he replied. "What's your problem?"

"The president wants me to look into used aircraft prices and . . . ."

"Oh, hell. Is he on that kick again!" the controller exclaimed. "I'll bet he wants your report for that Wednesday meeting with Chicago, too."

"As a matter of fact, he does."

"Well, come on in and let me give you a little advice," the controller said as he took off his coat and threw it across a corner of his desk. John took the chair in front of the desk as the controller looked down the hall and then closed the door. "Let me give you a little advice," he repeated. "I had to do the same thing you're doing last fall, right after the Globeaire bankruptcy. There's a lot of numbers around, but there's not much sense to be made out of them. I should know. I tried. You ought to go down there (he pointed to the president's office) and ask for at least a week and probably a month if you want to come up with anything. I worked for two weeks and didn't get anything except a bunch of numbers on used aircraft transactions."

"Do you still have the numbers?"

"Oh, sure," the controller replied. "They're in that file somewhere. He got up and began to search through a drawer in one of his filing cabinets. "Here we are." He opened the file and took out a sheet of paper marked "Used Aircraft Transactions" (Exhibit 1) and gave it to John.

"Where did you get the numbers?" John asked.

"Down at the CAB. They've got numbers on anything you might want to look at. The numbers are not very well organized though. I must have gone through a ton of paper to find this. All the airlines are required to report their purchases of aircraft and engines, and the reports covered everything from Cessna-150s to 747s. Even such minor things as $100 modifications to galleys were included." He reached into the file and pulled out another sheet of paper. "Here's a sample of the data I had to wade through." He showed John one of the forms on which airlines reported their transactions (see Exhibit 2). "Believe me, it really took some time to cull the data I wanted from that mess."

"Some of the purchases of used airplanes were not arm's-length transactions such as the planes American got from Trans-Caribbean in the merger, so they had to be sorted out. It took me almost a week to get the data in a form that seemed at all usable to me.

"There were some other problems with the data, too. The prices reported to the CAB did not include engines, while the new prices I

EXHIBIT 1. Used aircraft sales to trunk carriers*

(1) Aircraft type	(2) Buyer	(3) Used/new ratio	(4) Date of sale	(5) Age at time of sale (mo.)	(6) Age of design (mo.)	(7) Reference point in production span	(8) Industry load factor (%)	(9) 3 and 4 engine turbine sales	(10) Industry debt ($000,000)
B-720B	NW	0.9815	5-62	6	22	25	50.9%	121	$1,934
B-707-120	TWA	0.9645	6-60	10	21	19	56.0	198	1,507
B-707-120	TWA	0.9702	5-60	10	20	18	56.0	198	1,507
B-720B	NW	0.9325	10-62	12	27	31	50.9	121	1,934
B-707-320	TWA	0.9462	12-60	13	28	13	56.0	198	1,507
B-707-320	TWA	0.9326	12-60	13	28	13	56.0	198	1,507
B-707-320	TWA	0.9327	12-60	13	28	13	56.0	198	1,507
B-707-120	TWA	0.8664	12-60	18	27	25	56.0	198	1,507
B-707-120	TWA	0.8901	12-60	18	27	25	56.0	198	1,507
B-707-120	TWA	0.8961	12-60	18	27	25	56.0	198	1,507
B-707-120	TWA	0.8987	12-60	18	27	25	56.0	198	1,507
B-707-320C	TWA	0.8664	3-65	18	79	50	52.0	206	2,145
B-707-320C	TWA	0.8901	3-65	18	79	50	52.0	206	2,145
B-707-120	TWA	0.8810	12-60	19	27	25	56.0	198	1,507
B-707-120	TWA	0.8861	12-60	19	27	25	56.0	198	1,507
B-707-120	TWA	0.8849	12-60	19	27	25	56.0	198	1,507
B-707-120	TWA	0.8756	12-60	19	27	25	56.0	198	1,507
B-707-120	TWA	0.8779	12-60	20	27	25	56.0	198	1,507
B-707-120	TWA	0.8640	12-60	20	27	25	56.0	198	1,507
B-707-120	TWA	0.8685	12-60	21	27	25	56.0	198	1,507
B-707-120	TWA	0.8705	12-60	21	27	25	56.0	198	1,507
B-720B	PAA	0.8599	12-63	24	42	48	50.4	88	1,739
B-720	Braniff	0.7733	9-64	27	52	60	50.9	153	1,872
CV-880	TWA	0.6505	7-63	29	43	95	50.4	88	1,739
CV-880	TWA	0.6505	7-63	29	43	95	50.4	88	1,739
CV-880	TWA	0.6505	7-63	29	43	95	50.4	88	1,739
CV-880	TWA	0.6505	8-63	29	44	97	50.4	88	1,739
CV-880	TWA	0.6681	9-63	30	45	100	50.4	88	1,739
CV-880	TWA	0.6681	9-63	30	45	100	50.4	88	1,739
CV-880	TWA	0.6505	9-63	30	45	100	50.4	88	1,739
DC-9-14	Delta	0.5905	8-69	32	47	76	50.0	494	5,431
B-720B	PAA	0.7315	3-64	36	46	52	50.9	153	1,872
DC-8-20	National	0.6871	9-63	36	51	51	50.4	88	1,739

Model	Carrier	(3)	(4)	(5)	(6)	(7)	(8)	(9)	(10)
DC-8-20	National	0.7041	10-63	36	51	51	50.4	88	1,739
DC-8-20	National	0.7041	10-63	36	51	51	50.4	88	1,739
DC-8-20	National	0.6865	6-64	36	59	59	50.9	153	1,872
B-720B	PAA	0.7315	3-64	37	46	52	50.9	153	1,872
B-720B	PAA	0.7315	3-64	38	46	52	50.9	153	1,872
CV-880	TWA	0.2996	10-64	38	58	129	50.9	88	1,739
B-720B	PAA	0.6633	12-65	48	68	76	52.0	206	2,145
B-720B	PAA	0.6615	12-65	48	68	76	52.0	206	2,145
B-720B	EAL	0.6670	10-66	57	77	88	52.8	228	3,069
B-720B	EAL	0.6670	10-66	58	77	88	52.8	228	3,069
B-720B	EAL	0.6670	10-66	60	77	88	52.8	228	3,069
B-720B	EAL	0.6670	10-66	60	77	88	52.8	228	3,069
B-720B	EAL	0.6670	10-66	60	77	88	52.8	228	3,069
B-720B	EAL	0.6670	10-66	60	77	88	52.8	228	3,069
B-720B	EAL	0.6670	10-66	61	77	88	52.8	228	3,069
B-720B	EAL	0.6670	10-66	61	77	88	52.8	228	3,069
B-720B	EAL	0.6670	10-66	62	77	88	52.8	228	3,069
B-720B	EAL	0.6670	10-66	62	77	88	52.8	228	3,069
CV-990	Modern	0.1753	12-70	78	90	265	49.7	437	6,097
DC-8-30	United	0.6770	11-67	86	100	89	50.8	316	4,179
CV-990	Modern	0.1472	10-70	87	90	265	49.7	437	6,097
DC-8-30	United	0.7014	9-67	87	98	87	50.8	316	4,179
DC-8-30	United	0.6838	10-67	87	99	88	50.8	316	4,179
DC-8-30	United	0.6845	10-67	87	99	88	50.8	316	4,179
B-707-120B	TWA	0.4738	12-67	93	111	91	50.8	316	4,179
B-707-120B	TWA	0.5244	12-67	100	111	91	50.8	316	4,179
DC-8-50	United	0.6780	9-68	101	110	97	50.2	181	4,460
DC-8-33	Delta	0.3142	9-69	101	122	108	50.0	494	5,431
DC-8-30	United	0.6783	9-68	102	110	97	50.2	181	4,460
DC-8-33	Delta	0.3140	8-69	102	121	107	50.0	494	5,431
B-707-120B	TWA	0.5412	12-67	103	111	91	50.8	316	4,179

* Definitions of variables shown in the various columns:

(3) The ratio of used price of aircraft without engines to new price with engines.

(4) The month and year at time of sale.

(5) The number of months from date of production to date of sale.

(6) The number of months from date of production of first aircraft of that type to date of sale.

(7) The age of design (6) divided by the total number of months that model was in production expressed as a percent. If the reference point is greater than 100, the plane was no longer in production at the time of sale.

(8) The average industry load factor in the year of sale.

(9) The number of sales of new three- and four-engine turbine aircraft in the year of sale.

(10) The total debt of the 12 trunk line carriers in the year of sale.

EXHIBIT 2
Example of CAB form used by the controller to gather data

AIRFRAMES AND AIRCRAFT ENGINES ACQUIRED

Air Carrier __Delta Air Lines, Inc.__
Quarter Ended __June 30, 1971__

Date Acquired (1)	Date Placed in Transport Service (Airframes) (2)	Airframe License No. (3)	New or Used (4)	Number of Aircraft Engines Acquired (5)	Account No. (6)	Type, Model, and Cabin Design (7)	Max. Cont. Horsepower Pounds Thrust (8)	Aircraft Engines per Airframe (9)	Max. Seat Capacity (10)	Cost (11)	Reserve for Depreciation (12)	Estimated Residual Value (13)	Estimated Depreciable Life (Months) (14)	Flight Equipment Airworthiness Reserves (15)	Acquired From (16)	Line No.
4-14-71	4-17-71	N1281L	New		1601	McDonnell Douglas DC-9-32		2	89	3,806,368		380,637	120		McDonnell Douglas Corp.	1
5-12-71	5-14-71	N1282L	New		1601	McDonnell Douglas DC-9-32		2	89	3,868,944		386,894	120		McDonnell Douglas Corp.	2
6-11-71	6-15-71	N1283L	New		1601	McDonnell Douglas DC-9-32		2	89	3,867,649		386,745	120		McDonnell Douglas Corp.	3
6-24-71	6-28-71	N1284L	New		1601	McDonnell Douglas DC-9-32		2	89	3,870,136		387,013	120		McDonnell Douglas Corp.	4
					1601	McDonnell Douglas DC-9-32				9,363		936	120		Modification	5
					1601	Boeing B-747				386,082		38,608	120		Modification	6
					1601	Lockheed L-100-20				278,886		27,839	120		Modification	7
					1601	McDonnell Douglas DC-8-50				154,130		15,413	120		Modification	8
					1601	Convair CV-880				78,369		7,837	120		Modification	9
					1601	McDonnell Douglas DC-9-32				839,200		33,920	120		Modification	10
																11
																12
																13
																14
																15
																16
										17,158,917		1,715,892				17

Date Acquired (1)	(2)	Airframe License No. (3)	(4)	(5)	(6)	Type, Model, and Cabin Design (7)	(8)	(9)	(10)	(11)	(12)	(13)	(14)	(15)	Acquired From (16)	Line No.
																48
																49
Leased Airframes Returned to Lessor						Passenger										50
4-27-71		N8901E				McDonnell Douglas DC-9-14									McDonnell Douglas Corp.	51
																52
4-29-71		N8902E				McDonnell Douglas DC-9-14									McDonnell Douglas Corp.	53
																54
						Cargo										55
																56
5-31-71		N9262R				Lockheed L-100									National Aircraft Leasing, Ltd.	57
																58
																59
																60

* Denotes inverse amount.

SCHEDULE B-7

☆ U. S. GOVERNMENT PRINTING OFFICE: 1971—415-374

CAB Form 41

was working with did. I haven't included purchases by the supplemental carriers—because they weren't reported to the CAB—even though they buy most of the used airplanes.

"When I got back here I started thinking about how the data might relate to used aircraft prices, so I sketched out a few graphs. The dots were all over the place and didn't really seem to tell me much." He opened the file, took out several papers (Exhibits 3–8), and handed them to John.

"Thanks. Since I'm fairly new at this business, it would help me to know more about the characteristics of each of the aircraft types," said John. "Can you brief me a bit about that tomorrow?"

EXHIBIT 3
Used/new price ratio versus airframe age

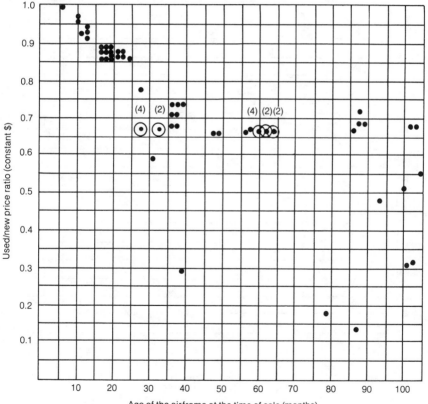

Age of the airframe at the time of sale (months)

Legend
· Single data point.
⊙ Multiple data point—the number of occurrences is indicated in parentheses next to it.

"You're lucky," the controller replied. "When I was trying to make some sense out of the data, I found a table summarizing the differences between the aircraft." He pulled the table (Exhibit 9) out of the file folder.

"This certainly will get me started," John replied. "I really appreciate your time."

"Glad to help, but I don't know what you're going to be able to do that I couldn't do. I tried and there are just too many things not in the data. As I told Harry (the president), the whole thing is a can of worms."

EXHIBIT 4
Used/new price ratio versus age of the basic design (measured in months from initial delivery)

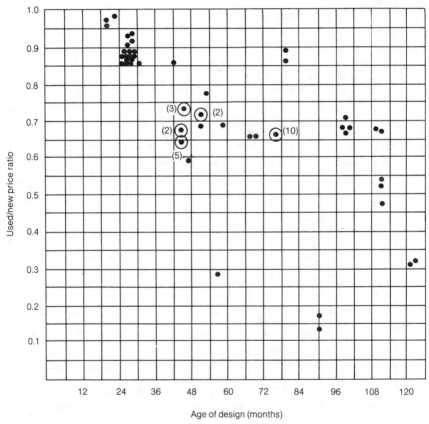

Age of design (months)

Legend
· Single data point.
⊙ Multiple data point—the number of occurrences is indicated in parentheses next to it.

"I'm not sure I can do anything, but I'd like to look at the problem."
"By the way," the controller said, picking his coat up from his desk,
"have you seen the March copy of *Fortune*? The article about United
says they have 29 of their 707s up for sale."
"Well, see you tomorrow."

EXHIBIT 5
Used/new price ratio versus the position in the production span at the time
of the sale

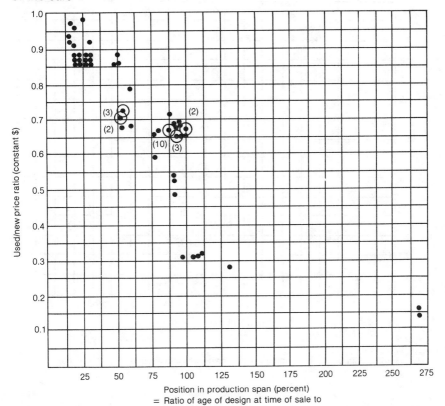

Position in production span (percent)
= Ratio of age of design at time of sale to
total length of production run*

* 100% = Plane sold just at the end of production run.

Legend
· Single data point.
⊙ Multiple data point—the number of occurrences is indicated in parentheses next to it.

EXHIBIT 6
Used/new price ratio versus industry load factor

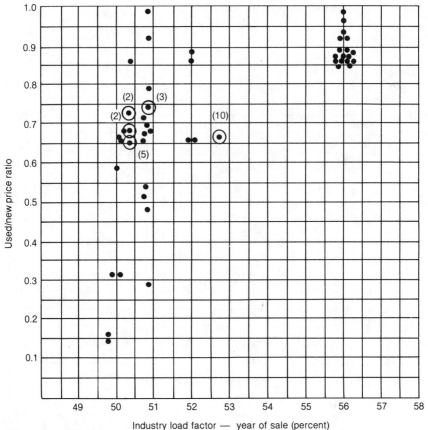

Industry load factor — year of sale (percent)

Legend
· Single data point.
⊙ Multiple data point—the number of occurrences is indicated in parentheses next to it.

EXHIBIT 7
Used/new price ratio versus three- and four-engine aircraft deliveries

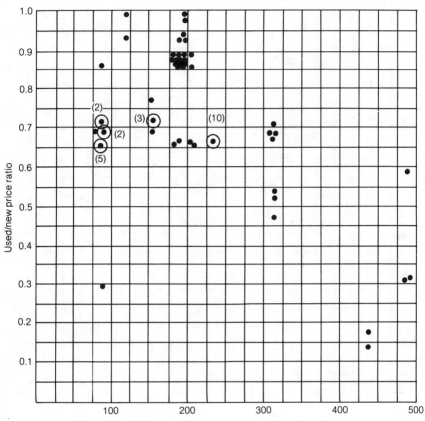

Three–and four–engine jets delivered in year of sale

Legend
  · Single data point.
  ⊙ Multiple data point—the number of occurrences is indicated in parentheses next to it.

EXHIBIT 8
Used/new price ratio versus industry debt

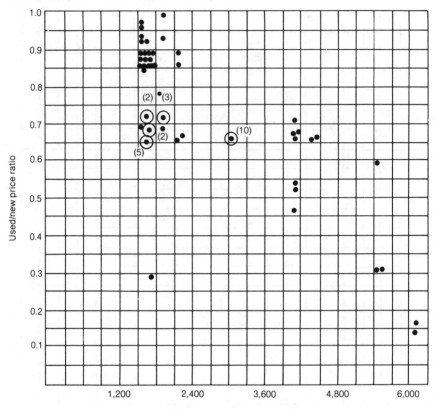

Industry debt in year of sale ($ millions)

Legend
· Single data point.
⊙ Multiple data point—the number of occurrences is indicated in parentheses next to it.

EXHIBIT 9
Comparative data on jet transport aircraft, 1971

	Cost new ($ millions)*	Number ordered†	Average available seats†	Cost per hour (dollars)‡	Cost per available seat-mile (cents)‡
Boeing					
707	$ 9	857	131	666	1.25
727	7	873	105	551	1.51
737	4.5	297	96	457	1.81
747	25	207	374	1,747	1.11
McDonnell-Douglas					
DC-8	10	539	160	776	1.14
DC-9	4.5	671	79	444	1.93
DC-10	22	223	270	1,279	1.12
Convair					
CV-880	4	64	96	780	2.13
CV-990	4.6	25	105	1,352	3.38
Lockheed					
1011	18.5	178	272	1,224	1.11

* Lloyd's Aviation Department, *Aircraft Types and Prices*, London, 1970.
† Jane's, *All the World's Aircraft*, London: S. Low, Marston & Co., 1972.
‡ Civil Aeronautics Board, *Aircraft Operating Cost and Performance Report*, Washington, D.C., U.S. Government Printing Office, 1971.

case 7–5

Xerox Corporation distribution system (B)[1]

SIMULATION OF REPAIR PARTS SUPPLY

The Information Systems Group (ISG) of the Xerox Corporation had become concerned about measurement of the performance of their repair parts distribution system in the early 1970s as competition in the plain paper copier/duplicator market began to mount. Although traditional measures of system performance indicated a fairly high service level on the average, individual cases often highlighted sig-

---

[1] This case was made possible by the cooperation of the Xerox Corporation. Selected names and data have been disguised to protect proprietary information.

360

nificant deviations from the norm. The source of most ISG revenues were leases of xerographic equipment which were based on the number of copies made. Therefore, long periods of machine downtime were of concern not only because an irritated user might switch to a competing copier, but because downtime represented lost revenue, i.e., copies which otherwise would have been made. Additionally, as the placement of faster xerographic copiers and duplicators increased, more and more copies and their attendant revenues would be forgone per unit of downtime.

The corporation had become increasingly cost-conscious as the growth of xerography had slowed from the hectic years of the 1960s. Consequently, the large ISG copier/duplicator repair parts inventory ($48 million in 1972) made improvement of repair parts flow an attractive area to look for cost savings. Further, the value of the repair parts inventory was expected to increase to over $90 million by 1977 as ever-faster "second-generation" xerographic copiers were introduced in the mid-1970s, while older, slower models were expected to continue to enjoy considerable popularity.

THE REPAIR PARTS PHYSICAL DISTRIBUTION SYSTEM

Physical flows through the repair parts distribution system are described in Exhibit 1. Stocking locations where strategic inventories of repair parts were maintained were the national distribution center (NDC) in Webster, New York, ten regional distribution centers (RDC), about 70 branch offices, and the luggage compartments of the company sedans used by the approximately 6,000 technical representatives (tech reps) employed by Xerox ISG in 1972.

EXHIBIT 1
Repair parts distribution system*

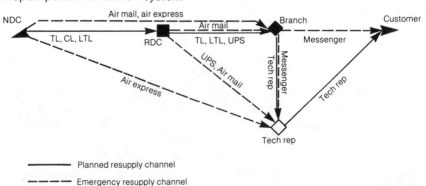

——————— Planned resupply channel

— — — — Emergency resupply channel

* In addition to the channels shown above, tech reps also could be supplied with repair parts on an "emergency" basis from branch offices and RDCs in other areas or regions than their own.

Tech reps operated out of the local branch offices. One of their primary functions was to respond to emergency service calls when equipment malfunctioned. On the average, there was one tech rep for every 60 xerographic copiers or duplicators, although this could vary widely depending on machine density and whether the tech rep was specialized on low-volume office copiers or high-volume duplicators. Even if the tech rep were specialized, it was likely that he would service several different types of copiers or duplicators including the newer second-generation models.

The corporation had traditionally placed considerable emphasis on the image projected by the tech rep. They carried their tools in a specially made kit having the appearance of a briefcase and were attired in a business suit. While Xerox paid for the purchase and operating costs of the tech rep's automobile, the tech rep enjoyed considerable latitude in specifying exactly which car he wished to buy. This freedom, in addition to the company policy of allowing the tech reps unlimited personal use of the automobile, were considered by many of the tech reps as one of their most desirable fringe benefits.

The trunk of the tech rep's sedan was an inventory stocking location where spare photoreceptors (selenium drums) and a small supply of repair parts (about 100 line items) were maintained. Each tech rep selected his particular supply of repair parts on the basis of experience with his particular machine population and by consideration of the criticality of a part to the functioning of a machine. In addition to this supply of "field repair parts" and spare photoreceptors, tech reps carried several PM (preventive maintenance) kits. PM kits were stocked more heavily by the tech reps who serviced the high-volume (and high-revenue) duplicator line, as strong emphasis had been placed on PM of these faster machines in recent years.

Branch offices were primarily a source of resupply for tech reps as well as providing backup inventory on parts which would take up an inordinate amount of space in the storage compartment of the tech rep's automobile but were high usage and/or highly critical. RDCs, in addition to providing backup inventories to branches and tech reps, were a repository of parts needed infrequently and which were of lower criticality. The national distribution center in Webster was a factory warehouse which provided backup inventory to tech reps, branches, and RDCs and stocked all repair parts including those used only very rarely. For the purpose of calculating stocking levels at each of these locations, the annual carrying cost of holding spare parts inventory was estimated to be 24 percent of the cost of the part. A breakdown on the location of spare parts inventory is found in Exhibit 2.

The most binding constraint on stocking repair parts at any of these levels of distribution was the space constraint faced by the tech rep.

362

EXHIBIT 2
Parts stocking locations and flows

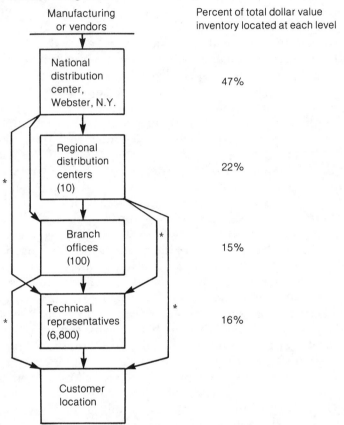

Manufacturing or vendors

Percent of total dollar value inventory located at each level

National distribution center, Webster, N.Y.	47%
Regional distribution centers (10)	22%
Branch offices (100)	15%
Technical representatives (6,800)	16%
Customer location	

*Primarily "emergency" flows moving via most expeditious mode of transportation—airfreight, United Parcel Service, messenger, etc.

He could not carry more parts than the luggage compartment of his automobile would hold. Company guidelines suggested an "intermediate" size automobile as appropriate for tech rep use, although in 1973 a report from corporate headquarters had suggested that several million dollars could be saved annually by requiring tech reps to drive compact cars as Xerox's response to that year's "energy crisis."

Luggage compartments in domestic intermediate-sized sedans ranged from 14 cubic feet to 19 cubic feet in size. Of the fleet of tech rep sedans, the average capacity of the luggage compartment was 16 cubic feet. Despite this constraint, the adequacy of the tech reps' stock in meeting emergency repair requirements was fairly high. When a repair part was required to complete a service call, the tech rep had the part over 70 percent of the time. If the tech rep did not have the required part with him (which occurred, on the average, twice a week per tech rep), he would place a call to his branch office which, if the part were stocked there, would send the part to the tech rep by the fastest means possible, usually a messenger service or taxi. If the part was not at the branch office, it would be ordered from either the RDC or the NDC, which would forward the part directly to the tech rep or, alternatively, to the customer's location. In 1972, about 90 percent of those parts ordered through this system on an "emergency" basis were in the hands of the tech rep within two hours of his initial call to the branch office. The overall system average of machine downtime resulting from parts delay was less than half an hour, including those repairs for which no parts delay was encountered (e.g., the tech rep had the replacement part with him).

SIMULATION OF THE DISTRIBUTION SYSTEM

Mr. Howard T. Fall, logistics planning specialist at ISG, described the decision to use simulation in an effort to rationalize the repair parts distribution system:

> There was considerable pressure on us to reduce costs and yet maintain and even improve the service levels in the system. Implementation of centralized refurbishing centers was a big step toward both of these goals (see Exhibit 3).[2] Yet we were faced with a staggering number of alternatives which we could possibly pursue which logically would seem to satisfy one or the other of these objectives. Also, as new products were introduced, the number of line items increased and so did the total inventory valuation. It was like swimming against the tide. We needed some tool to help us evaluate and choose from among this host of promising alternatives those courses of action which were best for the company as a whole.
>
> A traditional linear programming approach would have probably been too narrow and inflexible for the kind of analysis we were interested in. Further, necessary sensitivity testing would have been more difficult to perform and to interpret. Other forms of mathematical programming seemed to suffer from similar problems. So we were left with simulation. Although simulation of a system as complex as ours would be terribly expensive compared with these other techniques, we felt that the quality of the results and the size of the potential payoff would justify the additional investment. Therefore, we decided quite early in the game that the proper approach to the problem of modeling our repair parts supply system was simulation.

---

[2] Centralized refurbishing centers, where office copiers returned from lease were to be put in "as new" condition, were planned for each marketing region. Until these centers were operational, refurbishing was performed by technical representatives on a rotating assignment basis.

364

EXHIBIT 3
Centralized refurbishing centers, June 1972

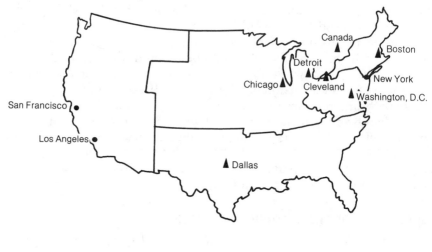

• Implemented
▲ Planned ·

Howard Fall went on to explain that there were two possible approaches to acquiring the necessary simulation model: Xerox could either develop the model internally or purchase an existing physical distribution model and adapt it to Xerox's repair parts supply system.

Among the simulation models available for purchase were IBM's Distribution System Simulator and LOGISTEK models and Systems Research Incorporated's Long-Range Environmental Planning Simulator (LREPS). The LREPS model was considered to be more comprehensive than either of the IBM models and, for a time, was seriously considered for purchase. Finally, however, the decision was made to develop a simulator internally, as this would assure that the model would be designed specifically to address Xerox's unique distribution problems. Further, it was felt that Xerox had the capability to develop a distribution system simulator internally, as Howard Fall had recently completed a doctoral thesis at the Pennsylvania State University which involved simulation of complex distribution systems.

THE ECHELON STOCKING MODEL

In August of 1972, Howard Fall began work on the development of a simulation model for the repair parts logistics system. As he envisioned the model, an optimal stocking scheme could be selected for each individual part by calculating the total costs of providing that part to the customer through exhaustive analysis of many different stocking schemes through every possible distribution channel. Costs included in the total cost analysis were:

1. Planned and emergency transportation costs.
2. Inventory holding costs: cost of capital, probability of obsolescence or loss.
3. Warehouse space costs.
4. Planned and emergency order-handling costs.
5. Machine downtime penalty per hour (waiting for parts): risk of cancellation and lost revenue.

Each echelon (NDC, RDC, branch office, trunk of tech rep's sedan) was defined as a specific stocking location served by specific modes of emergency and planned transportation with specific order cycle and lead times as well as specific handling and storage methods. For each repair part in each echelon, therefore, an optimal mix of emergency and planned transportation costs could be defined by consideration of each part's unique characteristics of usage (failure) rate, cost, criticality, and size. At each echelon, the optimal mix of emergency and planned costs could be determined for each part by selecting the lowest total cost stocking level from those simulated. This is illustrated conceptually by Exhibit 4.

EXHIBIT 4
Echelon cost trade-off

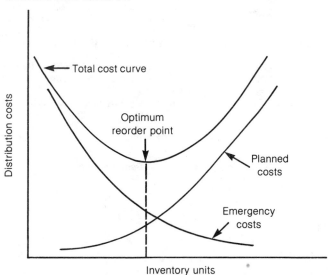

This simulation became known as the *echelon stocking model* (ESM) because of its aim to provide inventory policies at each echelon in the system. Howard Fall's approach to the simulation was to first define 11 echelon links with which to characterize all repair part movements into or out of the system as well as between echelons in the system. The planned and emergency transportation costs associated with movement of a repair part through each of these echelon links were collected along with estimates of the time elapsed for movement between echelons. By combining these echelon links or "laying them end-to-end" in such a way that there was both an entrance to and an exit from the system, seven complete channels or echelon chains were defined. Exhibits 5 and 6 describe this process.

Thus, each of the seven channels was defined as a specific sequence of echelons (inventory stocking locations) used for intermediate storage and movement of parts. The costs of moving a part through each of these channels was simply the sum of the costs for each echelon link

EXHIBIT 5

Echelon link definition

Number	Symbol	Meaning
1	→ NDC	Movement into NDC from manufacturing or vendors
2	NDC → RDC	Movement from NDC to RDC
3	RDC → BRA	Movement from RDC to branch office
4	BRA →	Movement from branch office to customer
5	BRA → TR →	Movement from branch office to tech rep to customer
6	RDC → TR →	Movement from RDC to tech rep to customer
7	NDC → RDC →	Movement from NDC through RDC to customer
8	RDC → BRA →	Movement from RDC to branch office to customer
9	→ NDC →	Movement through NDC directly to customer
10	EMRG R → B	Emergency movement from RDC to branch office
11	EMRG B → T →	Emergency movement from branch to tech rep to customer

Channel definition

Echelon chain	Echelon links
a	1, 2, 3, 4
b	1, 2, 6
c	1, 2, 3, 5
d	1, 2, 10, 11
e	1, 2, 8
f	1, 7
g	9

EXHIBIT 6
Echelon stocking model

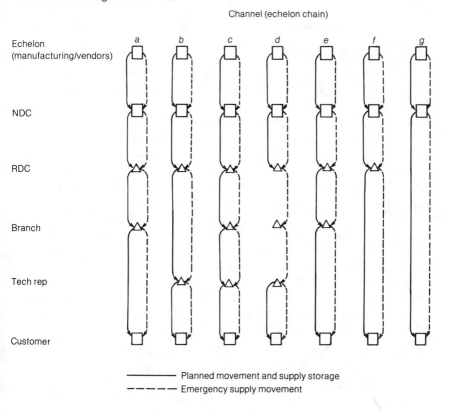

Channel (echelon chain)

— Planned movement and supply storage
––––– Emergency supply movement

movement and the inventory carrying costs at each echelon that made up the complete channel. These costs could be combined with the penalty costs associated with the service level of each channel arising from the downtime of machines awaiting parts flowing through that channel. This process was repeated for each of the seven channels. The channel having the lowest sum of distribution and penalty costs was then selected as the optimal channel for distribution of the part under study. The stocking policies at each echelon resulting in the lowest total cost would then be adopted as the stocking policy for that part.

IMPLEMENTATION OF THE ESM

As development of the simulation model progressed, Howard Fall decided that the first application of the ESM should be the simulation of the repair parts supply for the ARDRI duplicator. ARDRI was the code name for a soon-to-be-introduced, very fast xerographic duplicator designed to directly compete with offset copiers. Speed and cost per copy of the ARDRI machine were to be comparable to offset presses, and image quality was to be as high as any xerographic copier ever produced. Initial marketing plans for ARDRI called for placement of 1,320 of the machines and special training for 200 specialized tech reps who would service ARDRI along with other xerographic duplicators.

Engineers at the Webster Product Development Department were able to supply the necessary parts information including cost, size, criticality, and usage rates for ARDRI parts based on engineering data and information from the few prototype installations which had been made. With estimates of machine usage and proposed lease terms obtained from the Marketing Department, Fall was able to estimate that the average ARDRI machine would produce about $12 of revenue per hour. There was some question about applying the entire $12 to lost revenue, however, because the behavior of the customer with regard to ARDRI malfunctions was uncertain. Would the customer really not produce these copies (or switch to offset, for instance) or would he merely allow demands to queue up until the machine was repaired? Various opinions on this question were solicited by Fall:

ARDRI product manager: I believe that we have to assume that we will lose all of that revenue. After all, with ARDRI we are selling speed in duplication. If the machine is down, then obviously the customer will put ARDRI jobs on their old offset presses or have them reproduced on the outside by a service bureau. It is silly to assume that a customer who needs ARDRI's speed will allow jobs to queue up.

ARDRI market analyst: There is no doubt that we will in fact lose a hefty portion of that revenue. On the other hand, a lot of our customers will have little recourse except to wait for the machine to be fixed. Further, it is reasonable to assume that a lot of the work which is lost to ARDRI during downtime periods will be picked up by other Xerox operations, either other ARDRI duplicators or the higher-cost 3600s.

To resolve these different opinions, Fall decided that he would test the sensitivity of the results by making different simulation runs using different machine downtime penalty assessments.

RESULTS OF ARDRI SUPPLY SIMULATION

By September of 1973 Howard Fall had completed the simulation of the repair parts supply system for the ARDRI duplicator for each of the 1,540 parts unique to ARDRI using several different hourly machine downtime assessments. Fall discussed the result of these initial runs:

> The sensitivity analysis went pretty much as one would intuitively expect, with a higher penalty charge tending to push inventory down to the branches and tech reps and the very low penalties tending to collect inventory in the NDC and RDCs. The surprising result was the general insensitivity of the model to the amount of penalty once a threshold was reached. It didn't seem to make a whole lot of difference to most aggregate measures whether the penalty was $3 per hour or $12 per hour. For example, over that range, system parts availability changed only from 0.991 to 0.996, and the number of emergency orders went only from 0.56 to 0.37 per week (see Exhibit 7).

EXHIBIT 7
Echelon stocking model sensitivity analysis

Basic data: Number of machines: 1,320
Number of tech reps: 200
Demand: 29,200 parts
Demand: $327,800
Existing system configuration

	Downtime penalty charge per hour				
	$0	$3	$6	$12	$18
Cost ($000)					
Transportation	$ 6.8	$ 7.4	$ 7.6	$ 7.7	$ 7.8
Space	2.8	26.1	38.8	60.2	69.0
Handling	9.3	12.5	13.2	13.6	14.1
Holding	5.2	28.7	39.3	51.0	60.1
Emergency transportation	3.7	5.5	6.1	6.2	7.1
Distribution	$27.8	$ 80.2	$104.9	$138.7	$ 158.1
Capital costs	5.2	28.7	39.3	51.0	60.1
Downtime penalty	0.0	80.5	111.2	154.1	190.4
Total cost	$33.0	$189.4	$255.4	$354.8	$ 408.6
Inventory ($000)					
Tech rep	$ 0.0	$ 90.1	$142.0	$174.8	$ 262.2
Branch	0.0	49.2	92.9	131.1	133.9
RDC/NDC	46.4	87.4	84.7	84.7	84.7
Total inventory	$46.4	$226.7	$319.6	$390.6	$ 480.8
System service measures					
System availability	0.979	0.991	0.993	0.996	0.996
ARDRI emergency orders per tech rep per week	2.8	0.56	0.46	0.37	0.32
Delivery time (minutes)	960	83	62	46	42
Downtime (hours/machine-year)	240	20.2	14.0	9.7	8.0
Average tech rep inventory					
Dollar value	$0	$451	$714	$871	$1,295
Number of parts	0	302	356	522	535
Cubic feet	0	3	5	8	9

EXHIBIT 8
Inventory and total cost versus number of RDCs

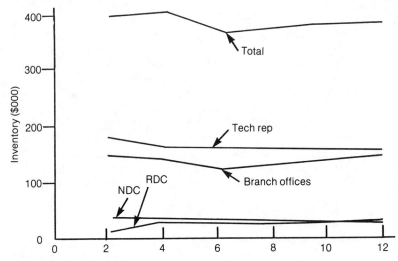

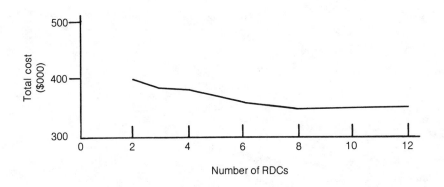

Number of RDCs

Holding the downtime penalty at $12, another set of sensitivity tests were run on the model to determine the system's response to adding or deleting particular stocking locations. In general, the model proved to be quite insensitive to the number of RDCs in the system (see Exhibit 8). Howard Fall commented on these results:

> It was apparent by this time that we did not have the optimal distribution system, at least for the ARDRI products. I was quite surprised to find that the ESM was insensitive to the number of RDCs in the system. Basically, what happened was that as the number of RDCs declined, the remaining ones were made larger by the ESM. Further, even as RDC

inventory was reduced by reducing the number of RDCs, the increased cost of emergency shipments from those remaining RDCs and the higher inventory at branches more than balanced out any savings. In fact, the total cost was slightly higher with fewer RDCs but not markedly so. System performance was even less affected. Machine downtime per year was essentially independent of the number of RDCs (see Exhibit 9).

EXHIBIT 9
Machine downtime versus number of RDCs

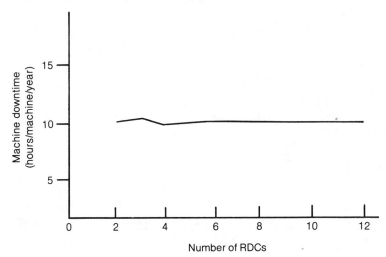

The result of still another set of sensitivity tests was quite the opposite, however. It turned out that the ESM model was highly sensitive to the number of branches. Another approach which we tried, on a very ad hoc basis, was to add a new class of echelon, a "mini-RDC" or "super branch" depending on how one looks at it. While the results were not definitive because of our lack of historical information on some of the input data, the results strongly indicate that selectively adding this new echelon will substantially reduce costs.

Another issue which we were able to address with ESM was distributing parts from logical shipping points, disregarding arbitrary region and branch boundaries. In our current system, for example, suppose we ship a part from Rochester to the RDC in New York City. This same part may go to fill a demand from a tech rep operating out of the Buffalo branch whose area extends to within about 50 miles of the Webster plant. This sort of thing goes on all over the country as a matter of routine. Not only does it consume a lot of transportation expense, it also takes a lot of time, especially in the case of emergency orders. Conservatively, we estimate a $150,000 annual savings by disregarding regional and branch boundaries and eliminating this sort of unnecessary circuitry.

THE FUTURE OF THE ECHELON STOCKING MODEL

It is clear to me that the echelon stocking model has a great deal of potential in assisting distribution planning here at Xerox. The effort which we put into making the model versatile has already paid dividends. This initial application has even suggested the need for some new channel structures which I am now working to include in the model. Beyond that, we are collecting data to expand the model to a simulation of repair parts supply for the entire product line and eventually into consumable items such as paper and cleaning fluid.

Xerography is basically a service industry, and a large component of that service turns out to hinge on efficient distribution practices. I think that Xerox would have had to develop something like the echelon stocking model eventually. It is fortunate that we did it as we move into this new regime of downtime costs. As revenues become concentrated in fewer machines, service becomes more important. What may be indicated is a complete reevaluation of our distribution system, and the echelon stocking model will be an invaluable aid in that process.

case 7–6

DYCO Chemical Corporation (AR)

On January 25, 1971, Walter Schroeder, assistant manager of the Economic Analysis Department of DYCO Chemical Corporation (pronounced "dye-coe"), was about to write a memorandum proposing that his department develop a computer model of the company for forecasting and financial planning. Developing a corporate model had been on his mind for some time, but his department had always been too busy to begin the project. Mr. Schroeder, having just returned from a seminar on cash flow computer models conducted by Data Resources, Inc., an economic consulting firm, now had new enthusiasm for the project.

DYCO INCORPORATED

DYCO, headquartered in Newark, New Jersey, was a diversified producer of chemicals with worldwide sales of over $470 million in

1970. The company was incorporated as the National Dye Company in 1914 to fill a void caused by the interruption of dye supplies in World War I. A German manufacturer of dyes and chemicals, I. G. Farben, had dominated the U.S. dye market with its strong patent position until 1914 when the patents were ignored and a new U.S. industry was created. With the U.S. entry into the war in 1917, the company began to manufacture gunpowder and explosives. National Dye diversified into chemicals and other products in the 1920s using the trademark DYCO on many of its products. In 1965 it changed its name to DYCO Chemical Corporation to better reflect its wider product line. It had plants in 27 U.S. locations and subsidiaries and affiliated companies in 17 foreign countries.

DYCO was organized into operating divisions which were responsible for the production and sale of products, and service divisions which provided services to the operating divisions and to the corporation as a whole. In 1970 there were eight operating divisions: Paint and Other Coatings, Explosives, Rubber Products, Plastics, Textile Products, Basic Chemicals, International, and Entrepreneurial Enterprises. The principal products and 1970 sales of each of these divisions are listed in Exhibit 1. The operating divisions were in turn divided into departments and product groups.

The service divisions were Accounting and Administration, Advertising, Computer Services, Engineering, Legal, Patent, Personnel, Purchasing, Traffic, and Treasurer. The expenses associated with these divisions were charged to the operating divisions as part of corporate overhead (with the exception of Computer Services which were billed on an as-used basis).

As the company diversified over the years and as its product line evolved, its organizational structure changed, the most recent reorganization being the 1970 consolidation of four of the ten existing divisions into two.

The company's sales had increased each year during the past decade, roughly doubling during the period. Although net income had been more volatile than sales, the company had been profitable in each of these years. DYCO ranked among the top 20 U.S. chemical companies in sales, profit margin, and return on investment. In 1970 it spent $13 million on R&D and $55 million on capital expenditures, and it ranked among the top ten chemical manufacturers in capital expenditures over the last five years. A ten-year summary of its key operating and financial statistics is shown in Exhibit 2. The percentage of business done in each of the principal industries in which the company sold commercial products is shown in Exhibit 3.

Paint and Other Coatings Division ($35 million)

Pigments: Inorganic and organic pigment colors, organic dyes, color lakes and toners, pigment dispersions, ceramic colors, cadmium colors, magnetic iron oxides

Coating materials: Nitrocellulose, chlorinated rubber, nitric acid

Industrial finishes: Enamels, lacquers, priming agents

Explosives Division ($83 million)

Industrial groups: Dynamites and gelatins, seismic explosives, blasting agents, fluidized explosives, blasting supplies, electric and regular initiators and detonators, explosives-grade ammonium nitrate, nitric acid, mixed oxides of nitrogen, smokeless powders for sporting use

Government sales: Gas generators, military ordnance, smokeless powders

Rubber Products Division ($87 million)

Automotive: Belts and belting, hose and tubing

Other: Latex foam rubber, coated fabrics

Rubber chemicals: Emulsifiers, para-methane and diisopropylbenzene hydroperoxides, synthetic rubber

Plastics Division ($56 million)

Resins: Acrylics, polyester, nylon

Plastic products: Plastic containers, speciality products—injected and formed foam—sheet and bun, industrial tape

Textile Products Division ($37 million)

Fibers: Nylon and acrylic

Film: Polyester and acrylic films

Basic Chemicals Division ($90 million)

Agricultural chemicals: Insecticides, pre-emergence and post-emergence herbicide, anhydrous ammonia, urea, prilled ammonium nitrate, ammonium nitrate and urea-ammonium nitrate solutions

Other chemicals: Plasticizers, pentaerythritol, methanol, formaldehyde, *para*-cresol, alpha-methylstyrene

International Division ($47 million)

Responsible for foreign sales, foreign investments, and the management of DYCO interests in foreign subsidiaries and associated companies in Argentina, Australia, Belgium, Denmark, England, France, Germany, India, Italy, Japan, Mexico, The Netherlands, New Zealand, Nicaragua, Spain, and Sweden

Entrepreneurial Enterprises Division ($45 million)

Responsible for initiating new business opportunities by commercializing new products from company research, purchasing or licensing technology outside the company, or by acquisition, merger, or joint venture

EXHIBIT 2
Ten-year financial digest

			Financial review ($000)			
Year	Current assets	Current liabil- ities	Gross	Fixed Assets*	Other assets	Reserves†
1961	82,160	33,121	199,331	96,847	26,224	34,754
1962	91,682	34,827	215,663	101,135	31,204	39,599
1963	106,417	36,379	231,243	103,414	33,053	43,755
1964	112,405	36,667	245,529	102,616	32,809	42,157
1965	113,590	39,475	283,277	123,861	42,937	41,741
1966	151,676	69,839	319,925	145,481	29,588	41,269
1967	141,544	61,560	390,686	200,400	45,265	38,749
1968	154,565	82,781	448,861	236,521	49,360	37,573
1969	164,880	88,868	481,483	242,986	52,134	36,850
1970	181,414	98,693	500,346	255,658	53,578	36,150

		Operating review ($000)		
Year	Net sales	Income before taxes	Income taxes	Net in- come
1961	247,752	38,398	20,830	17,568
1962	296,619	42,971	23,278	19,693
1963	313,756	42,458	22,008	20,450
1964	328,795	44,822	21,700	23,123
1965	330,676	47,274	21,228	26,046
1966	379,342	60,269	28,204	32,065
1967	385,575	51,220	23,237	27,992
1968	430,984	58,493	26,492	32,002
1969	447,595	48,711	22,345	26,366
1970	470,165	55,775	26,032	29,743

* Net after depreciation.
† Other than depreciation and doubtful accounts.

EXHIBIT 3
Breakdown of 1970 commercial sales to industries

Plastics	13%	Automotive and parts	4%
Rubber	10	Electrical and electronics	3
Synthetic fibers	10	Ordnance and accessories	2
Textiles	9	Soap and detergents	2
Protective coatings	7	Petroleum	2
Food	5	Paint	2
Agriculture	5	Stone, clay, glass	2
Miscellaneous chemicals	4	Construction	2
Mining and quarrying	4	Other industries	14

MANAGEMENT STYLE AND CORPORATE GOODS

One manager at DYCO described relationships among the top management as "gentlemanly." Problems were discussed as an exchange of ideas among peers, and persuasion rather than directive was used to affect performance. The top management of the company had known one another for a long time, and all but two had risen to their positions through the ranks.

The president of DYCO, William Reynolds, had joined the company as a research chemist in 1940, when he graduated from the University of Virginia. He moved up through a variety of supervisory and marketing positions until he became general manager of the company's Rubber Products Division in 1960, a member of the board of directors in 1963, and a corporate vice president in 1965. In December 1969 he was elected president and chairman of the executive committee. Articles in the trade press described him as "soft spoken and optimistic," a "calm, size-up-the-situation-before-making-a-move type," who was bent on guiding the company in new directions. This would be accomplished not only by upgrading its traditional chemical products but by entering new and unrelated product areas. Chemicals, which then represented close to 90 percent of total sales, were expected to represent 60–65 percent of the sales in 1980.

Mr. Reynolds thought of the company's traditional products as falling into three categories: "growth" products growing at more than 10 percent a year, which he expected to account for more than 50 percent of DYCO's sales and earnings by 1973; "cyclical" products such as phenol and formaldehyde, which he expected to grow in proportion to the gross national product; and "turnaround" products such as explosives and nitrogen, which he expected to rebound within the next three years or face the possibility of being divested. DYCO had recently divested itself of one of its turnaround product plants and had sold its joint venture interest in an unprofitable foreign subsidiary.

Soon after taking office, Mr. Reynolds visited all the company's U.S. plants and initiated a cost-cutting program aimed at increasing sales without a corresponding rise in indirect costs. He also expressed the opinion that market share should not be a deciding factor in future pricing policies; he was determined to get prices up in some of the company's important product areas.

THE ECONOMIC ANALYSIS DEPARTMENT

The role of the Economic Analysis Department, organized in 1937, originally was to make forecasts of the national economy. Always a department of the Treasurer's Division, its role gradually expanded first to industry and market forecasting, and during the early 1950s to consolidating long-range forecasts of the corporation's operations. In more recent years it had assumed the responsibility of evaluating proposals for large capital outlays and doing more detailed forecasts of DYCO operations. Its responsibilities included consolidation and review of the three-year strategic plan; preparation of one-month to three-year DYCO sales and profit forecasts; economic analyses and forecasts of industries, markets, and general business; analysis of DYCO performance; review of divisional financial data; analysis of real estate operations; financial analysis of appropriation requests; analysis of mergers and acquisitions; review of divisional budgets; special financial and economic studies; and maintenance of data for statistical analysis. In short, its role was that of collector, producer, interpreter, analyzer, and evaluator of forecasts, proposals, and information relating to strategic resource allocation by top management.

For example, the Economic Analysis Department evaluated all major capital expenditure and acquisition proposals involving more than $500,000 and filed a report to top management. The job of the Economic Analysis Department was to examine the assumptions, forecasts, and risks inherent in each of these proposals and to play a devil's-advocate role on behalf of top management.

As Mr. William Kirkpatrick, department manager, put it, "The operating divisions may be correct when they call us 'nay-sayers,' but we have a basis for each position we take. After all, they are out to sell and advocate their proposals and their egos are involved; someone has to keep them honest."

The Economic Analysis Department sometimes adjusted the forecasts presented by the divisions in their proposals and plans when it believed they were too optimistic. It was rare indeed when the forecasts of the divisions were deemed too pessimistic. It found that the divisions in rapidly growing markets tended to be too optimistic in their forecasts, while those in more stable markets were more realistic.

The department played an important role in the planning process; little planning information went to top management that did not also pass through it. Mr. Kirkpatrick also gave quarterly presentations to the board of directors on the national economic outlook. He felt that the Economic Analysis Department had a reputation with management for reasonable, well-thought-out analysis. Top management tended to call directly on the Economic Analysis Department for information and requests to do studies rather than going through the treasurer. Such calls were received at least several times a week and often daily. The same confidence existed within the Treasurer's Division; Mr. Kirkpatrick described the treasurer as "very supportive of our efforts and a very forward-looking guy."

In addition to forecasts designed for evaluating a specific proposal, the Economic Analysis Department was responsible for a hierarchy of general forecasts from very short range to long range. These were made for top management at regular intervals. In the short term the department made forecasts of sales and gross profit by product group three times each month: at the beginning of the month, at mid-month, and at the end of the month. (The actual monthly figures became

EXHIBIT 4
Accuracy of forecast by economic analysis department

Quarterly forecast of nongovernment sales
Deviation of forecast from actual (in percent)

Quarter forecasted	Four quarters ahead	Three quarters ahead	Two quarters ahead	One quarter ahead	Actual sales ($ millions)
1968					
1Q	2.6	1.5	−4.3	−4.6	85.3
2Q	3.7	0.4	−0.2	−2.4	95.6
3Q	−3.8	−7.9	−5.9	−2.5	98.8
4Q	−7.2	−10.1	−7.3	−4.6	100.7
1969					
1Q	−4.8	−4.3	−1.9	−1.1	96.4
2Q	3.6	−0.5	4.0	5.8	103.2
3Q	6.0	4.6	10.3	3.2	101.2
4Q	1.4	8.1	2.1	0.5	104.0
1970					
1Q	8.7	1.6	−0.2	0.5	103.0
2Q	4.5	3.7	−1.5	1.7	107.6
Average absolute deviation	4.6	4.3	3.8	2.7	

Long-range forecasts of annual earnings per share
Deviation of forecast from actual (in percent) for forecast of

Year forecasted	July 2, 1964	June 30, 1965	June 30, 1966	June 22, 1967	Jan. 15, 1968	Jan. 17, 1969	Feb. 6, 1970
1964	−4.0						
1965	−8.6	−6.3					
1966	−18.4	−19.1	−11.2				
1967	−1.7	−2.5	1.3	6.3			
1968	−8.2	−9.7	−5.9	6.3	6.7		
1969	18.1	20.4	22.6	41.6	33.5	29.0	
1970	9.2		16.3	40.2	39.8	27.5	4.4

available the middle of the following month.) These forecasts were used primarily to monitor the company's earnings-per-share record.

Every quarter the department forecasted income statements, balance sheets, and sources and uses of funds for each of the next four quarters for the corporation, divisions, and occasionally for the product groups. These forecasts were used for management of cash, receivables, inventories, and debt.

Finally, there were the long-range forecasts of corporate income statements and balance sheets extending three years into the future. These were used in long-range planning, including such things as financial management and new products. At each level of forecasts, short range, intermediate, or long term, management expressed strong interest in earnings per share. The department's record in forecasting is summarized in Exhibit 4.

THE DYCO "STRATEGIC PLAN"

Formal planning at DYCO consisted of developing the "strategic plan," a three-year forecast of activities of the corporation based on operating plans prepared by each division. Each year the operating plans were prepared and presented to the executive committee in a series of meetings which started in September and were held every two weeks until each division had presented its plans.

The steps in the formal planning process were designed to lead up to the executive committee presentations. Each operating division submitted its plans to the Economic Analysis Department during the summer and received the department's written critique before its presentation to the executive committee. The Economic Analysis Department found it hard to criticize the division's forecasts for individual products, but relatively easier to critique the aggregate sales figures. During the preparation of the plans by individual divisions, the Economic Analysis Department would provide information (such as industry forecasts or forecasts of corporate wage rates) when requested, but such requests were relatively rare. The format of a typical page in the plan is given in Exhibit 5.

Until 1970 the strategic plan had projected five years into the future. It was cut back to three years when the division managers complained that the last two years were a meaningless exercise. Evidence of their complaint was the fact that capital expenditure forecasts for the fourth and fifth years of the plan were always small because the division manager had difficulty visualizing specific projects that far into the future.

EXHIBIT 5
Sample page from the DYCO strategic plan

Forecast of DYCO performance, 1971–1973
Basic Chemicals

	Previous plan 1970	Latest estimate*	Current plan 1971	Current plan 1972	Current plan 1973

Net profit after taxes ($000)

	Previous plan 1970	Latest estimate*	Current plan 1971	Current plan 1972	Current plan 1973

Earnings per share ($)

Pesticides
Nitrogen products
Oxychemicals
Methanol-formaldehyde
Plasticizers
Adhesives
　　Total

Total operating assets ($ millions)

Return on operating assets (percent)

Pesticides
Nitrogen products
Oxychemicals
Methanol-formaldehyde
Plasticizers
Adhesives
　　Total

Net sales value ($ millions)

Pesticides
Nitrogen products
Oxychemicals
Methanol-formaldehyde
Plasticizers
Adhesives
　　Total

PROSPECTS FOR A DYCO PLANNING MODEL

The potential usefulness of a corporate planning model had been recognized by the Economic Analysis Department for some time. The primary motivation had been the need for a top-down forecast to temper the forecast that resulted from the bottom-up consolidation of the operating plans of the individual divisions. A second motivation was the rapid rate of obsolescence of the current long-range forecasts; a new procedure that permitted a relatively quick and inexpensive way of producing new forecasts seemed desirable. From time to time members of the department had discussed the possibility of a corporate model, but the press of other work such as special studies for top management had always postponed the model's development.

In April 1970 the Economic Analysis Department became a client of Data Resources, Inc. (DRI), a young firm founded by Harvard economist Otto Eckstein, former member of the U.S. Council of Economic Advisers, to apply time-shared computer technology to economic and financial analysis. DRI's services centered around on-line access to forecasts of the national economy, data banks, models, and statistical software. These services were supported by consulting, educational seminars, and supplementary contract research.

The heart of the DRI service involved use of the "DRI National Econometric Model" which is shown schematically in Exhibit 6. The model consisted of two parts, a national economic submodel, which took user-supplied assumptions about federal fiscal and monetary policies and from these projected various measures of national economic activity, and the industries submodel, which broke the economy down into 81 industry groups and captured the interrelationships and trans-

EXHIBIT 6
Schematic of the DRI National Econometric Model

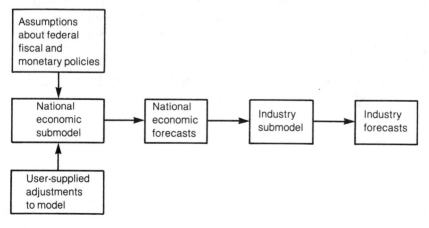

actions between these industries in an "input–output" matrix. It produced individual industry forecasts based on variables supplied by the national economic submodel. The model produced quarterly forecasts for two years of over 400 economic measures ranging from aggregate figures for the whole economy to the activity of individual industries.

Because the model was based on an historically observed normal balance within the economy, it was necessary to make adjustments for abnormal circumstances when these were expected. This was handled by user-supplied adjustments to the variables. In the case of a dock strike, for example, the model would overestimate imports and exports. By making adjustments to imports and exports, a user could input his estimate of the strike's impact. The adjustments would then affect other variables in the model, hopefully resulting in a more accurate forecast.

Consequently, there was a great deal of skill required in adjusting for current realities and in deciding upon a set of assumptions about federal fiscal and monetary policies. This managing of the model was done by a staff of economists at DRI. There were several hundred variables for which adjustments could be supplied and a smaller number of fiscal and monetary assumptions, including federal purchases for goods and services, transfer payments and social security taxes, federal tax receipts, the effect corporate tax rate (taking into account the investment tax credit and depreciation allowances), and the rate of growth of the money supply.

New forecasts based on DRI-supplied assumptions were made quarterly and whenever changes in the economic situation (such as the advent of price controls) warranted them. With each new run of the model, the DRI economists spelled out their assumptions in great detail. For example, in the September 1970 forecast, assumptions regarding future transfer payments and social security taxes were accompanied by a discussion of how the welfare reform issue would be resolved, and the assumptions regarding future tax receipts were supported by a discussion of when the import surcharge would be terminated. The documentation of a run from the model sometimes exceeded 100 pages, about 25 pages of which spelled out the assumptions and the reasoning behind them and the rest of which were forecasts and interpretation.

DYCO Chemical
Corporation (B)

In early January 1972, William Kirkpatrick, manager of the Economic
Analysis Department of DYCO Chemical Corporation, was reviewing
the company's new corporate simulation model with Walter Schroeder
and Peter Green, the men responsible for its development. The model,
completed in August 1971, had been developed by Data Resources,
Inc. (DRI), an economic consulting firm. The men were modifying and
checking the model prior to employing it in the Economic Analysis
Department's forecasting and financial planning.

THE EVOLUTION OF THE MODEL

The Economic Analysis Department had been interested in a corporate model for DYCO for some time, but special projects for top management had kept them from starting the project. Development of the
model had been given new impetus when Walter Schroeder attended
a DRI seminar on cash flow models in January 1971. When he returned
to DYCO he outlined his ideas for a corporate model in a memorandum which specified the output he thought the model should produce,
speculated on uses for the model, roughly sketched out the needed
equations, but also pointed out that there were various gaps to be
filled.

In his section on costs (reproduced below), he estimated costs and
suggested who should do the work.

> Two to four man-months would be a rough estimate of the amount of
> the Economic Analysis Department's time required to complete a pre-
> liminary model. Debugging and tuning could take another one to two
> man-months.
> The effort would draw on all of the people and resources of the de-
> partment on a part-time basis but it would be important that one person
> be responsible for its control, direction, and coordination. The model
> should be the principal responsibility of that person. Oscar North is one
> logical candidate, and Jim Dooley is another. Whoever it is would need
> the assistance of all of us.
> The DRI resources required would include use of (1) the DRI and
> DYCO data banks, (2) the DRI statistical analysis programs, (3) the DRI

model, and (4) the DRI model-building package. We would also have to call on Fred Bamber and possibly other DRI people for assistance.

The amount of DRI computer time required would probably be the equivalent of one to three months of our normal use of the DRI data and programs. Two to four of Fred Bamber's monthly visits might also be used on the model.

During the next few months, no work was begun on the model. Mr. Schroeder did, however, discuss his memorandum with Fred Bamber, DRI's consultant to DYCO, who visited the Economic Analysis Department one day each month.

In June 1971, DRI made an unsolicited proposal to the Economic Analysis Department to develop a model similar to the one outlined in Mr. Schroeder's memo. DRI offered to do the work for a fixed fee, plus the cost of computer time. The offer was accepted and the project was started at the end of June.

It was decided that three closely related models would be constructed in sequence, the first two being evolutionary steps toward the third. The first was an accounting model of historical financial relationships at DYCO. The second and third models made deterministic forecasts but each required different inputs. All three would produce the following output on a quarterly basis:

1. Income statement.
2. Balance sheet.
3. Cash flow statement.
4. A series of financial ratios.

They would be constructed on DRI's time-sharing computer. The three models were the following:

1. The *accounting identities model* would generate a set of quarterly financial statements from the first quarter of 1953 through the last quarter for which actual data were available, and would be updated over time as new data became available. The historical data in the accounting model would provide the basis for the relationships and estimating equations to be used in the forecasting models. The data would be adjusted to account for major acquisitions.

2. The *internal pro forma model* would extend the accounting identities model into the future for as many years as the user wished to supply data. This model's forecasts would be based on historical relationships (determined from the accounting identities model) between variables and on levels or rates of change of others of the variables. For example, the relationship between sales and direct costs might be based on historical data, while the level of capital expenditures might be assumed to change over time. The principal value of this model would be to allow the user to make assumptions about critical vari-

ables in the model and to learn how these changes might be reflected in the other accounts.

3. The *econometric model* would be used for forecasting by directly linking the DYCO model to the DRI model of the economy. The model would consist of a set of equations based on historical relationships that would relate variables in the DYCO model to each other and to variables in the DRI model. It was to be constructed so that judgment could be exercised in determining the effects of changes in the economy on DYCO; there would be many parameters that could be varied by the user. Development of this model was the primary objective of DRI's model-building efforts.

Programming for the model was to be performed by Suzanne Moot at DRI's Lexington, Massachusetts, office under the supervision of Fred Bamber. Peter Green was appointed liaison man from the Economic Analysis Department, and five people from the department spent two weeks early in the program gathering data.

The relationship between DRI personnel and Economic Analysis Department personnel, which had been very close prior to the model, remained close through heavy use of the telephone. DRI personnel were given free access to the necessary company data.

The accounting identities model was operational in early July, the internal pro forma model was operational on July 14, and the econometric model was available in preliminary version on August 5.

THE ECONOMETRIC MODEL

The Econometric Model was coupled directly to DRI's National Economic Model so that the user controlled it by varying some of the input parameters to the DRI model and some of the DYCO model parameters. The relationship between the two models is shown schematically in Exhibit 1.

The DYCO model made use of a number of variables from the DRI model as inputs. For example a combination of economic activity in the chemical and rubber industries was used to forecast DYCO sales (an accurate prediction of DYCO sales was extremely critical because so many variables in the model depended on it); the price index used to deflate the gross national product was used in forecasting DYCO direct costs; the DRI forecast of the interest rate of Moody's Aaa new issues was used in forecasting DYCO interest expenses (DYCO bonds were rated Aa); it was also used in forecasting receivables, since receivables tended to rise with interest rates; a measure of the tightness of the money supply was also used to help forecast receivables; and the DRI forecast of private nonfarm inventories was used to forecast DYCO inventories.

386

EXHIBIT 1
Relationship between DRI and DYCO models

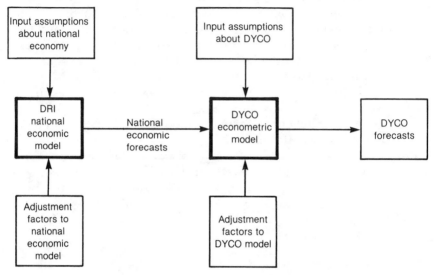

About 20 variables affecting DYCO were under the user's control. These included capital spending (based on a periodic forecast by the corporate Engineering Division), cash and marketable securities, projected quarterly dividends, the effective tax rate (including a factor for the investment tax credit forecasted by the Engineering Department), planned long-term debt, and government sales by the Explosives Division.

Compared to many corporate planning models, the DYCO model was a simple one, as evidenced by the small number of equations it contained. Forty equations produced the income statement, 35 more produced the balance sheet, 25 additional produced the funds flow, and 40 produced the financial ratios. The majority of these equations were accounting identities, and a large portion of the remainder were based on statistical analysis of historical relationships.

The output of the model was a simple forecast of the future with no statement of the uncertainty associated with the forecast. Sample output from a four-quarter forecast is shown in Exhibit 2; two-year forecasts were available if desired.

Work on the model since August 5

The Economic Analysis Department took delivery of the model on August 5 at a meeting at which Suzanne Moot and Don McLagan, vice president of DRI, gave a presentation at DYCO to Messrs. Schroeder and Green, the corporate treasurer, and two of the assistant treasurers.

Since August 5, Mr. Green, in consultation with Mr. Schroeder, had been refining and testing the model. Because he had been involved in its development, Mr. Green was satisfied that the basic equations were sound and that many parts of it were as refined as was practical. However, he felt that other parts could be improved.

To test the model he made forecasts with it and monitored the results. To differentiate between inaccuracies caused by the DRI model of the economy and those caused by the DYCO model, Mr. Green used a DRI-supplied set of data consisting of the actual economic results eight quarters back as control input to the DYCO model. He then compared the forecasted DYCO results with the actual and isolated errors due to the DYCO model.

On the basis of the results of the DRI control data, forecasts made since August with DRI projections, and his knowledge of the structure of the model, he was able to improve the DYCO model through use of alternate input variables and through changes in the model itself.

One example was the improvement in accuracy of forecasting sales that resulted from forecasting government sales separately from nongovernment sales. Formerly the two had been forecasted as a single number which depended on the level of activity in the chemical and rubber industries. However, since government sales were to a single customer under a few large contracts, the Government Sales Department of the Explosives Division was able to provide quite accurate forecasts. The model now combined management forecasts of government sales and statistical forecasts of nongovernment sales for increased accuracy.

In another example, investment tax credits had been handled by adjusting the average effective tax rate; in a revision, the tax credits were modeled explicitly.

Yet another example was the way interest charges on corporate debt were handled. Formerly interest on the entire DYCO debt was derived from certain economic measures. After modification, the interest rate on corporate Aaa bonds was used to predict the interest charges on a new Aa debt which were added to the actual charges on previous debt to get total interest charges.

Though he had many ideas about further work to improve the accuracy of the model, Mr. Green felt that two ideas were most promising. He observed that in time of economic expansion, indirect (GS&A) costs tended to lag sales growth, and similarly during downturns, the cutback in these expenses generally began after the start of the downturn. He guessed that reflecting this lag in the model would remove about 10 percent of the remaining error in forecasting. There was also great potential in improving the sales forecast by forecasting sales of each individual product group separately and then combining them to obtain a total nongovernment sales figure. However, he felt

EXHIBIT 2. Sample output from the DYCO model, DYCO Incorporated income statement ($000)

	1972:1	1972:2	1972:3	1972:4
Net sales				
Commercial	$117,308	$127,585	$130,216	$129,177
Government	12,797	13,738	12,997	12,840
Total	130,105	141,323	143,213	142,017
Cost of sales				
Commercial	81,209	87,681	89,611	91,110
Government	7,825	8,283	7,772	7,610
Total	89,035	95,964	97,382	98,720
Gross profit from sales				
Commercial	36,099	39,904	40,606	38,067
Government	4,972	5,455	5,225	5,230
Total	41,071	45,359	45,831	43,297
Indirect expense				
Commercial	23,428	24,046	24,719	25,262
Government	2,708	2,708	2,693	2,713
Total	26,136	26,754	27,413	27,974
Net profit from sales				
Commercial	12,671	15,857	15,886	12,805
Government	2,263	2,747	2,532	2,518
Total	14,935	18,685	18,418	15,323
Interest expense				
Short term	509	583	508	504
Long term	1,260	1,260	1,260	1,232
Total	1,769	1,843	1,768	1,736
Miscellaneous profit	388	1,483	382	504
Net income before taxes	13,553	18,245	17,033	14,091
U.S. and foreign taxes	6,609	8,210	7,665	6,341
Net income after taxes	7,454	10,035	9,368	7,750
Accrued dividends				
Class A and preferred	7	7	6	5
Common	2,987	2,990	2,995	5,397
Total	2,994	2,997	3,001	5,402
Retained earnings	4,460	7,038	6,368	2,348
Average shares outstanding	14,933,250	14,952,750	14,972,250	14,991,750
Earnings per common share	0.498	0.670	0.626	0.517
Dividends per common share	0.200	0.200	0.200	0.360

	1972:1	1972:2	1972:3	1972:4
Assets				
Current assets				
Cash and marketable securities	$ 14,716	$ 14,803	$ 15,004	$ 15,000
Accounts receivable	87,585	95,033	96,826	96,557
Inventories	82,164	83,020	84,007	85,121
Total current assets	184,465	192,856	195,838	196,678
Industrial revenue bonds held by trustees	2,580	2,580	2,580	2,580
Fixed assets				
Gross fixed assets	523,748	534,154	545,116	556,032
Depreciation and amortization	275,294	282,466	289,758	297,259
Net fixed assets	248,454	251,688	255,358	258,773
Investments in subsidiary and associated companies	26,356	27,556	28,756	29,956
Investments, other	12,659	12,496	12,461	12,360
Deferred U.S. and foreign taxes	7,454	7,454	7,454	7,454
Deferred charges and miscellaneous assets	7,984	7,969	7,950	7,950
Total assets	$489,952	$502,599	$510,397	$515,751
Liabilities				
Current liabilities				
U.S. and foreign income taxes	$ 18,361	$ 15,188	$ 18,884	$ 16,105
Notes payable	36,393	41,673	36,253	36,000
Other current liabilities	40,006	43,184	43,822	44,424
Total current liabilities	94,819	100,044	98,959	96,529
Long-term debt	78,634	78,634	78,634	77,038
Reserves				
Insurance	10,090	10,266	10,442	10,612
Pension	24,813	24,813	24,813	23,601
Other	0	0	0	0
Total	34,903	35,079	35,255	34,213
Stockholders' equity	273,503	280,871	287,570	290,248
Total liabilities	$489,952	$502,599	$510,397	$515,751
Balancing item (Total assets — Total liabilities)	8,093	7,970	9,979	17,724
Memo: Average total operating assets				
Commercial	$646,042	$659,934	$675,770	$688,400
Government	42,382	42,917	43,308	43,429
Total	$688,424	$702,852	$719,078	$731,829

EXHIBIT 2 (continued). DYCO Incorporated cash flow forecast, source and use of funds ($000)

	1972:1	1972:2	1972:3	1972:4
Source of funds				
Net income after taxes	$ 7,454	$10,035	$ 9,368	$ 7,750
Depreciation and amortization	8,003	8,141	8,286	8,521
Insurance	155	176	176	169
Deferred U.S. and foreign income taxes	0	0	0	0
Sales of fixed assets	0	0	0	0
Industrial revenue bonds	0	0	0	0
Long-term debt	−1,169	0	0	−1,596
Sale of capital stock	331	331	331	331
Subtotal	14,774	18,683	18,161	15,175
Change in working capital				
U.S. and foreign income taxes	2,993	−3,173	3,696	−2,779
Notes payable	778	5,280	−5,420	−253
Other current liabilities	178	3,118	638	602
Total current liabilities	3,949	5,225	−1,085	−2,430
Total source of funds	$18,722	$23,908	$17,075	$12,745
Use of funds				
Capital expenditures	$10,200	$12,600	$13,200	$13,200
Dividends	2,944	2,997	3,001	5,402
Investment in foreign subsidiaries	1,200	1,200	1,200	1,200
Investment, other	−35	−163	−35	−101
Capital stock reacquired	0	0	0	0
Deferred charges and miscellaneous assets	500	−15	−19	0
Other use of funds, net	−1,217	−1,225	−1,244	−1,264
Subtotal	13,642	15,394	16,103	18,437
Change in working capital				
Cash and marketable securities	−262	87	201	−4
Accounts receivable	1,437	7,448	1,793	−269
Inventories	670	856	988	1,114
Total current assets	1,845	8,390	2,982	840
Total use of funds	$18,722	$23,908	$17,075	$12,745
Balancing item (Sources − Uses)	$ 3,236	$123	−$2,009	−$6,533

EXHIBIT 2 (concluded). DYCO Incorporated financial-ratios (percent)

	1972:1	1972:2	1972:3	1972:4
Net sales (annual rate)/average TOA*				
Commercial	72.63%	77.33%	77.08%	75.06%
Government	120.77	128.04	120.04	118.26
Total	75.60	80.43	79.66	77.62
Gross profit/net sales				
Commercial	30.77	31.28	31.18	29.47
Government	38.85	39.71	40.20	40.73
Total	31.57	32.10	32.00	30.49
Indirect expense/net sales				
Commercial	19.97	18.85	18.98	19.56
Government	21.26	19.71	20.72	21.12
Total	20.00	18.93	19.14	19.70
Net profit from sales/net sales				
Commercial	N.A.†	N.A.	N.A.	N.A.
Government	17.68	20.00	19.48	19.61
Total	11.48	13.16	12.86	10.79
Net profit from sales/gross profit				
Commerical	35.10	39.74	39.12	33.64
Government	45.52	50.37	48.46	48.14
Total	36.36	41.02	40.19	35.39
Net profit from sales (annual rate)/average TOA				
Commercial	7.85	9.61	9.40	7.44
Government	21.36	25.61	23.39	23.19
Total	8.68	10.59	10.25	8.38
Net income before taxes (annual rate)/equity	19.82	25.98	23.69	19.42
Net income after taxes (annual rate)/equity	10.90	14.29	13.03	10.68
Net income after taxes (annual rate)/average TOA	4.33	5.71	5.21	4.24
Cash and securities/total current liabilities	15.52	14.80	15.16	15.54
Total current assets/total current liabilities	194.54	192.77	197.90	203.75
Long-term debt/equity	28.75	28.00	27.84	26.54

* TOA = total operating assets.
† N.A. = not available.

that this second refinement might require several months of data analysis to implement.

Mr. Green thought of the accuracy of the model in terms of forecasting earnings per share because of the great interest of DYCO management in those numbers. He told the case writer, "We've had a rather short experience with using the model for forecasts, so we don't have too many actuals against which to test our forecasts. But based on our short experience, my knowledge of what's in the model, and my best judgment, I'd guess we could hit annual earnings per share one year ahead to within ±10 percent. In my judgment the best we could ever hope for is ±5 percent given the current state of the art."

In his limited experience testing the model, Mr. Green had discovered that the DYCO model had to be managed through the use of adjustment factors just as DRI's model did. For example, he found that the third quarter 1971 sales forecast has exceeded actual, and upon review of the actual DYCO figures he noticed that international sales were off sharply. He then recalled the dock strike in that time period and concluded that he could have and should have corrected for the strike with an adjustment factor. Likewise, soon after the dock strike ended there would be pent-up demand, so an adjustment factor of the opposite sign would be needed temporarily to reflect this. Further, he decided that the lag in indirect expenses, mentioned above, could be handled temporarily through the use of adjustment factors or by using the budgeted figure.

Mr. Green estimated that about six man-months of effort by department personnel had gone into the model. About half of this occurred before the delivery of the model by DRI, including two man-months of data collection and one man-month of support work and of conferences with DRI. Since August Mr. Green had put in about two months refining the model and another half month taking trial runs. He estimated that about 40 percent of his time during 1972 would be spent working with and developing the model.

The DRI service during 1972 cost $25,000, not including model development, but including rental of the computer terminal and computer charges. The DYCO model was just one of many uses made of the DRI service. Mr. Kirkpatrick did not need the treasurer's approval before starting a new project such as the modeling effort provided he didn't exceed his budget. However, he did, as a matter of courtesy, keep the treasurer informed of all projects of any size.

Problems in developing the model

A number of problems were encountered in developing the model. Perhaps the most time-consuming was obtaining reliable and consistent historical data, since much of the historical accounting data had to be adjusted to account for intercompany sales, mergers, and acquisitions. (Among the larger acquisitions were a rubber belt company in 1956 having $13 million sales, a $25 million sales paint company in 1960, and a $22 million sales latex foam manufacturer in 1964.) These acquisitions were dealt with by generating pro forma financial statements for a half dozen of the largest acquisitions before they became affiliated with DYCO and then making adjustments in the acquired companies' accounting data to make them compatible with DYCO's accounting conventions.

A second problem was deciding on which of the 400 or more variables projected by the DRI model to use as a basis for making forecasts of various variables in the DYCO model. A good example was the forecasting of DYCO sales. Two kinds of variables from the DRI model could be helpful: projections of broad economic indicators such as GNP and industrial production and projections of the level of activities of the 81 different industry groups. Attempts to forecast sales based on the broad economic indicators were disappointing. Attention was then turned to the list of industry groups, a number of which could be arbitrarily eliminated (such as leather, iron, and steel). Others were thought to be related to DYCO sales, such as the lumber industry, but less so than some others. The list was narrowed to the chemical, paper, rubber, food and kindred products, textiles, and motor vehicles and parts industries. After considerable statistical analysis, only the chemical and rubber industries were actually used.

Another problem arose when reconciling output from the model with the company's accounting reports. Mr. Schroeder decided that output from the model would be presented in a format compatible with reports currently in use to facilitate communication with top management. When the results of the accounting identities model failed to match the historical funds flow reports exactly, a meeting was scheduled with the manager of accounting to reconcile the differences. "His comments at the meeting," Mr. Schroeder said, "indicated the maze of detailed accounting procedures required to satisfy the Accounting Principles Board, and we decided not to incorporate them in the model. This meant that while the format of the model and the currently used reports were identical, the results might differ by 5 percent."

USING THE MODEL

Running the DYCO econometric model used about $30 of computer time and an hour of Mr. Green's time at the time-sharing terminal. Once the first run was set up, additional runs could be made in ten minutes at a cost of about $20 each.

These figures assumed that the base-case forecasts from the DRI model were used; if a new run of the DRI model was made the cost increased by $10. Only rarely were changes made in the assumptions to the DRI model, since the modelers preferred not to outguess the DRI economic forecasts. Instead they concentrated on the assumptions for the DYCO model which were determined in face-to-face and telephone conferences with DYCO managers and by using their own judgment.

THE FUTURE OF THE MODEL

After Messrs. Kirkpatrick, Schroeder, and Green had discussed modifications to the DYCO planning model at their January meeting, their discussion shifted to uses of the model and to when and how it should be introduced.

Mr. Kirkpatrick emphasized the need for caution in introducing the model. "I doubt that the twelfth floor (the location of top management offices) knows about our model," he reminded the others. "They have had bad experiences in the past when untested tools were sold prematurely. We all know what happened when 'leading indicators' were touted as a forecasting device. The indicators fit past data well but were not sufficiently reliable as a forecasting tool.

"And we also know how complicated techniques can turn off top management. The risk analysis program developed by the Operations Research Department to analyze new investment projects is fantastically comprehensive for analyzing projects, but top management was slow to accept it. It's so complicated that it takes a long time even to set up a project analysis on the computer."

"But our model isn't all that complicated," interjected Mr. Green. "And we were able to do a pretty good job . . . and a quick one, too . . . in forecasting the impact of Nixon's new economic policy. I'm willing to bet that there isn't a better way around to study the implications of these new policies. I think we ought to consider introducing the model soon."

"We've got top management's ear and confidence, and our credibility with them is our most precious asset," Mr. Kirkpatrick replied, "and everyone calls here for information when they need it. We can't afford to risk our reputation on a possible bad experience with this model. Don't get me wrong, Peter; I'm as enthusiastic about using this new tool as you are. But, there's a limit to the rate of change any organization can stand, and using a model for forecasting is quite an innovation."

"Maybe what we should do is to begin to use the results of the model in conjunction with our current forecasting approach, and keep quiet about the role of the model," suggested Mr. Schroeder. "Then as we gain experience, we can tell top management about the model and begin to educate them in its use and interpretation."

"Regardless of when we do it, we're going to have to educate top management in the use of the model at some point so that they can use the results," said Mr. Kirkpatrick. "I'm sure that due to our good relationships we can get as much of their time as we need to bring them up to date *when* we are ready.

"Getting to your earlier point, I have my doubts that the model will ever supplant our current forecasting approach, but I can see it playing an increasing role in producing our forecasts. I think it will help the one-year forecast, but it will be even more helpful in forecasting the second year into the future. That's where our division management finds prediction difficult; they don't do badly at all on one-year forecasts. Another role it can play is to give us a quick turnaround in updating our forecasts when conditions suddenly change.

"I'm concerned about a conversation I had with the treasurer yesterday," Mr. Kirkpatrick continued. "He was asking how the model was coming along and though he didn't say so in so many words, I could tell he was hoping we would be putting it to use soon. I'd hate to be pressured into a move that we'd later regret."

The men then turned their attention to uses for the model and things they might do in the future. They had previously agreed that one of the main purposes of the model would be to provide a top-down bench mark for the total company forecast so that they would be in a position to constructively criticize the forecasts presented by the individual divisions. They also hoped to use the model to give management an idea of the ranges of things that could occur within the two-year period the model forecasted. They discussed the possibility of modifications to the model so that DRI's ten-year economic forecasts could be coupled with it to produce a longer-range forecast. This would require the assumption that certain key ratios remained constant within the company during the ten-year forecast, an assumption with which the men felt uneasy.

Looking further downstream they speculated on building similar models on a divisional basis and coupling these to the corporate model. Mr. Kirkpatrick also suggested the possibility of introducing probabilities for some of the uncertainties so that one could get a feel for the chances of various outcomes actually occurring.

Finally Mr. Kirkpatrick stood up and said, "Well gentlemen, let's knock off for today. It's all well and good to speculate, but our primary concern right now is getting something we have a lot of faith in."

Transit maintenance*

Late one afternoon in the fall of 1976, Jack Herringer and Paul Westlake prepared to leave their office. The two consultants unplugged the computer console, carefully packed away their latest set of numerical output, and locked the door marked "UMTA/MBTA Project." "Well, MASSTRAM's almost completed now," Jack said. "All that's left is to prepare the final user's manual. This project sure has been a lot of work. I hope the MBTA will make use of our model."

"Me too," said Paul. "But they've got so many problems, even in the maintenance area, that I wonder whether they'll consider MASSTRAM's implementation as a high priority. And even if they want to, I wonder if they can take all the right steps to make the best use of it? Guess we'll have to wait and see what they do, now that they have MASSTRAM over there to play with."

BACKGROUND

The Massachusetts Bay Transportation Authority (MBTA) is an independent state agency providing mass transit service to 79 cities and towns in the Boston metropolitan area. In 1975, the authority was beset with severe problems in virtually every area and had developed all of the characteristics of a dying enterprise: declining ridership and fare revenues, deteriorating service, and deferred maintenance. The existence of unions and weak management further contributed to the bleak outlook for this major transit operator.

In April 1975, in an attempt to reverse the fortunes of the authority, Governor Michael Dukakis appointed Robert R. Kiley, former deputy mayor of Boston, to the post of chief executive officer (CEO) of the MBTA. The post, created in 1975 by combining the roles of chairman of the board of directors and the general manager, was designed to provide strong leadership and direct accountability for costs and the quality of service. Kiley, with a reputation as a competent and politically skillful manager, was strongly supported by the state and municipal leaders responsible for paying the authority's deficit, and was committed to a major overhaul at all levels of the authority.

---

* Copyright © 1977 by the Trustees of Boston University.

Among Kiley's most severe challenges would be the revitalization of the rail vehicle maintenance departments, the major bottleneck in MBTA service. Although weaknesses in all operating departments were readily apparent, the drop in the quality of service during the previous decade could be attributed primarily to the deterioration of car maintenance. As one scheduling manager put it, "Back in the Boston Elevated days when we used to make a little money around here, we used to schedule the service for where the passengers were. Now we just schedule according to how many cars the maintenance departments can keep going. And every time we reduce the schedule to what we think they can produce, vehicle availability drops some more. I tell you—we talk about decreasing ridership—we're driving them away with bad service!"

SERVICES

The MBTA in 1975 served 79 municipalities with a total population of 2.8 million. It operated 37 route miles of heavy rail rapid transit, 43 miles of light rail streetcar lines, 3,538 route miles of bus service, and 8 route miles of trackless trolley. Over these routes, it operated three heavy rail rapid transit lines (the Red, Orange, and Blue lines), a light rail streetcar-subway line with four surface branches (the Green line), over 200 bus routes, and four trackless trolley routes.

In addition, the authority contracted with 17 private bus carriers for the operation of routes throughout the metropolitan area, and subsidized passenger service along ten railroad routes owned and operated by the Penn Central and Boston & Maine Railroads.

The quality of service depended largely on the available equipment and varied widely over the system. Exhibit 1 shows the composition of the MBTA's fleet of transit vehicles. In the rapid transit section, service was most reliable on the Blue line, although its cars were the oldest. The Red line had the newest cars and provided the swiftest and most comfortable rides, but the authority had trouble maintaining axle assemblies and a new signal system, so the line often broke down during storms. The Green line, the most heavily used, was the worst in the system. New cars expected in 1971 had not yet materialized, and the line's maintenance record was terrible.

The quality and reliability of bus and commuter rail service similarly varied. Some bus runs were slow and filled to capacity, while others ran quickly and were almost empty most of the day. Political influence in MBTA service planning had, over the years, led to the creation of a number of runs which could not be justified on the basis of their ridership.

EXHIBIT 1
Rail transit vehicles of the MBTA, 1976

	Number of vehicles	Year purchased
Green line: 291 vehicles, Pullman Co. Presidential Conference Cars (PCC)	7	1941
	80	1944
	94	1945
	36	1946
	50	1951
	8	1958
	16	1959
Orange line: 100 vehicles, Pullman Co. Standard	50	1957
	50	1958
Red line: 167 vehicles, Pullman Co. Standard	91	1963 (Bluebirds)
	76	1969 (Silverbirds)
Blue line:75 vehicles, Pullman Co. Standard	32	1923, refurbished 1951
	6	1924, refurbished 1951
St. Louis Co.,	37	1951

ORGANIZATION

The governing body of the MBTA was the five-member board of directors chaired by the CEO. Board approval was required for the hiring of some top-level department heads, the disbursement of major contracts, fare changes, bonding, and for the submission of the final budget to the MBTA's appropriating body, the advisory board.

The only major statutory check on the authority's power to spend was the advisory board, made up of representatives from each of the 79 communities served by the MBTA. Each community's vote on the board was proportional to its share of the previous year's MBTA assessment. (In recent years, these communities paid half of the annual fiscal deficit of the MBTA, while the remainder was contributed by the state.

The MBTA's line and staff departments, as reorganized by Kiley in early 1976, are shown in the organization chart in Exhibit 2. The major operating and maintenance functions were handled by four major departments, which included most of the authority's 6,400 employees:

1. Transportation Department, which was responsible for scheduling, traffic control, and manpower to operate service. All motormen, drivers, car shifters, guards, collectors, station masters, and other operating personnel were part of the department.
2. Engineering and Maintenance Department, which provided all maintenance to fixed property including buildings, tracks, structures, tunnels, power stations, transmission systems, etc.

EXHIBIT 2
Organization chart of the MBTA, January 1976

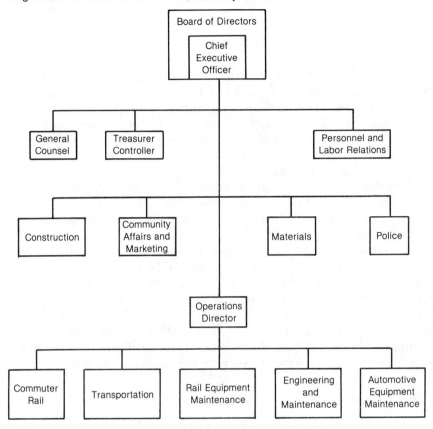

3. Automotive Equipment Maintenance Department, which provided ongoing repair for buses and trackless trolleys.
4. Rail Equipment Department, which was responsible for both light and heavy maintenance of all rapid transit vehicles and Green line cars. Ongoing light repairs and inspection work was done at carhouses on the lines, while heavy repair work took place at Everett shops.

These departments' budget levels (and authorized manpower) for 1975 were: Transportation—$54.6 million (3,440); Engineering and Maintenance—$19.5 million (1,051); Automotive Equipment Maintenance—$11.3 million (662); and Rail Equipment—$12.2 million (594).

The authority's major staff functions were handled by seven smaller departments: Law, Treasurer/Controller, Personnel and Labor Relations, Community Affairs and Marketing, Commuter Rail, Police, and Construction.

UNIONS

In 1975, the MBTA had collective bargaining agreements with 29 separate unions representing all but 450 of the authority's 6,400 employees. The most important union, Amalgamated Transit Workers Local 589, represented over 60 percent of the work force. Local 589 represented only the least skilled employees—the trades and middle management belonged to other unions—but it set the basic standards for all other bargaining agreements.

Outsiders described "Carmen's 589" as the strongest, tightest, most inured to criticism, and the most experienced in dealing with management of all public unions in Massachusetts. The membership included a great many extended families and close-knit groups. As an organization with strong internal bonds in a key service industry, 589 had been able to extend its power considerably. Over the years, it won contract settlements which included extremely generous wages and fringe benefits, plus a host of restrictive work rules which were generally believed to be costing the authority millions of dollars annually in productivity losses. Further, most of the authority's management personnel had come up through the ranks, and contributed to the strong identification of most employees with the "company family."

RAIL EQUIPMENT DEPARTMENT

In 1975, rail vehicle maintenance was handled by two separate departments, the Rail Equipment Maintenance Department and the Maintenance Shops Department. Rail Equipment Maintenance operated the rapid transit and streetcar "carhouses" located on each of the rail lines, and was responsible for cleaning, routine inspections and servicing, and repair of defective vehicles. Minor repairs were performed directly on the vehicle involved. But since the number of vehicles available for service was limited, the carhouses often quickly replaced an entire component system, such as an air compressor, with a working spare in order to rush the vehicle back into service. Maintenance Shops provided the components, and defective assemblies were returned to a major facility at Everett for overhaul. In addition to the machine component shop, Everett had a body shop whose tradesmen were responsible for all body work, whether performed in Everett or the carhouses. Both the body work and the component overhauls in Maintenance Shops were critical to the Rail Equipment Maintenance Department's day-to-day operations.

Sometimes it was difficult to pinpoint responsibility for maintenance problems since the two departments had complementary functions. The carhouses complained that Everett did not keep them adequately supplied with usable spare components, while Everett complained that the carhouses often had sufficient stock and didn't know it, and that they did not properly lubricate and service working vehicles.

In April 1976, Kiley's new director of operations, David Gunn, consolidated Rail Equipment Maintenance and Maintenance Shops into one unit, the Rail Equipment Department, headed by a new chief mechanical officer. Within the department, he gave greater responsibility and authority to managers of each of the four lines to strengthen line management accountability. The structure of the new department is shown in Exhibit 3.

HIBIT 3

ganization of the MBTA's Rail Equipment Department, 1976

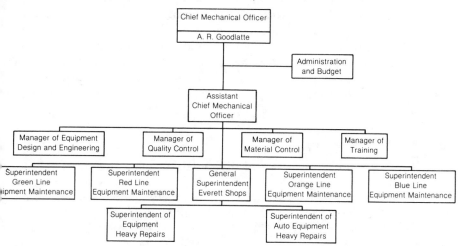

VEHICLE MAINTENANCE AND REPAIR

Maintenance work can be divided into two areas: (1) scheduled inspections and routine servicing, and (2) breakdown repair. The removal and return of cars either for in-service difficulties or for scheduled inspections required coordination between the Transportation and the Maintenance Departments, and there was much telephone contact between the two. The Maintenance Department was responsible for keeping cars in working condition. The Transportation Department determined when serviceable cars would be used and where they would be stored. When cars were due for routine inspections, the

Maintenance Department relied on Transportation to deliver them to the carhouse on schedule. Conversely, when the number of serviceable cars was less than the peak-hour requirement, the Transportation Department counted on Maintenance to complete its work on the needed cars in time to restore them to service.

Scheduled maintenance

Rapid transit vehicles were called in for inspection every 5,000 miles. Inspections were normally conducted during the day shift and often included minor repairs and adjustments. Teams of eight carhouse repairmen carried out the inspections and servicing, and covered four cars daily. Each team was broken into two truck men, two control men, one car-body man, one grease man, one axle man, and one insulator block man. Repairmen were supervised by an assistant foreman and a foreman of inspections. These periodic maintenance activities require an average of 20 to 25 man-hours of work per transit car.

Additional repairmen were often brought in during the inspection process to perform scheduled "modification" work—the planned repair or replacement of specific components in all vehicles of the fleet. Occasionally, repairmen were called in to make more extensive repairs identified during inspection, but foremen usually held these cars over until another shift.

Breakdown repair

In-service breakdowns were divided into four categories: (1) superficial problems such as a stuck hand brake, remedied at least temporarily by the vehicle operator without immediate involvement of the Maintenance Department; (2) minor breakdowns such as a defective windshield wiper, in which cars were able to reach the end of the line and, after brief work by repairmen located there, to continue in service; (3) breakdowns such as a defective motor generator, in which cars had to be towed directly to the carhouse for repairs; and (4) extreme instances such as derailments, fires, or major electrical failures in which repair crews were sent to the scene. For some breakdowns, such as failure of the controls, the diagnosis of a required repair could be quite extensive; for others, such as a broken window, diagnosis was a trivial part of the total repair activity. The frequency of breakdowns varied for the different parts ("subsystems") of the vehicle. Repeat breakdowns of the same subsystem on a single car was one indicator of unsuccessful repairs. Exhibit 4 presents illustrative data on breakdown frequencies.

EXHIBIT 4
Annual failure rate of selected vehicle subsystems

Vehicle subsystem	Total failures (per car per year)	New failures (per car per year)	Repeat failures* (per car per year)
Air brake	5.8	4.4	1.4
Control	9.9	5.5	4.4
Motors	0.7	0.6	0.1
Auto signal	2.0	1.7	0.3
Trucks	2.8	2.6	0.2
Door	3.9	3.2	0.7
HVAC	1.8	1.5	0.3
Other	11.6	11.4	0.2
Total	38.5	30.9	7.6

* A repeat is a failure which occurs within two weeks of a previous repair of the same subsystem.
Source: MBTA sample of 45 rapid transit line vehicles for the entire year 1976.

The duties of the two types of manpower—tradesmen and repairmen—were established separately, as the groups operated under different supervision and had separate unions. Tradesmen who were affiliated with the old Maintenance Shops Department became involved in direct repair on a vehicle only when their special talents were required in the carhouses, or when damage to a car was sufficient to justify its removal to Everett. The great bulk of their time was spent repairing damaged component systems for subsequent use as replacements for others which fail in service. Repairmen were part of the old Rail Equipment Maintenance Department and worked at the various carhouses.

DETERMINING DAILY WORK PRIORITIES

The determination of daily priorities was the responsibility of the carhouse supervisor. Scheduled inspections had the highest priority in the carhouses, and, occasionally, overtime was used to avoid backlogs in scheduled inspections. Other carhouse work was divided between scheduled repair of vehicles held over from previous days and unscheduled repair of newly arrived defective vehicles.

In-service breakdowns could not be anticipated, and, when only minor repairs were needed, were handled on a first-come-first-served basis. Major repairs (e.g., following a fire in a car) were backlogged until tradesmen became available. When there was a shortage of available cars for use during the next peak rush hour, cars requiring the easiest and quickest repairs were given top priority. When a line or carhouse faced a shortage, the use of overtime at time-and-a-half provided some flexibility, although, in 1976, the MBTA faced strong external pressures to limit it.

DEFERRED MAINTENANCE

Despite this emphasis on car availability and huge overtime expenditures in 1976, the Rail Equipment Department was unable to maintain enough vehicles in working condition to cover scheduled service. Exhibit 5 presents statistics on vehicle breakdowns and service

EXHIBIT 5
Illustrative data for MBTA rapid transit lines: Service summary and equipment availability*

Service summary		Reasons for canceled trips	
Trips scheduled	2,078	Vehicle not available	66
Trips canceled	96	Crew not available	2
Trips added	4	Vehicle disabled	22
Trips run	1,986	Accident	0
		Vandalism	0
		Weather	0
		Miscellaneous	6
		Total	96

Equipment availability	6:00 A.M.	8:00 P.M.
Peak requirement†	224	228
Over‡	4	6
(Short)‡	(14)	(10)
Available	214	224
Held§	110	100
Stored‖	18	18
Total	342	343

* Includes the Orange, Red, and Blue lines.
† Peak requirement is used for rush hours: Red line = 104, Orange = 76, Blue = 44 (48).
‡ While one line is short on vehicles, another may have more than its peak requirement.
§ Held signifies cars that are temporarily unavailable due to scheduled inspections or ongoing repairs.
‖ Stored signifies cars that are unusable but which have not been totally scrapped.

schedules. Vehicles that were placed in service could frequently break down, disrupting service and adding to the maintenance backlog. Behind this poor record was a long list of problems. C. W. England, superintendent of the Everett shops, commented as follows:

> Ever since the mid-1950s, we have been robbing Peter to pay Paul— pulling people out of Maintenance and into Transportation. Above all, remember, this has always been a very political organization. Without

strong leadership and with split factions, the outside political types have had a lot of influence. One result was that the "T" would do almost anything to keep service from dropping because that was the visible, politically sensitive part of the operation. And if you drop a driver you have to drop a route, so any belt-tightening always came out of maintenance. Nobody really noticed immediately if there were 36 or 37 rather than 40 repairmen in one of the carhouses or one less machinist in the shops, but eventually, of course, it caught up with us.

Since the late 1960s the MBTA has been caught in a failure-maintenance spiral. We have no time for programmed maintenance—just for putting out fires and trying to stay half a step ahead of the Grim Reaper. We aren't able to plan and schedule work—you know—every year a third of the older Red line cars should be overhauled, the axles on the Orange line cars should be repaired, there should be a systematized interior overhaul program, the lights should be changed on a regular basis—with manpower costs like ours, we have to get as much as possible out of every hour, and the only way to do that is through programmed maintenance. Otherwise, cars break down on the line, men have to be shuttled from stop to stop at $10 an hour—it's a very costly business. Take right now, we've got an emergency request for gearboxes on the Green line PCC cars. We always have an emergency request for something on the Green line. As a result, among other things, we haven't been able to systematically overhaul the silverbirds on the C-D (Cambridge-Dorchester) line. And now all their axles are breaking and the Red line is a disaster, so now we've got an emergency for axle assemblies, and the overtime is going out of sight.

One of the chief reasons for this, and you may think this is crazy, is that we have had too much capital money. At the same time that lines have been extended and rolling stock made more sophisticated, there has been a *real decrease* in the number of maintenance man-hours—not money, but man-hours—available.

Management's response to the failure-maintenance cycle generally involved attempts to attract additional resources. In past years, the MBTA had been very successful in getting its advisory board and the federal government to support special maintenance programs on grounds that if the authority were able to get out from under its deferred maintenance problem, it would be able to develop some long-run preventive maintenance programs. One manager remarked that "we've gotten some good things out of these programs. We would have had to do that work anyway, but we put it together in a special funding package and got some extra money. That's what really kept us alive." Some of the programs did produce—it was believed that Orange line vehicle availability in 1976 still benefited from maintenance work done in 1973. But the Rail Equipment Department had limited preventive maintenance programs, overtime was out of control, and the carhouses were not meeting their schedules.

WORK FORCE ATTITUDES AND CAPABILITIES

Contributing to the failure-maintenance cycle was the inability of past MBTA management to deal effectively with labor. A host of union work rules locked into the "589" contract interfered with the assignment of personnel, drove up overtime, and created inefficient jobs. For example, if a car repairman was unable to finish a job during his regular working hours, he had to quit and turn the job over to the most senior repairman who wanted overtime, even if that man couldn't do the job properly. Foremen often hired two or three men they didn't want in order to get down the seniority list to the one they needed. Other rules specified that two men be used on jobs where one was likely to be adequate, and carved out sharp "jurisdictions" for workers. In the trades, jobs were often delayed until an employee from a particular union could be sent over to perform "his" work.

The most damaging work rule, however, was the bidding system which provided the MBTA with car repairmen who did not possess necessary maintenance skills. Union contracts specified that repairmen would be selected from the ranks of car cleaners, who were usually former bus operators. Seniority was the sole qualification for the job, and repairmen were never disqualified for failure to demonstrate skills or aptitude in the authority's modest training course.

The relationships among repairmen, the union leadership, foremen and upper-level management also contributed to the problem. The vehicle availability crisis served the interest of the work force since it guaranteed extra overtime earnings. Dealing with union leadership on this subject was, therefore, difficult. One MBTA manager put it this way: "The union membership, especially the repairmen in the RTL carhouses, know they have a good thing going with overtime—they average over $4,000 a year. They have come to think of it as a normal part of their pay. Many have quit second jobs or bought a boat, or mortgaged their homes to buy cottages, and they are afraid to lose the extra pay. As a result, the union politicos try to outdo each other in virtually every area in ragging management to look as tough as possible."

The lengths to which union leaders and individual workers would go to support their interest were, at times, extreme. There were stories of intimidation of foremen and cooperative repairmen. At Everett, there were even rumors of "rat-holing" where components produced during the day were hidden to force overtime.

The foremen also had incentives to force overtime, and often had stronger ties to labor than to management. Foremen were on the weekly payroll and received little extra pay for their supervisory responsibilities. They were usually appointed to supervise the same people they had worked with for years, and usually retained their dues-paying membership and their seniority rights in Local 589 or a trade union. Many were "temporary charge" foremen who might be returned to repair duties at any time. And the foremen also received overtime pay at time-and-a-half rate with no competing incentive to complete work within normal working hours.

NEW TECHNOLOGY

The department's problems were further complicated by the introduction in the late 1960s and early 1970s of complex technical improvements. Operations Director Gunn felt that differences between the federal government's perceptions of transit needs and the operational capabilities of transit systems had created severe long-term problems.

The trap is that the Feds pour all sorts of money into the development of new hardware and support systems, and insist that you have to buy it, so everyone has been planning castles and letting the stuff we're operating fall down. Take the new light rail vehicles. We were supposed to have the LRVs three years ago, so maintenance on the old PCC Green line cars was deferred. We now have equipment falling apart, we have a seniority personnel system that says we have to bid out all our repairmen jobs among the bus drivers, collectors, and porters—you know, what the hell do they know about cars, no technical qualifications at all—so the only way we get a qualified repairman is by chance, and on top of that the Feds are coming down our backs with equipment that is fantastically complicated. It's here now—the LRV. To give you an idea of the problem: you can put the circuitry of a PCC car on one piece of paper, reduce it to one page, and it's legible. On an LRV the circuit book is 288 pages long. It is a maintenance man's nightmare. It's another case of the inventiveness of the salesman exceeding the system's engineering capability—the lack of a realistic evolutionary approach to building a railroad. You don't go out and build a system that only 1 percent of your maintenance force can work on.

On the Red line, we have another story. We have a brand new shop in the wrong place and we can't get to it. It was put there because there was a lot of local resistance (in other places) and now the Red line falls apart every time it clouds up. It's over behind South Station. You have to go down to Columbia Junction, go through a lot of reverse moves—because the newfangled signal system doesn't work, and we don't have enough qualified people to fix it, but that's still another story—to get to the shop. We've gone from a shop that was ideally suited for the line, albeit old, to one that is fantastic, modern, and jazzy but absolutely in the wrong place, with a signal system that ties up the whole line whenever you want to get in there. The problem is the Feds are parceling out grants to aircraft companies to develop sophisticated technology and requiring transit systems to include it in their specifications to get grant money. If the "T" had strong operations input at the time, they would never have gotten into this mess. It's technology for technology's sake. You've got the motorman there anyway, and he does a smoother job of running the train than the automatic signal system. In one step it obsoleted our whole force of maintenance men; the same with the LRVs.

MAINTENANCE PLANNING

The chaotic environment of rail equipment maintenance at the MBTA was not conducive to formal management analysis or planning. Limited staff capability and short-term operational crises constrained strategic planning in the maintenance area to occasional studies of facilities and equipment requirements. These studies were required to support requests for capital assistance from the Urban Mass Transportation Administration (UMTA) of the U.S. Department of Transportation. Even before the arrival of Robert Kiley as CEO, in 1975, some managers believed that there was a need for ongoing planning at the MBTA.

Perhaps that's why they were so receptive when, in the winter of 1974, a team of consultants approached them to try to define a high-priority management science project which might be eligible for federal funding. Of the several alternatives that were discussed, one clearly seemed to be of greatest mutual interest: the development of a computer-based model to aid MBTA management in evaluating the costs and benefits of different preventive maintenance schedules for rail rapid transit equipment. The purpose of the model would be to relate preventive maintenance strategies to vehicle breakdowns (and associated loss of transit service). It would keep track of labor and material costs associated with repair and maintenance of the many different vehicle subsystems. The model was to be used by MBTA management to calculate the overall cost and transit service implications from altering current maintenance schedules. Or it could be used "in reverse" to calculate the most cost-effective changes to current maintenance schedules in light of altered budgetary realities such as overtime constraints. As originally envisioned, the model would be programmed for interactive use on a computer terminal which would be located in the offices of top management of the maintenance function. These managers were hopeful that the proposed model would allow them to plan for improved preventive maintenance on the several rapid transit lines. It was also believed that projections from this model could provide persuasive backup for the department's budgetary requests. For the development and testing of the model, the Red line was selected.

Armed with this idea for a joint R&D project with the MBTA, the consultants prepared a proposal to develop the model which was to be named MASSTRAM. Exhibit 6 contains excerpts from the research proposal which was sent to UMTA in the spring of 1975.

A letter of sponsorship, signed by an official at the Maintenance Department of the MBTA, accompanied this proposal. The letter included the following passage:

> I believe that (this) tool will be useful to us and will be pleased to cooperate in (the proposed) venture. I am especially interested in developing a schedule evaluation system which will make use of the Computerized Maintenance Records System (CMRS) now being developed at the MBTA. . . . It would be most helpful to be able to use the proposed model to help develop maintenance schedules for the new MBTA vehicles currently on order.

Several months later UMTA reviewed and approved the proposed project which was to be conducted over a 12-month period. The consultants received a grant from funds that UMTA set aside for "research and investigations into the theoretical or practical problems of urban transportation." UMTA was especially interested in this project because it was designed to be of direct benefit to a particular transit organization in a key area of management. Maintenance managers at the MBTA were pleased with the launching of this project and promised their board of directors that the forthcoming model would help them to plan for more cost-effective maintenance of the railcar fleet.

Late in 1975 after the development of MASSTRAM was well under way, one of the consultants, Paul Westlake, was asked to review the project with the director of the Budget Office of the MBTA's advisory board. After describing the purpose of the project, Paul spoke of the progress the team was making and tried to distinguish MASSTRAM from other ongoing analytic efforts in the MBTA's maintenance area:

> Our team has completed an extensive review of MBTA activities in the ongoing maintenance and repair of rapid transit vehicles. We've also begun to explore some of the activities by which "crippled" cars are taken out of and returned to service. . . . Most of our work to date has been on the Red line although we have also spent considerable time looking at the Orange line. . . . This operational review has helped our model-building efforts. Now we're doing a very detailed assessment of the repair time and breakdown frequency of about 25 rail vehicle subsystems. These data are being assembled for the first time thanks to the cooperation of several key foremen and supervisors. We'll feed our initial computer model with these data as soon as it approaches a form that is suitable for operational use.
>
> Are you aware of the forthcoming Computerized Maintenance Records System, which is being developed for the Maintenance Shops

EXHIBIT 6
Excerpts from consultants' proposal to UMTA

STATEMENT OF THE PROBLEM

In general, equipment maintenance and repair work typically are of two interrelated types: "emergency" and "preventive." Emergencies arise when equipment breaks down, causing direct disruption to the production of goods or to the provision of services. For transit systems such "emergency" situations are particularly undesirable since they engender reduced public confidence in the reliability of the service, naturally upsetting patrons, many of whom have chosen to use public transit rather than their own automobiles. (In contrast to emergency breakdowns of production facilities, transit system stoppage is immediately apparent to the system's consumers. Indeed such occurrences are often reported by the media, thus having an indirect and perhaps profound impact on future public acceptance of the system.) And yet it is unreasonable to expect that such system breakdowns can be eliminated entirely; older equipment and uncontrollable events will always result in the need for some "emergency" maintenance. Nevertheless, it should be possible to reduce the frequency of emergency breakdowns by the implementation of a sound program of preventive maintenance.

The design of a suitable preventive maintenance program for transit vehicles is essentially a matter of balancing two types of costs: (1) the cost of scheduling inspections and then repairing or replacing different equipment components at specified intervals, and (2) the cost of experiencing an emergency breakdown between such intervals. The more thorough the preventive program (i.e., the smaller the inspection intervals), the less will be the likelihood of emergency breakdowns. But a preventive maintenance program itself can be costly, and ongoing fiscal pressures on transit operators make it difficult to expand indefinitely the size of the equipment maintenance work force. The management problem, then, is to develop a cost-effective maintenance schedule, specifying for a fleet of transit vehicles, when the cars, the subassemblies, and the individual components should be overhauled or replaced.

More specifically, the problem is to (1) determine whether to use preventive maintenance on a component of a transit vehicle or to wait until it fails; (2) evaluate alternative preventive maintenance schedules in terms of cost and number of disruptive failures; (3) determine when it may be economical to work on several subassemblies simultaneously; and (4) determine whether to replace an item or to repair it. . . . The purpose of this proposal is to develop a computer-based system to assist the management of urban transit systems in making (these) maintenance decisions.

To our knowledge there are no existing operational models which fulfill this function for transit maintenance managers today. Recent research and development activity in this general area has been restricted

EXHIBIT 6 (continued)

to the development of data processing systems which help to implement a predetermined maintenance schedule. The creation of such schedules at present is essentially determined by a combination of equipment manufacturers' guidelines and the experience of maintenance managers and engineers, tempered by the aggregate budgetary restrictions on the maintenance function. Although these maintenance schedules are sometimes partially based on the performance of existing transit vehicles, the use of such performance data is far from optimal. In fact, historical data of this sort are often too incomplete to provide a firm analytic basis for such decisions. We know of no transit operator who currently develops preventive maintenance schedules by systematically estimating the likely costs and benefits of different alternatives.

For the Massachusetts Bay Transportation Authority (MBTA), this problem of rail vehicle maintenance is of particular current interest. Due to a combination of several factors—the age and condition of the equipment, very long lead times on delivery of replacement components, and the necessity of manufacturing in-house certain components which are no longer available—there are currently substantial backlogs on needed maintenance and repair of existing equipment. Most important, the MBTA will be adding a substantial number of new vehicles (including the LRV) as well as some new maintenance facilities, thus requiring changes in the current maintenance operation. The proposed research is designed to provide this tool to the MBTA for their own use and to do so in a manner which could also be of value to other transit operators elsewhere who are faced with a similar need.

TECHNICAL APPROACH

There are several different aspects of the technical approach we plan to follow in the proposed project: (1) model formulation; (2) use of the model; and (3) integration of the model within a transit operator's overall maintenance system. Each of these subjects is discussed below.

Model formulation

Although it is premature to specify the precise methodology to be used in developing the proposed model, the major features of such a model can be anticipated. Technically speaking, the problem addressed by this project does not fit neatly into any single well-established theoretical framework. It does, however, share similarities with several familiar areas of management science: renewal theory, job shop scheduling, and production smoothing. A brief introduction to the theoretical strands which are likely to be relevant to our problem is provided below
. . . .

EXHIBIT 6 (*continued*)

Use of the proposed model: Man–machine interaction

In the absence of any significant changes to transit equipment usage, the proposed system would probably be used at periodic intervals (semiannually or annually) to reevaluate existing maintenance schedules. At this time all relevant statistical information, such as equipment failure rates and repair costs, would be updated. Naturally, the more differentiated the transit system (e.g., types of vehicles, numbers of transit lines), the more extensive will be these periodic uses of the proposed schedule evaluation model. We would also expect our model to be used on an as-needed basis to help transit managers evaluate the maintenance implications of additions or modifications to the fleet of transit vehicles or to the nature of its service. A further occasion for using the proposed model would be to help a transit equipment maintenance manager assess the implication of external changes to the maintenance schedules, ones which might be imposed, for example, by modifications to operating budgets or to labor union agreements.

With these types of applications in mind, we propose to design a computer-based model which is "conversational" in format: a manager will be able to sit at a remote computer terminal (in the offices of the MBTA, for example) and work directly with this model rather than requiring his own intervening staff of computer experts. Programming the model in "conversational" mode will facilitate the man–machine interaction that is desired for a model to truly be a decision-aiding tool of management. To insure that this conversational mode is successfully implemented, we plan to develop a prototype early in the course of this proposed project. Using this prototype the project's researchers and key managers of the MBTA will jointly identify needed improvements to the computer system's design. Implementing these improvements will be a crucial task in the latter part of the grant period. Following this process, we hope to become quite knowledgeable on the more general problem of how to integrate modern computer-based tools with ongoing transit management activities requiring different styles of decision making.

Integration of the proposed model within overall maintenance system

The evaluation of alternative equipment maintenance schedules, upon which this proposal centers, could serve as one piece of a larger system to aid transit management in their maintenance activities. This overall system should be capable of scheduling the jobs, maintaining time and cost for each job, and automatically updating inventories and reordering spare parts.

EXHIBIT 6 *(concluded)*

In our research project we intend to explore the crucial questions of how to integrate the proposed computer-based system for establishing maintenance schedules with other state-of-the-art computer systems which support the ongoing function of transit equipment service, inventory, and maintenance (but which accept the schedules as given).

We plan to work closely with managers and staff to the MBTA to insure that the proposed model will successfully interface with the other portions of their system, specifically the Computerized Maintenance Records System (CMRS) now being developed at the MBTA and with a computerized production and inventory control system that is to be developed by the MBTA.

Department? Don't get confused about the different functions of that system and our model. The CMRS is designed to collect, store, and report data on MBTA rail vehicle maintenance activities as an *information and control system*. It tells management day to day, week by week, what's been happening with regard to inspections, repairs, and break-downs. Our model looks ahead to evaluate different potential maintenance strategies. It's a *planning or policy tool*. It requires as input the kind of information which will exist in the files of the CMRS. So these two activities complement each other. In fact, without the CMRS, our model would lack an adequate supply of timely input estimates.

Another distinction is probably worth mentioning. I've heard that the MBTA is conducting a study of productivity of its maintenance operations. Our work has different immediate concerns compared with that study. We haven't attempted to evaluate current productivity. We just want to estimate actual current levels of effort required to accomplish various inspection and repair activities.

This spring we'll deliver the model to the MBTA. We're pleased with our progress so far. We're hoping the model can potentially serve a crucial managerial function. Between now and the end of our grant period, we'll do our best to help ensure that the model will turn out to be useful to the MBTA. Eventually we're hoping that this model and the data base will be used in strategic evaluations for all of the MBTA's rapid transit lines.

The development of MASSTRAM required that the consultant team work closely with MBTA staff and supervisors. Considerable time was spent at Cabot Center, the new Red line carhouse. The researchers paid special attention to maintenance and repair practices and procedures. They also became familiar with the kinds of records that were kept at the carhouse (see Exhibit 7). All of this information helped them to develop a reasonable set of test data for use on the new model.

EXHIBIT 7
Manual records available at MBTA maintenance carhouses

Log sheets: The most informative repair and maintenance records are the daily log sheets which are filled out by the foremen. On these logs are recorded troubles reported and repairs made. The information gathered by the foremen is entered in a chronological order.

Car histories: From the log sheets a record of individual car histories is created. It includes information on troubles, repairs, and inspections, although it is less detailed than the original.

Trip reports: A record is kept of the number of trips made by the cars as reported from the Transportation Department. These trip reports are posted daily by car on a sheet at the carhouse. The trip log is used for inspection scheduling decisions.

Dispatcher's summary sheets: The Transportation Department is responsible for the dispatcher's summary sheets, which report daily all incidents of vandalism and other troubles with cars. This list is distributed to carhouse supervisors, but there is no claim that it provides adequate detail or timeliness for guiding repairs. There is no comprehensive matching of items on this list with the condition of the cars that actually arrive in the shop.

By the summer of 1976, MASSTRAM was fully developed. The consultants met with officials at the MBTA to review the model with them. Among the topics covered were: the definition of a rail vehicle in terms of its respective "subsystems" (see Exhibit 8); data requirements for using MASSTRAM (see the list presented in Exhibit 9); and the need to view MASSTRAM as part of an ongoing process of analysis, management and control (see the chart in Exhibit 10). The presentation also covered some methodological points, especially the difference between data preparation for testing the new model and subsequent data needs for verifying the model. One of the researchers explained: "The availability of machine-readable input data is a fundamental assumption in the design and construction of MASSTRAM. Fully effective ongoing use of MASSTRAM requires an automated data collection and processing system. . . . To test MASSTRAM we pulled together some data for the Red line from a combination of interviews, sampling of your manual records, and from some special-purpose studies that you had previously conducted yourselves. Interviews with carhouse foremen gave us subjective estimates for much of the required data. This is how we began to calculate some relationships between maintenance intervals and failure frequencies for the different vehicle subsystems. And we used these statistics to help us develop and test our computer programs. We believe these input data

EXHIBIT 8
List of subsystems included in an MBTA application of MASSTRAM

Code	System	Subsystem
co01	Control	Motor generator
co02	Control	Compressor
co03	Control	Compressor motor
co04	Control	Compressor switch
co05	Control	Heat and fan
co06	Control	D-bar cable and button banks
co07	Control	Cineston
co08	Control	Relays and switches
co09	Control	Grids and connections
tr01	Trucks	Truck frame
tr02	Trucks	Wheels
tr03	Trucks	Contact shoes
tr04	Trucks	Emergency trips
tr05	Trucks	Hand brake and cable
tr06	Trucks	Drawbar
tr07	Trucks	Brake shoes
tr08	Trucks	Suspension
tr09	Trucks	Operating unit
ab01	Air brakes	Cineston and d-man control
ab02	Air brakes	Batteries
mo01	Motors	Traction motors
mo02	Motors	Brushes
cb01	Car body	General condition
cb02	Car body	Window glass
cb03	Car body	Destination signs
cb04	Car body	Door/light/crew signal equipment

to be reasonably accurate and feel comfortable that our findings are generally reliable. Still, MASSTRAM will be much more useful when your new data system's functioning."

At this point in the presentation, David Gunn, director of operations, asked for the status of the forthcoming information system, called CMRS. He was told that the engineer who had been working for the past two years on the development of that information system was having some difficulty in completing the project. Recently, that engineer had been temporarily transferred to another project having to do with the new LRV cars, but he would get back to working on the CMRS as soon as possible.

The presentation concluded with the review of a set of sample output from MASSTRAM. Exhibit 11 contains the materials that were handed out for this purpose. At the conclusion of the presentation, David Gunn, director of operations for the MBTA, asked: "What's the most significant finding from your analysis of our Red line's maintenance schedules?" The answer provided by Paul Westlake was: "This

EXHIBIT 9
Data input requirements of MASSTRAM

General operating statistics:
  Total mileage for all vehicles on the line during a specified time period.
  Total number of serviceable vehicles.
  Number of vehicles required for peak service.
  Average time to move a vehicle to the repair shop when it breaks down in service.

Maintenance and repair crew characteristics:
  Average annual hours worked for each type of repairmen (straight time, overtime).
  Number of workers available and average hourly wage rate for each type of repairman.
  Overtime pay rate.

Maintenance and repair-related activities and events (organized by subsystem):
  Number of workers in each category required for maintenance or repair of each subsystem together with the average elapsed time per worker to perform the particular task.
  Direct material cost attributable to maintenance or repair activities.
  "Held time" which is the average number of hours the car will be held if a subsystem must be repaired because of an in-service failure.
  Maintenance interval expressed in terms of the number of miles between the scheduled inspection of each vehicle subsystem.
  Failure rate (per 10,000 miles) which is related to the maintenance interval being used.
  Probability that when a subsystem fails the vehicle will need to be taken to the repair shop.

run of MASSTRAM shows that a savings of about 10 percent could be achieved by switching the maintenance frequency from its current rate of once every 5,000 miles for every vehicle subsystem to the 4,000 and 8,000 mile combined schedule shown in our optimal run of the model. But you must realize that all this is based on the data we were using, which may not be completely accurate, even though it's the best that's available." Gunn then asked his new chief mechanical officer, Richard Goodlatte, what he planned to do with the model. Goodlatte responded: "Let's send it over to Cabot Center where Frank Crowley, superintendent of Red line maintenance, can decide if he's interested in using it." James Burns, Goodlatte's assistant chief mechanical officer, suggested that Crowley ought to get better data by running some experiments. The group discussed this idea and it seemed rea-

EXHIBIT 10
MASSTRAM contributes to improved transit system management

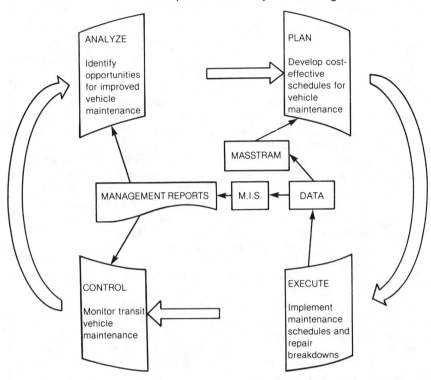

sonable to intentionally change the maintenance interval for selected
subsystems on a number of Red line rail vehicles. Experimenting with
a shorter maintenance interval would involve some additional cost but
no added risk. When a longer interval was attempted, the subsystem
would be closely monitored so that even though it was not maintained
at the old interval, when a failure appeared imminent, it could be
tallied as a failure and repaired at once. In this way, it was agreed,
longer maintenance intervals could be tested without increasing in-
service failures during the course of the experiment. This experimental procedure would provide systematic data for refining the failure
rate relationships and thereby improve the accuracy of a MASSTRAM
analysis. The meeting ended with the consultants promising to deliver
MASSTRAM and a computer console to Frank Crowley at the Red
line's Cabot Center, and David Gunn's thanking the outside team for
contributing their skills to an important problem area of the MBTA.

418

EXHIBIT 11
Sample output from MASSTRAM

As an introduction to MASSTRAM, a sample set of model output is presented below. While realistic, these outputs are only illustrative.

Table 1 illustrates a comparison between the "standard" schedule, where all subsystems are maintained at 5,000 miles, and a modified schedule using a maintenance interval of 4,000 miles for some subsystems and 8,000 for the others. The modified schedule is the least-cost schedule under the condition that the schedule can contain at most two different maintenance intervals. In this comparison, the modified case shows an expected annual net saving of 2,272 hours (about 10 percent) of maintenance labor. This modified case requires 855 hours (14 percent) less per year for scheduled inspections and 1,917 hours (8 percent) less for emergency repairs. The expected net annual savings of $34,000 (about 10 percent) in this illustrative comparison is due entirely to a reduction of overtime costs. (Parts costs which were ignored in these sample runs would tend to drive the system to more frequent maintenance.) The modified maintenance schedule not only costs less; it should also result in better service: There are 259 (8 percent) fewer vehicle in-service failures expected during the year, and annual "lost" vehicle hours are reduced by 16,233 hours. This results, on average, in having four more vehicles available for service on this line.

Table 2 shows the detailed subsystem evaluations for the modified schedule. Subsystem evaluations are listed in terms of the expected man-hours required for regular inspections (i.e., preventive maintenance) and emergency repairs, the estimated number of failures per year, and associated annual vehicle hours out of service. Note that subsystems are maintained at different intervals: some at a 4,000-mile interval, others once every 8,000 miles.

A comparison of Table 2 with a counterpart table for the standard (5,000-mile interval) program would show the expected net changes required for preventive maintenance and nonscheduled repairs. For each subsystem which has been shifted to a 4,000-mile inspection interval, the number of failures will decrease while the preventive maintenance effort will increase. The opposite occurs for those subsystems which have been shifted to an 8,000-mile interval. The total annual cost related to any particular subsystem, however, may either increase or decrease depending upon the net aggregate change between the preventive and failure-responding efforts. On balance, considering all of the vehicle subsystems together, this modified schedule represents a less intensive preventive maintenance program than the "standard" 5,000-mile inspection.

MASSTRAM can be used to examine a broad range of trade-offs between increased preventive maintenance and decreased in-service vehicle failures. A set of efficient schedules can easily be determined for

EXHIBIT 11 (continued)

which the expected number of failures is reduced with the minimum increase in the associated expected total cost. Table 3 presents such a set of results for schedules when 4,000 mile *or* 8,000 mile vehicle subsystem inspection intervals were the only ones permitted. For each line of the table, MASSTRAM will have determined a complete maintenance schedule (such as that shown in Table 2). As shown in Figure 1, a plot of this cost-failure frequency trade-off can also be generated by MASSTRAM. The cost increases shown in the plot and the table arise when some of the subsystems are rescheduled from an 8,000-mile interval to a 4,000-mile interval. The specific sequence of these changes is designed to be the most cost-effective way of achieving a particular reduction in the total number of failures. Management must then select the maintenance schedule which it feels will best serve the opposing cost and service objectives of the transit property during the current planning horizon.

TABLE 1
Sample MASSTRAM output, summarized run comparison

transit line evaluation

red line

	estimated labor hours required for maintenance					daily # of vehs. in serv.	veh hrs out of service	no. of vehicle failures
	straight	overtime	total	inspect	emerg.			
standard	17110	6844	23954	5967	17987	105	197771	3444
modified	17110	4572	21682	5112	16570	109	181538	3185

maintenance costs ($)
(000)

	labor costs				
	regular	overtime	total	parts	total cost
standard	222	102	324	0	324
modified	222	68	290	0	290

TABLE 2
Sample MASSTRAM output, subsystem evaluation

			subsystem evaluation				
		maint. interval	expected man-hours required for maintenance			veh. hrs. out of service	no. of vehicle failures
code	system description	(miles)	reg.	emerg.	total	per year	per year
ab01	cineston & d-man ctl	8000	83	73	157	122	5
ab01	batteries	8000	75	160	235	1523	23
cb01	general condition	4000	442	680	1122	9443	227
cb02	window glass	4000	233	678	911	2594	75
cb03	destination signs	4000	83	9	93	97	9
cb04	door/light/crew sig eqp.	4000	525	2475	3000	27831	619
co01	motor generator	8000	71	54	124	2520	42
co02	compressor	8000	71	206	276	4263	137
co03	compressor motor	4000	0	0	0	0	0
co04	governor switch	3000	63	33	95	1105	33
co05	heat & fan	4000	125	1936	2061	3228	242
co06	d-bar cable & button bks	8000	112	137	250	1246	91
co07	cineston	8000	79	201	280	2361	101
co08	relays & switches	8000	500	1803	2303	20193	451
co09	grids & connections	8000	75	561	636	3930	70
mo01	inspect trac motors	4000	508	2202	2710	11512	183
mo02	motor brushes	4000	0	0	0	0	0
tr01	truck frame	4000	600	1931	2531	14093	161
tr02	wheels	8000	292	572	864	2551	36
tr03	contact shoes	4000	250	2039	2289	23652	255
tr04	emergency trips	8000	150	189	339	1777	47
tr05	hand brake & cable	8000	83	81	164	1268	40
tr06	drawbar	8000	100	6	106	139	4
tr07	brake shoes	8000	125	20	145	1038	20
tr08	suspension	8000	192	309	501	5691	206
tr09	operating unit	8000	275	215	490	4412	108

TABLE 3
Sample MASSTRAM output, maintenance–failure trade-offs

Expected maintenance cost per year ($)	Expected number of failures per year
289768	3185
292271	3069
292637	3062
296130	3016
296995	3005
297899	2997
298736	2991
299799	2985
303416	2969
305236	2962
306024	2960
307835	2956
310929	2951
311941	2950

FIGURE 1
Plot of expected number of failures per year as a function of expected
maintenance cost per year

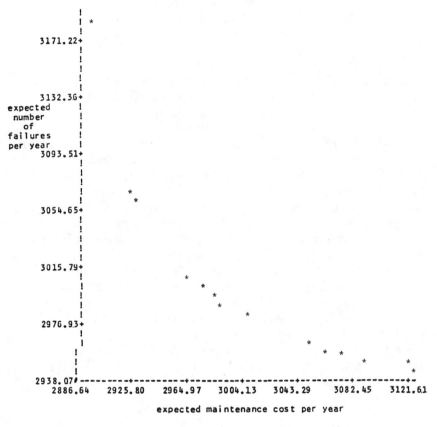

expected maintenance cost per year

x scale: 100.00   y scale: 1.00

Bennington Products, Inc.

In August of 1973, Mr. Eugene Kelley, president of Bennington Products, Inc., called Ms. Helen Newman into his office. Ms. Newman had been hired the previous May as a management trainee following her graduation from the University of Illinois with a business degree. Mr. Kelley proceeded to give Ms. Newman her first substantial assignment since joining the firm: "Helen, I received a consulting report on this Automated Scheduling Model (ASM) about the time you were hired. Since then the model has been mounted on our computer and debugged, and the model's output has been sent to Scheduling every month. Today I walked through the Scheduling Department and asked about the model. One of the schedulers looked at me like he didn't know what I was talking about. Then he said, 'Oh yeah. I remember that' and just smiled at me. When I asked Tony Reese, the department head, about it, he complained that the ASM hadn't been too helpful to his group. On the one hand, he said, the output was not detailed enough. On the other hand, it was cluttered up with a lot of numbers that didn't seem to apply to anything. There were some other problems too. What I want you to do is find out why the schedulers aren't using ASM and correct the situation. If half of the claims in that report are valid, we can't afford to let the thing sit."

COMPANY BACKGROUND

Bennington Products, Inc., was a medium-sized manufacturer of plastic household items, which ranged in size from forks and spoons to garbage cans. The company had been founded in Chicago in 1946 when rubber kitchen appliances were cured in a discarded oven in Thomas Bennington's garage and products were sold through a neighborhood hardware store. In 1955, Bennington bought it's first injection molding machine and entered the plastics manufacturing business. Expansion had been rapid throughout the 1960s, and factories had been opened in three other cities. Mr. Bennington withdrew from the business in the late 1960s and was replaced as president by Mr. Kelley, a long-time employee. In 1970, four regional divisions were formed, each headed by a vice president. Control of several functions remained centralized in Chicago, however, for reasons of efficiency.

The regional divisions were mainly oriented toward control of marketing and production operations.

Production

Bennington's products were manufactured on injection molding presses, which accepted plastic resin chips as raw material, melted the plastic, and forced it under pressure into a mold where the plastic cooled and resolidified. The completed product was then removed, inspected, trimmed, and packed for shipment or further processing in an assembly operation. Injection molding presses were quite flexible in terms of the range of products they would produce. Each press had a capacity limit above which it could not operate, but the largest presses could, in theory, produce any item in Bennington's line. For reasons of efficiency, the size of the product to be manufactured was considered a prime determinant of which machine would be assigned to produce it. For instance, if a very large press were assigned the task of producing a small item like a salt shaker, there would be considerable difficulty in setting the plastic feed on the press to inject just the right amount of plastic into the mold, leading to wasted press time, excessive labor costs for trimming, and a high reject rate. Also, the rate of production in such a situation would be far lower than a more appropriately sized machine could achieve, since the larger the press, the slower was the inherent cycle speed.

Bennington's four factories held a total of 85 presses of varying sizes (see Exhibit 1). Each plant manufactured the entire product line of 510 items. All shipments to customers were made through 16 distribution warehouses that also maintained all inventories of finished goods (see Exhibit 2). Each month marketing forecasts were generated for each

EXHIBIT 1
Production equipment location

Factory	Injection molding press size category						Total
	Mini	Light	Utility	Medium	Heavy	Super	
Newark	4	4	5	4	3	3	23
Chicago	4	5	5	4	4	4	26
Houston	3	3	3	3	3	2	17
Los Angeles	2	4	3	4	3	3	19
Total	13	16	16	15	13	12	85

EXHIBIT 2
Regional plant and warehouse location

Region	Plant	Warehouses served
East	Newark, N.J.	Boston, Mass. Albany, N.Y. Charleston, W.Va. Newark, N.J.
South	Houston, Tex.	New Orleans, La. Birmingham, Ala. Houston, Tex.
Midwest	Chicago, Ill.	Detroit, Mich. St. Louis, Mo. Denver, Colo. Indianapolis, Ind. Chicago, Ill.
West...................	Los Angeles, Calif.	San Francisco, Calif. Phoenix, Ariz. Portland, Oreg. Los Angeles, Calif.

item in terms of expected demand on each distribution warehouse. When these were aggregated for each factory and compared with inventory levels and safety stocks, they became the basis for production schedules the following month.

The Scheduling Department

The Scheduling Department consisted of 15 persons, two at each factory and the remainder in Bennington's central office in Chicago.

The schedulers assigned to each factory were mainly responsible for "rescheduling," that is, handling any deviations from the schedules that came from Chicago that might be necessary due to machine breakdowns, unexpected fluctuations in demand, and other problems. For example, a plant scheduler could recommend overtime production or the shifting of a product to a machine having excess capacity when unexpected demand materialized.

The schedulers in Chicago were specialized by machine capacity. A particular scheduler, for instance, would specialize on a particular size range of presses for all of Bennington's factories. He would thus become the scheduling "expert" on the products most efficiently produced on these machines.

Schedules were produced on a monthly cycle. After the marketing forecasts by plant had been formulated, which happened on about the tenth day of each month for the second following month, the schedulers would begin to make rough schedules for each of Bennington's 85 injection molding presses.

It usually happened that one or another machine classification would have excess capacity at some plant locations and be short at others. When this happened, it was often possible for a scheduler to specify a transshipment from a warehouse with excess inventory or increased production to a plant with excess capacity. By the 25th day of the month, the schedulers would have completed the rough scheduling of the machines for which they had responsibility. Near that date, each month the schedulers held a meeting to exchange information about which products still needed additional capacity and which machine classifications were not fully loaded. During and for several days after this meeting, the schedulers worked out mutual adjustments to their rough schedules, usually shifting products from smaller to larger presses to cope with as many of these problems as possible. By the end of the month, then, each scheduler in the Chicago office would know exactly how much of each product had to be scheduled on his or her presses in each plant.

From the first to the tenth of the month, detailed scheduling of the presses was accomplished. It was at this time that considerations of product color, run length, sequencing, and timing were combined to make the "final" production schedule for the ensuing month. These schedules were delivered to the plants by the 15th day of each month, by which time the schedulers were, of course, working on their rough schedules for the following month.

These detailed schedules were also distributed to the Purchasing Department. Using a formula that described the amount of resin in each product, the purchasing staff would order appropriate amounts of the 20 different types of plastic resin used in Bennington operations to maintain factory raw material inventories at about a one-month usage level.

Mr. Kelley, president of Bennington, had long recognized the extreme dependence of the company on the skills of the individuals in the Scheduling Department.

> Those fellows are incredible. It takes a special kind of person to, first, learn the operational details of this business and, second, have the mental agility to make the kinds of trade-offs they have to make when shifting products from one plant to the next the way they do. I figure it takes about eight years for a scheduler to really learn the job. For the first year or so, they'll serve a sort of apprenticeship here in the Chicago shop. Then we'll try them out as a plant scheduler for four or five years. That's rough work, but the good ones will be able to hack it. Then, as we have openings, we'll bring them back to Chicago and assign them to one of the

old hands who might be ready to retire. We plan on about six months' overlap to let the new scheduler get his or her feet on the ground and learn the job. If the trainee isn't ready then, he or she probably never will be. Typically, though, that assignment will be the last one. Employees usually retire from that job.

We've had some trouble lately, though, in getting the right kind of people to fill openings. The kind of person you can hire today doesn't seem interested in developing the necessary sort of craft skills for a scheduler's job. And its hard to tell immediately who would or wouldn't work out as a scheduler. We've had our share of personnel problems in the scheduling area, that's for sure. And the system doesn't have much built-in slack. Last year a plant scheduler in Los Angeles quit suddenly and we didn't have a replacement ready. Then, Charlie Ronald here in Chicago died. When we brought Doris White up from Houston, she was really flying blind for a year or so. Now, it looks like Tom Bower is serious about taking early retirement in January. Things are going to be hectic, that's for sure.

Part of the problem is that most of these people have grown up with the company over the last 20 years or so. They've been able to add to their skills gradually as Bennington expanded. To new people just coming in, however, the scheduler's job is a nightmare. And we in management haven't done a great deal to make their lives any easier.

THE AUTOMATED SCHEDULING MODEL

In January 1972, responding to the problems in the scheduling area, Mr. Kelley hired Carol Peterson, an independent management consultant, to study the problems in the Scheduling Department and make recommendations concerning possible management action. Mrs. Peterson spent a complete scheduling cycle in an apprenticeship role, learning the rudiments of production scheduling at Bennington Products. She also talked to the schedulers about the details of their jobs and the needs of the company. Finally, she followed the completed production schedule to the Purchasing Department, where she saw how they used the scheduler's information to generate raw materials requirements.

When Mrs. Peterson's six-week observation process was complete, she prepared a written report for Mr. Kelley. In that report she recommended that Bennington Products develop a linear programming model of the production process that would automate many of the scheduling and purchasing functions currently performed manually. Subsequently, Mrs. Peterson was retained to develop such a linear programming model.

As an initial step in developing the ASM, Mrs. Peterson met with the prospective users of the model. The Scheduling and Purchasing Departments were asked to list all of the information required or desirable in the monthly schedules the computer would prepare. A systems analyst was assigned to work with Mrs. Peterson for the purpose of ensuring that the ASM was compatible with Bennington's IBM System 360 computer. This analyst was also responsible for gathering data about machine capacities, transportation costs, production rates, and so forth for input to the model. He also began to define the different products' contribution margins as a first step in formulating the model's objective function.

Over the next 13 months, Mrs. Peterson developed and programmed the model using a time-sharing computer service. (Bennington's computer did not have the time-sharing feature, which can considerably ease the task of computer programming.) Her detailed knowledge of the scheduling process enabled her to work quite independently, making only occasional contact with the firm necessary. Approximately every 60 days, she would make a verbal report to Mr. Kelley about progress on the ASM when she presented an invoice for partial payments against her consulting fee.

In February of 1973, the ASM was completed and the systems analyst began the process of transferring the program to Bennington's computer. A few unforeseen technical difficulties arose in the transfer, but the ASM was running by late April, concurrent with delivery of Mrs. Peterson's final written report.

The ASM model generated production and distribution plans for each machine and warehouse. The model required demand forecasts as inputs, and from these, generated production requirements after consideration of excess or depleted inventory positions.

An exerpt from Mrs. Peterson's written report describes the ASM:

> The linear programming model was designed such that the best use would be made of the two most constraining resources: raw plastics and available press time. Since each item produced required different amounts and combinations of raw plastics and different amounts of press time on one of the six different types of injection molding machines, the formulation was a complex one. It was made more difficult because, in many instances, items could be produced on alternate molding machines but with reduced efficiency. The objective function was one of maximization of contribution to profit. The production variables (of which there were 720) defined the quantities of each item that would be produced on each of the presses. Stock transfer variables (1,440) defined the amounts of the six product classes that needed to be transferred from one distribution center to another.
>
> Beginning and ending inventories of each product at each distribution warehouse were recorded in a submodel that was not part of the optimization format. The reason these were excluded from the LP model was that to include them would have added 10,200 variables and increased process time unduly. Instead, a single constraint was placed on

the maximum value of total finished goods inventory equal to four weeks of Bennington's sales.

Finally, 510 "slack" variables indicating unused machine capacity (which could be used to produce for promotional purposes) complete the variable list. A total of 2,670 variables are thus included in the model.

Five basic classes of constraints were constructed for the model. The first set related to the availabilities of each of the raw plastics, while the second set related to the availabilities of press time. A third set of constraints specified upper limits on production due to maximum demand forecasts. Lower limits on the production quantities of certain items were specified in a fourth set of constraints. These were to ensure that a full line would be carried of some household items. A final set of constraints was constructed such that certain items would be produced in the same quantities as other items. These restrictions were necessary where items were packaged in sets, or where two or more items were later assembled. The total number of constraints in these five sets is approximately 2,000.

Although the formulation is fairly extensive, its solution is achieved in an hour of computer time using an existing efficient linear programming code. The model is easily understandable, and the results can be quickly interpreted even by lower-level management to guide the decision-making process. The solution to the monthly ASM problem will include the following results:

1. Regular time and overtime production levels for each product on each press.
2. Material and press time utilizations.
3. Excess units of raw material that need not be stocked.
4. Excess press time that would affect scheduling or be available for promotional production.
5. Excess packaging material that need not be stocked.
6. Stock transfers between distribution warehouses.
7. Excess inventory of finished goods.

Because of the ease of interpretation, management is capable of quickly communicating environmental and system changes to the model and reacting immediately to those changes, adding a new dimension to management's flexibility. Operating management in your firm will find that the utility of the model will exceed your initial expectations, and the results will put you in a better competitive position in your industry.

User reaction

In May of 1973 the Scheduling Department received the first examples of ASM output. Mrs. Peterson had received final payment for development of the model and, while she complained that she had "lost money on the project," she also felt that the ASM was the best management science project she had ever worked on. At about this time, the systems analyst who had worked on ASM left the company. Shortly thereafter, Ms. Newman was assigned to work on the project.

As Ms. Newman began work on implementing the model, she was disturbed to learn that Mrs. Peterson's documentation of ASM was far from complete. Further, she found that very little had been done to explain the system to the Scheduling and Purchasing Departments. Tony Reese, head of Scheduling, told Newman: "Just look at this output. How can you read it? It seems to tell us plenty about variables and shadow prices and so forth, but it really says very little about what we should produce. Furthermore, some of these machine assignments don't seem to make any sense. How did the model decide to make all of our salt and pepper shakers in Los Angeles and Houston but none in Newark or Chicago? When Peterson stopped by for a day to explain the output to us, it was the first time we'd seen her in a year. And the first time we'd seen the output too. Now we can't get hold of Peterson and, last month, we wasted a week trying to understand this stuff. I'm still trying to figure out how the ASM made these screwy assignments by working them out by hand, but I told the rest of the crew to get back to work. We've got four factories to schedule, you know."

At this point, Ms. Newman realized that she would have to educate herself about linear programming and the ASM system before she could hope to have much of an impact on the intended users. In the weeks and months that followed, Ms. Newman met frequently with members of the Scheduling and Purchasing Departments. In general, these discussions were about various details of the model, ranging from "unrealistic" assumptions of linearity to "obvious" errors in the objective function. Aside from these purely technical topics, however, Ms. Newman felt that the schedulers were uncomfortable with the "automatic" nature of ASM. Asking these schedulers to rely on a computer-based model, Ms. Newman realized, was somewhat like trying to make them believe in talking rabbits. The ASM was so foreign to their previous experiences and training that the easy thing to do was to pretend that it didn't exist. As the months passed, Ms. Newman was disturbed to realize that, although the computer solution was being produced each month, the Scheduling Department apparently was not basing its decisions on the ASM output.

The energy crisis

In December 1973, Bennington Products began to feel the effects of a worldwide shortage of oil and other petroleum products. The impact on Bennington was felt mainly as an increasing scarcity and cost of plastic resins, which were the major raw materials for Bennington's extensive line of injection molded plastic housewares. Most analysts felt that the shortage had been directly caused by an embargo of crude oil by the major oil-producing countries but agreed that a central contributing factor had been continued profligate use of oil products by large industralized countries like the United States.

In the words of Mr. Kelley, the resin shortages "couldn't have occurred at a worse time." Demand for Bennington's products had been growing at a moderate rate for several years but recently had spurted to new all-time highs for nearly every product. "This created a double problem for us," said Kelley. "Not only are our raw materials in short supply and their prices increasing almost daily, but we also have a severe capacity shortage problem. Our marketing people are continually fighting with each other and with the production schedulers about which products should be produced, when, and on which press, and everyone is unhappy with the purchasing agents who can't buy enough resin. The purchasers complain that the lead times they are quoted have lengthened from two weeks last summer to two months today. And, they say, there's every indication that the situation will get worse before it gets better."

Near the end of December, Mr. Kelley summoned Ms. Newman to report on her progress in implementing ASM. After Ms. Newman described her general lack of progress and the resistance of the schedulers to the Automated Scheduling Model, Mr. Kelley commented: "I know that the ASM situation isn't your fault and that you have basically run up against a brick wall there. What I want you to do now is to put ASM on a back burner for a while. Until this energy problem runs its course, I want you to get the marketing and production people together and help them figure out just how we should use the little amount of resin the Purchasing Department can get for us."

case 7–10

Everclear Plastics Company[1]

DECISION THEORY ANALYSIS OF A PRICING PROBLEM

The Everclear Plastics Company, with 1961 sales in excess of $300 million, was one of the nation's leading producers of plastics for industrial and consumer uses. One of the company's industrial products was a plastic called *Kromel*, which was used primarily in the fabrication of upholstery materials for automobiles, trucks, and other commercial upholstery applications. The product was priced at $1 per pound, a level which had been maintained since mid-1959. In early 1962, however, it appeared to Everclear's management that some weakness in Kromel prices could be anticipated within a year or two. Total demand had increased only slightly since 1959, and some increase in total industry production capacity was expected during 1962 and 1963. Some of the company's executives, especially Mr. Scott Carmichael, product sales manager for Kromel, felt that Everclear should reduce its price immediately. Others questioned the wisdom of a price cut on the ground that demand might not increase sufficiently to offset the lower revenue per unit. In order to gain a better perspective on the problem, Mr. Carmichael requested that a "special planning study" be made by Everclear's Operations Analysis Group. The study was carried out in April and May 1962, and a final report was presented to management in mid-June. Following this, Mr. Carmichael and several other company executives met to consider what action to take on the basis of the report.

THE PRODUCT AND ITS MARKETS

Kromel plastic had been developed by Everclear in the early 1950s and was basically a modification of an older and much more widely used plastic named *Verlon*. Kromel was superior to Verlon in several respects, including durability and appearance, but was somewhat

---

[1] This case is based on a paper by Paul E. Green, "An Application of Bayesian Decision Theory to a Problem in Long Range Pricing Strategy," presented at the 121st Annual Meeting of the American Statistical Association, December 1961. Dr. Green also supplied additional information regarding the organizational context of the problem. The name of the company, its personnel, the product, and the market data used in the case are fictitious, but the structure of the problem follows that of an actual marketing situation.

higher priced. The price spread between the two had been reduced gradually, however, and in 1962 Kromel prices were only about 10 percent above those of Verlon.

Both Kromel and Verlon plastics were sold to textile manufacturers who, in turn, sold upholstery materials to industrial users. These industrial users were classified into four major market segments:

Segment A: Automobile manufacturers, for use as original equipment (OEM) in automobiles.

Segment B: Truck manufacturers, for use as OEM in trucks and buses.

Segment C: Seat cover manufacturers, for use in replacement of seat covers.

Segment D: Miscellaneous users, including manufacturers of aircraft, boats, etc.

By far the most important market segment was the OEM automobile market, which represented about two thirds of the total potential volume.

During the late 1950s, the superior performance characteristics of Kromel had enabled it to displace Verlon to a large extent in all market segments except automobile manufacturers. Because of its continued dominance in this segment, total Verlon sales were more than double those of Kromel in 1961.

Everclear sales executives were sure that if the OEM automobile market could be penetrated, demand in the other three segments would increase substantially as a result. The reason for this was that, to some extent, upholstery was produced and carried in inventory to meet combined requirements for two or more end uses. Thus, for example, some of the major automobile manufacturers also produced trucks and had upholstery materials made up for both. Similarly, some of the manufacturers supplying the automobile companies also sold slip cover fabrics and found it economical to use the same materials for both uses. Because of the interdependence of the other market segments with the OEM automobile segment, penetration of this market was regarded by Everclear management as the key to expanding the total market.

Everclear was the largest seller of Kromel, with a market share in 1961 of about 40 percent. The three competing sellers were all large companies, and it was virtually certain that any price reduction made by Everclear would be met immediately by all competitors. Lower Kromel prices might not, however, lead to retaliation by Verlon manufacturers, since margins in the latter industry were already very low.

Kromel fiber was highly standardized and all four sellers offered virtually identical product quality, technical assistance, and terms of sale.

THE SPECIAL PLANNING STUDY

Responsibility for the special planning study was assigned to Dr. Alan White, head of the Everclear Operations Analysis (O.A.) Group. The Operations Analysis Group was a staff group within the Controller's Department of the Industrial Division of Everclear. A simplified organization chart depicting the relationships among Operations Analysis and the line departments involved is shown in Exhibit 1. The O.A. staff "sold" their services to line executives in all departments of the Industrial Division. Thus, for example, if the manager of one of the division's factories (Production Department) requested a study of a production scheduling problem, his factory was charged for the cost of

EXHIBIT 1
Simplified organization chart of Industrial Division

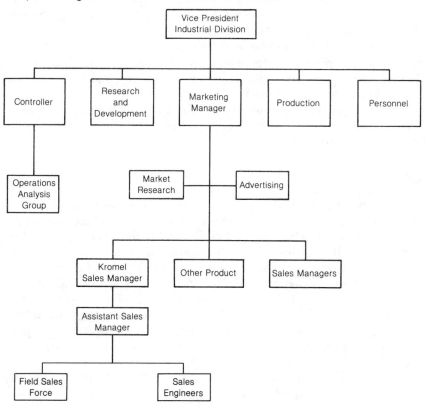

the study just as if an outside consultant had been retained. Charges were determined on the basis of the time required to complete a study plus any out-of-pocket expenses and an allowance for overhead costs.

Within the Marketing Department of the Industrial Division, there was a Market Research Group. This group made studies of various kinds to assist line executives in making decisions on sales and advertising problems. Most of the group's work involved either analysis of company sales figures (e.g., comparisons of actual versus predicted sales by region) or survey research, such as measurement of advertising recall. The Kromel product sales manager did not believe that information obtained by either of these means would be of much use in arriving at a decision on Kromel prices.

Dr. White began his investigation of the Kromel pricing problem by meeting with Mr. Carmichael, Mr. Carmichael's assistant, and the division marketing manager. In this meeting Dr. White sought to develop a reasonably specific definition of the problem. He explained that problem formulation "requires a certain amount of artistry and compromise toward achieving a reasonably adequate description of the problem while keeping the structure simple enough so that the nature of each input will be comprehensible to the personnel responsible for supplying the data for the study."

At the outset, Dr. White believed it was essential to have agreement on (1) what company objectives were involved in the pricing decision, (2) what alternatives were available to management, and (3) the period of time to be used in the analysis.

Discussion of these "ground rules" for the pricing study continued through two additional meetings beyond the first one, each session lasting about four hours.

Objectives

The basic objective which had been set by the top management of Everclear for all divisions and products was that of maintaining a rate of return on investment of at least 20 percent before income taxes. Mr. Carmichael felt that the pricing decision on Kromel might affect this objective in two ways. First, a lower price might permit expansion of total sales through penetration of the OEM automobile market, and the increase in sales might lead to greater total profits even though the profit per unit would be smaller. Second, a lower Kromel price might discourage the development of overcapacity in the industry and permit Everclear to maintain or even increase its share of total Kromel sales.

Whatever decision was reached regarding Kromel prices, no additional investment in production facilities for the product was planned, since a substantially higher level of output could be handled with present space and equipment. Hence, it was agreed that the proper criterion for comparing alternative prices was total dollar profits.

In discussion of the possible effects of a price reduction, it became apparent that the question of *timing* of profits had to be considered. A reduction in Kromel prices would undoubtedly lead to lower profits at least for a year or two, since some time had to elapse before the market would respond. Dr. White pointed out that differences in the timing of profits under alternative prices implied a need for a method of "compounding" all profits to put them on an equivalent basis at some future point in time. Only in this way, he said, could varying amounts of profit during different time periods be compared meaningfully.

No standard rate of "interest" had been adopted at Everclear, since comparisons of policy alternatives in these terms was not a regular procedure. As a result, some debate ensued regarding the rate of interest to use in the pricing study. Initially it was agreed that the rate of interest should represent an *opportunity cost* on potential uses of funds in a given time period. For example, if one price yielded, say, $100,000 more profit than another in Year 1 but $100,000 less profit in Year 2, the more immediate profits should be valued somewhat more than the later profits, since the money, if earned earlier, could be invested and would earn a return during the interim. It was not clear what this "opportunity cost" should be, since it was hard to anticipate just what use would be made of future earnings. Mr. Carmichael and his assistant suggested a rate of 6 percent per annum, a commonly accepted "conventional" rate of interest. The division marketing manager pointed out, however, that if the funds were invested within the company itself the return would, in fact, be considerably more than 6 percent. He believed that a rate of 10 percent should be used instead. After further discussion, no way of resolving the issue could be found. Dr. White then suggested that the analysis be made using both a 6 percent "interest" rate and a 10 percent rate. The results could then be compard to see if the interest rate made any difference. This approach was satisfactory to all concerned.

Alternatives

The basic question to be answered by the study was whether or not a price reduction should be made on Kromel. The possibility of *increasing* the price was ruled out immediately, since it was regarded as virtually impossible that competing sellers would follow suit if this were done. Dr. White said that, from the standpoint of keeping the analysis within bounds, it would be desirable to consider only a limited number of alternative prices. The reason for this was that he anticipated the necessity of estimating what they *thought* "would happen if . . . ." His experience indicated that it was difficult if not impossible for people to discriminate very small differences in making such estimates. Thus, for example, a salesman would probably predict the same customer response to a proposed price of 90 cents per pound as to a price of 92 cents. Consequently, he felt that the alternatives to be considered should be spaced far enough apart to elicit meaningful differences in predicted effects.

The lower limit of price alternatives was the variable cost per pound. As a practical matter, Mr. Carmichael felt that the lowest price worth consideration was somewhat above variable cost; he suggested $0.80 per pound as the minimum. Between the minimum of $0.80 and the status quo of $1.00, it was decided to consider two other alternatives, namely, $0.85 and $0.93 per pound.

Planning period

It was recognized that the effects of any decision reached on prices would be felt over at least several years in the future. Theoretically, the analysis could be made so as to cover an indefinite ("infinite") period, but it was not believed feasible to extend estimates of market behavior beyond a definite, fairly short time span. Mr. Carmichael and the other line executives agreed on a five-year period as a reasonable one to be covered by the analysis.

With the objectives, specific policy alernatives, and planning period agreed upon, it was possible to define the pricing problem explicitly as follows:

> Which of the four alternative prices—$0.80, $0.85, $0.93, or $1.00— would yield the greatest total net profits after taxes (valued at the *end* of the five-year period, using either a 6 percent or a 10 percent discount rate) over the next five years?

In the course of the initial discussion, another consideration affecting the formulation of the problem came to light. Apart from any price changes made by Everclear, it became apparent that sales of Kromel would depend on future growth in the *total* Kromel–Verlon market, which was determined by sales of automobiles, trucks, seat covers, etc. Lower Kromel prices would have a negligible effect on total market growth.

Predictions of combined Kromel–Verlon sales for the next five years had been made by the Everclear Market Research Group. Since the key variable in the market was automobile production, these forecasts were necessarily subject to considerable error. Three separate forecasts were available—an "optimistic" one, a "pessimistic" one, and a "most probable" one. It was decided to carry out the price analysis using all three forecasts and, as in the case of the compounding rate, compare the results to see how much difference the forecast would make.

APPROACH TO THE PROBLEM

Dr. White was attempting to develop a suitable method of analysis for the company's pricing problem during the course of the meetings with Mr. Carmichael, the marketing manager, and Carmichael's assistant. He saw the problem as a classic example of "decision under conditions of risk" as set forth in the literature dealing with decision theory. The essential features of decisions under risk were described as follows:[2]

1. A choice must be made among several (perhaps many) well-defined *alternatives*.
2. The consequences ("payoffs") of a given alternative depend on which of various possible circumstances or "states of nature" prevail or will prevail at some future time. Thus, in the Everclear pricing problem, the profits earned at a given price depend on how customers would respond to the price.
3. For a given alternative and a given (assumed) "state of nature," it is possible to estimate what the "payoff" would be. In the pricing problem, this meant that it was necessary to estimate the sales and profits of Everclear at each alternative price under a given set of assumptions about customer response, competitive retaliation, etc.
4. The actual "state of nature" that will prevail cannot be predicted with certainty, but it is possible to estimate the *probability* of each state assuming that a given alternative is chosen.

In order to implement this approach, Dr. White planned to obtain information on possible "states of nature" affecting the results of the pricing decision, on the probabilities assigned to each state of nature by management, and on estimated profit results for Everclear at various sales volume levels. The last point caused relatively little difficulty. Examination of accounting records showed that over a rather wide volume range, the total cost of Kromel sold could be estimated within a small margin of error by a simple equation of the form

$$\text{Cost} = FC + VC \times (\text{Sales volume})$$

---

[2] For an extended discussion, see Robert Schlaifer, *Probability and Statistics for Business Decisions* (New York: McGraw-Hill Book Co., 1959).

in which *FC* and *VC* were statistical parameters fitted by least-squares estimation. This meant that net profit could be derived for any given level of sales, and was equal to

$$\text{Net profit} = \text{Sales volume} \times (1 - VC) - F\dot{C}$$

Determination of the relevant "states of nature" and attendant probabilities posed a somewhat harder problem. In essence, what was needed was a prediction of what *might* happen if a given price reduction were made and estimates of the *likelihood* of each possible chain of events. In some problems it was possible to determine states of nature and their probabilities through systematic observation or experimentation. Thus, for instance, it might be possible to vary prices experimentally, observe the results, and (if enough trials were made) derive estimates of probabilities for the occurrence of each result. This approach did not, however, seem feasible for the Kromel price analysis. Since only a few customers were involved in the key market segment, it was not possible to change the prices charged these customers, wait for responses to work out, then change prices again, etc. Even if some indirect experimental procedure could be devised, Dr. White did not believe that any meaningful information could be secured in time to meet his deadline of 60 days. Consequently, he decided that estimates of states of nature and of probabilities of their occurring would have to be built up from the combined judgment of Everclear's own sales personnel. For this purpose, he scheduled a series of interviews with three groups: first, with Mr. Carmichael and his assistant, to define what *possible* responses could be expected from a price reduction; second, with a group of "outside" salesmen who had contact with Kromel customers; and finally, with a group of "inside" sales engineers who provided technical assistance to customers. The interviews with the two groups of sales personnel were intended to obtain estimates of probabilities for the various possible "states of nature."

POSSIBLE RESPONSES TO A PRICE REDUCTION

In the meeting with Mr. Carmichael and his assistant, Dr. White sought to trace out the various possible consequences of alternative Kromel price policies on the part of Everclear. The most important factors involved seemed to be:

1. Kromel penetration of the OEM automobile upholstery market. "Penetration" was defined as *any* significant amount of sales in

this market segment, if some minimum level of sales could be attained; it was believed that competitive imitation among the auto producers would lead to an expanding participation for Kromel.

2. The pattern of growth in Kromel sales to the OEM automobile upholstery market, once penetration had been accomplished.

3. Growth in Kromel sales to the other three market segments (a) if the OEM automobile segment *were* penetrated, and (b) if it were not.

4. Possible retaliation to a price reduction on Kromel by manufacturers of Verlon.

5. Possible reductions in Kromel prices by competing sellers, if Everclear did not reduce its price now.

Several possibilities existed for each of these factors, and the total number of possible *combinations* of factors was very large. For convenience in visualizing the problem, Dr. White drew a tree diagram of possible chains of events. A simplified version of this diagram is shown in Exhibit 2. Each "branch" of the "tree" represents one specific series of possible events. Thus, at stage 1, Everclear had four price alternatives. If one of these were followed—say, the stand-pat policy of

EXHIBIT 2
Simplified tree diagram of possible chains of events for alternative Kromel prices

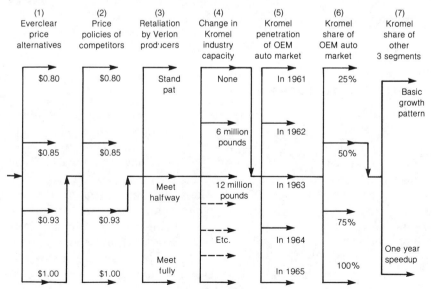

$1.00—then competing sellers of Kromel might reduce price to any of the alternative levels. (If any Kromel producer lowered his price, it was assumed that all would be forced to follow suit.) For any of these possible levels of Kromel prices, Verlon producers might retaliate by meeting the reduction fully, by meeting it halfway, or by standing pat. For a given combination of Kromel and Verlon prices, penetration of the key OEM automobile upholstery market might be achieved by 1961, by 1962, etc. Assuming this market segment *were* penetrated, the Kromel share of it might be as low as 25 percent or as high as 100 percent. Finally, for any given market share in the OEM automobile segment, Kromel market shares in the other three segments might follow a basic (predicted) pattern of growth or might be speeded up a year.

For any one of the possible series of events depicted in Exhibit 2, it was possible to trace out the sales and profit consequences for Everclear. There was, in effect, another set of "branches" (not shown in Exhibit 2) corresponding to the three alternative forecasts of total Kromel–Verlon sales over the next five years. Following any one of these forecasts and any one of the complete "chains" of Exhibit 2, it would be possible to arrive at a five-year forecast of Everclear's Kromel sales. As previously explained, costs were to be estimated in relation to sales volume, so that profits on Kromel sales could be derived from the sales forecasts.

With this formulation of the problem, Dr. White next sought to determine estimates of the probabilities assigned by Everclear sales personnel to each possible chain of events.

ESTIMATES OF PROBABILITIES

In a preliminary meeting with the "outside" field sales force of five men, Dr. White explained his approach to the pricing problem and asked the salesmen to start thinking in terms of likely consequences of various courses of action. Following this, an all-day session was held in which the salesmen were asked to make a series of estimates of relevant probabilities for specific situations. The term *probability* was defined in the sense of "how many chances in 100 do you think there would be that x would happen, if y were true?" Each salesman was given information on past sales of Kromel and Verlon to each market segment, along with prevailing prices for each material. The specific questions asked of the salesmen and their composite estimates of various probabilities are reproduced in Exhibit 3.

EXHIBIT 3
Estimates of probabilities of possible outcomes of alternative price strategies

---

The following estimates and probabilities can be conveniently framed in terms of a series of questions:

(a) If Kromel price remained at $1.00/pound and market segment A were not penetrated, what market share pattern for Kromel Industry sales would obtain in segments B, C, and D?

Base assumption, Kromel industry share

Year	Segment B	Segment C	Segment D
1961	57.0%	40.0%	42.0%
1962	65.0	50.0	44.0
1963	75.0	80.0	46.0
1964	76.0	84.0	48.0
1965	76.0	84.0	50.0

(b) If Kromel price remained at $1.00/pound, what is the probability that Kromel would still penetrate market segment A?

Composite estimate of probability of penetration, segment A

Year	Probability
1961	0.05
1962	0.10
1963	0.20
1964	0.25
1965	0.40

(c) Under price strategies $0.93/pound, $0.85/pound, and $0.80/pound, what is the probability of Verlon industry price retaliation; and, given the particular retaliation (shown below), what is the probability that Kromel would still penetrate market segment A?

Pricing case (entries are composite estimates of probabilities)

Verlon industry retaliation	$0.93 case	$0.85 case	$0.80 case
Full match of Kromel price reduction	0.05	0.15	0.38
Half match of Kromel price reduction	0.60	0.75	0.60
Stand pat on price	0.35	0.10	0.02

Given a particular Verlon retaliatory action, the probability that Kromel would still penetrate segment A (composite estimates)

442

EXHIBIT 3 (continued)

	$0.93 case			$0.85 case			$0.80 case		
Year	Full match	Half match	Stand pat	Full match	Half match	Stand pat	Full match	Half match	Stand pat
1961	0.15	0.20	0.35	0.20	0.40	0.80	0.75	0.80	0.90
1962	0.25	0.30	0.60	0.30	0.60	0.90	0.80	0.85	0.95
1963	0.35	0.40	0.65	0.40	0.65	0.95	0.85	0.90	1.00
1964	0.60	0.65	0.75	0.70	0.75	0.98	0.90	0.95	1.00
1965	0.65	0.70	0.80	0.75	0.80	0.98	0.95	0.98	1.00

(*d*) If penetration in market segment A were effected, what is the probability that Kromel would obtain the specific share of this segment in the (*a*) first year of penetration and (*b*) second year of penetration?

Share	First year	Second year
25%	0.15	0.00
50	0.35	0.00
75	0.40	0.00
100	0.10	1.00

(*e*) If Kromel penetration of market segment A were effected, what impact would this event have on speeding up Kromel industry participation in segments B, C, and D?

Segment B: Would speed up market participation one year from base assumption; point (*a*).

Segment C: Would speed up market participation one year from base assumption; point (*a*).

Segment D: Kromel would move up to 85 percent of the market in the following year and would obtain 100 percent of the market in the second year following penetration of segment A.

(*f*) Under the price reduction strategies, if Kromel penetration of market segment A were *not* effected, what is the probability that Kromel industry participation in segments B, C, and D (considered as a group) would still be speeded up one year from the base assumption; point (*a*)?

Composite estimates of
probability of speedup

Case	Probability
$0.93	0.45
$0.85	0.60
$0.80	0.80

EXHIBIT 3 *(concluded)*

(*g*) If Kromel price at the end of any given year were $1.00/pound, $0.93/pound, $0.85/pound, and $0.80/pound, respectively, *and* market segment A were not penetrated, what is the probability that present competitive Kromel producers would take the specific price action shown below?

Kromel price	Action	Composite estimate of probability
$1.00/pound	$1.00/pound	0.15
	0.93	0.80
	0.85	0.05
	0.80	0.00
$0.93/pound	0.93	0.80
	0.85	0.20
	0.80	0.00
$0.85/pound	0.85	1.00
	0.80	0.00
$0.80/pound	0.80	1.00

(*h*) Under each of the four price strategies, what is the probability that competitive (present or potential) Kromel producers would add to or initiate capacity (as related to the price prevailing in mid-1961) in the years 1963 and 1964? (No capacity changes were assumed in 1965.)

Competitor	$1.00/pound	$0.93/pound	$0.85/pound	$0.80/pound
R	0.50	0.20	0.05	0.00
S	0.90	0.75	0.50	0.20
T	0.40	0.10	0.05	0.00
U	0.70	0.50	0.25	0.00
V	0.70	0.50	0.25	0.00

Timing and amount available, beginning of year

Competitor	1963 (million pounds)	1964 (million pounds)
R	10	20
S	12	20
T	10	20
U	6	12
V	6	6

The procedure followed by Dr. White in obtaining probability estimates was as follows:

1. Each question was stated verbally to the group.
2. Each member of the group wrote down his own answer to the question. Because of the inherent difficulty of differentiating small

differences in estimated "odds," these answers were generally stated in multiples of 0.05, i.e., 0.05, 0.10, 0.15, etc.

3. The individual estimates and the reasons for them were discussed by the group. As a result of these discussions, differences in responses were resolved and a "group answer" was agreed upon. In almost all cases there was close agreement among salesmen in the group. In cases were differences existed the modal (most frequent) answer was usually adopted as the group estimate.

Following the meeting with the five "outside" salesmen, a similar all-day session was held with the company's two "inside" sales engineers. The same procedure was followed and a separate series of probability estimates was obtained.

Finally, a meeting was held with both the "outside" and the "inside" sales groups to resolve the two sets of estimates into a single set. Each participant was given a list of the figures derived from the two group sessions. Dr. White said that, if genuine and significant disagreements on the estimates still prevailed after this final discussion, it was possible to use separate figures in the analysis, as was to be done in the case of the interest rates and the sales forecasts. Most of the salesmen insisted, however, that a single figure be agreed upon for each of the probability estimates required in the analysis.

In most cases the estimates made by the two groups of salesmen differed only slightly, and compromises were readily achieved. The most serious discrepancy was that of question (f) in Exhibit 3. In this instance the two group figures differed by as much as 15 or 30 percentage points. The composite estimates shown were adopted only after long debate, and some of the salesmen still disagreed with them at the conclusion of the session.

COMPUTER SIMULATION OF ALTERNATIVES

Following the series of meetings with Kromel salesmen and sales executives, Dr. White had the decision model programmed for simulation of the various alternatives on an electronic computer. The calculations involved were not complex, but the large number of "branches" on the "decision tree" precluded manual computation of the results.

The procedure followed in the computer simulation was essentially as follows.

1. For each price alternative, the sequence of possible subsequent events was laid out, and the appropriate probability estimates were assigned to each event on the basis of the "composite estimates" given in Exhibit 3.

2.   Each price alternative was traced through to its possible results in terms of sales and profits. The total (cumulative compounded value at end of five years) profit associated with each outcome was computed from the equation

$$\text{Five-year profit} = \sum_{i=1}^{5} (1 + r)^{5-i}[(D_{ij} - Z_{ij})(K_{ij}M_{ij})]$$

where:

r = The rate of interest on profits—either 6 percent or 10 percent per annum.

D_{ij} = Kromel price (dollars per pound) in year i, under the jth outcome.

Z_{ij} = Total cost per pound of Everclear's Kromel in year i, under the jth outcome. This cost, as previously explained, was estimated as a function of total sales volume.

K_{ij} = Everclear's overall market share of Kromel sales in the ith year, under the jth outcome (K_{ij} assumed constant).

M_{ij} = Total Kromel sales (in pounds) in year i, under the jth outcome.

3.   Probabilities for each *final* result were computed by multiplying out the probabilities of the events leading up to it. At each branching point in the decision tree of Exhibit 2, the estimates of Exhibit 3 were used as *conditional* probabilities. The computation procedure is illustrated, for one portion of the complete tree, in Exhibit 4, which depicts some of the possible outcomes of the $1.00 price alternative. As shown in this diagram, if the price is kept at $1.00 the probability that Kromel would penetrate market segment A (the OEM automobile upholstery segment) was estimated at 0.05. This is derived from the responses given to question (*b*) in Exhibit 3. Following the left-hand branch corresponding to the assumption that segment A were penetrated, the probabilities assigned to various market shares of that segment [question (*d*) in Exhibit 3] were next multiplied by the 0.05 probability of penetration to derive the set of figures shown at the upper left of Exhibit 4. Thus, for example, the diagram shows that *if* market segment A were penetrated, then the conditional probability of attaining a 25 percent market share in 1961 was estimated at 0.15 (see Exhibit 3). Since the probability of penetrating segment A at a price of $1.00 was 0.05, the *joint* probability of achieving penetration *and* attaining a 25 percent share was computed by multiplying the two probabilities, i.e., 0.05 (0.15) = 0.0075. In a similar fashion, the joint probabilities of all possible sequences of events were determined by multiplying out the

446

EXHIBIT 4
Simulated experience, Kromel (portion of probability tree)

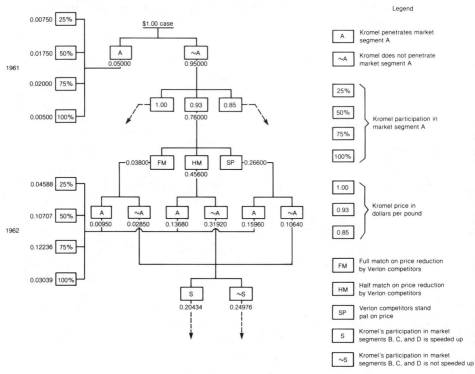

conditional probabilities at each stage. Following the branch down the middle of the diagram, if market segment A were not penetrated (probability 0.95), the probability of Everclear's competitors reducing price to 93 cents would be 0.80 [Exhibit 3, question (g)], and the joint probability 0.95 (0.80) = 0.76. The probability that these events would take place *and* that Verlon producers would meet the price reduction halfway was estimated at 0.456 = 0.76 (0.60); and so on.

The probabilities for each possible final outcome were determined by following the procedure depicted in Exhibit 4 for all of the many branches of the complete decision tree.

4. For each price alternative, the *expected* values of compounded net profits over the five-year planning period were computed, using the formula:

$$\text{Expected profit (price } k) = \sum_{j=1}^{n} \times P_j \text{ (five-year profit of } j\text{th outcome)}$$

in which P_j was the probability of the jth final outcome for the given price.

RESULTS OF THE SIMULATION

The computations yielded the following estimates of expected cumulative net profits for the five-year planning period:

Price	Total net profit, valued at end of period
$1.00	$6,625,000
0.93	7,575,000
0.85	8,475,000
0.80	8,725,000

Dr. White presented these results to a meeting of Everclear executives, along with certain supplementary figures. A series of charts used in this final presentation is reproduced in Exhibits 5, 6, and 7. Exhibit 5 depicts the probabilities of achieving penetration of the key OEM automobile upholstery market for each alternative price during each year of the planning period. Exhibit 6 shows the *differences* in estimated Everclear sales of Kromel for each price reduction as compared with the present price of $1.00, which was used as a reference point. Finally, Exhibit 7 reveals differences in compounded net profit for each price reduction, again in comparison with the status quo price of $1.00.

When the results were compared for the two alternative interest rates (6 percent and 10 percent) and for the three industry sales forecasts, it was found that differences in these factors did *not* affect the rank order of the four price strategies. Consequently, all of the results are given on the basis of a 6 percent interest rate using the "most probable" sales forecast.

These results clearly indicated that a price reduction on Kromel was desirable. Some uncertainty remained, however, about the validity of certain key assumptions used in the model. Most important, some of the executives were not convinced that an immediate price reduction would, in fact, be effective in discouraging the growth of total industry production capacity. Accordingly, Dr. White carried out a separate series of computations assuming that price reductions would *not* discourage additions to capacity—i.e., that the figures given in Exhibit 3, question (*h*), were the same for prices of $0.93, $0.85, and

EXHIBIT 5
Cumulative probability of Kromel's penetration of market segment A
(as a function of time and initial price)

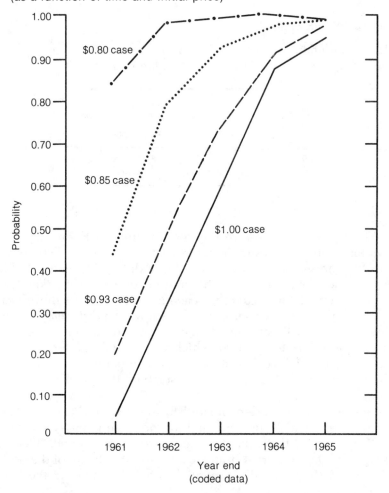

$0.80 as for $1.00. The estimated total net profits for Everclear, based
on this revised assumption, were as follows:

Price	Total net profit, valued at end of period
$1.00	$6,625,000
0.93	6,725,000
0.85	6,850,000
0.80	6,300,000

EXHIBIT 6
Kromel sales volume (incremental sales dollars generated over
$1.00 case)

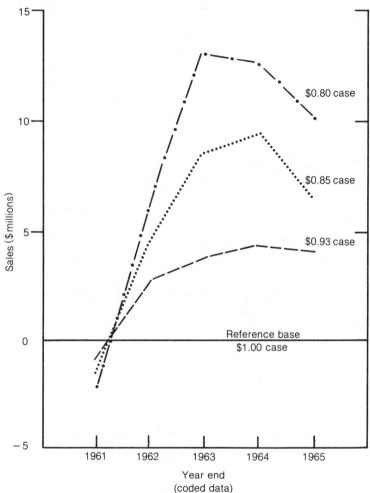

At this point it became clear that the key factor underlying the differences in total net profit previously estimated was Everclear's share of total Kromel industry sales. If it were assumed that a price reduction *would* discourage additions to capacity, then Everclear would probably achieve a higher share of the expanding market by reducing prices. On the other hand, if capacity were increased despite the price reduction by Everclear, the increased volume of sales— resulting from the penetration of the OEM automobile upholstery

450

EXHIBIT 7
Compounded year-by-year net profits of Everclear Plastics Co. (compound rate equals 6 percent annually)

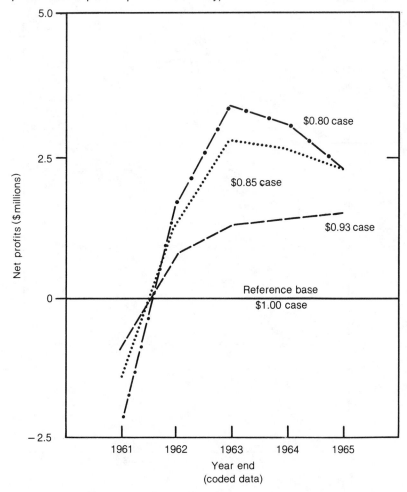

market—would just about balance the lower revenue per unit, and the expected payoffs of alternative price strategies would be much more nearly equal.

Mr. Thomas, the company's general counsel, then pointed out that if a price reduction had the effect of discouraging expansion by competitors and increasing Everclear's market share, he opposed any reduction. He expressed the opinion that if Everclear's market share, already 40 percent, were any greater, then the company might well be subject to investigation and possible conviction under the antitrust laws. Dr. White said that he had asked about possible legal constraints at the outset of the study but had been told not to worry about this factor.

chapter 8

Wisdom from the experts

Insightful articles on the processes of management science

Reading

8–1   Solving problems . . .
Ray Hyman and Barry Anderson

8–2   The process of problem finding . . .
William F. Pounds

8–3   On the art of modeling . . .
William T. Morris

8–4   The wizard who oversimplified: A fable . . .
Robert N. Anthony

8–5   Corporate models: Better marketing plans . . .
Philip Kotler

8–6   Management science and business practice . . .
C. Jackson Grayson, Jr.

8–7   Models and managers: The concept of a decision calculus . . .
John D. C. Little

8–8   Let there be light (with sound analysis) . . .
Cullom Jones

8–9   To tell the truth . . .
Charles J. Christenson

Solving problems

RAY HYMAN AND BARRY ANDERSON

Psychologists have been experimenting on thinking for more than 60 years. They have observed the problem-solving behavior of chickens, rats, chimpanzees, children, adults, mental defectives, psychotics, and so on. They have gathered data on how rats release themselves from puzzle boxes, how chimps employ tools to win bananas, how children combine colorless liquids to find the combination which produces yellow, and so on.

Is there anything that can be said, on the basis of this research, to help people solve practical and technical problems? When we—both of us experimental psychologists—first asked ourselves this question we agreed the answer was "No." It seemed to us that such studies were too far from naturalistic settings to have relevance for problem solving in "real life." But then we looked again at the outcomes of a number of experiments—and we were pleasantly surprised. It seems to us now that there may be a common thread between many of the laboratory experiments and many kinds of problem difficulties that crop up in our daily activities.

When we stand back and survey this heterogeneous body of data, we see one theme that appears again and again. In attempting to solve a given problem, the most typical difficulty is that humans fail to make use of the information *which they have.* Since most of this article will deal with laboratory experiments which are concerned with this difficulty, it may help at this point of we give two examples from "real life."

The first must be as old as the inner tube: It's the homely story of the truck which was stuck in an underpass. Various onlookers tried to be helpful by suggesting ways for extricating the truck, but all these suggestions involved reasonably major deformations—either of the truck or the underpass. Then a little boy suggested letting air out of the tires. Many such stories exist in science and invention. All serve to

Source: *Science and Technology,* September 1965, pp. 36–41. © 1980 by Cahners Publishing Company, Inc. Reprinted by permission.

show the same point: A solution, once stated, can be seen as "obvious."

A classic example involves the invention of the ophthalmoscope. The physiologist Brücke, interested in how the retina of the eye reflects light, devised an instrument to illuminate it. The famous physiologist Helmholtz, while preparing a lecture on Brücke's device, suddenly realized that the rays reflected from the illuminated retina could be used to view the retina itself. Helmholtz used a series of mirrors to reflect light into and out of the eye, and then used a lens to form an image with the light reflected from the retina. This was, as the mathematician Jacques Hadamard points out, "an almost obvious idea, which as it seems, Brücke could hardly have overlooked." But overlook it he did. Why? Here is Helmholtz' explanation: "In this, Brücke was within a hair's-breadth of the invention of the ophthalmoscope. He did not ask himself what optical images are produced by the rays that emerge from an eye into which a light is thrown. For his particular purposes it was not necessary to ask this question, but had it been posed, he would have been able to reply to it as quickly as I have."

Nobody should be surprised when people fail to solve problems for which they lack the necessary information. But it is curious indeed that they fail so frequently when they have all the necessary information.

How is it possible for a person to have the necessary information and not be able to use it? The answer seems to lie in the fact that the brain, like the computer, is divided into a storage unit and a processing unit. While the storage unit can hold a vast amount of information, the capacity of the processing unit is strictly limited. The average person is able to retain and repeat back immediately only about seven unrelated digits. This fact, along with other research, suggests that the processing unit can handle no more than about seven independent items of information at a time. Now any problem of any consequence probably involves more elements than can be handled by the immediate memory span. Unless the processing unit is guided by a systematic search plan, and unless it possesses perfect memory of where it has already looked, it can easily overlook elements or combinations for consideration. Furthermore, not only must the processing unit sift the relevant from the irrelevant—it must also organize the elements into larger units in order to deal with more items in its attempt to construct a workable solution pattern.

The limited attention span and the necessity of "chunking" items of information into larger organization units may contribute to an individual's failure to use available information. He may start his search by looking at the wrong elements. This will not necessarily lead him into trouble. But as he looks at any set of elements he is simultaneously placing them within a tentative organization. And this initial organization—no matter how tentative—serves as a guide to his search process. If it is not an appropriate construction, this organization may prevent him from looking in more appropriate directions. For example, think again of the truck: An inappropriate construction directs one's attention to the top of the truck, since this is where the problem is. And, if your thoughts are channeled by the inappropriate construction, this is where you look for the solution.

How can the problem solver be helped to look in the right direction? In one sense, we cannot answer the question, for we do not know in advance what the right direction is. But in another sense we can answer, by pointing out that the problem solver is more likely to hit upon the correct approach if he tries several approaches. What so frequently produces failure in problem solving is getting stuck on one approach and being unable to abandon it.

THE WORKING RULES

Let us look now at several precepts—or working rules—which may help in the problem-solving process. These precepts fall into two categories: Those intended to keep the problem solver from getting stuck on an incorrect line of attack and those which may be expected to help him get free when he is stuck. In other words, preventive rules and remedial rules.

Four considerations guided our choice of precepts. One, we agreed they must be relevant to overcoming the difficulty people have in making use of information. Two, they must be operational; that is, they should specify concrete actions that the individual can take. Three, they must be applicable at the time the individual finds himself confronted with a problem. (This forced us to exclude many precepts which might be classed as "preparation for problem solving" or "education for problem solving.") And four, they must have some support in psychological research.

Precept I: Run over the elements of the problem in rapid succession several times, until a pattern emerges which encompasses all these elements simultaneously.

This precept helps keep you from prematurely fixating upon a subset of the elements required for the solution. It also helps you get the "total picture" before you become lost in the details.

Descartes includes this precept in his *Rules for the Direction of the Mind*. He describes its application as follows: "If I have first found out by separate mental operations what the relation is between magnitudes A and B, then that between B and C, between C and D, and finally between D and E, that does not entail my seeing what the relation is between A and E, nor can the truths previously learned give a precise knowledge of it unless I recall them all. To remedy this, I would run them over from time to time, keeping the imagination moving continuously in such a way that while it is intuitively perceiving each fact it simultaneously passes on to the next; and this I would do until I had learned to pass from the first to the last so quickly that no stage in the process was left to the care of memory, but I seemed to have the whole in intuition before me at the same time. This method will relieve the memory, diminish the sluggishness of our thinking and definitely enlarge our mental capacity."

Compare this quotation with that of Helmholtz, some 200 years later: "It is always necessary, first of all, that I should have turned my problem over on all sides to such an extent that I had all its angles and complexities 'in my head' and could run through them freely without writing."

This precept serves to keep you from getting stuck on the first one or two interpretations that come to mind. When we jump too quickly from the problem statement to an attempted solution, we frequently get trapped into clinging to an inappropriate direction.

Precept II: Suspend judgment. Don't jump to conclusions.

Two examples: In teaching sixth-graders how to ask the right kinds of questions in order to discover the scientific principle underlying a physical event. Suchman found it important to train the children from prematurely guessing at the explanation, for once they had offered an explanation, these children had difficulty revising it or dropping it in the face of contradictory evidence. Bruner and Potter show this in another context: Their experiments show the fixating power of premature judgments. Color slides of familiar objects, such as a fire hydrant, are projected upon a screen and people try to identify the objects while they are still out of focus. Gradually, the focus is improved, through several stages. The striking finding is this: If an individual wrongly identifies an object while it is far out of focus, he frequently still cannot identify it correctly when it is brought sufficiently into focus so that another person—who has not seen the blurred version—can easily identify it. What this seems to say is this: More evidence is required to overcome an incorrect hypothesis than to establish a correct one. He who jumps to conclusions is less sensitive to new information.

Precept III: Explore the environment. Vary the temporal and spatial arrangement of the materials.

This precept serves to keep the mind "loose" by activating a variety of possibilities. It may also help uncover familiar patterns which were masked by an originally unfamiliar arrangement.

The difficulty in many problems frequently resides in the way the elements happen to be ordered. A rearrangement of the elements sometimes reduces the problem to a task that can be handled by standard procedures. The Scotch psychologist Hunter, for example, found his subjects had difficulty specifying the relation of George to Willie when he gave them these two terms: Harry is shorter than George; Harry is taller than Willie. Many 11-year-old children cannot handle this task, and the adult subjects took considerably more time to give their answers than when the problem was put in its logically equivalent (but more familiar) form: George is taller than Harry; Harry is taller than Willie. In fact, the evidence indicates that subjects actually solve this problem by rearranging the elements until they correspond with the familiar form: A is greater than B; B is greater than C.

Quite frequently, the solution to a difficult problem is suggested to the solver by a slight change in his physical relation to the elements in the problem. In Köhler's famous experiments on chimpanzees, one chimp was faced with the task of obtaining a banana which was beyond arm's reach through the bars of his cage. A stick was available to him, but the stick was behind him and out of his field of vision when he looked at the banana. Later, when he was idly playing with the stick, the banana and the stick accidently became part of the same visual field. When this happened, the chimp instantly made the connection between the stick as a tool for extending his reach and the obtaining of the banana.

REGAINING FLEXIBILITY

Now we shall turn from "preventive" precepts to others which can be looked upon as special operations for accomplishing the following more general precept: If you are getting nowhere on a problem, abandon your approach and try to find a new difficulty as a basis for solving the problem.

Let us begin with the word "direction"—a word employed by Maier to refer to the way in which an individual will attempt to solve a problem. The direction he takes, Maier tells us, depends on what he sees the problem to be. An example: In one of his experiments, Maier gives his subject the task of tying together the ends of two strings which are suspended from the ceiling; the strings are located in such a way that the subject cannot reach one string with his outstretched hand while holding the second string in his other hand. The typical person will see the difficulty as a shortness of reach. Consequently, his "direction" will be toward ways of lengthening his reach—by searching for a stick or hook, for instance. Another person will see the difficulty as a shortness of one of the strings. And consequently, this person will try somehow to make one of the strings longer. Now Maier arranged things so that these obvious solutions could not be used; he wanted to discover some things about "good" reasoners and "poor" reasoners, so he devised his test in a way that required a more imaginative solution: The solution he was looking for required that the subject see the difficulty in terms of getting the second string to come to him. Quite simply, if the subject tied something to the end of that string and then caused it to swing as a pendulum, so as to be grabbed as it swung toward the subject while he held the first string, then the subject would have solved the problem correctly.

The insight Maier gained from this test is this: He found that good reasoners do not persist in one direction if they are getting nowhere.

Rather, the good reasoner will jump from one direction to another until he finds a solution. Poor reasoners, on the other hand, persist doggedly in the same direction, even when the difficulty does not yield to their efforts. But he wanted to know more than this. For instance, as he watched people fumble along in the wrong direction he wondered whether this simply indicated that such people were incapable of better reasoning, or whether they were being blocked from considering new directions by some stubborn commitment to the old. To provide himself with an answer to this question, Maier performed another experiment. If people were being blocked as he suspected he reasoned that such people could reach solutions sooner if they were warned against continuing with an unsuccessful experiment. On the other hand, if such people simply were incapable of better reasoning, then such warnings would make little difference, since they would not be able to devise better alternatives anyway. Maier's experiment consisted of giving several hundred college students a one-hour test. Each was asked to solve three problems—one being the two-string problem of a moment ago. The students could do the problems in any order, and they could divide their time among the problems in any way they wished. With half the students, Maier provided the problems with no preliminary comments. With the other group, he prefaced the test with a brief introductory lecture which concluded with the following hints:

1. Locate a difficulty and try to overcome it. If you fail, get it completely out of your mind and seek an entirely different difficulty.
2. Don't be a creature of habit. Don't stay in a rut. Keep your mind open for new meanings.
3. The solution pattern appears suddenly. You cannot force it. Keep your mind open for new combinations and do not waste time on unsuccessful attempts.

As one might expect, this brief lecture produced a significant improvement in performance. The male students who heard the lecture, for example, solved an average of 62 percent of their problems, while those men who heard no preliminary comments solved only 51 percent of theirs. Among the young women, the same pattern appeared: 36 percent for those who heard the lecture, compared with 25 percent for those who did not.

From these tests and others, Maier concluded that the persistent and initially wrong directions that accompany problem solving actually prevent correct solutions from appearing. "Reasoning," he said, "at least in part, is the overcoming or inhibiting of habitual responses."

Precept IV:
Produce a second
solution after
the first.

This precept serves to shift the problem solver's orientation from solution-mindedness to problem-mindedness. In their studies of problem solving, Maier and Hoffman found that when an individual was seeking his first solution to a problem he was dominated by strong pressures to achieve that solution—in other words, he was solution-minded. When he was encouraged—after the first solution had been achieved—to go on to seek a second solution, the second solution was usually a more creative one. This was so, they concluded, because the individual was problem-oriented—he was no longer driven to find *a* solution, for he had already accomplished that; now he was, as Helmholtz would have said, "turning the problem over on all sides." Maier and Hoffman found this precept to increase "creative" solutions from 16 percent to 52 percent.

I want to insert a personal observation here—this is Hyman talking now: I have found that unless subjects are told in advance that they will have to produce a second solution, that second solution may be inferior to the first. But I do want to underline the importance of the Maier-Hoffman discovery by stating it again, in a somewhat different form: We can make much better use of the information we have at hand when we are *pushed to the limit*. An example from my own research: I asked a group of people to produce three solutions to the same problem. The problem related to the declining teacher-student ratio in higher education. I gave them statistics and information relevant to the problem and asked each person to write his first solution to the problem of maintaining high-quality education in the face of this declining ratio. Then I asked them to perform some other tasks, and after this interval they were asked again to reconsider the educational problem and write their second solutions. And after another interval I asked them again to produce their third solutions—but on this third go-round I deliberately blocked them from using ideas they were familiar with. I did this by giving each person a copy of his first two solutions, as well as a list of some of the most commonly offered solutions. And I said that these solutions, being already known, should not be considered for solution number three. What we wanted now were solutions that did not make use of any of these ideas. At this point, about one-quarter of the participants threw up their hands in despair. They could think of nothing to do or say. But the others! All were able to come up with at least adequate solutions—involving completely new ideas, in some cases to their own surprise. And as many as 25 percent of these people came up with truly creative and outstanding answers. They had been blocked from using obvious answers—they had been pushed to the limit.

Precept V: Critically evaluate your own ideas.
Constructively evaluate those of others.

This precept provides a heuristic for discovering new directions. Its purpose is to guard you against complacency in accepting your own ideas for solving a problem—and also, to help you get new ideas and insights from the attempts others have made at solving the same problem. Torrance, working with students, found that he could increase the creativity of term papers—in which students devised an original research project—by inducing attitudes of constructive evaluation of others' ideas.

I (Hyman) tested this precept with a group of 36 engineers. I asked them, individually, to devise a solution to an automatic warehousing problem. With half the group, I provided some solutions that other engineers had proposed—then I asked these people to list reasons why those solutions could *not* work. (This is the kind of critical task engineers seem well suited for. They willingly accepted it.) Following this task of critical evaluation, I asked each of these 18 engineers to write out his own solution to the problem. With the second group, I showed the same set of previous solutions, but I asked these men to list as many *strong* points as they could find within those previous solutions. Then, following this constructive evaluation task, these engineers wrote down their own solutions. My next step was to have these 36 solutions evaluated. I mixed them up, thus to prevent anyone's knowing the origin of any particular solution, and gave all 36 solutions to a committee of experts, who rated them for creativity. When the evaluations had been made, it turned out that the solutions of those engineers who had been asked to find strong points were significantly better—more creative—than those who had been asked to look critically at the solutions of others.

Before we can really pin down the extent of, and reasons for, these effects, we must have more information. But one thing that is suggested here is that a positive attitude—or a negative attitude—toward one's own ideas and toward the ideas of others can markedly affect the quality of the solution to a problem. More important, a constructive attitude can easily be induced by the simple expedient of causing the individual to look for weak points in his own first ideas and for strong points in the ideas of others.

Precept VI: When stuck, change your representational system. If a concrete representation isn't working, try an abstract one, and vice versa.

This precept takes advantage of the fact that relationships which are not easy to see in one representational system are often obvious in another. If you have been dealing with a problem in verbal terms, and if you are stuck, then try to switch to a picture, a model, a graph, numbers, or even to other words. If you have been dealing with the problem in nonverbal terms, try mapping the elements into words. A study, by Mawardi, of a group of professional creative thinkers bears this out. She taped sessions in which the group worked on a single problem. Then she classified these sessions into idea units—some were classified as abstract, others as instrumental, metaphor, orientation. She found a very strong tendency within the group to alternate between abstract and concrete modes of thinking.

Precept VII: Take a break when you are stuck.

This precept takes advantage of the fact that a dominant direction will usually weaken with time. Now, surely, to take a break when stuck is the most frequently given advice to problem solvers. But does it really do any good? In two experiments at Stanford, the evidence seemed contradictory: Irvine and Taylor found no advantage in taking a break, while Taylor and LaBerge—the second experiment—found a definite advantage. The difference was this: There was an advantage when the subjects were allowed to determine their own times for taking breaks. But what is the proper time? And with this question, we must face up to still another question: What is the meaning of "being stuck"? Let us look at the situation in this way: You are getting nowhere with a problem. Why? It may be that your plan of attack is inappropriate. Or it may be that your plan of attack is OK but your perception of the materials is such that they cannot be adapted to your plan. In either case, it is doubtful that a break will help you, for it may only cause you to return to an inappropriate plan or perception. On the other hand, if you have explored the possibilities of your present approach rather thoroughly—and if you cannot think of another approach to try—then you are "stuck" and this would seem a good time to take a break. Put it this way: If you are really stuck, then take a break. But if you simply have not given an approach sufficient thought, then the break won't help.

In talking with someone, you are forced to consider aspects of your problem which you might not otherwise have considered. You cannot take "shortcuts" here; you cannot jump across gaps that you might otherwise take for granted. You must return to fundamentals in order to communicate with your listener. And the presence of the listener provides a powerful feedback mechanism which quickly detects obscure or inconsistent points in your story. Where you have to communicate to another person, you have to put yourself in his shoes; this in itself is a powerful precept.

Further, the act of communicating any problem transforms that problem from a private to a public form. The Swiss psychologist Jean Piaget places great emphasis on this role of communication in the development of the thought process. Piaget has made monumental investigations of how thinking develops in children and he has concluded that thinking—as we recognize it in our society—would never develop in children if they were not forced by society to justify with reasons their behavior to adults and peers. (Quite independently, Russian psychologists have come to the same conclusion.) By being forced repeatedly to communicate his ideas to others, the child gradually masters public forms of representing the world. As he grows older, the child internalizes this public system of representation and thus can

Precept VIII: Talk about your problem with someone.

check his ideas by recasting them in this public form. For many kinds of thinking, he can now operate independently of the actual presence of others.

But for especially difficult problems, it still helps to communicate with someone. The importance of this precept is illustrated by an incident from contemporary medical research. Dr. Lewis Thomas, in a study involving the enzyme papain, noted a striking phenomenon when he injected the enzyme into the bloodstream of a rabbit: The rabbit's ears wilted dramatically. Thomas immediately interrupted his original investigation to try to discover why. He sliced and stained the rabbit's ears. He saw nothing unusual in the connective tissue—where he expected to find changes. He also looked at the cartilage, but he saw nothing obvious there. Like all physicians a few years ago, Thomas had looked upon the cartilage as inactive—he certainly expected to find no changes there. After searching in vain to solve the case of the floppy-eared rabbits, he gave up and returned to his regular work.

About seven years later, Dr. Thomas was teaching second-year medical students how to perform laboratory studies. He decided to demonstrate the floppy-ears phenomenon, feeling it would capture the students' interests. He went through the standard tests again, searching for the cause of the phenomenon. And this time he found it—in the cartilage. What made the difference? Here he was communicating to students; he did not skip or overlook incidental steps and precautions. In his own words: "Well, this time I did what I hadn't done before. I simultaneously cut sections of the ears of rabbits after I'd given them papain *and* sections of normal ears. This is the part of the story that I'm most ashamed of—the only way you could make sense of this change was simultaneously to compare sections taken from the ears of rabbits that had been injected with papain with comparable sections from the ears of rabbits of the same age and size which had not received papain."

Here we see, in striking fashion, how the necessity to rearrange his thinking led the investigator to take precautions he would normally overlook. The result was a discovery which he could have made years earlier.

By phrasing them in a very general form, our eight precepts can be reduced to two:

Look before you leap.

After you have leaped, if you find yourself bogged down, find out what you are doing and then do something else.

The usefulness of these precepts depends upon the manner in which they will be applied. And it also depends upon future research—psychological research. But let us add this much for psychological research: As a result of writing this paper, we have discovered that psychological research has more to tell about problem solving than even we had realized. And further—and this may testify to the fruitfulness of the precepts—in trying to communicate what we know to people of the "hard" sciences, we have come up with a number of ideas for doing experiments on problem solving.

The process of problem finding*

WILLIAM F. POUNDS

INTRODUCTION

As a result of research efforts over the past 20 years, a number of extremely effective analytical techniques are currently available for the solution of management problems. Linear programming is used routinely in the specification of optimum cattle feeds and fertilizers. Decision rules based on inventory models form the basis for production and inventory control systems in a wide variety of manufacturing companies. Simulation is evolving from a means for doing research on complex managerial problems to a process which can provide useful information to managers on a real-time basis.

Like other technological changes, these methods raise a number of social and organizational issues within the organizations which use them, but their net contribution is no longer seriously in doubt. As a result, in most large organizations and in many smaller ones, operating managers either are aware of these methods or have ready access to help and advice in their application.

But the manager's job is not only to solve well-defined problems. He must also identify the problems to be solved. He must somehow assess the cost of analysis and its potential return. He must allocate resources to questions before he knows their answers. To many managers and students of management, the availability of formal problem-solving procedures serves only to highlight those parts of the manager's job with which these procedures do *not* deal: problem identification, the assignment of problem priority, and the allocation of scarce resources to problems. These tasks, which must be performed

* Research for this paper was supported in part by a grant from NASA. The author gratefully acknowledges the many contributions of Professor E. H. Bowman to all phases of this study and particularly those he made to the planning and execution of the company study.

Source: *Industrial Management Review*, vol. 11, no. 1, Fall 1969, pp. 1–19. Reprinted by permission.

without the benefit of a well-defined body of theory, may be among the most critical of the manager's decision-making responsibilities.

This paper is concerned primarily with the first of these tasks—problem identification. It reviews some research relevant to understanding decisions of this type, presents a theoretical structure, and reports some results of an empirical study of the process by which managers in a successful industrial organization define their problems. Because this research was stimulated in part by an interest in the relationship between the so-called new techniques of management and what might be called traditional managerial behavior, similarities between these two modes of management which are suggested both by the theory and the empirical evidence are briefly noted.

BACKGROUND

Prior to 1945, our understanding of most cognitive tasks within industrial organizations was not much better than our understanding of the process of problem finding is today. Inventory levels were maintained, production schedules were determined, and distribution systems were designed by individuals who, through years of experience, had learned ways to get these jobs done. With few exceptions these individuals were not explicit about how they performed these tasks and, as a result, training for these jobs was a slow process and the development and testing of new procedures was difficult indeed.

So it is with the process of problem finding today. All managers have discovered ways to maintain a list of problems that can occupy their working hours—and other hours as well. They frequently find it difficult, however, to be explicit about the process by which their problems are selected. Consequently, the development of improved problem-finding procedures is difficult.

Since 1945, however, some progress has been made in understanding certain cognitive tasks in the areas of production and inventory control. Decisions rules have been derived from mathematical models of particular tasks, and in a number of cases these rules have performed as well as or better than the complex intuitive process they have replaced. The significant fact about these developments for this discussion is not, however, the economic impact of such rules, although it has been significant. Rather, it is the implication that the essential processes by which important decisions are made may be carried out satisfactorily by simple explicit decision rules which are easy to teach and execute and easy to improve through analysis, simulation, or experimentation.

Of course it is possible to discount these accomplishments by saying that inventory decisions were always rather simple ones to make. The validity of such arguments, however, seems suspiciously dependent on knowledge of what has been accomplished and on a lack of knowledge of inventory systems.

It is true, however, that mathematical analysis has been able only to suggest decision rules for a wide variety of managerial tasks. These tasks, including the definition of problems, seem to require symbols and analytical procedures not readily represented by standard mathematical forms. Some other means for discovering the decision rules by which such tasks are performed is clearly required.

Some progress in this direction has already been made. Encouraged both by the success of the analytical approach to decision problems, and by the availability of large digital computers, Newell, Simon, and others have been studying human decision behavior since the early 1950s. They have focused their attention primarily on tasks which would facilitate the development of a methodology for approaching decision situations not readily describable in mathematical terms. They have considered the decision processes involved in proving theorems in symbolic logic[1] and plane geometry.[2] They have considered decision processes involved in playing games like chess[3] and checkers.[4] They have worked on the assembly line balancing problem[5] and on trust investment.[6] The relevance of this research to problem finding can perhaps best be illustrated by considering the work on chess.

Research on chess

Chess is a game with rules simple enough for almost anyone to learn and yet complex enough that even the largest computer cannot play it by working out the consequences of all possible moves. Chess is a game of strategy in which individual moves can not always be evaluated without considering future moves. Chess moves are inconvenient to describe in mathematical terms and few people can be explicit

---

[1] A. Newell, J. C. Shaw, and H. A. Simon, "Empirical Explorations of the Logic Theory Machine," *Proceedings of the Western Joint Computer Conference*, February 1957, pp. 218–30.

[2] H. L. Gelernter, "Realization of a Geometry Theorem Proving Machine," *UNESCO Conference on Information Processing Proceedings*, 1959.

[3] A. Newell, J. C. Shaw, and H. A. Simon, "Chess-Playing Programs and the Problem of Complexity," *IBM Journal of Research and Development*, October 1958, pp. 320–35.

[4] A. L. Samuel, "Some Studies in Machine Learning, Using the Game of Checkers," *IBM Journal of Research and Development*, vol. 3, no. 3, July 1959, pp. 210–30.

[5] F. M. Tonge, *A Heuristic Program for Assembly-Line Balancing* (Englewood Cliffs, N.J.: Prentice-Hall, 1962).

[6] G. P. Calrkson, *Portfolio Selection: A Simulation of Trust Investment* (Englewood Cliffs, N.J.: Prentice-Hall, 1962).

about how they play chess. For these reasons and several others, chess was an attractive medium in which to attempt to unravel human decision processes that could not be modeled mathematically.

Three aspects of the work on chess-playing behavior are relevant to this discussion. First, simple explicit decision rules were discovered which make for very good chess play. This result has been tested by programming computers with such rules and observing the quality of play which resulted in response to the play of human experts. Second, the decision rules for chess playing were derived from observations, interviews, and the writings of chess masters. Thus, it is not necessary that simple, explicit decision rules be derived from mathematical or theoretical considerations. They can be abstracted from humans who have themselves never systematically considered the process of their own decision making. And, third, the decision rules by which humans play chess appear to be separable into three rather distinct classes: rules for defining alternative moves, rules for evaluating alternative moves, and rules for choosing a move from among evaluated alternatives. H. A. Simon has called these three classes of behavior intelligence, design, and choice, respectively,[7] and on the basis of his work both on chess and other decision-making situations has concluded that the process of intelligence or alternative definition is the key to effective behavior.

The work on chess and other complex tasks does not directly suggest how managers go about finding and defining the problems to which they devote their time. It does suggest, however, that tasks of this same order of complexity may be understood through careful observation of and abstraction from the behavior of human experts. It further suggests that, if useful insights into managerial problem finding can be gained, they may contribute significantly to managerial effectiveness.

AN EMPIRICAL STUDY OF MANAGERIAL PROBLEM FINDING

Since it was possible to gain useful insights into the process by which humans play chess by observing experts, it seemed likely that insights into the process of managerial problem finding might be derived from careful observation of successful managers. Arrangements were made therefore to interview, observe, and interrogate about 50 executives in a decentralized operating division of a large technically based corporation, which will be referred to as the Southern Company.

The study consisted of four relatively distinct activities. First, interviews were conducted during which executives were asked to de-

---

[7] H. A. Simon, *The New Science of Management Decision* (New York: Harper and Brothers, 1960).

scribe the problems they faced and the processes by which they had become aware of these problems. Second, observations were made of meetings during which problems were identified, discussed, and sometimes solved. Third, investigations were made of the source and disposition of several specific problems. And, fourth, a questionnaire was devised and administered to each executive who participated in the study.

As data began to accumulate from each of these activities, it became clear that a major objective of the study would be to discover some level of abstraction which would preserve what seemed to be essential details of the managerial situations being observed and at the same time provide a structure which would convert isolated anecdotes into data from which some generalizations might be drawn. This structure will be described in the following pages together with some of the observations it explains. Observations made outside this particular study will also be reported.

Theoretical structure

Like any number of other industrial tasks, the process of management can be viewed as the sequential execution of elementary activities. In describing their own work, executives find it easy to think and talk in terms of elementary activities like making out the production schedule, reading the quality control report, visiting a customer, etc. The attractive feature of this view of managerial work is that elementary tasks can be defined at almost any level of detail. Clearly the task of preparing a production schedule is itself made up of more elementary tasks like collecting data on orders and labor availability, which are themselves made up of even more elementary activities. On the other hand, one can aggregate elements like production scheduling into larger units of analysis like managing production.

A choice of some level of abstraction cannot be avoided. For purposes of this study, the level chosen was that which the managers themselves used in describing their activities. Thus, even at the theoretical level, advantage was taken of the fact that the managers' language had evolved as a useful means for processing information about their jobs.

Elements of managerial activity will be referred to as *operators*. An operator transforms a set of input variables into a set of output variables acding to some predetermined plan. For example, the operator "lay out a production schedule" takes machine capacities, labor productivities, product requirements, and other input variables and yields man, product, machine, and time associations covering some appropriate period of time. Since the action of an operator produces an effect which is more or less predictable, operators are frequently named for their effect on the environment. The operator "lay out production schedule" changes the production organization from one with no schedule to one with a schedule. The operator "hire qualified lathe operator" changes the size of the work force.[8]

The word "problem" is associated with the difference between some existing situation and some desired situation. The problem of reducing material cost, for example, indicates a difference between the existing material cost and some desired level of material cost. The problems of hiring qualified engineers and of reducing finished goods inventories similarly define differences to be reduced. Because problems are defined by differences and operators can be executed to reduce differences, strong associations are formed between problems and operators. The problem of devising a production schedule can ordinarily be "solved" by applying the operator "lay out production schedule." The problem of "increasing sales volume" can sometimes be "solved" by applying the operator "revise advertising budget." Since operator selection is triggered by the difference to be reduced, the process of problem finding is the process of defining differences. Problem solving, on the other hand, is the process of selecting operators which will reduce differences.

The manager defines differences by comparing what he perceives to the output of a *model* which predicts the same variables. A difference might be defined by comparing an idle machine to a production schedule which implies high machine utilization. In this case, the production schedule is the model used to define a difference. A difference might be defined by comparing a 10 percent reject rate in a department to a budgeted rate of 2 percent. In this case, the budget is the model. A difference might be defined by comparing available data to those required for a special report. The problem of understanding problem finding is therefore eventually reduced to the problem of understanding the models which managers use to define differences.

It should be noted that the theoretical framework proposed here has drawn on ideas discussed by Miller, Galanter, and Pribram,[9] who in turn refer to some basic work by Newell, Shaw, and Simon.[10] Figure 1 presents a flowchart of the process described in this section and, for comparison, the structures proposed by others.

---

[8] Because this paper is concerned primarily with problem finding, the process of operator selection and execution will not be discussed. The definitions are included only to complete the description of the theoretical structure.

[9] G. A. Miller, E. Galanter, and K. H. Pribram, *Plans and the Structure of Behavior* (New York: Henry Holt & Co., 1960).

[10] A. Newell, J. C. Shaw, and H. A. Simon, "Report on a General Problem-Solving Program," *Proceedings of the ICIP,* June 1960. Reprinted in: *Computers and Automation,* July 1960, as "A General Problem-Solving Program for a Computer."

FIGURE 1
Flowchart of managerial behavior

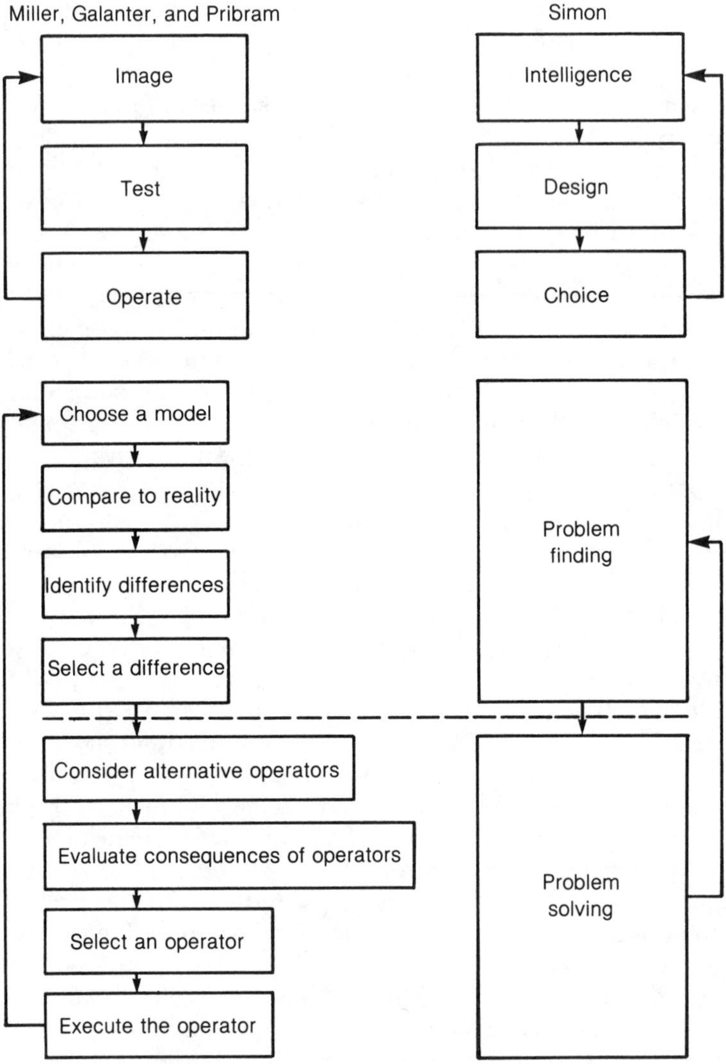

Miller, Galanter, and Pribram | Simon

(Image boxes: Image → Test → Operate; Intelligence → Design → Choice; Choose a model → Compare to reality → Identify differences → Select a difference → Consider alternative operators → Evaluate consequences of operators → Select an operator → Execute the operator; Problem finding; Problem solving)

MANAGERIAL MODELS FOR PROBLEM FINDING

Historical models

On the assumption that recent past experience is the best estimate of the short-term future, managers maintain a wide variety of models based on the continuity of historical relationships: April sales exceed March sales by 10 percent; Department X runs 5 percent defective product; the cost of making item Y is $10.50 per thousand; the lead time on that raw material is three weeks, etc. Because the manager's world is complex and these models tend to be simple, discrepancies frequently arise between the models' predictions and what actually takes place, Such discrepancies are a major source of problems to which managers devote their time. Why is our inventory account drifting out of line? Why is our reject rate so high this week? What has happened to make so many deliveries late? What can be done to reverse this trend in absenteeism? Why is our safety record suddenly so good? All these problems and a host of others like them are triggered by discrepancies from historical models and can keep a manager and his organization busy all day every day.

For the most part these models are non-explicit. The manager "carries them in his head" or "just knows." In a number of cases, however, these models are strongly supported by routine reports. Pieces of paper on which are printed monthly P&L statements, weekly reports of sales totals, daily reports of orders behind schedule, semiannual inventories, and many other items of interest flow across the manager's desk in a steady stream and, except in its historical context, each one has little meaning to the manager or anyone else.[11]

Recognizing this fact, most management reports in the Southern Company were prepared in such a way that current figures and recent reports of the same variables appeared side by side. Trends or sharp variations in any variable could be easily noted. The confidence placed in such analysis was clearly indicated by the fact that a large number of variables were added to routine reports following an unanticipated fluctuation in corporate profits. After several months, managers could review their history of "Return on Sales," "Return on Investment," and many other variables in addition to those previously reported.

The importance of routine reports as well as the use of an historical model to identify a problem were both illustrated when the rejection rate of one department moved past an historic high and thereby attracted attention to the Quality Assurance organization. A number of other examples could be cited. Out of 52 managers, 42 agreed with the statement that "most improvements come from correcting unsatisfactory situations," and, for the most part, unsatisfactory situations were defined by departures from historically established models of performance.

Departures of performance in a favorable direction—lower than historical cost or higher than historical sales, for example—were used to

---

[11] Budgets, which can also provide context for such data, are discussed in the next section.

modify the historical model not to define a problem *per se*. Several managers reported that better-than-average performance was frequently used as evidence of what could be accomplished when reduced cost allowances or increased profit expectations were being discussed. At the time of this study, the Southern Company was doing very well relative to its own past performance and a number of managers shared the sentiments of one who reported, "This year is going too well." They were clearly concerned about their ability to continue to meet what would become a new historical standard. Several were already working on that problem-to-be.

Besides serving as triggers for corrective and innovative problem solving, historical models are used extensively in the process of devising plans for future operations. These plans are in turn converted into budget objectives, and the budget objectives can sometimes serve as models which trigger managerial problem solving. Because of the complex process by which they are devised, managerial planning models will be discussed separately from the more straightforward historical ones.

Planning models

Managers in the Southern Company devoted substantial amounts of time to planning future operations. Detailed projections of operating variables for the coming year and less detailed projections for the coming five years were presented annually to corporate officers by each product department manager. When approved, perhaps after some modification, these projections were used periodically to evaluate managerial performance, and for other purposes as well.

In view of the importance attributed to planning by the Southern Company, it might be expected that planning models would constitute an important part of the problem-finding process. In fact they did not. Historical models were more influential on managerial behavior than planning models. To understand why, it is necessary to examine both the function of planning models and the process by which they were devised.

Among other things, plans are organizationally defined limits of managerial independence. So long as the manager is able to perform at least as well as his plan requires, he expects, and is normally granted, the right to define his problems as he sees fit. That is to say, as long as meeting his plan does not itself constitute a problem, the manager can use other criteria for defining his problems. If, however, he is unable to perform as well as he planned, he can expect to attract the attention of higher levels of management and to receive substantial assistance in problem identification. In other words, he will lose, perhaps only temporarily, the right to manage. One product manager put the matter this way, "The best way to remain in charge is to be successful." Other managers strongly supported this position. Success was defined relative to the predictions of the planning model.

In view of the fact that unfavorable deviations in performance were far more undesirable to managers than favorable deviations, it is not surprising that planning models were not simple descriptions of what the managers expected would happen. On the contrary, planning models represented the minimum performance the manager could reasonably expect if several of his plans failed or were based on the minimum organizational expectations of managerial performance, whichever was higher. Planning models were in general very conservatively biased historical models. For the most part these biases in plans were not injected surreptitiously. After approving a manager's plan, upper-level managers always inquired about how he would deal with various contingencies. At this point the manager would reveal some but usually not all of his "hedges" against uncertainty. If he could report a number of conservative estimates and contingent plans to back up the plan being proposed, this was viewed as highly desirable.

In aggregating departmental plans, further "adjustments" were made which led the plan to depart from expectations. In some cases, these adjustments shifted expected profits from one department to another to "make the package look OK." In other cases, already conservative departmental estimates were "rounded down" to cover contingencies further. Some of these adjustments were made explicit at higher levels.

Even with all its conservative biases, the Division's plan still exceeded the Corporation's minimum profit and volume expectations. It is not surprising, therefore, that the planning model was a far less important source of management problems than historical models. Extrapolations of past performance simply implied much larger levels of performance than the planning model called for. Only in those cases (not observed) where the corporate expectations required improvements over historical trends would one expect planning models to be important in the process of problem finding.

Other peoples' models

Some models which define problems for the manager are maintained by other people. A customer whose model of product quality is violated by the product he receives may notify the manager of the producing organization of this fact and thereby define a problem for him. A higher-level manager may lack information to complete an analysis and this discrepancy can define a problem for a lower-level manager. An employee may need a decision on vacation policy and his request will define a problem for his supervisor. A basic function of an organization structure is to channel problems which are identified by its various members to individuals especially qualified to solve them. Managers as well as other members of the organization do not always work on problems defined by their own models.

In the Southern Company, invitations to attend meetings, requests to prepare reports, and requests for projects of various kinds whether made by superiors, subordinates, or peers were rarely questioned by managers as appropriate ways to spend their time. While it was sometimes easy to get vehement testimony as to the uselessness of many of these activities, the behavior of managers clearly indicated the strong influence of other peoples' models. One reason for the influence of these models may be the cost to the manager of doubting them. Any attempt to validate each request made on him could easily imply a heavier work load on the manager than the simple execution of the work requested. In addition, by providing "good service" the manager builds (or at least many managers believe they build) a store of goodwill among other managers toward his own requests.

During the course of the company study, several clear examples of the influence of these models were observed. In a series of interviews, managers were asked to specify the problems currently faced by them and their organizations. Most of them mentioned from five to eight problems. Later in the same interview, each manager was asked to describe in broad terms his own activities for the previous week. In reviewing the data from these interviews as they were collected, it was noted that no manager had reported any activity which could be directly associated with the problems he had described.

In order to be sure that this result was not due to some semantic problem, this point was discussed with several managers—in some cases during the first interview with them and in other cases as a follow-up question. One manager found the point both accurate and amusing. He smiled as he replied, "That's right. I don't have time to work on *my* problems—I'm too busy." Another manager took a different tack in agreeing with the general conclusion. He replied rather confidentially. "I don't really make decisions. I just work here." In further discussion with a number of managers, the power of other peoples' models were repeatedly indicated. The influence of these models was also noted in the case of a rather involved project which was observed in some detail.

The Plant Engineering Department, using a quite different model, decided to look at the desirability of revising the management of the company's 21 fork trucks. Besides scheduling and other operating questions which were investigated by people within the Engineering Department, studies of the contract under which the trucks were leased and an economic evaluation of leasing versus buying trucks were also felt to be required. The manager of Plant Engineering called representatives of the comptroller's organization and the Legal Department to a meeting in which the project was discussed in some detail. This discussion clearly indicated that the project was risky both from the point of view of economic payoff and political considerations. The representatives accepted their tasks, however, and in due course their studies were completed. In neither case did the studies take much time, but the assumption that it was the job of the Accounting Department and the Legal Department to serve the Plant Engineering Department was clear. A problem found by someone in the organization carries with it substantial influence over the problems on which other parts of the organization will work.

Even clearer evidence of the power of other peoples' models was the time devoted by all the managers in the Southern Company to the preparation of reports "required" by higher management. These reports ranged in their demands on managerial time from a few minutes in the case of a request for routine information to several man-months of work on the preparation of a plan for the coming year's operations. In reply to the question, "If you were responsible for the whole company's operations would you require more, the same, or less planning?" four managers responded that they would require more planning, 32 said the same amount of planning, and 16 replied less. For many managers the expectations of the organization were consistent with their own ideas of the time required for effective planning. For a number of others, however, the influence of other people was clear.

In discussing these models as a source of problems, it is difficult to avoid a negative connotation due to the widely held ethic which values individual problem definition. Two points are worth emphasizing. First, the study was conducted to find out how managers do define their problems—not how they should do so—although that, of course, may be a long-term objective of this work. Second, both the organization and the individuals described here would, by almost any standards, be judged to be highly successful and this fact should be included in any attempt to evaluate their behavior.

Because historical, planning, and other peoples models require almost no generalization to make them relevant to particular events of interest to the manager, and because these three types of models can easily generate more problems than the manager can reasonably hope to deal with, it is not surprising, perhaps, that models requiring somewhat more generalization are less important elements of the process of problem finding. It is true, however, that on occasion managers draw on experiences other than their own to define problems for themselves and their organizations.

EXTRA-ORGANIZATIONAL MODELS

Trade journals which report new practices and their effects in other organizations can sometimes define useful areas for managerial analysis. Customers frequently serve the same function by reporting the accomplishments of competitors in the area of price, service, and/or product quality. General Motors is known for its practice of ranking the performance measures of a number of plants producing the same or similar products and making this information available to the managers of these facilities. The implication is strong in these comparisons that problems exist in plants where performance is poor relative to other plants.

In using all such extra-organizational models to define intra-organizational problems, the manager must resolve the difficult question of model validity. "Is the fact that our West Coast plant has lower maintenance costs relevant to our operations? After all, they have newer equipment." "Is the fact that our competitor is lowering its price relevant to our pricing policy? After all, our quality is better." There are enough attributes in any industrial situation to make it unlikely indeed that any extra-organizational model will fit the manager's situation perfectly. Judgments on the question of model validity must frequently be made by operating managers.

In the Southern Company one clear case was observed where two extra-organizational models were employed in an attempt to define a problem. A member of the Plant Engineering Department attended a meeting of an engineering society at which a technique called "work sampling" was discussed in the context of several successful applications in other plants. This model of a current engineering practice, which had not been employed by his department, led this man to consider the problem of finding an application for work sampling in the Southern Company. Clearly if this technique could be successfully applied, it would reduce the difference between his department and his extra-organizational model. A few days later this engineer noticed an idle, unattended fork truck in one of the manufacturing shops and he immediately thought that an analysis of fork truck operations might be the application he was looking for. He discussed this idea with his supervisors and they agreed that the project should be undertaken.

Because of the lack of direct responsibility for fork trucks, Plant Engineering was aware from the beginning of the project that its primary task would be to convince the product departments that their fork trucks indeed constituted a problem. To provide the department managers with evidence on this point, in addition to the internal work sampling study, a survey of fork truck operations was made in six nearby plants engaged in similar manufacturing operations. The explicit purpose of the survey was to define a basis (an extra-organizational model) on which internal fork truck operations could be evaluated.

The six company survey yielded in part the following results:

1. The number of trucks operated ranged from 6 to 50, with an average of 21—same as Southern Company.
2. Utilizations ranged from 50 percent to 71 percent, with an average of 63 percent—18.5 percent higher than Southern Company.
3. Responsibility for trucks was centralized in all six companies—contrary to Southern Company.
4. Trucks were controlled through dispatching or scheduling in five of the six companies (some used radio control)—contrary to Southern Company.
5. All companies owned rather than leased their trucks—contrary to Southern Company.
6. All companies performed their own maintenance of their trucks—contrary to Southern Company.
7. Three companies licensed their drivers, and assigned them full time driving—contrary to Southern Company.

The fact that the surveyed companies on the average operated the same number of trucks as the Southern Company was clearly cited as evidence supporting the validity of this extra-organizational model.

Because the six-company survey and the work-sampling study had defined the problem in aggregate terms, the analysis and recommendations proceeded at this level. The Plant Engineering Department decided to make their recommendation on the basis of an overall utilization of 60 percent (the average utilization found in the six-company survey) which implied a reduction of five trucks. They then looked at their work-sampling data and re-allocated trucks among departments to bring individual truck utilization figures as close to 60 percent as possible. The recommended re-allocation in fact supplied a saving of five trucks. The recommendation went on to suggest that Product Departments "compensate [for this reduction in trucks] by establishing sharing arrangements between departments."

The recommendation also proposed "permanent [full-time] licensed drivers" instead of production workers operating the trucks on an *ad hoc* basis as part of their regular duties. As a result of a study which had indicated that leasing was preferable to buying the fork trucks, no change in ownership or maintenance was proposed. The annual savings anticipated from the recommended changes amounted to $7,250.

It is interesting to note that the recommendations themselves constituted problems for the product department managers. The task of "establishing sharing arrangements among departments" had not been resolved by the study and remained a thorny problem. The task of transferring qualified production workers to full-time truck-driving duties involved not only complex problems of morale and labor relations but also economic trade-offs not evaluated by the study. The task of redefining departmental work procedures to relate to centrally controlled truck services was similarly unresolved. In return for these problems, the seven product department managers could expect to share in an annual saving of $7,250. Their response to the recommendation was less than enthusiastic. They agreed, after some bargaining, to return one truck to the leasing company but were not willing to pursue the matter any further.

Despite this rather negative conclusion, it is interesting to note that most managers considered the fork truck study a success. The validity of using the extra-organizational model derived from the survey as a means of defining the problem was never questioned and an evaluation of the existing policy on this basis was considered well-justified.

A more complicated use of extra-organizational models occurred in the case of several managers who had had personal experience in other organizations. In several situations they used this experience to define intra-organizational problems by emphasizing the personal element of this experience as evidence of its validity and by de-emphasizing (or not mentioning) where this experience was gained.

Extra-organizational models have a natural disadvantage as sources of problems because of the question of model validity which can always be raised against them. When extra-organizational experience agrees with local experience (historical model), it is seen as valid, but since it agrees with the local experience, it defines no problem. When extra-organizational experience disagrees with local experience and might therefore define a problem, the discrepancy itself raises the question of model validity. This attribute of extra-organizational models may serve to explain the fact that they were a relatively weak source of management problems in the Southern Company. Out of 52 managers, 47 agreed with the statement: "Most of our new ideas are generated within the company."

In the case of new organizations, of course, historical models are not available and extra-organizational models become more influential. One such situation was observed in the Southern Company. A promising new product was moving from the latter stages of development into the early stages of production and sales. A new product department was formed on an informal basis and the standard procedures of accounting data collection and reporting were instituted. No one expected the new department to be profitable immediately but after some months an executive at the product group level used a model not based on the history of the new department but one based on the performance of other departments to define a problem. He described the process this way:

"The numbers [on the monthly reports] were horrifying. I asked for a report and I got fuzzy answers that I didn't believe so I said, 'Fellows, I'm taking over the right to ask questions.'

"In asking questions I found I could pick holes in their analysis of the situation. Everything was loose.

"I analyzed their orders and found that with their overhead they couldn't make money.

"The department was reorganized."

In new organizations, extra-organizational models can be powerful sources of management problems.

SOME NORMATIVE QUESTIONS

The principal objective of this study was to find a relatively simple theoretical structure to explain the process of problem finding used by the managers at the Southern Company, and the set of four models just described represents that structure. These models, which range from ones maintained by other members of the organization, through simple historical and planning models, to those which apply the experience of other organizations to local situations, have been tested against the rather massive sample of data collected at the Southern Company and have been found sufficient to explain all these observations. That is to say, it is possible to trace all the observed behavior back to differences defined by one of these four classes of models. To this extent the study was successful.

But observations like these, even after abstraction into a theoretical structure, are only observations. They do not suggest the consequences of using other kinds of models or using these same models with different frequencies. They do not suggest how managers might behave more effectively than they do. Isolated observations cannot define differences. Observations must be compared to a model before normative questions can be answered.

One way to generate such comparisons would be to conduct comparative studies within and among a number of organizations. One could then answer such questions as: "Are these same models used by unsuccessful managers? If so, how can the difference in performance be explained? If not, what models are used? Do managers in other organizations use these models with different frequencies or under different circumstances? Are there systematic differences in the use of these models at different levels of the organization?" All such questions could be answered by careful study of several organizations or several levels of the same organization and these extra-organizational models might serve to suggest management improvements. Until such studies are completed, however, the only models which can be used to evaluate the behavior observed in the Southern Company are some which were not used there.

Scientific models

When compared to models used in the physical and social sciences for quite similar purposes, the models used by the managers in the Southern Company (and elsewhere) are almost startling in their naivete. In the same company, electrical engineers explicitly used quite complex theoretical models to help them define problems associated with the design of a relatively simple electronic control system. Similarly, mechanical engineers employed a variety of quite general theories in the design of new high-speed production equipment. In neither of these cases did the engineers base their predictions on their own experience except in a very general sense. They quite confidently applied theories derived from the observations of others and the equipment which resulted from their work required relatively little redesign after construction. Managers, on the other hand, based their expectations on relatively small samples of their own experience. Their rather simple theories, as has already been noted, yielded rather poor predictions, and managers therefore spent a substantial amount of time solving either their own problems or those defined by others.

The behavior of scientists (an extra-organizational model) suggests that there is an alternative to this rather frantic approach to a complex world. When discrepancies arise between a model and the environment, one can undertake to improve the model rather than change the environment. In fact, a scientist might even go so far as to suggest that, until one has a fairly reliable model of the environment, it is not only foolish but perhaps even dangerous to take action when its effect cannot be predicted.

If carried to an extreme, of course, the scientist's tendency to search for better models of the world as it is would leave no time for taking action to change it, and it seems unlikely that this allocation of time and talent would be an appropriate one for the operating manager. In the Southern Company, it must be remembered, those managers who based their actions on very simple models which took very little time to construct were judged to be quite successful by their organization. On the other hand, the increasing use by managers of more sophisticated modeling techniques like those mentioned earlier in this paper may suggest that the balance between model building and action taking is shifting. A number of companies now base changes in distribution systems, production and inventory control systems, quality control systems, advertising allocation systems, etc., on the predictions of relatively complex models which are based on substantial bodies of theory and empirical evidence. To the extent that these models fail to describe events which take place, they, like the simpler models they replace, can serve to define problems. To the extent that these more complete models take into account events which the manager cannot, or prefers not to, control, these models can serve to protect the manager from problems on which he might otherwise waste his energy.

While it may be true that these more explicit scientific models will gradually replace simple intuitive models, several reasons suggest that the change will take some time. First, many operating managers today find the language of the new techniques foreign, despite increasing attempts to change this situation through training. Second, the new techniques often involve even more generalization than extra-organizational models, and honest questions of model validity will tend to delay their widespread use. And third, the process of problem finding currently used will perpetuate itself simply by keeping managers so busy that they will find little time to learn about and try these new methods of problem finding.

More important than any of these reasons, however, may be one which, curiously, has been created by the advocates of management science. In most, if not all, of the literature describing them, model-building techniques are described as means for solving management problems. In their now classical book on operations research, Churchman, Ackoff, and Arnoff, for example, suggest model building as a step which should follow "formulating the problem."[12] The process by which the problem should be formulated, however, is left totally unspecified—and this is where managers as well as students of management frequently report their greatest difficulty. They can see the process by which these techniques can solve problems but they cannot see how to define the problems.

The theory which has been proposed here suggests that problem definition cannot precede model construction. It is impossible to know, for example, that a cost is too high unless one has some basis (a model) which suggests it might be lower. This basis might be one's own experience, the experience of a competitor, or the output of a scientific model. Similarly, one cannot be sure that his distribution

---

[12] C. W. Churchman, R. L. Ackoff, and E. L. Arnoff, *Introduction to Operations Research* (New York: John Wiley & Sons, 1957).

costs will be reduced by linear programming until a model is constructed and solved which suggests that rescheduling will lower costs. The imperfections of an inventory system are revealed only by comparing it to some theoretical model; they cannot be defined until after the model has been built. The logical inconsistency which suggests that problems must be clearly defined in order to justify model construction is very likely an important reason that scientific models will only slowly be recognized by operating managers as important aids in the definition of their problems.

Despite their current disadvantages, the so-called new techniques of model building are, as has already been noted, making significant contributions to management effectiveness. They represent, therefore, not only a means for evaluating current managerial behavior but also a new class of models which can be used by managers to define their problems.

THE PROBLEM OF MODEL SELECTION

The study of managers in the Southern Company indicates that concepts like image and intelligence which have been proposed to explain the process of problem finding can be made somewhat more operational. A rather small set of model classes has been defined which constitutes sufficient stimuli to trigger a fairly large sample of managerial behavior. This is not to say that future observations may not indicate the need for additional model classes or that future work is not required to make the process of managerial model building even more operational and testable. The study of the Southern Company represents perhaps only an encouraging start at understanding an important and little understood area of management.

Even with these initial insights, however, it is possible to see where major theoretical gaps still exist. Chief among these is the problem of model selection. As has already been noted, the requests of other people are sufficient to define a full-time job for many managers. The problem of investigating and taking corrective action on discrepancies from historical trends can keep any manager busy all the time. The construction of extra-organizational and/or scientific models and the actions which they trigger are similarly time-consuming. Even after the manager has constructed the models he will use to define his problems, he must somehow select from among the differences which are simultaneously defined by these models. Personal requests, historical discrepancies, extra-organizational ideas, and the stimuli of scientific models do not in general define differences one at a time. The choice of the discrepancy to attend to next may be as important a process as the construction of the models which define them. It seems clear, however, that we must understand the process by which differences are defined before we can worry seriously about understanding the process of selecting from among them. The study in the Southern Company, therefore, largely ignored the priority problem and concentrated on difference definitions only.

It is impossible, however, to observe managers at work without getting some rough ideas about how they deal with the priority problem. Telephone calls for example are very high-priority stimuli. A ringing telephone will interrupt work of virtually every kind. This priority rule is complicated sometimes by an intervening secretary but many managers pride themselves on always answering their own phone. One manager reported that he always worked on problems which would "get worse" before he worked on static problems. Thus, he dealt with a problem involving a conflict between a foreman and a troublesome employee before pressing forward on a cost reduction program.

Perhaps the most explicit priorities in the Southern Company were established by means of deadlines. Most problems defined by other members of the organization carried with them a time at which, or by which, the request should be satisfied. Certain reports were due monthly, a fixed number of working days after the end of the preceding month. Meetings were scheduled at stated times. Annual plans were required on a specified date. While a number of such requests might face a manager simultaneously, they almost never would have the same deadline and by this means the manager could decide which to do when. The fact that most problems triggered by other people's models carried deadlines may explain why these problems seemed to be given so much attention. When asked to indicate "Which problems do you usually get to first, time deadline, big payoff or personal interest?" 43 out of 52 managers indicated time deadline.

From a theoretical point of view, one could consider the flow of problems through an organization as analogous to the flow of jobs through a job shop and perhaps apply some of the theories which have been developed there to understand and perhaps prescribe the process of priority assignment. Managers, for example, must trade off relative lateness of their tasks with the duration of the tasks just as a foreman loading machines in a machine shop. Once the problem of problem definition is well understood it would appear that some theory is already available to structure the process of assigning problem priorities. The array of models used by and available to managers suggests that an understanding of the process by which problems are defined will not constitute a complete theory of problem finding. A process which assigns priorities to a set of simultaneously defined problems remains to be specified.

On the art of modeling

WILLIAM T. MORRIS

INTUITION IN MODELING

The process by which the experienced management scientist arrives at a model of the phenomenon he is studying is probably best described as intuitive. The term "intuitive" refers here to thinking which the subject is unable or unwilling to verbalize. Indeed, really effective experienced persons in any field typically operate in a largely intuitive manner and view with impatience attempts to make their methods explicit. The experienced management scientist may well consider questions as to how he selected the variables to be included in the model, how he decided which were to be regarded as random, and so on, as so trivial that they cannot occupy his serious attention or so non-trivial that they cannot be answered. He is perhaps willing to regard the abstraction and translation of a management problem into a scientific problem as an art in the sense that it must remain largely intuitive. Any set of rules for obtaining models could have only the most limited usefulness at best, and at worst, might seriously impede the development of the required intuition.

If one grants that modeling is and, for greatest effectiveness, probably ought to be, an intuitive process for the experienced, then the interesting question becomes the pedagogical problem of how to develop this intuition.[1] What can be done for the inexperienced person

---

Source: *Management Science*, vol. 13, no. 12, August 1967.

[1] Jerome S. Bruner, *The Process of Education* (New York: Random House, 1957). While this paper deals only with some crude attempts to meet the educational problem, there is considerable relevant literature. Some representative examples include:

Arrow, K. J., "Mathematical Models in the Social Sciences," in Daniel Lerner and Harold Lasswell, eds., *The Policy Sciences* (Stanford: Stanford University Press, 1951).

Beveridge, W. I. B., *The Art of Scientific Investigation* (New York: Random House, 1957).

Ghiselin, Brewster, ed., *The Creative Process* (Berkeley: University of California Press, 1952).

Hadamard, Jacques, *The Psychology of Invention in the Mathematical Field* (Princeton, N.J.: Princeton University Press, 1945).

who wishes to progress as quickly as he can toward a high level of intuitive effectiveness in management science? What can be done for the experienced person whose mind "draws a blank" when seeking to model some management problem? Can we say only, "Get more experience, for it is the chief source of intuitive development and the only recourse when intuition fails?" In what follows, an effort is made to verbalize about the process of developing models in a very limited fashion and to consider the role of such verbalizations in the educational process. In attempting to make the process of modeling explicit, it may be reasonable to suppose that one is raising hypotheses about the process and that one is providing a possible target for imitation when intuition is insufficiently developed. It does not appear reasonable, however, to suppose that one could provide a general "recipe" for making models, nor that one could do very much more than modestly enhance the process of developing intuition. It may well be that intuition or artistic skill is largely the product of imitation and practice, yet this process of development must have a beginning. Experience suggests that this beginning must include more than simply a familiarity with other people's models.

JUSTIFICATION AND DISCOVERY

A basic distinction that must be communicated to the inexperienced is the difference between the "context of justification" and the "context of discovery."[2] Management science (and all science) is reported and communicated in the form of a logical reconstruction which aims at providing a justification for the inferences produced. This logical reconstruction has little if anything to do with the psychological process by which the inferences were first obtained. It is the custom in science to report a piece of work by stating the assumptions of premises which determine the model, showing the deductive steps by which the relevant consequences of the model were obtained, and then reporting the design and analysis of the experiment aimed at testing the hypotheses suggested by the consequences of the model. All this is very much *ad hoc*. The danger for the inexperienced is that, finding little else in the literature of their science other than such justification, they will begin to assume that this is a description of the process of discovery.

Kemeney, John G., *A Philosopher Looks at Science* (Princeton, N.J.: Van Nostrand and Co., 1959).

Simon, Herbert A., "Some Strategic Considerations in the Construction of Social Science Models," in Paul Lazarsfeld, ed., *Mathematical Thinking in the Social Sciences* (Glencoe, Ill.: The Free Press, 1954).

[2] Hans Reichenbach, *The Rise of Scientific Philosophy* (Berkeley: University of California Press, 1959), p. 231.

The experienced scientist knows that the psychological process is very different, but he seldom attempts to verbalize it. One may wonder, however, whether even those with considerable experience do not sometimes practice a little delusion of themselves and their colleagues by tending to read *ad hoc* justifications as descriptions of the context of discovery. One often senses that a writer is implicitly saying, "See how logical, how methodical, how brilliantly inevitable was our progress in this study." Since all of the writing in a science is likely to be of this sort, one must conclude that the experienced persons in a field are not of great help to the inexperienced, so far as the art of modeling is concerned. In fact, the inexperienced may be lead far astray if they begin to imitate the logical process in seeking to develop their own intuitive skill. It is not at all clear that the teaching of models by exposing the inexperienced to the *ad hoc* contributes much to the development of creative model building ability. Indeed, this is the fundamental criticism that might be made of management science education. The teaching of modeling is not the same as the teaching of models. How then, is one to teach modeling?

Skill in modeling certainly involves a sensitive and selective perception of management situations. This, in turn, depends on the sort of conceptual structures one has available with which to bring some order out of the perceptual confusion. Models can play the role of giving structure to experience. Yet we seldom encounter a model which is already available in fully satisfactory form for a given management situation, and the need for creative development or modification is almost universally experienced in management science.

THREE BASIC HYPOTHESES

The approach to the development of model building skill which we have explored might be stated in the form of three basic hypotheses. It is of some importance to regard these statements as hypotheses, since no really systematic test of their effectiveness has been made.

The process of model development may be usefully viewed as a process of *enrichment* or *elaboration*. One begins with very simple models, quite distinct from reality, and attempts to move in evolutionary fashion toward more elaborate models which more nearly reflect the complexity of the actual management situation.

This seems harmless enough, yet it is of some importance to point it out explicitly to the inexperienced. The attempt to begin immediately with a rather rich model may become a serious source of frustration. Starting simply gets things moving and thus tends to relieve some of the tension. It does, however, require a certain amount of poise or "guts" to back off from a complicated problem and begin with a simple conceptual structure. It requires one to deliberately omit and distort certain aspects of the situation and to knowingly commit the sins of suppressing difficult considerations and suboptimizing.

Analogy or *association* with previously well-developed logical structures plays an important role in the determination of the starting point of this process of elaboration or enrichment.

Clearly, one point of teaching models is to provide such well-developed logical structures which can be utilized more or less directly as starting points. It must be emphasized, however, that they typically provide only the starting points. When one asks if a given management situation can be modeled in the framework of linear programming, or waiting-line theory, or inventory theory, what is really being asked if whether one of these structures will give a head start in the evolutionary process of obtaining a useful model. Sometimes the search for analogy calls forth broad general structures such as differential equations or probability theory, sometimes more specific and highly developed structures like waiting-line theory, and sometimes very specific models developed especially for another management problem. While analogies are central to management science, we are concerned here with what steps should be taken subsequent to the discovery of such an association or when none appears possible. This is perhaps another way of saying that management science is an emergent science and a long way from handbook engineering which uses "off the shelf" models.

The process of elaboration or enrichment involves at least two sorts of *looping* or *alternation procedures*.

1. The alternation between modification of the model and confrontation by the data. As each version of the model is tested, a new version is produced which leads in turn to a subsequent test.

2. The alternation between exploration of the deductive tractability of the model and the assumptions which characterize it. If a version of the model is tractable in the sense of permitting the attainment of the analyst's deductive objectives, he may seek further enrichment or complication of the assumptions. If the model is not tractable or cannot be "solved," he returns to purify and simplify his assumptions.

The importance of the first of these looping procedures is to make clear that the research need not be conceived as one grand test of a single model. Nor need one decide whether to develop the model first or "get the data" first. It is of considerable consequence in management science to note that a part of the data consists of the attitudes of the client, not only toward the management situation being studied, but toward the management scientist studying it. The role of looping here has been previously explored.[3]

The second of these alternations is the central concern of this discussion. Indeed, facility in modeling means, to a large extent, the selection and modification of basic assumptions which characterize models. Here again a certain poise is required to work with a variety of assumptions, some of which are more nearly in agreement with the analyst's conception of the management problem, while others may be productive of models more tractable from the viewpoint of his deductive abilities. The task is to discover a set of assumptions which are both usefully descriptive of the problem and deductively tractable. Implicit in this sort of proposition is the refusal to resort to simulation until a serious attempt at analysis has been made.

Whatever the relevance of these hypotheses for particular scientists, it has been our impression that conveying to the inexperienced the notion that modeling is a process with some such looping dynamics is essential. In the following section, the illustration of this in a particular instance is suggested.

SOME SPECIFIC HYPOTHESES

In the process of attempting to develop modeling ability in inexperienced persons for a number of years, several specific suggestions have emerged. We regard these as hypotheses in the sense that no claims can really be made as to their general effectiveness. In situations where persons are very inexperienced, these suggestions appear to be helpful. At least they are better than no explicit remarks whatsoever about procedure, since they do prevent the inexperienced from being completely at a loss as to how to respond to the challenge of developing a model.

In presenting these hypotheses in the context of an example, it is natural to choose an example which furnishes a good illustration of the ideas, but in doing so one once again introduces something of the flavor of an *ad hoc* reconstruction. Clearly, things will not always work out as in the example and thus the suggestions cannot be rigidly interpreted or applied.

Suppose one undertakes the problem of designing a transportation system which is to serve a network of terminals on a fixed schedule. The locations of the terminals are known and some data are available or could be obtained on the time pattern of demand for transportation

---

[3] William P. Morris, *Management Science in Action* (Homewood, Ill.: Richard D. Irwin, Inc., 1963).

among the terminals. We suppose also that the criterion for a good design involves some measure of service furnished in response to the demands, combined with some measure of the cost of obtaining and operating the equipment to be used in the system. Clearly, considerable effort may be involved in bringing the study to this point of definition, and there are well-known difficulties with making operational the criterion for a good system design. We will, however, suppress these considerations in order to emphasize the model-building aspects of the study. We suppose that it becomes clear to the designer that he may determine the schedule of arrivals and departures to be specified by the timetable and the number of vehicles to be available for running out the timetable. He may attempt to produce directly a model which will predict the level of service, investment, and operating costs for any choice of timetable and number of vehicles. He may search for analogies to this problem among the well-developed logical structures with which he is familiar. Suppose, however, that this effort is unsuccessful, and that he seeks to factor the system design problem into simpler problems for which models may be more readily obtainable. This is our first suggestion or hypothesis.

Factor the system problem into simpler problems

In this example the analyst might decide to consider:

1. The schedule design problem: Given a fixed fleet of vehicles, what schedule of arrivals and departures will give the highest level of service and still be within the capabilities of the available fleet?
2. The fleet size problem: If a schedule of arrivals and departures is given, what is the minimum fleet size which can accomplish it? (We have already allowed the assumption of homogeneous vehicles to creep in.)

An ideal factoring of the system design problems would yield simpler problems which could be modeled and would subsequently permit easy combination into a system model. When factoring occurs, the result is several problems whose solutions are sub-optimal or approximate from the viewpoint of the system model. For the inexperienced, this deliberate setting aside of the ultimate design objectives is often a very difficult step. Having done it, however, one may attack the simpler problems—for example, the fleet size problem.

Establish a clear statement of the deductive objectives

An essential early step would appear to be the achievement of a clear (but still tentative) statement of the deductive objective of the model. Do we want the model to predict the consequences of various policies? Do we want it to suggest an optimal policy? In the fleet size problem, suppose we take the deductive objective to be simply the determination of the minimum fleet size which can accomplish a given schedule of arrivals and departures. Such a statement provides the criterion for determining the deductive viability or tractability of the model. Yet in establishing such an objective, one should keep open the possibility that it may prove unachievable, or that different objectives may suggest themselves as the model is developed. The final deductive objective may be foreseen in advance or it may emerge as a surprising result of the study of the model.

Seek analogies

At this stage, as well as at any other stage in the process, one should seek opportunities to make analogies between the problem at hand and some previously well-developed logical structure. These analogies will often occur as a sort of intuitive leap. Is the problem a linear programming problem, a queuing problem, or an inventory problem? Is it usefully similar to one which has been modeled by someone else? Note that the possibility of an analogy ought to be considered even before the problem is very well defined, since analogies may well suggest the way in which the problem might tentatively be made more specific. We will suppose that the fleet size problem does not yield immediately to this search for analogies and it becomes necessary to take further steps.

We do not wish to give the impression here that the process of discovering analogies is easy or well understood, but only to suggest that it may be helpful to be somewhat self-conscious about it.

Consider a specific numerical instance of the problem

This is a key step for the inexperienced person. The specification of a simple instance of the problem is often difficult for the beginner, since it represents a retreat (hopefully temporary) from the generality and complexity which he ultimately seeks. The purposes of the specific example are at least three:

1. To lead the analyst to make statements about the assumptions which characterize the example. It is these assumptions which may be a useful starting point for achieving greater generality.
2. If the numerical instance can be "solved" by inspection, then perhaps the process of solution can simply be generalized.

3. The specific instance provides a workable starting point for establishing a symbolism and giving general expression to some of the obvious things which are noticed in the specific case.

Suppose for example, we consider a network consisting of terminals numbered 1, 2, and 3, which is to be served according to a timetable specified below. The timetable is based on an eight-hour clock and repeats every eight hours.

Departure times from terminal 1: 2, 5, 8
Departure times from terminal 2: 1, 3, 7
Departure times from terminal 3: 1, 4, 7

The routings are given as: 1 to 2, 2 to 3, 3 to 1, and the running times on these routes are 2 hours, 1 hour, and 2 hours, respectively. This permits the construction of the complete timetable:

Terminal 1		Terminal 2		Terminal 3	
Arrivals	Departures	Arrivals	Departures	Arrivals	Departures
1	2	2	1	2	1
3	5	4	3	4	4
6	8	7	7	8	7

At this point one might discover by "inspection" or by "trial and error" that this timetable can be run out with a minimum of four vehicles. By asking how such a result was obtained and then generalizing, one may find the key to a workable model for the problem. If this fails, however, the example provides a basis for making some explicit statements about the assumptions which it implies. For example, we seem to be assuming:

a. That the schedule must be met. No deviations from the specified departure times are permitted.
b. That the running times are inclusive in the sense that they include the times for a vehicle to load and unload.
c. That the running times are invariant. The possibility of breakdowns or delays is suppressed.
d. That the number of arrivals and departures at each terminal will be equal during each scheduling period.

Perhaps there are other assumptions as well, but these begin to define the sort of problem which has been established. If we fail to achieve the desired result with these assumptions, we can come back and modify or relax some of them for another try. In this sense, the assumptions that an analyst presents first in a journal article were probably actually discovered last—as he did the work. The task is to discover a set of assumptions which lead to a tractable model, and to do this typically requires a number of attempts.

Establish some symbols

Perhaps the next step might be to translate the numerical example into symbolic terms. For some reason this is often a difficult step. One wants to choose symbols which are suggestive of their interpretations, and to give careful definitions of each. The beginner often fails here, and carelessness at this point has serious consequences later on.

Suppose for example, we elect the rather conventional double subscript notation. Let:

$$a_{ij} = \text{The time of the } i\text{th arrival at terminal } j$$
$$d_{ij} = \text{The time of the } i\text{th departure from terminal } j$$

Now we are at a crucial point. What to do next? We suggest that in the absence of any useful insight, one simply writes down in symbolic terms some of the obvious things which can be seen in the numerical example. Our hypothesis is that giving expression to the obvious will be highly suggestive in terms of further steps in the development of the model.

Write down the obvious

What we have in mind are such things as conservation laws, input-output relations, ideas expressed in the assumptions, or the consequences of trivially simple policies. In the fleet size example, we might simply try to express the basic conservation law which states that the vehicles provided will spend their time either in making runs between terminals or sitting idle while waiting to depart. If we have a fleet of k vehicles available each scheduling period, we provide an input of kT vehicle-hours, where T is the length of the period. These vehicle-hours will be devoted to either idleness (let I = total vehicle-hours of idleness) or running (let R = the total vehicle-hours of running). Thus the conservation law is

$$kT = I + R$$

Hopefully such a simple statement will be suggestive. Perhaps in this case we notice that R is fixed by the specification of the timetable, and that to minimize k one must minimize I. What can one do to influence the amount of idle time? Since idle time is generated when a vehicle waits at a terminal for its scheduled departure, it must be that the way in which arriving vehicles are assigned to departures will influence idle time. At terminal 1, we might make the following matching of arrivals and departure times.

Vehicle arriving at	Departs at	Idle time
1	2	1
3	5	2
6	8	2

This matching generates a total of five vehicle-hours of idle time.

Before proceeding, it is worthwhile noticing a very important property of this system. So long as departure times are met, nothing which is done at one terminal can influence the idle time at the other terminals. This means the system can be "cut" in the sense that we can minimize idle time terminal by terminal, rather than having to consider the entire system at once. In symbolic terms the idle time at terminal j, I_j, is independent of the idle time at terminal k, I_k, and the idle time for the system is given by

$$I = I_1 + I_2 + I_3$$

The real objective of systems analysis is not simply to study larger and larger problems, but to find ways of "cutting" large problems into small ones, such that the solutions of the small ones can be combined in some easy way to yield solutions for the large ones.

Using the numerical example, one might try some other matchings of arrivals with departures. We notice that if at any time more departures have been scheduled than there have been arrivals, the excess departures will have to be made by vehicles kept over from the previous scheduling period. One can easily write out all of the possible matchings, and note that a matching which keeps no vehicles over from the previous period generates 5 vehicle-hours of idle time; one which keeps 1 vehicle over generates 13 vehicle-hours of idle time; one which keeps 2 over generates 21 vehicle-hours of idle time—and so on. Thus, keeping down idle time seems to be associated with keeping down the number of vehicles kept over from the previous period.

Now this same insight can be expressed symbolically:

$$I_j = \Sigma_i d_{ij} - \Sigma_i a_{ij} + A_j T$$

Here A_j is the number of vehicles kept over from one scheduling period to the next at terminal j. At this point the problem is "solved" in the sense that the minimum fleet size will result when we have minimized the A_j. Further examination of the numerical example may suggest that the A_j will be minimized when arriving vehicles are assigned to departures on a first-in-first-out basis. (There may be other policies which are as good, but there are none better than FIFO.)

All that remains is to compute the minimum fleet size. We may again return to the numerical example to compute the running time generated by the schedule. Using our symbolism, we might express this computation as

$$R = \Sigma_i \Sigma_j a_{ij} - \Sigma_i \Sigma_j d_{ij} + BT$$

Here B is the number of vehicles that depart in one scheduling period and arrive in the next.

Now the symbolism and the expression we have established begin to yield some interesting deductive consequences. It turns out that

$$kT = I + R = \Sigma_j I_j + R$$
$$= \Sigma_j A_j T + BT$$

and thus

$$k = \Sigma_j A_j + B$$

Thus we can suggest, "Find the minimum number of vehicles which must be kept over at each terminal using a FIFO assignment policy. Add to the sum of these minima the number of vehicles which are on route at the end of a scheduling period, and the result will be the minimum fleet size." This result was originally obtained by Bartlett.[4]

If we had not been successful, perhaps the next step would have been to return to the numerical example or to the assumptions, looking for ways to simplify and try again. As it is, we might wish to go on toward enriching or complicating the model.

If a tractable model is obtained, enrich it; otherwise, simplify

One might, in our example, wish to consider different types of vehicles, running times which are random variables, schedules which change from period to period, breakdown and maintenance time for the vehicles, and so on.

Generally speaking, one may simplify by:

Making variables into constants.

Eliminating variables.

Using linear relations.

Adding stronger assumptions and restrictions.

Suppressing randomness.

Enrichment may involve just the opposite sort of modification.

---

[4] T. E. Bartlett, *An Algorithm for the Minimum Units Required to Maintain a Fixed Schedule,* Management Science Research Group, Purdue University, 1956.

OTHER SOURCES OF MODELING SKILL

Sensitivity to certain other ideas appears also to be associated with the achievement of facility in modeling. For example, it is obvious that a feeling of being at ease with mathematics is important. One of the reasons that one studies advanced mathematics that will probably not be "useful" is to achieve a more comfortable and relaxed grasp of less advanced mathematics which is likely to be used. Some appreciation of the various purposes which models may serve is helpful. Illustrating the use of models to give quantitative predictions, to give qualitative predictions, as data collection plans, as research plans, as perceptual sensitizers, as devices for structuring knowledge, and so on, tends to broaden one's view of the sorts of models which are worth developing and the different directions their development might take.

Similarly, attempts to develop a consciousness of some of the characteristics of models appears helpful. Beyond the rough description of a model as "simple" or "complex," one might usefully consider:

Relatedness. How many previously known theorems or results does the model bring to bear upon the problem?

Transparency. How obvious is the interpretation of the model? How immediate is its intuitive confirmation?

Robustness. How sensitive is the model to changes in the assumptions which characterize it?

Fertility. How rich is the variety of deductive consequences which the model produces?

Ease of enrichment. What difficulties are presented by attempts to enrich and elaborate the model in various directions?

CONCLUSION

The test of such hypotheses as these is, of course, whether they appear to enhance model-building skills. In making such an investigation, it is important to present the model-building challenge or opportunity outside of any context which prejudices the result in an obvious way. Problems which are presented at the end of an extended discussion of some particular logical structure do not present the same kind of challenge as problems encountered outside of any such context. Similarly, exercises which require one to substitute numbers in previously developed models may help to bring familiarity with the models but they do not help to develop model-creating ability. A much more useful introductory device is to present a simple model and ask for enrichments in specific directions.

The central points, however, are that the teaching of models is not equivalent to the teaching of modeling, and that there is a difference between the context of justification and the context of discovery. We have attempted to raise here the hypothesis that some explicit suggestions can enhance the process of developing the intuitive skill associated with model building.

The wizard who oversimplified: A fable

ROBERT N. ANTHONY

In a certain kingdom, there was a school for the education of princes approaching manhood. Since the king and his court spent much of their time playing chess—indeed, chess was called the sport of kings—it was decided that the subject called "games" should be added to the curriculum of this school. A wizard was engaged to develop the course.

Never having played chess himself, the wizard was a little uncertain about what to teach in this course. (Only a *little* uncertain because his ignorance of chess was outweighed by his strong confidence in his general ability.) He sought the advice of a colleague in another kingdom and from him received the following communication:

"Above all else, a course in games should be rigorous and intellectually challenging. We wizards long ago concluded that chess, as actually played, is so complicated that it is impossible to formulate a body of principles and decision rules; these are essential to the rigorous analysis of any subject. We have therefore introduced a few simplifying assumptions. For example, in chess, the pieces move in a bewildering fashion—some forward, some on the diagonal, and some even at a right angle; we have tidied up this confusion by assuming that all pieces move according to the same rule. With such assumptions, we have been able, albeit with great difficulty, to develop a model, a set of principles, and decision rules which are teachable, and intellectually challenging. A 700-page treatise describing these is enclosed."

The wizard was much impressed by the 700-page treatise, and used it in his course. He found that it was teachable, and that the task of learning this model and solving problems with the decision rules was indeed rigorous and intellectually challenging, as proved by the fact that good students did well on their examinations, while poor students failed them.

Source: *The Quarterly Journal of Economics*, vol. 79, no. 2, May 1965, pp. 209–11. Reproduced with permission.

The wizard maintained an active correspondence with wizards in other kingdoms about the model and its decision rules. In this correspondence, the game was referred to as "chess" although this was solely for convenience of expression; it was taken for granted that everyone knew that their game was not quite like chess as played in the real world. Eventually, some of this correspondence came to the king's attention. Although he didn't understand the formulas and the jargon, he did notice that the word "chess" was mentioned, so he commanded the wizard to appear before him.

At this audience, the wizard asked, "How can I serve you, O King?"

And the king replied: "I understand that you are teaching the princes how to play chess. I wish to improve my own game. Can you help me?"

"What we call chess may not be exactly like your game, your majesty. So before answering your question, I must analyze the problem. Please describe chess as you play it."

So the king explained the game of chess. As he did so, the wizard noted that it had the same physical layout, the same number of pieces, and apparently the same objective as the game he taught in school. It seemed clear therefore that the solution was simply to apply the decision rules for this game, although he of course did not immediately reveal this fact to the king for he wanted to preserve his reputation for wizardry. Instead, he said thoughtfully: "I will study the problem and return in 90 days."

At the appointed time, the wizard appeared again, carrying a crimson pillow on which lay a spiral-bound report with a Plexiglas cover. It was a paraphrase of the 700-page manuscript. "Follow the rules in this report, your majesty, and you will become the best chess player in the world," he said.

The king avidly studied the report, but soon ran into difficulty. He summoned the wizard again. "I see reference to kings, and men, and squares, which are familiar terms to me; but what is all this about 'jumping,' and 'double jumping,' and 'countervailing force,' 'suboptimization'; and where do you mention queens, rooks, bishops, and knights?"

"But your majesty, as I have clearly explained in the introduction, it was necessary to simplify the environment a trifle. I doubt that these simplifications lessen the practical usefulness of what I have written, however."

"Have you by chance watched some chess players to find out?" asked the king.

"Oh, no, your gracious majesty, but I do carry on an extensive correspondence with other wizards. This is better than observing actual practice because it is generally agreed that wizards are smarter than chess players."

"And your princes. Are they equipped to play chess in the real world because of what they have learned in your course?"

"No offense intended, sir, but we wizards do not believe this to be a proper question. The purpose of our course is to teach princes to think, not to prepare them for a mere vocation."

At this point, the king lost his patience, but since he was a kindly king, he sent the wizard back to his school room rather than to a dungeon.

Moral for economics professors: An education in checkers does not prepare one for a life of chess.

Moral for operations researchers: Half a loaf is not necessarily better than no bread; it may be only chaff.

Moral for businessmen: A consultant who wants to play his own game rather than yours is worthless.

Corporate models: Better marketing plans

PHILIP KOTLER

The market planner's task may seem no more onerous or complex than that of the plant manager who must plan the best utilization of the company's labor, equipment, and raw materials, or of the financial officer who must plan the flow of company funds. These other managers, however, generally work with better data, more measurable and dependable input-output relationships, and more direct control.

In marketing, information is poor, expenditures affect demand and costs simultaneously, and human factors play a large role. Thus it is no wonder that marketing management is considered essentially an art by both its practitioners and its critics.

The need to make order out of this chaos may be answered by one of management science's newest and most promising developments—the corporate marketing planning model, which is:

Computerized.

Industry-specific.

Data-based.

Comprehensive.

Designed for developing and evaluating alternative company marketing plans.

In this article, I shall describe and illustrate a specific, seven-step procedure for mapping and programming such a marketing model for a typical company. Then, in the Appendix, I shall present some broader background information about the evolution and current state of development of corporate marketing models.

CHARTING THE SYSTEM

Every company is a pioneer in this area because it must start fresh to create its own concepts, data base, and means of validation. I have found the following seven concepts and tools to be basic to any such system:

1. Core marketing system model.
2. Comprehensive marketing systems model.
3. Input-output models.
4. Functional relationship models.
5. Four-quadrant profit-forecasting and -planning model.
6. Mathematical sales and profit model.
7. Computer model and output.

Before discussing these concepts in detail, I think it is important to emphasize that the development of a marketing system (or, indeed, of any system) must be undertaken with the full participation of the marketing and other company executives who will be the future users of the corporate marketing model. Education is one of the important by-products of model-building activity, and participation will help to expose the blind spots of various executives about the overall operation of the marketing system.

Executives in the same company tend to see the marketing system in different terms. It is not exceptional to find executives omitting or deemphasizing critical elements in the marketing system. The cooperative attempt to build a corporate marketing model should yield, as one of its major products, a comprehensive and consensual view of the company's marketing system.

CORE SYSTEM MODEL

The most elementary marketing system is made up of a company and a market. The company is related to the market through a set of four basic flows, those shown in Exhibit 1. The company dispatches goods, services, and communications to the market; in return it receives dollars and information. The inner loop is an exchange of money for goods; the larger, outer loop is an exchange of information.

A modern marketing system includes additional institutions that play a crucial role in the operation of the system. For instance, the behavior of suppliers has many direct and indirect effects on the company's marketing program and its ability to serve its customers. Furthermore, the company typically faces competitors who are seeking to satisfy the same market needs. Between the company and its market stands a host of selling, facilitating, and consulting intermediaries who

504

EXHIBIT 1
An elementary marketing system

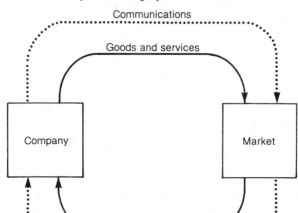

add time, place, form, and possession utility to the marketplace. Finally, all of these institutions interact with the larger social forces of public policy, economics, technology, and culture.

To illustrate these concepts, let us examine each one in relation to an actual, but disguised, company. We will assume that the company is a leading candy producer, and we want to develop the marketing model for one of its major products—a soft-centered chocolate-covered candy bar.

A diagram of the company's core marketing system can be constructed, showing the company, the market, and the linking channels of distribution (see Exhibit 2).

We assume that the company has already made a major *product-market decision* to produce and sell this candy bar. Such a decision is not made lightly or frequently; it is, rather, a *strategic* decision that is followed by sizable resource commitments to its pursuit. Only at long-run intervals will the company evaluate and decide whether to continue or drop the product.

The right side of the diagram attempts to expand the generic market underpinnings of this particular product. It can provide clues to spotting other opportunities and also to understanding the sources of competition. Thus:

A candy bar is part of a larger market, the candy market, which contains many other forms of candy that may constitute potential opportunities or threats.

EXHIBIT 2
Core marketing system model

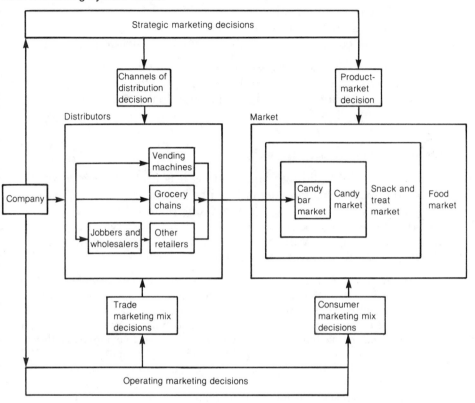

In turn, the candy market itself is embedded in a much larger market, known as the snack and treat market, which represents all
products that provide nourishment or taste satisfaction between
major meals. Seen in this light, candy is in competition with such
sundries as potato chips, soft drinks, pastry, and chewing gum.

Finally, the snack and treat market represents only a small part of
the food industry. The company must see itself as primarily in the
food business. Further analysis will reveal that the product is also
deeply involved in the pleasure market as well.

To reach candy bar consumers, the company some time ago decided
to use the three major channels of distribution shown in Exhibit 2. The
channels-of-distribution decision is another *strategic* decision that
will have a major effect on current operations. The relative importance
of these various channels has been changing through time, and management will want to periodically evaluate the channels with respect
to at least five measures of performance:

1. Relative sales volume.
2. Relative profit volume.
3. Expected growth in sales.
4. Expected growth in profits.
5. Degree of control and adaptability of each distribution channel.

Within the context of these two major strategic decisions on the product market and the channels lies the whole area of *marketing operations planning*. This company has the dual problem of developing marketing plans for the trade and for the consumers.

Strategic versus tactical decisions

From a model-building point of view, it is useful to recognize the distinction between strategic marketing decisions and tactical marketing decisions (in the marketing operations planning area). It may be that quite different models have to be built for these two categories of decisions. A General Mills executive recently articulated his view of the difference between the two as follows:

> At General Mills, our marketing activities can be classified in two basic ways. The first of these would be the *tactical operations* which are continually going on with the objective of getting the right balance between elements in the marketing mix. This type of operation can result in spending efficiencies, proper tactical responses to competitive thrust, etc. To a certain extent, you might classify it as the money-saving end of the marketing business as opposed to the money-making end of the business.
>
> We feel that the second basic marketing activity, *strategic innovation*, is probably more likely to create major increases in profit than optimizing tactical operations. At General Mills the responsibility for strategic innovation is primarily shared by the marketing groups and the R&D groups. We feel most strongly that only by creating major discontinuities in established marketing patterns are we going to be able to grow in profit at our targeted rate.[1]

Clearly, if strategic innovation involves changing the system itself, the model necessary for its evaluation may be quite different from that required for evaluating marketing operations planning that takes place within a stable system.

COMPREHENSIVE SYSTEM MODEL

The next step is to diagram the company's marketing system more comprehensively to show other marketing entities and decisions and

---

[1] H. B. Atwater, Jr., "Integrating Marketing and Other Information Systems," a paper presented to the National Industrial Conference Board, New York City, October 18, 1967, p. 7.

EXHIBIT 3
Comprehensive marketing system model

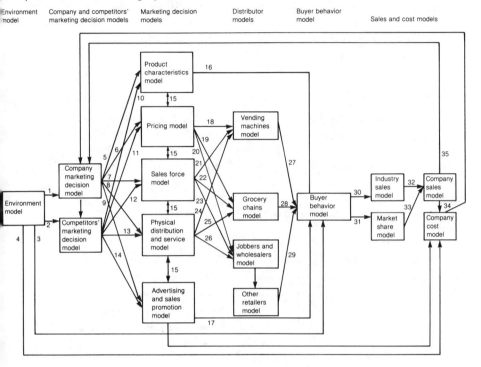

the feedback-control relationships. Exhibit 3 illustrates how such a model could be constructed for the candy company. The system is logically divided into six aspects:

1. The environment, or, more precisely, those forces in the environment that affect candy demand, such as population growth, per-capita income, attitudes toward candy, and so on.
2. The company and competitors' marketing decision models.
3. The major categories of decision making in this market—product characteristics, price, sales force, physical distribution and service, and advertising and sales promotion.
4. The three major distribution channels that the company uses for this product.
5. The buyer behavior model which shows customer response to the activities of the manufacturers and the distribution channels, as well as to the environment.
6. Total industry sales and market shares for each company.

The various arrows show the flows which connect the major elements in the marketing system. The flows are numbered for ease of reference by the company subsequently. Flow 5, for example, would refer to a detailed diagram and description showing types of product characteristic decisions, the inputs used to influence each of the decisions, the sources of data for each of the inputs, and so forth. Using this device, the company can develop a detailed documentary analysis of its marketing system.

INPUT-OUTPUT MODELS

At this stage the marketing system is further refined by preparing diagrams of the inputs and outputs shown in the boxes of Exhibit 3.

As an illustration of this technique, consider the company marketing-decision box which is singled out and featured in Exhibit 4.

EXHIBIT 4
Input-output model of company marketing decisions

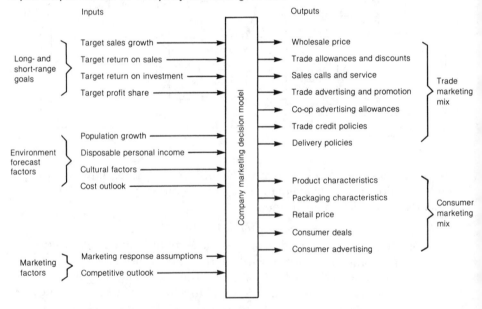

To obtain the information shown in such an exhibit, company executives are asked to list the major types of marketing decisions made in the company. A variety of answers can be expected, which again emphasizes the fact that managers in the same company carry in their heads only partial models of the total marketing system.

Note that their answers generally seem to relate to either trade decisions or consumer decisions. The two kinds of decisions are called outputs and are listed on the right side of the exhibit. To influence the trade, the company uses the wholesale price, trade allowances, sales calls and service, trade advertising, co-op advertising allowances, credit policy, and delivery policy. To influence the consumer, the company uses product characteristics, packaging characteristics, retail price, consumer deals, and consumer advertising.

Having identified the major decision outputs, management then lists the various inputs and influences on these decisions, which fall into one of three groups:

1. The company's long- and short-range goals for sales growth, return on sales, and return on investment.
2. Forecastable factors in the environment, such as population growth, disposable personal income, cultural factors, and the cost outlook.
3. Various assumptions about the sales effectiveness of different marketing instruments as well as expectations concerning competition.

The inputs listed at the left represent one possible way to classify the factors affecting the company marketing decisions listed at the right. Each input and output can be elaborated further. For example, in the area of cultural factors, it is possible to isolate three such factors that will have a significant effect on future candy consumption:

Weight-consciousness—if there is any relaxation of the pressures in American society toward the idea that "slimness is beautiful," and we return to a Peter Paul Rubens view of feminine beauty, this will lead to a substantial increase in the sales of candy.

Cavity-consciousness—as better dentrifices are developed, people will worry less about the negative effects of sugar on their teeth, and this will reduce their inhibitions against eating candy; nevertheless, worry about sugar may remain a factor, and some companies will see this as an opportunity to develop a tasty, sugarless candy which will offer the double appeal of not contributing either to tooth decay or to overweight.

Cigarette consumption—as people reduce their cigarette consumption in response to the publicity given to the health hazards, we can expect candy, gum, and other "oral" gratifiers to take the place of cigarettes.

All this adds up to the fact that the traditional economic-demographic factors used in marketing forecasting should be supplemented whenever possible with forecasts of cultural factors. Cultural forecasting, like technological and public policy forecasting, is a field that is just beginning to be developed.

510

Flow of information

Having identified the major inputs and outputs of the company marketing decision model, we now proceed to trace how these data feed into other parts of the system. Consider the output described as the trade marketing mix. This output now becomes input into each of the distribution channels—for example, the grocery chain model (Exhibit 5).

EXHIBIT 5
Input-output model of grocery-chain decisions

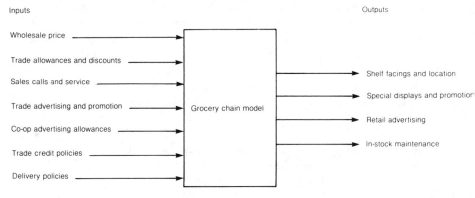

Inputs

Wholesale price

Trade allowances and discounts

Sales calls and service

Trade advertising and promotion

Co-op advertising allowances

Trade credit policies

Delivery policies

Grocery chain model

Outputs

Shelf facings and location

Special displays and promotion

Retail advertising

In-stock maintenance

The next step is to consider the major outputs of the grocery chain model—that is, the decisions which grocery chains independently make that affect the purchase rate of this candy bar. These include:

The amount and location of shelf facings that will be devoted to this candy bar product.

The extent of store cooperation in special displays and promotions.

The amount of retail advertising of this candy product that each store decides to undertake.

The policy of the stores toward maintaining good inventories and keeping the shelves filled with the product.

These are store decisions that vitally affect the sales of this candy bar through the stores, especially considering that candy bar sales have a large impulse component. The manufacturer, however, has no direct control over the stores' decisions in this area.

This is why it is vitally important to identify the factors on the left, since they represent the "handles" the manufacturer can use to influence the store decisions shown on the right. That is, the manufacturer will develop wholesale price, trade allowances, sales calls and service, trade advertising, cooperative advertising, credit policies, and delivery policies in such a way as to exert the maximum amount of influence on the grocery chains to feature its product.

The influence of the dealers' decisions on the final consumers is shown in Exhibit 6, along with influences coming from other parts of

EXHIBIT 6
Input-output model of buyer behavior

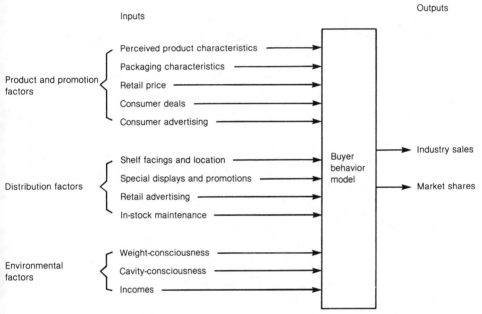

the marketing system. The various influences are classified into product and promotion factors (outputs coming from the company marketing decision model), distribution factors (outputs coming from the channels of distribution models), and environmental factors (outputs coming from the environment model). These factors shape consumers' buying behavior to bring about a certain level of industry sales and brand share sales of candy bars.[2]

FUNCTIONAL RELATIONSHIPS

I have illustrated how each model component can be analyzed in greater detail to define its inputs and outputs, and how the outputs of

[2] For a review and comparison of some recent buyer behavior models, see James F. Engel, David T. Kollat, and Roger D. Blackwell, *Consumer Behavior* (New York: Holt, Rinehart & Winston, Inc., 1968), chap. 3.

one component become the inputs to other components. The next task is to measure the functional relationships between various key elements. For instance, it is obvious that the retail price and advertising affect the rate of consumer purchase; the real task is to measure by how much.

Let us look at two examples of measured functional relationships. Part A of Exhibit 7 shows the estimated effect on candy bar sales of an important characteristic—i.e., the relative amount of chocolate (mea-

EXHIBIT 7
Functional relationship models

A. Relationship between chocolate weight percentage and sales

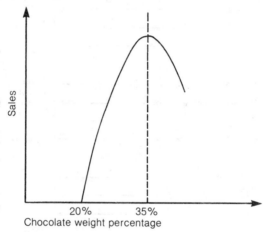

B. Relationship between deal level and sales response of different channels

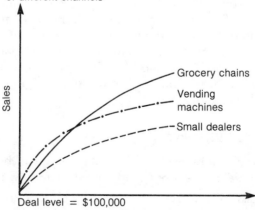

sured as a percent of the total weight of the candy bar). In our case example, the candy bar is chocolate-covered, and the question is: How thick should this chocolate covering be?

The company would like to keep this percentage down because chocolate is an expensive ingredient compared with the ingredients that make up the soft center. However, consumer tests reveal that, as the chocolate content of the bar is reduced, preference and sales decline. The soft center begins to appear through the chocolate in places and leads the average consumer to feel that the bar is poorly made. Furthermore, his palate desires more chocolate to offset the soft center.

Surprisingly, when the layer of chocolate gets too thick (above 35 percent of the weight of the bar), consumer preference for the bar also falls, but for a different reason. The consumer begins to think of this, not as a soft-centered candy bar, but as a chocolate bar with "some stuff in it." He relates this bar to pure chocolate bars, and it suffers by comparison.

To the best of management's knowledge, then, sales have the parabolic relationship to percentage chocolate weight that is shown in Part A of Exhibit 7.

Given this functional relationship, what is the optimum level of chocolate? If the company wishes to maximize sales, then chocolate should constitute 35 percent of the candy bar's weight. However, since the company is primarily interested in maximizing profit, management needs the ingredient cost functions, as well as the sales response function, to determine the profit-maximizing amount of chocolate.

Part B of Exhibit 7 shows another functional relationship—namely, the one between the amount of trade allowance (deal level) and sales. It appears that the channels of distribution differ in their response to deal offers. Small retailers are less responsive to deals than are other channels. They do not handle as high a volume, nor do they calculate as closely the profit implicit in various deals. The grocery chains, on the other hand, are quick to take advantage of deals. These functional relationships can be useful in determining the optimal allocation of deal money to the different distribution channels.

PROFIT-FORECASTING MODEL

At some point, the various functional relationships must be put together into a model for analyzing the sales and profit consequences of a proposed marketing plan. Let us first look at a graphical method of integrating major relationships in the marketing model. Then, in the following section, we will use this to develop a computerized version of the marketing model.

514

EXHIBIT 8
Profit-forecasting and planning model

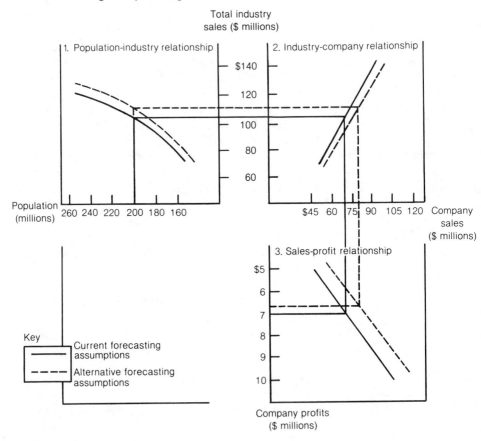

The graphical-analytical device is shown in Exhibit 8. It has been adapted for the candy company example from an idea of Robert S. Weinberg's.[3]

Quadrant 1 shows the relationship between population and the total sales of chocolate-covered soft-centered candy bars. (We are assuming for the sake of illustration that the only important environmental variable is population. If two or more environmental variables are involved, a weighted combination of them may be portrayed on this axis, or a mathematical analysis can be substituted for the graphical one.)

---

[3] "Multiple Factor Break-Even Analysis: The Applications of Operations-Research Techniques to a Basic Problem of Management Planning and Control," *Operations Research*, April 1956, pp. 152–186. (This idea has an even earlier origin in macroeconomic literature for analyzing equilibrium levels of investment and savings.)

The functional relationship shows that sales tend to increase with population, but at a decreasing rate. The part of the curve describing candy consumption for stages where the U.S. population was under 200 million is historically derived through least-squares regression analysis. The part of the curve showing sales for future sizes of the U.S. population is extrapolated and is influenced by anticipated cultural and economic trends. The curve indicates that a population of 200 million consumes approximately $105 million of soft-centered candy bars.

Quadrant 2 shows the relationship between total sales of soft-centered candy bars and company sales. When industry sales are $105 million, this particular company enjoys sales of $70 million, i.e., a market share of 67 percent. The part of the curve toward the lower level of industry sales is derived from historical information; the part toward the higher levels of sales is extrapolated on the assumption that there will be no dramatic changes in company and competitors' marketing efforts.

Although the function is linear, it does not necessarily indicate that the company expects its market share to remain constant. This would be true only if the line started at the 0,0 origin of this quadrant (not shown). Actually, the line indicates that the company expects its share of market to fall slightly as total sales increase. For example, when industry sales are $140 million, the expectation of company sales is $90 million, or an estimated market share of 64 percent, as compared with 67 percent now.

Quadrant 3 shows the relationship between company sales and company profits. Here, again, the company assumes that the relationship is basically linear. At the present time, profits are $7 million on company sales of around $70 million, or 10 percent. If company sales go up to $105 million, the company expects profits of approximately $10.2 million, i.e., 9.7 percent.

This kind of graphical device, which assumes that all the underlying relationships have been combined and expressed in terms of three basic relationships, allows us to visualize the effect of a particular level of an environmental factor and continued marketing program on company sales and profits. To this extent, it is a forecasting device.

Its use extends beyond this, however, into marketing planning as well. Suppose, for example, that the company expects the new anti-smoking campaign to have a big impact on candy bar sales, shifting the curve in Quadrant 1 higher (see Exhibit 8). Furthermore, suppose the company is considering intensifying its marketing effort to increase its market share even further. The anticipated effect of this on company market share can be seen by shifting the function in Quadrant 2 to the right. At the same time, the company's marketing costs increase, and that shifts the sales-profit curve to the right, as shown in Quadrant 3.

What is the net effect of this complicated set of shifts? The result is that, although sales have increased, profits have fallen. Apparently, the cost to the company of attaining a still higher market share exceeds the profits on the extra sales. The company would be wise not to intensify its marketing effort, at least according to the specific plan it is considering and its estimated effects.

MATHEMATICAL PROFIT MODEL

The four-quadrant profit-forecasting and -planning model helps one to visualize the impact of a complex set of developments on final company sales and profits. It is also a very useful device for explaining a forecast or a plan to others in the company. At the same time, however, it is quite limited with respect to the number of factors that can be handled directly. For more detailed modeling, we need a mathematical formulation of the candy company's marketing system.

A simplified version of such a model is shown in Exhibit 9. The starting point for any marketing planning model is an equation that expresses profits as a function of the variables under the company's control. Equation #1 shows a profit equation for Company i where profit is gross profit margin $(P - c)$ times quantity (Q), minus the fixed costs (F), advertising and promotion expenditures (A), and distribution expenditures (D). It is possible to spell out the profit equation in greater detail, but this form will suffice for illustration.

Typically, the most difficult variable to estimate is company sales (Q_i). The model builder's skill comes into play here as he tries to formulate an explanatory and predictive equation for company sales. Equation #2 is such an equation. It appears that the model builder took the easy way out by defining company sales as the product of company market share (s_i) and total sales of soft-centered candy bars (Q). However, when doing this, it is necessary to account for the two new variables, total sales and market share.

To explain total sales, we formulate the relationship shown in Equation #3. Total soft-centered candy bars sales are the products of the population (N), the per-capita candy consumption rate in pounds (k), and the ratio of soft-centered candy bar sales to total candy sales (m). But now it appears that we have traded the variable Q for three new variables. Fortunately, the three variables are fairly easy to account for exogenously. The ratio of soft-centered candy bar sales to total sales is a fairly stable number. The per-capita candy consumption rate is expected to rise asymptotically in the United States from its present level $(t = 1)$ of 18 pounds per capita to 24 pounds per capita, which

EXHIBIT 9
Mathematical sales and profit model*

#1 Company i's profit equation

$$Z_{i,t} = (P_{i,t} - c_{i,t})Q_{i,t} - F_{i,t} - A_{i,t} - D_{i,t}$$

#2 Company i's sales equation

$$Q_{i,t} = s_{i,t}Q_t$$

#3 Industry sales equation

$$Q_t = m_t k_t N_t$$

where

$$m_t = \text{Parameter}$$
$$k_t = 24(1 - 0.25^t)$$
$$N_t = 200(1.03)^t$$

#4 Market share equation

$$S_{i,t} = \frac{R_{i,t}^{e_{R,i}} P_{i,t}^{-e_{P,i}} (a_{i,t}A_{i,t})^{e_{A,i}} (d_{i,t}D_{i,t})^{e_{D,i}}}{\sum_i [R_{i,t}^{e_{R,i}} P_{i,t}^{-e_{P,i}} (a_{i,t}A_{i,t})^{e_{A,i}} (d_{i,t}D_{i,t})^{e_{D,i}}]}$$

---

* Variables:
$Z_{i,t}$ = Profits in dollars of Company i in year t
$P_{i,t}$ = Average price per lb. of Company i's product in year t
$c_{i,t}$ = Variable cost per lb. of Company i's product in year t
$Q_{i,t}$ = Number of lbs. sold of Company i's product in year t
$F_{i,t}$ = Fixed costs of manufacturing and selling Company i's product in year t
$A_{i,t}$ = Advertising and promotion costs for Company i's product in year t
$D_{i,t}$ = Distribution and sales force costs for Company i's product in year t
$s_{i,t}$ = Company i's average market share in year t
Q_t = Industry sales of soft-centered candy bars in year t
m_t = Soft-centered candy bar poundage as a share of total candy poundage
k_t = Per-capita candy consumption in lbs. in year t
N_t = Millions of persons in United States in year t
$R_{i,t}$ = Preference rating of Company i's product in year t
$a_{i,t}$ = Advertising effectiveness index
$d_{i,t}$ = Distribution effectiveness index
$e_{R,i}$ = Elasticities of preference, price, advertising, and distribution, respectively, of Company i
$e_{P,i}$
$e_{A,i}$
$e_{D,i}$

happens to be the per-capita candy consumption level of the highest candy-consuming country in the world, Great Britain. The population itself (N) is rising at the rate of 3 percent a year.

The other variable in the company's sales equation, market share, is typically the hardest of the elements to formulate; yet it is crucial in that it will reflect all of the assumptions about the company marketing decision variables.

There are several ways to formulate the equation for market share.[4] Equation #4 is one example. It shows market share as the ratio of the weighted value of the company's marketing mix to the sum of all candy companies' weighted marketing mixes. The weighted value of a marketing mix is the product of the company's effective preference level, price, advertising, and distribution raised to their respective elasticities. Further refinements can be introduced to reflect the carryover effects of past promotions. The market share model, whatever its form, must synthesize the functional relationships described earlier.

Additional refinements can and should be introduced into this model. For example, cost per pound (c) may not be constant but, rather, may vary with the scale of sales (via production), the preference rating for the company's product (to the extent that this involves better quality ingredients), and time itself, because of inflation. This means some formulation of $c = f(Q,R,t)$ would be desirable. Furthermore, fixed costs may not be independent of the level of sales and production, and therefore some formulation of the form $F = g(Q)$ might be necessary. These and other refinements are introduced as part of the evolution of the model into an increasingly accurate instrument for forecasting and planning.

The model not only must be formulated, but also must be fitted and updated according to the best available information and statistical techniques. Objective data are preferred, but, when they are not available, carefully collected subjective data may be used. The effect of uncertain data inputs on the results can be tested through sensitivity analysis.

COMPUTER MODEL AND OUTPUT

At some stage the model should be programmed for the computer and made available to management, preferably on an on-line basis. Marketing planners should be able to sit at a terminal, type in the latest research data, along with specific proposed settings of the marketing decision variables, and get back an estimate of the plan's expected sales and profits. The computer program should also contain, if possible, a subroutine which can search for the best plan possible.

For an illustration of the printout from one such computer program, see Exhibit 10. The particular model that underlies this output is much simpler than the one discussed earlier. Instead of using a sales model to derive sales estimates from planned levels of marketing decision variables, management supplies subjective estimates of sales.

---

[4] See, for example, Doyle L. Weiss, "The Determinants of Market Share," *Journal of Marketing Research*, August 1968, p. 290.

EXHIBIT 10
Sample printout from computer program

```
           INTERNAL RATE OF RETURN (AFTER TAXES) = 45              PCNT

                              TIME HORIZON = 7                     YEARS
REMAINING UNDEPR. P&E INVEST. AT BEGIN. YR.1 = 900000             DOLLARS
REMAINING NO. OF YEARS OF P&E DEPRECIATION   = 3                  YEARS
REMAINING UNDEP. BLDG INVEST. AT BEGIN. YR.1 = 210000            DOLLARS
REMAINING NO. OF YEARS OF BLDG DEPRECIATION  = 21                YEARS

      DEPRECIATION HORIZON FOR P&E INVESTMENTS  = 10              YEARS
      DEPRECIATION HORIZON FOR BLDG INVESTMENTS = 30              YEARS

      OPPORTUNITY COST (AT BEGINNING OF PERIOD) = 2.E+06         DOLLARS
                          WORKING CAPITAL = 13                   PCNT SALES
              SALVAGE VALUE (AT END OF PERIOD) = 10              X EARNINGS
```

	1 RET.PRICE($)	2 RET.MAR.(PCNT)	3 WHOLE.PRICE($)	4 WHOLE.MAR.(PCNT)
YEAR				
1969	.577	18	.473	0
1970	.602	18	.494	0
1971	.621	18	.509	0
1972	.639	18	.524	0
1973	.659	18	.54	0
1974	.675	18	.554	0
1975	.698	18	.572	0

	5 FACTORY PRICE($)	6 VARIABLE MAN. COST($)	7 VARIABLE MAN. COST(PCNT)	8 VARIABLE MKTG COST(PCNT)
1969	.473	.191	40.4	5
1970	.494	.196	39.7	5
1971	.509	.202	39.7	5
1972	.524	.208	39.7	5
1973	.54	.214	39.6	5
1974	.554	.221	39.9	5
1975	.572	.227	39.7	5

	9 CONTRIB. TO FIXED COSTS AND PROFIT ($)	10 (PCNT)	11 FIXED MAN. COST($)	12 FIXED MKTG. COST($)
YEAR				
1969	.258	54.6	915000	4.25E+06
1970	.273	55.3	971000	4.9E+06
1971	.282	55.3	1.028E+06	5.5E+06
1972	.29	55.3	1.31E+06	5.75E+06
1973	.299	55.4	1.386E+06	6.25E+06
1974	.305	55.1	1.471E+06	6.85E+06
1975	.317	55.3	1.824E+06	7.6E+06

	13 P&E INVEST.	14 BLDG.INVEST.	15 DEPREC.EXPENSE
YEAR			
1968	850000	0	
1969	0	0	395000
1970	0	0	395000
1971	850000	1.E+06	395000
1972	0	0	213333
1973	0	0	213333
1974	850000	1.E+06	213333
1975	0	0	331666

	16 INDEX OF COMPANY SALES	17 COMPANY SLS(UNITS)	18 INDUSTRY SLS(UNITS)	19 MARKET SHARE
YEAR				
1969	1	3.E+07	1.166E+09	2.6
1970	1.1	3.3E+07	1.182E+09	2.8
1971	1.2	3.6E+07	1.198E+09	3
1972	1.3	3.9E+07	1.215E+09	3.2
1973	1.4	4.2E+07	1.23E+09	3.4
1974	1.5	4.5E+07	1.247E+09	3.6
1975	1.6	4.8E+07	1.265E+09	3.8

	20 MKTG EXP.(PCNT SLS)	21 P.A.T.(PCNT SLS)	22 P.A.T.($)	23 CSH FLOW(A.T.)
YEAR				
1968				-2.85E+06
1969	34.9	7.7	1.097245E+06	-353001
1970	35.1	8.4	1.370807E+06	1.493337E+06
1971	35	8.8	1.610162E+06	-110272
1972	33.1	9.9	2.014062E+06	1.953967E+06
1973	32.5	10.4	2.361914E+06	2.281351E+06
1974	32.5	10.4	2.591395E+06	667228
1975	32.7	9.9	2.723974E+06	2.722089E+06
1976				

The printout shows the inputs and expected payoffs for a seven-year plan being considered for a cereal product. (This plan calls for the continuation of the past marketing strategy; other plans were also considered.)

The first item printed out is the calculated internal rate of return after taxes for the particular plan. (The computer program is set up to give two other payoff measures—i.e., the present value of the after-tax cash flow, and the sales and market share needed to achieve a 10 percent ROI after taxes.)

The next line shows that this calculation is for a seven-year planning horizon. Some details are then printed out on the initial value of the undepreciated plant and equipment and building investment devoted to this product line and the remaining number of years of depreciation. The depreciation horizons are also printed out, as well as the current opportunity cost of this investment and its expected salvage value at the end of the period.

The rest of the printout shows the expected or planned year-to-year levels of important variables that ultimately affect the internal rate of return. Column 1 shows the retail price per unit, which is expected to rise from $0.58 to $0.70 in the course of seven years. Column 2 shows that the retail margin for this product (18 percent) is not expected to change. Column 3 shows the resulting wholesale prices. Since this company sells direct to the retailers, there is no wholesale margin (Column 4), and the factory price (Column 5) is the same as the wholesale price.

Column 6 shows estimated variable manufacturing costs, and they too are expected to rise over the period, from a present level of $0.19 to $0.23 in 1975. The ratio of variable manufacturing costs to factory prices is shown in Column 7, followed by the planned ratio of variable marketing costs to factory prices (Column 8). Subtracting variable manufacturing and marketing costs per unit from the price, the result is the contribution to fixed costs and profits, which is shown in dollar and percentage form in Columns 9 and 10, respectively.

The next step calls for estimating fixed manufacturing costs and fixed marketing costs over the next seven years, which are shown in Columns 11 and 12. The symbol E + 06 is computer printout shorthand and means that the reader should move the decimal place, in the associated number, six places to the right. Thus $1.028E + 06 means $1,028,000. Columns 13 and 14 show the anticipated investments in plant, equipment, and building over the next seven years, and Column 15 shows the estimated total depreciation expense.

We now arrive at the estimated sales and profits. Columns 16 and 17 show management's estimates of sales (in percentage and in unit terms, respectively) over the next seven years. The figures indicate that management expects company sales (in units) to rise at the rate of about 10 percent a year, on the basis of its planned levels of marketing expenditures. Column 18 presents management's estimates of industry sales for the next seven years.

The figures in Column 19, market share, are derived by dividing estimated company sales (Column 17) by estimated industry sales (Column 18). We see that management expects market share to grow from 2.6 percent to 3.8 percent over a seven-year period. Column 20 expresses total marketing expenditures (Columns 8 and 12) as a percent of sales, and this percentage is expected to fall. Examining this more closely, we see that management expects sales to rise faster than marketing expenditures; hence it is assuming an increase in marketing productivity.

Columns 21 and 22 are a derivation of the implied yearly profits after taxes in percentage and dollar terms. The computer program uses the following formula to calculate dollar profits after taxes:

$$Z = (1 - T)(CQ - F - D)$$

where

Z = Profits after taxes
T = Tax rate
C = Contribution to fixed costs and profit
Q = Sales in units
F = Fixed manufacturing and marketing costs
D = Depreciation

For example, the profits after taxes for 1969 are: $(1 - 0.4944)$ $[(\$.258)(30,000,000) - \$5,165,000 - \$395,000]$, or $\$1,097,245$.[5]

Column 23 shows the results of the conversion of profits after taxes to cash flow after taxes. The formula for cash flow can be expressed as

$$L = Z + D - W - Y$$

where

L = Cash flow after taxes
Z = Profits after taxes
D = Depreciation
W = Working capital in dollars (i.e., working capital as a percent of sales, times wholesale price, times sales in units)
Y = New investment expenditure

---

[5] This figure is the computer output and differs slightly from the arithmetic result of the formula as presented, because of certain simplifications of input data.

For example, the cash flow after taxes for 1969 is: $1,097,245 + $395,000 − [0.13($0.473)(30,000,000)] − 0, or −$353,001.[5]

Having calculated the cash flow after taxes, the computer now calculates the internal rate of return implicit in the cash flow in Column 23. This is found by taking the opportunity cost at the beginning of the period and searching for the interest rate that would discount the future cash flows so that the sum of the discounted cash flows is equal to the initial opportunity cost; this rate turns out to be 45 percent.

Thus computer programs such as this one enable the marketing planner to determine the financial consequences implied by a particular set of costs, investments, and sales. He can easily calculate the impact on profit of any alterations in his data or assumptions. This particular computer program could be improved further by:

Including separate estimates of each marketing decision variable, rather than lumping them together as total marketing expense.

Incorporating a sales model that estimates sales analytically from the marketing plan variables and from environmental and competitive assumptions, instead of requiring direct estimation.

Introducing a subroutine for planning territorial allocations of the marketing budget.

Introducing risk explicitly into the program by including pessimistic, optimistic, and normal estimates.

Introducing a profit-maximizing algorithm which will search for the best marketing plan in the light of the assumptions and data.

CONCLUDING NOTE

In this article I have outlined one rational approach to building a model for determining and evaluating marketing strategies. With such a model for a given product within its total environment, the marketing executive can experiment with any number of detailed plans to determine the best one. While computerized models will not guarantee success in marketing, they are likely to produce better results than intuition alone.

Marketing plans will always be subject to unknown risks and so must be tempered by the judgment and experience of the decision maker. But a systematic analysis of market forces and their probable effects on a particular product will go a long way toward keeping the risks within tolerable limits.

APPENDIX
Background on corporate marketing models

For the comprehensive corporate marketing planning model, the primary source lies in the *general* model-building tradition in management science. It also has two *specific* sources that give sharp focus to the idea—the corporate financial model and the marketing game.

THE CORPORATE FINANCIAL MODEL

The corporate financial model represents a company's operations in financial terms. The concept originated in early efforts to computerize manual accounting procedures so that management would have a more efficient way to prepare and check budgets, income statements, and balance sheets.[1] The accounting relationships would be expressed in a series of equations which could be run through the computer. Soon it became clear that the computerized accounting model could be used for a number of additional purposes:

It would facilitate the preparation of alternative short-term budgets and profit plans. Many companies had previously avoided preparing alternative budgets because of the substantial man-hours required.

It also could aid in forecasting the financial effects of different long-term investment strategies. This use was picked up quickly by the electric utility companies that needed a tool to help estimate the financial consequences of alternative capacity expansion plans. Early models were built for the Boston Edison Company[2] and the Philadelphia Electric Company.[3] More recently, companies in the oil industry, particularly Sun Oil[4] and Standard Oil of New Jersey,[5] have pioneered large-scale corporate financial models.

---

[1] See Richard Mattessich, "Budgeting Models and System Simulation," *Accounting Review*, July 1961, p. 384.

[2] John M. Kohlmeier, *An Analysis of Some Aspects of Capital Budgeting Policy, A Simulation Approach,* an unpublished doctoral dissertation at the Harvard Business School, 1964.

[3] Joseph K. Furst and Marvin H. Porter, "Computerized Corporate Planning Model," a paper presented at the ORSA/TIMS Joint Meeting, San Francisco, May 1–3, 1968.

[4] George W. Gershefski, "Building a Corporate Financial Model," *Harvard Business Review*, July–August 1969, p. 61.

[5] D. K. Abe, "Corporate Model System for Planning," a paper presented at the TIMS International Meeting, New York, March 27, 1969.

THE MARKETING GAME

The other source of the corporate marketing model idea is the marketing game. Such games were originally developed as a pedagogical tool to put players through a simulated business experience. It was expected that the players would gain a number of insights into business decision making not available through textbook study or case discussion.

More recently, investigators have realized that gaming could serve research purposes as well. Benefits could arise both in attempting to design realistic marketing games and in studying the organizational and decision behavior of the players during the game. From this, it was a small step to recognize the potential conversion of complex games into company planning models.

The early marketing games were very simple in design, consisting usually of one product, one territory, and only a few marketing instruments, such as pricing and advertising. The sales response functions were artificially developed. More recently, however, games have been designed around specific industries and have been backed up by considerable research into the industries' behavior.

The first version of such a game will usually strike actual decision makers in the industry as oversimplified and sometimes behaviorally incorrect. The game designers will then revise it, and, after several cycles of criticism and revision, the final game will emerge as a complicated and realistic model of the industry. It is at this point that some executives will begin to recognize the potential uses of the game for marketing planning purposes.

Following are brief reviews of two outstanding games which show the variety of mechanisms and approaches that can be taken.[6]

Carnegie Tech's marketing game

One of the first and most fully developed business games is the Carnegie Tech Management Game, created by faculty members at the Graduate School of Industrial Administration, Carnegie-Mellon University.[7] A special version, called MATE (Marketing Analysis Training

---

[6] In addition to the two games described, several others deserve mention: D. C. Basil, P. R. Cone, and J. A. Fleming, *Executive Decision Making through Simulation: A Case Study and Simulation of Corporate Strategy in the Rubber Industry* (Columbus, Ohio: Charles E. Merrill Publishing Company, 1965); R. E. Schellenberger, *Development of a Computerized, Multipurpose Retail Management Game* (Chapel, Hill, Graduate School of Business, University of North Carolina, 1965), Research Paper No. 14; W. B. Kehl, "Techniques in Constructing a Market Simulator," in *Marketing: A Maturing Discipline*, ed. Martin L. Bell (Chicago: American Marketing Association, 1961), p. 85.

[7] Kalman J. Cohen, et al., *The Carnegie Tech Management Game.* (Homewood, Ill., Richard D. Irwin, Inc., 1964).

Exercise) and developed by Alfred A. Kuehn and Doyle L. Weiss,[8] shows the marketing operation in more detail while simplifying the production and financial aspects of the original game.

MATE involves three companies in the packaged detergent industry, operating in four geographical regions. Each company may market from one to three brands of detergent in each of the four regions. Once a month the company may establish or alter price, advertising expenditures, sales force size, call-time allocation to the brands, and retail allowance.

The company may also purchase market survey reports containing estimates of total retail sales and market shares, of retail distribution and stockouts, and of competitive advertising expenditures. These estimates are subject to an amount of error that varies with the funds appropriated for each survey and with chance factors. Furthermore, the company can invest in product research to find new and better products or to imitate competitors' products, with the results also depending on how much it invests and on chance factors.

On the nonmarketing side, the company owns one factory and a factory warehouse, and rents factory space in each marketing region. Products may be shipped directly from the factory to the regional warehouses or stored in the factory warehouse, with the decision depending on the respective costs. Each month the company decides how much to produce, subject to availability of funds to pay for this level of production and subject to capacity limitations. The company may seek additional funds to augment its working capital, and this must be approved by the game administrator. At the end of each month the decision makers receive financial and accounting information on monthly sales, cost of goods sold, and operating expenses and profit.

M.I.T. marketing game

The M.I.T. Marketing Game also models a complex and realistic marketing environment.[9] Involving electric floor polishers for household use, this game requires the players to determine product quality, price, dealer margins, channels of distribution (including number and type of dealers), market area, advertising expenditures, advertising media and appeals, number and deployment of salesmen, and promotions within the retail store.

Like the Carnegie Tech game, the M.I.T. game is designed as a training device, specifically for use in advanced marketing manage-

---

[8] "Marketing Analysis Training Exercise," *Behavioral Science*, January 1965, p. 51.

[9] Peter S. King, et al., "The M.I.T. Marketing Game," in *Marketing: A Maturing Discipline*, p. 85.

ment courses. But, in contrast to most other business games, the M.I.T. simulation requires the players to make some qualitative as well as quantitative decisions. For example, players of the M.I.T. game must develop advertising plans and copy for their product which are subsequently given a quantitative rating by a control team.

Industry sales are determined by adjusting exogenously determined "normal sales" for the effects of price, promotion, and retail margins. Market share for each company is a function of competitive prices, distribution policies, and advertising. Company sales are determined by multiplying total industry sales by market share.

The control team ratings enter the model through certain "effectiveness functions" that adjust the sales figures for the quality of the respective company marketing programs. While the control team's ratings are subjective, they provide an analogue of the subjective appraisal of real marketing programs by real customers. This overcomes a criticism that has been directed at most business games—that they stress only the dollar allocation dimensions of competition and not the bright ideas that could make for a brilliant advertising campaign or marketing strategy.

CORPORATE MARKETING MODELS

The example provided by corporate financial models and industry-based marketing games has led some companies to attempt to construct a corporate marketing model. One of the best-known examples is the Xerox Corporation's work on MARS (Marketing Analysis Research System). See Figure A, where the overall model, which consists of six component models, is shown. MARS as a whole is still under development, and many adjustments and changes will no doubt

FIGURE A
Xerox marketing analysis research system for MARS project

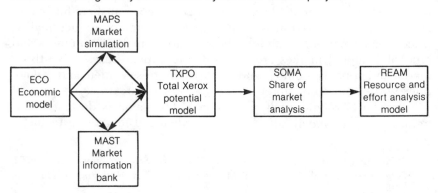

be made before it becomes fully operational. Nevertheless, its designers testify to many benefits that have already been yielded in decision making and information gathering by the effort to design this model.

Here are a few other corporate marketing models:

The Minute Maid Company's forecasting planning model for frozen orange concentrate relates sales to such marketing variables as the case price, advertising budget, and sales commission rate.[10]

The Arthur D. Little Company helped develop a market model of the fertilizer industry for forecasting long-run demand for different fertilizers.[11]

Henry J. Claycamp and Arnold E. Amstutz helped develop for the LaRoche Company a complex model for simulating the effect of different marketing plans, involving detail men, media promotion, and direct mail promotion, on the rate of prescription drug sales for specific products.[12]

A. M. Economos describes a model for evaluating the future of the computer-leasing business in view of the uncertainty of such factors as the rate of market growth, the year of the introduction of fourth-generation computers, and the year of the decision of computer manufacturers to impede the growth of the leasing industry.[13]

E. I. duPont de Nemours & Company has developed several simulations of specific markets and marketing plans under the general name of venture analysis.[14]

---

[10] Stanley Buchin and Ray A. Goldberg, "A Model of the Florida Orange Industry for Minute Maid Planning" (Boston: Harvard Business School, December 1968), AI 270.

[11] George B. Hegeman, "Dynamic Simulation for Market Planning," *Chemical and Engineering News*, January 4, 1965, p. 64.

[12] "Simulation Techniques in the Analysis of Marketing Strategy," in *Applications of the Sciences in Marketing Management*, ed. Frank M. Bass, et al. (New York: John Wiley & Sons, Inc., 1968), p. 113.

[13] "A Financial Simulation for Risk Analysis of a Proposed Subsidiary," *Management Science*, August 1968, pp. B-675–82.

[14] Sigurd L. Andersen, "Venture Analysis: A Flexible Planning Tool," *Chemical Engineering Progress*, March 1961, p. 80.

Reading 8–6

Management science and business practice

C. JACKSON GRAYSON, JR.

"What we need to do is humanize the scientist and simonize the humanist." This dictum is a popularization of C. P. Snow's view of science and the humanities as two distinct cultures, and it is all too true when applied to management. Managers and management scientists are operating as two separate cultures, each with its own goals, languages, and methods. Effective cooperation—and even communication—between the two is just about minimal. And this is a shame.

Each has much to learn from the other, and much to teach the other. Yet, despite all kinds of efforts over the years, it seems to me that the cultural and operating gap which exists between the two is not being closed. Why?

I can offer some explanations, based on my years as an academician, consultant, businessman, and, most recently, head of an organization with control over a large part of our economy—the Price Commission. I can also suggest a way to build the bridge so badly needed between the two cultures and the people who make them up. This bridge must span the gap between two quite different types:

The management scientists. As people, they want to help managers make decision making more explicit, more systematic, and *better* by using scientific methodology, principally mathematics and statistics. They can be found largely in universities and in staff operations of enterprises. They may belong to any of a number of professional associations, such as The Institute of Management Sciences (TIMS), Operations Research Society of America (ORSA), and the American Institute for Decision Sciences (AIDS).

The managers. They make and implement decisions, largely by rough rules of thumb and intuition. They are the operating executives, found principally in the line.

The lines of distinction are never so pure, but most people, I believe, understand what I mean.

What I have to offer to the management scientists is a few bouquets and then a load of bricks. First, the bouquets:

Management scientists have had *some* impact on real-world operations and managers.

Some management science tools have been successfully applied in accounting, finance, production, distribution, and weapons systems.

Managers do tend to give a little more conscious thought to their decision making than in previous years—but still precious little.

By indicating how abysmal our knowledge is about decision making, management scientists have highlighted areas for further research.

Both the faculty and the students at business schools have gained some added prestige in the business and academic communities for being more "scientific."

And now the bricks. The total impact of management science has been extremely small. Its contribution looks even smaller than it is if one compares it to the revolution promised for management offices in the early years. And the "wait-until-next-generation" theme is wearing thinner and thinner.

Let me quickly acknowledge that there are *some* management scientists who operate effectively in both cultures. But they are rare birds. Most management scientists are still thinking, writing, and operating in a world that is far removed from the real world in which most managers operate (and in which I personally have been operating). They often describe and structure nonexistent management problems, tackle relatively minor problems with overkill tools, omit real variables from messy problems, and build elegant models comprehensible to only their colleagues. And when managers seem confused or dissatisfied with the results of their activities and reject them, these scientists seem almost to take satisfaction in this confirmation of the crudity and inelegance of the managerial world.

Have I overdrawn the picture? Only very slightly.

WHY THE GULF?

I do not mean to say that management scientists have purposefully created this cultural gap. Most of them feel that much of what they are doing today is really helpful to managers. But I'm afraid it simply isn't so. Others argue that much of what they are doing is "pure research," which will be useful one day. I do not discount the value of pure research; some of it is needed. But the fact remains that only a small fraction of management science "results" are being used.

Those management scientists who do acknowledge a gap often excuse it by one of two reasons:

"The manager doesn't understand the power of the tools."

"He isn't sympathetic to systematic decision making and would rather fly by the seat of his pants because this is safer for his ego."

I myself am a counterexample to both these excuses. I have had some fairly good training in management science. I have done research in the area and written a book urging the use of more explicit decision tools in a specific industry—oil well drilling.[1] I have taught various courses in the area, for example, in statistics, management control systems, and quantitative analysis.

And yet, in the most challenging assignment of my life—putting together the Price Commission—I used absolutely *none* of the management science tools explicitly. One might think that in the task of developing an organization of 600 people (mostly professionals), creating a program to control prices in a trillion-dollar economy, and making decisions that involve costs, volume, prices, productivity, resource allocations, elasticities, multiple goals, trade-offs, predictions, politics, and risk values, an expert would have found ways to use his familiarity with management science to advantage. I did not.

A defender of the faith will quickly say that, although I did not use them explicitly, I probably used them *implicitly*, and that they helped to discipline my approach to decision making. I agree that this is probably true. But I nevertheless think it is a damning indictment that I can identify *no* incident of a conscious, explicit use of a single management science tool in my activities as head of the Price Commission.

Further, my conscience is clear. To my mind there are five very valid reasons for my rejecting the idea of using management science.

Shortage of time

Although I thought about using management science tools on many occasions, I consistently decided against it because of the shortage of time. Management scientists simply do not sufficiently understand the constraint of time on decision making, and particularly on decisions that count; and the techniques they develop reflect that fact. They may write about time as a limitation. They may admonish managers for letting time push them into a "crisis" mode. They may recognize the

---

[1] *Decisions Under Uncertainty* (Boston: Division of Research, Harvard Business School, 1960).

constraint of time with a few words and comment on its influence. They may say that they, too, experience time constraints. But their techniques are so time-consuming to use that managers pass them by.

Does this mean that all management science work ought to be thrown into shredders? No, it simply means that management scientists (a) need to get out of their relatively unpressured worlds and *experience* the impact of time on the decision-making process, and (b) need to build the time factor into models instead of leaving it as an exogenous variable.

Inaccessibility of data

The second reason for ignoring management science in practice is related to the time problem. A manager will ordinarily use data or a management science tool only if both are conveniently, speedily accessible. If he is told that the needed data are buried in another part of the organization, or that they must be compiled, or that the model must be created, nine times out of ten he will say, "Skip it." I did, ten times out of ten.

True, many management scientists would say that I must have developed "trade-offs" in my mind, weighing the cost of obtaining data or building a model against the probable opportunity payoff, and that my mental calculator ground out negative responses on each occasion. This is perfectly plausible. Unconsciously I probably did build a number of such informal investment-payoff models.

But where does this leave us? It leaves us with management scientists continuing to construct models that call for substantial investments in design and data collection and managers discarding them. The statement is made ad nauseam that most data are not in the forms that most models call for, or that they are not complete; yet the management scientists go right on calling for inaccessible, nonexistent, or uncompiled data to suit "theoretically correct" models. And hence managers continue to say, "Skip it."

Instead of asking a manager to lie in the Procrustean bed of the theoretically correct model, why shouldn't the management scientist design a realistic model, or a realistic part of a model, or come up with a realistic data prescription? The result might be extremely crude; it might embarrass a theoretician; it might be shot down by the purist and the theoretician. But it just might be *used*.

Resistance to change

The third reason that I did not use management science tools explicitly is that educating others in the organization who are not familiar with the tools, and who would resist using them if they were, is just too difficult a task. Management scientists typically regard this problem as outside the scope of their jobs—at most, they remark on the need to educate more people and to change organizations so they become more scientific. Or, if they *do* recognize the problem, they grossly underestimate the time and organizational effort needed to "educate and change." I suggest that management scientists do two things:

1. They should build into their models some explicit recognition of the financial and emotional cost of change of this kind and make explicit allowance for the drag of change resistance. I am quite aware that some change techniques are being used: sensitivity training, Esalen-type devices, management by objectives, quantitative analysis courses for managers, and so on. I have used them myself, and I know that they help. But the magnitude of time and energy required to install them is not generally appreciated—certainly not by management scientists—and their impact is highly overrated.

2. They should get themselves some education and direct experience in the power, politics, and change-resistance factors in the real world of management so they can better incorporate the imperfect human variables in their work.

Long response time

Fourth, few management science people are geared up to respond to significant management problems in "real time." Management science people in universities live largely by the school calendar, and if they receive a request for help, they are likely to respond in terms of next semester, next September, or after exams. And once again the manager is likely to say, "Skip it." Even most management science personnel in staff positions of live organizations operate in a time frame that is slower than that of the line managers. It is their nature to approach a problem in a methodical, thorough way, even when the required response time dictates that they come up with a "quick and dirty" solution.

Invalidating simplifications

Fifth, and finally, it is standard operating procedure for most management science people to strip away so much of a real problem with "simplifying assumptions" that the remaining carcass of the problem and its attendant solution bear little resemblance to the reality with which the manager must deal. The time constraints, the data-availability questions, the people problems, the power structures, and the political pressures—all the important, nasty areas that lie close to the essence of management—are simplified out of existence so that a technically beautiful, and useless, resolution may be achieved.

This is somewhat paradoxical since management science originated in wartime Britain, when many interdisciplinary talents were forced into combination to grapple with the problems of total mobilization. That situation tolerated no fumbling around. But in subsequent years management science has retreated from the immediate demands for workable results. It has increased its use of the hard sciences of mathematics and statistics, hardening itself with methodological complexity, weakening its own reliance on the softer sciences of psychology, sociology, and political science, and losing the plain, hardheaded pragmatism with which it started out.

Realizing this, many managers think it pointless to turn the really important problems over to management science. Their experience has shown them the impotence of emasculated solutions.

At the risk of repeating a tired joke, let me recall the story of the man who said he had a way to destroy all the enemy submarines in the Atlantic during World War II: "Boil the ocean." Asked next how he would do this, he replied, "That's your problem." Similarly, when managers ask management scientists how to solve a problem, they too often say, in effect, "Boil the company." They leave it to the manager to worry about shortages of time, inaccessibility of data, resistance to change, slow response times, and oversimplified solutions.

FIRING THE FURNACE

At the Price Commission we operated, I think fairly successfully, without getting the data we "should" have had, without using any explicit decision tools, without once formally consulting a management scientist, and without building models of our decision-making processes. I am not especially proud of these facts; I am a member, and an intellectually loyal member, of ORSA, TIMS, and AIDS. I believe in the general direction in which these organizations want to go. But I also have a personal dedication to action, a sense of the urgency and immediacy of real problems, and a disbelief in the genuine responsiveness of management science models to my managerial needs.

I have asked myself the question whether we might have done better by using some management science models, and my honest answer is *no*. Using models would have slowed decision making. It would have frustrated most of our personnel. Given the fact that most models omit the factors of time, data accessibility, people, power, and politics, they simply would not have provided sufficient predictive or prescriptive payoff for the required investment of energy.

Consider the severity of the demands that were made. Establishment of the Price Commission required fulfillment of seemingly impossible tasks and directives:

Create and staff a fully competent organization.

Work out regulations worthy to bear the force of law.

Keep the program consistent with policies established in Phase I and the current state of the economy.

Work in conjunction with the Pay Board, the Internal Revenue Service, and the Cost of Living Council.

Control the prices of hundreds of millions of articles and commodities in the world's largest economy.

Do not inhibit the recovery of the economy.

Do not build a postcontrol bubble.

Do all of this with a regulatory staff of 600.

Have the entire operation functioning in 16 days.

A natural first reaction to such demands might well have been General McAuliffe's famous one-word response: "Nuts!" It would have been very easy to point out, for example, that:

Nobody could begin to do the job of price control with 600 people, even with the services of 3,000 Internal Revenue Service agents to help with enforcement. It had taken 60,000 people to handle the assignment in World War II and 17,000 in the Korean War.

To do the job right would require a thoroughgoing study of what was involved—the resources and kinds of personnel required, the most efficient way of actually controlling prices, the optimum method of working in concert with other federal agencies—as well as the accumulation of data about the economy and the testing of various models.

The 16-day period was too short. There was not enough time to get the Price Commission appointed, let alone to build, organize, and house the right kind of staff, promulgate regulations, and get it all functioning.

I might have pointed out these things and many others. I did not. I simply starting bringing in staff, renting quarters, creating an organization, framing regulations, and developing a modus operandi. In 16 days the organization was accepting requests for price increases from U.S. business; the staff was at work—in some cases eight to an office, four to a telephone, and a good many spending up to 20 hours a day on the job.

I cite this record not to boast. Our achievement did not grow out of extraordinary capability. It was simply a matter of orientation and intuition—orientation and intuition toward action. But just as managers incline toward intuition and action, management scientists incline toward reflective thinking. They tend to be scholarly, less action-oriented, and averse to taking risks—even risk of criticism from their peers. They dissect and analyze, they are individualistic, and they are prone to trace ideas much as one can trace power flows in a mechanical system, from gear to belt to gear. They have not cared much about firing the furnace that makes the steam that drives the gear in the first place.

The manager offers an almost complete contrast. He integrates and synthesizes; he sees situations as mosaics; his thoughts and decision processes are like electrical circuits so complex you can never be sure how much current is flowing where. At the core of his value system are depth and breadth of experience, which he may even permit to outweigh facts where the whole picture seems to justify it.

For his part, the management scientist tends to optimize the precision of a tool at the expense of the health and performance of the whole. He has faith in some day building ultimate tools and devising ultimate measurements, and this lies at the foundation of his values and beliefs.

The problem, then, boils down to two cultures—the managers' and the management scientists'—and not enough bridges between them. Somebody has to build the bridges.

WHO SHALL BUILD THE BRIDGES?

Closing any gap requires that one or both cultures change. It is my strong belief that the management scientist must move first, and most. *The end product is supposed to be management, after all, not management science.* Further, as a philosophical point, I think science has greater relevance to our world if it moves constantly toward art (in this case the management art) than the other way around. Then, instead of moving toward increased and separated specialization, both evolve toward a mature symbiosis, a working and dynamic unity of the kind found in successful marriages, détentes, and mergers.

The management scientist is not going to find it easy or comfortable to change, and yet it is he who must change most in attitude, action, and life style. He is going to have to think in terms of the *manager's* perceptions, the *manager's* needs, the *manager's* expectations, and the *manager's* pressures—that is, if he wants to have impact in the real world of the manager. If not, he will go on missing the mark.

What, concretely, can be done? Let me offer a few suggestions to the management science people and the managers they are supposed to be helping.

Inside operating organizations

First, top management should not isolate the management science people but sprinkle them throughout the organization in situations where they can really go to work. It should give them *line* responsibility for results. Their natural tendencies will cause them to flock together at night or on weekends to compare and refine tools, and that, again, is as it should be; but their prime responsibility should be to the line unit, not to a management science group. To put the matter another way: management should not think of having an operating person on a management science team—it should think of having a management scientist on an operating team.

Second, managers, should demand implementation by management scientists; they should not tolerate "package" solutions that leave out the complicating factors. In that way, managers can avoid simplistic, unworkable solutions that ignore the factors of time, data accessibility, unwillingness of people to change, power, and so on.

Third, even when professional management scientists are brought into companies as consultants, they are often given the easy, old problems, for the reasons that I have named. This expectational cycle has to be broken.

At the university

The same general approach is valid within universities.

First, both management science faculty and students have to get out of the isolated, insulated world of academe. They must go beyond structured cases and lectures and become directly involved in real-world, real-time, live projects, not as a way of applying what they know, but as a way of learning.

It is a mistake to teach the student linear programming or decision theory and then search for a problem to which the tool can be applied. That creates the classic academic situation from which managers are revolting—the tool in search of a problem. Instead, tackle the *real* problem. This will be frustrating, but the frustration of trying to reach a *workable* solution can be used to teach the management scientist or student in a way that is useful both to him and to the business or government unit. The solutions thus derived may not be so elegant as they might be, but they may be used. The student who wants to reach for higher, more sophisticated theories should be treated as a special case, not the general case.

Second, management science people should stop tackling the neat, simple problems, or refining approaches to problems already solved. These projects may be easier, but working and reworking them will not help bridge the cultural gap I am talking about. Instead, tackle the *tough* problem. The management of time pressure and the use of the persuasion and negotiation required by a real, tough problem will give both the faculty member and the student some salutary discipline in convincing others to follow a strange idea, to cooperate, and to listen.

The best example of what I am describing occurred at Case Institute in the early days of Russell L. Ackoff, E. L. Arnoff, and C. West Churchman. There, faculty and student teams worked on real problems in real time in real business settings. That example does not seem to have caught on at other universities, partly because of the difficulty of doing it, and partly because it flies against the nature of the management science personality that I have described. The process is messy, people-populated, schedule-disrupting, time-demanding, and complicated by power and politics. That is exactly as it should be.

Third, faculty members should plan to get out of the university, physically and completely, for meaningful periods of time. They should plan their careers so that they schedule at least a year, periodically, in which they get direct, real-world experience in business, nonprofit organizations, or the government.

One helpful device with which I am familiar is the Presidential Personnel Interchange Program of the federal government, now in its third year. So far this year it has brought 60 business executives into government work and 18 federal government managers into business. These numbers should be expanded tremendously, and the organizations involved should include universities. The universities could well join in a three-way interchange, or start their own program with business.

Finally, universities should bring in real managers and involve them directly in problem-solving and joint-learning sessions. Doctors expect to return to medical school as part of their normal development; so should managers. The universities can offer managers an update in science; corporate managers can offer universities an update in management.

These are some of the ways to build bridges. There are other ways to tear them down, or to maintain the gap. Jargon, for example, will drive away managers. So will intellectual snobbery toward "intuitive" decision making. Management scientists should dispense with both. Managers can maintain the gap by continuing to refer to past disillusionments and never allowing management science people to tackle executive-suite programs. Managers should recognize that. In fact, defensive behavior on the part of either group can block reconciliation and progress.

People *do* exist who effectively bridge the two cultures. Such people do not always bear an identifying brand; one cannot distinguish them by their degrees, university course credits, titles, experience, or even home base. But they do have one strong, overriding characteristic—they are *problem- and action-oriented.* They are essentially unicultural; they employ a healthy mix of science and intuition in their decision making.

WORDS TO THE WISE

I am not suggesting that the two specializations—management science and management—be destroyed. Primary bases and modes of operation can be preserved, provided that both groups are receptive to and understanding of the other's basic orientation, and that they work together in harmony, not in dissonance. And all should remember that the problem is the thing, not the methodology; the function, not the form.

My slings and arrows have been directed mostly toward management science—rightly so, I think. But managers must assist in the bridge-building process:

They should stop recounting tales of how "they never laid a glove on me" in encounters with management scientists. They should make it a point of future pride to use management science.

They should make available the real nasty, complicated decisions to management scientists.

They should not expect a lot.

They should not deride small gains.

They should hold any management science approach or individual accountable for producing *results,* not recommendations.

The management science people must play their part, too:

Get out of the monasteries, whether these are universities or staff departments.

Submerge the paraphernalia (journal articles, computer programs, cookbooks) and rituals ("sounds like a linear programming program to me" or "we need to get the facts first").

Put people, time, power, data accessibility, and response times into models and create crude, workable solutions.

Learn to live with and in the real world of managers.

Again, I submit it is the management science people who will have to change most. They should take the first step toward closing the gap between the two cultures. The consequences can only be better for managers, for management science, and for the problem itself.

Models and managers: The concept of a decision calculus

JOHN D. C. LITTLE*

1. INTRODUCTION

The big problem with management science models is that managers practically never use them. There have been a few applications, of course, but the practice is a pallid picture of the promise. Much of the difficulty lies in implementation and an especially critical aspect of this is the meeting between manager and model. I believe that communication across this interface today is almost nil and that the situation stands as a major impediment to successful use of models by managers. Furthermore I want to suggest that the requirements of the interface have implications for the design of the model itself.

As an area to illustrate the ideas presented, we shall use marketing. This field well demonstrates the problems and opportunities at hand. Marketing has high managerial content in the sense that decisions are often non-routine and usually require a bringing together of people, ideas, data, and judgments from diverse sources. Although something is known about underlying processes, much uncertainty remains to confront the manager. Data are prolific but usually poorly digested, often irrelevant, and some key issues entirely lack the illumination of measurement. At the same time, marketing is of interest for its own sake. This is not only because of its key and sometimes controversial role in the society but also because fundamental knowledge in market-

* This is the eighth in a series of 12 expository papers commissioned by the Office of Naval Research and the Army Research Office under contract numbers Nonr-4004(00) and DA 49-092-ARO-16 respectively. The underlying research was supported in part by a grant from the Mobil Oil Corporation and in part by the Army Research Office under contract number DA-31-124-ARO-D-209. The author wishes to acknowledge the contribution of several unidentified product managers who provided their time and enthusiasm for the example reported. An earlier version of the paper was delivered at the TIMS/University of Chicago Symposium on Behavioral and Management Science in Marketing in June 1969.

Source: *Management Science*, vol. 16, no. 8, April 1970.

ing has application beyond business into the marketing-like activities of governments, universities, hospitals, and other organizations.

The terms "manager" and "decision" will be used frequently. Let it be noted now that a "manager" is frequently a fuzzy, shifting mix of people and a "decision" is usually a murky event, identifiable only in retrospect.

The paper is organized under the following headings: (1) Introduction, (2) What's wrong? (3) How do managers use models? (4) What might be right? (5) An example from marketing, (6) What happened to science? and (7) Conclusions.

2. WHAT'S WRONG?

Some of the reasons that models are not used more widely by managers appear to be:

1. *Good models are hard to find.* Convincing models that include the manager's control variables and so contain direct implications for action are relatively difficult to build, particularly in the areas that are of greatest concern. Some progress, however, is certainly being made. In marketing, for example, see Montgomery and Urban.[1]

2. *Good parameterization is even harder.* Measurements and data are needed. They require high-quality work at the design stage and are often expensive to carry out.

3. *Managers don't understand the models.* People tend to reject what they do not understand. The manager carries responsibility for outcomes. We should not be surprised if he prefers a simple analysis that he can grasp, even though it may have a qualitative structure, broad assumptions, and only a little relevant data, to a complex model whose assumptions may be partially hidden or couched in jargon and whose parameters may be the result of obscure statistical manipulations.

Typically the manager is willing and eager to accept flawless work that delivers the future to him with certainty. Unfortunately as he digs into any study performed by human researchers in an ordinary OR group, he finds assumptions that seem questionable, terminology that is confusing, and a certain tendency to ignore a variety of qualitative issues the manager feels are important. The manager feels that to get deep into the model and find out what is really going on is totally out of the question because he lacks the time and background. The solution to this predicament is often for him to pick on some seeming flaw in the

---

[1] D. B. Montgomery and G. L. Urban, *Applications of Management Science in Marketing* (Englewood Cliffs, N.J. Prentice-Hall, 1970).

model, usually a consideration left out, and make that the basis for postponing use into the indefinite future.

In this situation the operations researcher's response is often to conclude that his model is not complete enough. Therefore he goes back to work to make things more complicated and probably harder to understand. Meanwhile the manager continues to use intuitive models that are much simpler than the one rejected.

I might point out the professional OR/management science fraternity also escalates the model builder into complexity. A favorite pastime in the trade is to tell a model builder, "You left such and such out."

Some people have asked why it is necessary for a manager to understand the models he uses. After all, most of us drive cars and few of us understand the details of an internal combustion engine. An R&D manager is not expected to follow the technical niceties of the work being done in his labs. However, I would argue that the kind of understanding that is required is defined relative to the job. As drivers we had better understand what will happen when we turn the steering wheel even though we do not need to know how to repair the brakes. The R&D manager had better be able to tell effective teams from ineffective ones, but this will not usually require him to be a specialist in laboratory technique. The marketing manager should understand a marketing model in the sense of knowing very well what to expect from it but need not know the details of its computer program.

4. *Most models are incomplete.* Having complained about complexity as a bar to understanding, I now decry incompleteness. This means that I hope we can invent simple models that have the capacity to include quite a few phenomena.

Incompleteness is a serious danger if a model is used for optimization. Optimization can drive control variables to absurd values if critical phenomena are omitted. One popular answer to this difficulty is not to optimize. Sometimes this is the right thing to do—we should say out loud the model provides only part of the decision-making information and that the rest must come from elsewhere. However, in most cases we want to be able to evaluate and compare. This is embryonic optimization and incompleteness can be a pitfall.

The above list of obstacles of implementation could be extended but should suffice to ward off complacency.

3. HOW DO MANAGERS USE MODELS?

Here is an impression, albeit anecdotal, of how managers actually use models.

The OR Group of a major oil company recently did a survey on the use of mathematical programming in production scheduling at their refineries. Refinery scheduling was a pioneer application of mathematical programming and has been an active research area for 10–15 years. At one refinery the dialogue between the interviewer and the local OR analyst went somewhat as follows:

Interviewer: Do you make regular mathematical programming runs for scheduling the refinery?

Analyst: Oh yes.

Interviewer: Do you implement the results?

Analyst: Oh no!

Interviewer: Well, that seems odd. If you don't implement the results, perhaps you should stop making the runs?

Analyst: No. No. We wouldn't want to do that!

Interviewer: Why not?

Analyst: Well, what happens is something like this: I make several computer runs and take them to the plant manager. He is responsible for this whole multi-million dollar plumber's paradise.

   The plant manager looks at the runs, thinks about them for a while and then sends me back to make a few more with conditions changed in various ways. I do this and bring them in. He looks at them and probably sends me back to make more runs. And so forth.

Interviewer: How long does this keep up?

Analyst: I would say it continues until, finally, the plant manager screws up enough courage to make a decision.

What is the plant manager doing here? Before speculating on this, let me recount some experiences with people using MEDIAC, a media planning model developed by L. M. Lodish and myself.[2] The first step in using the model is preparing the input data. This requires a fair amount of reflection about the problem at hand, a certain effort spent digging out numbers, and usually subjective estimates of several quantities. Thereafter, the model is run and a schedule is generated.

The user looks at the schedule and immediately starts to consider whether it makes sense to him or not. Is it about what he expected? Sometimes it is and, if so, usually that is that. Oftentimes, however, the schedule does not quite agree with his intuition. It may even differ substantially. Then he wants to know why. A process starts of finding

---

[2] J. D. C. Little and L. M. Lodish, "A Media Planning Calculus," *Operations Research*, vol. 17, January–February 1969, pp. 1–35.

out what it was about the inputs that made the outputs come out as they did. This usually can be discovered without too much difficulty by a combination of inspection, consideration of how the model works, and various sensitivity analyses.

Having done this, the user decides whether he is willing to go along with the results as they came out. If not, he can, for example, change the problem formulation in various ways or possibly change his subjective estimates. Sometimes he finds outright errors in the input data. Most of the time, however, if he has been careful in his data preparation, he will agree with the reasons for the answers coming out as they did and he has, in fact, learned something new about his problem. The whole process might be described as an updating of his intuition. The model has served the function of interrelating a number of factors and, in this case, not all the implications of the interrelations were evident to him when he started.

Notice, incidentally, that he has by no means turned over his decision making to the computer. He remains the boss and demands explanations from his electronic helper.

I believe the same type of process is going on with the plant manager in the earlier example. He is involved in an analysis-education-decision process built around man-model-machine interaction in which the man does not lose responsibility or control and instead of understanding less, understands more.

Such an interaction should, I believe, be the goal for much of our normative model building.

Further advice to scientists about managers has been reported by Mathes.[3] He asserts that managers and scientists have different approaches to problem solving and that this fact hinders communication between them. Managerial people analyze problems on the basis of differences or changes in situations. Scientific people look for similarities or common elements.

Certainly the model builder by the nature of his role is seeking generalizations that fit many problems. And certainly the manager looks at differences: this year vs. last year, his organization vs. the competition, forecast vs. actual, etc. Pounds has observed that such mechanisms form one of the manager's principal means of problem finding.[4] The same idea is supported by control theory: action in control systems is usually triggered by a discrepancy between observed and desired results.

[3] R. C. Mathes, "'D' People and 'S' People" (letter), *Science*, vol. 164, May 9, 1969, p. 630.

[4] W. F. Pounds, "The Process of Problem Finding," *Industrial Management Review*, vol. 11, Fall 1969, pp. 1–19.

The model builder can take advantage of the idea of working with differences by having his model give and receive much of its information in these terms.

The following quotes from Mathes may (or may not) be helpful to any group of managers and management scientists working together to apply models:

> The difference (managerial) people know only two degrees of probability, zero and one, and the similarity (scientific) people recognize every degree of probability except zero and one.
>
> The difference people tend to act before they think, if they ever think; whereas the similarity people think before they act, if they ever act.

4. WHAT MIGHT BE RIGHT?

If we want a manager to use a model, we should make it his, an extension of his ability to think about and analyze his operation. This puts special requirements on design and will often produce something rather different from what a management scientist might otherwise build. I propose a name to describe the result. A *decision calculus* will be defined as a model-based set of procedures for processing data and judgments to assist a manager in his decision making.

From experience gained so far, it is suggested that a decision calculus should be:

1. *Simple*. Simplicity promotes ease of understanding. Important phenomena should be put in the model and unimportant ones left out. Strong pressure often builds up to put more and more detail into a model. This should be resisted, until the users demonstrate they are ready to assimilate it.

2. *Robust*. Here I mean that a user should find it difficult to make the model give bad answers. This can be done by a structure that inherently constrains answers to a meaningful range of values.

3. *Easy to control*. A user should be able to make the model behave the way he wants it to. For example, he should know how to set inputs to get almost any outputs. This seems to suggest that the user could have a preconceived set of answers and simply fudge the inputs until he gets them. That sounds bad. Should not the model represent objective truth?

Wherever objective accuracy is attainable, I feel confident that the vast majority of managers will seize it eagerly. Where it is not, which is most of the time, the view here is that the manager should be left in control. Thus, the goal of parameterization is to represent the operation as the manager sees it. I rather suspect that if the manager cannot control the model he will not use it for fear it will coerce him into actions he does not believe in. However, I do not expect the manager to abuse the capability because he is honestly looking for help.

4. *Adaptive.* The model should be capable of being updated as new information becomes available. This is especially true of the parameters but to some extent of structure too.

5. *Complete on important issues.* Completeness is in conflict with simplicity. Structures must be found that can handle many phenomena without bogging down. An important aid to completeness is the incorporation of subjective judgments. People have a way of making better decisions than their data seem to warrant. It is clear that they are able to process a variety of inputs and come up with aggregate judgments about them. So, if you can't lick 'em, join 'em. I say this without taking away from the value of measurement. Many, if not most, of the big advances in scientific knowledge come from measurement. Nevertheless, at any given point in time, subjective estimates will be valuable for quantities that are currently difficult to measure or which cannot be measured in the time available before a decision must be made.

One problem posed by the use of subjective inputs is that they personalize the model to the individual or group that makes the judgments. This makes the model, at least superficially, more fragile and less to be trusted by others than, say, a totally empirical model. However, the model with subjective estimates may often be a good deal tougher because it is more complete and conforms more realistically to the world.

6. *Easy to communicate with.* The manager should be able to change inputs easily and obtain outputs quickly. On-line, conversational I/O and time-shared computing make this possible.

Every effort should be made to express input requests in operational terms. The internal parameterization of the model can be anything, but the requests to the user for data should be in his language. Thus, coefficients and constants without clear operational interpretation are to be discouraged. Let them be inferred by the computer from inputs that are easier for the user to work with. Expressing inputs and outputs as differences from reference values often helps.

On-line systems come through as being very effective in bringing the model to the manager. Some writers, for example Dearden,[5] have belittled the importance of immediate response. They argue that decisions made once a year or even once a month hardly require systems that deliver the answers in seconds. Anyone who has used a conversational system perceives that this argument misses the point. Practically no decision is made on a single computer run. A person develops his understanding of a problem and its solution as he works on it. The

---

[5] J. Dearden, "Can Management Information Be Automated?" *Harvard Business Review*, vol. 42, March–April 1964, pp. 128–35.

critical time is not that of the decision deadline but of the next step in the user's thinking process.

Perhaps equally as important as the operational convenience of conversational programs is their contribution to learning. Good on-line models are user-instructing and introduce a person to the issues of the problem and the model much faster than would otherwise be possible. A person can rapidly get a feel for how the model works through direct experience. This is in sharp contrast to batch processing with its long time lags and imposing tribal rituals of punched cards, systems programmers, and computer operators.

In summary, we are learning techniques of model design and implementation that bring the model to the manager and make it more a part of him. We are calling such a model a decision calculus.

5. AN EXAMPLE FROM MARKETING

An on-line marketing-mix model for use by product managers is currently being developed. The present version emphasizes advertising budget decisions. It will be described below in an inductive, narrative way. Its mathematical specification is given in the Appendix.

The product or brand manager is an ideal customer for a decision calculus. He has substantial responsibility for all of the marketing control variables for a brand. He is busy and will not use a model unless it does something for him. He is at ease making judgments and, being a single person accountable for results, he can gather inputs and make judgments without the elaborate coordination required in many other complex decision processes.

The work is being done in cooperation with three different product managers at two different companies. The variety in companies and managers has been helpful for getting perspective on the man-model interface and in keeping the model structure general. The development has proceeded in evolutionary steps. First a very simple advertising budgeting model was brought up and used to demonstrate concepts. Then a more complex model for advertising budgeting, one with sufficient detail to be of practical value, was brought up. This version will be described here. Experience with it is influencing the design of a more elaborate model.

5.1 Model structure

We seek a simple, robust, easy-to-control model of sales response to advertising. As a first step brand sales is partitioned into product class sales and brand market share. That is, we separately model what is happening to the whole industry or product class of which the brand is a part and what is happening to the brand's share within the class. Such a breakdown has a number of advantages, not the least of which is that marketing people usually think this way. Consider a given time period. We suppose:

1. If advertising is cut to zero, brand share will decrease, but there is a floor, *min*, on how much share will fall from its initial value by the end of one time period.
2. If advertising is increased a great deal, say to something that could be called saturation, brand share will increase but there is a ceiling, *max*, on how much can be achieved by the end of one time period.
3. There is some advertising rate that will maintain initial share.
4. An estimate can be made by data analysis or managerial judgment of the effect on share by the end of one period of a 50 percent increase in advertising over the maintenance rate.

Figure 1 gives a pictorial representation of this information. The same data can also be represented as four points on a share response to advertising curve, as in Figure 2. A smooth curve can then be put through the points; for example, the function

$$\text{Share} = \text{Min} + (\text{Max} - \text{Min})(\text{Adv})^\gamma / [\delta + (\text{Adv})^\gamma] \qquad (1)$$

The constants *min*, *max*, δ, and γ are implicitly determined by the input data.

FIGURE 1
Input data for fitting a sales response to advertising function

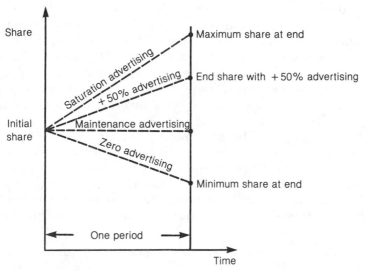

FIGURE 2
A smooth curve of share versus advertising put through the data of form
shown in Figure 1

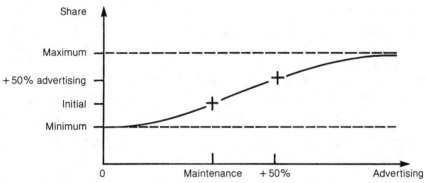

Equation (1) represents a versatile but nevertheless restricted set of response relations. Actually I am willing to use anything. The curve could go down or up or loop the loop for all I care. It should be changed when and if a product manager wants it changed. Meanwhile, he can give four numbers, each of which has operational meaning to him and which together will specify a curve. It is doubtful that, as of today, we could specify a sales response curve in any greater detail than represented by a smooth curve through four appropriately chosen points.

I now claim that the above structure is robust. Suppose we do a two-level spending test and run a regression that is linear in advertising in order to estimate response. Such a regression might make reasonable statistical sense but by itself would have absurd normative implications (advertising = 0 or ∞); it would not be robust. However, if the regression results are used to estimate the +50 percent point and a reasonable *max* and *min* are chosen we can expect reasonable answers. This would be difficult to prove in general, but with a specific manager and product it can usually be demonstrated satisfactorily by sensitivity analysis.

To be sure, more sophisticated models and data analyses can easily be suggested. A quadratic term could be put in the regression, for example, but its coefficient would almost certainly be unstable and normatively alarming. A Bayesian analysis or an adaptive control model might restore order,[6] but the intellectual cost of such complications is high. Even if more sophisticated studies are done, they could

---

[6] J. D. C. Little, "A Model of Adaptive Control of Promotional Spending, *Operations Research*, vol. 14, November 1966, pp. 1075–98.

probably be translated into a set of operational terms like the above. In any case we should start simply.

A person might well ask: Is the structure too robust? Conceivably a model could be so constrained that output would be almost decoupled from input. This is hardly the case here. The value specified for the share increase with +50 percent advertising is certain to be an important determinant of advertising rate. The values of *max* and *min* play the role of keeping changes in a meaningful range.

Incidentally, the sketch in Figure 2 shows an S-shaped curve. This is not required by (1). If $\gamma > 1$, the curve will be S-shaped, for $0 < \gamma \leq 1$, a concave function. The particular γ will depend on the input data.

A major omission in the description so far is consideration of time delays. To take these into account, the model assumes:

1. In the absence of advertising, share would eventually decay to some long-run minimum value (possibly zero).
2. The decay in one time period will be a constant fraction of the gap between current share and the long-run minimum, i.e., decay is exponential.
3. The decay determines *min* for the time period.
4. The advertising affectable share $(max - min)$ stays constant.

Let *long-run min* denote the long-run minimum and *persistence* denote the fraction of the difference between share and long-run minimum that is retained after decay. Under the above assumptions:

$$\text{Persistence} = (\text{Min} - \text{Long-run min})/(\text{Initial share} - \text{Long-run min})$$

$$\text{Share } (t) - \text{Long-run min} = (\text{Persistence})[\text{Share } (t - 1) - \text{Long-run min}] + (\text{Max} - \text{Min})[\text{Adv}(t)]\gamma/(\delta + [\text{Adv}(t)]\gamma) \quad (2)$$

This is a simple dynamic model. It is explainable and it behaves reasonably. It could be further generalized by permitting some of the constants to change with time, but that does not seem desirable at the moment.

But now what is meant by advertising? Dollars? Exposures? A product manager worries about spending rates, media, and copy. Let us construct two time-varying indices: (1) a media efficiency index, and (2) a copy effectiveness index. Both will be assumed to have reference values of 1.0. The model then hypothesizes that the delivered advertising, i.e., the adv (t) that goes into the response function is given by

$$\text{Adv } (t) = [\text{Media efficiency } (t)][\text{Copy effectiveness } (t)][\text{Adv dollars } (t)] \quad (3)$$

The media efficiency and copy effectiveness indices can be determined subjectively, but better alternatives exist. Copy testing is helpful and data on media cost, exposures by market segment, and relative value of market segments can be used to develop a media index.

So far we have taken up share response to advertising, media efficiency, copy effectiveness, and share dynamics. Consider next product class sales. Two important phenomena here are seasonality and trend. These and any similar effects can be combined into a product class index that varies with time. Thus

Product class sales (t)
    = [Reference product class sales][Product class sales index (t)]

In addition there may be a product class response to brand advertising and corresponding time lags. The treatment of this is analogous to that for share. Details are given in the Appendix.

A variety of other factors affect share and therefore indirectly or directly can affect the product manager's thinking about the advertising budget. Some of these factors are: promotions, competition, distribution, price, product changes, and package changes. These factors are all treated, but in a simple way, not unlike the way a product manager might handle them without a model.

Upon examining the factors, we find that the product manager has a definite idea about what various changes are likely to do for him. If he plans a promotion he does so with the expectation that something will happen to his sales and share. The same holds for a product change or price change. Therefore we ask him to construct an index of how he believes these factors will affect brand share in each period. The process can be formalized by filling in a table such as Table 1, listing all factors deemed by the product manager to be relevant. The composite index of nonadvertising effects is simply the product of the numbers in each column. Brand share will then be the product of the nonadvertis-

TABLE 1
Developing a composite index of nonadvertising effects

Index of effect on share	Period			
	1	2	3	4
Promotions	1.00	1.10	0.98	1.00
Price	1.00	1.00	1.00	1.00
Package	1.00	1.05	1.05	1.05
Competitive action	1.00	0.98	0.95	1.00
Other	1.00	1.00	1.00	1.00
Composite	1.000	1.132	0.978	1.050

ing effect index and the share developed from the advertising response relation. For clarity the latter will be called the unadjusted share:

Brand share (t) = [Nonadv effects index (t)][Unadj share (t)]

People often ask how product managers can make judgments like the above. The answer is that managers make such judgments all the time but in a less formal and less numerical way. Whenever they take an action they form some belief about what will happen. As a result, it has not proven difficult for them to make estimates which they feel reasonably comfortable with.

Essentially, the model is now specified. However, as we have added time-varying effects such as media efficiency and the nonadvertising phenomena, we have created a problem for the inputs that determine share response to advertising. What values of the time-varying effects are assumed in the share response inputs? To deal with this question we introduce the concept of a reference case. The reference case is a standard set of values against which changes can be measured. The reference case includes a reference time period. This is not one of the numbered time periods of the calculation but one set apart to serve as a standard. It can be patterned after a real period or can be constructed as a "typical" period. In any case each time-varying effect is assigned a value in the reference period. From this data the sales response parameters *min*, *max*, γ, and δ are then inferred.

To summarize the model:

1. *Share*

   Brand share (t) = [Nonadv effect index (t)][Unadj share (t)]
   Unadj share (t) = Long-run min + [Persistence]
       [Unadj share $(t - 1)$ − Long-run min]
       + (Max − Min)[Wtd adv (t)]$^{\gamma}$/
       $\{\delta +$ Wtd adv $(t)]^{\gamma}\}$
   Wtd adv (t) = [Media efficiency (t)][Copy effectiveness (t)]
       [Adv dollars (t)/
       [Reference value of numerator]

2. *Brand sales*

   Brand sales (t) = [Reference product class sales]
       [Product class sales index (t)][Brand share (t)]

3. *Profits*

   Contribution to profit after adv (t)
       = [Contribution per sales unit (t)] · [Brand sales (t)]
       − Adv dollars (t)

The units situation has not been developed in detail here and we have omitted the effect of brand advertising on product class sales. These details are treated in the Appendix.

The basic equations defining the model are really quite few. Nevertheless the structure permits consideration of share response to advertising, copy effectiveness, media efficiency, product class seasonality and trends, share dynamics, product class response to advertising, and a variety of nonadvertising effects such as promotion, distribution, and price. I feel that the structure meets the criteria of simplicity, robustness, and ease of control.

5.2 Conversational I/O

We have said that the model should be easy to use. It must be easy to put data into the computer, easy to find out what is in there, easy to change it, easy to make output runs, easy to search over control variables and make sensitivity analyses. Clerical errors should be quickly correctable. The mechanical operating details should require as little training as possible.

The best way to show how these issues are being approached would be by demonstration at a computer terminal. Short of this we can provide an example. Table 2 shows the trace generated by a person putting in data for "Groovy," a struggling brand in the treacle market. Table 3 shows an input summary printed back by the computer. Table 4 shows an output run.

Some of the options open to the user are: saving data in the computer for later use, changing individual data items, and printing selected items of input or output. He can choose between long descriptive questions or terse questions that type quickly. An important facility is the search option: Any variable or parameter of the model can vary from an arbitrary minimum to an arbitrary maximum in any number of steps. At each step a set of user specified output items is calculated and printed. Thus a search might be made over a control variable to look for improved profit. Or a search might be made over an input parameter to find that value which conforms best to manager's feeling about the parameter's effect on sales.

The traces of Tables 2–4 are largely self-explanatory, except that the item SLOPE in Table 4 needs clarification. This item is intended to answer the question that a user is most likely to ask: Which way should I change advertising to increase profit? But we must ask: What profit? Profit in that period or, since sales changes persist into the future, profit over several periods? We have chosen to anticipate the answer to be "cumulative contribution after advertising" in the last period of the

TABLE 2
Trace of a user putting input data for GROOVY into the computer; all user responses are circled

---

(GO /ADBUDG/)

ADBUDG II—A MULTIPERIOD ADVERTISING BUDGETING MODEL

1 COMPUTER ASKS QUESTIONS IN STANDARD FORM
2 COMPUTER ASKS QUESTIONS IN SHORT FORM
ANS = (1)
1 ENTER NEW DATA
2 USE SAVED DATA
ANS = (1)

BRAND NAME: (GROOVY)

NO OF TIME PERIODS(MAX=8) : (4)

LENGTH OF PERIOD: (QUARTER)

NAME OF FIRST PERIOD: (1 ST Q 70)

GEOGRAPHIC AREA: (US)

   BRAND DATA FOR REFERENCE PERIOD.
   SEASONALITY, TREND, OR OTHER NON-ADV.
   EFFECT REMOVED.

MARKET SHARE AT START OF PERIOD (% OF UNITS): (1.86)

ADVERTISING THAT WILL MAINTAIN SHARE

(DOLLARS/PERIOD): (486900)

MARKET SHARE AT END OF PERIOD
IF ADV REDUCED TO ZERO: (1.77)

MARKET SHARE AT END OF PERIOD
IF ADV INCREASED TO SATURATION: (2.25)

MARKET SHARE AT END OF PERIOD IF ADV INCREASED
50% OVER MAINTENANCE RATE: (1.95)

MARKET SHARE IN LONG RUN IF ADV REDUCED TO ZERO: (0)
INDEX OF MEDIA EFFICIENCY (E.G. AVERAGE EFFICIENCY=1.0): (1.0)

TABLE 2 (*continued*)

INDEX OF COPY EFFECTIVENESS (E.G. AVERAGE COPY=1.∅): (1.∅)

UNITS IN WHICH SALES ARE TO BE MEASURED
(TO BE USED FOR BOTH BRAND AND PRODUCT CLASS.
E.G.,POUNDS,GALLONS,CASES,THOUSANDS
OF DOLLARS,ETC.): (HOGSHEADS)

CONTRIBUTION PROFIT (BEFORE ADV EXPENSE)

EXPRESSED IN DOLLARS/SALES UNIT: (.68)

AVERAGE BRAND PRICE (DOLLARS/SALES UNIT): (1.812)

  OTHER BRAND DATA

MARKET SHARE IN PERIOD PREVIOUS TO PERIOD 1: (1.86)

  PRODUCT CLASS DATA FOR REFERENCE PERIOD.
  SEASONALITY, TREND AND OTHER NON-ADV
  EFFECTS REMOVED.

NAME OF PRODUCT CLASS: (TREACLE)

PRODUCT CLASS SALES RATE AT START OF PERIOD
(UNITS/PERIOD): (29∅∅∅∅∅∅∅)

CONSIDER RESPONSE TO PRODUCT CLASS ADV ? (NO)

AVERAGE PRICE FOR PRODUCT CLASS (DOLLARS/SALES
UNIT): (1.88)

TIME VARYING DATA. IF TIME VARIATION NOT SPECIFIED,
REFERENCE DATA WILL BE COPIED INTO ALL PERIODS.

PRODUCT CLASS SALES RATE HAS SEASONAL OR OTHER NON-ADV
TIME EFFECT ? (YES)

INDEX OF PRODUCT CLASS SALES (REFERENCE CASE=1.∅∅) FOR
PERIOD:
1: .943
2: 1.∅12
3: 1.∅65
4: .959

TABLE 2 (concluded)

BRAND SHARE HAS A NON-ADV TIME EFFECT ? (YES)

INDEX OF NON-ADV EFFECTS (REFERENCE CASE=1.00) FOR PERIOD
1: (1.0
2: 1.05
3: .98
4: 1.0)

MEDIA EFFICIENCY VARIES ? (NO)

COPY EFFECTIVENESS VARIES ? (NO)

CONTRIBUTION VARIES ? (NO)

AVERAGE BRAND PRICE VARIES ? (NO)

AVERAGE PRICE FOR PRODUCT VARIES ? (NO)

BRAND ADV RATE VARIES ? (YES)

BRAND ADV (DOLLARS/UNIT) IN PERIOD
1: (486000
2: 606000
3: 876000
4: 414000)

1 SAVE.DATA
2 PRINT DATA
3 CHANGE DATA
4 OUTPUT
5 RESTART
ANS = (1)

DATA FILE NAME: (GROOVY-70)

calculation. But which advertising? We expect the question might be asked about advertising in any period. Thus we calculate

SLOPE (t) = The change in cumulative contribution after advertising in the last period, per unit change in adv. dollars in t

A positive SLOPE indicates that advertising increases will be profitable (in the above sense); negative, unprofitable; and zero, indifference.

TABLE 3

Summary of input data for GROOVY brand; it has been stored in a file named /GROOVY-70/; the letter M stands for millions

---

```
1 SAVE DATA
2 PRINT DATA
3 CHANGE DATA
4 OUTPUT
5 RESTART

ANS = ②

1 STANDARD PRINT
2 ONLY SPECIFIED LINES

ANS = ①

/GROOVY-7Ø/

1 BRAND NAME: GROOVY
2 NO. PERIODS: 4.ØØØ
3 PER. LENGTH: QUARTER
4 FIRST PER.: 1ST Q 7Ø
5 AREA: US
    REFERENCE PER.-BRAND
7 INIT. SHARE (% OF UNITS): 1.86Ø
8 MAINT. ADV (DOL./PER.): .486M
9 MIN SHARE AT END: 1.77Ø
10 MAX SHARE AT END: 2.25Ø
11 END SHARE WITH + 50% ADV: 1.95Ø
12 LONG RUN MIN SHARE: .ØØØ
14 MEDIA EFFCY: 1.ØØØ
15 COPY EFFECT: 1.ØØØ
16 SALES UNIT: HOGSHEADS
17 CONTRIBUTION (DOL./UNIT): .68Ø
18 BRAND PRICE (DOL/UNIT): 1.812
    OTHER BRAND DATA
19 STARTING SHARE: 1.86Ø
    REFERENCE PER.—PROD. CLASS
21 PROD. CLASS NAME: TREACLE
22 INIT. CLASS SALES RATE (UNITS/PER.): 29ØM
29 CLASS PRICE (DOL/UNIT): 1.88Ø
    TIME VARIATIONS
    PERIOD                    1       2       3       4
30 CLASS SALES INDEX:
                            .943   1.Ø12   1.Ø65    .959
31 NON-ADV EFFECT INDEX:
                           1.ØØØ   1.Ø5Ø    .98Ø   1.ØØØ
```

TABLE 3 (continued)

32 MEDIA EFFCY:				
	1.000	1.000	1.000	1.000
33 COPY EFFECT:				
	1.000	1.000	1.000	1.000
34 CONTRIBUTION (DOL/UNIT):				
	.650	.680	.680	.680
35 BRAND PRICE (DOL/UNIT):				
	1.812	1.812	1.812	1.812
36 CLASS PRICE (DOL/UNIT):				
	1.880	1.880	1.880	1.880
37 BRAND ADV (DOL./PER.):				
	.486M	.606M	.876M	.414M

5.3 Applying the model

One might think that ways to apply the model would be obvious. Not really. The model has to be worked into the user's system. There are a number of ways in which this can and should be done. I shall describe one which we have just been through: The model was used to assist in the quarterly review of a brand plan.

The usual pattern of operations with a consumer product is to construct a brand plan. This is done once a year. The plan lays out the whole marketing program in considerable detail. However, as the year progresses and various parts of the program are carried out, changes get made: new opportunities arise, actual results come in and are not quite as expected, and generally a variety of unforeseen circumstances occur. Consequently, a series of review and replanning points are scheduled, usually quarterly. This does not preclude actions at other times, which in fact take place, but it does at least schedule times in which changes are definitely considered or, if already made, are consolidated in a revised forecast of results.

Our goals in applying the model were to start from a "brand plan" view of the market, modify it to accommodate the new information contained in year-to-date results, then evaluate new strategies and repredict future outcomes. Here is what we did:

Step 1. Setting up the model according to the annual brand plan. A set of input data was developed which would reproduce as model output the results found in the original brand plan. (If the brand plan had been constructed using the model, this step would not have been necessary.) The product class was identified. The seasonality and trends in product class were worked out. The input data for sales response to advertising were estimated by a combination of judgment

558

TABLE 4
Output for GROOVY

```
1 SAVE DATA
2 PRINT DATA
3 CHANGE DATA
4 OUTPUT
5 RESTART

ANS = ④

1 STANDARD OUTPUT
2 EXCLUDE SPECIFIED LINES
3 INCLUDE SPECIFIED LINES ONLY

ANS = ①

1 CALCULATE CURRENT CASE
2 SEARCH
3 FINISHED

ANS = ①
```

		1	2	3	4
1 OUTPUT FOR	GROOVY				
2 PERIOD LENGTH:	QUARTER				
3 STARTING PERIOD:	1ST Q 70				
4 AREA:	US				
5 SALES UNIT:	HOGSHEADS				
6 DATA FROM FILE:	/GROOVY-70/				
8 PERIOD		1	2	3	4
9 MARKET SHARE: (% OF UNITS)		1.868	1.999	2.002	2.009
10 PROD. CLASS SALES(UNIT/PER)		273M	293M	309N	278M
11 PROD. CLASS SALES(DOL/PER)		514M	552M	581M	523M
12 BRAND SALES (UNITS/PER)		5.89M	5.87M	6.18M	5.59M
13 BRAND SALES (DOL/PER)		9.22M	10.6M	11.2M	10.1M
14 CONTRIBUTION (DOL/PER)		3.46M	3.99M	4.20M	3.80M
15 BRAND ADV (DOL/PER)		.486M	.606M	.876M	.414M
16 CONT. AFTER ADV(DOL/PER)		2.97M	3.38M	3.33M	3.39M
17 CUMULATIVE CONT. AFTER ADV		2.97M	6.36M	9.69M	13.1M
23 SLOPE		1.634	1.169	.228	−.379

and the examination of past time series of advertising and sales data. (In this case there were no spending levels test data but one of the side consequences of our study is that the company is seriously considering such tests for the future.) A promotion was planned for the second quarter and estimated to have a certain effect on share. A copy test, using two different areas of the country, was under way. The brand plan proposed that the test be continued for the year and so the copy index was held constant at 1.0. Similarly no substantial media changes were anticipated and the media efficiency was held at 1.0. A certain set of spending rates for advertising was envisaged and they were put into the model. A package and price change was under consideration but it had not gone into the plan.

The assembled data were put into the model and fine adjustments were made in the parameters until the model predicted the brand plan results exactly. We then took the model as a reasonable indication of the product manager's feelings about how the market worked as of the time the brand plan was written.

Step 2. Udating the model on the basis of year-to-date results. Our analysis was done after the first quarter data were in. Two principal events had occurred. First of all, sales were off from their forecast value. Second, media expenditures had been lower than originally planned. The first question to be asked was whether the lower sales could be attributed to the decreased media expenditures. Therefore, we ran the model with the new first quarter's advertising level. According to the model, the change would account for some but not all of the sales differences. The question then arose whether the advertising had a greater effect on sales than we originally thought or whether some other factors were causing sales to be off. The product manager's opinion was that other factors were probably responsible. The next question was whether the factors would continue to operate and he felt that there was no reason to believe otherwise.

Consequently we adjusted the nonadvertising effects index to account for the loss in sales observed in the first quarter and not otherwise attributed to the advertising decrease. The same adjustment was then continued through the year.

At this point it was possible to rerun the brand plan with the new parameters. It put forth a rather pessimistic view of the year.

Step 3. Evaluation of new strategies. In the meantime, a number of new strategies had been proposed. First of all, because of the lower sales in the first quarter and the implied poorer profit position, the advertising levels for the rest of the year had been reduced. Secondly, the package and price change under consideration had been decided upon and was scheduled to begin in the third quarter. In support of that, the trade promotion was changed from the second quarter to the third quarter. Finally, more results were available on the copy test and a sufficient difference had shown up between the two areas that it was planned to implement the better one nationally in the fourth quarter. An estimate of the effect of the new copy on the copy index was made using the results of the test.

All these changes were made to the input. Furthermore a rough brand plan for the following year was put into the analysis. Then the new plan was run. This suggested there would be a substantial improvement in sales and profit compared to the previous case. It also showed that certain reallocations of advertising spending during the year and certain changes in the budget might well be warranted.

Step 4. Predictions of future results. After the above runs were made, a few further adjustments to strategy were decided upon. Thus the whole plan was run again. This run then became part of the quarterly review.

The above application illustrates the general way we expect the model to enter into the product manager's operation. However, each application is somewhat different. The previous one was very much of a team operation with the product manager being supported by specialists with marketing research and operations research skills. Although this is usually to be expected, in another case the product manager has run the model and made his recommendations almost single-handed. He found that it took two or three concentrated exposures to the model to become comfortable with it. In between he was pulled away by the press of other activities for a month or so at a time. Finally, however, he was confronted by a specific budgeting problem and sat down to work with the model intensively. Out of this effort came a report and a specific set of budget recommendations. His particular concern was the conflict between a strategy of budget cutting, short-range profit taking, and possible erosion of market position and a strategy of maintaining or increasing budgets to try to protect or build share. He worked out sets of assumptions about market behavior and alternative company actions and, using the model, traced out their projected consequences. Finally he wrote it up with his recommendations.

The following conversation then took place between himself and his boss, the group product manager. They went over the report at length and, finally the group manager said, "All right, I understand what the model says, but what do you *really* think?"

This is a good question because it uncovers certain important issues. First, has product manager lost control, i.e., does the model really reflect his view of the market? Second, the question may contain some implications that product manager is using the model in a partisan way to make a case for a particular position. Third, has the next level of management lost any control when the product manager's case is buttressed by this new tool?

The product manager was a little surprised by the question but his answer was: "*This* is what I really think. I've spent a lot of time considering the assumptions and results and feel they express my view of the market." As for the issue of whether the report might be partisan, it must be remembered that the product manager system is an advocate system, i.e., each man is supposed to look out for his own brand. It appears, however, the use of models may temper this partisanship because assumptions and data are explicit and subject to examination and relatively easy consideration of alternatives. For the same reason, although the next and higher levels of management need to understand the basic model ideas, once this is accomplished, the explicitness of the model and its inputs can actually make communications between levels more effective.

6. WHAT HAPPENED TO SCIENCE?

Science is concerned with describing nature with fidelity and economy. We have proposed that the managers describe the world as they see it. Can we really afford to pass over issues like: How does the world really work? What is the best way to describe it in a model? How accurate is a given model? How do we measure accuracy?

Clearly these are important issues, although there is a fairly tenable position that says we can gain value from models, even if they do not contain real-world measurements. One can argue that a quantitative model can be used as a qualitative device to aid qualitative thinking. In this role there is no need for a one-to-one correspondence between real-world quantities and quantities in the model.

However, that is not the intention here. We aspire that the model represent the world well. The standard of comparison, however, will not be perfection but rather what the manager has available to him now. If you look at his present situation you find that he has practically no predictive models beyond simple extrapolation of the past, so that complex models and detailed fidelity are not yet required. Nevertheless let us hope that careful research will lead us through a series of increasingly accurate and useful models which at the same time are able to be understood and controlled by the user.

Most of the models we are proposing here tend, at least initially, to be overparameterized with respect to the available data. That is, we tend to put in more phenomena than we know how to measure, but do so anyway because we believe they are important. As a result, by suitably picking parameters we can often fit past data fairly easily. Therefore it may be difficult to develop a good a priori measure of the accuracy of the model.

We should, however, evaluate the model by tracking performance, if this is at all applicable. As decisions are made, we usually forecast the future with the model. We should see whether actual performance differs from the forecast. Ordinarily it will. Then the task is to determine why and correct the model parameters and sometimes the model structure. This process will be greatly facilitated if the model contains a variety of touch points with the real world, i.e., contains quantities which are observable in the real world. The process will also be aided if we design and implement special measurement programs. One of the most obvious side benefits of model use is the pinpointing of critical measurements that should be made.

The task of parameterizing the model is, of course, difficult and important. A good methodology for this is the one used by Armstrong for forecasting.[7] After he had specified what he hoped was a satisfactory structure, he proceeded as follows: First, all the parameters were set by judgment. Then, he tried to estimate each through data analysis. He used as many independent data sets and approaches to analysis as he could invent and separately appraised the accuracy of each. Then he combined the results up to that point by formal methods. Using the now parameterized model, he made forecasts and devised various means of evaluating their quality. One way was to make forecasts from new data. Having done this, he readjusted his parameters to use the information from the new data. The same sequence of initial parameterization, model use, new data collection, and updating the parameters is an adaptive procedure appropriate for most applications of models to ongoing operations.

7. CONCLUSIONS

In many respects, the biggest bottleneck in the managerial use of models is not their development but getting them used. I claim that the model builder should try to design his models to be given away. In other words, as much as possible, the models should become the property of the manager, not the technical people. I suggest that, to be used by a manager, a model should be simple, robust, easy to control, adaptive, as complete as possible, and easy to communicate with. Such a model, consisting of a set of numerical procedures for processing data and judgments to assist decision making, has been called a decision calculus.

---

[7] J. S. Armstrong, "Long-Range Forecasting for a Consumer Durable in an International Market," Ph.D. thesis, M.I.T., 1968.

The model is meant to be a vehicle through which a manager can express his views about the operations under his control. Although the results of using a model may sometimes be personal to the manager because of judgmental inputs, the researcher still has the responsibilities of a scientist in that he should offer the manager the best information he can for making the model conform to reality in structure, parameterization, and behavior.

Although it is really too early to tell, I would like to predict how such a model will enter these companies and how the companies will organize to make use of it. First of all, the managers have to learn how to use the model. This requires technical assistance and a teaching program. Technical assistance is required for problem formulation and data analysis. As for a teaching program, our experience suggests that the best approach is to lead the potential user through a sequence of models of increasing scope and complexity. This is essentially what we have done with the model above and it is what Urban has done with his new product model, SPRINTER.[8] Often a user, having learned a simple model, will start to ask for just the additional considerations found in the advanced models.

As for organization, a matrix form seems to be indicated. Under this setup the manager has line responsibility but also has a commitment from operations research and/or market research in terms of somebody assigned to his area. The manager needs a person to whom he can address questions about model behavior and a person or persons who can help design measurements and do data analysis.

One of the most evident consequences of the experience to date has been that a model is a stone in the shoe for better data. Under present planning procedures many measurement problems are glossed over or suppressed. The model forces explicit consideration of every factor it contains and so pinpoints data needs.

APPENDIX
ADBUDG model

s_t = Brand sales rate in period t (sales units/period)
h_t = Brand share in period t
c_t = Product class sales rate in period t (sales units/period)

$$s_t = h_t c_t \tag{A1}$$

$\bar{h}_t$ = Unadjusted brand share in t

---

[8] G. L. Urban, "SPRINTER: A Model for the Analysis of New Frequently Purchased Consumer Products," Sloan School of Management Working Paper 364–69, M.I.T., Cambridge, Mass., 1969.

564

n_t = Nonadvertising effects index in t

$$h_t = n_t \bar{h}_t \qquad (A2)$$

α = Persistence constant for unadjusted brand share
β = Affectable range of unadjusted brand share
γ = Advertising response function exponent for brand
δ = Advertising response function denominator constant for brand
λ = Long-run minimum brand share
w_t = Weighted, normalized brand advertising in t

$$\bar{h}_t = \lambda + \alpha(\bar{h}_t - \lambda) + \beta w_t^\gamma/(\delta + w_t^\gamma) \qquad (A3)$$

e_{1t} = Brand media efficiency in t
e_1^* = Brand media efficiency reference value
e_{2t} = Brand copy effectiveness in t
e_2^* = Brand copy effectiveness reference value
x_t = Brand advertising rate in t (dollars/period)
x^* = Brand maintenance advertising rate (dollars/period)

$$w_t = e_{1t}e_{2t}x_t/e_1^*e_2^*x^* \qquad (A4)$$

d_t = Product class sales rate index in t
c_t = Unadjusted product class sales rate in t (sales units/period)

$$c_t = c_t d_t \qquad (A5)$$

α' = Persistence constant for unadjusted product class sales
β' = Affectable range of product class sales rate (sales units/period)
γ' = Advertising response function exponent for product class
δ' = Advertising response function denominator constant for product class
λ' = Long-run minimum product class sales (sales units/period)
v_t = Normalized product class advertising rate in t

$$\bar{c}_t = \lambda' + \alpha'(\bar{c}_{t-1} - \lambda') + \beta' v_t^{\gamma'}/(\delta' + v_t^{\gamma'}) \qquad (A6)$$

v^* = Maintenance advertising rate for product class sales (dollars/period)

$$v_t = (v^* - x^* + x_t)/v^* \qquad (A7)$$

m_t = Brand contribution per unit in t (dollars/sales unit)
p_t = Brand contribution rate after advertising in t (dollars/period)

$$p_t = m_t s_t - x_t \qquad (A8)$$

σ_t = Cumulative contribution after advertising for periods 1 to t (dollars)
T = Number of periods considered

$$\sigma_t = \Sigma_{s=1}^t p_s \qquad (A9)$$

$\sigma_T(x_t)$ = Value of σ_T as a function of x_t

η_t = The rate of change of σ_T with x_t, called SLOPE, and calculated by:

$$\eta_t = [\sigma_T(x_t + 0.05x^*) - \sigma_T(x_t)]/0.05x^* \tag{A10}$$

The parameter sets α, β, γ, δ, λ and α', β', γ', δ', λ' are uniquely determined by the reference case data in the input. In the reference case $n_t = 1$, $e_{1t} = e_1^*$, $e_{2t} = e_2^*$ and referring to Figure 1, the items in Table 3, and A2–A4, we obtain the following determining relations: λ = (item 12); (item 9) = $\lambda + \alpha[(\text{item } 7) - \lambda]$; (item 10) = $\lambda + \alpha[(\text{item } 7) - \lambda] + \beta$; (item 7) = $\lambda + \alpha[(\text{item } 7) - \lambda] + \beta/(\delta + 1)$; (item 11) = $\lambda + \alpha[(\text{item } 7) - \lambda] + \beta(1.5)^\gamma/[\delta + (1.5)^\gamma]$. A similar set of relations determines the primed parameters. If the option not to consider the effect of brand advertising on product class sales is chosen, $\bar{c}_t$ is set to the initial product class sales rate of the reference period (item 22).

Let there be light
(with sound analysis)

CULLOM JONES

The pharaoh had had a troublesome dream, and no one could interpret it for him. Joseph, who had languished in an Egyptian dungeon for two years, was summoned to provide an interpretation. He shaved and changed his clothes, then went to the emperor. According to the Book of Genesis, this is what Joseph heard from the pharaoh:

"In my dream behold, I was standing on the bank of the Nile; and behold, seven cows, fat and sleek, came up out of the Nile; and they grazed in the marsh grass. And lo, seven other cows came up after them, poor and very ugly and gaunt, such as I had never seen for ugliness in all the land of Egypt. And the lean and ugly cows ate up the first seven fat cows. Yet when they had devoured them, it could not be detected that they had devoured them, for they were just as ugly as before. Then I awoke. I also saw in my dream, and behold, seven ears, full and good, came up on a single stalk; and lo, seven ears, withered, thin, and scorched by the east wind, sprouted up after them; and the thin ears swallowed the seven good ears. Then I told it to the magicians, but there was no one who could explain it to me."[1]

Whereupon Joseph gave his interpretation. His methodology was revelation from God. A modern analyst may have other methodology and technique, but in the same fashion as the prisoner, he describes the present or projected situation, defines the problem, and points out its implications. Joseph said: "Pharaoh's dreams are one and the same; God has told to Pharaoh what He is about to do. The seven good cows are seven years; and the seven good ears are seven years; the dreams are one and the same. And the seven lean and ugly cows that came after them are seven years, and the seven thin ears scorched by the east wind shall be seven years of famine.

Source: *Harvard Business Review*, May–June 1976. Copyright © 1976 by the President and Fellows of Harvard College; all rights reserved.

[1] *New American Standard Bible* (Chicago: Moody Press, 1971).

"It is as I have spoken to Pharaoh: God has shown to Pharaoh what He is about to do. Behold, seven years of great abundance will be forgotten in the land of Egypt; and the famine will ravage the land. So the abundance will be unknown in the land because of that subsequent famine; for it will be very severe. Now as for the repeating of the dream to Pharaoh twice, it means that the matter is determined by God, and God will quickly bring it about."

Then Joseph took a simple step—one which, despite its importance, eludes many persons in analysis of problems. He proposed action!

"And now let Pharaoh look for a man discerning and wise, and set him over the land of Egypt. Let Pharaoh take action to appoint overseers in charge of the land, and let him exact a fifth of the produce of the land of Egypt in the seven years of abundance. Then let them gather all the food of these good years that are coming, and store up the grain for food in the cities under Pharaoh's authority, and let them guard it. And let the food become as a reserve for the land for the seven years of famine which will occur in the land of Egypt, so that the land may not perish during the famine."

Some eager planners and analysts give the impression that they are a library of techniques and methods in search of a problem. But good solutions come when the technique flows from the situation, not when a situation is forced to fit the technique. For example, it would be blind devotion rather than good practice to insist on installing a discounted cash flow system in a company simply because it had not used DCF before.

If Joseph had been bound to the technique, he might have proposed the establishment of a chain of Dream Diagnostic Centers. But no, he looked beyond the technique to the need of the organization—to the plight of Egypt.

Joseph's plan made allowances for organizational change. This step—"Let Pharaoh look for a man discerning and wise and set him over the land of Egypt"—along with the next—"Let Pharaoh take action to appoint overseers"—provided the administrative structure to ensure the completion of the job.

SUCCINCT AND CLEAR

How an analysis is presented will greatly influence its acceptance. Joseph did not go into the theory of dream reading. He was not hung up on documentation or justification of the method used to arrive at his conclusions, even though the conclusions were of life-and-death importance. He simply stated the result of his evaluation unequivocally and in terms meaningful to the pharaoh. Joseph made sure his conclusions would be understood. Note the repetition:

"Pharaoh's dreams are one and the same; God has told to Pharaoh what He is about to do."

"It is as I have spoken to Pharaoh: God has shown to Pharaoh what He is about to do."

"Now as for the repeating of the dream to Pharaoh twice, it means that the matter is determined by God, and God will quickly bring it about."

Unfortunately, not every analysis communicates so clearly. Some are long, boring, and hard to follow. Some are theoretical; the purpose seems to be more to educate the manager receiving the report than to solve his problem. Some attempt to establish the importance of the analyst's function instead of helping to solve the problem. Some seek to satisfy idle curiosity rather than come to important conclusions.

Joseph's proposed solution had the added virtue of simplicity. Consider his tax program: "And let him extract a fifth of the produce of the land of Egypt in the seven years of abundance." He dealt in round numbers. The proposal was not "extract 19.53 percent of the produce as indicated by the risk model." While Joseph's proposal entailed sweeping changes, he covered the major points—the organization, the amount of tax, the need for security, and the need for providing storage facilities—in a few sentences. He did not get lost in details that could obscure the thrust of the program.

The last part of the proposal spelled out the benefits of the program. Largely because of Joseph's good analytical work, the program was adopted:

"Now the proposal seemed good to Pharaoh and to all his servants. Then Pharaoh said to his servants, 'Can we find a man like this, in whom is a divine spirit?' So Pharaoh said to Joseph, 'Since God has informed you of all this, there is no one so discerning and wise as you are. You shall be over my house, and according to your command all my people shall do homage; only in the throne I will be greater than you.' "

Joseph's analysis was accurate; the famine *did* occur. He justified the promotion given him by the pharaoh. Joseph was willing to be held accountable for the implementation of his plan and the results. Egypt survived and the pharaoh prospered, so in the audit of the program Joseph came through with shining colors. So should the modern analyst whose work is up to the standard set by Joseph.

To tell the truth

CHARLES J. CHRISTENSON

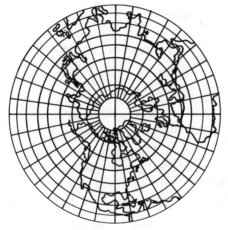

Map no. 1: I am the map of the world.

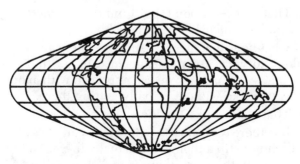

Map no. 2: I am the map of the world.

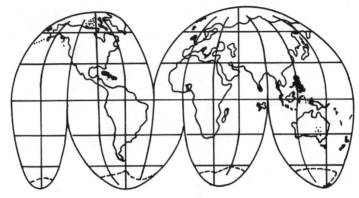

Map no. 3: I am the map of the world.

Contestant: This is all very confusing! You resemble each other a little, but you're all different. Would the *real* map of the world stand up, please?

Globe: (Appearing from behind the curtains.) They're *all* imposters; they're flat! The *real* world is more spherical, like me.

Contestant: Aha! Then you're the real map of the world?

Globe: To tell the truth, no. The real world isn't *exactly* a sphere like I am; it's a little flattened at the poles. And then *it* has a rather irregular surface—mountains, valleys, oceans—and mine's more smooth. And if you want to get picky, France isn't really purple all over.

Contestant: Well, where *is* the real map of the world, then?

Globe: Let me ask you this—what do you mean, *real* map?

Contestant: That's a good question. I hadn't thought of it. I suppose I mean one that's as much like the real world as possible.

Globe: If it were *exactly* like the real world, how would you know which was the map and which the world?

Contestant: That's a clever point, but I didn't say *exactly* like the real world, I said *as much* like it as possible.

Globe: And what does that mean? I suppose one way to interpret it is by analogy to what a mathematician calls a "limit" or a "limit point"—that's a point that you can approach with another point as closely as you like without actually getting there.

Contestant: That sounds like the idea.

Globe: But then there *is* no closest point—you can always find another one that's closer still although not actually there. And I suspect it's the same way with maps—there is no "closest" one.

Of course, this argument is only an analogy. If I wanted to make it rigorous, I'd have to prove, among other things, that the real world (the limit point) exists. Philosophers have been fooling around with that one unsuccessfully for too long for me to try to tackle it now.

Besides, from one point of view, the question of whether the real world exists is not susceptible to proof one way or the other; it's not even a valid question. "Proof" is applicable only within logic or mathematics, and the real world isn't part of logic or mathematics.

Contestant: That's a relief. I'd hate to think that whether the real world existed depended upon whether I could prove it, because I certainly can't. But say, I started out looking for the real map of the world, and all of a sudden we're talking philosophy, logic, and mathematics.

Globe: That's not too surprising. After all, a map is really nothing but a mathematical model of a certain territory.

Contestant: *You're* a mathematical model? You look more like a picture to me, a picture with a certain shape—and with certain shapes *on* you.

Globe: Didn't you ever study geometry? It deals with shapes too, and it's part of mathematics. What makes it mathematical is that it has certain definite and logically related rules for manipulating and comparing shapes.

Contestant: OK, I'll buy that. Now let's come back to the point about how close a map is to the real world. Granted that there may be no such thing as a "closest" map, it still seems to me that I ought to be able to compare two maps and determine which of the two is "closer." Isn't that so?

Globe: To tell the truth, no. Let me draw you a picture to illustrate. Here is a limit point, *L*, and two neighboring points, *X* and *Y*.

Which point is closer to *L*: *X* or *Y*?

Contestant: There must be a trick here, but I'll guess *Y* anyway.

Globe: Wrong! Actually you're right about there being a trick. You assumed that the scale of distance is the same in all directions from a point like *L*. That's true in the Euclidean geometry you studied once, but it's not necessarily true in *every* geometry. In fact, it's not usually true on a map of the world, for example. Check me out on this if you don't believe me.

Now take the picture above again. Assume L represents the "real world" (although, remember, I don't think the "real world" is part of mathematics). X represents a map that agrees with the real world in all details except one, and on that one it differs by an amount that I have represented by the distance XL. Y represents another map that agrees with the real world in all details except another one, and here the difference is represented by YL. Now, can we *really* compare XL and YL in terms of which is "larger" or "smaller"? That would be like adding apples and oranges— they're two different things.

And *that's* why you can't usually compare two maps in terms of which is "closer" to the real world. It just doesn't make sense.

Contestant: That's all too abstract for me. It probably doesn't happen that way too often in practice.

Globe: Wrong again! It happens all the time! Look at maps no. 1, no. 2, and no. 3. Which one is "closer" to me? They're *all* different, but in different ways. Each one has tried to be "close" to me in some respects (such as preserving the shapes of the continents), but in the process of doing this while staying on a flat sheet, each one has had to compromise in other respects.

Contestant: This *is* very disturbing! Are you telling me that there are no standards? Is any map as good as any other one?

Globe: Well, that's a difficult question. There are standards, and not every map is as good as any other one. In one respect, I am the standard. In the final analysis, though, *you* are the standard.

Contestant: That *is* confusing. You'd better elaborate.

Globe: OK. To start with, will you agree that I'm a closer approximation to the real world than maps no. 1, no. 2, and no. 3?

Contestant: Of course. As you said yourself, they're all flat and the world is more spherical, like you.

Globe: Can you *prove* that I'm a closer approximation?

Contestant: Well, let's see. As I said, at least you're spherical. Everywhere else I can see a difference, you seem to me to be closer to the real world.

But wait a minute—why are you asking for proof? Didn't you tell me yourself that the relationship between a map and the real world isn't a matter of proof? I forget how you put it—that the real world isn't *really* a limit point?

Globe: You're learning! And you've hit on the respect in which *you're* the standard. In the last analysis, in judging how well a map "fits" the real world, it's up to *you* to discern the differences on the various attributes and to decide which attributes are relevant and how they should be compared with one another.

Contestant: That sounds awfully subjective. Couldn't I be making a big mistake? Suppose I thought that a flat map represented the real world? I'd be wrong, wouldn't I?

Globe: Well, you do that all the time, don't you? Take a flat map as representing reality, that is. The danger of subjectivity is there, as you say, but unavoidable. As the philosopher Wittgenstein put it, "The difficulty is to realize the groundlessness of our believing." To realize, for example, that there *is* no *real* map of the world. But that realization is precisely what you need to protect yourself against subjectivity. If you recognize your map as only a working approximation that differs from reality in ways you may not even be aware of, much less able to specify, then you leave yourself open to new information that may overthrow your old map. Otherwise, you may try to keep the map and reject the new information.

Let me give you a new piece of information, for example. You probably didn't notice that my scale of distance is *smaller* than any of these three flat maps. In that respect, at least, I'm *less* close to the real world than they are.

Contestant: You're right. I didn't notice that. But I don't think scale or size is relevant in judging resemblance anyway. In fact, since you brought up geometry, isn't it true that triangles can differ in size and still be "similar"?

Globe: Right—and that's a good analogy, for reasons I'll come to.

Now let me talk about how *I'm* the standard. Or maybe a better word is "paradigm," in its literal meaning of "pattern," because I am the "pattern" from which any "correct" flat map is obtained. So far you've essentially argued that, so far as you're concerned, *any* globe is a better representation of the real world than any flat map, assuming that the globe shows all the detail that the flat map does.

Contestant: Right.

Globe: Now flat maps can be obtained from a globe by a *purely* mathematical operation called "projection." The idea here is related to the projection of an image onto a screen. You can visualize the process, in fact, by imagining that the globe which is to be your paradigm is transparent except that the land masses are painted on it in opaque paint. Inside there is a light bulb and outside there is a flat piece of paper (rolled up, perhaps, into a cylinder or cone). The land masses will be "projected" onto the paper as shadows.

Their exact shapes and relative sizes and locations will be *determined* by the locations of the light bulb and paper relative to the globe.

What I'm saying is this: The relationship between a flat map and a globe is *not* a matter of subjective judgment in the way that the relationship between the globe and the world is. Rather, it's a matter of logical *necessity*—the flat map can be *calculated* from the globe. That's the sense in which *I'm* the paradigm for any flat map. (I'm also the paradigm for any other globe of any size, by the way, because they can also be obtained from me by projection. That's why you're right in feeling that scale is unimportant in judging resemblance. Change of scale is purely mathematical.)

What this means is, if you accept me as the paradigm to which all flat maps (and globes) are to be compared, and if a given flat map *can't* be obtained from me by some mathematical projection, then you must logically judge that map to be "incorrect."

Contestant: I think I follow that. Now let me ask you this. Would the method you're describing enable me to compare maps no. 1, no. 2, and no. 3 with each other *directly?* I suppose what I mean is, could one of these maps be obtained from another one by a mathematical projection?

Globe: As a rule, *no.* You see, some of the information I contain about relationships in the real world may be lost or distorted in the projection and can only be recovered by coming back to me, the "original." It's like making a copy of a copy—you can't make it better and you might make it worse.

It's usually nonsense, for a similar reason, to argue about whether one flat map is a "closer" approximation to the real world than another. Each one, if mathematically "correct," has been obtained by a method of projection which has sacrificed some attributes of resemblance in favor of others. A rigorous statement of how these trade-offs have been made can be given only by comparing each of them with a globe.

Contestant: I see. So coming back to the beginning of our discussion, instead of wondering which of the three flat maps was the "real" map of the world, I should have recognized that each one could be a "correct" map, provided it was derived by a mathematical projection from a globe *I* accepted as a standard or paradigm.

Globe: You've got it.

Contestant: Well, thank you very much. [Globe leaves.]

Host: Would the next group of panelists identify themselves, please?

Theory no. 1 (behaviorist): I am the theory of business activity.

Theory no. 2 (economist): I am the theory of business activity.

Theory no. 3 (strategist): I am the theory of business activity.

Contestant: You can't fool me this time! There *is* no *real* theory of business activity. A theory is only a mathematical model, like a map.

Actually, you all *do* resemble business activity somewhat, so I suspect that you're all shadows of some global theory who's hiding there behind the curtains. If I could compare each of you with him, I'd have a better idea of what you show and how you are different. So would you come on out, global theory?

[When nothing happens, contestant gets up and looks behind the curtains.] There's no one there!

Title index of materials for discussion

Accounting Model, Development of the, 22
ALPHA Concrete Products, Inc., 334
Art of Modeling, On the, 486
Atomic Model, Development of the, 18

Bennington Products, Inc., 422
Bill French, Accountant, 54
Bob Mogielnicki, 46
Bud Mathaisel, 24

Central Steel, 285
Corporate Models: Better Marketing Plans, 502

DYCO Chemical Corporation (AR), 372
DYCO Chemical Corporation (B), 383

Edgartown Fisheries, 239
Elegance and Relevance of Mathematics, The, 2
Engle Company (A), The, 326
Engle Company (B), The, 333
Everclear Plastics Company, 431

Family Health Center (A), 176
Family Health Center (B), 185

General Leasing Company (A), 346
Grimbel, The, 282

Hawthorne Plastics, Inc., 210
Hinkle Automotive Products, 205
Hollingsworth Manor Apartments, 291

J. B. Robinson Fertilizer and Explosives, Inc., 195
J. B. Robinson Fertilizer and Explosives, Inc. (P), 237

Law School Question, The, 94
Let There Be Light (with sound analysis), 566
Lockbourne Company, The, 112

McGowan Paint Company, 115
Management Science and Business Practice, 528
Marketronics, Inc., 244
Models and Managers: The Concept of a Decision Calculus, 539

Nancy M. Hohman, The, 173

Petro Enterprises, 202
Process of Problem Finding, The, 466

R. C. Blake Company, 49
Red Brand Canners, 91
Rubicon Rubber Company, 103

Solving Problems, 453
Stephen Douglas, The, 248
Super-Rite Meats, 97
Synergistic Systems Corporation, 279

Tauride Transportation Company (A), 296
Tauride Transportation Company (B), 300
Technotronics Corporation, 204
To Tell the Truth, 569
Transit Maintenance, 396

Weatherburn Aircraft Engine Company, 278
Weston Manufacturing Company, 191
Wizard Who Oversimplified: A Fable, The, 499

Xerox Corporation Distribution System (B), 359

Index of text

A

Absolute error, 169–71
Abstraction, 4, 16; *see also* Model building
Accountant's concept of cost, 37
Accounting records as data source, 38, 40
Acquisition cost, 37; *see also* Cost
Act selection, 122; *see also* Decision theory
Additivity, 76
Adjustment factors, 166
Allocation of fixed cost, 43
Allocation of resources; *see* Linear programming
Alternate optimal solution, 87; *see also* Linear programming
Analysis, 16; *see also specific topics*
Analyst, role of, 14, 320
Anderson, Barry, 453
Anthony, Robert, 499
Average; *see* Decision theory, probability distribution, measures of
Averages player, 233–34; *see also* Preference theory

B

Babbage, Charles, 1
Backward induction, 130
Ball point pen example, 62–75; *see also* Linear programming
Bayes theorem, 139n
Boston University, 396 n
Bottom-up, approach to modeling, 319
Brackets, used to approximate probability distribution, 147–49
Brown, Rex V., 315 n, 321 n

C

Carter, E. Eugene, 315 n, 318 n
Case method
    answers, 8–10
    class using, 7

Case Method—*Cont.*
    cost of developing, 9
    educational purpose, 6
    ethics of, 8
    how to prepare, 7
    learning by the, 5
Certainty, assumption of linear programming, 76
Certainty equivalent, 222, 231–32
Change, rates of, 3
Collectively exhaustive, 124
Computers
    time sharing, 322
    use of
        in linear programming, 70–75
        in simulation, 273
Conditional probability, 139
Consequences; *see* Decision theory, event outcomes
Constraints
    linear inequalities as, 64–67
    linear programming formulation of, 70–72, 78–79
    optimal solution location, 67
    simplex, 69–72
    trade-offs along, 64–70
    transportation method, 78
Continuity, assumption of linear programming, 76
Contribution margin, 40–43; *see also* Objective function
Correct probability, 127
Cost
    accountant's concept, 37
    acquisition, 37
    classification of
        by product, 38
        by variability, 38–39
    direct, 39
    economist's concept, 37
    fixed, 38
        allocation of, 43
    future, 37
    historical, 37

Cost—*Cont.*
opportunity, 37
of excluded route, 81–83; *see also*
Linear programming, transportation method
overhead, 39
period, 39
period, 39
prime, 39
relevant, 37–40
sunk, 40
variable, 38–39
Cumulative probability, 145–47; *see also*
Decision theory, probability distributions

D

Data access, 314–15
Decision diagrams; *see* Decision theory
Decision theory
decision diagrams
act forks, 121, 125
act selection, 122
backward induction, 130
Bayes theorem, 139 n
conditional probabilities, 139
event
consequences, 129
evaluating, 125–26
forks, 121, 125
outcomes, 123
selection, 122
expected monetary value, 129
expected value of perfect information,
132–36
forks, 121, 125
imperfect tester, 136–41
joint probabilities, 138–39
sensitivity analysis, 130–32
time sequence of, 121–22, 125
frequency, long-run relative, 161
preferences, 129, 215–37; *see also* Preference theory
probabilistic forecasts, assessing
with distinguishable data, 165–71
with indistinguishable data, 158–65
with no data, 153–58
probability
equivalent gamble, 155
manager's judgment about compared
to true or correct, 127
probability distributions
continuous, 145–47
approximation using brackets,
147–49
discrete, 143–44

Decision theory—*Cont.*
probability distributions—*Cont.*
measures of
extremes, 155–56
fractiles, 151–52, 156–57
mean, 150–52
median, 151, 154
mode, 150–52
uncertainty principle, 119
Decisions under uncertainty; *see* Decision
theory
Decreasing risk aversion, 234–35
Degenerate transportation problems, 81 n,
84–85
Diebold Corp., 320
Direct costs, 39; *see also* Cost
Direct overhead, 39; *see also* Cost
Dorfman, Robert, 88 n
Drake, John W., 311 n, 315 n, 318 n, 320 n
Dual value; *see* Linear programming,
simplex method, shadow price
Dynamic equilibrium, 3

E

Economist's concept of cost, 37–43
Educational purpose of case method, 6
EMV; *see* Expected monetary value
Equivalent gamble, 155
Ethics of case method, 8
Event; *see* Decision theory
Event based simulation; 269
EVPI; *see* Expected value of perfect in-
formation
Excluded routes; *see* Linear programm-
ing, transportation method
Expected monetary value, 129; *see also*
Decision theory
Expected value of perfect information,
132–36
Extreme values, assessing, 155–56; *see
also* Decision theory, probability dis-
tributions

F

Failures of models, 311
Feasible area, 63; *see also* Linear programming
Fixed costs, 38; *see also* Cost
Forecasting; *see also* Decision theory,
probabilistic forecasts
error, absolute and relative, 169–71
example, grocery wholesaler, 165–68
models, 168–71
Forks, 121, 125; *see also* Decision theory
Format, model inputs and outputs, 317–18

Formulation, of linear programs, 70–72, 78–79
Fractiles, 151–52, 156–57; see also Decision theory
Funk, Thomas C., 97 n
Future costs, 37; see also Cost

G

Gambler, 234; see also Preference theory
Gragg, Charles I., 8
Grayson, C. Jackson, 316 n, 528
Green, Paul, 431 n
Guelph, University of, 97 n

H

Harvey, Allan, 315 n, 316 n, 320 n
Heisenberg, Werner, 119
Historian, accountant's role as, 37, 40
Historical costs, 37; see also Cost
Historical data, used for forecasting, 158–71
Hyman, Ray, 453

I

Imperfect tester, 136–41; see also Decision theory
Implementation, responsibility for, 315
Implicit cost; see Shadow price
Improving transportation programs, 83–84
Included route; see Linear programming, transportation method
Independence
    assumption of linear programming, 76
    simulation, of events in, 254
Inequalities, 64–67
Initial solution
    simplex method, 69, 72
    transportation method, 78–80
        number of included routes, 81
Innovation, importance to modeling, 316
Input to models, format, 317–18
Interquartile range, 157
Introduction, backward, 130
Intuitive models, 12
Involvement in modeling
    management, 13, 315–16
    user, 14, 317
Iterative nature of modeling, 15–18, 313

J–K

Joint probabilities, 138–39
Jones, Cullom, 566

Judging models, 12
Judgments about probabilities, risk attitude separate from, 228
Kotler, Philip, 502

L

Lazarus, Mitchell, 2
Linear programming
    assumptions of
        additivity, 76
        certainty, 76
        continuity, 76
        independence, 76
        linearity, 76
    constraint, 64, 70
    definition of, 61
    example applications of, 61–62
    objective function, 61, 68, 71
    optimality defined, 61
    simplex method
        dimensionality, 75
        example, two-product mix, 62–75
        feasible area, 63
        formulation
            constraints, 70
            objective function, 71
            resources, 71
            variables, 70
        graphical analysis, 75
        initial solution, 69, 72
        linear inequalities, 64, 67
        optimum, location of, 67
        right-hand-side, range of, 73
        shadow price, 72–73
        simultaneous equations, 70
        slack variables, 71–72
        technological coefficients, 70, 78–79
        transportation method, related to, 77–79
    transportation method
        alternate optimal solution, 86–87
        degeneracy, 81 n, 84–85
        excluded routes, 80–89
        improving feasible solutions, 83–84
        included routes
            alternative combinations, costing of, 81–83
            number of, 81
        initial solution, 78–80
        northwest corner method, 80
        optimal solution, 84
        shadow price, 86–87
        simplex method, related to, 77–79
        slack variables, 78
        technological coefficients, 78–79
Little, John D. C., 319 n, 539

M

Management science, defined, 1
Manager; see Model building, modeling
    unit
Marshall, Alfred, 1
Mathematical modeling, 3; see also Model
    building
Mathematicians, musicians compared, 4
McKinsey and Co., 312 n, 317
Mean; see Decision theory, probability
    distributions
Median; see Decision theory, probability
    distributions
Mode; see Decision theory, probability
    distributions
Model builder; see Model building, model-
    ing unit
Model building
    iterative nature of, 15–18, 313
    model world, 16–17
    modeling unit
        manager, 13, 315–16, 320
        model builder, 14, 320
        user, 14, 322
    models
        computer, 273; see also Computers
        decision trees; see Decision theory
        defined, 11
        failure of, 311
        intuitive, 12
        judged, 12
        linear programming; see Linear pro-
            gramming
        management support of, 315
        misuses of, 324
        objectives of, 257, 317
        preference; see Preference theory
        simulation; see Simulation
        updating of, 322
        use of, 311–25
    process, 15–18, 312–13, 323
    real world, 17
    steps in, 15–18, 312–13, 323
    user involvement in, 317
Model world, analyst's enchantment with,
    17; see also Model building
Modeling unit; see Model building
Morris, William, 486
Musicians, mathematicians compared, 4
Mutually exclusive, 124

N–O

Northwest corner, 80; see also Linear pro-
    gramming, transportation method
Novelty example, 122–41; see also Deci-
    sion theory

Objective function, 61, 68–71; see also
    Linear programming
Observation, 16
Opportunity costs, 37, 81–83
Optimal solution, 67, 84, 86–87; see also
    Linear programming
Optimality defined, 61; see also Linear
    programming

P

Perfect information; see Decision theory,
    decision diagrams, expected value of
    perfect information
Period cost, 39; see also Cost
Pfeiffer, Wayne, 97 n
Pounds, William, 466
Pratt, John W., 235 n
Preference theory
    analysis using, 229–31
    benefits of, 228–29
    certainty equivalent, 222, 231–32
    limitations of, 236–37
    preference curves
        assessing, 225
        characteristics, 224
        reference consequences, 224
        types
            averages player, 233–34
            gambler, 234
            risk averter, 233
        using, 223
    questionable alternatives to
        coefficient of variation, 220
        conservative estimates, 219
        worst case analysis, 219
    risk attitude
        decreasing risk aversion, 234–35
        need to separate from probabilities,
            228
    zero illusion, 235
Prime cost, 39; see also Cost
Probabilistic forecasts; see Decision
    theory
Probability; see Decision theory
Probability distribution; see Decision
    theory
Problems, analyst's approach to, 16
Programming; see Linear programming
Purpose of text, 4

Q–R

Quartiles
    interquartile range, 157
    lower, 156
    upper, 157

Random number
  generator, 260–61
  table, 276–77
  use of, 261–62
Rates of change, 3
Real world, 17
Reference consequences; *see* Preference
  theory
Relative error, 169–70
Relative frequency, 161
Relevant cost, 37–40; *see also* Cost
Resource allocation; *see* Linear pro-
  gramming
Resources, 71; *see also* Linear programm-
  ing
Responsibility for implementation, 315
Riddle of St. Ives, 40
Right-hand-side, 73; *see also* Linear pro-
  gramming
Risk
  attitude; *see* Preference theory
  aversion; *see* Preference theory
  profile, 259, 263–67
Role definition, 13–15, 320–22
Ronstadt, Robert, 8
Roulette wheel example, 134–35

S

St. Ives, riddle of, 40
Saturation, 3
Schlaifer, Robert O., 225 n
Sensitivity analysis
  decision theory, 130–32
  right-hand-side range, 73
Shadow price; *see* Linear programming
Simplex method; *see* Linear programming
Simplicity, need for in modeling, 318
Simulation
  computers used in, 273
  end point sampling, example, 257–67,
    272–73
  problems with, 274–75
  random numbers; *see* Random number
  risk profile, 259, 263–67
  time, treatment of, in
    event based, 261
    time slicing, 261
  trials, proper number of, 263
  uniqueness of each, 257
  waiting line example, 267–73
  what if questions, 256, 272–73
Simultaneous equations, 70
Slack variables; *see* Linear programming
Smith, Adam, 1
Stanford University, 91 n
Sunk cost, 40; *see also* Cost

T

Table of random numbers, 276–77
Taylor, Fredrick, 1
Technological coefficients, 70, 78–79; *see*
  also Linear programming
Terminal positions, 125–26; *see also* Deci-
  sion theory
Tester, imperfect, 136–41
Testing, 17; *see also* Model building
Text objectives, 4
Time-sharing computer, 322
Time slicing, 269; *see also* Simulation
Top-down, approach to modeling, 319
Transportation method; *see* Linear pro-
  gramming
Trials; *see* Simulation
True probability, 127; *see also* Decision
  theory
Two-product mix example; *see* Linear
  programming

U

Uncertainty; *see* Decision theory
Uncertainty principle, 119
Unfair die example, 159–62; *see also* De-
  cision theory
Uniqueness of each simulation model, 257
Updating models, 322
Upper quartile, 157
User of models, 14, 317, 322
Utility theory; *see* Preference theory

V

Value
  expected monetary, 129; *see also* Deci-
    sion theory
  extreme, assessing, 155–56
  of perfect information, 132–36
Variable; *see* Linear programming,
  simplex method formulation
Variable cost, 38–39; *see also* Cost

W–Z

Waiting line example, 267–73; *see also*
  Simulation
What if questions; *see* Simulation
Wheelwright, Steven C., 334 n
World War II, 1
Worst case analysis criticized, 219
Xerox Corporation, 359 n
Zero illusion, 235; *see also* Preference
  theory